SOMETHING *SENSATIONAL* TO READ IN THE TRAIN

SOMETHING
SENSATIONAL
TO READ IN THE TRAIN

*The Diary of
a Lifetime*

GYLES BRANDRETH

JOHN MURRAY

First published in Great Britain in 2009 by John Murray (Publishers)
An Hachette UK Company

The diary extracts comprising 'Part Five' are an abridgement of material first published in
Breaking the Code: Westminster Diaries (Weidenfeld & Nicolson, 1999)

2

A CIP catalogue record for this title is available from the British Library

Hardback ISBN 978-1-84854-311-9
Trade paperback ISBN 978-1-84854-239-6

Typeset in Fournier by Servis Filmsetting Ltd, Stockport, Cheshire

Printed and bound by Clays Ltd, St Ives plc

John Murray policy is to use papers that are natural, renewable and recyclable products and made from wood
grown in sustainable forests. The logging and manufacturing processes are expected to conform to the
environmental regulations of the country of origin.

John Murray (Publishers)
338 Euston Road
London NW1 3BH

www.johnmurray.co.uk

For Benet, Saethryd and Aphra
who made the journey worthwhile

Contents

CONTENTS

PART FOUR: Under the Jumper

PART FIVE: Member of Parliament

PART SIX: After the Fall

Miss Prism: You must put away your diary, Cecily. I really don't see why you should keep a diary at all.

Cecily: I keep a diary in order to enter the wonderful secrets of my life. If I didn't write them down, I should probably forget all about them.

Miss Prism: Memory, my dear Cecily, is the diary that we all carry about with us.

Cecily: Yes, but it usually chronicles the things that have never happened, and couldn't possibly have happened.

. . . .

Algernon: Do you really keep a diary? I'd give anything to look at it. May I?

Cecily: Oh no. You see, it is simply a very young girl's record of her own thoughts and impressions, and consequently meant for publication. When it appears in volume form I hope you will order a copy.

. . . .

Gwendolen: I never travel without my diary. One should always have something sensational to read in the train.

Oscar Wilde,
The Importance of Being Earnest

Introduction

My father, Charles Daubeney Brandreth, was born at Hoylake, in Cheshire, in July 1910, eight weeks after the death of Edward VII. He always regretted not being an Edwardian. He was the son of a lawyer and a housewife and, after a public school education in Kent and three years at Oxford University, he became a lawyer himself. In the winter of 1936, in London, he met my mother: Alice Mary Addison. She was born in April 1914 in Rawalpindi in India (as it then was), the daughter of an Indian Army officer and a missionary. She had come to England to read law at London University, but never completed her studies. She married my father in March 1937 and gave birth to three daughters in quick succession: Jennifer, Virginia and Hester, my three sisters.

During the Second World War, my father served in the Intelligence Corps. After it, as part of the Allied Control Commission, he was stationed in Germany where he served as a senior magistrate. I was born in Germany, on 8 March 1948, in the British Forces Hospital in Wuppertal. This note from my father to my mother was written on the day that I was born:

Düsseldorf
8 Mar 48

My beloved,

Miss Prince has been making enquiries for me at the hospital and they say I ought not to come up tonight. But I'll be with you in the morning, or as soon as they'll let me see you.

Dearest sweetheart, I am at your side now in spirit helping you bear up in your pain. Neither of us will get much sleep tonight!

I have just seen that Ki has had a baby girl (Patricia Rosemary), so you'll be in the fashion with a daughter.

I care more for you, my darling, than for anyone else and my only prayer is that you are soon safe and well again. God bless you, my dearest ducky.

Your C

Gould is waiting to take this note. I am hoping he may bring some small message from you. My only one to you is I LOVE YOU!

As I type this, my father's note – written on a small visiting card in his clear, elegant hand – sits propped up against my computer screen. I have it – and the envelope in which it was delivered to my mother – because my father kept all his papers. To the side of my desk sit three of my father's metal deed boxes, stuffed to overflowing. There are several more in the basement. The ones here in my study are marked (in my father's hand): 'Gyles – memorabilia'.

Every aspect of my life has been recorded. From the moment of my birth onwards, my father kept everything: notes, cards, correspondence, medical records, school reports, photographs, press cuttings, *everything*. And what he didn't keep for me, from quite a young age, I kept for myself. It's all here – in trunks and boxes (more than one hundred quite substantial boxes) and scores of scrapbooks, notebooks and files.

I have kept souvenirs of my life from the age of six or seven. (My daughter Saethryd has spent the past several months sorting and filing the material for me. She has filled forty-nine cardboard cartons – 47 cm x 37 cm x 30 cm – to date.) From the age of eleven, when I first went away to boarding school, I have kept a daily diary. I have also kept a series of separate journals relating to specific interests or projects – reviews of plays seen, accounts of plays produced, etc. – as well as, occasionally, a more personal record, a second diary that I marked 'Private'. It seems that I have been writing, every day, since I was nine or ten years of age. I have written hundreds of thousands of words each year for more than half a century. I am a writer. Oddly, that's not how I think of myself. Probably, that's not how you think of me. But that's what I am. That's what I have done.

The book you are now holding is culled from my daily diary. It represents roughly a fiftieth of the material – two per cent. (Yes, my unexpurgated diaries would run to fifty volumes of at least this length!) What have I included? What have I left out? Why have I done it?

I hope I have included enough to give you a flavour of the pattern of my life, and the little world in which I have lived, without overwhelming you with detail. I hope I have chosen extracts that are representative of the whole. The years covered run from 1959 to the dawn of the twenty-first century. Part Five deals with my time as a member of parliament and government whip and includes material first published in my book, *Breaking the Code: Westminster Diaries* (1999). In the present volume, at my publisher's suggestion, I have focused on diary entries that touch on events in the outside world as well as my own and I have given more emphasis to some aspects of my life (e.g., my childhood, entertainment, politics, royalty, gossip) than to others (e.g., holidays, my business life, prison reform, charities, notably the National Playing Fields Association). Inevitably, I have cut out whole areas of my existence and tried to keep control of the number of characters featured in the story. Several of my closest friends do not get mentioned in the published diary at all. (They may be relieved.)

At my wife's request, I have kept the references to our marriage and to her and to our children to a minimum. I have also – in the interests of space and family harmony – included very little about my three sisters, my younger brother, and their families. I regret this principally in the case of my sister, Hester, whose roller-coaster life story, while including many fewer famous names, was, at a human and dramatic level, rather more remarkable than mine.

I am an enthusiastic reader of the diaries of others. My five favourite diarists are Samuel Pepys, Virginia Woolf, Noël Coward, Harold Nicolson and Sir Henry 'Chips' Channon. In his diary, Channon remarked: 'What is more dull than a discreet diary? One might as well have a discreet soul.' I am not sure about the state of my soul, but I hope that my published diary is, in fact, reasonably discreet. I hope I have not betrayed the trust of others. I do not want anything in the pages that follow to hurt anyone. I do not believe it will.

'I wonder why I do it?' Virginia Woolf asked herself in her diary. What is this compulsion to record one's own life? Is it simply vanity – an assertion of self? 'Here I am. Look at me. This is what I've done.' Or is it, in fact, more about self-protection than self-aggrandisement? 'To become a spectator of one's own life is to escape the suffering of life,' observed my hero, Oscar Wilde.

I keep a diary because, on the whole, I am happier talking to myself than to other people. I think, too, that writing it makes me feel more alive, more aware of what is happening to me, more real. It's like checking in a mirror to make sure you are still there – and reasonably comfortable with what you see. (Though I may not seem it, I am very insecure.) I do it, too, because I have been fascinated always by famous people (the achieving, the celebrated, even the notorious) and I still find it exhilarating to get a close-up snapshot of a famous name. I like to observe them but, I suppose, I also hope for a touch of glory-by-association. I am wanting some of their magic to rub off on me. James Boswell, Dr Johnson's great biographer, freely admitted that he kept his journal with immortality in mind.

'My wife, who does not like journalizing, said it was leaving myself embowelled to posterity,' he confessed, 'but I think it is rather leaving myself embalmed. It is certainly preserving myself.'

Well, here, in one volume, is a slice of the preserved life of Gyles Daubeney Brandreth, born 1948, author, broadcaster, sometime MP, husband, father, diarist. Thank you for having the book in your hands. Thank you for thinking of reading it. Thank you for being interested at all.

PART ONE
Schoolboy

Prep School Boy

April 1959 – July 1961

Tuesday, 28 April 1959

I have arrived at my new school. It is called Betteshanger School, near Deal, Kent (telephone: Eastry 215). There is a long drive and the school is in a big, old building owned by Lord Northbourne. The uniform is grey shorts with blue shirts for everyday and white shirts for Sunday. Maroon tie. Grey socks and brown sandals. All my clothes are marked with Cash's name tapes with my name in brown: Gyles Daubeney Brandreth. There are eighty boys and ten teachers at the school. The two headmasters are called Mr Stocks, who is very old, and Mr Burton, who came with us on the school train.* The train left Charing Cross Station at 4.10 p.m. Ma and Pa came to see me off.† Ma cried, but I didn't, of course. They have chosen Betteshanger because I need to pass my Common Entrance which they don't do at the Lycée.‡ Also Betteshanger is a prep school where they don't have beatings. And it is quite near Broadstairs, scene of my last triumph!§

Wednesday, 29 April 1959

My bath nights are MWF. MWF = Mondays, Wednesdays, Fridays. Next term they will be TTS. TTS = Tuesdays, Thursdays, Saturdays. One of the matrons is called Angela Corfield. Before bed we have to line up and show her our teeth,

---

* Charles Stocks, who founded the school, was 81 in 1959; Ivor Burton, the joint head-master, was in his early fifties.
† GB's parents lived in London. Charles Brandreth (1910–82) was a solicitor and Alice Brandreth (née Addison, 1914) a housewife and, later, a Montessori nursery-school teacher.
‡ GB's first school was the French Lycée in South Kensington.
§ GB's family took an annual summer holiday at Broadstairs in Kent where, according to a certificate from the Broadstairs and St Peter's Urban District Council Entertainments Department, 'Gyles Brandreth, aged 10, was placed first in the Children's Talent Competition held at the Broadstairs Bandstand on 18 July 1958.'

our hands and the bottoms of our feet. My dormitory is called Brackenbury. The bathroom I use is called Ganges. I am writing this in bed. I am at the bottom of the bed using my torch with the three colours to see with. I have got it on green because when it is on white the light shows through the blanket. The tuck shop is open on Wednesdays and Saturdays. I went and bought Rolos. They don't have Aeros or Spangles, but can order them if enough people want them.

Sunday, 3 May 1959

I forgot Jen's birthday.* After church, letter-writing. We all sit in the Maths Room at our desks and write home. I sent Ma and Pa my news. The school play is *Tom Sawyer* but I am not going to be Tom Sawyer after all. It is a musical play and Mr Burton says that my singing is not strong enough because we are going to do the play out of doors, either in the Dutch Garden, down by the church, or on a special stage on the path outside the Maths Room. I don't mind. (I do mind.) Everything else is quite toodly-pip. On Sundays we get pats of butter at breakfast instead of margarine. My teachers are:

Mr Harkness – English and music
Miss Loewen – Art and geography
Major Douch – Latin and history
Colonel Thomas – Mathematics
Mr Gargiulo – French

Mr Gargiulo is quite strange. Jenkins is going to be Tom Sawyer. He is 13 and taller than me and he is in the choir.

Sunday, 24 May 1959

Today is Empire Day, but from this year it is going to be called Commonwealth Day. We had a special service at church. It is now letter-writing. Colonel Thomas is in charge so we have to be very quiet. I have written to Ma and Pa and Auntie Edith and Grandpa. Later I am going to be writing my play. It is called *Just His Luck*, a play in three acts for thirteen artists. It is set in the offices of the late Lord Arthur Grimsby's lawyers. As the curtain rises all Lord Grimsby's relations are seen seated round the room chatting. It is a comedy with a twist in the

---

* Jennifer (b.1 May 1938), the oldest of GB's three sisters, then studying modern languages at London University.

4

tail. At lunch yesterday I sat on top table next to Mrs Stocks. Her name is Olive and she always wears olive-coloured hats. No one has EVER seen her when she wasn't wearing one of her olive hats with a pheasant's feather in it. She is nice but quite grand. After tea we had a whole school detention given by Mr Gargiulo. Three boys flicked butter pats up at the paintings in the dining room, trying to see who could score a direct hit on the faces, but didn't own up. We all stood in the gym in our house lines. We had to stand completely still for ten minutes, but every time anybody moved Mr Gargiulo started the ten minutes all over again. We were standing in the gym for a very, very, VERY long time!

Sunday, 7 June 1959

I have bought an Airfix model from the tuck shop for half-a-crown. It is a German fighter, a Messerschmitt Me-109. I am going to build it after letter-writing in the sunshine outside the Maths Room window. That's where we do all the model-making on Sundays. If the sun is bright enough, Jenkins can make balsa wood burn using his magnifying glass. Later we have *Tom Sawyer* rehearsals. I am in the chorus with Babington-Smith, Barda, Browne, Cumming-Bruce, Demery, Wainwright and Rule. Last night I told Cumming-Bruce my S.*

Wednesday, 17 June 1959

Gin's birthday.† In chapel I am now helping Mr Harkness with the organ. I work the bellows at the side of the organ while he plays. I have shown him my new play which he likes very much. It is called *One Step Up*. It is in two acts and has a small cast: Sir Felix Thistlethwaite, Gustave (his butler), Slippery Sam (a thief), the Inspector and two policemen. It is a lot funnier than *Dixon of Dock Green*!‡ I had tea with Mr Harkness in his room. We had lemonade and soft white rolls, with real butter and tinned crab. Delicious!

Sunday, 21 June 1959

Tom Sawyer was a Huge Success. Most of the parts were played by boys, but Mr Burton was the Reverend Minister, Mr Gargiulo was Old Catfish, the

---

* In the early part of the diary, the letter S stands for 'secret'. In this instance, the secret was that GB's baby brother, Benjamin (b.22 April 1958), was adopted.

† GB's second sister, Virginia (b.17 June 1939), was then a student nurse at the Middlesex Hospital, London.

‡ *Dixon of Dock Green*, 1955–76, the long-running television drama starring Jack Warner and Peter Byrne, was, in fact, a Brandreth family favourite.

schoolmaster (very funny), and Miss Corfield was Aunt Polly (S).* The weather was good and the audience clapped loudly. Ma and Pa came and thought that I did the scene when we painted the fence particularly well!

Sunday, 28 September 1959

Important News. There is going to be a general election on Thursday 8 October. We are going to have a mock election at school and I am going to be the Liberal candidate.† Mr Harkness is going to help me with the campaign. Our leader is Mr Jo Grimond.‡ Our colour is yellow. Our message is 'People Count'. We are going to win!

Friday, 9 October 1959

We lost the election quite badly!! The Conservatives won, Labour came second, we came third.§ Mr Harold Macmillan (Supermac!) is back as Prime Minister.¶ I think we fought the best campaign, but the people were not listening to us. And tomorrow we have a wet run. This has not been my lucky week!

Thursday, 31 December 1959

According to today's newspaper, *Wagon Train* is the most popular television programme in the country, followed by *Take Your Pick* and *Sunday Night at the London Palladium*. Because we don't have ITV I haven't seen them. We are going to get ITV next year. These are my all-time top TV programmes:

1. *Hancock's Half-Hour*
2. *Billy Bunter*
3. *Whack-O!* with Jimmy Edwards
4. *The Lone Ranger*
5. *The Cisco Kid*
6. *Circus Boy*

---

* In this instance, the 'secret' was a rumour, widely circulated among the older boys, that Miss Corfield did not wear knickers at the weekend.

† GB's mother was a lifelong Conservative, but his father had been a prospective parliamentary candidate for the Liberal Party.

‡ Joseph Grimond (1913–93), MP for Orkney and Shetland, 1950–83; Leader of the Liberal Party, 1956–67 and 1976; later Baron Grimond of Firth CH CBE.

§ Nationally, the Conservatives secured 49.4 per cent of the vote and 365 seats; Labour 43.8 per cent, 258 seats; Liberals 5.9 per cent, 6 seats.

¶ Harold Macmillan (1894–1986), Conservative MP between 1924 and 1964; Prime Minister, 1957–63; later 1st Earl of Stockton OM.

7. *What's My Line?*
8. *Crackerjack*
9. *Pinky and Perky*
10. *Lenny the Lion*

Ma's favourites: *The Billy Cotton Band Show* and the *Black and White Minstrels.* Pa's favourites: *Panorama* and *Tonight*. I think the girls like *The Grove Family* and *Six-Five Special*.

Friday, 1 January 1960
New Year's Day. Bank Holiday in Scotland. Annual Motor Licences renewable

Pa broadcasting on BBC Network 3, *Motoring and the Motorist.** Get present for Hester.† For a New Year gift I was given a record, *High Society*, 33⅓ rpm. Yesterday I went to the British Drama League talk on Actors Preparing at Wyndham's Theatre and then to the Mermaid Theatre for *Treasure Island*. Happy New Year!

Sunday, 3 January 1960

Carol service at St Stephen's.‡ I had a reading, Genesis chapter 3, verses 8 to 15. It wasn't easy because the word 'bruise' was in the last sentence TWICE and I say 'bwuise' when I want to say 'bruise'. Never mind. T. S. Eliot was there and told me that I read very well!§ I told him that I am going to learn his poem 'Macavity the Mystery Cat' by heart. He was pleased. He put his hand on my head. I like him and he likes me.

Sunday, 10 January 1960

Go to evensong and benediction at St Stephen's. Server and boat boy. Good things this week: 1. Went with Hester to the Schoolboys' Own Exhibition. Very good. 2. Went with Foss (from school) to see *The Hostage* by Brendan Behan. 3. Went with Foss to see the film of *Gigi*. Very, very good. 4. Went swimming with Ma at Fulham Baths. She didn't swim. 5. Went with Pa to the Harrods Sale. Pa

---

* GB's father was legal adviser to the Automobile Association and a regular broadcaster on motoring law.

† GB's youngest sister, Hester (b.4 January 1941), was then working as a stable girl in Hereford.

‡ GB was a server and altar boy at the High Anglican church, St Stephen's, Gloucester Road, and a chorister at Holy Trinity, Brompton.

§ Thomas Stearns Eliot (1888–1965), poet and playwright, was a sidesman and regular worshipper at St Stephen's.

bought a suit. We saw Randolph Churchill* in the street. I am collecting famous people – Charles de Gaulle, John Masefield, etc.† Who next?

Sunday, 17 January 1960

Was feeling poorly, but served at evensong and benediction. (The smell of the incense made me feel better.) On Friday I ran to Gapps [the local grocery store] and back in three minutes. Pa was on the radio at 7.30 p.m. and 9.00 p.m. Yesterday went to see *Dick Whittington* at Streatham Hill. V good show. Back to school on Tuesday.

Thursday, 21 January 1960

Played my first game of rugger. It was quite fun but rather cold. Read *Miranda* in the Art Room. It is a play about a man who meets a mermaid on the Thames embankment and falls in love with her. Very good. Had first music practice in Mr Harkness's room. X.‡

Saturday, 30 January 1960

Had first 'cello lesson with Mr Reid. Not very good. He is old and serious. He wears a wig. You can see that it's a wig because of the very clear parting right down the middle. It looks as if it is going to fall off. Watched men hunting in the grounds in the afternoon. It was quite good fun. They only caught one pheasant while we were there. News. I am now doing Skylarks and Nightingales. Four boys sing a hymn or psalm together on the main landing early in the morning before we get up (Skylarks) and last thing at night before lights out (Nightingales). Mr Harkness conducts. He has a little tuning fork so that we get the first note right. After Nightingales, X.

Saturday, 13 February 1960

Visiting Weekend. It is snowing slightly. Ma and Pa arrived, one hour early. We had a lovely time. Went to cinema. *Babette Goes to War* with Brigitte Bardot. I have finished the first scene of my play, a stage adaptation of Colette's novel, *Gigi*, in two acts. It is going quite well. Because it is Visiting Weekend, tomorrow we have an anthem in church.

---

* Randolph Churchill (1911–68), journalist son of Sir Winston Churchill.
† President de Gaulle (1890–1970) visited the French Lycée, when GB was a pupil there, and John Masefield (1878–1967), Poet Laureate, was a worshipper at St Stephen's.
‡ X in the diary is code for 'He kissed me'.

Saturday, 20 February 1960

We had a free morning after break in honour of the Queen's child!* There was no games (hurrah!) and I have got to the third scene of *Gigi*. Listened to some records, including 'What do you want if you don't want money?' (Adam Faith), 'Voice in the Wilderness' (Cliff Richard) and 'Rawhide' (Frankie Laine) and then went to the Art Room to read a book, *Shakespeare and his Stage*. I am planning a production of *A Midsummer Night's Dream* and have drawn a picture of the set. The whole play will be centred round a huge tree like the ilex tree at the bottom of the lower lawn.

Tuesday, 1 March 1960
Shrove Tuesday

Haven't thought of anything to give up during Lent yet. On Sunday saw a film, *The Titfield Thunderbolt*. Quite good.

Saturday, 5 March 1960

Elvis Presley has gone back to America after two years in Germany in the army. He changed aeroplanes in Scotland! At 5.00 p.m. we had the Institution and Induction of the new rector of St Mary the Virgin, Betteshanger. The service was conducted by The Most Reverend and Right Honourable the Lord Archbishop of Canterbury.† Mr Harkness asked him to sign my Form of Service for me and he signed it 'Geoffrey Cantuar'. X. (Mr Harkness, not the Archbishop of Canterbury! Tee-hee.)

Tuesday, 8 March 1960

Happy Birthday me! I am twelve today. Ma, Pa and Ginny came on Sunday with my presents. They left a chocolate cake for me to have today. Auntie Hope sent me ten shillings. No games, good. Haircut, not good. My hair is now so short my ears really stick out. I look like a monkey. Mr Harkness says he likes the way I look. X.

Monday, 25 April 1960

Saturday was St George's Day and Shakespeare's birthday, of course. On Sunday I went to St Stephen's for evensong and benediction and Pa went to a dinner at

---

* Prince Andrew was born on 19 February 1960.
† Geoffrey Fisher (1887–1972), Archbishop of Canterbury, 1945–61.

the Garrick Club in honour of Sir Michael Redgrave.* They ate *Suprême de Volaille à la Kiev* and drank Château Magdelaine St Emilion 1953 and Pa got Sir Michael to sign his menu for me. Thanks, Pa! Today, after a Wimpy, I went with Foss to see *Follow That Girl*, the musical by Dorothy Reynolds and Julian Slade who wrote *Salad Days*. My kind of show!

Saturday, 30 April 1960

Summer term. Form V. My desk is in the second row by the window. My dormitory is Northbourne. The school play is going to be *As You Like It* and Mr Burton says that I am going to be either Jacques, Touchstone or Celia. In English, Mr Harkness is reading *My Family and Other Animals* by Gerald Durrell to us. He is wearing blue suede shoes. (Dark purple really.)

Friday, 6 May 1960

On Major Douch's TV we watched the wedding of Princess Margaret, the Queen's sister, to Antony Armstrong-Jones. He is a photographer and has his birthday on the day before mine!† Mr Burton has decided that I am going to play Celia in *As You Like It* and I have started to learn my lines.

Wednesday, 18 May 1960

Guess where I am? In Canterbury Hospital, gazing at a tank full of goldfish! On Monday I woke up with a horrible stomach ache. The doctor came and I was brought here in an ambulance with appendicitis. Yesterday I woke up with a bandage around my stomach feeling rather poorly. Pa came from London to see me and Miss Woodhouse [the school matron] has been to visit me too, bringing grapes. Pa brought me the *Beano*, the *Dandy*, the *Topper*, the *Beezer* and the *Stage*. Ma and Pa will take me back to school on Saturday. At least there'll be no more games for a while!‡

Sunday, 5 June 1960

Whit Sunday. V nice service, no anthems, but good hymns. Ten days to the dress rehearsal and Mr Burton has just told me that I should swap my part with

* Sir Michael Redgrave (1908–85), actor.
† Tony Armstrong-Jones, 1st Earl of Snowdon, was born on 7 March 1930.
‡ GB's recollection is that he invented the stomach ache to get out of games and, when in hospital after the operation, was shown his 'unswollen appendix' in a bottle and told by one of the nurses that there had been nothing wrong with him. Unfortunately, the diary offers no corroboration for this version of events.

Bremner. Bremner is going to play Celia and I am going to play Rosalind! I am going to get a lot of lessons off so that I can learn the part and have extra rehearsals with Bremner, Demery (Touchstone) and Strecker (Orlando).

Sunday, 12 June 1960

Stormy weather. Thunder. I hope it clears up because we are doing the play out of doors in the Dutch Garden. I know all my lines and the two costumes I have for Rosalind are very good indeed.

Saturday, 18 June 1960
Anniversary of the Battle of Waterloo, 1815

The Day, 1960. Met Ma and Pa after rehearsal and went out to lunch and came back for the performance at 2.45 p.m. The weather was perfect. It went extremely well.

Cutting from the Betteshanger Chronicle *pasted into the diary:*

> Brandreth's Rosalind was a delightful creation, appealing to the eye whether as young woman or young man, gay yet poised, fluent in speech as in action, managing everybody in the play and cheerfully sensing the possibility of managing the audience too! One knew that here was an enthusiastic natural actor delighting in his first big part. As Celia, Bremner made an excellent foil to Rosalind, easily acceptable as a girl when dressed in that most becoming costume and head-dress. He benefited very much from his rehearsing with Brandreth and their scenes together were among the best in the play.

There you are!

Sunday, 19 June 1960

Had a v good service with anthem, 'The Heavens Are Telling'. Then went to Broadstairs with parents. Picnic lunch and film in the p.m. *School for Scoundrels* with Ian Carmichael and Terry-Thomas. Excellent, especially Terry-Thomas.

Sunday, 3 July 1960

V good service, with christening during it. Good week with v good music lesson with Mr Reid. Best thing was my stall at yesterday's fête. I ran it with Webb. My idea was a game called 'Highwaymen'. We started work at 2.30 p.m. and got a nice lot of money in: £3 4s 5d!!! Bought books for Pa's birthday on the 11th. Must get him a card.

Wednesday, 13 July 1960

Did sports practice. Hurdles and racing starts. My present reached Pa safely. Letter arrived from him today:

> *Dearest Gyles,*
>
> *Just to thank you for your delightful card and very well chosen books. Nothing could have pleased me more. I gave Uncle Wilfrid lunch at the Garrick today. Among others, we saw the Leader of the Opposition, Mr Hugh Gaitskell. I am just about to meet Mummy for a meal before going to the new Royalty Theatre where Mummy has bought us stalls for the play there. It has been a lovely birthday. I'm afraid that for the next five years or so you'll always be at school on July 11th – but afterwards wherever you may be you must promise to come to London to have lunch with your old Pa – at the Garrick, of course. God bless you and thank you again for your gifts, card and splendid newsy letter.*

Friday, 5 August 1960

Roller-coaster week – in every sense! On Bank Holiday Monday went with Ginny to the Battersea Fun Fair. V good. On Tuesday saw *Oliver!* at the New Theatre. Excellent. V good setting and costumes. V good boys. On Wednesday, intended to see Laurence Olivier film of *Hamlet* (again!), but no seats so went instead to see film of *Pollyanna*. Hayley Mills is lovely. I think we can forget Juliet now!* On Thursday disaster. Car stolen during the night. Pa parked it in the street outside our flat as usual. In the morning it was gone. Really ghastly. Went with Pa to the police station. Friday (today) 1.00 p.m. dentist. Two fillings.

Monday, 8 August 1960

Had my hair cut. Did Launderette. Went to collect passports at Passport Office at Petty France, St James's. In the evening went round the streets looking for the car with Pa. No luck.

Thursday, 11 August 1960

All's well. AA have lent us a car! Up at 3.30 a.m. to get to Dover for departure at 10.45 a.m. for Dunkirk, then on to Bruges and Ghent and Düsseldorf.

* As a small boy, GB had seen Juliet Mills (b.1941) as Alice in a stage production of *Alice Through the Looking-Glass*. GB first saw her younger sister Hayley (b.1946) on screen in 1959 in *Tiger Bay*, the film that made her a child star. Initially the lead role in *Tiger Bay* was to have been played by a boy and, in 1958, GB was one of the boys considered for the part.

Later

In Bruges wonderful walk in flower market and supper at Le Cornet d'Or – *Sole Meunière* and then chocolate mousse. The best meal I have ever had!

Sunday, 14 August 1960

Staying with the Paices in Düsseldorf.* I have found a copy of *Lolita* by Vladimir Nabokov in my bedroom and I am reading it. It is about an old man who falls in love with a girl who is 12. I am 12. Interesting. 'Lolita, light of my life, fire of my loins. My sin, my soul. Lo-lee-ta: the tip of the tongue taking a trip of three steps down the palate to tap, at three, on the teeth. Lo Lee Ta.'!!!

Wednesday, 17 August 1960

We are in Bavaria in the village of Oberammergau and we have seen the famous Oberammergau Passion Play. It lasted seven hours. The benches were quite hard, but it did not matter because the play was marvellous and superb. The villagers of Oberammergau have been performing the play since 1634. They started doing it as part of a pact with God to stop the bubonic plague. It worked! Now they perform the play every ten years in a huge open-air theatre, the Passionspiel Theater. Everyone in the village takes part and members of the same family play the same roles, down the generations. The house we are staying in belongs to a family who have cousins who always play the part of Judas Iscariot.

Saturday, 20 August 1960

No rain today. Had a super walk with Pa in the afternoon. We descended the Wallbergbahn at Tegernsee with lots of slips and falls resulting in Pa having a twisted ankle. The car has also gone *kaput*, but it is being repaired so everything will be all right. After here we go to Innsbruck where, on Monday, I will take the six o'clock train to Paris for my holiday.†

* John Paice, GB's godfather, was stationed in Düsseldorf with the British Army on the Rhine.
† From 1955, when he was just seven, GB was sent every year on his own to spend part of his holiday in Switzerland or France, sometimes in a hostel for young people, usually with a family. Even at the age of seven, he travelled to and from his destination unaccompanied. In 1960, he stayed with a French couple in their apartment on Avenue Wagram, Paris XVII.

Tuesday, 13 September 1960

Yesterday I had a bad headache and went to bed with a temperature of 39.4. I sweated badly, soaked the sheets and blankets and ruined Madame's velvet bed cover. Up and better today and taking my plane back to London as planned. I bought my return ticket here last Tuesday. Everything has been good, especially *Le Bourgeois Gentilhomme* at the Théâtre Français and Gounod's *Faust* at the Opéra. Also good: the Louvre (went twice), the Bois de Boulogne (long walk), Notre-Dame (climbed on the roof with an English girl from Hull – I stood near the *flèche*, VERY high), the Aquarium, the Musée Grévin waxworks, the Emperor Napoleon's tomb at Les Invalides. At the Eiffel Tower I climbed on foot up to the second floor – that's all that could be done. At Prisunic I bought a black watch strap for 200 francs.

Thursday, 15 September 1960

Yesterday I had a day in bed recovering from my great illness in Paris. Ma gave me my favourite tea: Marmite and tomato sandwiches with chocolate Nesquik. I also had two Lyons chocolate cupcakes. As usual, I pulled away the silver foil without damaging a single one of the chocolate ridges! (Ma had a lemon cupcake.) Feeling much better today and took Ben to his first day at nursery school with Pa and Jen. Now I have to start packing all my books and toys and junk I have collected down the years into orange boxes. We are on the move! We are leaving our flat at 42 Kensington Mansions, Trebovir Road, London SW5 (FREemantle 5915) and moving to Baker Street. When I come back from school our new address will be 5H Portman Mansions, Chiltern Street, London W1 (WELbeck 1750). We will be on the third floor, with a lift! Here we are on the top floor, with 89 stairs!

Monday, 19 September 1960

Finished all my packing and tidying. My room is empty. Everything is in boxes – typewriter, books, records, gramophone, drums, toy theatre, puppet theatre, glove puppets, Pelham puppets, magic things, make-up box, hats, wigs, costumes, papers, scrapbooks, the lot. All done. Goodbye Kensington Mansions! Term tomorrow. 3.41 p.m. from Charing Cross. Tonight we are going as a treat to Ma's and my favourite film, *Pride and Prejudice* with Laurence Olivier and Greer Garson. (Favourite Shakespeare film: *Richard III*. Favourite comedy: *The Court Jester* with Danny Kaye. 'The pellet with the poison's in the vessel with the pestle, the chalice from the palace has the brew that is true!' Favourite cartoon film: *Pinocchio*.)

Friday, 23 September 1960

Tonight I passed my Royal School of Church Music Blue Badge test. I will get my chorister's badge with three other boys at mattins on Sunday 2 October. Mr Harkness is very pleased. X. This term I am going to start writing my new book, *The Life of William Shakespeare*. Preparing for the move to Baker Street, I am reading *The Hound of the Baskervilles* by Sir Arthur Conan Doyle. Excellent. First few days of term have been fine, except that there is a boy in my dorm called Bowden who is only six and cries himself to sleep every night. I am trying to cheer him up.

Saturday, 5 November 1960

Guy Fawkes Day. Lots of fun after free day spent building the bonfire. In the evening after tea we all got warmly clad and, armed with torches, bangers, Roman candles, etc., we paraded out to the games pitch where we watched the 'Burn the Bomb' Guy go on the fire. Then we had the firework display – Vesuvius erupted, the Sputniks flew and it was very jolly. At 8.00 p.m. we had a singsong and then to bed with hot soup. Eight mugfuls for me!! S – LCL.[*]

Sunday, 4 December 1960

Yesterday my copy of *Lady C.* arrived and was confiscated! In the morning when the post arrives it is all put out on the dresser in the front hall for everyone to collect and Mr Burton must have come along and seen the Penguin Books label on the parcel and thought 'Aha!' I had to go to his study/sitting room to see him. Mrs Burton was there. Mr Burton told me that he understood why I wanted the book because of all the fuss in the newspapers, but it is not a suitable book for boys to read! He is not going to tell Mr Stocks or my parents about it because I have done nothing wrong. The Advent calendar from Ma arrived in the same post and was NOT confiscated!

Today the weather is ghastly. We plodded down to church in pouring rain. After v good service, Mr Harkness and I brought 28 big hymn books back up to school in a howling gale. We both got soaked. (The smudge on the top of the page is a drop of water from my hair!!) Just as we reached the building, Mr

---

[*] In 1960 Penguin Books attempted to publish an unexpurgated paperback edition of D. H. Lawrence's 1928 novel, *Lady Chatterley's Lover*, and were prosecuted under the Obscene Publications Act, 1959. The trial at the Old Bailey in London ended on 2 November with a verdict of Not Guilty from the jury of three women and nine men. GB sent a postal order for four shillings to Penguin Books for a copy of the book.

Harkness slipped with twenty hymn books and I fell backwards down the steps nearly turning the umbrella I was holding inside out and dropped all my books. CALAMITY!!

This afternoon the choir is going to Challock to the parish church to sing carols, so Christmas is really at hand. Next Sunday we go to Northbourne church to sing and then during the week to two old ladies' societies and then on Thursday 15th we have our service here. My favourite carol is 'In dulci jubilo', arranged by Pearsall. I have sent Ma and Pa my list of ideas for Christmas presents, including two records: 1. *Follow That Girl!* 2. Mendelssohn's Overture to *A Midsummer Night's Dream*. I think Pa might be amused to have the record of Peter Sellers and Sophia Loren singing 'Goodness Gracious Me'. (Not Charlie Drake and 'Mr Custer'!) I think Ginny would like Cliff Richard or Connie Francis or Johnny Mathis.

Last night when I went upstairs two boys in my dorm were crying (Bowden and Lewington) so we chatted quite a while, till everybody was laughing, and then they were soon all off to sleep.

Sunday, 1 January 1961

Happy New Year!
 Important Events of 1960:

1. John Fitzgerald Kennedy is elected 35th President of the United States of America – the first Roman Catholic President.
2. Adolf Eichmann, the German Gestapo Chief, is captured in Argentina. He will be put on trial in Israel.
3. *Sputnik V*, the Russian spaceship, orbits the earth seventeen times with two live dogs on board.

Important Events of 1961:

1. The farthing is no longer legal tender – as of today. (I am keeping one as a lucky souvenir.)
2. I am taking my Common Entrance exam.
3. I am being confirmed – on 19th February by the Bishop of Dover. (Why not by the Archbishop of Canterbury? That's what we want to know!)

Friday, 13 January 1961

Friday the thirteenth – unlucky for some. Back to school after excellent Christmas holiday. Excellent Christmas theatre including:

1. At Streatham Hill Theatre, 'Jack Hylton and Emile Littler present The Laughter Pantomime *Cinderella*' – with Frankie Howerd as Buttons. Good fun.
2. *Emil and the Detectives* at the Mermaid Theatre (Stalls 15/-). Good story. Not a bad show.
3. At the Princes Theatre, Shaftesbury Avenue, Bridget D'Oyly Carte's season of Gilbert and Sullivan operas. We saw *The Mikado* and *The Yeoman of the Guard*. Excellent, especially John Reed who does the patter songs. (In my stocking I got a book of the lyrics of the Gilbert and Sullivan songs. I am learning some of them by heart. 'When you're lying awake with a dismal headache and your sleep is taboo'ed by anxiety . . .' etc.!)
4. At the Old Vic (Stalls 8/-) *A Midsummer Night's Dream*. Alec McCowen as Oberon, Gwen Watford as Titania, Judi Dench as Hermia, Tom Courtenay as Puck (my part!*), Douglas Campbell as Bottom (not nearly as good as Frankie Howerd†).
5. Best of all, *Romeo and Juliet* at the Old Vic, directed by Franco Zeffirelli, with John Stride and Judi Dench as R and J, Alec McCowen as Mercutio (my part, one day!) and Peggy Mount as the Nurse. All excellent. Just wonderful. My best Shakespeare to date.

I went to the British Drama League talk at the Criterion Theatre on 2 January and Judi Dench told a funny story. One night she came out onto the stage for the balcony scene and said her famous line, 'Romeo, Romeo, wherefore art thou Romeo?' and a woman in the fifth row of the stalls shouted out, 'Down there, ducks, underneath yer balcony!'

Sunday, 19 February 1961

Today I was confirmed by the Lord Bishop of Dover in St Augustine's Church, Northbourne, Kent. It was a good service and felt as special as I hoped it would. As he confirmed me, the Bishop rested his hand on my head. It was quite a heavy hand! Afterwards, he gave me *A Book of Prayers for Men and Boys* which he signed for me: 'Lewis Dover'. Tonight I shall use it for my evening prayers – page 15:

* In the late 1950s, when GB had hopes of becoming a professional child actor, his audition piece was a speech of Puck's.
† GB saw Frankie Howerd (1917–92) play Bottom at the Old Vic in 1957.

Forgive, I pray, whatever has been wrong this day.

Ask yourself: How have I behaved at home? How have I behaved at work? How have I behaved with my friends? How have I behaved alone?

Grant that there may be nothing in my life to hinder Thy purposes, but teach me to do Thy work and to esteem it a great thing to be Thy faithful servant; through Jesus Christ our Lord. Amen.

When you have got into bed, say:
Into thy hands, O Lord, I commend my spirit,
and go to sleep.

Monday, 20 February 1961

For my confirmation Grandpa and Auntie Edith sent me *Great Souls at Prayer*. I think it will be my best confirmation present. It has prayers by all sorts of people from St Augustine to Robert Louis Stevenson. So far I think the prayers by Christina Rossetti are best. Mr Burton has given me *A Diary of Private Prayer* which is really good too. It is like a diary and there is room on every left-hand page for you to write your own special prayers. I shall do so. I have already written something wise in the book: 'He who prays belongs to two worlds. He who prays not belongs to one.'

I am keeping my new prayer books with my Bible and torch etc. in my bedside locker along with the four books that I have been given by the old man in the boiler room. He used to work at Betteshanger Colliery and the books are National Coal Board notebooks, Ruled Feint, 400 pages in all. In each book in blue ink he has written out wise and interesting things – e.g. Sentiments of de la Bruyère, Thoughts of Marcus Aurelius Antonius, Juvenal's Tenth Satire, Geological Tables, poems by Thomas Hood, the History of Canterbury Cathedral, etc. I am learning some of the Maxims of de la Rochefoucauld by heart – e.g. 'He who lives without folly is not as wise as he imagines.' 'We easily excuse in our friends those faults that do not affect us.' 'The pleasure of loving is to love and we are much happier in the passion we feel than in that we excite.' These four books are the boiler man's most treasured possessions. He has spent YEARS writing them and now he has given them to ME! I will treasure them all my life.*

Sunday, 26 February 1961

Last week we had to prepare a speech for Mr Burton on a famous person. As I wanted to be rather different from the other boys I decided to make my speech

---

* GB has them on his desk to this day.

on Adam and Eve and also to make it rhyme – which I did. It was 4 minutes 45 seconds long. I got a star for it. My star total at the moment is 13. We had a history test on Friday on the Boer War, First World and Second World Wars and I got 25 out of 30. In art I have painted three pictures: 1. A television studio. 2. Inside a country house. 3. For a competition organised by Brooke Bond Tea something that could be called 'The Arrival'. I have painted a pianist on the concert platform arriving at his grand piano. There is at the moment going round the school *chicken pox* and two boys, Lewington and Boult, from my dorm have got it. Several others in the school have it and only 17 more will be able to get it as the rest of us (such as poor me!) have had it before. This afternoon we had a film, *Where No Vultures Fly*. TTS bath night (Ganges) then Nightingales with Mr Harkness. XX. (He always smells of cigarette smoke and Old Spice and I smell of it now. I am writing this at the bottom of my bed with my torch on. I am going to say my prayers now. Goodnight.)

Saturday, 15 April 1961

This week's news. Ma had her 47th birthday on 10 April. The trial of Adolf Eichmann began in Jerusalem on 11 April. The Soviet cosmonaut Yuri Gagarin became the first human being in space on 12 April. He orbited the earth for 1 hour 48 minutes in the spaceship *Vostok*. History is being made! And history is being made here too because this is the last day of our Easter holiday break at the Norfolk Lodge Hotel, Canford Cliffs, Bournemouth. It cost 8 guineas per person per week, but because I am just 13 I cost only two-thirds: £5 12s 0d. It has been quite fun because I have been working as a waiter at every meal (breakfast, lunch and supper) and tonight 'Uncle Charles' [the hotel's proprietor] gave a 'Gala Dinner in honour of Master Gyles Brandreth' to thank me for my efforts. The meal included *La Fondue, Potage de Poireau*, Dorset Duckling Cooked in Red Wine, Sauce Montmorency, Steamed Rice, Garden Peas, Bean Sprouts, *Glace Napolitaine, Crème*, plus Cheese Board. (Tea and Coffee served in the lounge 1/- extra.) All the guests signed the menu for me.

Sunday, 30 April 1961

This is my last term at Betteshanger! A new system has been devised for the servers and leaders, starting this term. There are only going to be three boys who have any authority in the school and they are Webster, Wallace and myself. We are in charge downstairs, in the corridors, in the changing rooms, etc. We are the only boys who can use the head boy's stairs, leading straight from the dorms down to outside Mr Stocks's study, and we are to be given a special tie – maroon with a silver stripe. (They haven't been bought yet.) A few boys object a little to me being made 2nd head boy as they were much senior last term and I wasn't even a probationer-server then, but all is well. I am allowed now to go to bed at last bed-bell which is at 8.30 p.m. (In the summer all bells are twenty minutes later than in winter.) My dorm is Brackenbury, where I was my first term, and there are ten boys: Bornoff (naughty), Tuckett ii (naughty), Burns (good), Anderson (naughty), Demery (good), Yeats ii (fair), Read (fair), Donald (fair) and Coackley (naughty) – and me. At first they were dreadful, but now they are behaving much better. The school play is going to be *Twelfth Night* and I am to be Feste the jester. Mr Harkness is pleased because I shall have two songs ('O mistress mine, where are you roaming?' and 'When that I was and a little tiny boy') and he will be accompanying me!

Saturday, 27 May 1961

President Kennedy has announced that the Americans are going to land a man on the moon before the end of the decade – and I am not doing any art until I have done my CEE [Common Entrance Exam]. I am doing extra Latin instead! I have learnt my lines for Feste and rehearsals are going well, but I have a lot of CEE work to do – history, science, geography, scripture, French, arithmetic, algebra, geometry, etc.! I am using the turquoise ink that Mr Harkness has given me. I like it. And I am practising my signature. I can't decide between 'G. D. Brandreth' and 'Gyles Brandreth'. (Should my stage name be 'Gyles Daubeney'?) I had tea with Mr Harkness in his room. I sat on the bed. T.*

Sunday, 18 June 1961

Twelfth Night has been and gone and I survived! I thought I wasn't going to. My voice was half gone. I was croaking badly, but the show must go on – and it did. Everyone seemed pleased and liked my black and white jester's costume with cap and bells. Common Entrance is tomorrow!!! There has been a bad train accident in France with 24 people killed.

Friday, 30 June 1961

Two important things to report. 1. My Common Entrance done and dusted, I am now definitely going to go to Bedales, which is what I hoped. This is good news. 2. Not such good news. Mr Warren [the games master] walked me round the gravel path this afternoon and asked me about Mr Harkness. He asked lots of

* Code for 'He touched me'.

questions. Lots. I said nothing. I said there was nothing to say. I think he believed me. (TTIHLM. IDM. INTBL.*)

Saturday, 15 July 1961

On Thursday we had the choir outing to Folkestone and, as on all my previous choir outings, it rained! We ate our packed lunches in the bus and then groups of boys set off, each with 8/6d in his pocket to find some form of entertainment. A lot went to see a film, *Sink the Bismarck*, which is showing with *When Comedy Was King* (with Charlie Chaplin & Co.) which Pa and I saw together and enjoyed. Others saw *VIP* with James Robertson Justice which is also meant to be extremely good and very funny. I, however, confined myself to looking around the shops and spent nothing! I shall go home with 30/- savings at the end of term.

Yesterday, *le quatorze Juillet*, in the dining room on the French table at lunch we had a really gay meal, with, besides our school fish, tomato salad, cheese, fruit and WINE. The wine was Spanish! *Vive la France!* (On the French table everyone has to speak French.)

Mr Harkness is leaving at the end of term.

Monday, 24 July 1961

My last Sports Day. I ran – as fast as I could. (Not fast enough!) I did the relay – and didn't drop the baton. It was a sunny day. Ma and Pa came with all the other parents. Mr Burton asked Ma to present the prizes which was an honour. Tonight I am going home. Goodbye Betteshanger. I will not miss Mr Warren, the gym, the changing rooms (they smell!), PT, cricket, etc. but I will miss Mr and Mrs Stocks, Mr and Mrs Burton, Major and Mrs Douch, Colonel Thomas, Miss Loewen, Willy Wardale [who ran the school tuck shop and general stores], the Art Room, the chapel, the boiler room, the ilex tree, the Dutch Garden, the church. Lots in fact. This is the end of an era! 'Come, come! No time for lamentation now, / Nor much more cause . . . Tomorrow to fresh woods, and pastures new!'†

---

* Code for 'The truth is he loves me. I don't mind. It's nice to be loved.'
† GB, at 13, was not a Milton scholar. These quotations from *Samson Agonistes* and *Lycidas* were favourite lines of his father's, who had played Manoa in a production of *Samson Agonistes* at Oxford in the late 1920s.

Pastures New

September 1961 – December 1962

Thursday, 14 September 1961

Launderette. Haircut. Finish packing trunk.

Lovely postcard from Mr Stocks: 'We shall be absolutely lost without you next term! So much music, and fun, and goodness! But may you enjoy Bedales,[*] and the lovely downs nearby, very much. Have an aim – really hard work. Hard workers are always happy.'

Monday, 18 September 1961

Apart from my stupid twisted foot and cracked ankle bone (almost better now – I can run down three stairs at a time as opposed to my usual five!), a good summer holiday (esp. Paris) with some good shows and films. My top ones (in order):

1. *The Parent Trap*. Film at Studio One with Hayley Mills. In the film Hayley plays twins! XX.[†]
2. *Dr Faustus* at the Old Vic with Michael Goodliffe as Mephistopheles – excellent. Michael Goodliffe's son Nicholas, who was in my class at the Lycée and my best friend (sort of), was there and sat just in front of us. We were in Row R, 8 and 9 (Stalls 7/-).
3. *La Vache et Le Prisonnier*. Lovely, moving film with the very funny Fernandel who has an amazing face and is my favourite French film actor. (I love Brigitte Bardot, of course, but that's a bit different. X.)
4. *L'Avare* at the Comédie Française. I also bought the text of the play. Harpagon is my kind of part!
5. *The Merchant of Venice* at the Old Vic (Gallery, 4/-). Robert Harris as Shylock, Barbara Leigh-Hunt as Portia.
6. *Bye Bye Birdie*, musical at Her Majesty's with Chita Rivera, Angela

---

[*] Independent, progressive coeducational boarding school, founded in 1893, located in the village of Steep, near Petersfield, close by the Hampshire Downs.
[†] These kisses were in GB's head. He did not meet Hayley Mills for several years.

Baddeley and Marty Wilde. Fun. (A24, front row of the balcony, my favourite place, 5/-).

7. *The Rehearsal,* play by Jean Anouilh at the Globe. V well done. Maggie Smith funny. (Went with Mr Harkness. Last time I'll see him I think. All over.)

Now going to Woolworths for assorted bits and pieces. Then going to the Zoo for the afternoon. Then end-of-holiday celebration supper with family at the Deerstalker [restaurant in Baker Street]. Tomorrow the Bedales term starts. I am on the 2.57 p.m. train from Waterloo to Petersfield. A new age dawns!

Sunday, 24 September 1961

I am writing this in the dorm at Lithcot, the house where I have my dorm. To get to it you have to walk across the Memorial Field from the main school buildings. I'm sharing with four other boys – Stephen Levinson, Hugh Wills, Andrew Flood, Gino Henry, all okay. Everything is okay here so far, except rugger. Routine as follows:

7.15   Getting-up bell

7.45   Everyone has to be up

7.55   Go for walk round the orchard, rain or shine

8.00   Breakfast

8.30   Bed-making

9.00   Morning school – five periods – with break halfway at 11.10. We have break in the Quad. Milk, tea, biscuits, bread. (I am making interesting bread sandwiches: two slices of white with a slice of brown as the filling. Delicious!)

1.00   Lunch

1.30   Siesta – my diary time.

2.15   Change for Games or Outdoor Work

2.45   Games or Outdoor Work. Ugh!

4.00   Tea. Aah!

4.35   Afternoon school – three periods

7.00   Supper

7.30   Evening Activities

8.15   Evening Assembly. This is in the Lupton Hall.* A piece of music,

---

* Built in 1911, the Lupton Hall, and the adjacent library (1920, with furniture by Ernest Gimson), are the school's architectural highlights and reflect its close association with the early-twentieth-century English Arts and Crafts movement

followed by a reading. Then the whole school files out – all 238 of us – with every single pupil shaking hands with every member of staff. All the staff line up by the door and we walk pass them, shaking hands with each one, and saying 'Goodnight Mr So-and-so, Goodnight Mrs So-and-So'. It is an old Bedales tradition.

Sunday night (tonight) instead of Assembly we have something called 'Jaw'. It's like Assembly, but longer! And there is a proper talk/sermon, the 'jaw' bit. Tonight it was about Dag Hammarskjoeld.[*] He had a one-word prayer, the most powerful prayer in the world: 'Yes!'

A lot of Bedalians, including staff, were at the Ban the Bomb demonstration with Canon Collins, Bertrand Russell, Vanessa Redgrave, etc.[†] Mr Gillingham (who teaches me Maths) is the leader of the Bedales CND brigade. He is also producing *The Mikado* with the local Gilbert and Sullivan Society! I am going on 2 December.

Sunday, 8 October 1961

11.27 a.m. I am writing this in the Library. I am up in the gallery in an oak-beamed alcove. This is my favourite place.

I have had quite an amusing letter from Mr Harkness. He says: 'I quite understand how you feel about the rugger. Seldom does the true artist enjoy that sort of thing. Unfortunately, in life we find we can't *always* be doing the things we like best, and then we just have to struggle like mad to make some sort of job of it. Otherwise it gets on top of us and makes us even more fed-up.'

Actually, this week even the rugger hasn't been too bad, helped by the fact that Mr Bennett (the Lithcot matron's husband) has got me some new boots. I take size 9 and the old ones were size 6!

On Wednesday and Saturday afternoon we are allowed to walk into Petersfield. It's about twenty minutes, all downhill. Last Saturday some of us went to see Peter Ustinov in *Romanoff and Juliet*. It was great fun – and very cheap. You can sit anywhere in the cinema (children under 14) for one shilling! Yesterday, I went on my own to see HM [Hayley Mills] in *Whistle Down the Wind*. Wonderful.

---

* Swedish Secretary General of the United Nations, killed in an aeroplane accident on 18 September 1961.

† The Campaign for Nuclear Disarmament, chaired by Canon Collins, organised a demonstration in Trafalgar Square on 17 September 1961. There were more than 15,000 demonstrators, 3,000 police and 850 arrests.

Last night, as on every Saturday, we had 'entertainments'. They were five art films, extremely interesting, especially the ones on medieval painting and on Reg Butler the sculptor.*

Ma has sent me some 'jeans' which will be useful for 'Outdoor Work', not my favourite.

Thursday, 19 October 1961

On Tuesday, as the weather wasn't too good, instead of 'Outdoor Work' I went on what is called 'Wet Run'. It was fairly short and only took about twenty minutes. Adam Reeves (who is in my block, wears Billy Bunter gig-lamps and plays the double bass) showed me round. (He's even more of a weed than I am!) Yesterday I went to Petersfield and bought some Bournville dark chocolate at Woolworths (Pa's favourite and mine) and had my hair cut very nicely (and very short) for 2/6d. Then I went and did some bell-ringing in Steep Church where one of the older boys began me on my first lessons – not very difficult. This afternoon two other boys and I tried to cut a branch off a rotting tree in 'Outdoor Work'. We were at it for nearly two hours and finally left before lessons without it being down!!

This weekend, on Saturday we will have an Old Bedalian giving a talk on the magazine *Which?* and on Sunday at 11.00 a.m. Sir Basil Henriques† is giving a talk on his work in the 'East End' which should be interesting. No more now as my biro has run out.

Sunday, 12 November 1961

Remembrance Sunday. Augustus John‡ has died. Apparently, whenever he met a small child he would pat it on the head in case it was one of his!

On Wednesday Mr Bellis, the gym master, asked me if I would touch-judge an 'away' match against St Edward's so I could not get down to see the film *Parent Trap* or buy my paper [the *Stage*]. The match wasn't at all bad though a little cold. I made myself look very sporty and cheered madly throughout. We did brilliantly the first half then they caught up and won.

Yesterday, however, I got to see Hayley Mills as the film was showing all week. The cinema was packed with a long queue outside. I managed to get in for the beginning and stayed to see it half through again.

---

* Reg Butler (1913–81), one of the best-known British sculptors of the 1950s.
† Sir Basil Henriques (1890–1961), Jewish philanthropist. He died six weeks after his visit to Bedales.
‡ Augustus John OM RA (1878–1961), British painter.

For 'entertainments' last night we had a man, C. E. Ellis, to talk about his sailing trips around the world showing slides. It was nothing to shout about.

Friday, 29 December 1961

Hes[ter] is not very well.* This evening she was on all fours in the front room, barking. Ma didn't know what to do, so retreated to the kitchen. Pa didn't know what to do, so I went with him next door to find our neighbour, Dr Schindler [a Freudian psychoanalyst]. Dr Schindler came over and tried to to talk to Hes, but she turned on him and tried to bite his ankle. He ran back to his flat terrified! Hes seemed a lot better after that and was quite normal by supper-time.

Saturday, 30 December 1961

My Bedales report came and Ma and Pa let me see it. Bits to note: Height at the end of term 5′ 4 ½″. Weight, 7 st 6 lb. Average age of form: 13.11. All good really, except for Outdoor Work. Look:

> Outdoor Work is obviously not his *métier*. Nevertheless there has been a marked lack of effort and concentration. His repartee is amusing and diverting but there is too much of it.(!!!)

That was David Sykes, the Outdoor Work master. He loves Outdoor Work. He is an Old Bedalian. Outdoor Work is at the heart of the Bedales 'ethos'. This is Mr Gill's form report:

> Giles has become a confident member of the school and has achieved good results, by and large, in his academic subjects. He is amusing and sociable. His contemporaries enjoy his eye-rolling melodramatic impressions; so do I. But it would be a pity if he shirked manual jobs on the estate. There is much of practical use to be learnt there and pleasure to be had.

Note spelling of 'Giles'!!

Tuesday, 16 January 1962

Tomorrow, back to school, 4.22 from Waterloo. Good Christmas holiday. I may be nearly 14, but I still like the crackling noise of my stocking (actually pillow case) at the end of the bed on Christmas Day! (Not a good Christmas for every-

---

* GB's sister suffered from mania and depression and received a variety of psychiatric treatments from pre-adolescence onwards. Eventually, time cured her – completely.

one, of course. Adolf Eichmann is going to be hanged. And in Peru thousands of people have died in a landslide.)

Good Christmas shows. We did not get to see *Beyond the Fringe* after all, but on Monday we saw *The Mousetrap* at the Ambassadors' (the longest-running play of any kind in the history of British theatre, now in its tenth year – X did it!*) and tonight we are going to *Old King Cole* at the Palladium with Charlie Drake ('Hello my darlings!'). *Wizard of Oz on Ice* was fun at Wembley and we had a box at the Royal Festival Hall for *The Nutcracker* on Boxing Day. (Well done Pa sorting that out!) But best of all was *Critics' Choice* at the Vaudeville with Ian Carmichael (very stylish and funny) and super-best Christopher Plummer and Eric Porter in *Becket* by Jean Anouilh at the Globe. Directed by Peter Hall. Really good.

I have renewed my membership of the Homosexual Law Reform Society and the Albany Trust and have received a letter from Antony Grey personally.† The magazine is very interesting and worthwhile.

Sunday, 21 January 1962

As last term my form is 3C. My form includes Gay Parsons, John Wicksteed, Alison Ball, Chris Irwin, Sian Bennett and a few others. The purpose of the form is to meet occasionally on Sunday afternoons at Mr Gill's house (form master) and generally chat. The complete block which consists of about 45 is divided into three sets, A, B and C. I am in A for everything, except Maths (B) and Science (C). The Science C set is for all the people who have to catch up with work they have missed. I have dropped the 'cello (despite my beautiful bowing wrist!), but I am striving away at the piano. My dorm is now on Boys' Flat in the main school where we have lights out at 9.30 p.m. For this term only I and about eight others have to get up at 7.30 a.m. to lay the breakfast tables. We lay two each and miss the morning walk. This morning I ordered the *Sunday Times* (7d) and it was delivered TO MY BED at 7.00 a.m. by a boy who goes out every Sunday and collects all the newspapers from Petersfield railway station at 5.30 a.m.! We get cooked breakfast (sort of) from Monday to Saturday, but Sunday breakfast is definitely my favourite: soft white rolls, butter, honey and Marmite. (Honey and Marmite together is a delicacy that I much recommend.)

---

* In the original diary, GB reveals the perpetrator.
† Antony Grey, pseudonym of Anthony Wright (b.1927), treasurer and later secretary of the Trust formed to campaign for the implementation of the reforms recommended in the 1957 Wolfenden Report, principally the repeal of legislation outlawing homosexual acts between consenting adults in private.

Sunday, 18 February 1962

The *Sunday Times* now comes with a 'colour supplement' each week. V good. James Hanratty has been found guilty of the murder of Michael Gregsten on the A6 at Deadman Hill and is to be hanged. Not good. I am against the death penalty. This morning we have a talk about Tristan da Cunha and the evacuation of all the islanders following last year's volcanic eruption. Should be interesting. This afternoon I am having tea with Rachel* in her sitting room at Steepcote. If I get there first I have to put on the fire! She is entering me for a national verse-speaking competition and we are going to decide what poems I will learn – something by Masefield definitely, and probably 'To a Snowflake' by Francis Thompson. For my 'free choice' I want to do 'Lord Lundy' by Hilaire Belloc. Rachel is a funny old thing, but I am in her good books at the moment and I want it to stay that way because she is important to me. (And I like her really.)

Sunday, 4 March 1962

Yesterday we caught the 9.30 train from Petersfield, changed at Haslemere and reached Waterloo at 11.00 a.m. We took the tube to St John's Wood (Bakerloo Line, no changing) and walked to the George Eliot School on Marlborough Hill where the competition was taking place. Rachel gave us good advice before we got there: 'Don't make audible rude comments about other people's speaking – you never know who you may be sitting next to!' It went well, but not perfectly. I came second in both my sections and got two certificates. For our choric effort ('The Pobble who has no toes had once as many as we' – E. Lear) we came third. We will do better next year!

   I stayed the night at 5H, going back on the 5.27 this evening. I am reading Pa's copy of *Famous Trials: Oscar Wilde*. It is gripping stuff:

Mr Carson: Do you drink champagne yourself?
Oscar Wilde: Yes. Iced champagne is a favourite drink of mine – strongly
   against my doctor's orders.
Mr Carson: Never mind your doctor's orders, sir.
Oscar Wilde: I never do.

Oscar Wilde's older son, Cyril, was a pupil at Bedales.† For my fourteenth

---

* Rachel Cary Field joined the staff in 1941 and spent her entire career teaching speech and drama at Bedales.
† Cyril Wilde, later Holland (1885–1915), was at Bedales at the time of his father's arrest in 1895. He was killed in action in France on 9 May 1915.

birthday (Thursday!) I am hoping to receive a special edition of *The Complete Works of Oscar Wilde.*

Sunday, 29 April 1962

Going today with Ma and Pa to Bristol to see Hester in her mental hospital. She is having electric shock treatment and may be in a straitjacket so it could all be a bit grim. Poor Hes!

Yesterday went to *Write Me a Murder* at the Lyric. James Villiers & Co. Great fun. Other holiday highlights: *The School for Scandal* at the Theatre Royal, Haymarket, with Ralph Richardson, Margaret Rutherford, John Neville, Daniel Massey, Anna Massey, directed by John Gielgud. Wonderful, wonderful. It's such a brilliant play and done *con brio.* Also at the Haymarket, Joyce Grenfell with her songs and monologues. Funny and good. Ma really loved it. Went with Pa to *Rear Window* at the Plaza – Hitchcock and v good. Also the film of *Julius Caesar* with Gielgud, Marlon Brando, James Mason at the Baker Street Classic – really, really good. And not forgetting my puppet show for brother Ben's fourth birthday party on Saturday 14th – a brilliant success! Of course!

Family pride. Cousin Beryl's work will be featured when the new Coventry Cathedral is consecrated next month.* I am not going to St Stephen's, Gloucester Road, any more. I am going round the corner to St Marylebone Parish Church just opposite Madame Tussaud's. It is famous as the church where Elizabeth Barrett of Wimpole Street and Robert Browning got married when they ran away together. I have been going to the 8.00 a.m. Communion service on Sundays. I miss St Stephen's. I liked being the boat boy and carrying the dry incense for the thurifer. I miss the smell of the incense. I miss kneeling on the hard floor in front of the altar and looking up at the altar when everyone else bowed their heads at the ringing of the Angelus. I miss Father Howard. (He showed me my first dead body – in a coffin in the room behind the vestry.) But we're in Baker Street now. Time for a change.

Wednesday, 2 May 1962

The newspapers are full of pictures of Peter Paice!† According to the *Daily Mail*: 'A red heron aircraft of the Queen's Flight, piloted by Prince Philip, took off from

---

* Beryl Dean MBE (1911–2001) was GB's father's first cousin and a leading ecclesiastical embroiderer.

† Son of John Paice, GB's godfather, Peter Paice, then 17, was Guardian or head boy at Gordonstoun.

Lossiemouth at 1.40 p.m. yesterday. A few minutes later it swooped over Gordonstoun, waggled its wings, then headed for the North Sea and Holland. This was Prince Philip's parting salute to his son, who yesterday became a Gordonstoun schoolboy.' Peter Paice is photographed in his shorts and pullover showing Prince Charles around the school. PP is grinning, but poor Prince Charles looks rather sad and serious. And his ears are even bigger than mine! (We will learn more in more detail from PP in due course, but I don't envy Prince Charles. There's lots of Outdoor Work and team games at Gordonstoun! And it's always raining in the Moray Firth. And though officially ragging isn't allowed, the new boys are always put under the cold shower fully clothed. Not the way we do things at Bedales!)

Also in today's *Daily Mail,* a wonderful conversation between Judy Garland and Noël Coward. Noël on the secret of success: 'In our profession the thing that counts is survival. Survival. It's comparatively easy, if you have talent, to be a success. But what is terribly difficult is to hold it, to maintain it over a period of years.' Judy talks about people who use her as a kind of court jester –

> *Noël*: Oh, yes, and after you've done your number, darling, without any rehearsal and no lighting and no rest, someone says, 'My, doesn't he look *old.*'
>
> *Judy (laughing)*: Or fat.
>
> *Noël*: But, of course, it is no use ever expecting society to understand about showbusiness or entertainers because they never do, do they?

Friday, 18 May 1962

I am feeling very pleased as I have been elected to take over from Christopher Irwin to be school council representative for my form, 13 votes to 1 – so, as you can expect, I am (he is) not on the best of terms with him (me)!*

The dress rehearsal for our Junior Play, *Elizabeth Refuses,* has gone wonderfully well. The play is only one episode from *Pride and Prejudice* so Mr Darcy doesn't appear, otherwise I like to think I would have been playing him!! As it is, I am playing Mr Collins and making him very oily and creepy and everyone seems to think it is very funny. Caroline Bullock as Lady Catherine de Burgh is also excellent.

Did I say that I have had my first cricket match? My side was fielding so I haven't had a go at batting yet. Something to look forward to!! (Cricket balls are very, very hard.)

---

* GB and Christopher Irwin maintained both their friendship and rivalry throughout their school years. Irwin went on to work for the BBC and became managing director of Guinness World Records in the 1990s.

Tuesday, 29 May 1962

I am going with Roslyn Payne. She is 17 and in Block VI. And very keen on sport and sailing! We went to the haystack beyond the orchard during activities and stayed so long (XX!) that we almost missed evening Assembly. We ran to the Lupton Hall and walked in at exactly 8.15 p.m. We were the very last two people to walk to our places and I didn't know it until afterwards but I had straw all over my back. There were lots of sniggers. I thought it was because we came in together and were last, but it was because of the straw!! None of the staff said anything so that's all right.

Wednesday, 30 May 1962

Went with RP up Butser Hill and lay right at the top on our backs on the grass looking up at the sky. It was sunny and the sky was blue and we watched the clouds. XX. STHTO.*

Tuesday, 12 June 1962

9.15 a.m. I am in the San! Suffering from German Measles, only quite mildly though, so I shall hope to be up and about in a few days and I am using this as an opportunity to catch up on my diary.

I have seen the school doctor who I have to say is no Dr Kildare! He is more Dr Gillespie (Ma's favourite), old and grumpy.† Nobody likes him very much. The girls say that he takes his time putting his stethoscope across their chests and is quite creepy!

We have had a heat-wave during the last week and I'm getting quite a tan (!!) and since the swimming pool was opened on Wednesday I have been in twice. The pool is three times the size of the one at Betteshanger and has twice as many boards, and also seems warmer (joke!).

On Saturday I went to an extremely interesting and good talk on the newly opened Chichester Festival Theatre (not far from here) and have a lot of fascinating literature and am hoping to be able to go and see some productions this term.

My little radio is invaluable and in constant use and I have now acquired an

---

* 'She took her top off.'

† The NBC TV series, 1961–6, was a Brandreth family favourite. Richard Chamberlain, the star, had a hit record in June 1962 with a song based on the *Dr Kildare* theme tune. GB's mother, who spent her adolescence in Toronto, was a particular admirer of the Canadian actor, Raymond Massey, who played Dr Gillespie.

earplug so can listen to the News and *Today* with Jack de Manio[*] in the a.m. without disturbing others.

I have just finished reading *How Green Was My Valley* by Richard Llewellyn (which I loved) on the advice of Mr Stocks. I will write to tell him.

RP [Roslyn Payne] – RIP.

Wednesday, 25 July 1962

I am on the 5.55 p.m. train from Chichester to London. I have just been to see *Uncle Vanya* by Anton Chekhov at the Chichester Festival Theatre. This is the finest play I have ever seen. It is funny and powerful and very moving. The in-the-round production by Laurence Olivier is wonderful. The set by Sean Kenny is modern, but you feel completely that you are in Russia. The acting is the best acting I have ever seen. It is full of stars. Dame Sybil Thorndike is the old nurse and her real husband, Lewis Casson, is the old man, Waffles. The girls are Joan Plowright and Joan Greenwood who are both excellent and very moving. (I love Joan Greenwood's husky voice!) Laurence Olivier, of course, is my hero and he is brilliant as Astrov, the doctor. He is amazing, let's face it. But let's face it also: Michael Redgrave as Uncle Vanya is even more amazing! He was completely and utterly real, heartbreaking and wonderful. This is the best acting in the world and I was there! Exciting.

Thursday, 16 August 1962

I am in Paris and staying with Madame Caumont. It is not a family this year, but a house that takes students. I am the youngest by quite a bit. They are mostly 16–20, but there is one older man (26?) who thinks he is the bees' knees and is making a play for all the girls. There are lots of girls! There is also a very pale, pasty English boy, 17, who shares my room and all he talks about is saving up enough money to go to a prostitute in Montmartre! I shall be going to Montmartre also – to the Sacré Cœur!

Friday, 17 August 1962

The French papers are full of Algeria and Marilyn Monroe.[†] I went to Café Mephisto and bought an airmail edition of *The Times*. Laurence Olivier is to be the director of the new National Theatre when it opens. Renate Lepp XX. She is German! (*Mein Deutsch ist schrecklich, aber . . .*)

---

[*] Jack de Manio (1914–88) presented the BBC Radio programme, *Today*, from the year of its inception, 1958, until 1972.

[†] France had recently given Algeria her independence and, on 5 August, Marilyn Monroe was found dead in her Hollywood bungalow.

Pastures New

Saturday, 25 August 1962

Renate has gone. She gave me a lovely little wooden box as a present. François, the 'older man', has been asked to leave. I am glad. I don't know why he was here in the first place. We are all doing French lessons. He is French! I didn't like him and he didn't like me. (Though I can see that he was quite amusing and clever.) I think he also really did behave quite badly towards some of the girls. I am taking Monika to the station this morning. She is going home. St Lazare. I will get my own ticket at the same time.

Sunday, 26 August 1962

Picnic! Brigitte. X.

Wednesday, 29 August 1962

Hugh says he went to a prostitute near the Moulin Rouge last night. I don't believe him. He had no details to offer, just tried to look pleased with himself. I shall not be sorry not to be sharing a room with him any more. Home next. St Lazare 9.55. Dieppe 13.05. Victoria 18.29.

Monday, 24 September 1962

B Dorm this term, the biggest and, in some ways, the best dorm on flat, with a very pleasant, 'arranged' group (i.e. we asked to be together) including my particular *copains*, Robert Booth and Julian Langinger (both Block VI). Robert has wonderful black boots that cover his ankles and he 'treats' them with a bone before polishing them to keep them supple. He is *très* elegant! Also in the dorm, Syphilis Erlich,* John Wicksteed, Chris Tomlinson (all in Block IV with me) and two new boys (from Block III). Anthony Gillingham (Maths, CND and G & S) is my form master. When not marching, he is producing *Princess Ida* with the local amateurs this term. I have been elected form representative for school council again. Also I'm in charge of 'Clocks' which consists of checking all the electric school clocks.

All the subject sets are much smaller (no more than five people) and my main teachers are as follows:

French: George Smith (fat, jolly, nice, good, smells of tobacco)
Latin: Cyril King (old – *very* old, he has been teaching at Bedales since 1923; also very dotty and eccentric and nice. When he wants you to start

* The nickname given to a boy called Michael Erlich. The Nobel prize-winner Paul Erlich (1854–1915) pioneered research into the disease of syphilis, but, in fact, was no relation of the young Bedalian.

work he says, 'Carry on with your labours!' At first I thought he was saying, 'Carry on with your neighbours!' – which led to some confusion. He is the brother of Cecil King, the head of the *Daily Mirror*, and is married to Mrs King, who is another Old Bedalian.)**

Maths: Anthony Gillingham (He has six children, five daughters and a son. I think he and Mrs Gillingham must be vegetarians! Mrs G is like a faded rag doll, but very nice, an OB herself and part of the Great Bedales Heritage. Her father was a Bedalian in 1896, taught here, etc. etc. She is also v CND.)

English: George Bird (new this term and v interesting. He is very tall and thin and walks with huge strides, leaning forwards with a stoop. They say he used to be a spy. He looks like one of the spies in *Mad* magazine and he speaks Russian.)

German: George Bird (as above)

History: Tim Slack (new this term and v v interesting. He is the new head-master. He is 34 and comes with the blessing of Kurt Hahn . . . I think we know what that means.*)

** Mrs King was head girl at Bedales when Mr King first met her, but they did not get married until afterwards. Staff–pupil relationships are not allowed. And, while we are on the subject, just for the record, you are 'going' with someone according to the Bedales tradition if you are seen walking across the Quad holding hands. You get into the Bedales Record Book, kept in the first bay of the Library on the left (right-hand side, bottom shelf), as an official 'couple' if you are going with someone for eight weeks or more. Holding hands and 'light kissing' are allowed. According to Mr Slater, the boys' housemaster, the unwritten rule is 'Nothing below the waist'. According to Miss Caiger-Smith, the girls' housemistress, the rule is 'Nothing below the neck'.

PS: Today I played my first rugger game of the season and *scored the only two tries of the game*!

Sunday, 7 October 1962

This year the Senior School Play is to be T. S. Eliot's *Murder in the Cathedral* (male cast of eight; the chorus will be all girls). I have auditioned for the part of Herald (32 lines) and if I get it, which I have a feeling I will, I will be the youngest person ever to get a speaking part in the S.S. Play.

* Tim Slack (b.1928) had been an assistant master at Salem School in Germany, run by Kurt Hahn (1886–1974), the founder of Gordonstoun.

Currently I am preparing sketches for the 'Merry Evening' entertainment planned for 20 October. I have three lined up: two black-out sketches and 'Three little boys from school are we', music from *The Mikado* with new words by GDB. I am also to play the triangle in a musical quiz devised by Anthony Gillingham! Last night for 'entertainment' Mr Slack gave a talk on Burma, dressed in their national costume. Not very informative, but amusing and spirited.

Yesterday I went into Petersfield to get my watch mended and Liz Overton (Block VI) gave me a lovely pencil drawing she has done of me. It's a head and shoulders portrait and she has made a little frame for it. She has given me beautiful long eyelashes. Perhaps I *have* beautiful long eyelashes?!

Wednesday, 24 October 1962

News:

1. I have got the part of the Herald in *Murder in the Cathedral*; only 32 lines but an unprecedented achievement in the history of Bedales school plays. Becket will be played by Ben Powell (18), First Knight Robert Booth (18), First Priest Julian Langinger (18).

2. The end of the world is nigh! President Kennedy says that Russia has missiles sites on Cuba and has imposed an arms blockade. There could be a nuclear war! Everyone here is taking it VERY seriously, especially Mr Gillingham and all the CND crowd. (At Bedales that's virtually everybody!) I say that it is because we have nuclear weapons that we are safe, but no one is listening to me! All over school people are working out where to hide in the event that the Bomb gets dropped – in cupboards, under the oak dining-room tables, etc. I think the stone dressing rooms under the Lupton Hall will be the safest place, but I am not very worried. We have a nuclear deterrent. It will deter!

3. Went to Pefe.* Haircut. Woolworths. Watch.

4. Sent epistle to Jackie.†

Sunday, 28 October 1962

1. The 'Cuban Missile Crisis' is over! Mr Krushchev has announced that the Russian missiles based in Cuba will be dismantled. President

---

* Bedales slang for Petersfield.
† Jackie Reid (b.1947) was in the year above GB and his first serious girlfriend. She and her sister, Susan, were the daughters of a member of staff, Jane Reid, the matron of one of the girls' houses, Foxcot.

Kennedy has promised that America will not invade Cuba and is lifting the blockade. CND are planning demonstrations. Bedalians will be on the march! (Not all of us, of course.)

2. Excellent play-reading yesterday. *An Inspector Calls* by J. B. Priestley.
3. Jackie XX.
4. Have just finished *Pacifique* by Jean Mortet (French novel) and *Where Angels Fear to Tread* by E. M. Forster. Both excellent.

Sunday, 11 November 1962

On Wednesday E. Martin Browne* came down. He has produced all T. S. Eliot's plays, including the first production of *Murder* at Canterbury, and is *the* expert. He gave a long and interesting talk to the cast, and Rachel has, I feel, taken a lot of tips from him.

I am taking tips from Mr Bird (English). I have shown him some of the poetry I have been writing. He thinks it is 'too personal' for publication! He has written me a long note. He says, interestingly:

> When the muse stirs in us, it almost always to begin with, produces thoughts on what touches us closely. The developing poetic talent soon transmutes the fruit of personal experience into an utterance of general appeal and significance. I think the novelist does much the same. *Passage to India*, for example, might well have been just another travel book – but it's far from that. *War and Peace* could have been *Mrs Dale's Diary* of the Napoleonic invasion of Russia, but it's far, far more and almost timeless in its general appeal (cf. the classical tragedies). *Anna Karenina* could have been a sordid, personal tale of adultery, a kind of *Room at the Top*, but Tolstoy transmutes its value and raises it far above this.
>
> All this is v heavy and it's not meant to be discouraging or disparaging. When I look back at my own stuff, I still can't raise it from the narrowly personal – that's because I'm not a poet. There are signs that you may soon do so, esp. in the non-strictly personal poems, 'I Am' and 'Why?'

I think this is good criticism. He has gone through each poem very carefully and doesn't pull his punches. This is what he says about the opening of 'Last Night':

---

* E. Martin Browne (1900–80) directed and taught modern and medieval religious drama, most notably Eliot's plays and the revived medieval York Cycle.

Same problem of weak and colourless words coming in strong places or places unsuitable to the rhythm. Here's an example of the sort of juggling that can sometimes straighten the trouble out eventually:

Version (a) 'Last night as awake I lay,

　　　　　　Thinking . . .' *Too artificial, almost comic*

Version (b) 'Last night as I lay sleepless . . .' *Too like 'Lost Chord'. Is 'Last night' perhaps the trouble?*

Version (c) 'Wakeful at night I thought of you

　　　　　　And heard a voice, like yours,

　　　　　　Ring out . . .' *Not bad, not bad at all! Let's keep it for a moment. But does her voice ring out like a Knightsbridge hostess?*

It's a good principle to aim at being one hundred per cent concrete and vivid all the time, making every word contribute towards this effect, though fifty per cent success is all that's necessary or possible. 'But you didn't give me any love' isn't vivid or concrete – 'didn't' and 'any' being particularly windy, gutless words. 'But me you gave no love at all', I suggest not as an alternative but as an example of an attempt to exclude the windy and the weak.

I like his suggestions and shall attempt to act accordingly.

Sunday, 30 December 1962

Best things of the year 1962 – top ten.

1. Wonderful report! Best ever. 'Excellent', 'impressive', 'full of intelligence'. Lo and behold, Outdoor Activities: 'At long last he has forsaken the role of jester during the afternoons. For the first time I really feel he has made some measurable contributions.'!! But there is a WARNING from Mr Gillingham which I note: 'He is a very cheerful and friendly boy, perhaps rather pleased with himself, but becoming more seriously concerned with and involved in the community around him. He has a delightful vitality and bonhomie which I hope will develop under reasonable control.'
2. Monk (with v good wig) and Herald (with v good 32 lines!) in *Murder in the Cathedral.*
3. Jackie. Eight weeks yesterday!
4. Mr Bird.
5. My typewriter.
6. My room. I have rearranged everything. It is looking v good, esp. the bookshelves. All books now arranged alphabetically by type.

7. Theatre. *Uncle Vanya* with Michael Redgrave and Laurence Olivier.

8. TV. *That Was The Week That Was*. New and v interesting and v controversial. Esp. gd, B. Levin arguing about everything with everybody!*

9. Music. Everybody else has bought 'Stranger on the Shore', 'Telstar' and 'Return to Sender' (Elvis). I haven't! My top records are *My Fair Lady*, *Edith Piaf* and *Noël Coward in Las Vegas*!

10. Quotations of the Year. (I am collecting quotations in a new book.) Top two: i) 'We're eyeball to eyeball and the other fellow just blinked.' Dean Rusk, American Secretary of State on the Cuban Missile Crisis. ii) 'Greater love hath no man that this, that he lay down his friends for his life.' Jeremy Thorpe MP on Mr Macmillan's Night of the Long Knives.†

* The journalist Bernard Levin (1928–2004) was featured in a topical debate each week in the BBC's ground-breaking Saturday-night satire show, launched in November 1962, hosted by David Frost and produced by Ned Sherrin.
† In July 1962, following by-election setbacks, Prime Minister Harold Macmillan sacked seven Cabinet colleagues, including the Chancellor of the Exchequer, Selwyn Lloyd.

Sex and Politics

January – December 1963

Wednesday, 2 January 1963

2.30 p.m., Aldwych Theatre, Upper Circle A6. *King Lear* with Paul Scofield as Lear and Alec McCowen as the Fool, directed by Peter Brook. Magnificent. Strong and swift and angry and then desperate and pitiful.

Saturday, 5 January 1963

To Launderette with Ben. (We took the basket-on-wheels with the sheets etc. and two pillow cases full of shirts etc.) To Harrods Sale with Pa, followed by tea and iced buns at ABC, Gloucester Road. (Ma in King's Road at Josephine's getting hair done.) Hester home for her birthday meal last night. All's well. Christmas thank-you letters – must do. Taking decorations down tomorrow – Twelfth Night. Jackie, 10 weeks.

Monday, 14 January 1963

JPR [Jackie] came to London yesterday and we ended it, after 78 days . . . we are going to be 'friends'. A sad and difficult afternoon, to be followed today by a silly and fun afternoon. I am taking Ben [now nearly five] to see *Noddy* on stage! We love Big Ears! Back to school tomorrow. Waterloo, 4.20 p.m.

Saturday, 19 January 1963

I shouldn't really be writing the diary as I have a 500-word article on *King Lear* to write, type and find photos for before this afternoon. The reason being that a 'wall magazine' (a weekly magazine by members of the school to be pinned up on a large board in the Quad) has been started by Mr Henschell – senior history – and I have been chosen editor of Drama, Television, Films, Religion and small Obituaries! This week I am writing on *Lear* and *That Was The Week* . . . Next week Olivier and 'television today', and so on. I have been able, because of this lark, to get off all snow-clearing – so seven free afternoons a week!

The Entertainment this evening is a play-reading – a dozen people sit (or stand) on stage and read a play to the rest of the school. We are doing Dylan Thomas's *Under Milk Wood*. I am Second Narrator.

Other news. 1) President de Gaulle ('*Français, Françaises* . . .') has told the world that he does not want Great Britain to join the Common Market and he does not like our decision to take Polaris missiles from the Americans. 2) Hugh Gaitskell has died. (Sister Ginny will be v sad about this. She has been nursing him at the Middlesex and says that he is/was a wonderful man.)*

Friday, 1 February 1963

I am in the San. I have the flu. I am not well, but I have not been idle. I have been writing articles, essays, letters! I wrote to Jackie and she came to see me last night. She wasn't allowed into the San, but she stood at the window and waved at me and blew kisses. I got a nice letter from her this morning. She says, 'I hope I will be able to pull my socks up and stop being such a bloody fool and let myself fall in love with you again soon.'!! She has added a funny PS:

> Must write something horrid about matron just in the hope that she reads it.
>
> Oh, sorry, I forgot you're mad about her. What's the new nurse like?

Sunday, 10 February 1963

Last night, jiving.

This afternoon, tea with Mr Gillingham.

In between, I'm a recovered and a busy boy: since leaving the San, two articles, two poems, letter to Mr Stocks, letter to Ma and Pa, school council meeting, play-reading (*Lord I Was Afraid* by Nigel Balchin), more *Pelleas and Melisande* rehearsals (our producer, Judith Earnshaw, 17, who adapted the play from Maeterlinck, is supposed to be the cleverest English student Bedales has ever known, but Peter Brook she ain't!) and extra work for Religious Knowledge! I am practically learning St Matthew, St Mark and all the Apostles off by heart!! AND – yes, here is the news – Jackie says she loves me. XX MT.† (Since you ask, on the mats in the storeroom in the gym!)

---

* GB's sister Virginia trained as a nurse at the Middlesex Hospital where the Leader of the Opposition died of Lupus disease on 18 January 1962, aged 56. On 14 February, he was succeeded as Leader of the Labour Party by Harold Wilson MP.

† MT = much touching.

Sex and Politics

Saturday, 23 February 1963

Sex is in the air – and sex at Bedales is in the newspapers!! Mr Slack (headmaster) has written to all parents (and prospective parents!) about the article that appeared in *Sixth Form Opinion* under the headline 'Is chastity outmoded?' It seems that some Bedalians – notably my friend, Judith Earnshaw, the producer of the ill-starred *Pelleas and Melisande* – think it is! The *SFO* article has been picked up by *The Times, Herald, Sketch, Mirror*, etc. and Mr Slack is 'extremely sorry for the distress which parents will have suffered'.

I am extremely sorry for the distress suffered by the cast of *P and M*! Judith Earnshaw is practically in a state of collapse and the fuss Mr Slack has made has only made matters worse. Reporters and photographers are now continually prowling round the school grounds, mostly trying to get hold of Judith, who has been forbidden all visitors and has her post checked before she sees it. Mr Slack tried to get hold of a *Daily Express* cameraman's camera after he had taken a photograph of him in a furious temper!

Friday, 8 March 1963

My 15th birthday. Phoned home. All's well. *P & M* dress rehearsal went okay. GE X.*

Wednesday, 13 March 1963

Pasted into the diary, a note from Jackie:

> Do you really hate me so much that you have to ignore me completely and glare at me as if all this is my fault and that I'm to blame for you being such a spineless two-faced bastard. Anyway, I love you. You've crushed my heart into little pieces, do you have to take so long scattering the bits? Since you haven't said anything I presume from your silence that the whole thing is at an end, though I can't bear leaving it in mid-air like this. Please confirm, in words *not* in writing. Please.

It's over. I have told her.

Also pasted into the diary, a review of Pelleas and Melisande *from the school 'wall magazine':*

> *This was an unfortunate play to choose for juniors, or indeed for any children, as only mature professionals could convey Maeterlinck's symbolism to its proper degree. The*

* Gail Engert, who turned 15 in April 1963, was in the same class as GB.

best performance in this extremely difficult play came from Gyles Brandreth, who for-
tunately played down his usually melodramatic style, and the only lapse in an otherwise
outstanding performance was when for one moment he became Gyles and not
Goloud, so losing his sincerity.

Saturday, 16 March 1963

Long letter from Jackie. Harsh and bitter. 'You cannot fall in love until you can learn to love someone more than yourself.' She is very angry with me, which I understand. She is nice about Gail! 'I genuinely hope that she will make you happy. I'm sure she will.' She wants me to go to supper at Foxcot [the girls' house where her mother was matron] and ends, 'Good luck with the speech comp. I'm sure you will do brilliantly without my ring.' Well, as it happens . . . I did come first.

Sunday, 17 March 1963

Went to supper at Foxcot. Jackie XXX. All on again.

Began rehearsals for *Our Town* by Thornton Wilder. I'm playing Mr Webb. My first part with an American accent. Should be fun.

Sunday, 24 March 1963

I love Jackie. Jackie loves me. I love Gail. Life is complicated! And I am not alone . . . A member of the Cabinet, Mr John Profumo MP, Secretary of State for War, has told the House of Commons that he has NOT been having a love affair with a model called Christine Keeler! Three Labour MPs (George Wigg, Richard Crossman and Barbara Castle) have suggested that Mr Profumo has been in a 'relationship' with the model (aged 21) who at the same time was in a relationship with the Russian naval attaché, one Captain Ivanov! Mr Profumo made a 'personal statement' to Parliament on Friday denying all the allegations: 'There was no impropriety whatever in my acquaintance with Miss Keeler and I have made the statement because of what was said yesterday in the House by three honourable members whose remarks were protected by privilege.'*

According to Mr Profumo, he and his wife (the actress Valerie Hobson) met Christine Keeler at Lord Astor's home, Cliveden in Berkshire, in July 1961. They were guests of Dr Stephen Ward, a London osteopath, who has a country cottage on the Cliveden estate. Also there were Miss Keeler and Eugene Ivanov of the

---

* John Profumo (1915–2006) threatened to sue for libel if the allegations were repeated outside the House of Commons. His statement on 22 March 1963 bought him just ten weeks of respite.

Russian embassy. The allegation is that Christine Keeler could have passed on state secrets (*nuclear* secrets) that she had learnt from Mr Profumo (British War Minister) to Captain Ivanov (Soviet spy) ... Mr Profumo denies EVERYTHING, but our Mr Bird (who was also a spy, remember) tells me that George Wigg MP has his nose (and his very large ears) very close to the ground and, whatever Mr Profumo says, something FISHY has been going on! Mr Henschell says I can write about it for *Roundabout* [the school wall magazine].

Wednesday, 27 March 1963

End of term. 8.22 a.m. train from Petersfield. Waterloo 10.50 a.m. Will the line survive Dr Beeching?* The chairman of British Railways wants to close 2,128 stations, including Ballater, the station the Queen uses when she goes to Balmoral. Is nothing sacred?

Last night, school film: *The Mouse That Roared* with Peter Sellers playing three different parts. Quite funny. Afterwards, Jackie XX but no T. 'I wish I could explain why I don't want to, but I can't because I don't even know myself. I promise you that next term, if you still love me, everything will be all right.'

Tuesday, 2 April 1963

Selfridges. Get gramophone mended. Buy shoes. Lunch with Pa at Fanum House in Leicester Square. Miss Webb† is making more mistakes than ever! Pa showed me the carbon copy of one of her letters and there were seventeen corrections!! 2.30 p.m. Interview with Mr Maxwell Park about the summer job at Thomas Cook headquarters in Berkeley Square. It is right by Gail's father's camera shop, Engert Photography. Writing to Gail tonight. She is very beautiful.

Sunday, 7 April 1963

I am at Foxcot for the weekend, staying with Jackie and her mother. Sue‡ is on holiday in Cornwall. Ups and downs, but all good really. Last night we went by train to Portsmouth and saw two wonderful films, *Room at the Top* and *A Taste of Honey*. (Both certificate X, but we got into the cinema without any questions being asked.) I say the films were wonderful, but that's the wrong word. They were very well made, but they were sad and painful. There is lots of sex in *Room*

---

* The line survived, but as a result of Dr Beeching's report, *The Reshaping of British Railways*, published on 27 March 1963, many others did not.
† GB's father's long-serving and loyal secretary.
‡ Sue Reid, Jackie's older sister (b.1944), later married to David (now Lord) Sainsbury.

at the Top (and, of course, I liked Donald Wolfit as the north country father), but I preferred *A Taste of Honey* and found it more real and more moving. Rita Tushingham and Murray Melvin really excellent.

Wednesday, 10 April 1963

Ma's 49th birthday. As a special treat, we went to the first night of *An Evening with Maurice Chevalier* at the Saville Theatre. He is 75 and superb! He gave us all the favourites – 'Thank Heaven for Little Girls', 'Louise', 'I'm Glad I'm Not Young Any More', etc. – and was a true star from start to finish. A night to remember.

Sunday, 14 April 1963

Easter Day. Went to St Stephen's, Gloucester Road, a.m., then letters in afternoon. Jackie has sent three letters this week. All lovely. She doesn't believe in God, but she says she is going to church today: 'I will pray not to anyone or anything, but for you and for us.' I have written to her and to Jane [her mother] and now I'm going to write to Gail. It's her birthday on Friday.

All good here. Pa is excited because Raymond Baxter is coming to the flat this week to film an interview with him for *Panorama*. It is all about the arrival in the UK of the American phenomenon of parking meters and because Pa is the nation's Number One motoring lawyer they are going to be talking to him.

I shall be following the Aldermaston March on the TV news in the hope of catching sight of Mr Gillingham other Bedalian CND supporters.*

Saturday, 11 May 1963

What a day! ITV have been here at school for the past two days filming for a programme on British education. The programme is every Wednesday at 6.45 p.m., called *Here and Now*. We are, of course, representing coeducation.

This morning, during lessons, there was an hour-long 'sit-down' in protest against a new regulation concerning the types of sandals that might be worn by boys. The boys want to wear any kind of sandal, but Mr Slack says we must wear sandals with heels and closed toes and we must always wear socks. During the protest, there was lots of chanting: 'Down with Slack!', 'Closed Sandals Mean Sweaty Feet!' and so on. The sit-down took place in the Quad and the head boy

---

* In the original Aldermaston March in the 1950s, demonstrators protesting against nuclear weapons walked for four days over the Easter weekend, from London to the Atomic Weapons Research Establishment near Aldermaston in Berkshire. From 1959, the route of the march was reversed and ended in Trafalgar Square.

and I were the only two boys in the entire school who did not take part. The ITV people lapped it up and I was asked why I didn't take part!! It's doubtful whether they'll use it as Mr Slack had a word with them.

Roundabout goes well. I have joined the editorial committee, writing for the Conservative Party. I'm going to have some difficulty this week!! Things are not going well for Mr Macmillan and people are calling Mr Wilson 'the British President Kennedy'. (Kennedy and Wilson are having their first meeting at the White House.) Others news: Sir Winston Churchill is retiring. He is 88 and has been an MP for sixty years.

Other news here: In Sports we have a House Competition where you score points for your House by getting standards. I got my first yesterday: 220 yards in 28 seconds. And Jackie will be 16 on Tuesday. I am giving her a love letter, a poem and some red roses.

Saturday, 18 May 1963

That was the (most hectic) week that was – and it's not over yet! On Monday I was drawn into the French Junior Play – due to be performed tonight – to look after props. But true to my spirit I have now taken charge of the whole evening and turned it into a 'Soirée Française'! I've organised a band – I'll conduct! – to play the Marseillaise. I'm introducing the programme and singing a song!

Also: *Our Town* rehearsals continue and I'm doing the props for that and typing out the programmes. I now have five standards: hurdles, 100 yds, 220 yds, 440 yds and 880 yds. I'm trying for the Mile on Monday. The ITV programme won't be on for some weeks – they're coming to do some more filming tomorrow. The music staff want me to give up the piano now – hurrah! It fits in with both their timetable and mine. On Wednesday went to tea with Mr Henschell (senior history, in charge of *Roundabout*) and we had an interesting discussion, contrasting the current situation in Birmingham, Alabama, with the 1958 Notting Hill race riots in London.*

Saturday, 25 May 1963

Tomorrow *The Admirable Crichton* (I am doing props and programmes); tonight *Our Town* (props, programmes, playing Mr Webb with wonderful make-up and costume); yesterday the South Hampshire Area Sports (I was roped in for some

---

* On 18 May 1963, President Kennedy ordered US Federal troops into the state of Alabama to quell the riots and violence that had followed protest marches against segregation.

unknown reason to do the 220 yds and the relay);** tomorrow Jackie and I mark our eight-month anniversary. *Boum! Quand notre cœur fait Boum, / Tout avec lui dit Boum, / Et c'est l'amour qui s'éveille!*

** In the 220 I came fourth in my heat and sixth in the final (out of eight!!). We didn't do too well in the relay. Someone trod on my foot with their spiked shoes. However, I looked very smart in my (borrowed) track suit!!

Saturday, 8 June 1963

Sports Day today, Parents' Day today, *Our Town* today in the Lupton Hall, but let's face it – what everyone is really interested in is THE PROFUMO CASE.

Mr Profumo resigned from the Government and from Parliament this week [on 5 June]. He confessed that he had lied to the Prime Minister and the House of Commons on 22 March. He *had* been having an affair with Christine Keeler, but he insisted there was no breach of security. Mr Macmillan is on holiday in Scotland and has written to Mr Profumo: 'This is a great tragedy for you, your family and your friends.' The Government is in chaos and the newspapers are going wild!

Friday, 28 June 1963

Celebrations last night: GDB and JPR = 9 months. Celebrations today: GDB has a letter published in *The Spectator* – my first appearance in print in the national press. It is a letter about the Profumo case:

> Sir – In beginning your leading article last week, 'It is not and never has been a moral crisis,' you automatically separate morals and politics into two very distinct water-tight compartments. Yet surely to every political problem there is also a moral aspect. Spying, racial discrimination and the Bomb, all have their moral as well as political sides; as does the Profumo affair . . . &c. &c. for three paragraphs.

Anyway, the point is: it's there (followed by a letter from Bertrand Russell OM!) and I'm very pleased.

Wednesday, 3 July 1963

Interesting letter from Pa about my *Spectator* letter:

> You can now tell your friends that you have broken into print in the journal made famous by your ancestor on the maternal side – i.e. Jos. Addison who

* Charles Trenet (1913–2001) was GB's favourite French singer and 'Boum!' and 'Que reste-il de nos amours?' his two favourite Trenet songs.

'made' the original *Spectator* by his essays. Will certainly be sending a copy to the Accrington Addisons.*

Also I hope that Jack Profumo will not connect you with *me* – because I forgot to tell you that I'm handling his speeding case at Brentwood tomorrow. You know I looked after Valerie, his wife, recently and then last week his secretary rang me for advice re his summons. On Friday last Profumo himself rang me and we talked for half an hour. I'd better not recite to you all he said. I had drafted a plea of Guilty – pleading 'stress' (it happened 24 hours after his resignation) but he insisted he would keep to his present line of *not* asking for sympathy in any direction. So we have cooked up something pretty non-committal. Anyway you may possibly read all about it tomorrow if the press finds room for it among the revelations of Mandy & Co.

It seems that Mandy Rice-Davies, 18 and also a 'model', is Christine Keeler's flatmate and was having an affair with the osteopath, Stephen Ward. Ward seems to have brought down the pack of cards by writing to the Prime Minister (and to Mr Wilson!) to tell them 'the truth' about Mr Profumo and Christine Keeler and Captain Ivanov. Now Dr Ward is being charged with 'living off immoral earnings'.

Other news – is there 'other news'? Yes! I am deep in revision and President Kennedy has been to West Berlin and declared: 'All free men, wherever they may live, are citizens of Berlin. *Ich bin ein Berliner!*'

Sunday, 21 July 1963

The exam results are all in and I have the highest average in the block (68 per cent) and have 'been to Mr Slack' for good exam results. Maths was the worst, though the top mark was only 61 per cent and my result, though not good (40 per cent) hasn't caused Mr Gillingham much anxiety. He says that if I carry on like this I am bound to end up at the Treasury! I was first in English, second in History and French (Jessica French came first – how apt! I did a careless *dictée*), and, amazingly, third in Latin – on a very stiff paper, or so it seemed to me.

A week ago today the annual Dramatic Society meeting took place. I was proposed as a new member and got in, *nem con*. The meeting was adjourned till yesterday. So last night I attended for the first time and we discussed next term's

---

* Sadly, there is no evidence of Joseph Addison being a forebear of GB's maternal grandfather, Colonel Lance Addison, who, when he retired from the Indian Army in 1947, went to live with his maiden sister in Accrington, Lancashire.

School Play. Gradually it was narrowed down to a Shakespeare, then a Shakespeare comedy, then to *Twelfth Night* and *A Midsummer Night's Dream.* Mr Gardiner – senior English – and I were the only ones for the *Dream* – my objection to *TN* being that it only has three speaking girls' parts. But a vote was taken (Rachel, who will be producing, abstained) and *Twelfth Night* it is! I shall try for Aguecheek and Feste – and pray not to be landed with something feeble like Valentine or Curio! I expect, if I get anything, it will be Feste again. Such is life!

Trouble (of a sort) in store for me on Tuesday. At School Council, each of the Committee reports will be read out. I am in charge of the Breakages Committee – deals with loss, damage etc. to school property. And so as to relieve the monotony of these reports I have composed mine in verse! It's a fairly pleasant rhyming piece, which contains *all* the facts, yet somehow one of the staff members on the Committee – George Smith, French – objects, because he feels it's a waste of words. I have the backing of the rest of the Committee – three pupils, one other staff – and so am going through with it. But George Smith is a member of the School Council and is, I am told, going to make a big fuss and dismiss me from the Committee for 'deliberate disobedience'. Should be fun!

Trouble (of a different sort) with Jackie. She has sent me a very moving and lovely seven-page later. It is full of beautiful things and I will treasure it always. She is full of love, but also very hurt and upset and angry – and she says: 'I suppose you are too young to be anchored to one person, a basic difference between us.' Yes. I have written her a long reply. I am also having tea in a minute with Pobs in the Block II hut.* (Should be fun!)

Later

It was!! It was amazing. Pobs is lovely. And very funny!

Monday, 29 July 1963

Today in Moscow, the Third Man, Kim Philby, became a Soviet citizen,† while today, in London, Gyles Brandreth became gainfully employed for the first time – upstairs in the railway reservations department at Thos. Cook & Son, Berkeley Street, Piccadilly. It is just a holiday job, of course, but I am to receive a weekly

---

* Jackie was a year older than GB and 'Pobs' (Jennifer Webber) was two years younger.
† Philby (1912–88) was a high-ranking officer in British Intelligence who was later revealed to be part of a Soviet spy ring that included Donald Maclean, Guy Burgess, Anthony Blunt and John Cairncross.

salary of £5 plus a London Allowance of 11/6d per week. My hours are 9.00 to 12.30 and 1.30 to 5.30. They are very friendly and the first day went well.

Thursday, 1 August 1963

Work is going well. I can get it all done by lunch-time! They let me off early yesterday so I went to the Academy Cinema in Oxford Street to see Olivier's *Hamlet* – again. I'm off early again today, but tonight will not be so rewarding. I am going for extra coaching to a Maths tutor (John Batty – good name) in Highgate, N6.

News. Stephen Ward, the osteopath in the Profumo case, has attempted to commit suicide. He is in hospital unconscious. The jury have found him guilty of living off immoral earnings, but sentencing has now been postponed.[*] The trial has been gripping stuff and the newspapers are having a field day. Ward admits to being 'a connoisseur of love-making', but denies that he was in it for the money. He says that the Establishment wants to destroy him because of his part in the Profumo affair. He did live with Christine Keeler, but didn't have an affair with her, he says. As well as Mr Profumo, it turns out that Christine Keeler was also having an affair with Peter Rachman, the slum landlord. When Christine Keeler moved out of Ward's flat, Mandy Rice-Davies moved in! Mandy R.-D. did have an affair with Ward – and with Mr Rachman, but not with Mr Profumo! During the trial when she was in the witness box and the prosecuting counsel told her that Lord Astor denied having an affair with her or even having met her, she answered, 'Well, he would, wouldn't he?' (Another one for my Dictionary of Quotations!)

And all this took place here in Marylebone, at addresses only a short walking distance from where I am writing this now!

Friday, 9 August 1963

Theatre. Last Saturday I went with Jackie to Chichester and we saw *Saint Joan* by Bernard Shaw with Joan Plowright as Joan and Robert Stephens as the Dauphin. It was magnificent – a wonderful production of a powerful play. Last night, I went to the first night of *The Ides of March* at the Theatre Royal, Haymarket, starring Sir John Gielgud. It was a disaster. We were up in the gallery (only 3/6d) and people near us BOOED! Yes, the greatest classical actor of his generation is playing Julius Caesar and the audience booed! In fact, Gielgud spoke very well. The problem was the way the play was put together – it's been adapted from a

---

[*] It never took place. Ward died on 3 August 1963, without recovering consciousness.

novel by Thornton Wilder and it's very wordy and not very interesting. It's all about the last days of Caesar, but they are wearing modern dress, with little togas on top. Ridiculous. But at least I can say: I was there!

News. There has been an amazing train robbery. The Glasgow to London mail train was ambushed and thieves have stolen more than £1 million in used banknotes. (This reminds me that I must get on with my stories about Cyril Playfair, the gentleman confidence trickster. So much to do – including extra Maths and extra German!)

Chinese supper out tonight. Sweet and sour pork and special fried rice. Yum yum.

Sunday, 15 September 1963

I spent this morning with Francis Arnold (and his mother). We drank vodka and orange juice (lots of it), so will what I am writing now make sense?

I like Ham.* Some people think he's obnoxious, but then we can't all be liked by everybody all the time. (There are some people at school who call me 'Supercilious Simpson'! When it's abbreviated to 'Super' I don't mind.) Ham's parents are divorced. His father is a children's author living in the US – Arnold Arnold. His mother is a world-famous photographer based in London – Eve Arnold. She is a small woman, looks just like Ham, with grey hair done up in a bun. She is very American, but nice. She told us stories about Marilyn Monroe, whom she knew well and photographed many times, and we discussed Martin Luther King and the march on Washington. She said that she believes that his speech will be regarded as one of the greatest speeches ever made – alongside Abraham Lincoln's Gettysburg address and Winston Churchill's wartime speeches.†

I was going to write my review of the summer holiday plays, but I haven't really got time now. In brief, the best were *Saint Joan* at Chichester with Joan Plowright and *Oh What A Lovely War* at Wyndham's produced by Joan Littlewood and quite perfect. It's about the Great War and very moving. One of the best things I have ever seen. Also good: *Man and Boy* by Terence Rattigan at the Queen's Theatre with Charles Boyer. I went on the first night (Upper Circle, 10/-) and it was good to 'collect' Monsieur Boyer who is a huge star and has much style and charm and authority. (That's what we want – style, charm

---

* Francis Arnold (b.1948) was an American boy in the same year as GB. He was nicknamed 'Ham' by fellow Bedalians because of his supposed physical resemblance to 'Ham the Astrochimp', the first hominid launched into outer space, in January 1961.
† This was Martin Luther King's 'I have a dream' address at the civil rights demonstration in Washington DC on 28 August 1963.

and authority!) Also good: *Six Characters in Search of an Author* (Pirandello) at the new May Fair Theatre and *Where Angels Fear to Tread* (E. M. Forster) at the St Martin's. At my favourite theatre (because it's the traditional home of *Peter Pan*, my favourite play not by Shakespeare) I saw the National Youth Theatre production of *Hamlet* which I much enjoyed, though the critics didn't. ('Young Ones Right Out of Their Depth', Milton Shulman, *Evening Standard*.)[*]

Last week I went back to Thos. Cook to see them all. They were pleased to see me, but all the reorganisation I had done was undone! I had improved all the systems in the department so that the whole week's work could be done in half the time – or less! They have changed everything back to the way it was before I arrived!!

I have written to Pobs.[†]

I am now going to clean the typewriter and put in a new ribbon. I like having the red and black ribbon, because the red is useful sometimes, but the problem is that if I type very fast (and even with one finger I do!) the bottom of the black letters appear in red! I am going to use an all-black ribbon in future.

Back to school on Tuesday. Block V. An important term awaits . . .

Wednesday, 2 October 1963

Wednesday is my best day this term because all I have on Wednesday morning is Latin in Period 5, so I can spend the rest of the morning here in the Library catching up on everything – work, letters, diary, reading. I read *The Times* every day, and *The Spectator*, *New Statesman* and *New Society* every week. I look at the cartoons in *Punch*. (They don't get *Theatre World* for the Library: I buy that for myself in Petersfield.) I am following the Party Conferences with interest. It can't be denied: Harold Wilson (also Pisces!)[‡] is doing rather well. He is promising a new Britain 'forged in the white heat of the scientific revolution'. Forged is the word!

---

[*] The NYT *Hamlet* featured many young actors whom GB later got to meet, including Simon Ward (as Hamlet), Giles Block, Neil Stacy, Hywel Bennett, Bill Kenwright and Helen Mirren. Alan Allkins, who played Guildenstern, eventually became GB's brother-in-law, marrying Virginia Brandreth in 1968.

[†] She replied: 'I knew from the beginning it wouldn't last more than a week or so at the most . . . You say that you are too self-loving. Well, that is no complaint as I believe that everyone is, however much they pretend not to be . . . In your letter you have made everything seem far more tragic than it can be. I am sure it can't be quite so complex. See you next term. Love, Pobs.'

[‡] Harold Wilson was born on 11 March 1916 (d.1995); Leader of the Labour Party, 1963–76; Prime Minister, 1964–70, 1974–6.

Sunday, 6 October 1963

The nation is gripped by Beatlemania – 'She loves you – yeah, yeah, yeah' etc. GDB is gripped by *Twelfth Night* fever. Today I learnt, as I had expected and hoped, that I had got Malvolio. The agony of waiting now over, the agony of waiting to get down to work on the play begins.

Monday, 7 October 1963

This morning I received the greatest shock of my career. Rachel's note commenting on my audition shocked me out of my complacency and made me realise how far I have to go. She said that I was 'not right or ready for Malvolio' at present. (I know that Peter Harris, Block VI, would have got the part if he hadn't been ill.) She complained that I played from the outside in and now it must be from the INSIDE OUT! No guying or funny business, 'but a real person, important (to himself), dignified, self-righteous, but not Gyles Brandreth'. She says that I have got into the trick of raising my right shoulder, which I must lose; that often I tend to make everything significant and lose the importance of simplicity; that I should start using my natural voice and stop putting on 'funny ones'. I can see that she is right, but I am lost as to how to begin. She spoke of her criticism being a compliment to my being good enough to take it; she also said that she admires my stage sense, enthusiasm and good humour, and my help with everyone at the auditions; so at least we're fighting the same battle, yet I am so afraid we may lose.

Tuesday, 8 October 1963

I have been so unhappy and worried over the prospect of playing Malvolio that I went to see Rachel at her place this afternoon. I am more than glad I did. She retracted nothing (though she was sorry if I had had a miserable day!) and added little, but gave me back some confidence. We talked about Malvolio, and my style, and she said that she was glad I was a little lost and that it would come in time, but it must come from within: Malvolio, a real person. She stressed that I should not play about with my voice and gave me a book (*Old Vic Prefaces* by Hugh Hunt) to look at. I am much relieved and shall bide by her ruling now: sincere, and naturally comic, no artificial guying, Malvolio from within. We start rehearsals tomorrow afternoon. I shall keep a daily record of progress.[*]

---

[*] He did. It runs to many thousands of words. The reader will be spared.

Thursday, 10 October 1963

The Prime Minister has resigned! The Conservative Party is in a state of confusion! High drama! Much excitement! (And I have Latin, German, Maths this morning, followed by Gym!)

Edith Piaf has died, aged 47.

Sunday, 13 October 1963

News of the week. Harold Macmillan is in hospital in London and announced his resignation from his bed of pain. The Conservative Party is in conference in Blackpool and running riot! Everybody wants to be the next leader! Rab Butler is the Deputy Prime Minister and the obvious choice,* but he made a poor speech at the conference and people seem to think that his moment has passed. (Seize your moment – that's the lesson!) Except Lord Hailsham (whom I rather fancy) seized his moment, but did it a bit too obviously! He announced from the conference platform that he is going to renounce his peerage and seek a by-election.† He has been photographed kissing babies, eating candyfloss and distributing badges marked Q for Quintin – not the behaviour we expect from a Tory statesman. Lord Home (pronounced Hume), the Foreign Secretary, is emerging as the unexpected favourite.‡ He may have a lisp and a face like a skull (think of an albino version of the Green Meekon in Dan Dare in the *Eagle*!), but he is a gentleman to his fingertips and I reckon could turn out to be our man.

Saturday, 19 October 1963

The 14th Earl of Home has kissed hands with Her Majesty on his appointment as Prime Minister. The Queen chose him on the advice of Mr Macmillan, having taken 'soundings' from Sir Winston Churchill and others. Unlike the Labour Party, the Conservative Party does not elect its leader. He 'emerges' after

---

* R. A. Butler (1902–82), MP for Saffron Walden, 1929–65; Home Secretary, Chancellor of the Exchequer and Foreign Secretary, but said to lack the 'killer instinct' necessary to take him to Number Ten.

† Quintin Hogg (1907–2001) was the son of the 1st Viscount Hailsham, Lord Chancellor under Stanley Baldwin. He was able to renounce his hereditary peerage under the 1963 Peerage Act. In 1970, he was given a life peerage and as Lord Hailsham of St Marylebone served as Lord Chancellor, 1970–74 and 1979–87.

‡ The 14th Earl of Home (1903–95) renounced his peerage and, as Sir Alec Douglas-Home, fought a by-election in November 1963, serving as Prime Minister until October 1964. He was Edward Heath's Foreign Secretary, 1970–74, and given a life peerage, as Lord Home of the Hirsel, in 1974.

consultation within the party. This may change. Some MPs are not at all happy with the present system and two of them (Iain Macleod and Enoch Powell) are refusing to serve in Lord Home's administration as a consequence.

The *Twelfth Night* rehearsals are gathering pace. We went through the 'Sir Topas' scene for first time today. *Pas mal* . . . I find Feste a little slow, but I expect he'll liven up in time. The serious characters are all a bit stodgy at the moment. I have yet to see Aguecheek and Fabian in action.

Friday, 25 October 1963

Friday night 'civics' in the Old Music School. We had a talk from Kurt Hahn, the founder of Gordonstoun. I am going to write it up for *Roundabout*. He looks a bit odd and gnome-like and he is not a great orator, but he was v interesting nonetheless. He talked about the danger we are in as a society. He believes that young people are being affected by a five-fold decay:

the decay of fitness
the decay of initiative and enterprise
the decay of care and skill
the decay of self-discipline
the decay of compassion

He said that the curriculum at Gordonstoun – and at Bedales – is designed to combat this decay. He paid a special tribute to The Chief.*

I asked several questions and told him I knew Peter Paice! He asked me if I knew Prince Charles!!

Sunday, 27 October 1963

JPR [Jackie]. Anniversary. One year. (With some ups and downs!)

Yesterday I read *A Man for All Seasons,* the play by Robert Bolt, and a perfect gem of a book by Denys Blakelock, *Advice to a Player*, a small collection of good advice in the form of letters to a 'Walter Plinge'. I mention this mainly because of his references to playing 'inside out' and the final paragraph which ends: 'You wouldn't like, in the middle of your best scene, to hear a voice call out, "But we don't believe you, dear boy!"' This is my task – pray God I succeed. Never must

---

* John Haden Badley (1865–1967), the founder of Bedales, known as 'The Chief', still lived in the school grounds, in a bungalow attached to the sanatorium.

I be able to fear the voice from the back of the Lupton Hall calling out: 'But we don't believe you, dear boy.'

Sunday, 3 November 1963

Half-term weekend. Yesterday morning I went with Ginny to Selfridges to buy wall-paper for Ma and Pa's room. In the afternoon I went to the Aldwych to see the controversial play by Rolf Hochhuth, *The Representative*. It's about Pope Pius XII and the Second World War and the degree to which he did or didn't collaborate with the Nazis. The play is not sympathetic to His Holiness! It was well done (wonderful set), but a bit heavy-going and sometimes difficult to follow. Today we are papering the bedroom. We are going to do it all by 7.00 p.m. and then have a Chinese supper out as our reward! Tomorrow the Beatles are appearing at the Royal Command Performance and I'm going back to school.

Sunday, 10 November 1963

I am writing this in D Dorm at the end of a very long weekend. It started on Friday night with a civics talk in the OMS [Old Music School] – Joan Quennell MP.[*] She is an OB [Old Bedalian] but doesn't seem like one. She is very awkward and stiff, in tweed suit and hat, and not an inspiring speaker. As just about the school's only active Conservative I did my best to support her and asked helpful questions, but it was not a great success. However, Jackie on Saturday was wonderful. XXXX. Also rehearsals v good – see separate diary. And I'm just in from watching the Royal Command Variety Performance on the goggle box in [the housemaster] John Slater's room. It was quite a party. We had chocolate milk and my favourite biscuits (the ones where each biscuit features a different sport) and the show was really good – Max Bygraves, Buddy Greco, Marlene Dietrich, Tommy Steele, Pinky and Perky (my favourites!), Steptoe & Son (very funny) and, of course, The Beatles! It has to be said they were very good and Paul McCartney and John Lennon were both very funny introducing the songs. Before they did 'Twist and Shout', John Lennon said, 'For this song I'm going to need your help. Will the people in the cheaper seats, please clap your hands. Everyone else, just rattle your jewellery.' The audience went wild.

Friday, 22 November 1963

Jane [Jackie's mother] has sent me a letter asking me to be supportive to Jackie this week while she is doing her O Level retakes. She was expected to pass them

---

[*] Joan Quennell (1923–2006), Conservative MP for Petersfield, 1960–74.

last time and it seems that I may be the reason she didn't! Jane doesn't like to interfere, and she knows I am preoccupied with the play, but she would be grateful if I could be kind to Jackie between now and next Friday. She doesn't want Jackie to know she has written to me. It is a very nice letter and must have been difficult to write and I will certainly do my best to be a loving and supportive friend this week. I'm doing O Level French on Thursday. *Roundabout* article this afternoon. Civics talk on Chad this evening.

Later

President Kennedy assassinated.

Saturday, 23 November 1963

The whole world is in a state of shock.

We were in the Old Music School listening to the talk on Chad when the news came though. Everyone was completely stunned. A lot of people cried. This morning a lot of the girls are wearing black arm-bands that they must have made overnight. We had a special Assembly and stood in silence. Except for a couple of girls who keep blubbing loudly in the Quad, everything everywhere is very quiet. Nobody knows what to say, except how terrible it is. Lessons as usual (Singing, French, Maths, Gym).

Later

I have just come back to the dorm from John Slater's room where we were allowed to stay up late to watch a special edition of *That Was The Week That Was*. It was very moving – none of the usual jokes, just a tribute to the President. Dame Sybil Thorndike did a lovely reading and Millicent Martin sang a quite amazing song about the assassination.[*] We were all in tears.

Sunday, 24 November 1963

'The Whole World Mourns Murdered President' is the headline right across the front page of my *Sunday Times*. I have never seen a headline going right across the page before. Under it is the first picture of the moment of the assassination, with President Kennedy bringing his arm up towards his face and two bodyguards behind him turning round to see where the shots are coming from. Under the picture is a second big headline, 'Duke of Edinburgh and the Premier going to US to join in last tributes':

* 'In the Summer of His Years' by Dave Lee and Herbert Kretzmer.

As plain men and women of all races across the world mourned the death of President Kennedy, Heads of State and Government everywhere yesterday prepared for the journey to Washington. In London it was announced that the Duke of Edinburgh will represent the Queen at the memorial service for the President in Washington tomorrow.

With the Duke will be the Prime Minister, Sir Alec Douglas-Home, Lady Douglas-Home and Mr Harold Wilson, Leader of the Opposition. They are leaving London this afternoon.

More than 1,000 miles from Washington in Dallas, Texas, a white-faced young man, by turn frightened and wildly defiant, was being charged with the murders of President Kennedy and a policeman who tried to detain him. The man, Lee Harvey Oswald, aged 24, declared his innocence through a ten-hour interrogation. But the District Commissioner said: 'I think we can prove he committed both murders.'

There is a picture of Lee Harvey Oswald facing a crowd of newsmen in Dallas after being charged. He looks very calm and very ordinary. 'Case against Oswald is a cinch' says the headline on page two, alongside pictures of Mr Krushchev signing the book of condolence at the US Embassy in Moscow and General Eisenhower, the last US President, talking with the new President, Lyndon Johnson, in Washington. Nine pages of the paper are given over to the assassination. There is a powerful leading article under the heading 'In the line of Heroes'. It ends:

A great comfort and inspiration is gone, but a great inspiration is still there all the same. The combination of judgement and courage was unique – the United States will no more find another Kennedy than Britain will find another Churchill or another Chatham. Yet it was a wonderful life, wonderfully lived; and the example of courage is never wasted.

I must speak to Mr Henschell about how we are going to cover all this in *Roundabout*.

Meanwhile, life goes on. I see that Prince Christian of Hanover, aged 44, brother of Queen Frederika of Greece, was married in Salzburg yesterday to Mireille Dutry, aged 17! And, according to the Court Circular, the Queen and the Duke of Edinburgh spent yesterday quietly at Luton Hoo, home of Sir Harold and Lady Zia Wernher, and Princess Margaret and Lord Snowdon were guests on a pheasant shoot at Hever Castle. The shoot was led by Lord Astor's son, Mr Gavin Astor.

Flying in to London Airport today: Mr Christopher Soames, Minister of Agriculture (from Rome). Flying in to London Airport tomorrow: Sir Charles Maclean, the Chief Scout (from New York); Mr Julian Amery, Minister of Aviation (from Paris). And flying off to *Twelfth Night* rehearsals, right now: Mr Gyles Brandreth, 15, Malvolio (from Dorm D).

Wednesday, 27 November 1963

French O Level today, 9.00–10.30 and 2.15–4.15. *Pas mal! On verra . . . Twelfth Night* – rehearsal at 4.45 p.m. and news of costumes: black tunic, balloon pants and tights, white collar and cuffs; then nightdress and cap; then yellow and black tunic and pants, and yellow stockings, of course, plus cross-gartering. It's going to be good. Make-up (by Mr Crocker, physics): smooth, hook nose. (I am supposed to be 49.) Wig: straight back and jet black. I like the look!

Went to see Mr Gillingham's *Iolanthe* in Pefe last night. Excellent, but audience subdued because of the assassination. Pictures in all the papers of little John Kennedy, who was three on the day of the funeral, saluting his father's coffin. Jack Rubinstein (Jack Ruby) has been charged with the murder of Lee Harvey Oswald. His lawyer says he should be given the Congressional Medal of Honour!

Wednesday, 11 December 1963

First night of *Twelfth Night*.

'An actor cannot be merely someone, somewhere, at some time or other. He must be I, here, today.' Constantin Stanislavsky.

Sunday, 15 December 1963

What a wonderful week! What a wonderful last night! What now? What next?

Before we move on, we are allowed a moment to feel happy about the way it went. The audiences were wonderful. They couldn't have been warmer or more generous – and Rachel kept me in check throughout! Ma and Pa came on Friday night and sat just behind Michael Hordern. Apparently he harrumphed loudly every time I came on, but he has played the part himself![*] Joanna [Hordern] was excellent as Olivia and Felicity [Sherwood] was lovely as Viola. (She is v beautiful.) I am doing my best to look nonchalant about my success!

Jackie. 58 weeks.

* Sir Michael Hordern (1911–95) was a noted Malvolio at the Old Vic. His only child, Joanna, was in the year above GB at Bedales.

Monday, 23 December 1963

This morning I went Christmas shopping and took brother Ben. This evening I am going to the Automobile Association Christmas Party with Pa at the Regent Palace Hotel. There will be Twiglets – my favourite. At the moment, I am sitting at my desk in my room at 5H, looking at a copy of the *Hampshire Telegraph* dated Thursday, December 19, 1963. The review is sensational – 'Gyles Brandreth – a superb performance . . . the changes in mood and tone . . . his understanding of the character was remarkable' etc., but the best bit is the headline. It is huge and stretches right across the top of the page:

MALVOLIO STOLE THE SHOW

This is not a headline designed to make me popular at school. Indeed, I fully appreciate that I am probably the only person in the world who will enjoy it – and I do. I shall now paste it into my scrapbook and never mention it again. (But I know it's there.)

Merry Christmas!

Lessons Learnt

January – December 1964

Wednesday, 1 January 1964

A lovely start to the new year: a lovely school report for last term. It is all good stuff – especially History and English and even PE and Outdoor Work! Rachel ends hers with this: 'Full marks for his modesty offstage and for a lovely perform-ance on stage.'!! Ruth Whiting (form teacher) says: 'Gyles appears to be a person of boundless energy and enthusiasm . . . I am sure that the effort he is making to show greater self-control is much appreciated by his contemporaries.'!!! John Slater (housemaster): 'He fills his life with a multitude of activities, and the stand-ard and enthusiasm which he brings to each is impressive. I hope there is no danger of his overcrowding his time – but I think he is aware of this problem.' He is. And is it a problem? As Mr Stocks tells us, 'Busy people are happy people. Hard work is the secret of a happy life.' I am seeing Mr Stocks tonight at the Betteshanger Old Boys' Reunion at the Royal Overseas League Club – cocktails, 6.00–8.00 p.m., 7/6d! Tomorrow I am going to the Aldwych to see Donald Sinden and the Royal Shakespeare Company in *The Comedy of Errors*, 10/6d. They say it's a very funny production.*

Sunday, 5 January 1964

No *That Was The Week That Was* on the gogglebox last night. The BBC have cancelled the series planned for the New Year because there is likely to be a gen-eral election in the coming months and the BBC must not be seen to be poking fun at politicians in the run-up to the election. And no *What's My Line?* on the box tonight. That's over for ever, apparently. The end of an era. I have watched it from the beginning.† Eamonn Andrews is an excellent host, but my favourites

---

* It was. Directed by Clifford Williams, with music by Guy Woolfenden, whose brother Peter would marry GB's sister Jennifer in 1969.

† This cannot be the case, as the quiz show started its life on BBC Television in 1951 when GB was three years old and the Brandreths did not acquire a television until the year of the Queen's coronation, 1953.

on the programme are: Gilbert Harding (we all love his bad temper), David Nixon (charming), Cyril Fletcher (funny) and Lady Isobel Barnett (a doctor and a lady with style and true class). Pa's favourite, of course, is Katie Boyle – because she is so beautiful and because he has represented her in court. We only watch the Eurovision Song Contest so Pa can say, 'There's my friend Katie!' We do not watch it for the songs. *Nul points.*[*]

Let's face it, ours is not a musical household. I have given up the piano. I have given up the 'cello. I hardly ever use my drum set now. (I still play the triangle rather well.) We don't listen to music on the wireless. I don't listen to it on my crystal set. Ma listens to *Music While You Work* when she is doing the ironing – and at Christmas she listens to her Bing Crosby LP over and over and OVER again – except that this year it was the Perry Como Christmas album and 'Dominique', the Singing Nun! We have not bought any of the Beatles' records, but it doesn't matter because everybody else has! The Beatles are selling a million records a week. I am still listening to *Salad Days* and on Saturday night we had a box at the Savoy for *The Pirates of Penzance* (G & S) and *Cox and Box* (music by Sir Arthur Sullivan, words by Maddison Morton and F. C. Burnand).

Our new TV favourite is *Steptoe and Son* by Galton and Simpson who wrote my all-time favourite, *Hancock's Half-Hour*. I do quite a good impersonation of Harold (Harry H. Corbett) and, when he takes his teeth out, Pa is excellent as Dad (Wilfrid Brambell).

Wednesday, 8 January 1964

Jackie has come to London for a few days. She is staying at her sister's flat and has tempted me over for lunch there with promises of chocolate mousse! Her last letter was quite grumpy. She does not like me typing my letters to her. She says typewritten letters are 'impersonal' – 'I'd far rather you wrote in your own handwriting even if it does irritate you.' She said she was feeling depressed, thinking back to last April when we were properly in love, but added that she'd love to see me 'and would like to go to anything you'd like to go to – it's up to you (like everything else) . . .' Well, I took her to *Gentle Jack*, the new play by Robert Bolt at the Queen's Theatre, Shaftesbury Avenue (Upper Circle, C17 & 18, 12/6d).

[*] Katie Boyle (Caterina Irene Elena Maria Imperiali Di Francavilla) (b.1926), multilingual model, actress, author and television personality, presented the Eurovision Song Contest on several occasions from 1960. GB's father represented her when she was charged with motoring offences – always successfully.

It's an odd play, mixing fantasy and reality, but worth seeing for the stars: Dame Edith Evans, who has such a presence and that amazing swooping voice, and Kenneth Williams,* who plays a kind of strange woodland sprite in the play. He isn't as funny as the audience hoped he would be, but he is very *compelling* – you keep watching him, wondering what's going to happen next – and I think Jackie enjoyed it. It was a good thing to go to because it gave us lots to talk about. Her real love is music. She was given a new gramophone for Christmas and six new records. Her mother can't really afford it. Jackie knows that. (I hope to be rich one day – not just so that I can have a chauffeur-driven car (I don't mind the Piccadilly Line!) but because it's clear that 'money worries' get people down. Jackie's mother is always thinking about money.)

As I write this it is midnight and I am at my desk in my room and Pa is sitting next door at the kitchen table, smoking his Olivier cigarettes, with a cup of tea going cold, and all around him all the bills set out in piles across the table. He is trying to work out which bills to pay first – starting with the school fees! Whenever the girls are on the telephone (all the time!) he stands right by them, tapping his watch, because he is thinking about the cost of every call. His favourite pictures are the two drawings in the hallway outside my room of the Victorian gentleman in his nightcap sitting in his counting house, spectacles on nose, quill pen in hand. In one picture he looks so happy; in the other he is utterly downcast: 'Balance on the right side – happiness', 'Balance on the wrong side – misery'.

Friday, 10 January 1964

Tonight I took Gail to *Poor Bitos* at the Duke of York's, St Martin's Lane (Stalls, 10/6d). It is Jean Anouilh's play about the French Revolution with Donald Pleasence being utterly superb as Robespierre. It was a good evening but I know that G doesn't really love me. She says she does to be kind. I think she thinks I'm funny and a bit different from other males so she doesn't want to let go, but she doesn't LOVE me! And perhaps I love her for the wrong reasons. I love her golden hair, beautiful and long (she can sit on it!), I love her nose, I love her freckles, I love her eyelashes. (I think she's Alice in Wonderland and she thinks I'm the Mad Hatter.)

Saturday, 18 January 1964

Plenty to report:

---

* Kenneth Williams (1926–88), already well-known for his appearances in *Hancock's Half-Hour*, *Round the Horne* and the *Carry On* films.

1) My French result has arrived. This is what it says: 'Brandreth, G. Ordinary Level. French. Grade 1.' I couldn't have done any better! Three girls and myself got 'ones'; the rest varied from '2' to '6', with about two failures. The only disadvantage of having got a 'one' is that I bet someone ten shillings I wouldn't, thinking I hadn't done terribly well.

2) I have been made editor of *Roundabout*, alongside Chris Irwin (my opposite number in the Socialist camp. He has curly hair and ideas that aren't quite straight either!) This is an unexpected but welcome development. We have just had our first meeting and we haven't just been talking. We have cleared the whole office and planned the design and contents of our first issue. We are considering making a complete break with the old and renaming the magazine 'The Phoenix'.

3) I am taking the Conservative message to the people – with new posters and articles on my Conservative Party board in the Quad. This week I am going to have to write an attack on Iain Macleod.* He has written a three-page article in *The Spectator* on the Conservative leadership 'crisis' and the way in which Sir Alec was chosen instead of Rab Butler. He denounces what he calls the 'magic circle' that chooses the leader and makes it clear he thinks the wrong man got the job. I shall deal with him!

4) Heard the excellent production of *Richard II* (with Gielgud, Richardson and Goodliffe) on the Third Programme last night – preceded by *Motoring and the Motorist* beforehand with Pa on the air (on road safety) and in good form. (Everyone else on the programme has to come with a prepared script to read out. It's a strict BBC rule, but Pa is allowed to speak off the cuff, from notes!)

Much more to report, but no time. Rushing as ever. I have two articles AND A PLAY TO WRITE! (The play is going to be rather good, I think! '*A Study in Sherlock*: a forgotten fragment from the memoirs of John H. Watson MD'.)

Saturday, 1 February 1964

Work report. Work goes well and is quite tolerable, especially English Lit where I'm doing Chaucer. (I have Mr Gardiner for English now and he reads Chaucer

---

* Macleod (1913–70) became editor of *The Spectator* on his resignation from the Government in October 1963. MP for Enfield West from 1950, he held a variety of ministerial offices and was briefly Chancellor of the Exchequer before his death, aged only 56, in 1970.

out loud as if he had been born in 1343! On the page, Chaucer is difficult. Out loud, he is totally comprehensible.) English Lang also good. I'm doing (as a special privilege) Congreve, touching on other late-Restoration comedy (incl. Garrick's adaptations of Shakespeare – of which the Library has an original copy, 1766). French is fine – I'm studying the plays of Anouilh. Maths and German are all right. Latin is frightful – my worst and *the* worst.

Speech Comp report. I am doing a bit of Milton, a W. H. Auden ('Look, Stranger') and possibly Lewis Carroll, 'The Walrus and the Carpenter'. For my Shakespeare solo, Rachel wants me to do a bit of Malvolio, but I have in mind part of Richard Gloucester's long soliloquy from *Henry VI Part 3* or, following a strange dream I had a few nights ago, a bit of *Hamlet* – 'O, that this too too solid flesh . . .' or 'Speak the speech, I pray you . . .' We shall see.

Political report. We Tories (sorry – Conservatives!) are fighting the good fight, taking every opportunity to swipe at the Socs – especially following the admirable speech of our great leader at Swansea last Monday. The speech, needless to say, is at present prominently displayed, with a large photo of Sir Alec, on our board!

Saturday, 8 February 1964

This is difficult to write about, but I will. On Thursday evening ST and I kissed. We were together until midnight. We were together again yesterday and all today. I know it is wrong because she is a member of staff (and she has a fiancé!) and we can get into a lot of trouble. I know it is stupid, but it's also wonderful and I don't want to stop and nor does she. She thinks I'm amazing and I think she is rather special too! It's madness, of course, but how old was Romeo? (I know. Juliet wasn't a member of staff!!!) Help.

Later

We talked and talked. And talked! She likes to hear me talking. She let me look at her. We touched. She let me touch her. It is wonderful – exciting and beautiful. She feels guilty about her fiancé. They are getting married in the summer.

Sunday, 9 February 1964

Disaster. This is very, very bad. How it got out I really do not know. Did I say something? I know inside my head I was boasting about it, but I did not say anything out loud. I honestly – *honestly* – don't think I did. Were we seen? Perhaps we were. Anyway, it is dreadful, ghastly, terrible. Truly terrible. I do not know what is going to happen now. After lunch I was told to go and report to John

Slater [housemaster]. I went up to his room. He was very friendly, asked me to sit down, and said, 'A little bird tells me something that's not quite right'!!!! Anyway, he said what he'd heard and asked me if it was true. I said straightaway that it was. I told him everything. Everything. He told me to go the Library and do some work. That's where I am now, writing this. I have got to go back to see him again at 5.45 p.m. He was very friendly. He said several novels had been written on this theme! He said if everyone was sensible everything would be all right, but I am quite frightened, to be honest.

Monday, 10 February 1964

It's all over. At 4.15 p.m. this afternoon I went to see TWS [Tim Slack, the headmaster]. I was very nervous. I was shaking. I have been thinking about nothing else. I have done no work today. Since seeing JS [John Slater] last night I have talked to no one. Anyway, I got to the headmaster's study at exactly 4.15. I pressed the bell, waited for the green light that says 'Enter' and went in. He was very friendly. He made me sit down in an armchair. His secretary brought me a cup of tea and biscuits! He pulled his chair around from behind his desk and sat leaning towards me with his elbows on his knees. He asked me what happened. He asked me to tell him everything. When did it start? Who started it? How far did we 'go'? Had I written to her? Had she written to me? I was in there for an hour, exactly.

When I had finished, he told me not to worry. He told me that I had done nothing wrong, but that it *was* wrong because I was only 15 and she is a member of staff. He said that he had spoken to her and that she is very sorry. He said that since it hadn't 'gone too far' the best thing now is to forget all about it. I must not see her privately or ever speak to her again, or write to her. She is leaving at the end of term anyway to get married. He said it is much worse for her than for me. He said he didn't think he would have to tell my parents and he was sure I had learnt a lesson. By the end of it all, we were laughing! He is very nice. He is wonderful actually. He made it very easy and I am very grateful. He isn't going to tell Hopalong[*] either. He says that I must not talk about it to anyone. And I won't. IT'S ALL OVER.

Just back in the dorm from having cocoa with John Slater. He told me about a play called *Young Woodley*. He says I should read it. It was banned when it was

---

[*] The nickname given to Ruth Stewart, one of the music staff and GB's form teacher that term. She was called Hopalong by the children because a limp gave her the walking gait of a cowboy.

written in the 1920s. He thinks that I would enjoy playing the hero.* I have to say that he (JS) and TWS have been wonderful. I am very, very relieved. I want to write to ST, but I am not going to. It will be difficult when I see her at hand-shaking and across the Quad, etc., but that's life. I have learnt my lesson – I hope!!

Saturday, 15 February 1964

V interesting 'Civics' last night on prisons and prison reform.

Today I have started something new to join the rest of my activities. I am taking a course in how to instruct children to take the National Bicycling Proficiency Tests. It means learning all the patter, the mechanics of a bike, details of the tests and suchlike. It gets me off a run and an Outdoor Work and enhances my reputation, so it seems worthwhile. Also it will help the children! I will begin teaching next term, starting with all the Block IIs and Block IIIs who have bikes.

School readings tonight. I am doing a bit from *Le Bourgeois Gentilhomme* with Mark Kidel (Orsino in *Twelfth Night*) and, needless to say, play 'Monsieur' – supercilious, self-important and all the rest.

This afternoon more casting for the Junior Play I am producing, *A Study in Sherlock*. Whoever I choose has to be approved by Rachel. Tomorrow I am start-ing a week of getting up at 6.30 a.m. to do an hour of Vergil revision before breakfast. Mocks begin on Thursday.

Saturday, 7 March 1964

Home for the weekend, by kind permission of TWS, headmaster and new best friend. (I may be the only boy in the school who likes him. He is very unpopular. Apparently, new heads always are. Anyway, I like him. Of course, I have my reasons!!)

Yesterday, School Cross-Country Run. Not a lot of fun, but I survived! And didn't come in last (quite). Today, on the train to London for the National Speech Comp, Rachel told me that she approves of my casting for *A Study in Sherlock*. This is Good News. I am very excited with my Sherlock Holmes. He is key to the whole thing, of course, and I feel that I have found a star in the making. He is 13 and quite small, but he can do it. He is called Simon Cadell,

---

* The play, by John Van Druten, is about a 17-year-old schoolboy who falls in love with his housemaster's young wife.

was at Dunhurst [the Bedales Junior School] and comes from a theatrical family.*

Tomorrow I shall be 16 years of age. Tonight I am going to Fielding's Music Hall at the Prince Charles Theatre in Leicester Square to see the great Sir Donald Wolfit perform 'The Death of Bill Sikes'.

Did I mention the Speech Comp? I didn't? Well . . . I came first.

Tuesday, 31 March 1964

> *Woodpeckers Guest House,*
> *in the middle of NOWHERE*
> *(actually, somewhere near Canterbury)*

If God had meant us to live in the countryside, he would have given us gumboots. The country is hell! It is cold! It is wet! It is muddy! There is NOTHING TO DO. We arrived here on Friday – Good Friday, except there was nothing good about it. We were supposed to stay here for three weeks, while Pa goes to the Royal London Homeopathic Hospital in Great Ormond Street to have his varicose veins removed, but I have persuaded Ma to let me go home today. I need to work and I need to be in London.

Thursday, 16 April 1964

Ma and Pa and brother Ben are still at Woodpeckers. Pa recovering well from his op. Last night I went to the Regent Palace Hotel in Piccadilly for dinner with Ginny and Mr Bagram, an Indian gentleman of riper years who was very nice but who I do not think Gin thinks suitable as a *beau*, let alone as a husband! Pa will be disappointed. (He wants his daughters to be married! He needs to get them off his hands! They are 25, 24 and 22 and getting long in the tooth! 'Who will rid me of these costly daughters?' This is Pa speaking, not me. 'In India they'd all be brides by now!')

And speaking of young brides, I went to the 1954 film of *Romeo and Juliet* at the Baker Street Classic last night. Okay, but not a classic. Unlike *Who's Afraid of Virginia Woolf?* by Edward Albee (with Uta Hagen and Arthur Hill) – so powerful.

I am taking Jackie to *Hedda Gabler* at the St Martin's on Monday. She wrote me a letter out of the blue. She said: 'I just want to make sure that you might

---

* Simon Cadell (1950–96), the son of John Cadell, a leading theatrical agent (whose clients included Donald Sinden), and Gillian Howell, actress and later head of the Guildhall School of Drama. Simon's paternal grandmother was the character actress Jean Cadell (1884–1967), whose films included *Pygmalion* and *Whisky Galore!*

speak to me again and that we can still talk naturally and always will be able to. After all, it's only three months and I'm not all that good at forgetting things! Anyway now that we've done our best and worst and parted etc. I didn't think there would be any harm in writing. You'll probably write back and tell me to go jump in a lake and forget everything – the which I will accept with grace, but I hope you don't.' I didn't. I am looking forward to seeing her.

Thursday, 23 April 1964

Letter just in from Jackie: 'It was lovely to see you on Monday. Thank you for a super evening. You know when you kissed me goodnight it was for the first time in three and a half months – 14 weeks 1 day! I shall probably have to wait even longer for the next one. And still I love you just as much now as I did then – stupid isn't it?'

Today is the 400th anniversary of the birth of William Shakespeare. (Of course, we can't be sure of that. We know he died on 23 April 1616. We know he was baptised on 26 April 1564. We can *surmise* that he was born on 23 April, St George's Day.) We began our Shakespeare celebrations yesterday at the Mermaid Theatre, Puddledock, not a mile from where Shakespeare's own theatre would have been. We went to the first night of *Macbeth*. I rather enjoyed it, but the critics did not – e.g. this morning's *Daily Mail*:

> It will be many years before we recover from the celebrations attendant on the 400th anniversary of Shakespeare's birthday. I suspect productions like *Macbeth* at the Mermaid might well put back the appreciation of the Bard some 400 years.

I, however, will be giving the production a reasonably good review.[*] The harshest notices are being reserved for Josephine Wilson (Mrs

---

[*] Seeing himself as the natural successor to Kenneth Tynan (the celebrated theatre critic who had become literary manager of the new National Theatre), GB wrote full reviews of most of the productions that he saw. In 1964, these included, at the Mermaid, *The Canker and the Rose* and *The Maid's Tragedy*; at the National Theatre at the Old Vic, *The Recruiting Officer* (with Olivier's memorable Captain Brazen), *Hobson's Choice* (with Michael Redgrave and Joan Plowright), *Andorra* by Max Frisch, *Play* by Samuel Beckett and *Philoctetes* by Sophocles; as well as *Othello*; at Chichester, *The Dutch Courtesan* and *The Royal Hunt of the Sun*; at the Théâtre National Populaire in Avignon, Corneille's *Nicomède*; at the Aldwych in London, the Royal Shakespeare Company production of *Endgame* with Patrick Magee; and at the Royal Court, *Inadmissible Evidence* by John Osborne with Nicol Williamson. GB's collection of theatre programmes, cuttings and reviews fills many books and boxes. The present reader is being spared.

Miles)* who plays Lady Macbeth and is somewhat plummy-voiced and non-stop screechy! But, as we know, in private life the poor woman has quite a lot to put up with. (Peter Harris told me that his sister – who works at the Mermaid – told him that Bernard Miles often sleeps with young actresses in his dressing room. Apparently, he can be 'at it' with a girl when the stage manager calls him for his next entrance. He just gets up, pulls up his britches and walks straight out onto the stage!)

We also splashed out on supper in the Mermaid Restaurant. I have kept the menu for my archive. I had Chef's Pâté (2/6d), *Omelette Fines Herbes* (8/6d) and Fresh Sliced Pineapple (4/-) – Pa had it with Kirsch (2/6d extra). There was no chocolate mousse!

I took Jackie to Wimpy's. We like Wimpy's. In her letter she says: 'I hope you enjoy *Othello* – but of course that's a foregone conclusion with his lordship in the title role!' She is right. He is my hero.

Saturday, 25 April 1964

Olivier is my hero. I have made a scrapbook that covers his whole career – every performance. But whatever he has done before cannot equal this. Last night I saw Olivier's Othello – the greatest performance of our age. Whatever Kean and Irving were to their time, Olivier is to ours. It was so daring, so brilliant, so beautiful, so true. It was utterly extraordinary. He looked the part, he walked the part, he *was* the man. *This* was Othello. There was power and glory and laughter – and then heart-breaking tragedy. This was bravura acting to catch your soul. Astonishing. And yes, ladies and gentlemen, I was there.

(And now, you may like to know, I am going to spend the day creating a pastiche mural on our lavatory wall and painting the back of the lavatory door! Back to school on Tuesday.)

Monday, 18 May 1964

News update:

- Letter from home. Ma is one degree under; Jen is lower than a snake's belly; Hes is having treatment; Gin is going to America; Ben is making a nuisance of himself. (Happily, all's well here!)
- Mods and Rockers are running amok on the beach at Margate. There is

* Josephine Wilson was married to the actor and director Bernard Miles (1907–91), the founder of the Mermaid. He was later knighted and, in 1979, became the second actor, after Laurence Olivier, to be given a life peerage.

'gang' fighting all along the south coast. Fortunately, so far Broadstairs has been spared!

- Mr Gillingham has lent me one of his pipes for Sherlock Holmes to use in the play. I have been obliged to make three alterations in the cast – including my Watson. Annoying, but there we are. On we go!

- This week's *Roundabout* is very insipid. David Kremer (fellow Tory) is editing, but it's washed out and uninspired.

- I am writing this badly because I've just returned from some beastly running practice since I'm entering the South-East Hants Sports next Tuesday, doing the 220. Am most *un*enthusiastic. Never mind, it puts me in the authorities' good books.

- A splendid portrait of Will [Shakespeare] now hangs above my bed in G Dorm, next to my own personal bedside light and elegant home-made bookshelf – two old drawers nailed together!

- O Levels loom. The horrors of Vergil and multiple factors!! German Oral on Friday.

Saturday, 30 May 1964

In the Lupton Hall at 7.40 p.m., the world premiere of *A Study in Sherlock*, dramatised and produced by GDB. It was a considerable success, I am proud and relieved to report, and will be repeated on Parents' Day. My Holmes [Simon Cadell] is quite excellent and will one day be the doyen of Bedales Drama.

Mr Nehru has died. Ma will be sad.*

Wednesday, 8 July 1964

O Levels over – excellent. (The O Levels weren't excellent – Latin was a nightmare. Excellent that they are over.)

Workshop: coffee table completed – excellent. (Well, Grinling Gibbons it ain't, but all my own work it is, and the mortise and tenon joinery is not bad, though I say so as shouldn't.)

* GB's mother was born in Rawalpindi in what was then British India in 1914. In the 1930s she went, first to Canada and then to England, to go to university, but in her heart she never left the Indian subcontinent and asked for her ashes to be scattered there. Jawaharlal Nehru (1889–1964) had been Prime Minister of India since the country's independence in 1947.

Lessons Learnt

At the Donkey Cart in Pefe (with tea and a toasted teacake!) I finished reading *Confessions of Felix Krull* – more than excellent. It's my story!*

Saturday, 18 July 1964

1. I have been made a Dorm Boss. 2. I have been made a Librarian. 3. I have been asked to join the *Chronicle* [the school magazine]. All good.

I saw Rachel about next term's school play. (She wants to do *The Physicists* by Friedrich Dürrenmatt and needs my support.) I had coffee in Pefe with Helen Levinson. (I like her.) I had supper at Foxcot with Jackie. (I love her.)

Senator Barry Goldwater of Arizona has been chosen by the Republican Party to stand against LBJ in the US presidential election. He can't win.† He can't possibly win. Why on earth did they choose him?

Thursday, 13 August 1964

We are in Dinard. Pa is going home tonight and I am staying here with Ma and Ben for ANOTHER TWELVE DAYS. I am staying very reluctantly and only after ghastly scenes. I want to be in London where I have WORK TO DO and PEOPLE TO SEE. I have been in France since 29 July and I am now more than ready to go home. Besides I have just endured TEN DAYS IN HELL. I have been to ten countries in ten days. It might sound like fun. It was anything but!

What happened was this: Ma, Pa and Ben stayed in Dinard, enjoying the sun and sand, while I was sent off in the family Ford Consul to spend ten days travelling around Europe with, as my driver and sole companion, my 18-year-old cousin from Canada. He is a very nice chap and all that, I'm sure, but HE AND I HAVE NOTHING IN COMMON – and he eats with his mouth open, making the most revolting noises. As we travelled I wanted to visit theatres and cathedrals and buy books. He wanted to find 'Hitler's bunker' ('Hitler's bunker'!!! In every one of the ten countries we visited!!!) and the ONLY THING he wanted to buy was picture postcards of big-busted beauties in bikinis sitting on beach balls! These cards he duly sent to his assorted girlfriends back in Canada.

The whole thing was a nightmare. On the first day we drove to Nantes and picked up a Dutch hitch-hiker called Jan who persuaded us to drive to the coast

---

* *Confessions of Felix Krull, Confidence Man: The Early Years* by Thomas Mann was published in 1954. The story remained unfinished because of Mann's death in 1955. The novel has been described as 'the tale of a morally flexible yet irresistible confidence trickster'.
† He didn't. On 3 November 1964, President Lyndon B. Johnson won comfortably, taking 61 per cent of the vote to Goldwater's 39 per cent.

to a bar in Pornic where he said we would find Jean-Paul Sartre because he is always there. He wasn't! The three of us slept sitting up in the car in a side street!! The next day we drove to Tours where – thank the Lord! – I found Jackie (as planned) and stayed (secretly) in her room. After that, for the next ten nights, we spent every night SLEEPING IN THE CAR. I slept on the back seat, but the seat wasn't long enough – so I had to sleep with my feet sticking out of the window. There is now a permanent ridge on the back of my ankles. Cousin Johnnie spent the nights in a sleeping bag beside the car looking at disgusting magazines and doing unspeakable things. He is obsessed. (In Marseilles he drove us round and round the red light district honking the horn trying to make the prostitutes come out of their flats to wave at him!!!)

The ten countries: 1. France. 2. Spain (we fled the country almost as soon as we arrived, thinking we were being pursued by the police – Cousin Johnnie STOLE a painting from a street market in Llansa, ran down the road with it, jumped into the car and off we went!) 3. Monaco. 4. Italy. 5. Switzerland. 6. Austria. 7. Germany. 8. Holland. 9. Belgium. 10. Luxembourg. *The driving never stopped* – but our conversation did. I came to HATE HIM SO MUCH that after a while I couldn't bear to sit next to him in the car. I sat directly behind him instead. We played a word-game for hours on end and I cheated – using a dictionary behind his back – so that I won every time. It drove him mad – but he was driving me mad! Literally.

I didn't spend any of my spending money. I saved it all, so that on Monday, in Paris, at Magasin Réunis, I was able to buy all the books I wanted: Baudelaire, Molière, Sartre, Cocteau – in each case, the complete works. That's something. And in the interests of total accuracy, there was one good day. On Saturday 1 August, near Aix-en-Provence, I visited Paul Desorgues [a former French teacher from Bedales] on his family farm and, after lunch, tasted the sweetest, juiciest, most perfect peach you can imagine. It was the taste of a lifetime. And in the evening in Avignon I went to see *Nicomède* at the Palais des Papes. (Johnnie went looking for Hitler's Bunker!)

Tuesday, 25 August 1964

I am going home. Hallelujah! I am on the SS *St Patrick* from St Malo, reaching Weymouth at 4.30 a.m. Pa has sent me £2 so that I can buy him some cigarettes. He knows what he wants: '25/- worth – 200 FILTER tips. They have DU MAURIER in the upper bar only. Du M for preference, otherwise STUYVESANT.' What happened to Olivier? (I can keep the change!)

Tuesday, 8 September 1964

O Level results: fail Latin and German. Not good. Retakes in November. Bristol Old Vic production of *Love's Labour's Lost* at the Old Vic. Very good. Near perfection. It may now be my favourite play.

Friday, 25 September 1964

The new term has started with a bang! A starting pistol in fact . . . The general election has been called. Nominations open on Monday. Polling day is set for Thursday 15 October. I am to be the Conservative candidate in the mock election at school. Chris Irwin for the Socialists. Liberal still to be confirmed. (I shall probably ignore the Liberal altogether!) It is going to be good – and a close-run thing. However, we can win!

I am going to see Mrs Gunning tomorrow [the local Conservative Party activist] to discuss what I can do for her in Steep village – put up posters, deliver leaflets, etc. I have all the campaign material I require. I shall start working on my speeches now! We are to have hustings in the Quad, debates organised by John [Slater, the housemaster], etc. DCK [David Kremer] will be my campaign manager. 'Prosperity for a Purpose – and a Power for Peace' – these are our themes. Onward!

Sunday, 11 October 1964

So far so good, but it isn't in the bag. According to today's *Observer*, 'Labour nose ahead on the last lap', 'Tories in mood of weariness'. Not so on the Brandreth campaign! We fight on and we fight to win! I think my Quad speeches have gone okay. There's been some heckling, but that's been fun. And Master Irwin's speeches have not been good – too full of boring detail and complicated arguments that nobody understands. I have been putting up posters everywhere – and changing them regularly to keep them fresh. I have also been writing new messages for the policy board every day – even managing to include some of the 'Wit and Wisdom of Sir Alec'!!! ('The 14th Mr Wilson' is still my favourite.)[*]

Other news: 'The Queen set foot in French Canada today, under the strongest guard ever thought necessary anywhere for a British sovereign in this century. She was greeted with freezing indifference by the citizens of Quebec.' And here,

---

[*] Harold Wilson, the Labour leader, had mocked Alec Douglas-Home for having been the 14th Earl of Home. Home responded: 'Well, Mr Wilson, when you come to think about it, is the 14th Mr Wilson.'

yours truly has been cast to play Newton in *The Physicists* – the part played on stage by Michael Hordern and on TV by Michael Goodliffe. Chris Irwin is Einstein; Peter Harris, Möbius.

Tuesday, 13 October 1964

I'm just in from supporting our candidate, Joan Quennell, at her public meeting in Steep Village Hall. It went quite well, but I don't think we can pretend that Miss Quennell MP is ever going to set the Thames alight. Her only claim to fame is that she is responsible for an amendment to the Rating and Valuation Act, 1962, affecting agricultural buildings cooperatively owned!!

We will win in the Petersfield constituency because this is rural Hampshire – but nationally I'm not so sure. 'Thirteen Tory wasted years' is a line that can be rebutted quite easily (in my opinion!) but 'Time for a change' is a more difficult nut to crack. On we go. I have my final batch of leaflets ready.

Thursday, 15 October 1964

We lost. The Bedales poll closed after supper and the results were announced at 8.40 p.m.:

> Labour 115
> Conservatives 98
> Liberals 72

I had only prepared a victory speech – so I gave it anyway!

Saturday, 17 October 1964

I am writing this in the first year sixth common room. I have made myself some toast (slightly burnt, as I like it), with butter and Marmite, and a mug of tea, and I am sitting on the (disgusting) sofa underneath the window studying the general election results in *The Times*. With just two seats still undeclared this is the picture:

> Labour 317
> Conservatives and Associates 302
> Liberals 8
> Non-Party (The Speaker) 1

At 48, Harold Wilson is the youngest Prime Minister of the century.

He is in by a whisker, but he is promising 'strong government' regardless of his tiny majority and has announced one hundred days of 'dynamic action'. He has begun to form his Cabinet. Mr George Brown,[*] the 'character' of the election campaign, gets a new post as Secretary of State and Minister for Economic Affairs. He will also act as Deputy Prime Minister. It has to be said, it's all looking good for Labour and we are looking pretty sad. Already there's 'The Question of Sir A. Home's Future' . . . According to *The Times*: 'The Conservative Party, historically, does not spare the feelings of leaders who have served their turn.'

Yes, time to move on. By seven o'clock last night I had removed ALL our posters and every other trace of the campaign. I'm now going to concentrate on the play and the *Chronicle*. I have joined the *Chronicle* committee and I have plans to change it COMPLETELY! It's not just in Moscow that change is afoot.[†]

I should add that the paper is full of news besides the election. 'Krushchev Associates Dismissed'. 'Chinese Explode Their First Atomic Bomb'. 'Americans Continue to Dominate Tokyo Olympics'. President de Gaulle is back in Paris after his four-week state visit to ten Latin American countries, the British Museum has a lantern lecture on English watercolours today, and Mr Cole Porter has died.

Barny[‡] has arrived with photographs he has taken of the campaign trail. I must go.

Sunday, 25 October 1964

I have had to cancel tea with Mr and Mrs Cox. They are the old couple that I am now visiting each week at Merries, their bungalow in the village. They are very nice people: he is timid and serves the tea; she is large, strong-willed and does most of the talking. (They are very much Mr and Mrs Jack Spratt.) I like them and they like me. I am supposed to do a bit of gardening for them first (Voluntary Work/Outdoor Work) but really we just have tea and he sits quietly while Mrs Cox tells me about the struggles of women in Victorian England! (I am also now regularly having tea and playing Scrabble with The Chief [Mr Badley, the school's

* George Brown (1914–85); Labour MP, 1945–70; Deputy Leader of the Labour Party, 1960–70; various ministerial offices, including Foreign Secretary, 1966–8; later Lord George-Brown.
† Nikita Krushchev, the Soviet leader, had been deposed in a Kremlin coup on 15 October 1964.
‡ Barny, or Barnabus, the nickname of David Kremer (b.1946) who was one of GB's closest friends at school and university. He was a keen photographer and went on to work as a television director and BBC executive with a particular interest in religious affairs.

founder], so that my first-hand knowledge of all things Victorian is considerable. The Chief, incidentally, wins every Scrabble game we play. He uses words that are obsolete, claiming that he is allowed to use them because they were current when he learnt them nearly one hundred years ago! His favourite word is 'jo' – a Scottish term for 'a sweetheart'. My favourite word is 'yex' = a hiccough.)

I've cancelled the Coxes because I am having lunch at Foxcot for Jane Reid's birthday. (Jackie, 2 years anniversary on Tuesday.) And then I have *Physicists* rehearsals. At half-term I shall be making my first visit to Nathan's, theatrical costumiers of Covent Garden, to see Miss Dolly and have my Isaac Newton wig fitted. I am also meeting up with Biddles the printers to discuss the printing of the *Chronicle*. I am now Business Manager and plan to change everything – look, layout, the lot. For a start, we are going to take advertising and if Biddles aren't biddable we shall look elsewhere!

Must dash. Toodle-pip.

Tuesday, 3 November 1964

I had lunch with Pa at the AA. I'm now on the train back to school reading about the Queen's Speech in the *Evening Standard*. 'Immediate moves to raise retire-ment pensions; sick, unemployment and widows' benefits; to abolish prescription charges and to restore rent controls are promised.' Also nationalisation of steel and other 'strong Socialist medicines for industry'. And the supersonic Anglo-French airliner Concord is to be scrapped. I shall get back to school in time to watch the US Election Day programme 'by satellite' with Richard Dimbleby & Co. on John [Slater]'s TV, but too late to catch *Compact* or *Here's Harry*. (NB: I never watch *Compact* or *Emergency – Ward 10*, but I do like Harry Worth.)

Sunday, 29 November 1964

I have a letter published in this week's *Spectator* – good. I have written countless letters to potential *Chronicle* advertisers – good. I have learnt my lines – good. I am up to speed with Latin revision – *bene*. (And important.) I have had a long walk and talk with Jackie. Not good!

Tuesday, 15 December 1964

The term has ended wonderfully well. The play was a great success. I survived an attack of cramp mid-performance! TWS [the headmaster] has asked me to be in charge of the celebrations for The Chief's 100th birthday – quite a compli-ment, given the Chief is 100 and I am 16! I had lunch at Foxcot on Sunday and Jackie and I are going to be friends. I had tea with The Chief yesterday. Today it's Gonda's tea after Library checking.* Last night was the school dance. I am with Pobs again!!! (Thank you, Pobs.)

Thursday, 31 December 1964

The post has brought a letter from Jackie (typed!) and my school report.
   Jackie:

> Here's to next year – let's hope it will be a happy one. Not that '64 has not been happy. On the contrary – granted, it has contained some of the worst moments and hours of my life but I think it has been the happiest year that I can remember; and most thanks to you, happiness and unhappiness alike. This year all my dreams of the beginning of the year came true (proof in my diary); it is just a pity they had to be shattered again at the end. But as you say – such is life.

And the school report. First, John Slater, housemaster:

> Gyles has accepted the responsibility of being a dorm-boss with unruffled good sense. He has already shown himself aware, in a kind and perceptive manner, of other people's problems. He also has authority without being authoritarian.

Now, Rachel Cary Field, speech and drama:

> I admire enormously his energy, enthusiasm, savoir faire and diligence. His heroism when suffering cramp was magnificent. What I think he finds difficult is getting away from himself in a part. He needs to *observe others* more. He has much technical skill but is a little afraid, I believe, of the heart underneath . . .

Next, form mistress, Ruth Stewart:

> Gyles's zest for life and its various experiences is immensely refreshing and this does not prevent him from being genuinely interested in other people although I think he can be too carried away by the volition of his own activity to really understand what other people's doubts and difficulties are . . . I find this difficult to say and a little puzzling as he could not be a more friendly, cooperative member of the form.

---

* Gonda Stamford had been the school's librarian since 1958. A pupil at the school in the 1920s, she was one of GB's favourites among the staff and especially helpful to him with the arrangements for the school's founder's centenary celebrations.

Finally, T. W. Slack, headmaster:

> A very active and successful term in many directions as usual. But the reports on his approach to his part in the play and from his form teacher are most perceptive. I think he is still being carried away by his own cleverness to an extent where he does not consider enough its effect on others who may be more deeply sensitive.

What do you make of that?

Triumph and Exhaustion

January – December 1965

I had tea today with Mr Badley. We had lemon sponge cake with butter icing and talked about Winston Churchill and Oscar Wilde. The Chief said that Churchill [who had died on 24 January, aged 90] was the greatest Englishman of our time. 'He possessed the cardinal virtue,' said Mr Badley, 'courage.' According to the Chief, Churchill's speeches during the Second World War were much more than brilliant pieces of well-crafted oratory: 'They were expressions of courage that got into the national bloodstream and gave us courage too.'

I asked him who were the greatest speakers he had heard in his long lifetime – the Chief was born ten years before Churchill! He said Sir Winston, David Lloyd George and the Chief's friend, Rabindranath Tagore.* I said that Bernard Shaw described Oscar Wilde as 'the greatest talker of his time – perhaps of all time.' The Chief said that Shaw was right – but that Wilde was a conversationalist, not an orator. He also told me that much of Oscar's famous 'wit' wasn't spontaneous. It was worked on, rehearsed and studied. He recalled staying at a house-party in Cambridge with Oscar and travelling back with him to London by train. Assorted fellow guests came to the station to see them on their way. At the moment the train was due to pull out, Wilde, standing at the carriage window, delivered a wonderful farewell quip, then the guard blew the whistle and waved his green flag, the admirers on the platform cheered, Oscar sank back into his seat and the train moved off. Unfortunately, it only moved a yard or two before juddering to a halt. The group on the platform gathered again outside the compartment occupied by Oscar and Mr Badley. Oscar hid behind his newspaper and hissed at the Chief, 'You talk to them now. They've had my parting shot. I only prepared one.'

---

* The Indian philosopher and poet (1861–1941) wrote one of his most memorable poems, 'Speak to Me of Him', following his visit to Bedales in 1920.

Saturday, 30 January 1965

I went to watch the Churchill funeral at HEG's house.* There were a dozen of us and we sat on the floor in their small sitting room, perched on the arms of the sofa etc. I felt bad for HEG and Mrs Gardiner because people were fidgeting and chattering and the Gardiners wanted to concentrate on the service. HEG became quite snappy: 'Be quiet. This man saved your country. If you don't want to watch, you can leave.' No one left. It was moving to see how moved the Gardiners were.

And it was moving to watch the ceremony. The pageantry was impressive and the commentary by Richard Dimbleby was just right. (He is so good at it: he has a wonderfully rich voice and his tone and timing are always spot on.)†
It was a state funeral – the only one given to a statesman this century. The great man's coffin lay 'in state' in Westminster Hall for three days while 300,000 people (including Pa) filed past. The funeral was held at St Paul's Cathedral, with the Queen and all the royal family and Harold Wilson and the prime ministers and presidents and representatives of more than one hundred and ten nations in attendance. We watched from ten to twelve, until the nineteen-gun salute and the RAF fly-past when Churchill's body was taken to Tower Hill and piped aboard a launch to go up the Thames to its final resting place in the graveyard at Bladon, near Blenheim. It was a morning spent watching history happen and, thanks to TV, it was seen 'as it happened' all over the world.

Sunday, 21 February 1965

Today is the 100th birthday of John Haden Badley, the founder of Bedales. He is in good heart and good health and he certainly seemed to enjoy the show last night. At least, he said he did! He looked very smart and upright: he wore a tie (unusually) and a white shirt with a large floppy collar. We called the show the Badley Beano (he said he didn't want anything too solemn: 'I'm not dead yet!') and did it twice, once on Friday for OBs and invited guests, then yesterday for the school. The Chief had asked for Shakespeare, so Part Two was the last act of the *Dream*, directed by Kate Slack [the headmaster's wife] and Part One was the

---

* Harold Gardiner had been teaching English at Bedales since 1952. He went on to become an Inspector of Schools.
† Richard Dimbleby (1913–65) was the most celebrated and highly regarded broadcaster of his time. This was the last state occasion that he covered for the BBC. He died of cancer in December 1965.

variety bill with assorted generations of Bedalians doing turns. This was the bit I devised and compèred and I think/hope a good time was had by all. There was much cheering anyway and the opening moment – small child walking down the aisle to hand The Chief a bunch of snowdrops – worked a treat. Not a dry eye in the house.

Sunday, 28 February 1965

The month is at an end already and what have I achieved? My ten top activities this term:

1. Helping HEG with his 'Jaw' in memory of T. S. Eliot [who had died on 4 January]. (I performed 'Macavity' and managed *not* to mention that I knew the great man or that T. S. Eliot is an anagram of Toilets!)
2. Being Business Manager of the *Chronicle*. I have secured the advertising and the new printers and today I will be sitting down with Mark Kidel (co-editor) to finalise the content.
3. I have turned 'interviewer'. My first 'Face to Face' for the *Chronicle* is with the Reverend Snelgar, vicar of Steep. 'Why do you believe in God?' 'Because he is ultimately unavoidable.' (Good question! Good answer!! Good interview overall, I hope. Barny has taken excellent shots of us wandering among the gravestones, BBC-style.)
4. I am running the Paperback Bookshop – a new venture of mine. I love choosing and ordering the stock, mainly from Penguin and Pan. I love the smell and feel of the new books when they arrive – the smell especially. I love it when we make a sale!
5. I am running the Cycling Proficiency Tests and have the local police coming in ten days to see us in action.
6. I am giving a talk on Homosexual Law Reform.
7. Finance Committee
8. Library
9. Speech Comp
10. The Badley Beano

And while I'm here (up in my favourite bay in the Library) and 'reviewing the situation', who are my top ten friends? 1. Jackie; 2. Pobs; 3. Gail. (This is in no particular order.) 4. Miranda Harrison (Skinny's younger sister. History should know that Skinny Harrison was the most beautiful girl in the school – even though she wore glasses! Interesting, is that not? History does not need to know that I gave Skinny a rose one Sunday after Jaw – and I think she threw it away!

Ah well . . .) 5. Julia Wake (who is beautiful too); 6. Ali Ball (who is fun); 7. Antonia Burrows (I like the way she doodles in biro on her thighs and shows me during class!); 8. Di Ambache; 9. Louki Healing; 10. Willow Greenwood; 11. Stephanie Clare (I'm not sure why I've put her in the list. She's a new girl and she's crazy. She keeps sending me mad love notes across the dining room in the middle of meals. Perhaps that's why I'm including her. I hardly know her, but I like her hair and her funny crooked nose. I like her madness and devotion!)

Okay, that's more than ten and you have noticed that they are all girls. (And, of course, many of my favourites – Beetle, Tessa Ventris, Helen Levinson, etc. – have now left.) My male friends (top five): Peter 'Fumbly' Harris, Mark Kidel, Chris Irwin, Ham Arnold, Barny . . . Speaking of Barny, in assembly last night he said, 'Have you noticed how as the girls walk out for hand-shaking the boys only look at their breasts?' I hadn't. He may be right. I shall study the matter.

And – this is true! – today I heard Jonathan 'Bex Bissell'* Hyman ask: 'Are couchettes prostitutes?'

Friday, 5 March 1965

The night before last it snowed, many inches, and the roads are blocked, the post delayed (no letters since the 3rd), food running low, and too much time spent with shovels almost knee-deep in the wretched stuff. Last night, for over an hour we were without electricity and so fumbled our ways to bed by candle and flickering torch light. This morning, my splendid Selfridges alarm clock woke the world – or at least our little corner of it – at six and I stumbled down to this machine. I have 'commandeered' the Careers Room on the first landing overlooking the Quad and am using it as my 'office'! No one seems to mind.

What's the news? Everything here trundles along much the same . . . Busy-bee-business all day long: up early, down late, work and pleasure, just as it always is. So, as I approach my 17th birthday, life's pleasant and I'm happy. I have been feasting myself on early birthday treats from home: thirty-six inches of Maison Lyons chocolates (that's the length of the box), fudge and tanjies. I am saving the nuts, Twiglets and cake for the weekend. On Sunday I shall have lunch at the Reids' (Jackie's household) and tea with Martin Sorrell, the French teacher, who celebrates his twenty-third birthday on the seventh, the day before mine. Special note: the menu for Sunday will include chocolate mousse – so will my tea with Mr

---

* The nickname came about because his hair was said to resemble a Bex Bissell brush. His father was the businessman and Viyella tycoon Joe Hyman, much admired by GB.

Badley on the 8th. (Mr Badley's housekeeper, Anne Cook, looks after me well!) I very much like the idea of marking my seventeenth birthday by taking tea with a centenarian who knew Oscar Wilde.

Wednesday, 10 March 1965

Goldie, the London Zoo Golden Eagle, has been recaptured after ten days of freedom. I am in my 'office' with a lemon curd tart and a mug of tea preparing my notes on Oscar Wilde. The Chief told me that the reason that Oscar was such a wonderful conversationalist is that 'he could listen as well as talk'. We exchanged our favourite Wilde witticisms.

Mine: 'After a good meal one can forgive anyone – even family.'

The Chief's: 'Murder is always a mistake. A gentleman should never do anything he cannot talk about at dinner.'

The Chief said: 'Wilde always put himself out to be entertaining. He was a delightful person, charming and brilliant, with the most perfect manners of any man I ever met. Because of his imprisonment and disgrace he is seen nowadays as a tragic figure. That should not be his lasting memorial. I knew him quite well. He was such fun.'

Tuesday, 6 April 1965

I will not make this mistake again. I am on holiday in Cornwall. I have come down here with a group of 'younger' teachers and some fellow Bedalians and we are renting a house. We drove down from Jackie's on Saturday (Martin Sorrell driving) and eventually found the village of Lerryn where we are staying. The village is 'unspoilt', just south of Lostwithiel, on the river that turns into the sea at Fowey. Cornwall is very beautiful, but we are lost in the heart of nowhere. Life is pleasant enough, but idle – which is tedious. The air and the company are not conducive to work. I've done little reading, less writing. (I have decided that next term I am going to undertake a complete survey of English Lit from 1550–1660 – starting with drama. I shall read everything!)

On Sunday I took a six-mile walk, which was satisfying if exhausting. In the evening, Margaret van den Pant – 27-year-old potter, teaches once a week at Bedales and Lancing – and I went to evensong locally. A disappointing service for such a lovely church. We have driven to Fowey (very 'touristised') and Mevagissey and are going to Padstow. This afternoon we drove to the Atlantic coast and wandered along the deserted beach. I may well return to town earlier than planned if I run out of interesting walks, books and patience. The truth is: I AM HATING IT HERE.

I have managed to follow the Budget.* In *some* respects very Conservative – but Callaghan put up a very poor, amateur, show when he was interviewed. 'I have a heart you know. I've already hit the motorists in the autumn!' Hoho. Not impressive. (Unbelievably, the *Daily Mail* is the best paper available in either Lerryn or Lostwithiel. I doubt very much that I will be able to get hold of a *Spectator* on Friday. This really is the end of the world. Never again. NEVER.)

Monday, 12 April 1965

A fine edition of *The Times* today. On the front page, the usual notices – with the Personal Column headed by some wise words from St Matthew: 'Watch and pray that ye enter not into temptation: the spirit indeed is willing, but the flesh is weak.' On the back page a fine portrait of the Prince of Wales on his pony in Windsor Great Park yesterday when he played polo – the Duke of Edinburgh also took part in the game. And in between, at the very centre of page 11, a robust contribution to the debate on the Budget from one G. D. Brandreth of 5H Portman Mansions, London W1 – my first letter to *The Times*. It looks good and reads well!

Also in *The Times* and of interest: on the facing page reports of Mr Wilson handling hecklers in Reading and 'feeling fine' and Mr Brown in Derby having 'a busy day' (travelling 250 miles and holding five meetings) and also feeling fine – alongside a dramatic (very dramatic) photograph of United States Marines landing near Da Nong, South Vietnam, to help defend the air base. Also interesting (to me), on page 6, from Our Political Correspondent: 'In a day or two backbenchers in the Commons will have been enjoying the benefits of their salary rise from £1,750 to £3,250 for a full six months, and it is not too early to begin noting the effects that the change has had, or is likely to have, on the proceedings of the House and the attitude of its members to their work. There is already little doubt that the payment of better salaries is quickening the process of turning membership of the Commons into a full-time job.'

This is a day for celebration. I have bought a new typewriter at Selfridges, £24 15s od. Excellent. I have phoned Pobs. Also excellent.

Monday, 26 April 1965

I have just got in from another of my nights as a 'Debs' Delight'. I don't think it is my natural *métier*! I dress the part – dinner jacket, evening shirt, cufflinks, black

---

* James Callaghan (1912–2005), Labour MP, 1945–87, had become Chancellor of the Exchequer in October 1964. This was his second Budget.

bow tie. I sound the part – 'What ho! Good evening, Sir! How *good* to meet you! And your lovely wife!' But I don't feel the part. I've got into this because of Penny Wilson. I met her at the Speech Comp. She is lovely. I really like her, but she lives in a strange world. A lot of braying goes on! (And smoking.) She has introduced me to her 'set' – all girls from Francis Holland and Queen's Gate, Roedean, Benenden, etc.* They really do whinny like horses! In the minibus tonight – taking our 'party' from the 'drinks' at 1 Upper Harley Street (chez Diana Ferguson – '*such* fun!') to Hurlingham for the Easter Egg Ball – the big-busted girl squashed next to me said, 'Have you ever seen a match burn twice?' I said 'No' and she proceeded to light a match and hold it up saying, 'Look – it's burning once!' Then she took the burning match and stubbed it out on my knuck-les!! 'Look – it's burning *twice*!' She guffawed and guffawed and *guffawed* until I thought she was going to wet herself. The burn was very painful.

Wednesday, 28 April 1965

Tonight I took Penny to *Present Laughter* at the Queen's Theatre. Wonderful – Nigel Patrick so stylish; Richard Briers hilarious as the lunatic young playwright. And Penny liked it too. (I spared her *The Night of the Iguana* last week and *The Crucible* tomorrow night. I don't think Tennessee Williams and Arthur Miller are really what she's looking for!) The evening began awkwardly. I went for supper at their flat. I did my best to entertain her very nice parents – in my best Debs' Delight manner. Then I let slip that I proposed taking Penny to Shaftesbury Avenue by Underground. As we set off, her father pulled me to one side in the hallway and pressed a ten shilling note into my hand, 'A cab, I think, for Penny, don't you?' And he winked at me!

Sunday, 9 May 1965

The holidays ended with one of the golden theatrical experiences of my lifetime – the Franco Zeffirelli *Much Ado*.† The term begins with me embarking on an ambitious theatrical enterprise of my own. Because so many people in the lower blocks have asked to be in a Junior play, I have agreed to produce something.

---

* Knowing this set would prove very useful to GB exactly forty years later when he came to write *Charles & Camilla: Portrait of a Love Affair*. Camilla Shand was a pupil at Queen's Gate School in the early 1960s.

† The cast in the National Theatre production included Maggie Smith and Robert Stephens as Beatrice and Benedick, with Albert Finney, Derek Jacobi, Ian McKellen and Frank Finlay as the other principals. Playing minor roles were Lynn Redgrave, Edward Petherbridge, Ronald Pickup and Michael York.

Yesterday I put up a notice asking people interested to sign down and I now have over forty names! I am going to stage *Thirty Minutes in a Street*, an unusual farce with *twenty-three* speaking characters. I will find roles for everyone who wants one.

This afternoon I am going to the OB Society meeting to explain the *Chronicle*'s financial situation – surprisingly good as it happens. I can't really believe it, but we have a balance in hand of £160.

Yesterday afternoon I went to a Labour Party meeting in Petersfield addressed by the Parliamentary Private Secretary to the Ministry of Agriculture. It was attended by more Tories than Socialists. Plenty of angry farmers – and their Jags!

Tomorrow evening – under the new system evolved at our Religious Discussion meetings last term – I am taking Assembly. I haven't quite decided on my reading.

I am relaunching *Roundabout* – now as sole editor. And I might join the choir!

And just in from one of my new regular duties for Mr Slack – taking prospective parents round the school. Today, it was an actor, Donald Sinden – very charming, full of energy and theatrical sparkle.* Oh yes, it's all happening here!

Sunday, 30 May 1965

Have I written about 'Walks' before? 'Walks' is what we are required to do on a Sunday afternoon – take a walk out of doors, out of the school grounds, for at least an hour and a half. I sometimes go with Barny or Adam Reeves, but usually with a couple of girls. I prefer going with the girls because we have more fun gossiping and because I have developed a rather charming game for us to play . . . What happens is this: on our walk we spot a house that looks inviting – and we see if we can get invited in. Our usual trick (my idea) is to ring the doorbell and ask whoever answers if one of the girls might be allowed to use the lavatory – the girl tries to look embarrassed as though it is something embarrassing that needs to be attended to! While the girls go off to the lavatory, my job is to charm our way into the house!! It doesn't always work, but today we had a very nice tea with a charming lady called Mrs Plumbridge!

I have been reading the Denys Blakelock book [*Making the Stage Your Career*] – fascinating, if a little disturbing. He claims that the only way to get

---

* GB later became a friend of Sir Donald Sinden (b. 1923), and his family. Whether or not as result of the Brandreth tour, in the event, the Sindens' sons did not go to Bedales.

onto the stage is through drama school. The advantages: proper training in all the required skills, from voice production to dancing and fencing, and the fact that managers and agents are more interested in ex-drama school actors because they can rely on basic skills and knowledge. The unions make trouble too, apparently. The advantages are obvious and it does seem by far the safest course. Still . . . I shall consult the powers-that-be here. I'm quite divided.

The play [*Thirty Minutes in a Street*] is progressing. Problems: time – not enough of it. And the wretched monkey suit which one of the leads (Simon Cadell) has to wear. We can't afford to hire one, so Rachel is writing round to her friends enquiring after one. Also the set's a problem: building and painting the house for the street is taking forever. But good news: I am hoping to get a proper letter-box from the BBC. My wardrobe mistress (Sally Henry) and stage manager (Gino Henry) are persuading their BBC designer father (*Z Cars* etc.) to lend us one. (Sally H., by the way, I think X.)*

Saturday, 12 June 1965

Last night: up late, typing up the programme and rolling it off on the Gestetner machine in the school secretary's office.

This morning: Parents' Day. Sports at 11.30 a.m. (modest contribution to relay. And I didn't drop the baton!) Lunch with Pa and Ma – picnic in car (sandwiches: tomato, Marmite and Kraft slices; lemon barley water; chocolate mousse).

This afternoon at 3.00 p.m. in the Lupton Hall: *Thirty Minutes in a Street*. A wonderful triumph. Perhaps the happiest thirty minutes of my life.

Thursday, 17 June 1965

I am reading *A Moveable Feast* by Ernest Hemingway and then going to Pefe for haircut, envelopes and stamps. I shall not be writing to the newspapers outraged by the Beatles' MBEs – awarded for services to exports and quite right too – but I am writing to the Port of London Authority. When we went on the recent school trip and were walking around the docks I saw what appeared to be blatant racial discrimination: public conveniences marked 'Asians Only'.

Wednesday, 30 June 1965

Tea and Scrabble with Mr Badley. He has given me a signed copy of his book, *The Bible As Seen Today*. It is the Bible, in modern English, rearranged in historical sequence – his life's work in three volumes.

* Sally Henry (1950–84) became GB's longest-lasting teenage girlfriend.

I am working on a play that's a satire on the theatre of the absurd, kitchen sink drama and the rest. There are plenty of pauses and tramp-like characters sitting in dustbins – and a sort of philosophy: 'Try to forget the cant and the hypocrisy, the tangerine toenails and unread *Encounters*, and smile a little. Laugh a little. Don't think about "life" too much, too often, too seriously: it gets depressing. Laugh with life. Wink at it.'

And I'm analysing bestial imagery in *Othello* – line by line. Very revealing. Was Shakespeare doing it consciously – thinking I'll give these characters rats and toads and goats and monkeys to speak of? Or did it come instinctively as he wrote?

Thursday, 1 July 1965

I have received this reply from the Port of London Authority:

> In reply to your letter of 17th June, you were quite correct in saying you have noticed special lavatory facilities for Asiatics in the docks.
>
> It is customary to provide specially designed lavatories at the berths where the ships' crews include Asiatic seamen because, mainly due to the dictates of their religion, European lavatories are unacceptable to them.
>
> The basic feature of the Asiatic lavatories is that a 'Baroda' pan and a 'Lucknow' squatting plate are installed at floor level. Further details of the design can be obtained from Messrs Doulton & Co. Ltd, Potters, Albert Embankment, SE1.

Thursday, 22 July 1965

I am exhausted. Utterly. On Tuesday I caught the 3.05 p.m. boat train from Victoria, reaching Folkestone at 5.25 p.m. and Calais at 7.19. Then I crossed France, changing again and again and *again*, until I reached Sion in the Valais canton of southern Switzerland at 8.34 yesterday morning. I am lying on my bunk bed in my little room up in the hills above Sion, in the village of Arbaz, on the second day of my holiday job as English tutor and companion to the children of Brigadier Maurice Juilland. He turns out to be the head of the Swiss Army!

That's why I'm exhausted. This morning the entire family was up at 5.00 a.m. so that the Brigadier could lead us out into the woods to gather mushrooms for breakfast! He explained that each of us has to eat the mushrooms that he or she has picked. He told me that he had found this rule very effective in ensuring that his troops learnt quickly and correctly which fungi were poisonous and which were not.

He is obviously very tough. He is quite old but quite jolly, so long as you do exactly as he says. Madame Juilland is his second wife and much younger. She and I are going to be friends. The children seem okay. I think it's going to be all right.

Significant news from home: Sir Alec has resigned as Leader of the Conservative Party. There is to be an election for the new leader – the first election in the party's history. I am cut off from newspapers here, but we are able to get the BBC World Service.

Wednesday, 28 July 1965

'LONDRES: TED HEATH NOUVEAU CHEF TORY: il doit être élu aujourd'hui après le retrait de M. Maudling'. In the *Gazette de Lausanne,* Mr Heath's victory is front-page news. Heath: 150 votes; Maudling: 133; Enoch Powell: 15. Maudling was the front-runner, but Heath was my man from the start. He looks new (he's the youngest leader the party has had for a century), he is a grammar school boy (which is good for us), and he comes from Broadstairs – need we say more? I am delighted. (We are swimming in Sion where I have bought the newspaper.)

Saturday, 31 July 1965

Today is Sally Henry's 15th birthday. She is camping in a tent in France (poor girl!), but has written me a wonderful letter. She writes beautiful letters – very warm and real and full of detail. (She awoke on the day she sent her letter to find a frog in her tent – a little creature, not one of the locals.) She loves music and dress-making and sun-bathing (she says she always turns puce before she goes brown). Oh yes, she also (so she says) loves me. I have just sent her an epistle running to eleven sides to thank her for doing so!

Yesterday we all went on a picnic – a *raclette* at Evolène. And I saw my first glacier. Tomorrow is the Swiss National Day and the Brigadier as *Commissaire des Guerres en Chef* will be away taking the salute somewhere. The day after we set off, *en famille,* on our national tour. We shall be going to Altdorf, Bern, Interlaken, etc., both taking in the sights and visiting military installations – including a complete 'invisible town' that has been built inside a mountain. It's a secret headquarters for the military – complete with streets, houses, hospitals, everything – ready for use in the event of invasion.

The Brigadier has been explaining Switzerland's 'citizens' army' to me and encouraging me to advocate something similar in Britain. They have adopted the idea in Israel where he has been to advise them on how it works. Here, at 20, according to the Swiss Civil Code, the adolescent becomes a citizen and the citizen becomes a soldier. He remains a soldier for thirty years. Beginning with four months' national service, he must return each year for three weeks until he reaches the age of 50. Only priests are exempt. According to the Brigadier, 'We have not been invaded in Switzerland because we have an army that is ready for war at any time. Because every citizen is also a soldier, with his uniform, weapons and ammunition, sometimes even his jeep, kept at home, we can mobilise an army of 700,000 by tomorrow. Not bad for a country of five million.' What he says is true: I have seen the automatic rifles in people's houses, hanging on the back of the kitchen door.

The Brigadier also believes that his kind of national service helps create a classless society – and avoid 'the physical degeneration that will end in the collapse of Western civilisation'. He says that young people today rely too much on machines. 'In a hundred years' time your grandchildren will be breaking rocks on some Tibetan mountainside because they won't be physically strong enough to defend themselves.'

Friday, 13 August 1965

Friday the thirteenth – a lucky one for me. Letter from Mr Slack asking me to be a prefect. Letter from Rachel telling me that next term's play is to be *A Passage to India* and that she has a part in mind for me that will challenge me to play for 'truth' rather than 'effect'. Letter from Sally telling me that she loves me very much and is missing me desperately!

A lucky day and a memorable one too. I have just been playing cards with the President of Switzerland! I won – which I now realise was probably a mistake. Monsieur Paul Chaudet is 60 and looks like a friendly version of Adolf Hitler: he has warm eyes, but Herr Hitler's toothbrush moustache and unfortunate hairstyle. He is the Swiss Defence Minister and one of the country's seven Federal Councillors – they take it in turns to be President. He is an old friend of the Brigadier's and has spent the evening with us here at the chalet. Madame Juilland has been all of a twitter having such an important visitor and, as a consequence, at dinner the atmosphere was a little forced. When the Brigadier gave me some wine and it was the last drop in the bottle, he said I should kiss the bottom of the bottle – 'it's an old Swiss custom and means you'll be married before the end of the year'. Madame was very shocked by this! After dinner, she was also very anxious to get us away from the card table and down into Sion. She had arranged for a special command performance of the Sion *son et lumière*. The President and the Brigadier wanted to carry on drinking and playing cards. So did I! Madame, however, insisted that we all clamber into the presidential limousine (flags flying on bonnet) and sweep into town. It really was a command performance: there were just eight of us to see the show. We sat on two wooden benches for a very long hour listening to the incredibly dreary *son* and watching the far from exciting *lumière*. It was not a jolly experience – and when it was over, though pressed to come back up to the chalet for a nightcap, the President and his wife decided to go home. Madame was mortified, the Brigadier was disappointed, the President was insistent – and that was that.

Tuesday, 21 September 1965

The end of a good summer holiday and the arrival of a wonderful school report. 'Quite outstanding' is Mr Slack's charming summary! And hark at HEG in my Form Report:

> For someone who gives so unstintingly to the life of the school, Gyles has had a very good year in his academic work. He really is good for us – a rebel against so many Bedalian conventions, he is gracious and polite, neat and an enthusiast. I find him more aware of the moments when he almost caricatures himself – and well able to take a joke and make a joke against himself . . . I am very pleased, in fact, to have so many points of association with him, and to have such a frank and friendly relationship. It is boys like Gyles who give me grounds for hope.

I am honoured by what he says and will endeavour not to disappoint him.

Actually, everything has been WONDERFUL this summer. When I left Switzerland, Madame Juilland (Gaby!) gave me one of her most precious possessions: her own signed copy of Jean-Louis Barrault's autobiography, personally dedicated to her by the great man. She added a lovely inscription of her own.* She was an actress before she married the Brigadier and Barrault, of course, is France's greatest. When I got back to England I saw a joyous *Trelawney of the 'Wells'* at Chichester and the Berliner Ensemble at the Old Vic – *The Threepenny Opera* and *Coriolanus* with Helene Weigel (Mrs Bertolt Brecht) as Volumnia. This week I have been catching up with friends: a walk in Richmond Park with Pobs, lunch in Notting Hill with Jackie, supper with Penny at her parents' in Kensington, and fun and games on several days with Sally in East Putney. (Her parents are very nice. And Pobs's parents are charming too. Mr Webber gave me

---

* *'Vous avez 30 ans pour devenir le Monsieur Heath des temps futures! Profitez de l'immédiat pour mettre en pratique les conseils de ce livre et devenir un Laurence Olivier . . . avec ou sans resemblance!'*

a lift to Hammersmith – apparently unheard of. He normally hides in his study when Pobs's friends appear. And, according to Pobs, since my departure her mother has done little but praise my 'grand social manner' and ask Pobs why she doesn't bring home more boys like me!)

At home, all's much as ever. Ma's under the weather and in bed with a hot water bottle and lemon tea. Pa is in the kitchen sorting through the bills. (Money worries have got worse now that Ben's gone to Ashfold [a boys' prep school] – more fees to find!) Gin is as high as a kite and looking for love. Jen is lower than a snake's belly and looking for love! Jen and Hes have fallen out. Very badly. They had a horrible fight (which I witnessed) with kitchen knives drawn and glass broken. Hester is a girl who likes girls (Figgy in particular!) and Jen thinks it's 'disgusting' and 'immoral'. I must read Chekhov's play, *The Three Sisters*!

Sunday, 26 September 1965

A letter from Tim Slack, headmaster, awaited me on my return to school and began: 'My dear Gyles, The ideas contained in your letter are very exciting . . .' The 'ideas' contained in my letter (which has been shown to several staff, head boy and girl, etc.) are all to do with creating activities for Block II – the youngest year in the school. At present they are given very little to do: I propose to change all that! I have already made a modest start. I have squeezed a plump £6 out of the Finance Committee towards the cost of getting them a hut of their own and, on Wednesday evenings, Di Ambache and I are organising a Dancing Activity for them – teaching the little darlings to dance! From the waltz to the jive, simple rudiments only! (Di is giving *me* a lesson this afternoon. We have been friends ever since Mr Payne apparently ordered her out of his chemistry class – and sheepishly she went towards the door until I explained to her that he hadn't said 'Come on, Di, outside!', he'd said, 'Carbon dioxide'! He is very Scottish.)

I am taking on more, I know, but then this term I have more time. Prefects have four 'late nights' a week when we don't need to go to our dorms until ten. I have on my desk wise words taken from the Library calendar on 31 July:

> 'Opportunities are swarming around us all the time, thicker than gnats at sundown. We walk through a cloud of them.' Van Dyke.

Saturday, 16 October 1965

As part of my programme of 'involving' Block II, Sally and I took two of the tiddlers to tea in Pefe this afternoon: Patrick Cadell (younger brother of my friend, Simon) and Tomás Graves (youngest son of the poet, Robert Graves).

Tomás is particularly amusing. He's twelve, but very charming and cheeky and keeps inviting me to come to stay with the family in Majorca. (I rather like the idea.) Patrick is just like Simon, but without the theatrical trimmings! (Simon is now my best friend. We spend a lot of time listening to Flanagan and Allen and Noël Coward and planning our thespian futures. He is only 15, but his way with wine and women is a wonder!)

Tuesday, 9 November 1965

Everything went wrong with Sally last week. My fault. I was difficult. I am difficult. Today she sent me a long and loving letter:

> I am here if you want me, when you want me, and not unless you want me. I love you. I trust you. It may be hard to believe, but I do, and this love will weather *anything*. I know I don't often say it – in time I will get over my shyness . . . Meanwhile, I don't mind the little girls on our supper table, I don't mind walking over to Steephurst alone eight nights a week, I don't mind forgoing any of the pleasures that convention and Jo Boyden say I ought to have – because I prefer it the way it is. I would rather you show your love *your* way, as and when you feel it, instead of keeping to any rules.

History ought to know about these strange Bedalian 'rules'. By tradition long established, a 'couple' at Bedales becomes established when the boy asks the girl if he can 'take her over' and she agrees. 'Taking over' means walking with her from the main school to Steephurst, the girls' house. 'Taking over' happens after breakfast, lunch and supper. It is fun in the evening, when you chat and kiss before saying goodnight, but it is also very time-consuming when you have a crowded diary as I do! Sally says that she is happy 'for paradise to be restricted' to Steepcot [where she worked on the costumes for the school plays] and whatever else we can manage – 'the supper table, after brekky, exchanging letters'. If I involve her in some of my projects we can have more time together. I think that's the best way forward.

Tuesday, 16 November 1965

A good evening on BBC1:

7.30 p.m.	Eric Sykes and Hattie Jacques
8.00 p.m.	*Z Cars*
8.50 p.m.	*The News*
9.00 p.m.	Play of the Month: *A Passage to India*, with Cyril Cusack

(wonderful) in my role (Mr Fielding) and Sibyl Thorndike as Mrs Moore.

10.50 p.m.   *Twenty-Four Hours* with Cliff Michelmore & Co.

11.20 p.m.   *Bonjour Françoise*, French lessons.

11.45 p.m.   Weather and Close Down

We were tuning in tonight because of *Passage to India.*[*] The only programme we get to see regularly during term time (in John Slater's room, in pyjamas, sitting on the floor, with chocolate milk and biscuits) is *Danger Man*. (When I am not Laurence Olivier in *Pride and Prejudice*, Danny Kaye in *The Court Jester*, Pitt the Younger or Felix Krull, I am ready to settle for being Patrick McGoohan in *Danger Man*!)

Tuesday, 30 November 1965

Tonight I took part in the Petersfield Rotary Club Schools' Public Speaking Competition and, happily, came first. (The prize was three guineas. I had to give a speech on road safety as the Minister of Transport.) Have I also recorded that I have won the MacDonald Senior Essay Prize – given by Malcolm MacDonald, ex-Bedalian, ex-MP, diplomat, son of Ramsay MacDonald? The junior prize went jointly to Elizabeth Bingley and Sappho Durrell. (Sappho is 14, very beautiful, amazing hair and eyes. She is difficult to 'know', but she thinks I'm funny and we're friends. She has invited me to meet her famous father.)[†]

I am recording these TRIUMPHS not in the spirit of boasting, but because I do try to note everything down!! (From the Library calendar for Friday 8 October, now on my desk: 'There is something noble in hearing myself ill spoken of when I am doing well.' Alexander the Great.)

Friday, 31 December 1965

Richard Dimbleby who has died (the Big C) is to have a memorial service in Westminster Abbey.[‡] As usual, the Brandreth household will be seeing in the

---

[*] A party from the school had been to watch the recording being made on 15 October 1965.

[†] When Sappho Durrell (1951–85) committed suicide, some said that the writings she left behind suggested an incestuous relationship with her poet and novelist father, Lawrence Durrell (1912–90).

[‡] The broadcaster died, aged 52, on 22 December 1965. Cancer was always referred to euphemistically in the Brandreth household as 'the Big C'. Dimbleby was probably the most mourned man in the history of British broadcasting: more than four thousand people attended his memorial service.

New Year in front of the gogglebox, first footing with Andy Stewart and fellow members of the White Heather Club. All's well on the home front. The year has ended charmingly, in fact, with the arrival of my report. Mr Slack has clearly forgiven me for the Merry Evening 'impression' I did of him: 'His contributions all round have been quite remarkable. Much of the excellent tone at present prevailing in the school is due to his good sense and enthusiasm.' And I'm happy with the look of the *Chronicle* too. I probably shouldn't have included my play in its entirety (!) or the photographs of me and Sally outside the Natural History Museum (Barny at his best!) or the references to yours truly on every other page, but I am happy with my interview with the President of Switzerland:

> *Brandreth*: Monsieur Chaudet, in Switzerland women do not have the vote. Can you tell me why?
>
> *Chaudet*: Because men and women are not equal.
>
> *Brandreth*: Do you really mean that?
>
> *Chaudet*: Yes, I do. The sexes may be complementary, but they are certainly not equal. Man is absorbed in his professional, political, social and military life, while the woman's place is in the home.

Brigadier Juilland told me that in Switzerland when they last had a general referendum on the matter of women's suffrage, he locked his wife in the bathroom from breakfast-time until the polls closed!* Happy New Year.

---

* Swiss women did not gain the right to vote in Federal elections until 1973.

Several Lives

January – December 1966

Monday, 10 January 1966

I feel that I am leading several lives. (1) I am Sally's boyfriend – and more than that. We are so close: we have no secrets. But when we are together (and I've seen her almost every day this holiday) I am quite different from when I am being (2) A Debs' Delight – I have seen Penny several times (we went to the Organ Grinder's Ball at Chelsea Town Hall – what larks! Actually rather ghastly) and I've been to 'drinkypoos' with Caroline Gill and Cordelia Fraser and been charming (I hope) to their 'mummies' and to their 'papas' (esp. Lord Strathalmond [Cordelia's father]). But when I'm with them (and I do like them) you'd never know that my real love is (3) The Theatre – I've seen Gielgud's *Ivanov* and Michael Redgrave's *A Month in the Country* this week and playing those parts (producing those plays), that's what I *really* want to do. Or do I want to change the world? Who am I? Answers on a postcard please . . .

Family news. On Saturday night at midnight Pa and I were sitting in the kitchen having cocoa when we got a call from St James's Hospital, Wandsworth. Hes and her friend Figgy were there – one of them had taken an overdose. High drama. Pa and I raced over to Wandsworth in the car – rain pouring, windscreen wipers swishing. Before we got to the hospital we went to their flat. Pa, at speed but very calmly, went through all the cupboards and drawers and flushed all the pills and drugs etc. down the WC – 'in case the police come looking'. Pa, being a lawyer, knows about these things!! At the hospital, all was fine. We brought Hes home. She's fine. (V dramatic and, let's face it, quite exciting too.)

World news. The Indian Prime Minister, Mr Shastri, has died in Tashkent. He had been at a dinner with the Soviet Prime Minister, Mr Kosygin.

Saturday, 22 January 1966

The Vietnam War is worsening. The Americans have launched their biggest offensive – 8,000 troops have attacked a single Viet Cong stronghold with mass casualties. I went to a meeting addressed by Connie Zilliacus (Labour MP) at

Petersfield Town Hall. He was convincing: I am pro-American, but what can the war hope to achieve?

Civics last night. Joe Hyman, Chairman of Viyella, talked to us about business and enterprise: be clear about your product, identify your market (is it big enough? will it last?), deliver ideas, energy, quality, consistency and follow-through. He was inspirational. I gave the vote of thanks and had coffee with him afterwards at Mr Slack's. He has olive skin, tight curly hair and gleams. He crackles like electricity.

I have cast the Junior Play I am producing – Terence Rattigan's *Harlequinade*. As last year, I am finding a part for everyone who has asked to take part. Forty-three in the company to date, with ten backstage. I have strong leads: Simon Cadell (excellent) and Katy Chapman (pretty and charming).

Saturday, 5 February 1966

From today's Library calendar: 'But now let it pass, 'tis nothing strange: it hath happed before; and if thou live longer it will happen again.' Thomas à Kempis.

Work. A Levels. I have reread *Le Rouge et Le Noir*, making notes. I have reread *Andromaque* making (rather good) notes. English: I got a pleasant B++ for a not (to my mind) outstanding essay on John Whiting and I am enjoying the Henry Fielding (*Joseph Andrews*) greatly. HEG is a wonderful teacher.

Play. I have replaced Katy Chapman with my Sally. Simon isn't well and has gone home and isn't going to be available for rehearsals before Sunday 13th. Damn and blast – but we have time on our side at the moment.

Tuesday, 22 February 1966

From today's Library calendar: 'No one ever did anything worth doing, unless he was prepared to go on with it long after it became something of a bore.' Bishop Steere.

I have replaced Simon (who is covered in boils and still at home sick) with Mervyn Riches (student teacher and both jolly and willing). I thought of playing the part myself, but Rachel vetoed that. (She was right.) Mervyn is excellent and it's going to work out fine, I think. Everyone is working incredibly hard: marshalling a cast of forty-plus is no picnic, but we're getting there.

Saturday, 12 March 1966

Harlequinade – a triumph. (I know it's what I always say, but it usually is! And in this case it really was. My youthful band of players delivered the goods in full measure and to see their delight – and the delight of their families watching – was wonderful.)

National Speech Comp – a triumph. (Well, almost: I came first in Drama and second overall.)

18th birthday – a bit of a non-event. (Birthdays don't feel exciting any more. I got some excellent books from Ma and Pa – esp. a biographical dictionary of English and American poets – and shortbread and chocs and 10/- each from Aunts Edith and Helen, but I did not 'mark' the day. It did not feel 'special'.)

General election – a bit of a non-event also. The local candidates are unremarkable: Miss Quennell is a dry old stick – we had her going through her paces at Steep Hall last night: she was as inspiring as a damp flannel. At least the Labour candidate has a name that looks familiar on the posters: she is called Lady Wilson. Nationally, Mr Wilson is making all the running – wily words and gimmicks galore. He is promising 'A New Britain' and folk seem to like the sound of that! Our programme is more straightforward – get the economy straight: check rising prices and restore expansion; reform the trade unions; remodel the welfare state; restore respect for Britain and lead her into Europe. Mr Heath is sound and our slogan is strong: Action not Words – but if they're not interested they're not interested. I'm beating the drum here, but to no avail. And we're not having a mock election this time because the poll is during the holidays, on 31 March[*] – the day I'm off to Paris.

I am writing a letter to *The Spectator* about prison reform. I've been reading Tony Parker's account[†] of the man who had been convicted eight times for thefts totalling £178 and had spent twenty-six years of his life behind bars, with an average period of eleven weeks between sentences. Within a few hours of his release from seven years' preventive detention he was arrested for attempting to steal from some mailbags at King's Cross Station and sentenced to ten years' further imprisonment. Clearly the previous seven years had taught him nothing! Currently our prisons are places where we hide our criminals: we do not really attempt to cure them or prepare them properly for the world they must face on release. We must change all that.

Thursday, 7 April 1966

14 Avenue Carnot, Cachan, Seine

Distressing financial news. I am very happy in my suburban student boarding house, but this morning I made a discreet enquiry into the cost of board and lodg-

---

[*] The result: Labour 363 seats; Conservatives 253; Liberals 12; Others 2. Harold Wilson secured an overall majority in the House of Commons of 96.
[†] In *The Unknown Citizen*, 1966, which GB had just ordered for the school Paperback Bookshop that he was still running. GB's long interest in prison reform dates from this period. He is uncertain what prompted it.

ing: 30 fr per day – rather more than I had bargained for. I arrived on the night of the 31st and, at present, I plan to leave on the evening of Wednesday 20th April. This will mean a twenty-day stay, costing 600 francs or £43 17s 0d!! I have £30 uncashed traveller's cheques. I also have a £5 note and £1 in French currency – but next Wednesday I go by train to Caen (to the prison there) which will eat further into my petty cash. I have no choice but to write home for more funds – £10 (or £12 if Pa wants me to get duty-free cigarettes).

Quick summary of past seven days – full journal *à la Gide* to follow.

Friday 1st. I watched the evening news – *Télésoir* – and it began with this: 'There has been a surprise change of affairs in the British elections today.' They said the Tories had just scraped in and showed pictures of Ted Heath arriving at Downing Street, cheered on by the crowds. For a moment my heart thumped, until I realised it was an elaborate April Fool.

Saturday 2nd. Walk to Paris from here after lunch: 2.30 p.m.–6.00 p.m. non-stop! Buy paper, '*M. Wilson va remanier son cabinet*', buy theatre tickets, look about. Return exhausted to excellent supper. (I can't now remember what it was. This is why it's essential to write the diary on the day. I know it was good because we've only had one unpleasant meal: '*betterave*' salad, frankfurter sausages and potatoes.)

Sunday 3rd. Day of study – that's why I'm here! *Tempest* in the morning. Camus' *La Peste* in the afternoon. V funny French film on TV in the evening.

Monday 4th. To Paris after lunch. Visit Administration Pénitentiaire in the Place Vendôme: long discussion with gentleman who agrees to fix prison visits for me next week. On Tuesday at Fresnes – Paris outskirts – I shall go to a centre where prisoners are 'sorted' before being allocated a prison. On Wednesday out to Caen to a '*prison longue peine*'. He also gave me a fat book of statistics and told me to come back in the summer to see their marvellous new prison in Corsica!

Tuesday 5th. Day of study: touch of Chaucer, then Camus. In the evening *Chat en Poche*, an hilarious Feydeau farce taken at great pace and at quite a volume – at the Edouard VII, a gem of a theatre named in honour of our Edward VII. I sat in cheap seats (5 fr – 7/6d) but saw most excellently. *Weds.* More Camus, then in the evening to J. L. Barrault's Théâtre de France for Claudel's spirit v. flesh four-cornered-triangle, *Partage de Midi*. Subsidised theatre, vast and packed. My seat was 3 fr (cheapest) though I stood for most of the performance as that was the best way to see it all. Barrault overdid it, but it was good to see the fabled Edwige Feuillière.

Today. I plan to go to Paris this afternoon to sort out my return flight. I came on Skyways Coach Air – bus from Victoria then a short hop from Lympne to Beauvais, not bad and £9 8s od return. Then I'm off to the Louvre (incredibly full of foreigners when I went on Monday) and might run to one more theatre ticket. Curious how all the theatres in this good Catholic country give extra performances on Sunday – matinee and evening. And performances tomorrow which is Good Friday! (Madame, who is the housekeeper here by day, by night works as an *ouvreuse* at the Opéra: one of the fierce little bodies who unlock the door to your box and show you to your seat – with a grasping hand ever open. It's the one aspect of French theatre I really hate.)

I have been getting the airmail edition of *The Times* most days and *Le Monde*. The French view is that Britain won't enter the Common Market under Wilson. Heath is liked here because he is a European. André Fontaine in *Le Monde* quotes the remark General de Gaulle made just before the '64 elections: 'The Socialists will get in for a short and unhappy spell, before the Tory party under Ted Heath wins. It will be Heath who brings Britain into Europe.'

I reckon the election result in the UK can be explained very simply. During the first eighteen months of Wilsonism:

> Production up 2%
> Prices up 5%
> Wages up 9%

So people only doing 2% more work are getting 9% more money, while prices have only increased by 5%. People feel better off. If prices had gone up 9% and incomes only 5% then Heath would be PM. Elections are governed by what people have in their pockets. The present ratio is good for the individual, but bad for the country as a whole. (An oversimplification, I know, but there's something in it.)

I am sorry Humphrey Berkeley lost his seat. He was good on homosexual law reform. I am amused that one of the few Tory members to increase their majority was Miss Joan Quennell of Petersfield!

Wednesday, 4 May 1966

One of the advantages of being a senior librarian is that you get first pick of the quotations on the Library calendar. I was able to go through all the ones from the holiday period and I have chosen two for my collection:

'Is this true or only clever?' Augustine Birrell. (Read and mark, Brandreth.)

'My observation is that whenever one person is found adequate to the

discharge of a duty by close application thereto, it is worse executed by two persons, and scarcely done at all if three or more are employed therein.'
George Washington

Friendly letter from Nigel Lawson, editor of *The Spectator,* saying that an article on the French prison service will probably be too specialised for him, but suggesting I try Timothy Raison of *New Society.*

I am liking the new look to *The Times.**

Friday, 6 May 1966

Trouble – serious trouble – and I am in part responsible. One of the girls in my block is having a relationship with MS – and I have been helping her. Their affair is illegal because she's a pupil and he's a teacher, but they are in love and I have 'assisted' them by acting as a decoy – being seen going over to his room arm in arm with her (apparently to do French revision!) and then leaving her in his room alone while I've sat *cave* outside the door . . . Anyway, it seems that she is now pregnant. He is going to have to leave – and I don't know what's going to happen to her. She's got exams etc. I think she'll leave to have the baby and then come back to take the exams. They are going to get married.

It's quite funny. Whenever outsiders ask about Bedales, they always want to know if we are all sleeping with one another. I say, 'No – it's the staff we're sleeping with!'

PS: I have just heard on the Home Service news that Ian Brady and Myra Hindley, 'the Moors murderers', have been given three and two concurrent life sentences apiece at Chester Assizes. It is horrific cases such as these that make it next-to-impossible to engage public sympathy for the cause of prison reform.

Friday, 20 May 1966

I have just had a half-hour session with TWS, beloved headmaster. (Well, I like him, even if others don't. Most people think he's too 'bouncy' and 'keen'. 'Bouncy' and 'keen' are not Bedalian virtues!) Anyway, the point is, over coffee and biscuits, we have planned my 'university career'. This is the outcome: Oxford (definitely not Cambridge for me for some reason) and New College, reading PPE (Philosophy, Politics, Economics). The reasons: he sees me going a long way in the Union [the debating society] rather than the OUDS [the university dramatic society]; the social life is good at New College, 'but not too Evelyn

* On 3 May 1966, *The Times* started printing news in place of personal advertisements on its front page.

Waugh'; PPE is not a limiting course, will be suitable for more things – civil service/politics/journalism etc. – afterwards than, say, English (which is heavy) or Law (which is hard).

I think I'm to take it as a compliment that TWS himself read – yes! – PPE at – right again! – New College. He feels the college 'knows and likes' Bedalians and that, with good A Levels, and the right write-ups from him and others, I should make it. It's comforting he's so hopeful.

Pa will be disappointed that dear old Exeter College, his *alma mater*, is not in the running, but I know that, from his point of view, making it to Oxford, *tout court*, will be enough. According to Gin, Pa needs his morale boosted at the moment. She's written to report that Ma gave him a clip over the ear as a consequence of one of his 'witty asides' at her expense. Ma has now gone off to what Pa calls one of her 'fat farms', a two-week 'slimming holiday' involving high colonic irrigation and a diet of carrot juice. (The diet is unlikely to work because, as usual, Pa will be visiting at weekends, with chocolate éclairs and cold lamb chops secreted about his person.)

Gin in high spirits because Princess Anne has been a patient in her hospital and, while Gin didn't get her own horny hands on the royal personage (PA was on the floor above), she did get sightings of brothers Andrew and Edward with paternal grannie, Alice of Greece. For the six days of the royal hospitalisation, the press maintained a 24-hour vigil, but HRH's departure was discreetly managed. The hospital announced she would be leaving by the front door at 5.00 p.m. She slipped out of a side door at 4.00 p.m.

Saturday, 28 May 1966

Predictably enthusiastic reactions to the prospect of New College from the home front. Pa has written (from the kitchen table at 5H): 'I notice how poor old Exeter College is brushed aside, but I don't care at all about that, nor over the possible expense . . . I think you ought to feel flattered that TWS regards you so highly. You owe so much to Bedales – tho' I know B owes a lot to you – but I think you'd agree that no other school could have allowed you to develop as you have. You "owe" them the sequel which is a dazzling Oxford career. All you must do is safeguard your health. I *am* a little concerned about that, tho' I believe you inherit a strong constitution. Please avoid emotional tangles. (It was funny how Peter Paice whom we saw at Oxford* was so concerned over possible liaisons you

* Peter Paice, a few years' GB's senior, had gone on from Gordonstoun to St Peter's College, Oxford.

might get involved in. I told him that your economical turn of mind was alone enough to deter you!) But this isn't a Lord Chesterfield effusion. After all you haven't got anywhere yet! And unless you do justice to yourself in examinations you won't get anywhere at all! I know you realise this and that the old Daubeney charm is just not enough. From the little I saw of your Paris work, I don't think you need any advice there. (My trouble over you is that I just think you're doing marvellously: you need only our appreciation – which you have!).'

Dear old Pa. He's on his lonesome at the flat, 'tuckered out' by problems at work and money worries. Ma has written from a bench in the Shakespeare Memorial Garden in Stratford-upon-Avon. (Pa says she sneaks into Stratford from the fat farm to find sustenance at the Cobweb Tearooms!) She writes:

> Knowing your temperament, I know just how pleased you must be to have the year ahead mapped out for you – *now* all you have to do is get down to the *work*. Whatever it is to be – a place – an exhibition – or even a scholarship! – you know how happy we shall be for you. No matter what ups and downs we have had with the girls, we are indeed grateful for the eighteen years of pleasure and satisfaction you have brought us. Pa specially needs a measure of sheer joy in your progress – for it is but a lull before I have to start dragging forward my anxieties as regards Ben.[*]

She has lost 8 lbs so far and, lucky thing, has a 30/- Stalls ticket for David Warner's *Hamlet*.

Sunday, 5 June 1966

I will be brief because my A and S Levels begin this week and a touch of last-minute revision is required. Oddly, I am quite looking forward to the exams – both to doing them and to having got them done. We do them in the Old Music School, where it is very calm and very quiet and the sun filters in through the windows and across the wooden floor and makes it all feel rather Edwardian and very safe. All will be well, if I pace myself, if the ink flows (I have broken in a new pen, but will have the old one 'on hand' just in case) and I am not sitting between a girl who sniffs and a boy who scratches (as I have been in the past!) . . .

Update:

[*] GB's adopted younger brother, then aged 8, had been diagnosed as suffering from dyslexia and the nature and cost of his education was to be an issue for several years to come. GB's mother, who later that year opened her own small Montessori nursery school in the family flat off Baker Street, went on to become a much-admired teacher specialising in children with reading difficulties.

1) Sal – first anniversary TODAY.

2) An interesting new addition for my autograph collection: Colin Jordan, leader of the British Section of the World Union of National Socialists. A nasty piece of work, but we interviewed him for the *Chronicle* and he's sent a letter asking for a second copy. On his notepaper is a large swastika printed in bright red. It is chilling just to see it. I feel almost uncomfortable keeping it in my archive.

3) Anne Cook [Mr Badley's housekeeper] tells me that The Chief did not really enjoy the scene from the *Dream* that we performed for his 100th! All a bit 'coarse' and 'obvious'. I will *not* report this to Kate Slack who produced it! Anne wonders if we could do another Shakespeare as the post-A Level play and perform it for The Chief. He is nearing his end. It would be the final thrill of his life. (He saw Irving in his prime!)

4) Library calendar quotation (1 June): 'Censure is the tax a man pays to the public for being eminent.' Jonathan Swift.

Friday, 17 June 1966

Well, if the exams turn out to have been disasters, it won't be for lack of sustaining goodies in between them. Ma sent a huge parcel of Stratford-upon-Avon humbugs, Vienna biscuits and home-made fudge – meteors amid the empty heavens of exam existence! I have appeased my dorm-mates with a few humbugs, but guarded the Viennas and the fudge to myself (some of the very best I can remember) and nibbled noiselessly at them under my pillow while listening to 'the latest' every night from ten o'clock on the Home Service. And I can't blame outside distractions either – Sal has been away all week in Wales with the Block IV camp.

The essence of what I have to report is that I think/hope/pray the worst is over. The horror of the week was the first French paper on Tuesday. Reasonable essays, but a nasty dictation (everyone agreed) and a horrid bit of Graham Greene to translate into French. I got stuck on 'the street lamp', 'the vacuum cleaners' and 'to hum' – all of which I should have got. I don't think I've failed, but I think we're looking at a D or an E. (The marks run from A to E, F being for near miss, H being Hard cheese try again next year and O being an O Level pass.) If I do really good answers in the Literature paper (next Tuesday) and two nigh-perfect French to English translations (Wednesday) I'm still in with a chance of a B. Not so with the English, I fear . . . We had Shakespeare on Tuesday afternoon. The paraphrases were reasonably easy and I wrote one good essay on forgiveness in *The Tempest* – but annoyingly I gave a good quote from Blake re forgiveness to a girl just before the exam and we both used it. All the papers from here go to the same examiner, so it won't look original, which is a shame since it was! But the weakest essay should have been the strongest: my beloved *Othello*! And today I felt I did a fair essay on *Samson Agonistes*, but on reflection I'm not sure I answered the question sufficiently!!! We could be in C/D territory. Bah. How I sympathise with Ma's observation that beautiful notes do not necessarily lead to the best result! My notes are acknowledged as the finest and clearest, but sadly they never reach the eyes of the examiner. . .

Ah well, if the worst comes to the worst, there's always a short stint on the *Northern Echo* before a couple of years at drama school and a century at Sullypoole Rep.

Das ist tout pour now. *Andromaque* calls.

Saturday, 2 July 1966

The exams are done, the die is cast. I have been riding high. Literally. This morning, at 11.00 a.m., I bounced on the school trampoline. (A surprisingly pleasant sensation.) At 1.00 p.m. I joined the Cadell family for an excellent lunch at the East Meon Hut. Wonderful Ralph Richardson stories. Mrs C. was in his company when Simon was born and he is Selina's godfather.* I said I'd loved *You Never Can Tell* and asked if he was as eccentric as he seemed. 'More so!' is the answer. Mrs C. told a lovely story of finding him on all fours in a stage box after a poor performance. The great actor was scrabbling about on the floor, apparently looking for something. 'Has anyone seen my talent?' he wailed. 'It's very small, but it used to be quite shiny.' According to Mr C., it was George VI who said of RR: 'I don't know his name, but he's got a face like half a teapot.' Simon and I spent lunch trying out our Richardson impressions.

This afternoon in the Speech and Music programme in the Lupton Hall, I gave my (non-Richardson) reading of *Peer Gynt* (we know it's a bit fey, but this is Bedales) and now I'm off to open up the Paperback Bookshop, 5.00–6.00 p.m. Buy now, while stocks last.

Tuesday, 19 July 1966

The last day of the last summer term in my last year at Bedales. I'll be here next week, of course, for the International Arts Festival, but I've packed my trunk and this sunny day marks the official end of an era.

---

* Richardson appeared in *The Heiress* with Gillian Howell (Mrs Cadell), Peggy Ashcroft and Donald Sinden, directed by John Gielgud, in 1949. Simon Cadell was born in 1950; his twin brother and sister, Patrick and Selina, were born in 1953. GB had been to see Sir Ralph in *You Never Can Tell* in March 1966.

This evening I'm off to Chichester for the first night of *The Cherry Orchard*. This morning I went to Pefe with HEG [Harold Gardiner] for a farewell coffee at the Donkey Cart. Last Tuesday, we had our 'Henry Fielding Dinner': sherry at HEG's house, followed by a dinner for five of us at the Wyndham Arms – good fare (chops etc.), fine ale and fruity eighteenth-century chatter in honour of the great man.

What else has my last week had to offer? On Monday, my forty-minute lecture on crime and punishment – well prepared, well delivered, well received (though all said by myself). On Wednesday, my second lecture, on crime and cure, less well prepared and rather more diffuse. I had been distracted, trying to learn my lines for the A Level Play – *Ring Round the Moon*. I do play the lead and it is two parts! On Thursday Sir Lawrence Bragg FRS[*] came and gave a lecture on science. He is the youngest man ever to receive a Nobel Prize and he ran the laboratory where Crick and Watson determined the structure of DNA. I shook his hand. (I like to shake hands with history.) On Friday there was frantic line-learning before tea and Scrabble with Mr Badley. Good tea, but unsuccessful Scrabble – the 101-year-old won both games! At 7.30 p.m., *Ring Round the Moon* in the Lupton Hall. Beautiful set, attractive costumes, uninspired production – but, irony of ironies, GDB does not falter once, nor need to be prompted, while those word-perfect for weeks dry up.

Less triumphant, let's face it, was my contribution to the end-of-term dance. A cabaret was called for and, over supper, seeing the shaving cream that's served on the fruit salad, I decided to use two huge bowls of it in an improvised slapstick sequence that involved me and the head girl performing a doctors' sketch that culminated in my stripping down to long johns and running riot with the shaving cream. All this to the accompaniment of live drum rolls and a record of Frank Sinatra singing 'Strangers in the Night'. Not everyone was equally amused.

The day has flown and is still flying. I must go, but before I do I need to record this. I asked The Chief for the three quotations that he had found most valuable during his long and remarkable life. He gave me these:

'Labour, Art, Worship, Love, these make men's lives.'

'I am come that they might have life and that they might have it more abundantly.' Jesus Christ.

'O let me learn to do what is possible.' Goethe.

---

[*] Sir William Lawrence Bragg CH, OBE, MC, FRS (1890–1971), best known for his work on X-ray diffraction, won the Nobel Prize for Physics in 1915, with his father. He was later director of the Cambridge Cavendish Laboratory.

Sunday, 31 July 1966

The sun is shining, though none of it reaches my room. I don't mind. I'm very happy here. It is the thirty-first of July 1966, Sal's 16th birthday. I love her and she loves me. She understands me, too, which is very nice. This evening I'm going over to Putney to her house for a birthday supper. It will be charming.

Meanwhile I'm here at my desk, having just completed my 5,000-word 'diary' of the CIS Arts Festival.* I'm editing the souvenir magazine (of course) and, now all the contributions are in, it's clear that the star of the show was Mr Antony Hopkins,† who conducted the orchestra, and swept in and out of the school grounds in one or other of his E-type Jaguars. (One has the number plate, AH 600; the other 1 CAH – I see Antony Hopkins. How could you miss him?) 'Music is like a group of men who do not understand a word of French watching a film of Brigitte Bardot – it has its compensations,' he declared before raising his baton to take the orchestra through a Lennox Berkeley Divertimento. Some thought him vulgar and unnecessarily noisy. Others were bowled over. It ain't easy being a star.

Highlights of the festival for me (apart from my French Ham in the trilingual production of *Noah*) were discovering the poetry of Robert Frost and meeting Mr and Mrs Cecil Day-Lewis.‡ They gave a wonderful poetry reading and were delightful – indeed a very nice letter from Jill D.-L. has arrived this morning. I also made new friends – especially Jessie Sayre from Washington DC (daughter of the Dean of Washington Cathedral and granddaughter of President Woodrow Wilson's daughter, Jessie) and Sibella Dorman of Badminton School and San Anton Palace, Malta GC. She has invited me to stay!§

I got back from the festival yesterday morning. Yesterday afternoon, I joined the rest of the nation (if not the world) in front of the TV to watch the Football World Cup: England v. Germany. We won! 4–2. It was the first football match I have ever watched from start to finish and, I admit, it was quite exciting! The stars of the day: Alf Ramsey, the wonderfully dry team manager, Bobby Moore,

---

* The ten-day festival, under the auspices of the UNESCO-affiliated Conference of Internationally Minded Schools, involved 120 young people, aged 16 to 18, from six different countries. George Smith, senior French master at Bedales, was honorary secretary of the CIS.

† Antony Hopkins CBE (b. 1921), composer, conductor, broadcaster remembered for his long-running BBC Radio series, *Talking About Music*.

‡ The poet Day-Lewis (1904–72), and his actress wife, Jill Balcon (1925–2009) subsequently sent their children, Tamasin and Daniel, to Bedales.

§ Sibella's father, Sir Maurice Dorman, was Governor General of Malta. Her subsequent claims to fame included being an early girlfriend of the Prince of Wales.

captain, Martin Peters, who put England ahead with his goal, and Geoff Hurst, who scored the other three. I like to think it was the fact that I was watching that helped us to win.*

From my point of view it was a memorable day for a different reason. In the evening I went with Ma to see Noël Coward in his double bill at the Queen's Theatre in Shaftesbury Avenue. The plays are not his best, but his presence is amazing – his speed of speech extraordinary, his panache unbeatable, his style unique. He is sixty-six and by all accounts not well. Last night was the last night – it was Noël Coward's farewell to the stage – and, yes, ladies and gentlemen, I was there.

Saturday, 6 August 1966

This is hell and I am HATING it. I am in Kent at something called the St Mary's Bay Camp organised by Lady Astor and the Children's Country Holiday Fund. It is a worthy cause – giving deprived children a seaside holiday – but the children are ghastly (really ghastly!) and the place is grim, grim, grim. The huts are horrible – torn lino on the floors, no curtains, cold water, disgusting lavatories. The food is uneatable – quite revolting. The 'organisation' utterly hopeless. I am a 'volunteer helper' and I DEEPLY REGRET letting Ma push me into this. I blame her wretched Black Bombers!† She is on manic overdrive.

Sunday, 7 August 1966

I am on the five o'clock from Folkestone, going home. I did the two and a half hour walk to Romney Marsh this morning and then pleaded sick. I know this is feeble, but I could not stand it any longer. I am returning to London (my natural habitat!) and I'm going to see Sal. (Do not reproach me, dear reader. If you had a choice between spending time in a squalid 'holiday' camp with a bunch of lawless 8-year-olds or falling into the gentle arms of a beautiful, blonde 16-year-old with breasts like pomegranates, which would you choose? I rest my case, m'lud.)

Monday, 8 August 1966

It is clear that I was *meant* to come home. I arrived to find a wonderful letter from Sal waiting for me. She sent it on the 6th, when we thought we weren't going to meet up again until she gets back from France. I love the way it begins:

---

* GB has not watched a football match since; nor has England won the World Cup since. He rests his case.
† GB's mother had been prescribed strong antidepressants that came in the form of large black capsules.

My dearest,

First and foremost – how empty and unexciting it all is without you. I miss you already and six weeks of it seems unbearable. Almost unbearable. Two things help – one, I know you like to be missed, and two: you always seem to love me better when I'm not there.

I love it all, in fact. I love her, in fact. Today, I'm 'resting', playing Scrabble with sister Virginia, working on my theatre programme scrapbooks, polishing off the material for the festival magazine before I send it to the printer. Tomorrow, at 11.00 a.m., Sally will be here!

Thursday, 11 August 1966

Cabinet reshuffle. George Brown becomes Foreign Secretary! He switches places with Michael Stewart who now goes to the Department of Economic Affairs. This is Wilsonian manoeuvring to reward Brown for staying on board when he threatened to quit over the wages freeze last month. But the volatile Mr Brown, 51, is famously pro-Europe so it may be good news for the nation! (That's the view of GDB. *The Times* thinks otherwise.)

Also on the front page today: Mr Heath was turned away from a reception in honour of the Deputy Prime Minister of South Vietnam at the Dorchester Hotel last night because the security men thought his invitation might be a fake. The US have conducted an underground nuclear test in Nevada and a Lunar Orbiter has been launched from Cape Kennedy to take photographs of the moon's surface. The Monopolies Commission says that Unilever Ltd and Procter and Gamble Ltd should reduce the selling price of household detergents by twenty per cent. And foot-and-mouth disease is spreading across the countryside . . . which is why I'm living in Baker Street.

Sal will be here at 4.30 p.m.

Monday, 15 August 1966

Refreshed by my beautiful girlfriend and boosted by my A Level results just in – straight As for the As and a 1 and a 2 for S Level – I have returned to the horrors of the St Mary's Bay Camp to do my duty . . . Tomorrow at dawn we take a coach to Dover and *walk back*: it's twenty-one miles and I will have four snivelling and unruly urchins in my care. It can and it will be done!

'When we get up tomorrow morning we may well be able to do without our tragic awareness for an hour or two, but we shall desperately need our sense of the comic.' Eric Bentley.

Friday, 19 August 1966

Suddenly, just now, I thought of Betteshanger and singing Nightingales: 'The day thou gavest, Lord, is ended . . .' It has been a long, long day. It began at the camp, with us checking all the huts and every child and their luggage to uncover any stealing (there had been quite a bit – the girls as bad as the boys), then the buses left in convoy for the long journey back to Ladbroke Grove. I didn't enjoy one minute of it, but I am glad I didn't chicken out entirely. And tonight I had my reward: I joined Gin and boyfriend (he's not yet popped the question!) for dinner at Beoty's and I had my favourite: a very tasty *Sole Meunière*. And for my next treat: the Whitehall Theatre on Wednesday to see the beautiful Mr Danny La Rue and the delightful Miss Barbara Windsor in *Come Spy With Me*! Now *that's* my idea of a fun night out.

Sunday, 11 September 1966

I am sitting with a cup of tea in the Festival Club, 54 George Street, Edinburgh. This has been my base all week – where I've written up my notes, etc. My weekly club membership (15/-) expires today and I am on the twelve o'clock train home, reaching King's Cross at 7.54 p.m. It has been a satisfying week, though a bit lonely (which is odd since I've been busy-busy-busy all the time). I have been to twelve shows (see separate notebook for my reviews) and seen some of our great actresses giving their all – notably Gwen Ffrangcon-Davies and Wendy Hiller, and Flora Robson as Hecuba. (Jane Asher was Cassandra – and also a perfect Perdita in *Winter's Tale*. She could be the new love of my life, but she appears committed elsewhere!)* I also went to the ABC [cinema] and saw *Dr Zhivago* and fell in love with Julie Christie – she is *so* beautiful. And back in the real world, I made a lovely new friend who made me feel less lonely: Honey Blake. (I love her name!) We had supper here on Friday and I took her out for a Chinese last night. I wonder if I will see her again? Probably not.

Wednesday, 28 September 1966

This is my last term at Bedales. Eight weeks from now I will be taking my Oxford Entrance exams. This time next year I shall be starting at university – if not Oxford then somewhere else, Cambridge, Bristol, York, Sussex, Reading . . . I have the interviews coming up shortly. And then what? Strange to say, I don't

---

* Jane Asher (b.1946) was then, famously, the girlfriend of one of the Beatles, Paul McCartney. In the summer of 1966, the group, then at the height of their popularity, undertook their final world tour.

believe that I am going to be an actor after all. I think I realised that for the first time in my life today – this very afternoon – when I was walking with Simon [Cadell] through the orchard on our way down to Pefe for tea at the Donkey Cart. Simon knows he's going to be an actor. It's his destiny. That's what he lives for. That's *why* he's alive. Olivier says that if you want to be an actor, don't be. If you *need* to be an actor, then be one. I want to be a whole variety of things – but suddenly I'm thinking an 'actor' *tout court* probably isn't one of them. (Secret truth: I'm not sure that I'm quite good enough to be a *great* actor and if you can't be that, what's the point?)

Later

We talked about 'great acting' and 'star quality'. We talked about David Warner's Hamlet. It's all the rage – Hamlet, the contemporary student prince in his college scarf etc. – and it's a fine performance in an interesting production (Peter Hall), but, despite the brouhaha, do we reckon it's one of the all-time greats? No. David Warner is a wonderful actor, but does he have that 'little bit extra' – as per the story of Dame Edith Evans and the young director who had spent day after day of rehearsal telling her where to stand, when to sit, how to say this line and that ... Eventually, Dame Edith turned to him: 'Young man, when are you going to give me a moment to do that little extra something the audience has come for?' On Saturday the school film was *All About Eve*. George Sanders has that 'little bit extra'. (If I could be as good as George Sanders I'd be an actor.) He was a Bedalian!*

Simon and I are planning some sketches for the next Merry Evening – including one about us, set forty years from now, in which Simon has become a great star and I've become a down-on-his-luck waiter, and I'm serving him a drink and he doesn't recognise me. Funny we hope – and poignant!

Saturday, 5 November 1966

The highlight of half-term – the highlight of the year, of the *decade* possibly! – was 8.30 p.m. last night at the Golders Green Hippodrome. Simon and I went to see Miss Marlene Dietrich and she was, indeed, sensational. We knew that she would be, of course – but the reality exceeded our expectations. The delayed start; the sense of anticipation; the prolonged overture; the rustling of the curtains; the completely manufactured but nonetheless real anxiety: will-she-

---

* George Sanders (1906–72) was at Bedales, 1915–19. He won an Academy Award as Best Supporting Actor for his performance in *All About Eve*, 1950.

won't-she-be-appearing . . . and, suddenly, she does! We find her, in a spotlight, in *that* dress, in that outrageous floor-length fur, with those eyes and that teasing smile and we *roar* – we stand and we cheer – and she laughs at us and takes it as her due! *Formidable* in every sense of the word. Every element of the evening was impeccable: her appearance, her face, her hair, her arched eyebrows, her voice, her banter, her timing, her repertoire, her arrangements . . . take a bow, Mr Bacharach – I want my *life* arranged by you!

In the programme, there is a note about her by Ernest Hemingway: 'I think she knows more about love than anyone. I know that every time I have seen Marlene Dietrich ever, she has done something to my heart and made me happy. If this makes her mysterious then it is a fine mystery.' The mystery to me is how the magic is contrived. From start to finish, there are tingles up your spine. She is extraordinary. Never mind love, I think she knows more about *theatre* than anyone.

When it was over, the *moment* it was over, Simon said, 'Follow me!' We raced into the street and round to the stage door. A crowd was already gathering and a car was waiting. Simon said, 'That'll be the decoy car – let's wait at the front.' So we did. And we were duly rewarded – after about half an hour another limousine appeared and drew up in the street in front of us. A policeman appeared and then another. There was a flurry of movement around the theatre doors and suddenly she was there, before us, within touching distance. She was small and looked so gentle – and she smiled at us. As she walked towards the car, from around the building a crowd came surging – men and women, young and old – and just as I thought she was about to be trampled underfoot I realised that two men – her driver and one of the policemen – were lifting her bodily onto the roof of the limousine. They held her as she struggled to her feet (she was wearing a sort of leather miniskirt!) and, on spindly high heels, she then began to teeter about the roof of the car – her arms outstretched to maintain her balance. She looked down at us, laughing, as we began to cheer. As she mouthed the words 'I love you!' her driver held up a sheaf of photographs for her – already signed – and she took them and, wobbling to and fro on the roof, began to distribute them to the adoring fans. When the pictures were all gone, she revolved slowly, surveying the scene one final time before lowering herself onto her bottom and edging herself towards the side of the car – and me. This was Golders Green at midnight and Marlene Dietrich was coming off the roof of her limousine into my arms. Her legs were thrust towards me. As the policeman helped her to the ground, for a never-to-be-forgotten moment in my hands I held Marlene Dietrich's left thigh.

Monday, 28 November 1966

I have just emerged from three hours of General Paper I of what is described as 'The Examination of the Men's Colleges of the University of Oxford for Admission and Entrance Awards'. We were faced with a six-page essay on authoritarianism by Hannah Arendt. I answered the question, 'What sort of evidence do you find for or against the view that "we are in fact confronted with a simultaneous recession of both freedom and authority in the modern world"?' I have no idea what I said or why.

Wednesday, 30 November 1966

I came out of this morning's (okayish) English Literature examination and was summoned to Mr Slack's study at 12.45. He was beaming and hopping from foot to foot the way he does. He asked if I'd like to be head boy. I said, 'Yes, of course, thank you very much.' He said, 'You don't seem very pleased. It's only for a few weeks, until the end of term.' I said, 'No, I'm delighted, thank you.' 'We didn't ask you before,' he said, 'because we thought you were so busy with all your activities, with the things you do for Block II and so on.' 'That's fine,' I said, but I could see that he was surprised that I wasn't as pleased as he expected me to be. 'And you didn't need to be head boy to get into university,' he went on. I said thank you again and we shook hands. 'I didn't realise it was important to you,' he said.

That's what I think is interesting. He didn't realise that it would matter to me. Of course I wanted to be head boy. And now I am, it's too late and it doesn't mean a hill of beans.

Monday, 5 December 1966

This morning: Petersfield 8.30 – Guildford 9.24 – Reading 10.13. Interview with someone from the English Department [at Reading University]. He was youngish, bespectacled and bearded. He had a tiny room, not much bigger than a coffin, a desk piled high with papers, a small window and on the back of his door a huge poster of W. H. Auden. We talked about the lines on Auden's face – so many of them, criss-crossing his features like tram lines. It was not an interesting or promising encounter. I know they won't offer me a place and I can't say I'm sorry. I came back on the 2.34 and got to Pefe at 4.30. I'm now in the Library – the one place here that I'll really miss. I love it in here – the beams, the smell of beeswax, the absolute silence, the copy of Caroline Spurgeon's tome on Shakespeare's imagery that no one else seems to know about . . . I'm upstairs in the gallery looking down. At one end I see the giant globe, at the other the Library calendar. I'll miss the calendar!

Yes, for their sustaining philosophy some turn to the Bible, some to the Koran. I go to the Library calendar. Here is my latest batch of wisdom, my favourites from November:

5 November: 'Idleness leads to languor, and languor to disgust.' Amiel's Journal.

7 November: 'Always laugh when you can; it is cheap medicine. Merriment is a philosophy not well understood. It is the sunny side of existence.' Lord Byron.

13 November: 'If I were ambitious, I would desire no finer epitaph than that it should be said of me, "He has added a little to the sweetness of the world and a little to its light."' Havelock Ellis.

21 November: 'Perhaps the most valuable result of all education is the ability to make yourself do the thing you have to do, when it ought to be done, whether you like it or not.' T. H. Huxley.

Friday, 16 December 1966

I'm on the train back from Oxford. I'll write it up properly later – dreaming spires etc. For now, this is the essence: it didn't go wonderfully well. The disaster was the Big Interview with three senior New College dons. It was led by Mr Quinton* – well-built, beaming, genial, very much the man running the show. He thought to put me at my ease by starting off with some questions about my much-vaunted interest in prisons. I burbled rather boastfully for a minute or two, when I heard him ask: 'Mr Brandreth, what is a "star" prisoner?' I didn't know. 'It's a term quite commonly used in the English Prison Service,' he said pleasantly. 'It means a first-time prisoner.' 'Oh,' I said, 'I didn't know.' From then on I was completely thrown.

Damn and blast. Reading here we come!

Saturday, 17 December 1966

I've been doing the rounds saying my goodbyes. Gonda [the librarian], Rachel [the drama teacher], The Chief. I will miss our games of Scrabble. He says he will too! (I shall miss Scrabble and tea with Mr and Mrs Cox as well.) I'm trying to see everyone because when it's over it's over. I shall not come back.

I must add this. I've been getting letters and notes from the Block II people –

---

* Anthony Quinton (b.1925), now Baron Quinton of Holywell, political and moral philosopher, Fellow of New College from 1955, Fellow of All Souls and Master of Trinity, 1978–87.

lovely letters and notes, lots of them. (So many I think it must have been coordinated.) They're all going in the archive. 'May I thank you for being so kind and generous to me. The school shan't be the same when you leave. In fact, it will be much quieter. Yours faithfully, James.' 'Thank you very much for letting me be on your supper table. I have enjoyed it very much. Well, goodbye Gyles. Lots of love, Biddy (or Bridget if *you* prefer.)' &c.

I'm off to the dance now. MC and cabaret. I'm doing a soft-shoe-shuffle with the headmaster. I'm imitating him and he is imitating me.

Tuesday, 19 December 1966

This telegram came today, sent from Oxford at 3.40 p.m.:

AWARDED SCHOLARSHIP NEW COLLEGE CONGRATULA-TIONS

= QUINTON

Thursday, 22 December 1966

I'm meeting Sal at Tottenham Court Road tube at 4.00 p.m. We're going to Foyle's to buy Christmas books and then having tea at Lyons – with toasted teacakes, I hope.

The post has brought this letter from HEG – Harold Gardiner, my English teacher and the best of men.

> *Ridge Cottage,*
> *Steep,*
> *Petersfield, Hants.*
> *20 Dec. 1966*

My dear Gyles,

> *What an extraordinary thing, that, at the last moment, neither of us felt capable of facing the other; and so the congratulations are by the more formal medium of a letter. They are none the less heartfelt, and of the warmest. You have deserved every grain of success, for the way you have done everything one could have hoped for, and then still found the time and the drive to do more. I don't think a swelled head is a serious risk, and so I can say how much more pleased I am for your success than for any other pupil's whom I have ever taught, or whom I am ever likely to teach.*
> > *Aye,*
> > > *Harold*

PART TWO
'Child of the Sixties, Man of the Seventies'

The American Way

February – October 1967

Friday, 17 February 1967

I'm in Baltimore, Maryland, USA. I'm alone, upstairs, in a large house on Ridgedale Road. It's a long road – the house is Number 5700. It's a fine house, with large rooms and an easy, slightly ramshackle feel. This is going to be my home for the next few months while I'm here teaching English and French at the Park School, Baltimore. The house belongs to Jack and Sydney Ramey. I met Jack at the CIS Festival last summer and I like him very much. I'm tapping this out on his typewriter, sitting at his desk in the room he calls his 'library'. It's a fine library, a library he uses – the shelves, the chairs, the floor, the grand piano, are all piled high with books. Jack is 36 (a little more, perhaps), short, dark, plump-ish, a talented pianist and occasional composer who teaches music and Latin at Park and has done so for the past thirteen years. Sydney is his wife (her sister is called Robin!): she works at the school, too, on the administration side. She is a large lady with close-cropped hair and a heart of gold. Their children are Jack Arthur (aged 7) and Mark (6): they make my brother Ben look positively saintly. The noise from their bedroom this morning was horrendous and started at the crack of dawn. Eventually they were silenced by their father who, standing on the landing just outside my bedroom, hollered up to them: 'Shut it, kids, and turn on the boob-toob!'

The boob-toob is clearly central to the American way of life. At 10.00 a.m. today, after an excellent breakfast – cereal, 'Beep' (an orange juice of sorts), scrambled eggs, toast and coffee – I watched *Divorce Court*, an extraordinary programme in which real divorce cases are re-enacted with 'legal conferences' and emotional outbursts stage-managed to allow time for the commercials to be shown. I'm now in here writing this because snow has been falling all night – thick and fast – and Baltimore's Snow Emergency Plan (Phase I) has been called into action: across the city there is NO SCHOOL today. The past two days have been memorable, to say the least.

Just forty-eight hours ago, on Wednesday at 12 noon, accompanied by Ma and Pa and Gin, I arrived at London Airport. At 3.00 p.m., London time, Flight TWA 701 for New York and Washington took off on schedule. I was well placed in a window-seat behind the wing with an excellent view of the world and its clouds. Soon after take-off, newspapers and a tasty chicken lunch were served. I had no immediate neighbour, but a sweaty all-American paunch was two seats away and I had to clamber over it each time I wanted to get to my free TWA soap and dentifrice. The seven-hour flight was smooth all the way. I didn't pay my two bucks for the movie (*The Russians Are Coming*) but slept right through it, waking to enjoy a 'snack, served with mustard – to add zest to eating'.

JFK Airport in New York was not a happy place. Immigration and Customs were neither welcoming nor courteous. Finding my way to the connecting flight was a nightmare, but I managed it. Others didn't. When the flight took off, in a plane for 108, there were four hostesses and four passengers. Even so, the service wasn't up to much. We reached Dulles, the international airport serving Washington DC, at around 8.30 p.m. local time and were driven directly from the door of the plane to the airport building in a fantastic contraption called a 'mobile waiting lounge'. Jack Ramey – bless him! – was there to meet me. We collected my baggage, looked round the magnificent but empty airport (magnificent because new, empty because it's twenty-five miles from Washington proper and DC already has two other airports) and set off for Baltimore. The drive was eventful. On America's newest and most deserted highway, we ran out of gas! (Jack is a musician not a mechanic.) Happily, the second car that passed us stopped and *from his car* the driver *telephoned* a garage who sent a man to help us!

By 12.30 a.m. US time (5.30 a.m. in London) I was in bed, but six hours later I was up again and three hours after that I found myself on a school bus joining a party of senior Park School students on a day-long outing to Washington DC. Within twenty-four hours of my arrival, I had been on a guided tour of the World Bank, the International Monetary Fund, the Folger Shakespeare Library (the finest collection of Shakespeare papers in the world) and the Library of Congress! Welcome to America, Mr Brandreth . . .

I think I'm going to like it here. I shall miss Sal, I know. She is going to write me at least a paragraph a day and promises to be my 'devoted and ever-faithful angel'! We are both going to be faithful and concentrate on our work. Park is a large school – five hundred pupils, ninety-five per cent Jewish and all of them wealthy (the older kids drive to school in their own Cadillacs: the teachers arrive in Volkswagens!). I'm hoping the teaching will work out okay. They 'just lurve' my English accent – and the 'Oxford scholar' thing goes down a treat, so fingers crossed. I am certainly expected. There is a charming piece about my arrival in *The Postscript*, the school's weekly newspaper:

> The British are coming! Don't be startled if some long-haired stranger (speaking the Queen's English beautifully) stops you in the Hall on February 15 asking for directions. It will only be Gyles Brandreth, the tall, dark, blue-eyed eighteen-year-old bringing the charm, tradition, refinement and modness of our mother country to Park . . .

They will be disappointed in the short-back-and-sides I acquired in Baker Street on Tuesday. I look nothing like a Beatle.

Thursday, 2 March 1967

Extraordinary. Last night I went to Nancy Eisner's house – for port (at 6.30 p.m.!) followed by a formally served and very splendid dinner. About twenty minutes into the meal, Mr Eisner turned to me and said, 'Would you like a job, Gyles? My advertising agency is always on the look-out for talent. I want you to join my team of copy-writers. I believe you could go all the way.' Assuming he was in jest, I said, 'When do I start?' He replied, 'Tomorrow!' He was in earnest! He has read what I have written for *The Postscript*, he has seen the CIS magazine, he says I 'speak pure copy', some of the 'smartest copy' he's ever heard. He has spoken with his friend, the principal of the upper school at Park, and the school is ready to release me. Apparently the money will be fabulous and 'the sky's the limit'!

That's what I keep hearing. It's the phrase of the season. Just before I came out here I met up with the monkey-faced boy from Stowe.[*] 'We shall conquer the world!' he kept saying, dancing around me like a whirling dervish. 'Come and join us, Gyles. The sky's the limit! *The sky's the limit!*' I made my excuses and left. I shall decline Mr Eisner's kind offer as well. But it's nice to feel wanted.

Friday, 3 March 1967

I am in the heart of Manhattan, sitting on a stool in Woolworths, with a Coke and a hamburger, having just bought myself a $6 pair of grey trousers. I drove up last

---

[*] Richard Branson (b.1950) was launching a magazine for young people, *Student*. From Stowe he had written to GB when GB was editing the school magazine at Bedales. When they met, Branson suggested they go into business together and begin a publishing empire. GB declined.

night with Jack Ramey. We arrived at the Statler Hilton on 33rd Street at six o'clock and, at 8.00 p.m., in the vast and thickly carpeted Georgian Room, I addressed the massed ranks of the National Association of Independent Schools. My theme: last summer's arts festival and how we need more of them. JR is staying at the Hilton, while I am staying in Brooklyn with Agnes and Aunt Polly and a rum assortment of the McSkimming clan.* Cousin Agnes is a good woman (courageous and kind – and so spruce: she was in the US Navy, flies the flag on her porch and her lavatory bowl is filled with bright blue water, amazing!). Aunt Polly is 85: she has had both a stroke and a heart attack in recent days,' but appeared to appreciate the china roses I brought as a belated birthday present.

This has been a good day. The sun is brilliant, but the wind is sharp. I like New York. It's my kind of town! The centre of it, where I've been wandering, Third to Seventh Avenues between 38th and 47th Streets, is fun – a mix of Piccadilly Circus and Tottenham Court Road at Christmas time. The skyscrapers *are* incredible. I have just emerged from the Radio City Music Hall. $1.35 but what a show! Crooning singers, symphony orchestra (oh yes!), funny man on trampoline, full-scale ballet, then the endless chorus line of high-kicking Rockettes in a spectacular finale before the movie – *The 25th Hour*, a heart-clutching Second World War *Dr Zhivago*. (Cousin Agnes would have loved it.) And now back to Brooklyn. I mustn't be late. Apparently, Aunt Polly is keeping her teeth in until she sees me.

Wednesday, 8 March 1967

My 19th birthday. Sydney Ramey is baking a chocolate cake as I write and, before I go to babysit for the Kleins (for $2), it's birthday drinks (and presents) at the Boltzes. And yet . . . I'm not feeling birthday-like. I'm feeling sad – see below. And I'm feeling anxious. I don't like the way my head sticks forward and my ears stick out. I don't like the fact that I haven't once looked at any of the Economics textbooks I brought out with me. I don't like the constant worry about money. The school was going to pay me an 'honorarium', but there's been no mention of it yet. I'm babysitting as often as I can, but unless the honorarium materialises I'm going to end up working for Mr Eisner!

I'm sad because this morning I received a birthday telegram from Sally at Bedales in which I learnt of the death of Mr Badley. This isn't really a surprise – he was 102! – but it marks the end of an era and, for me, the end of a special friendship. At least I can say that I shook the hand that shook the hand of Oscar

---

* Cousins of GB on his mother's side of the family.

Wilde! I have spent the afternoon writing a long letter to Sal with instructions for our memorial magazine.* I'd like to fly home for three weeks to sort it out, but I simply can't afford to.

I can't really afford the $13 it'll cost me to get to New York tomorrow. I'm going back to Brooklyn because this morning, during a French class with the twelve-year-olds, I was called away to the telephone. Aunt Polly died last night and the clan would like me to represent the English side of the family at the funeral. I have written to Ma and Pa with the news. I'd have sent a cable, but I simply don't have the dollars and cents.

Thursday, 9 March 1967

The honorarium – $10 per week – WILL be forthcoming. And Mr Klein (Vice President, Allegheny Pepsi-Cola) says that, as far as babysitting goes, 'The sky's the limit!'!!

Much comforted, I blew $12.90 on the Trailways bus from Baltimore to New York city. Via subway and bus and a long, long walk I reached the McManus Funeral Parlour in Brooklyn at 6.00 p.m. As soon as I arrived, I was ushered into the Chapel of Rest and immediately startled by the number – and volubility – of my black relations! The room was dimly lit, stifling hot and crowded with overweight Negroes, weeping and wailing. It took me a moment to register that I had been shown into the wrong chapel. Eventually, I found the right place – but the scene that greeted me there was no less strange. The room was packed with a variety of grotesques (my relations!), a number of them dressed in elaborate, flowing white robes. Cousin Agnes is a Mason and the Service of Last Rites was to be conducted by members of the Lodge of the Eastern Star.

Before the service began, I joined the line snaking past Aunt Polly's casket. It was an open casket. Dear dead Aunt Polly was sitting up in it looking better than she has done in years. Evidently, the morticians had had a field day. (I expect Agnes said, 'The sky's the limit!') The old lady was barely recognisable. As Agnes remarked sweetly, 'Mom never wore lipstick during her life, but we think it kinda suits her in death. She'd have wanted to look her best to meet her Maker.'

The service was bizarre, conducted by a Scottish parson and enlivened by weird chanting and ritualistic gyrations from two men and six women (Agnes

---

* In anticipation of Mr Badley's death, the Bedales Society had asked GB to edit a memorial magazine in his honour. *John Haden Badley, 1865–1967, Bedales School and its Founder*, edited by Gyles Brandreth and Sally Henry, was published later in 1967.

among them) dressed in the druidical garb of the order of the Eastern Star. When it was over, we all filed past Aunt Polly again and then set off for 2160 Coleman Street and the wake . . . It was not a pretty affair.

Friday, 10 March 1967

I retired to bed as early as I decently could. I slept remarkably well, considering . . . Yes, cousin Agnes tucked me up in the very bed in which dear Aunt Polly died just seventy-two hours ago. 'We've changed the linen, of course, Gyles.' I shared the room with a Canadian called Wally and his ten-year-old son. I hope we are not related, but I fear that we may be.

I was up at 8.00, good breakfast, cooked by Agnes for us all (she is a good, good woman), and at 9.00 the limousines arrived to whisk us back to the funeral home. There we had a last sighting of Aunt Polly before the closing of the casket and the long drive (an hour and more) to the cemetery at Port Washington. I was in the second limo and sat in the back row with Betty and Sloan – a mistake, in one way: Sloan is huge (I was squashed all the way to the graveside); useful in another: they invited me down to stay on their boat in the Bahamas, whenever I want and for as long as I want.* The best bit of the drive was the limo's electric windows: the interment was a wash-out. We got to the cemetery at 11.00 to find that the graves had all been flooded. After a powwow between Agnes, the Scottish parson and the cemetery officials, it was agreed that we would 'bury' Aunt Polly temporarily in a vault. When a suitable grave dried up, she would be moved to it. No extra charge.

In the event, we were only in the cemetery for a matter of minutes. We then all piled back into the limos for the return to Brooklyn. En route, I caused something of a drama by needing a 'comfort break'. The funeral cortege all parked up outside the roadside Rest Room was quite a sight. Sloan was much amused. (And relieved. He joined me in the Gents. 'We writers must stick together.') Back at Coleman Street the wake resumed, with the Scottish parson leading the feasting and drinking. (It was incredible the way that man quaffed and sluiced!) I chatted with Sloan, about women and himself (his principal preoccupations), the war in Vietnam and the family. I like him. At two it was time to set off and, as I departed, Agnes came up to me and pressed a $20 bill into my hand. 'From Aunt Polly. She wanted you to have it. I know she did. She couldn't talk after the stroke, but if she could have done she'd have said so.'

---

* GB's cousin Betty was married to Sloan Wilson (1920–2003), a popular American author whose books included *The Man in the Gray Flannel Suit* (1955) and *A Summer Place* (1958), both of which were made into movies.

Wednesday, 22 March 1967

This has been my best day in America so far. New England is very beautiful. The snow has been falling thick and fast: there is picture postcard loveliness all around. Sydney is the easiest travelling companion* and today her mother (who glories in the name of Mrs Clapp) has taken us in the family Jeep on a tour that included South Deerfield (where they make pickles), Old Deerfield (where they make young gentlemen – there's a men's college there and a 300-year-old village 'perfectly preserved'), Amherst (where we visited the home of Emily Dickinson) and Northampton (the home of Smith College, Sydney's *alma mater*). Highlights of the day: the Robert Frost Library at Amherst College and the Kirby Theatre there, a jewel. I wore my duffel coat (thank you, Ma) and overshoes (thank you, Mrs Clapp) and stayed dry and snug all day. We're back in Conway now. I have been reading Robert Frost and Emily Dickinson by the fire. Later I shall join the ladies to watch Cassius Clay's latest bout on the boob-toob.† Tomorrow, we go to Boston, 'cradle of liberty', and then on, with Sydney's horn-playing sister, Robin, to Cambridge, to Harvard University where, wait for it, at the Sanders Hall, tomorrow night I will be attending a lecture on European Defence being given by the Rt Hon. Edward Heath MP.

Friday, 24 March 1967
Good Friday

Mr Heath's lecture did not set the Potomac on fire. It *was* interesting and I was pleased to see the great man in the flesh – he was much more relaxed and convincing than when giving his fireside chats on British TV – but it was not a barrelload of laughs. Whereas horn-playing Robin and her trumpeting husband Malcolm are very jolly. Their flat is tiny (by US standards) and made tinier by the sound-proof 'practise chamber' – a booth the size of a telephone box – that sits in the middle of their sitting room. Malcolm is a professional musician and so, by definition, poor, but music and 'the life of the mind' are what drive them and they are special people as a consequence. (There is a drawback: their ghastly minah bird, brought back from their travels in South America. Shades of Mitou.)‡

* GB and Sydney Ramey were taking a week-long Easter break in Massachusetts and New York.
† Cassius Clay (b.1942), so-called by GB though he changed his name to Muhammed Ali in 1964, was fighting Zora Folley at Madison Square Garden in New York. He beat Folley with a technical knock-out. This was Ali's last bout for three years, following his refusal to be drafted into the US Army.
‡ The Brandreth family parrot, released over London by GB's father in 1957.

Good Friday and I'm not going to church. Odd when you think of the endless hours I spent at St Stephen's, Gloucester Road, and Holy Trinity, Brompton. (Happy hours.) Pa still gets down on his knees by the bed every night to say his prayers. I sometimes say them in my head, but I'm not sure that anybody's listening.

Today we're off on the Freedom Trail. (They are quite ambivalent about their relationship with 'the Old Country'. And they are utterly convinced that *they* won the war!)

Monday, 27 March 1967

Another day, another parrot. On Saturday I made my way to Candlewood Farm, Ipswich, Mass., to take lunch with an old man who is an old friend of Sal's mother. He is called Mr Burrage. He is 80, small, nut-brown (as a consequence of many a Jamaican winter) and lives alone in a fabulous house on a great estate. He made a splendid entrance, coming down the central staircase with a parrot perched on his shoulder. His English butler was everything you could have wished for: as old as his master, but terribly pale, with sunken cheeks and wispy white hair. Hemcliff (that was his name – I promise) mixed the cocktails (gin & vermouth), announced luncheon and served it. I acquitted myself reasonably well, I think. I did not mistake the fingerbowls for cold lemon soup, but I wasn't quite sure about the knife rests. Should I or should I not have returned my knife to the knife rest after use?

I'm now in New York and just in from the official tour of the *New York Times*. A fascinating experience – exhilarating and possibly inspiring. (Well, what *am* I going to do with my life?) We were shown every aspect of the newspaper-making process. In the newsroom – the open-plan journalists' enclave – I even had a sighting of the great Harrison E. Salisbury at his desk.[*] He looked satisfy-ingly like a newsman played by James Stewart. The talk here is entirely of the war in Vietnam and everyone I know (other than my cousins in Brooklyn) is now opposed to it. The Rameys and the Clapps and their kind also talk of 'culture' and European culture in particular. They are tremendous Anglophiles. The Third Programme and the BBC World Service loom large in their lives. They all say I must, must, MUST see *Blow-Up* with Vanessa Redgrave and David Hemmings. (I will, but I'm set on seeing Lynn Redgrave in *Georgy Girl* first.)

---

[*] Salisbury (1908–93) was a distinguished *New York Times* foreign correspondent and his reports from North Vietnam in 1966 fuelled mainstream opposition to the US war in Vietnam.

Sunday, 2 April 1967

I am out every night and exhausted! I'm Baltimore's novelty British teenager and a little weary of being expected to produce an endless stream of witty repartee coated with modest charm. I'll be glad when the end of term comes. I need to move on. How am I to fund my travels? With difficulty. I am hoping to do more poetry readings and I am fund-raising for Bedales, but will it be enough?*
Greyhound buses have dropped their $99 for 99 days offer. Just getting to California and back will cost $200 plus. Heigh-ho. These are the vicissitudes of this our sublunary existence.

I am missing Sally, but staying faithful.

Saturday, 15 April 1967

I have before me the final edition of today's *Baltimore Evening Sun*. The headline: 'NY Peace Marchers Hear King Call for Halt in Viet Bombing'. The story: 'Thousands of peace marchers jammed into United Nations plaza today to hear Dr Martin Luther King repeatedly call on the United States to "honor its word" and "stop the bombing" of North Vietnam.' I was one of them! At 7.00 a.m., with a small party from Park, I climbed aboard one of the six buses taking the Baltimore protesters to New York for the day. It was a memorable – and moving – experience. We walked in our thousands along the avenues of Manhattan with a sense of purpose: we felt we were doing something worthwhile and important. The war is wrong. I saw Dr King way, way in the distance. The loudspeakers destroyed the power of his oratory, but it didn't matter. It just felt good to be part of such a huge crowd and to know that we had right on our side.

I am spending most of my time, of course, with the faculty members at Park – liberal, Jewish, intellectual.. We all admire Dr King. Others feel differently. In the last presidential primary here in Maryland, George Wallace (the pro-segregationist white supremacist whose *wife* is now Governor of Alabama) secured 42 per cent of the vote.

Friday, 21 April 1967

Yesterday I went to the Maryland State Penitentiary, a disheartening experience. Had I hoped to find ideas for reform and progress, Baltimore is not the place. The food was good (they gave me lunch with the men) but that was all. The

---

* GB was being paid for giving occasional poetry readings to schools and local women's groups and could claim travelling expenses if he visited US-based Old Bedalians to solicit their support for the Bedales School Development Fund.

overcrowding is terrifying, with two men in cells for one in almost every instance – except for sex offenders, those in the punishment block and those on Death Row. One of the most alarming aspects is the way that all the prisoners are thrown together – from teenage first offenders to old lags, murderers, rapists, the lot. The attitude prevails that a man should 'pull himself up'. He doesn't get to have a different job, or get parole or take classes or play sports if he doesn't get himself up and do it. This means that those really in least need of help progress the fastest while the incapables sink further and further down.

Seeing how the death penalty is administered certainly confirms my view that execution is obscene. They use a gas chamber here – it looks like a small space capsule. The prison officer showing me round, pulled open the door, pointed to the metal chair within and said, 'Try it for size.' I was quite frightened. When they have executions, up to fifteen 'witnesses' are required to watch. Apparently, members of the public apply in droves. What's almost worse than the legalised slaughter itself is the way they operate Death Row: a series of isolated cells on a corridor leading to the gas chamber. One of the men I met has been on Death Row, alone in the same cell, and completely idle, for more than ten years.

On to jollier things: today is my last day at Park and (O joy, O rapture!) the school has given me a check (that's how they spell it) for $150. And I have another check for $8 from the Valley School where I've been doing the odd morning teaching French. This morning the 9th Graders (ages 14/15) gave me a surprise cookies and Coke party and tonight there's to be a dinner in my honour with the outgoing principal, the incoming principal, Uncle Tom Boltz and all. The new head has kindly asked me to stay on for the rest of the year and told me there's a job for me here whenever I want it. I don't think it's for me. I'm okay as a one-off novelty – I can hold a class for fifty minutes – but to be a *real* teacher you need staying power.

Konrad Adenauer[*] has died.

Tuesday, 25 April 1967

Busy busy. Dumbarton Oaks (with Hugh Wills from Bedales); Washington Cathedral (with Jessie Sayre – it's modelled on Canterbury Cathedral, but it's *bigger* than Canterbury, of course; they have a herb garden: the way Jessie calls it 'an urb garden' is very sexy!); the Smithsonian Institution (with David Schuchat[†]);

[*] Konrad Adenauer (1876–1967), first Chancellor of the Federal Republic of Germany, 1949–63.
[†] A Park School alumnus and friend of the Rameys, who put up GB in his Washington DC apartment.

and, tonight, I'm just in from a very plush four-hour candlelit dinner at '1786'. My hostess was Miss Emily Brown, a lovely lady, a *lonely* lady, born 1906, at Bedales in the early twenties, at the British embassy here since 1949. I was very flirtatious (Felix Krull!) – she is very lonely – and I agreed to see her again . . . She began by telling me that her years at Bedales were the worst of her life and ended by giving me £150 for the Bedales Development Campaign! (Am I feeling guilty? Just a touch.)

She drank six martinis. I drank wine. Delicious wine. Goodnight.

Sunday, 30 April 1967

I took the Greyhound bus, leaving Washington DC at 5.15 p.m. I reached Toronto at 9.10 a.m. Never again. I shall not to be crossing America by bus! I shall be going by air: half-price student standby. Uncle Jack was waiting for me.* He put me on the local bus for Etobicoke where Aunt Ede was waiting too – hair redder than ever, a little dumpier than I remember, all of four feet off the ground, wearing her white gangster raincoat and dark glasses. She started talking the moment I arrived. Seventy-two hours later she hasn't stopped. It's been fine – in its own extraordinary way, an alcohol-fuelled weekend during which I imagine I am the only one in the entire household to have drawn an even vaguely sober breath. They drink from dawn to dusk – and through the night. Uncle Jack had a flask with him for the wedding rehearsal. He is droll: around the house he wears nothing but a kimono and does nothing but sit in front of the boob-toob, glass and bottle in hand, watching the hockey and occasionally shouting 'Shut it, woman!' when Aunt Ede in the kitchen gets too voluble.

The wedding was fine. Uncle Jack travelled with a bottle and a glass in the bridal car! The ushers wore tuxedos, the bridesmaids were in yellow, the bride's outfit was simple and effective. The supper was dry, tough and served at six. There was a fizzy rosé for the toasts (cries of 'Where's the hard stuff gone?') but the moment the speeches were done (mercifully few and brief) the dancing and the serious boozing began. You have never seen anything like it! The music was Rolling Stones and similar; the bar was open and free. I did my jigging and poking to 'entertain' the crowd and each time Jack or Ede stumbled past they cried, 'Just wait till your parents hear about this, hic!' Eventually we got home and that's when the REAL drinking started – and it didn't stop until 5.00 a.m.!

* GB was visiting his mother's brother's family in Toronto to attend a family wedding. GB's grandmother took her two children, Jack and Alice, from India to Canada in the early 1930s. While GB's mother came to England to go to university, his uncle stayed in Canada where he worked for the Bank of Nova Scotia.

(Let's be fair: 4.00 a.m. – summertime began last night.) Giggling, gurgling, tippling, tumbling, belching, burping, I have never, EVER seen anything like it.

And this morning when I emerged they were already at it – the ladies, in curlers with cold cream covering their faces, tossing pancakes while tossing back Bloody Marys; the men in kimonos watching the hockey (there is always hockey on TV here – every hour of every day) each clutching his bottle to his chest. Johnnie (much improved since our European tour) proposed that I join him ground-hawk hunting and I'm glad he did. We escaped the House of Booze and drove into some fresh and lovely countryside and spent the whole afternoon wandering through the woods. It was really quite magical – streams, glades, spring flowers, horses running free . . . Nothing to shoot, however. At four, Johnnie set up some old tin cans and did a bit of target practice. I took a few pot shots and at least managed to hit the right hillside.

Wednesday, 3 May 1967

The Vietnam War can take a back seat. Elvis Presley has married Priscilla Beaulieu.

Last night I dined (beautifully) with Dr Edward Murphy and his wife. He is an Old Bedalian and the son of J. T. Murphy, the British Communist leader in the 1920s. Dr Murphy, who is taking me today to visit the Toronto Sick Children's Hospital where he works, showed me a photograph of himself on his father's shoulders in 1926. In the photo the little boy is holding hands with a familiar-looking figure. Yes, I can now say that I have shaken the hand that shook the hand of Joseph Stalin.

A letter has come from Sloan Wilson [the author, married to GB's cousin]. I asked him what lessons life has taught him. He said he'd think about it. He has – and here they are:

1. Liquid shoe polish doesn't work.
2. A man who wants time to read and write must let the grass grow long.
3. Beware of people who are always well-dressed.
4. The hardest part of raising children is teaching them to ride bicycles. A father can run beside the bicycle or stand yelling directions while the child falls. A shaky child on a bicycle for the first time needs both support and freedom. The realisation that this is what the child will always need can hit hard.
5. Children go away and live their own lives, starting when they are about eighteen. Parents who accept this as a natural part of the order of things will see their grown children surprisingly often.

6. Friends are fun, but they are more dangerous than strangers. Strangers ask for a quarter for a cup of coffee, while friends ask for a thousand dollars, no questions asked if you're a *real* friend. Some friends also have a roving eye for your wife and daughters.
7. Despite all the advice about how to achieve connubial bliss, a happy marriage is usually an unearned miracle. The reasons why some people get on so well together are as mysterious as the reasons why other people fight.
8. When things break around the house, call a handyman. No intelligent man is capable of fixing anything unless he has made home repair his business.

Saturday, 20 May 1967

Do not come to the greyest capital in the Western world for there is nothing to see – except grey civil servants in grey suits making their way to grey offices in tall grey buildings. The place is so dead it has a morbid fascination.

Where am I? Ottawa, of course, where the good souls are all tucked in bed by ten and up, eating porridge, well before 7.00 a.m. For nightlife, you go to neighbouring Hull. For shopping you go to Montreal. To sleep, you stay at home. I am with the Wises – lovely people: he is the son of Mrs Cox from Steep; she is a keen Christian Scientist. The liveliest part of my visit to date has been a Christian Science meeting. I have also been to the National Gallery. I recommend Simon Vouet's *The Fortune Teller* (c.1620) on the second floor. And in the half-empty Capitol Cinema I caught the Bristol Old Vic on tour – with a poor *R & J* and a fun *Measure for Measure* which I could just about hear above the coughing, chatting, tittering and rustling of sweet papers around me. I don't think they appreciate Shakespeare here. He wasn't Canadian and in this centennial year that's really all that counts.*

A lovely letter today from Sal – her 28th. We are numbering them so we know where we are. I miss her. I would like to be playing with her tonight.

Tuesday, 23 May 1967

Last night, at the end of the Victoria Day holiday, Dr Wise drove me downtown to Parliament Hill to witness 'the symbolic giving of centennial medallions to Canada's youth'. Today, in Montreal, just now – minutes ago – I was in the

---

* The birth of modern Canada dates from 1867 when British imperial rule ended and the 1867 Constitution Act brought about a new Confederation, creating 'one Dominion under the name of Canada' on 1 July.

Youth Pavilion at Expo '67 where the exhibits celebrate the young as the great idealists and world builders of the future! This fawning on us young is rather nauseating. I contrasted the huge romanticised photographs of 'youth in action' with the real thing all around me – bored, pimply and nose-picking.

To my surprise, Expo '67 is a messy success. See separate journal for my pavilion-by-pavilion account. For the record here, it *is* an amazing experience – and only $2.50 for the day. In the French, Canadian and Russian pavilions there's simply too much to absorb; Thailand, Israel, India, Egypt each tell a simple story well – without any politics. The Cuban pavilion is all propaganda, with a giant picture of a stout lady looking very like Mrs Krushchev in a black bathing suit illustrating 'Cubans at Play'. The British pavilion is best – it really is. You begin standing on a conveyor belt being taken on 'A Journey Thru Time' and end up in 'Britain Today', illustrated by film clips, moving models, records, puppets, etc. I felt quite proud and homesick. When Expo is over it should be transported to London brick by brick.

The food in here is outrageously expensive. I knew it would be. Mrs Wise has kindly equipped me with cheese sandwiches and an apple (carried in the blue duffel bag I won at Bingo in Broadstairs all those years ago). I am sitting on the grass by an artificial stream reflecting on the genius of Karsh of Ottawa. Every one of his photographs – Churchill, Kennedy, Picasso, Olivier – packs a punch. They're the best thing by far in the Canada pavilion.

Thursday, 8 June 1967

War rages.* And while it rages, life goes on. That's the message from my new friend, Richard Leacock, Old Bedalian documentary film-maker and pioneer of 'direct films', films that show us life 'as it is'.

In New York in the past twenty-four hours, while I've been following the news and feeling almost 'involved' because the United Nations is here, life has indeed been going on. I've seen three films – *Blow-Up, Fahrenheit 451* and *Deadlier than the Male* – and a play, *Black Comedy* at the Barrymore Theater on West 47th, and now I'm on the train coming back from a memorable day with a raft of long-lost relations. I have been upstate, to Ossining, to the hometown – to the home, in fact – of the last Brandreth to make any serious money (and the first,

---

* The Middle East 'Six Day War' broke out on 5 June 1967 when Israel launched 'pre-emptive strikes' against Arab forces, destroying 374 planes. On 10 June the fighting ended when Israel, having gained considerable territory, agreed to observe the United Nations ceasefire.

too!): 'Dr' Benjamin Brandreth, pioneer of Brandreth Pills. 'Dr' B. (the medical qualification was self-awarded) set off from Liverpool in 1835 determined to make his fortune. He succeeded. When he died in 1880 the *New York Times* credited him with a stack of real estate (including a mansion on Fifth Avenue) and cash in excess of a million dollars. He achieved it all with a simple laxative – an unremarkable patent medicine that when marketed by Dr Brandreth became a powerful cure-all. Each packet of pills (I now have several, as fresh as they were a hundred years ago!) came with a promise: 'That Brandreth's Pills, in all future time, are warranted to possess and contain those purgative, those cleansing and innocent qualities, which they have always heretofore possessed in so eminent a degree.' Whatever your problem – pleurisy, inflammation, fever, heart complaint, the Big C – Brandreth's Pills would help not hinder. 'The great advantage of using Brandreth's Pills in sickness is that they *never make any mistakes*, often prolonging, never shortening life.' To prove the point, the great man published a book packed with hundreds of testimonials from satisfied patients and their awestruck physicians. Fox Brandreth Connor, who runs the family business now, has kindly presented me with a copy.

We must get a proper family tree done. Dr B. had two wives and fourteen children and working out who is descended from whom is not exactly easy. Obviously I know I'm descended from Henry Brandreth who was sent back to Liverpool to run the European end of the business (and, as we know, ran it into the ground!) but where all the rest have ended up I am not entirely sure. Eleanor B., who lives in one of the family houses and served me sherry and slivers of cheese before I left, appears to have inherited handsomely, so I'm not quite sure why we haven't! The Pills still sell – mainly to the Arabs (pronounced *A-rabs*) – but the business has diversified and Fox Brandreth Connor now does best out of the Brandreth Have-a-Heart traps: humane animal traps – 'catch any creature, from a mouse to a moose without causing it harm'. What you do with the creature once trapped is *not* specified.

Later

I bought the *Daily News*, 8 cents. The banner headline: 'ISRAELI VICTORY!' Stories on pages 3, 4, 5, 6, 7. But below the massive headline an unexpected picture filling two-thirds of the front page: a very frosty-looking Queen Elizabeth II meeting the Duke and Duchess of Windsor at the unveiling of a memorial to the late Queen Mary. 'Thirty Years Later: Royalty Accepts "The Woman I Love" – Wally Is Given The Royal Nod.' 'The Duchess of Windsor, slender and appearing much younger than her 70 years, wore a deep blue shantung coat with blue pillbox hat.' They are fascinated by Wallis Simpson over here. We don't forget she hails from Baltimore!

Saturday, 1 July 1967

Count your blessings, Mr Brandreth. Ten good things that have happened this week:

1. Dinner with Suzy Blaustein. (She is fourteen and very lovely. Truly beautiful. And her grandfather is the richest Jew in America. He gave $1 million to Israel this week.)
2. Dinner with Emily Brown, who is neither fourteen nor beautiful, but is rather fun and a generous hostess. We dined very grandly at the Carriage House: succulent steaks, creamed spinach, European wines. (Tomorrow we are going Chinese: Nanking on P Street.)
3. A swim in the Washington Hilton pool. (Well, it was good at the time. How was I to know I'd get a heat rash?! The itching, O Lord, the itching! The heat here is horrendous.)
4. The reception given to my talk on 'progressive education in the Summerhill tradition'! (This was for Mrs Bloom who had already given me $50 for my hour-long poetry reading to her Chi Chapter of Pi Lamba Theta group. More please.)
5. Reading *Scoop* by Evelyn Waugh.
6. Good work on the proofs of the Badley memorial magazine – corrected, cut, pasted, returned. Posted at 2.00 a.m. at the DC Post Office – followed by coffee at the all-night Georgetown café. (This is what I like doing best: completing a project.)
7. Arranging my meeting with James V. Bennett, long-serving director of the Federal Bureau of Prisons – the man who really knows.
8. Taking tea (and then cocktails), with Betty Ducat, vaudevillian friend of Pa's friend, 'Wee' Georgie Wood. Miss Ducat has a dance school and created a dance troupe, 'The Fabulous Ducats' – four girls and a boy – who were 'a complete sensation' on *The Ed Sullivan Show*.
9. Lunching with Dr Ackerman at the Cosmos Club at 2121 Massachusetts Avenue. It's a club for gentlemen and explorers – they don't allow black people in the place, except to wait at table. (Incredible, but true.) Dr A. is so civilised: cool, calm, courteous. At the end of the meal, in his pocket diary he made a note of my interests and what I'd eaten. He does that every time he meets someone: 'helps place them,' he

explained, 'and next time we meet they're pleased with the details I appear to have remembered.'

10. Getting my hair cut in the barber's shop at the United States Senate. Oh yes. And meeting Robert Kennedy in the lift. (I didn't know it was an elevator for Senators Only. I truly didn't.)

I think this week sums up all that I like best in life – a beautiful girl, a performance that goes well, fine food, interesting people, *top people*, theatre people, prisons, politics, projects . . . and a good book. (*Scoop* is a very good book.) Now I'm off to meet David Schuchat at Dupont Circle. We are going to take a beer and a burger and observe the kooks and hippies who congregate there. Should be interesting.

Thursday, 6 July 1967

3359 Chevy Chase, Houston, Texas

I flew here yesterday morning, via Atlanta. Maurice, the Symonds' houseman and chauffeur, met me at the airport. He is a charming man, black (as all the servants are), gracious and devoted to the family. He has been with them for eighteen years. In the car I sat next to him until we reached the gates of the estate (in River Oaks where the money and the mansions are) when he pulled up and suggested I might prefer to sit in one of the back seats: 'That's what Mr Symonds would expect.'

My cousin H. Gardiner Symonds, 63, is an oil man – and a successful one.* He is chairman and chief executive of the Tenneco Oil Co. and keeps a house in Mexico, a ranch in Texas, an apartment in New York, a place at Brandreth (in the Adirondack Mountains) as well as the palatial home where I am now. Gardiner's grandmother was the first child of the great Pill man's second family. Gardiner and his wife have five children, from 40 to 23. As a family they have more than that number of cars: I have only seen five, but I know there are more. The number plates go S1, S2, S3 etc. and today at the Tenneco building I came across S12.

The house is a marvel: my suite's not bad – large bedroom, larger sitting room, boudoir and bathroom with vast square bath. (The bath is actually too big: sitting in the middle you can't reach the taps or the sides.) When I arrived I asked for a telephone (installed instantly) and a typewriter (brought out from Tenneco); my bed is made by the maid; my clothes are laundered and replaced

---

* Under Symonds's leadership Tenneco developed into an industrial complex of diversified interests reporting assets of over $4 billion in 1970, the year before his death.

before I know it; in a moment I may go for a swim in the pool, beneath the palms on the patio. When I arrived Mrs Symonds greeted me quite formally and gave me lunch – Mexican food, hot and good, served by Maurice – and then Quita appeared. She is 23 (Susan is her proper name), attractive, intelligent and, though to the right of Duncan Sandys, a raving radical by local standards! (The radio blares out: 'We need a great deal more of Jesus and a lot less rock and roll!' That's how they feel in these parts.) Quita has been my good-humoured Houstonian guide. (Is it legal to marry your cousin?!) Yesterday afternoon she drove me through town to visit the magnificent campus of Rice University to see the Astrodome (the largest stadium in the world, on a complex covering 260 acres, at a cost of $31 million, with six thousand tons of air conditioning and a two-million-dollar scoreboard) and the medical centre (again the largest in the Western world, with ten hospitals and almost as many medical schools). Tomorrow she is taking me to the Humble Building (the tallest in town, if not in the world) to lunch with her brother, David, in the Petroleum Club on the 43rd floor. It's a club for oil men. The workers eat in the cafeteria below – known as the Linoleum Club.

Everything here is biggest and best – including the prison. And that's the strange thing. What the Texas Department of Corrections has created at Huntsville really is impressive. I'm just back from a day there. I began at the Diagnostic Center – where the prisoners first arrive and where their needs are actually assessed. The main jail is for recidivists and, amazingly, there are proper education and training programmes on offer. The men aren't just cooped up in their cells all day: things are *happening*. I was able to talk with the men quite freely. When they discovered I was English they wanted to know if I'd met Twiggy. They seemed quite taken with Twiggy! ('Swinging London' is something everyone is aware of in America – even the poor unfortunates on Death Row. The one thing that worries them is the way we treat the Union Jack. The idea of using the national flag to decorate underpants is deeply shocking. Here there is a federal law to protect the stars and stripes from insulting behaviour.)

Saturday, 8 July 1967

It is two in the morning (it's Sunday in fact) and I am sitting on the floor in New Orleans Airport waiting to board Delta Flight 121 to Los Angeles. It's scheduled to depart at 4.31 a.m. I have had a long, long day, all of it memorable.

I started the day with Quita's friend, John Shanahan, a good man. He took me around the poor areas of Houston – he's one of the directors of the Federal Poverty Program there. We concentrated on an area known as 'The Bottom' because that's exactly what it is. We went into 'homes' that were no more than dilapidated shacks, I saw a single room where a family of ten was living in filthy conditions, without a bathroom or a kitchen. They didn't even have a TV – and in the US a TV is a necessity. The heat was unbearable, the squalor truly desperate. The poverty is not only among the Negroes, though they are the largest group, but among Mexicans and Whites – according to John, these last are the most difficult to help.

I flew out of Houston at 4.25, marvelling that so much poverty and so much wealth could exist side by side. (If I married Quita I'd have enough money to do something about the poverty!!) Fifty minutes later I landed in New Orleans. I put my luggage (briefcase and duffel bag) in a locker and boarded a bus to go downtown. (On bus, little white girl points at little black girl and says, 'Mommy, look – a baby maid!' . . . the joke – which Quita told me – doesn't quite work because you rarely see a white child on a bus!) I got off at Canal Street – 'the nation's widest, most brilliantly lighted thoroughfare' – and walked into the French Quarter, the Vieux Carré. I wandered down Chartres Street to Jackson Square. The charm is real: small streets, overhanging houses with intricate lace railings. It reminded me of Bruges. I bought a newspaper and wandered across Jackson Square, over a disused railtrack and up a slight hillock – and there it was: the Mississippi. I stood for quite a while gazing at the huge, still river. (Sometimes I think I'm not me, but a character in a novel – Felix Krull or Julien Sorel in *Le Rouge et Le Noir*.) I wandered back towards the French Market and into the beautiful Basilica of St Louis, then across to Bourbon Street to see 'the girls'. That's what Bourbon Street is famous for. On my way I stopped for a Coke and opened the paper. I read of the death of Vivien Leigh.[*] I was stunned – and surprised at my own distress. And amazed, too. I was in New Orleans and reading of the death of Vivien Leigh. I wandered around town until I found it – and I did: a streetcar named Desire.

I decided to go to the movies – and I went to *Spartacus*, for no other reason than Sir Laurence Olivier was in the cast! It wasn't bad – a lot better than *Khartoum*. When the show was over, I decided to take a cab out here to the airport, thinking that New Orleans late on a Saturday night is not the best place for a stranger to be hanging around a bus stop. (Good public transport in this country is pretty much non-existent. The black people really are treated as second-class citizens.)

---

[*] Vivien Leigh (1913–67), actress and film star, especially remembered for playing Scarlett O'Hara in *Gone with the Wind*, 1939, and Blanche du Bois in *A Streetcar Named Desire*, 1951; married to Laurence Olivier, 1940–60.

The airport is completely deserted. I have been thinking about Sal, as well as Quita and Suzy Blaustein. I've just bought a copy of T. H. White's *The Making of the President, 1960*. I am going to start it now. I know I should be reading *An Introduction to Positive Economics*, but I just can't face it. I had a chocolate malted for supper. Tasty.

Thursday, 13 July 1967

Yesterday I visited Saint Sophia Greek Orthodox Cathedral, the most beautiful church I have ever seen, full of light and extraordinary colour. Then I went to the area of Los Angeles called Watts, home of the race riots of '65 (thirty-four people were killed) — it's a depressing district: the Negro poverty and dissatisfaction have not gone away. I spent some time looking at Watts Towers, a huge series of 'statues' (oil derricks? Gothic cathedral?) created, over thirty-three years, by one Simon Rodia — made out of broken glass and junk and cement because 'I wanted to do something for the United States because I was raised here you understand. I wanted to do something for the United States because there are nice people in this land.'

And I'm with some of the nicest of them now. I'm on the beach at South Laguna, looking out over the Pacific Ocean, watching the orange sun go down. Laguna is a vacation beach and an 'artists' colony'. South Laguna is much less spoiled: it's a kind of earthly paradise. And the crowd I've fallen in with are giving me a flavour of 'alternative America'. My hosts are delightful: he (Bill) is a mild-mannered Jewish doctor from Baltimore; she (Christina) is unorthodox Greek, stout, funny, somewhat crude, 'earthy', messy, a Georgy Girl with enormous buck teeth and bare feet. Her brother is Ike Pappas, the CBS newsman I've often seen on TV. He was there when Jack Ruby shot Lee Harvey Oswald. He's the man who said: 'Oswald has been shot! Holy mackerel!'* Her father lives with them — Nestor Pappas: he has great charm and just potters about, drinking beer, writing home to Greece and sleeping. They have two little girls, aged 2 and 4 — and a babysitter, aged 13. The babysitter does all the work! Also here — this is an eccentric beach party — is an exhausting Catholic lady (a mother of seven) who wants a break from her husband and children and a middle-aged 'hippie' who glories in the name of Rusty de la Rosa. She has abandoned her husband in New York, dresses strangely, takes drugs, and has brought her two daughters out West in search of freedom and enlightenment. The two daughters are called

---

* In fact, he said: 'There's a shot! Oswald has been shot! Oswald has been shot! A shot rang out. Mass confusion here, all the doors have been locked. Holy mackerel!'

Michelle (aged 12 and fat) and Kim (aged 10 and enchanting). I have fallen in love with Kim. Completely. If I am Peter Pan and Sal is Wendy, Kim is Tinkerbell.

There has been much talk of *The Feminine Mystique.**

Wednesday, 19 July 1967

San Francisco is another world: it is the Western city I had been promised, the Paris of the Pacific – except that it is full of 'hippies' and Chinese. Chinatown here is the largest Chinese community outside the Orient and the hippies are *everywhere*. San Francisco is their Mecca and the Haight-Ashbury district (where I am writing this) is their holy of holies. (I have just tried to take a discreet photo of one of the hippies – he has a halo of frizzy hair that must be three feet in diameter. I do not exaggerate.) How would I describe hippies to the man in the moon? Well, they are beardy-weirdies bedecked in beads: long-haired and youthful mostly, they live communally, take drugs (some harmless, others not), have bare feet and (I think) can be divided into two groups: the 'drop-outs', intellectual, social failures by mistake or design; and the 'radicals', angry and rejecting the current 'values'. They are all over San Francisco, slouching and sleeping, selling their newspaper, smoking their pot, dancing and singing:

> 'I don't believe in Jesus,' the hippie said to me
> 'Trust no one over thirty – and Christ was thirty-three.'

Friday, 21 July 1967

Yesterday, San Quentin – a traditional penitentiary getting predictable results: no one emerges better from the experience. Today, a fascinating morning in one of the municipal courts with Judge Harry Low, recently appointed and the first Chinese judge in California. (Here it is a political appointment: Low's appointment was one of Democrat Pat Brown's last acts as Governor; Ronald Reagan would never have chosen him.)† I sat on the bench, next to the judge. The day began at nine with all the drunk and disorderly charges. The judge dealt with forty-five cases in thirty minutes: all but one pleaded Guilty: most regular offenders were given thirty to sixty days in the county jail, others were given suspended sentences, a few were fined, a few put on probation, three sent to Alcoholic School. Judge Low admitted freely that this is rubber stamp justice and does no

---

* The best-selling book by Betty Friedan, published in 1963, that brought to light the lack of fulfilment in many American women's lives.
† Actor and Republican Ronald Reagan (1911–2004) succeeded Pat Brown as Governor of California in January 1967.

one much good, though he does try to look out for the first and young offenders. He admitted that his usual sentence to the county jail is meaningless, particularly so since it's run by a sheriff with a known fondness for the bottle . . . For the rest of the morning Judge Low sat in his criminal court with a typical list of cases, from shoplifting to prostitution. A number of hippies appeared, having marijuana and sleeping in the park. The judge went easy on them.

Wednesday, 26 July 1967

The good news. Yesterday I travelled from Seattle to Tacoma (one and a half hours each way) via the Boeing works (these aircraft are *the* business of Seattle) to the Cascadia Diagnostic and Reception Center for Juveniles (8 to 18). Here they receive all the kids committed by the courts, study them in depth for six weeks, then decide what they should do with them. The recidivist rate is wonderfully low: twenty per cent this year. I was impressed and will be writing it up properly.

The bad news. I got back to Seattle to read the headline: DETROIT AFLAME. Paratroops have been flown in to quell the worst race riots in years. I have just bought the special 6 a.m. 'souvenir' edition of today's *Seattle Post-Intelligencer*. The front page has dramatic pictures of burning buildings, rioting and looting in Detroit, Wilmington, Grand Rapids, Maryland and New York and pictures of President Johnson and Martin Luther King looking solemn and in 'deep thought'. The headline reads: AMERICA TODAY – HOW DID IT HAPPEN? I think we know the answer: right across the country, for generations, the Negroes have been treated as second-rate citizens – and they've had enough.

Monday, 14 August 1967

I am writing this on board TWA 704 bound from Washington DC for London. We left at 8.00 p.m; we land at 8.05 a.m. Dinner has been served, the lights are being dimmed and I am reflecting on the past six months. I have travelled well over one hundred and fifty-eight thousand miles and I am returning home slightly weary, slightly tanned, slightly less stooped, slightly heavier, slightly changed.

Without consulting my notes, what are the highlights of my time in America – what are the ten moments or places that come *instantly* into my mind?

1. Last week, flying into Chicago, with eighty soldiers fresh from Vietnam – so fresh they hadn't slept since leaving Saigon. They were

full of the horror of the war and the glory of it. However, they all believed in what they were doing. They talked a lot about the money they earned and how they spent it – mostly on prostitutes. 'The girls cost $20. The inflation in Vietnam is terrible.'

2. Still in Chicago: the Baha'i Temple at Wilmette.

3. In LA, sitting on top of the hill looking down over the Hollywood Bowl, watching Barbra Streisand effortlessly hold an audience of seventeen thousand in the palm of her hand.

4. Up in British Columbia, going up Howe Sound to Squamish. Normally, I'm not one for 'nature', but the beauty of this was overwhelming. (More memorable than the Niagara Falls.)

5. The Forest Lawn Memorial Cemetery – it was everything that Evelyn Waugh led us to expect and more.* And Disneyland – it was everything Uncle Walt led us to expect and more. (I *really* liked both. They are ridiculous, but wonderful.)

6. Sitting on the hot sand drinking an iced chocolate malted on the beach at Coney Island.

7. Drinking so many martinis with James Bennett, head of the Federal Prison Service, that when I left him I could barely stand!

8. The Shakespeare Garden in the Golden Gate Park – featuring each and every flower mentioned in Shakespeare.

9. Lunch in the Senators' dining room at the US Senate. (Of course.)

10. Rescuing Kim de la Rosa from the Pacific Ocean. She had disappeared beneath the waves. It was my heroic moment, my finest hour. I dived in and brought her out in my arms! (And that I could do so is all thanks to those cold afternoons at the Fulham Baths. Thank you, Ma! And the swimming lessons were followed, I remember, by a cup of hot Bovril seated on a high stool in the Fulham Baths café. I can picture the counter I sat at and the advertisement for 7-Up that was my constant reading.)

Tuesday, 15 August 1967

The plane landed on time. I took the bus to the Victoria terminal. Ma and Pa were there, waiting for me. We had coffee and they told me 'the news'. Hes has had a baby – a little girl called Polly. They didn't say who the father was or

---

* Forest Lawn was the inspiration for Evelyn Waugh's satirical novel *The Loved One*, 1948.

where he was. There was no question of Hes marrying him. She thought about an abortion, but didn't want that. (Pa could have arranged it.)* She thought about adoption, but didn't want that either. The baby was born in the Middlesex [Hospital] – Hes was the only unmarried mother there. There was some hostility from some of the nurses and other mothers kept asking where her husband was, but she coped. She's coping well, apparently. Ma and Pa are coping, too. They seem very happy to be grandparents. And proud. They say Polly is a lovely baby. I'm going to see her on Sunday.

I am going to sleep now. But before I do (I am going to sleep all day!) I must report that there was a letter waiting for me from Sally:

Dearest Gyles,

I have nothing to say that cannot wait till I am with you again, except welcome home my darling. I am as sure as is possible after all this time that I love you and will forever. The rest, and there is much of it, must wait. I got your letter 58 this morning – thank you . . . I am going to the Prom tonight to stop myself thinking, but I shall long to hear tomorrow evening. Till tomorrow, I love you. I am yours – what more can I say?

Sally

I am glad to be home.

Friday, 25 August 1967

Met Sal at Waterloo at 1.30 p.m. We lunched at the Festival Hall, took the tube to London Bridge, found Medway Ltd at Winchester Wharf, where I bought a grey two-tier filing cabinet for £8 10/-. Got driven back to 5H [the Brandreths' flat] by van, had tea with Hes and baby Polly in kitchen, then Sal and I *walked* to Charing Cross. Saw *You Only Live Twice* at the Odeon, Leicester Square. Supper at Lyons + chocolate. Took Sal home. A very happy day.

Tuesday, 29 August 1967

I have seen Sal every day – except for Sunday with Simon Cadell and the Rev. Peter Delaney.† It has been perfect – especially yesterday at her house. Full

---

* Abortion was legalised in England in July 1967, three months after GB's niece was born.
† The Ven. Peter Delaney MBE (b. 1939), Archdeacon of London since 1999, was curate of St Marylebone Parish Church, 1966–70, and officiated at the marriages of GB's sisters.

details in my Secret Diary, now safely under lock and key in my handsome new filing cabinet. (No snooping!) All I need to say here, for posterity, is that we play together and it is wonderful.

I'll put this letter here for the moment, but I think, in future, I am going to keep all the letters together in the filing cabinet.

23.viii
12.40

My darling boy,

I am home in bed and longing for you. I simply want to say thank you – for waiting six months, for wanting me, and for this wonderful day. You can be quite sure that I am certain now – you are right to remember that moment coming out of the Odeon. I think it was then that I fully realised that this must continue forever. We have been so contented today. 1.30 seems a lifetime away and yet you, at each moment of the afternoon, are still alive in me now. I could go on – I won't. Simply know I am waiting for 3 tomorrow, that I love you and that this day has been very beautiful.

Thank you – believe me –

Your Sally

Tonight we are meeting at 6.45 p.m. at Tottenham Court Road and going to the Berkeley Cinema to see *Le Bonheur* and *Un Homme et Une Femme*.

Sunday, 17 September 1967

A perfect day, a perfect night – a perfect month in fact. It was our last night together for a while. We watched the Last Night of the Proms on TV at her house. It was a moving occasion because of what happened at the end. Colin Davis, the conductor, ended his speech saying to the audience: 'Now I have a surprise for you. Sir Malcolm Sargent is in the hall and I am going to get him for you.' The Promenaders went wild – and when Sargent appeared, thin, drawn, but, as ever, oh-so-elegant and dashing, and stepped lightly onto the podium, we all had tears in our eyes. It was absurdly theatrical and totally wonderful!*

This morning we had brunch and listened to the radio. Pa was on *Pick of the Week*!

---

* Sargent (1895–1967) was chief conductor of the Proms from 1948. He died of pancreatic cancer on 3 October, two weeks after his valedictory appearance at the Royal Albert Hall.

Tuesday, 19 September 1967

Sal has gone back to Bedales and I have come back to Betteshanger. This may prove to be a mistake. I am here to do two weeks' teaching and earn some money which I need. I have just had tea with Major Douch – he hasn't changed. And now I'm going to see Mr Burton to discuss the timetable. I'm teaching English, Drama and French. Saying goodbye to Sal and coming down here on the train, I had that awful lurching feeling in the stomach.

Sunday, 1 October 1967

I am not sure that returning to Betteshanger was a good idea. ('If I start looking behind me and begin retracing my track, I'll remind you to remind me, we said we wouldn't look back.')* I think I've helped little Ian Jones, the new boy who is so desperately homesick, but apart from that I don't feel that I have contributed much. The £25 is useful and, of course, there has been Brian How!

Brian How is extraordinary and when I write my version of *Decline and Fall* he will certainly be a leading character. He is Bacchus, Mr Toad, Buddha, Mr Pickwick all rolled into one. He is 54, but looks years older. He drinks like a fish and talks non-stop. Of course, he has ended up teaching Latin in an English prep school! He is a wonderful raconteur – the best I have met – and all his stories (however far-fetched) have the ring of truth to them. Tangiers, Hong Kong, Rome, Hollywood – he was there. 'I have splashed my sperm across three continents. Shall I tell you about it?'

Pa telephoned last night because it turns out that he knew Brian How in Germany after the war and remembers him well. When Pa was chief magistrate BH was one of his colleagues. He says he was 'highly intelligent, but lazy', a dandy and 'a great *poseur*'. He had a German servant who wore a white jacket and gloves to serve dinner! And another German servant, a female, who was supposed to look after me when I was a baby, but neglected her duties to the extent that Pa 'boxed her ears until her curlers fell out'! Pa especially remembers the girl in Brian How's life: Maggie. According to Pa, she was a Rank starlet of surpassing beauty and a mistress rather than a wife.

In fact BH tells me they *were* married. It happened like this: in 1947 Brian was having a complicated affair with a Polish lady who was getting awkward – 'Drop 'em when they get awkward, Gyles – that's my advice. No use hanging on to a woman if she's awkward. It only ends in tears.' Anyway, he went

* From *Salad Days* by Dorothy Reynolds and Julian Slade. GB had the original cast album and knew all the lyrics by heart.

to England on a brief leave, encountered this Rank starlet, aged nineteen, and married her in six days! He returned to Germany without her at first and carried on with the Polish lady. Eventually, he brought Maggie over, but things didn't go too well. She didn't want children for a start. 'Why else get married?' says How. When, eventually, they returned to England, financial problems arose and she was unsympathetic – indeed she even insisted on an expensive London Clinic nose job because her profile was all wrong. In 1951 they parted: he was 39, she 24.

He has taken me through quite a number of his other affairs – particularly the story of the love of his life, *the* woman, Mrs Cyril Connolly. Most of his stories are unprintable and in his cups he is ridiculous. Last night, *in the staff room*, he dropped his trousers and tucked his private parts between his legs to show me how the boys in Hong Kong disguise themselves as girls and create 'a totally convincing *mons Veneris*'. 'Does it look like the real thing or what?'

Monday, 2 October 1967

Letter from Pa: Jen is in excellent form – 'She's quite her old self.' She is 29 and still unmarried. Pa wants his daughters married! 'Would she appeal to Brian How, I wonder – for I'm certain he's lost Maggie and probably needs young female company even if he *is* my age, or almost. I'd love to see him again though he's an old *flâneur*.'

I mentioned this to Brian. Yes, he'd go for Jennifer. 'I still enjoy the best material,' he chortled, with a smack of the lips, a wobble of the purple chins and a roguish twinkle of the yellowing dilating eyes. He thinks his next affair will probably kill him, however. He fears he will drop dead of a heart attack with too much exertion. He said to me sadly, when we were still drinking at 2.00 a.m. the other night, 'Teaching here is very trying.' I don't think he'll last long.

Sunday, 8 October 1967

Met Sal at Guildford Station at 11.30 a.m. She came from Petersfield. I came from London. We went to Lyons for tea, lunch and coffee till 3.00 p.m. Then we returned to the station and I tried on the red velvet waistcoat she has made for me. We decided we couldn't part and that we'd risk her being late. We walked and sat in the castle gardens. We had tea. We talked and talked. It was lovely. We parted at 6.00. She had brought one of the quotations from the Library calendar for me – from 20 September:

'I learnt that it is possible to create light and sound and order within us, no matter what calamity may befall us in the outer world.' Helen Keller.

Tuesday, 10 October 1967

I finished the US leaflet and sent it off to the printers.*

Tomorrow the Oxford Michaelmas term begins and I have to report to New College by 5.00 p.m. Today I had lunch with Pa – we bought me my dinner suit and then ate at Littlewoods. Oxford was everything to Pa – *everything*. I know what he wants for me: the Union, *Isis* OUDS.† We'll see.

Meanwhile: haircut.

---

* GB planned to return to the US during the Christmas vacation and hoped to pay for the visit by giving talks and poetry readings. The leaflet was designed to drum up business.

† GB's father was at Exeter College, Oxford, 1929–32, when an ambitious undergraduate's goals might have included becoming President of the debating society, the Oxford Union, editor of the university magazine, *Isis*, and a leading light in the university dramatic society, OUDS.

Listen with Mother. GB aged four

GB's father, Charles Brandreth, around the time of GB's birth

GB at Betteshanger, the first summer, 1959. Taken by Mr Harkness

In Mr Harkness's study, Betteshanger, summer, 1961. Taken by Mr Harkness

GB at Bedales, April 1963. Taken by Jackie

Jackie at Bedales, April 1963. Taken by GB

Sally, Bedales, 1965

The *Badley Beano*, Bedales,
20 February 1965

GB losing the 1964 General Election, Bedales

GB aspiring to the Presidency of the Oxford Union, 30 May 1968. Future parliamentary colleagues William Waldegrave and Edwina Cohen [Currie] look on

GB in his rooms in New College, 1969. Noël Coward and Lenin look on.

The first Zuleika Dobson competition with the winner, Lady Annunziata Asquith,
12 June 1968. Michèle Brown sits first on the left

Making a splash. GB's first centre spread, *Daily Mirror*, 13 June 1968

After picking the beauty contest winner, the judge
walked off in a sort of daze

It looked like being a beautiful day for
Gyles Brandreth. In his first year at
Oxford and poised at 29 on the
threshold of life, he was invited to organise
a beauty contest.

With the quiet satisfaction of a chap
who knows when he's on to something
good, he donned his dinner suit, rounded
up eight university lovelies and whipped
them off to Christchurch Meadows for a
champagne lunch.

While cameras recorded the event for a
BBC television show called "Through
One Pair of Eyes," he explained about
the Zuleika Dobson Award for 1968.
Punctuating his patter with a knowing
wink later, at an engaging male these.

He bestowed the title on Lady Annunziata Asquith of Somerville College. And
that's when it happened.

Young Brandreth looked into her eyes
and, suddenly, turned away in a daze.
Seeing no more the wondrous woodland,
nor long no more the scent of summer, he
walked plumb into the river and vanished.

Indeed a dry reality. Such a promising
lad. But there it is. These girls do have
the strangest effect on a virile young
man.

Pictures by ARTHUR SIDEY

Bemused he walks .. straight into the river

Winning beauty Lady Annunziata Asquith .. with the judge Gyles Brandreth

His suit is ruined .. but he plods on .. to emerge safely after this final scene

Opening Night, *Cinderella*, 12 November 1968. From left to right: Diana Quick, first female president of the Oxford University Dramatic Society, Sir Michael Redgrave, who performed the Prologue, Archie Harradine, who wrote the pantomime and GB, who produced it

POST OFFICE

TELEGRAM

WHAT FUN ACCEPT WITH GREAT PLEASURE SUGGEST 12TH OPENING NIGHT = REDGRAVE +

How to show a girl a good time. GB and Michèle Brown at the ABC, Baker Street, Christmas 1969

GB looking to the future. Publicity shot for *Child of the '60s*

Review by Richard Last, *Daily Mirror*, 27 December 1969

Gyles—man of the 'seventies

GYLES BRONDRETH—shattering assurance

AT THIS time of year it is customary to make rash prophecies. I forecast, without too m u c h trepidation, that probably by the end of 1970, certainly not long after, we shall have a new all-purpose t e l l y personality named Gyles Brandreth.

Mr Brandreth is a third-year undergraduate at New College, Oxford, reading French and History ("Rather nice things to read, I thought").

President

For the past year he has been President of the Oxford Union. But when you've said that, you still haven't started to identify him.

He is also the extremely witty speaker, a sort of 1960-ish Noel Coward, who competed with F r a n k Muir and Norman St John Stevas in televised Union debates.

By RICHARD LAST

He writes copiously for magazines like Honey, Punch and Vogue, earning, he says, "more than the average man with two children."

Mr Brandreth d o e s poetry readings in the States (at 60 dollars a go), visits prisons, has directed university dramatic productions and given the staid old Union a jazzy new look.

Tonight he makes his debut as a TV "anchor man" in the Day - Frost - Muggeridge tradition in a 90 m i n u t e programme from London Weekend, A Child of the Sixties.

Chosen

He was chosen by Peter Morley (producer of the Mountbatten series) to select news film of the decade, add his own commentary, and interview a panel consisting of Ian Macleod, Michael Foot, Lady L o n g f o r d, and American TV pundit Fred Friendly.

The format is a useful variation of the inevitable look-back-at - the - Sixties

theme What's remarkable is the shattering assurance of 21-year-old Gyles as he quizzes his distinguished guests.

I can think of hardened pros who might envy his blend of fluency, aplomb, and nicely-judged deference.

It will be surprising if some telly tycoons are not reaching for their 'phones on Monday morning. Indeed some already have.

"I've had one or two very flattering suggestions," Gyles admitted. "But I'm not doing anything about them yet. I think at this stage I should rather let everyone overtake me. Anyway I have another two terms to go at Oxford."

Gyles is not exactly a typical student. Son of a prosperous lawyer (his father is legal adviser to the A A), he went to the French Lycee in Kensington and co-ed boarding school.

He might be described as a middle-of-the-roader politically (anti-Vietnam, pro-Kennedy, pro-Biafra, Family) and sartorially too: he favours "mod" but non-extreme dress and hair styles.

Shares

He shares with more radical contemporaries a certain youthful contempt for the political set-up. This doesn't stop him wanting, ultimately, to be an MP, on the Tory side.

Apart from his other gifts, Gyles is a tremendously hard worker. He says he gets up about 6 a.m., does a three hour writing stint, and often catches the train to London to attend to journalistic or TV commitments before r e t u r n i n g to Oxford.

He is also a trained acrobat and can do a somersault or stand on his head at a moment's notice. Should be useful for a politician.

GB interviewing the Archbishop of Canterbury, Michael Ramsey, 27 July 1970

Anything to declare?

Longford's sex books go safely through the Customs

By COLIN MACKENZIE
Picture: DAVID CAIRNS

IT was without doubt a consignment of blatant pornography.

But Lord Longford had the best of motives in bringing the dozen Danish "blue" magazines through the Customs at Heathrow Airport last night.

In the line of duty it was necessary for Customs officers to examine them with care.

But on Lord Longford's assurance that the magazines were for research only, the literature was allowed through.

Lord Longford and his pornography investigation team were returning from their two-day examination of Copenhagen's "anything goes" sex industry.

The team insisted that although their reaction to sex shows had varied, there was no split in the group.

Lord Longford, surrounded by his team, sorts through 'blue' magazines in the airport lounge

" Actually, I'm not even on the committee ! "

Press cuttings from the *Daily Express*, *Evening Standard*, *Daily Mirror* and the *Sun*, August 1971

THE Sun

WARD WITH THE PEOPLE 3p   Friday, August 27, 1971

My life with the porno rebel

BY HIS GIRL FRIEND MICHELE

MICHELE BROWN, girl in the life of Gyles Brandreth, rebel of Britain's "Porn squad," talked last night of their life together.

Michele, 14-year-old freelance TV reporter, has been living with 23-year-old Brandreth since they graduated from Oxford.

And she holds views on marriage which might shock Lord Longford, leader of the Commission investigating the effects of pornography.

"Marriage?" she said. It's a bit like pornography isn't it?

"It depends what you get."

Liberal

Brandreth, publisher and TV personality, is already fallen out with Lord Longford.

The division came while they studied the question at first hand in the porn capital of the world, Denmark.

Lord Longford found it disgusting," Brandreth didn't.

Yesterday, at home in Hanwell Hill, North London, Michele speaks "People make the mistake of thinking that because Gyles speaks with a frightfully upper-class accent

he is an old reactionary.

"He actually has very liberal views about most things."

Brandreth, son of the AA's legal adviser, once courted his girlfriend by bringing an aircraft full of champagne to fly over Oxford on her birthday.

Michele said: "Lord Longford phoned up Gyles one day and asked him if he would like to join a commission on pornography.

"Gyles knew Lord Longford's son at university, and agreed.

" It's a pity that Lord Longford won't listen to the evidence, although it must be hard for him as it strictly brought-up Catholic."

And her own views on pornography?

"Like most people, I don't really know what it means.

" Some of the books

Michele ... " Marriage? It's a bit like pornography."

REPORT: IAIN WALKER   PICTURE: JOHN PICKERING

I have seen would probably be pornography to Lord Longford but I cannot see how they would deprave anyone.

" Children should be protected, though.

"I don't think they should be exposed to books like I Was A Teenage Flagellator when they go to buy bubblegum."

Lord Porno Row to—Page 3
Jon Akass—Page 6

Brandreth ... porn rebel

LORD LONGFORD IN PORNLAND

Lord Longford excuses to a pink bench to consult his sex-books' hardback

Inside the full-frontal world of nudes, sex and smut

Story: MICHAEL RELLIGAN
Pictures: ERIC PIPER

WHY is Lord Longford's expeditionary force into Pornland coming to grief? This is the extraordinary—and mostly hilarious—record of their two nights of porn-storming in the world's sexiest capital.

SHOPPING AROUND

AND NOW FOR THE NAKED TRUTH

Woman, September 1972

'Modern as tomorrow, he still has a lot of time for yesterday . . .'

THIS IS GYLES BRANDRETH

He's twenty-four years old and has already made his mark as a writer and broadcaster on such vastly differing subjects as pornography and pantomime. He's got a keen eye open for all that's amusing or touching, lovable or deplorable. Modern as tomorrow, he still has a lot of time for yesterday. His ideas are wide-ranging; the words in which he expresses them are thought provoking; and we are pleased that every week he's going to be expressing them for us.

Recording the *son et lumière* for Royal Greenwich, 1973. From left to right: Peter Howell, GB, Dame Peggy Ashcroft, Cyril Fletcher, Michèle Brown

Oxford
October 1967 – December 1968

Wednesday, 11 October 1967

The city of dreaming spires stuff will have to wait. No time for purple prose. Cutting to the chase: I arrived at 4.00 p.m. I found my room and my staircase – in the back quad by the library. It's a plain, rectangular room, overlooking the street, but that's fine. I met my scout, Jack. Old boy, but very friendly. He'll make the bed, wash up, sort the laundry, etc. The chaplain's room is next door. That's not a problem, according to Jack! And the Home Secretary's son[*] is going to be on this staircase, too.

Hall is grand, high-ceilinged, oak-panelled, adorned with oil paintings of former Wardens and the like. The food, however, is unremarkable. Had post-supper coffee with assorted other freshmen, then drinks at 11.00 with Barnabus and friends.[†] So far so good. And my kettle works!

Thursday, 12 October 1967

Meeting with Moral Tutor, Dr Merlin Thomas, at Savile House. He is round, smooth, amusing, teaches French – makes jokes, but doesn't give a lot away. I think he thought I talked too much. I think I thought I talked too much!

Lunch with Xan Smiley, amusing fair-haired Old Etonian. His father is a sort of latter-day Lawrence of Arabia. Get gown from Jack. (Because I'm a scholar I get a longer, fuller gown than the commoners!) Tour Union – wonderful building, especially the debating chamber and the Library, with murals by Rossetti, William Morris and Edward Burne-Jones. Chaplain's sherry – dry (both the event and the sherry!). Sup and coffee with Victor Bulmer-Thomas (his father is an MP and Church Commissioner).

[*] Charles Jenkins (b.1949), son of Roy Jenkins (1920–2003), Labour MP and later Social Democratic Party MP, Home Secretary, 1965–7 and 1974–7.
[†] David Kremer and Peter Harris were Bedalians who had arrived at New College the year before.

Friday, 13 October 1967

Addressed in Hall by Warden, Dean and Domestic Bursar. The essence of the Warden's message: look up while you are here – look around at the buildings. Unless you choose to live in Venice, you are unlikely to live in such a beautiful city again.

Addressed on PPE by Quinton, Nicholas and Opie. (Have I chosen the right subject??!!)

Chat and lunch with Peter Torry. Coffee with Mark Kidel. Call on Peter Adamson, editor of *Isis*. Discuss article possibilities. Not discouraging. Coffee with Barnabus.

Saturday, 14 October 1967

Coffee with Peter Harris – he has returned from his travels in the East with dysentery and worse, poor fellow. Coffee with Victor Bulmer-Thomas. Change for 'Inauguration of Freshmen': signing the register, mumbling Latin phrases, shaking hands with the Warden.* Sherry afterwards, plus chat with Sir William. V amiable and gossipy: talk of Kim Philby ('there was always something slightly doubtful about him, you know') and Harold Macmillan (he's the University Chancellor: Sir William had favoured Clement Attlee). Chinese lunch with parents and Ben – special fried rice, as always, and sweet and sour pork. Freshmen's Fair. Sup and coffee. Look at papers in Junior Common Room. Letters – incl. long letter to Sal. (She worries that I tell lies – not to her, but to the world. I don't tell her lies. She knows that. She worries that my only real world is the world inside our heads.) Visit from Kevin Pakenham (Lord Longford's son) who wants me to write an article on prisons for the new magazine he is editing. It's all going to be fine.

Monday, 23 October 1967

It is 1.00 a.m., so it is Tuesday in fact. I've just come from a 'mystical experience'. A group of freshmen gathered around a table with a wine glass to communicate with 'the other side'. Quite amusing, though the line was mostly busy!

This must be brief because seven hours from now, Jack will wake me. In eight hours, matriculation in the Sheldonian Theatre. In ten, a lecture – my first. In thirteen, I shall be deep in the study of consumer equilibrium, Alexis de Tocqueville and the complexities of the 1905 Russian revolution. Meanwhile I need to report on the major event of my Oxford career to date: my speech at the

---

* Sir William Hayter (1906–95), Warden of New College, 1958–76, had been British Ambassador to Moscow, 1953–7.

Union Freshmen's Debate on Sunday night. In short, it was a resounding success. True, the other paper speakers were fearful, but nonetheless I am bound to say (!!) it was cheers and laughter all the way. I spoke for ten minutes and was received by the three hundred or so present with very long and gratifying applause. As I sat down the President passed this note: 'Splendid: a Churchill tank fitted with flails, doubling as a semaphore machine! Robert Jackson.'* The word 'semaphore' isn't that, but I can't decipher it. Leastways, I sense I am off to a good start at the Union. Of course, preparing the wretched thing took most of my thinking time at the weekend, together with lengthy discussions with my opposite number in the debate: William, Viscount Lewisham (son of Lady Dartmouth, grandson of Barbara Cartland) – not too bright, a slight stammer, not a good speaker but well-intentioned. He has a refrigerator in his rooms! And his buddies are caricatures of the Christ Church aristocracy. I called in for claret (hah!) on Thursday and enjoyed (hah again!) the company of a pretentious idiot (though very brilliant they assure me) Charles Cecil (pronounced Cicil!) and one Max Wyndham (milder and nicer), the son of Macmillan's former private secretary, Lord Egremont.

Went to my first Crime Society meeting (I'm the New College rep) and had pleasant chitchat with Brigadier Maunsell, Inspector General of Prisons. Auditioned for New College play and rather hope I don't get anything because I'm already horribly busy. My first piece of Oxford writing appears on Wednesday. It's called 'The Breast'. I thought I should be a bit outrageous to ensure they noticed it and used it. They have! (I am rather dreading its appearance now!!) On Saturday afternoon I christened my new crockery by giving tea to a gaggle of Bedalians and a lonely Old Etonian. In the evening I joined Barnabus and his parents and elder sister at the Elizabeth restaurant (Oxford's finest) for a super dinner on the occasion of his 21st birthday. Needless to say, he didn't mention anything about it being his birthday beforehand . . . It was a very grand but rather a sad and lonely affair.

Bed. I have my own wash-basin etc. here, but the baths are in the basement, down two flights which is a bore. The water is hot and I usually time my bath to coincide with the ten o'clock news.

Sunday, 29 October 1967

Just in from meeting with the editor of *Isis*. My piece on 'The Breast' appears to have gone down well – provoking a little controversy, some disgust and some

---

* Robert Jackson (b.1946), Fellow of All Souls from 1970, MP for Wantage, 1983–2005.

amusement. As it should be. He has plenty more he wants me to do, starting with something on Death Row.

Rehearsals for the New College play have now begun: Pinter, *A Night Out*. I've got a predictable part: urbane middle-aged businessman. The only interesting member of the cast appears to be one human horse: Eliza Manningham-Buller, daughter of our former Lord Chancellor.* She's jolly and I like her.

Life here is beginning to take on a definite shape – except when it comes to the matter of *work*! However, I do have plans – a schedule to take me through from now until Prelims on 14 March. As soon as I've finished tapping this, I am off to discover the charms of the Demand Curve, its shape, constraints and elasticity . . .

Saturday, 4 November 1967

Durham. What a nightmare! Four hours and twenty-five minutes on the train to get here – for what? A truly hideous evening! The President of the Oxford Union was invited to speak at the Durham Union and sent me instead! Toady that I am, I came! 'This house believes it has the answer to who we think we are' – that was the motion. A pointless motion, a silly speech, a lukewarm reception. I can't wait to leave. The only high spot has been meeting John Wells,† schoolmaster turned professional satirist, who also spoke and who was very nice – waspish in debate, charming privately. The other consolation: Sally is here (Bedales half-term) so at least I have a shoulder to cry on.

Monday, 20 November 1967

High drama. The pound has been devalued. I am an economist: I should know what this means! Harold Wilson has explained it to the nation, but we are none the wiser. Perhaps when I see my Economics tutor [Roger Opie] he will take me through it. Whenever I go into his room he is always just coming off the phone to Number Ten – he makes that very clear. (I assumed it was 10 Downing Street and perhaps sometimes it is. Usually, I now realise, it is Number 10 Great Turnstile – the offices of the *New Statesman*. RO is a regular contributor.)

Play rehearsal tonight – dire. No lines learnt. My focus is now on Thursday. I'm Tellering for the Noes in the debate 'that the Roman Catholic Church has no place in the twentieth century': the Reverend Dr Ian Paisley versus Norman St

---

* Elizabeth Manningham-Buller (b.1948) was the daughter of Reginald Manningham-Buller, 1st Viscount Dilhorne. She joined MI5 in 1974 and served as Director General, 2002–07

† John Wells (1936–88) wrote for *That Was The Week That Was* before becoming a performer and actor.

John Stevas MP.* Normally, nobody would stay to hear the Tellers' speeches, but this debate is being broadcast on BBC2 live and in colour from 9.05 to the close at 11.30 p.m., so the audience will stay and I should be heard. Robert Jackson (the Union President, a good man, a lonely man, right, I think, for the academic life he plans) tells me I must be SERIOUS.

Thursday, 23 November 1967

It went well. (It went *wonderfully* well.) Being last up helped. Having the hall full to bursting helped. The lights, the cameras, the sense of occasion – they all helped. Ian Paisley was the star turn: his argument is monstrous. His theatricality alarming – he produced a communion wafer and snapped it in two saying, 'They dare to call this biscuit the body of Christ – this *biscuit!*' But he has a power and a presence that cannot be denied. Stevas was silky, smooth, amusing. It was a tremendous evening. At dinner (Lobster Mornay, roast pheasant, *Marrons Glacés*) I sat with Dick Francis from the BBC. Afterwards I had a drink with Desmond O'Donovan and Giles Playfair who were 'commentating'. There was much congratulation and happy prognostication. A good night – one of the best.

Friday, 1 December 1967

Another lovely review for my speech just in (another rave, in fact!). Last night at the Union was less enjoyable, but possibly more historic. Miss Geraldine Jones has just been elected the first woman President in the 144-year history of the Union. I like her: she doesn't *inspire* me, but she has made a little bit of history and you can't argue with that. Well done her.

Not so well done, the New College Drama Society. The play was NOT a banging, smashing, walloping hit. Actually, it was something of a mitigated disaster – mitigated because all the others were quite as bad as I was.

Work improves slightly. Opie's one-word comment on the *thirteen sides* I did for him last week on Money Supply was 'good'.

Wednesday, 6 December 1967

A.m. Opie tutorial. Work on speech. Meet Harold Gardiner for Chinese lunch – not inspired. (Mustn't look back.) Afternoon. Sharon Churcher's tea party at

* Ian Paisley (b.1926), founding member of the Free Presbyterian Church of Ulster, Democratic Unionist Party MP from 1970, First Minister of Northern Ireland, 2007–08; Norman St John Stevas (b.1929), now Baron St John of Fawsley, leading Catholic, Conservative MP for Chelmsford, 1964–87 and a Cabinet minister under Margaret Thatcher.

LMH [Lady Margaret Hall, one of the women's colleges] – not inspired. Got soaked in snow. Ugh.

P.m. Party at the Adamsons' flat in Walton Street. Peter [the editor of *Isis*] is a good man: rough but dignified, and very straightforward. I arrived at eight and left at 3.00 a.m. – mostly talking to Lesley, Peter's wife. (She is 21, I think. Married undergraduates are VERY unusual.) Also talked to Philip Maxwell, the *Isis* business manager. I like him. He's an odd mix: shy and bombastic at the same time. He arrived with two bottles of champagne which some thought a bit show-off, but why not? His father* is helping to fund the magazine, so he is a power in the land.

Thursday, 7 December 1967

Union Farewell Debate: '*Quales artifices perimus*' – the dying words of the Emperor Nero when he had fled from Rome and was making preparations for his own suicide. I think the idea was to celebrate the genius of our outgoing President. I did my best. It seemed to work. Opposite me was a very strange fellow: Leofranc Holford-Strevens, a sort of genius *manqué*, a Union fixture. He has a wonderful mind and a mad, uncoordinated body. When he gets excited his arms flail and he froths at the mouth. This is no exaggeration. (He would be a Fellow of All Souls, but for his table manners. Robert Jackson will be a Fellow of All Souls: his table manners are impeccable.) The visitors were Basil Boothroyd (of *Punch* magazine) and Robin Day† (ex-President) who was best by far. We got on well: he went out of his way to be friendly and kindly agreed to let me interview him next term for *Isis*. After the debate, there were unexciting eats on offer. I didn't linger. It's best not to linger.

Friday, 8 December 1967

Letter published in *The Times* – on BOAC and their pricing policy. (See separate scrapbook.)‡ Coffee with Geoff Lean. Amiable and balding, though he's not much older than me. He is still an undergraduate, but he wants to be a journalist

---

* Robert Maxwell (1923–91), MP for Buckingham, 1964–70, publisher and newspaper proprietor.
† Sir Robin Day (1923–2000), television journalist and pioneer of the abrasive political interview.
‡ GB kept published letters to newspapers in one set of scrapbooks; articles by him in a second set of scrapbooks; articles about him in a third. As well as his daily diary and his 'secret diary', he kept journals covering certain subjects and projects, and filed all the correspondence he received (alphabetically by surname of correspondent) in a series of ring binders.

and sells stories to *The Times* Diary for £5 a time. We cooked up something together. Met up with Peter Adamson at the Union for a drink – discussed an *Isis* column (he's going to give me one next term!) and Lesley. Lunch at Merton (a beautiful college) with Denis Matyjaszek* [one of the *Isis* editorial team]. Lesley was there. (Am I falling in love with her?) Tea with Barnabus – dull, though the anchovy toast at the Union is very, very tasty! Bought a copy of *The Oxford Dictionary of Quotations* as a present for the Adamsons. Failed to go to the Union Ball. (I had a ticket, but I didn't go. I have decided that it's best to stay away. Don't let them get to know you too well – they may see through you if they do!)

Monday, 15 January 1968

All a bit testy at home. Ma is upset because her school has had to close – the landlords aren't happy with the flat being used as a place of business and the neighbours aren't too keen on a dozen toddlers plus pushchairs cluttering up the stairwell. Pa is worried about money – as ever. I'm worried about Sal. We had two hours at Paddington Station together, before I took the 1.15 p.m. to Oxford.

Went to New College, then straight round to Walton Street to see the Adamsons. We talked about my *Isis* column, went out to tea at Fullers (my favourite), went back to Walton Street to sup. Returned to New College, unpacked, sorted. I've just finished my first article.

Tuesday, 16 January 1968

Today I worked – in a haphazard way.

·   I also had lots of cups of coffee. (Post-luncheon with ultimatedium, David Walter.† Then Julian Radcliffe,‡ Old Etonian, Territorial Army enthusiast, tall, thin, Sir Andrew Aguecheek to the life. Then Peter Torry.§ Then . . . oh, the list goes on! Too much time here is spent around the coffee cup.)

At 10.30 p.m. Pa arrived, exhausted, bringing all my luggage. I gave him coffee and then found that he had been locked in! (The college gates are closed at 11.00 p.m. After that you have to climb in or out. I have climbed into Wadham a couple of times – not my idea of fun. Pa at 57 was not inclined to climb out!! The

---

* Denis Matyjaszek (b.1948), later changed his name to Denis MacShane; Labour MP for Rotherham from 1994; Foreign Office Minister under Tony Blair.
† Later a good friend of GB, a political journalist and Liberal Party press officer.
‡ Also a good friend; later an international security consultant.
§ Now Sir Peter Torry GCVO KCMG, former UK Ambassador to Germany and Spain.

wall where you climb out from here really is quite high. Eventually we found a very grumpy porter and Pa was released to return to the St Giles Hotel where I shall join him at breakfast. They maintain the old values at the St Giles Hotel. Gentlemen are automatically given *two eggs* at breakfast: women only get one.)

Friday, 19 January 1968

Fruitless day at work. Nothing else.

Saturday, 20 January 1968

Try to work during morning.

2.00–5.00 p.m. Disastrous 'Collection' in Economics. Feel inadequate and depressed. Contemplate changing subject. (If I do, will I lose my scholar's gown?!)

Tea with Andrew Ingram (handsome) and David Graham (nice). Cheered a bit.

7.30 p.m. Picked up by car for the Maxwell party at Headington Hill Hall, the Maxwell family pile. Went with Peter and Lesley and the *Isis* crowd. (Held Lesley's hand in the car.) The party was beautifully done: drinks, dinner, dancing. (I danced with Lesley.) The house is huge, Victorian, pillared, very palatial but a touch gaudy in the decoration. (Shelves of false books etc.) I met our host, Robert Maxwell, MC, MP and chairman of Pergamon Press. He put his arm around my shoulder in a jovial and slightly menacing way. I told him that I was honoured to be visiting Headington Hill Hall – especially because Oscar Wilde had come to a ball at the house when he was at Oxford. Oscar came dressed as Prince Rupert of the Rhine. 'And who have you come dressed as, young man?' he growled. (The house used to be owned by the Morrell family. Now it belongs to Oxford City Council. 'It is the best council house in the land', according to Mr M.)

Coffee at the Adamsons' afterwards. (Can't take my mind off Lesley.)

Thursday, 25 January 1968

Tea at Union with Geraldine [Jones] and her parents. GJ very upset because Jeremy Thorpe[*] ratted on her at the last minute and phoned to say he couldn't turn up for tonight's debate – her first. Lots of tears.

The debate (on the abandonment of Britain's military presence east of Suez) was tedious. Julian Radcliffe spoke and was laughed at mercilessly.

---

[*] Jeremy Thorpe (b.1929), MP for North Devon 1959–79, had become Leader of the Liberal Party the year before.

Oxford

Monday, 5 February 1968

Lunch with Philip Maxwell. Nice man. Serious man. He is concerned about the flippancy of *Isis*.

2.30 p.m. Visit HM Prison, Oxford. Tour and talk with Mr Dermot Grubb, the governor. We are sharing a platform at the Crime Society meeting on Saturday – alongside R. K. Leslie, governor of Spring Hill Open Prison, Grendon.

P.m. Write *Isis* columm. Write Swiss feature. Take them to 142 [Walton Street]. Write prison editorial. Write notes for piece for *Oxford Tory*.

2.30 a.m. Late-night visit from Peter Adamson and Mike Palmer [from *Isis*]. Apprehended by chaplain. Not amused.

Tuesday, 6 February 1968

Piece and pic in *Sun* newspaper, based on the interview I did two weeks ago. It's a whole page: 'The Tomorrow People'. Jill Guyte visited 'two widely differing universities, Oxford and Newcastle-upon-Tyne', and this is the result. I get the top photograph and a quote from me as the headline: 'I'd like to be a sort of Danny Kaye and then Home Secretary'. The interview is slightly embarrassing, but there we are. Under the stuff about me is a pic of Mike Rosen,[*] 21, playwright, and a piece about him and Diana Quick,[†] 21, 'generally talked about as the best actress at Oxford for years'.

All day: work, lecture, tutorials, off and on.

See chaplain and dean about Peter and Mike's visit last night! Severe rap over knuckles.

Talk with Kevin Pakenham about doing an article about alcoholism for his magazine, *Cover*.

Friday, 16 February 1968

Last night was good. I dined at the Union 'as friend of the President'. Good debate on censorship. I didn't speak, but somehow got referred to – pleasantly by Viscount Lewisham, disparagingly by Jonathan Sumption. The guests were Brigid Brophy – tough and good: we got on well – and Kathleen Raine, poetess,

[*] Michael Rosen (b.1946), broadcaster, children's author and poet; Children's Laureate, 2007–09.
[†] Diana Quick (b.1946), actress, first female President of the Oxford University Dramatic Society, still best remembered as Julia Flyte in the television adaptation of *Brideshead Revisited*, 1981.

a sort of milder version of Rachel Field from school. We talked at some length and she gave me two quotes to treasure:

'He who would do good to another must do it in minute particulars.' William Blake.

'The best lack all conviction while the worst are full of passionate intensity.' W. B. Yeats.

Tonight not so good. Terrible in fact. Pete and Les [Adamson] called to work on the television play that Pete and I are writing together and it all got out of hand. Pete was in a silly mood. Went back with them to Walton Street. Was rude to Alasdair Lidell. Oh dear.

Saturday, 17 February 1968

Noon. Les comes over. Talk, hold hands, go shopping.

P.m. Party at Pete and Les – quite pleasant. Try to be nice to Alasdair and avoid Les – too ostentatiously. Kiss her on leaving.

Donald Wolfit dies.

Sunday, 18 February 1968

Just catch 8.30 a.m. train to London. Go to 5H. Pleasant morning with parents and Polly who is delightful. An ex-convict called Norman is there doing paintwork.

Meet Sal, 2.00 p.m. Waterloo. Go to Festival Hall for tea. Mutual recognition that 'love' was dead. Agree to part after two years, six months and thirteen days. Feel curiously numb, empty and middle-aged. She was obviously, almost hurtfully, relieved! At least it died a natural death. She had nothing to say, but wanted to return the ring melodramatically. Felt remote, so not unhappy to say goodbye. To be 'free' after all this while will be strange.

Sup at 5H with family. Hes in. Everyone talks loudly and at once. Hes full of horrors at Springfield Hospital, the psychiatric hospital where she is now a nurse. (They like to have staff who have been patients!) She is v funny about it all – dropping the tray of false teeth and having to work out, by trial and error, which teeth belong in which mouth; smoking in the laundry cupboard and setting the towels alight; giving the tranquilliser injections to the patient who needed the antidepressant and vice versa, etc. It really is *Carry On at the Loony Bin*!

10.00 p.m train to Oxford.

Saturday, 2 March 1968

142 Walton Street at 11.30 a.m. BBC film unit from *Panorama*, including Robin Day, came to talk to a quartet of us from *Isis* about Roy Jenkins[*] for a pre-Budget programme. We were filmed outside the Radcliffe Camera. Fairly successful.

Lunch at Randolph Hotel as guests of BBC. Robin Day aggressive throughout – and conceited in a defensive way. That said, he was very pleasant to me! I seemed to amuse him. I think he thought I was like he was when he was here.

Tea with Les. Difficult. Must come to terms with inevitable situation. She is married to someone else! And he is my friend!!

Quiet evening. Pete and Les called round just before eleven. Rather nice.

Friday, 8 March 1968

Ember Day. Seems appropriate. My 20th birthday – alas! (I have liked being a teenager. Very much. I'm not sure about being twenty.)

Last night I went to the presidential debate. Tony Bird was so much better – firmer and funnier – than William Waldegrave,[†] but Waldegrave won. Geraldine asked me to speak in her Farewell debate. It's going to be televised.

I met up with Les at 8.30 a.m. She came in for coffee before going to school. She missed her car lift on purpose. She gave me a present – a beautifully wrapped book about Olivier and his Shakespeare films. (I love her.)

Les in at 4.15 p.m. Tea then out shopping for party. On to 142. Pete in strange temper.

Party from 8.30 onwards: some nice people, my friends. Spent almost whole time with Les. After party, 12.30–1.30, alone with Les.

Thursday, 14 March 1968

A.m. French prelim – not bad. P.m. Economics prelim – simple stuff, but badly done by me, I fear.

6.45 p.m. To Union. Sherry. Dinner. Sat next to amusing bald English tutor and novelist, Rachel Trickett.[‡] 9.00 p.m. Spoke first in the televised debate: '*Vive la difference!*' They all laughed. The guests were Miriam Karlin (actress),

[*] Jenkins was Chancellor of the Exchequer, 1967–70, succeeding James Callaghan who had resigned after the devaluation of the pound in November 1967.
[†] William Waldegrave (b.1946), Conservative MP, 1979–97, Cabinet Minister under John Major; now Baron Waldegrave of North Hill.
[‡] Rachel Trickett (1923–99), Principal of St Hugh's College, 1973–91.

funny and nice; Clement Freud* (grandson of Sigmund), very funny, very dry, dared to tell his stories very slowly (wonderful control of his material); and Frank Muir† (scriptwriter), completely delightful – not as funny as Freud, but because he was friendlier (he twinkled) the audience liked him more. Max Beloff likened my contribution to those of Philip Guedella and F. E. Smith which was gratifying.‡ Pleasant drinks afterwards. Much congratulations, but I felt somewhat empty.

Friday, 15 March 1968

George Brown resigns as Foreign Secretary.

Parents' 31st wedding anniversary.

History prelim – not bad.

See Dr Thomas (Moral tutor) to discuss changing my subject.

Evening: call in at Walton Street. Pete and Les out.

Lots of nice notes about last night's speech – from Geraldine, from Rachel Trickett ('best speech of the night'), from Edwina§ (reporting lovely reaction from her parents), etc.

Typewriter. My one possible buyer for this machine has fallen through, so I'm going to hold on to it a while longer – perhaps get it 'overhauled' in the holiday.

Term ends tomorrow. I'm glad.

Friday, 29 March 1968

11.30 p.m. last night. By-election result. Tories sweep in.

Today. Hear of Pass at Prelims. Pleasant relief. (Will make it easier to change subject without losing scholar's gown!)¶ Go to Victoria: fix ticket for Paris. Visit Peter Harris at Hospital for Tropical Diseases near Mornington Crescent. Easy conversation. Meet Sal at Waterloo. Disappointed (relieved?) to find her unattractive. Pleasant enough lunch at Royal Festival Hall, but not much to say. (Once she was everything. Now there's nothing. Will the day

---

* Sir Clement Freud (1924–2009), author, broadcaster, restaurateur, Liberal MP for the Isle of Ely and North East Cambridgeshire, 1973–87.

† Frank Muir (1920–98), comedy writer, broadcaster, television executive.

‡ Philip Guedella (1889–1944) and F. E. Smith (1872–1930) were distinguished former Union presidents noted for their oratory.

§ Edwina Cohen, later Currie (b.1946), an undergraduate at St Anne's College and Oxford Union officer; Conservative MP, 1983–97.

¶ GB was allowed to change subjects, from PPE to History and Modern Languages, without forfeiting his Open Scholarship.

come when at least I remember 'something'? I hope so. Or is this what comes of love? NB: The world will be spared any poetry from me on this theme!)

On to Piccadilly: get francs at bank. Sit for a while in Green Park. Return home.

Achieve nothing concrete today. Feel poorly.

Monday, 1 April 1968

Meet two (cankered) rosebuds on train to Paris, real innocents abroad. Once arrived, coffee with them, take them to Alliance Française, find them hotel in rue Rousselet. Lunch at self-service, Vaneau.

Call at Administration Pénitentiaire, Ministry of Justice. See same man as two years ago. Distressed at own jerky French. Get literature and promise of attempt to arrange the prison visits I'm wanting. On to Comédie Française to book tickets for Thursday.

Read of Lyndon Johnson's decision not to run for US presidency again in November and of his moves to secure some sort of peace in Vietnam. LBJ not standing is a major surprise and leaves the Democrat spot open for Robert Kennedy.

Doze in Les Tuileries, then decide to get to grips with correspondence. Lovely letter from Suzy Blaustein, now 16 but not liking it. ('I feel so old!') She wrote to LBJ and got a reply within six days. I wrote to Samuel Beckett and he sent me a lovely handwritten reply. He won't be interviewed: 'I don't know any of the answers and am not interested.' But he'll meet me: 'It would be grand to see you in Paris if you don't mind not interviewing me.'

Thursday, 4 April 1968

2.30 p.m. Comédie Française. Excellent seat. *L'Etourdi* – highly stylised and amusing. *Le Médecin Malgré Lui* – delightful set, production predictable and safe.

6.00 p.m. Champs-Elysées. *Vie Privée* with Brigitte Bardot. She is still gorgeous (gorgeous) but the film is *awful*.

I came out and heard the news. Martin Luther King has been assassinated – gunned down in Tennessee. I walked back along the banks of the Seine. Everybody was quiet. Everyone here feels affected by this.

Saturday, 6 April 1968

It's gone midnight. I am on the boat going home. It is very cold. I have been reading Voltaire – one of the two books I bought yesterday on my walk along the boulevard St Michel before seeing *Tom Jones* in the tiny cinema near La Madeleine. The film was great fun. I needed cheering up.

I could do with cheering up now. It is *so* cold and I am hungry. I had supper at the Wimpy at Gare du Nord about five hours ago. I bought the English papers to read about Martin Luther King. He was only 39. He was shot on a hotel balcony in Memphis – apparently by 'a well-dressed white man' who fled in a car. The Reverend Jesse Jackson was standing with him when a single shot was fired from an automatic rifle. He said King's last words were, 'Sing "Precious Lord" tonight and sing it well.' President Johnson has asked every citizen to 'reject the blind violence that has taken Dr King' but rioting is already breaking out all over the US.

Sunday, *14 April 1968*

Easter Day. I don't go to church any more. Heigh ho. Aimless days these – postponing things till late evening and then being too weary to complete them. Getting about one thing done a day.

Letter published in the *Sunday Times* today – on prisons. Sent off a letter to *The Times* on the Chicago execution of teenagers. I hope not too melodramatic.

Planning a jolly week of cheer-me-up entertainment – to include *Flubber* at the Ionic Cinema, Golders Green, tomorrow. *Mrs Wilson's Diary* with John Wells at the Criterion on Tuesday (supposed to be very funny). *Around the World in Eighty Days* again (it never fails) and *Cabaret* at the Palace on Saturday with Judi Dench. (Ma is in hospital having her appendix out. Have I already reported this?)

Friday, *26 April 1968*

Lunch with William Waldegrave at 5 Foley Bridge [in Oxford]. It's very comfy, but then he is the son of an earl. And an Old Etonian, effortlessly courteous and unselfconsciously charming. (I am self-consciously charming: there is a difference, alas.) He is also highly intelligent. I like him and we agree that Enoch Powell's 'river of foaming blood' speech on immigration was unacceptable and that Heath had no choice but to sack him from the Shadow Cabinet. What Powell says may be what half the population thinks, but it doesn't make it right.[*]

[*] On 21 April, in a speech in Birmingham, Powell said that Britain must be 'literally mad as a nation' to allow 50,000 dependants of immigrants into the country each year. 'I am filled with foreboding,' he said. 'Like the Roman I see the river Tiber foaming with much blood.' Edward Heath, the Opposition leader, relieved him of his post as shadow Defence Secretary.

Oxford

Thursday, 2 May 1968

Her Majesty Queen Elizabeth II visited the Oxford Union today. As a consequence, Trinity term at the Union should have begun with a bang. In fact, the event was such a damp squib there was barely a whimper. Her Majesty came in to wild applause and happy cheering – Harold Macmillan twinkling at her side. But when the cheering stopped, a sudden chill filled the atmosphere. There was a silence, and a palpable awkwardness, in the hall. There were eight hundred of us there, I suppose, and because of the presence of the Queen none of us could be 'normal'. The debate itself was dismal – dull as ditchwater: so restrained, everyone on best behaviour. It was actually a rather dreadful evening. Once the excitement of seeing the Queen at close quarters had worn off, tedium set in.

Afterwards I reprimanded William for not carrying Her Majesty's umbrella for her as he escorted her across the courtyard. He told me, 'The Queen insists on holding her own umbrella – always. If someone else holds it, the rain trickles down her neck.'

Thursday, 9 May 1968

My day in Paris has been memorable. I landed at Le Bourget at 8.50 a.m. As I emerged, first off the plane, I was gratified to find a crowd of several hundred well-wishers corralled on the other side of the tarmac waving and cheering. Whistles blew, flash bulbs popped and then the noise subsided. It turned out they were not waiting for me on my way to interview the Aga Khan – but for Ho Chi Minh, due to arrive from North Vietnam today for the Paris peace talks.

It's all happening here. There are armed police on every street corner, but north of the Seine it is relatively calm and much as normal. Go south of the river, though, and you are suddenly in a city in the middle of a revolution – burnt-out cars, pulled-up paving stones, streets closed off. Around the Sorbonne, there are barricades and tanks and armoured vehicles everywhere you turn. At the start of the week there was full-scale rioting. I saw no fighting, but – for safety's sake – I took a taxi and, crossing the boulevard St Germain, we had to negotiate our way through a throng of protesting students on the march. The taxi proceeded quite slowly and, at first, all was well – then, suddenly, our car seemed to catch the attention of a group of the protesters and they turned on the vehicle and, chanting and jeering, began to rock it to and fro. I looked out of the window, desperately trying to show them that I was a student too. The driver pressed on, honking his horn, and eventually the students let us pass. It was an alarming few minutes.

The Ile de la Cité appeared deserted. You would never have known that *les événements* were taking place half a mile away. At 6.20 p.m., as instructed by Miss Bishop, Secretary to HH Shah Karim, Aga Khan IV, I made my way down a squalid backstreet to 10 rue Chanoinesse. I rang a bell, climbed to the third floor and was admitted to a plush suite of offices. I waited and Miss Bishop appeared. 'You haven't brought a tape-recorder have you?' 'No,' I said. She looked relieved: 'His Highness won't want you to have a tape-recorder.' She smiled. 'You will only ask the questions we agreed?' 'Of course,' I said. She took me down into the street and showed me a little alleyway leading to rue des Ursins. 'When I get there, do I ring the doorbell?' I asked. 'There's no need,' she said. 'Good luck.'

When I reached the house I couldn't see a doorbell or a knocker. The front door was wooden, covered with heavy metal studs. As I climbed the steps, it swung slowly open. A servant in a white jacket stood within. *'Monsieur Brandreth? Son Altesse vous attend.'* The house was entirely lit by candlelight – a blaze of candlelight.

I followed the servant along a corridor, up a winding staircase, along another corridor, to a double door. Without knocking, the flunkey pushed opened the doors and bowed low, murmuring as he did so: *'Altesse! Monsieur Brandreth, Altesse!'*

The Aga Khan is 31, slim, lithe, handsome, though the hairline is receding. He was sitting on a chaise longue facing the door. He got to his feet at once and bounded towards me, smiling, hand outstretched. 'Gyles, welcome! Come in. So good to meet you.' He is a direct descendant of Mohammed the Prophet – through Mohammed's daughter, Fatima. I was very pleased to shake his hand. I was very pleased to meet him.

At once he said, 'What would you like to drink?' I couldn't think what to say. My mind went blank. Then I blurted out, 'An orange juice.' He didn't respond. I thought I had said the wrong thing – until five minutes later when, from behind a tapestry in the far corner of the room, another white-jacketed flunkey emerged carrying a silver salver with, on it, a huge glass of freshly squeezed blood-red orange juice. (The Aga Khan definitely did not order the drink: the man must have been hovering behind the arras listening.)

His Highness showed me round the room. We looked at family photographs. We stopped by a huge globe and I asked him to show me some of the countries where his people live. He is the leader of fifteen million Ismaili Moslems around the world and what he says goes. (Because they were in danger of persecution, three thousand Moslems left South Africa at his command.) My interview was about his life and work as a spiritual leader. I said that in the West fewer are committing themselves to religion. He said the reverse was true in the Moslem world. 'There is now more attendance at mosque and equal devotion.' He was softly spoken, very gentle, earnest and sincere. He was frequently self-deprecating – he talked several times about his 'lack of self-assurance'. I stayed with him until gone eight o'clock. Knowing that this was his first-ever interview, I asked him why he had agreed to see me. 'Because you are a student,' he said, 'and you wrote a very persuasive letter.' I left feeling that I had been in the presence of a special human being. Writing up the interview won't be easy.

Thursday, 16 May 1968

Diana Quick is 21, dark, beautiful, pouting, and the first female President in the history of the Oxford University Dramatic Society. When I went to meet her for the first time she was wearing a *leather* miniskirt! We had a drink in a pub: she was both exciting to be with and a bit alarming. But she encouraged me in my ambition to direct an OUDS production at the Playhouse and today I went for the audition – and got the job! I am quite surprised. I had to rehearse a scene in front of the OUDS Committee. Diana played the girl in the scene. I think it was asking her to suggest desire by putting her top teeth over her lower lip that clinched it! Anyway, I'm delighted. They want me to do a traditional Victorian pantomime. Should be fun.

Lunch at the Taj Mahal with Fred Burnley, BBC TV director. I liked him at once, though I'm not sure what he made of me. He is making a TV film with Kenneth Tynan.[*] It's for a series called *One Pair of Eyes* and will be about Oxford twenty years ago (when Tynan was here and the wunderkind) and Oxford now. Apparently I'm to feature in the film as the Tynan of my generation! (I send out my letters in bright orange envelopes: Tynan used peacock blue.)

Union debate: 'This house regrets the invention of television.' I joined the speakers for dinner: John Wells (good to see him) and David Frost (friendly, unctuous, very bad skin).

Letter in response to mine from the director of the Department of Public Safety in the State of Illinois. The executions of Cannon and Cochran[†] have been stayed pending appeal.

---

[*] Kenneth Tynan (1927–80), the most admired theatre critic of his generation; literary manager of the National Theatre when it opened; the first person to say 'Fuck' on television, 1965; the creator of the erotic revue, *Oh! Calcutta!*, 1969.

[†] Cannon and Cochran were teenage murderers, members of a gang called the Dell Vikings; they were due for execution but were granted a reprieve.

Friday, 24 May 1968

Yesterday: Lunch with Diana Quick (great name, great girl) and Michael Coveney.* He is to be my choreographer on the pantomime. Tiny, slight, very pleasant. (I have settled on *Cinderella* – Byron's *Cinderella*. No, not Lord Byron: H. J. Byron, Victorian playwright and humorist, the man who observed that life is too short for chess.)

Tea with Venetia Thomas at Somerville. (She is lovely.)

Union: chat with Tariq Ali.† I can understand why he might think me a touch ridiculous, but he has no idea why I might think the same of him. ('The best lack all conviction, while the worst are full of passionate intensity.')

Midnight–4.00 a.m.: write History essay

Thursday, 30 May 1968

Day working on speech. Genial lunch with Clive Syddall.‡ A nice man and *generous* – not something we see a lot of in Oxford!

7.00 p.m. to Union for the Eights Week 'Funny' Debate: 'A little sincerity is a dangerous thing, but a great deal of it is absolutely fatal.' The speakers: me, Viscount Lewisham, the Earl of Arran (Boofles to his friends), James Robertson Justice, Michael Beloff and Christopher Hollis. A nice dinner. I sat next to Justice (a wonderful companion) and opposite Diana Quick who looked (and was) enchanting. The debate was something else. Both the BBC and German TV filmed my speech.§ The house was appalling – so sticky, refusing to laugh. The speech was not a total flop, but a great disappointment – though the others fared no better. I suppose/hope that once edited it'll look okay. I saw Venetia there. I was pleased she'd come, but I'm sorry it was such a dead affair. At least it's over now. Soon forgotten, too, one hopes.

Saturday, 1 June 1968

In France, de Gaulle is standing firm. He will concede nothing to the protesting students – nor anyone else. He has been elected. He is in command. *L'état c'est moi.*

* Michael Coveney (b.1948), later theatre critic of the *Financial Times*, *Observer* and *Daily Mail*.
† Tariq Ali (b.1943), student activist and, later, political campaigner, writer and film-maker.
‡ Clive Syddall (b.1945), later award-winning television director and producer.
§ A German TV company was making a separate documentary film about Oxford, also featuring GB.

In England, Brandreth is down by the river, affecting to enjoy Eights Week for the benefit of the BBC and German film crews. Boating and quaffing Pimm's are not really for me – and it probably shows.

Brecht is not really for me either. I rehearsed my scene for Tim Maby's show, *Bert Lives* – devised from Brecht's writing. A pretentious shambles.

Tuesday, 4 June 1968

The fourth day of the *Cinderella* auditions. I'm holding them in New College cloisters, in the music room. It's a wearying process. I am looking for the girl of my dreams, a fairy-tale princess – and perhaps, at last, I have found her? Michèle Brown, St Anne's, came today: 21, dark hair, beautiful. She could be a perfect Cinders. She has the look, but does she have the voice or technique?

Sally has sent me a lock of her hair.

Thursday, 6 June 1968

Lunch with William Waldegrave, a thoroughly nice person. He is very cut up about the Robert Kennedy assassination.[*]

Plan to film *Cinderella* auditions foiled. Forbidden by Warden: 'we have had enough of Mr Brandreth's antics'.

Sherry party in my room for potential Zuleikas. A pretty motley gang, but Fred [Burnley] seems happy with the look of them.[†] We are filming the 'crowning' on the banks of the Isis next Wednesday.

Saturday, 8 June 1968

6.15 p.m.: Garden cocktails at Corpus Christi College. Take Michèle: already enchanted. Drink pretty potent.

On to party on the St Catherine's barge. BBC filming it, but the evening's a failure. I danced a lot with Kathleen Tynan. Tynan himself was in a filthy humour throughout. Robin Day turned up for a while; I chatted to him; he was very merry. When I talked with Tynan he was very scratchy, told me to go off and dance some more with his wife. He kept saying, 'This is boring. Nothing's happening.' Nothing was. He produced a £5 note from his wallet and held it up,

---

[*] Senator Robert Kennedy was shot and fatally wounded at the Ambassador Hotel in Los Angeles, hours after winning the California US presidential primary.
[†] In Max Beerbohm's satirical novel about Edwardian Oxford, the divinely beautiful Zuleika Dobson scorns her many undergraduate suitors, driving them to suicide. GB proposed a 'Zuleika Dobson competition' to find a modern Zuleika and chose eight girls as 'finalists'.

saying he'd give it to any girl who would take off her top for him. 'I want to see some young tits! I want to see something *happening*.' Fred was upset 'cos Tynan was upset. 'There's nothing to film because there's nothing to see.' The girls all sensibly kept their tops on, so, to be obliging, at midnight, fully clothed, I threw myself off the barge and into the river.

Sunday, 9 June 1968

Breakfast with Fred at the Randolph. He wasn't much happier. Talked briefly with Robin Day. He was very full of himself. He felt he had had 'a successful row' with Tynan the night before – 'just what I enjoy.'

Rehearsing the appalling *Bert Lives*.

Monday, 10 June 1968

Phone national newspaper picture desks to alert them to Zuleika filming on Wednesday.

More auditions.

Dinner with Michèle – a bad first meal really: stilted. We went for a Chinese. I paid, but I asked for the bill thinking I could give it to the BBC or the German TV company and claim expenses. Michèle was not impressed. All the usual stuff fell flat. I asked her questions she wouldn't answer. Ended up holding hands and kissing. Unsatisfactory. Curious.

Tuesday, 11 June 1968

7.30 a.m. Rehearse *Bert Lives*. Brecht before breakfast! Can you believe it?

Lunch with Diana Quick.

2.00 p.m. Record interview with William Waldegrave and Ken Tynan in Union President's office. Some of it goes well, but I was pompous when William was so natural. Tynan is not a comfortable creature: he smokes all the time, holding his cigarette out affectedly. He is sex-obsessed and never anything but spiky. I wanted to talk to him about Olivier and Marlene Dietrich (of course) but he only wants to talk about 'who we fuck and how'.

Evening: Michèle.

Wednesday, 12 June 1968

A.m: Filming Zuleika Dobson Award. Eight girls: Annunziata Asquith, Charlotte Gray, Kathy Henderson, Rosalind Erskine, Melanie Sandiford, Kirsty McLeod, Liz Davey and Michèle – the most beautiful girls of their generation, all in evening dresses. Self as judge – in dinner jacket. Set off together from my room at 10.15 a.m., down Rose Lane in a procession of vintage cars, led by a horse (ridden by Julian Radcliffe). We filmed the luncheon table sequence, I made a short speech and gave Annunziata the crown. (Annunziata was Fred's choice. He was adamant. Clearly Annunziata attracts the older man!* Unaided, I would certainly have picked either Michèle or Kirsty.) Presentation over, the girls all left. I then walked into the river.

Boring lunch with Xan Smiley and friends.

Successful production meeting at Playhouse.

Dinner at Randolph with Fred and the BBC crew and Michèle and two of the girls and Julian and David,† two good, decent and selfless men.

Oh, and yes, I think I have a History essay to write. It's coming up to midnight. I'd better start it now!

Thursday, 13 June 1968

Good picture of the Zuleika Dobson event on page 4 of the *Daily Mail*. And amazing centre spread in the *Daily Mirror* under the headline: 'After picking the beauty contest winner, the judge walked off in a sort of daze.' There are six pictures: one of me and Annunziata, the rest of me walking straight into the river, submerging, disappearing . . . 'Young Brandreth looked into her eyes and, smitten, turned away in a daze. Seeing no more the wondrous woodland, smelling no more the scent of summer, he walked plumb into the river and vanished. Dashed pity, really. Such a promising lad.'

Lunch with Rona Bower. She agrees to play Cinderella. (I have offered Michèle a part in the chorus. She has declined. She is going to play Viola in the Queen's College production of *Twelfth Night*.)

Friday, 14 June 1968

Lunch: Michèle.

Kevin Pakenham comes round with a man from Independent Television who has an interesting filming job for me – a series. Could be exciting. I have to go for a meeting in London on Monday.

Union election: get elected Secretary. The folk in the Union bar booed when the result was announced, but the figures showed quite a convincing victory.

---

* Lady Annunziata Asquith (b.1948), daughter of the Earl of Oxford and Asquith, later model, biographer and partner of Patrick, 5th Earl of Lichfield.
† David Graham (b.1948), later international banker, helped GB find the girls for the competition.

I suppose this must be reckoned the most successful week of my life: some good TV filming, a centre spread in the country's biggest-selling newspaper, election as Secretary of the Oxford Union, and Michèle. All things I dream about – and now it's happened, I feel just the same. Luckier perhaps, but no happier. Odd.

Saturday, 15 June 1968

It turns out that the man from Independent Television who came round yesterday was nothing of the sort. It was a hoax, a rather mean practical joke conjured up by Kevin Pakenham.

To the Maxwell Ball at Headington Hill Hall – 9.00 p.m. to 3.00 a.m. It was beautifully done – with drinks in the house, dinner in the marquee, dancing and breakfast on the lawn. It nearly went awry in the Maxwell drawing room: I was 'entertaining' the crowd with my 'impression' of Robert Maxwell, hunched forward, gurgling and growling, when, suddenly, I felt a heavy hand on my shoulder. I turned around – and it was him! He gazed at me steadily and then, slowly, he began to chuckle.

I've never been to a party like it. We all had formal dance cards (with little pencils attached to them with red string), telling us to choose five *different* partners for five special dances. There was a band, a pop group, a discotheque – and steaks and ribs served at the barbecue between dinner and breakfast. A fantastic spread. It could have been perfect – and would have been but for an unpleasant moment when Peter Adamson accosted me and told me to keep my hands off his wife . . .

Saturday, 22 June 1968

Note from Rona Bower: she can't play Cinderella. Her tutors have told her she's got to work. It's bad news, but I don't feel desperate. I have Nigel Osborne as my musical director. He is going to be very good.[*]

With Michèle to New College Boojums party at noon. On to perform *Bert Lives* at Oxford Prison. The inmates liked it! (They really did.) Sent telegram to Michèle.[†] Evening with Michael Coveney. Saw Germans re filming New College Ball. Julian [Radcliffe] is in charge of security so it will be *tight*.

[*] Nigel Osborne (b.1948), later composer and Reid Professor of Music at Edinburgh University.
[†] GB regularly sent telegrams to Michèle, even though New College and St Anne's were only a mile or so apart and there was a twice-daily messenger service that delivered letters between colleges.

Sunday, 23 June 1968

Join Michèle at St Anne's at noon. Lunch at the Ox in the Cellar. Stay in all afternoon.

6.00 p.m. Drinks with Michèle's friends, including Christopher Hampton who wrote *When Did You Last See My Mother?*[*] He is very charming, a true writer who lives for his writing. Get a little drunk. Sup at ghastly pub. Back to M's until the curfew [at 11.00 p.m.]. She is determined somehow to remain a rolling stone: I'll fight it.

Return to New College after eleven strange/wonderful hours with her.

Monday, 24 June 1968

Sitting in room contemplating essay on the collapse of the Russian Duma when Christopher Hampton called round with Bob Kidd[†] who is directing Jane Asher in *Summer* at the Playhouse. They wanted New College Ball tickets for Jane and possibly Paul McCartney, her Beatle boyfriend. Said I'd do what I could to help.

5.00 p.m. Go join Michèle at St Anne's. Eat in pub. Perfect girl. Reach Ball at 11.00 p.m. Julian manning the barricades as though New College was the bridge at Arnhem. Report to German film crew as planned – but everybody irritable. Shoot three sequences. Find Jane Asher and Bob Kidd. No sign of Paul McCartney, but signs that Bob has his eye on Jane. They are an enchanting couple: she's so freckled. We talked a lot. I asked her to play Cinders for me. She'll think about it. And she's going to let me have her recipe for a perfect chocolate mousse. She was tired so I left her to sleep in my bed. (Yes, I can now say that Jane Asher has slept in my bed.) We parted at about 5.30 a.m.: agreed to meet on Wednesday for *Summer* at the Playhouse. It was a wonderful night – Jane and Bob, young and amusing and appreciative and gentle; Michèle, perfect.

Wednesday, 26 June 1968

Tony Hancock has died. He has committed suicide in Sydney. Very sad. At his best he was the best. Completely brilliant.

---

[*] Produced at the Royal Court Theatre in 1966, when Hampton was just 20, later transferring to the Comedy Theatre, so making him the West End's youngest-ever playwright. He went on to write plays, translations and screenplays, winning an Academy Award for *Dangerous Liaisons*, 1988.
[†] Robert Kidd (1943–80), theatre director particularly associated with the Royal Court and the early plays of Christopher Hampton and David Storey.

Gillian Cooke, the editor of *Honey* magazine, called. Small, bouncy, eager: she didn't want to chatter – she simply wanted to ask me to write a regular column: a man's eye on the dollies! I said I'd do a dummy for her. Marvellous if it happens. (I don't think it was a hoax!)

Joined Michèle at St Anne's, supped at pub, joined Bob Kidd and Chris Hampton at Gloucester Arms, got comps for *Summer*. The play was whimsical, and quite funny, but I don't think it'll run. Gathered afterwards for a drink. Bill Gaskill* there – rather smooth, but kind. Jane, gentle and lovely.

Thursday, 27 June 1968

Joined Michèle at 9.30 a.m. – helped her with her luggage. Train to London, via Pa in Leicester Square to BBC Television Centre, where Fred [Burnley] met us and gave us lunch. He said he'd been dining with Cyril Bennett, head of London Weekend Television, who wants to give me my own show! (This is not a hoax! And, if it happens, it will change everything.) Watch the rushes of the Tynan film – the interview is not so bad as I feared. Fred was all charm, but not uncritical. He says I am far too 'mannered' and not at all 'modern'. He asked me what was top of the pops this week. It seems the answer is 'Jumping Jack Flash' from the Rolling Stones, but I had no idea. He suggested I start reading *New Musical Express*.

Took Michèle to Charing Cross to catch her train to Ashford [in Kent, where her family lived]. I do adore her so. Sent her a telegram.

Thursday, 4 July 1968

General de Gaulle has won a landslide victory in the French general election. Lone yachtsman Alec Rose has landed in Portsmouth after taking a year to circumnavigate the globe. I have had lunch with Pa at Buck's Club as the guest of Harry Middleton, number two at BBC Outside Broadcasts who is going to introduce me to the heads of Features and Current Affairs.

Coming out of Buck's, we stumbled into Frank Muir, now head of entertainment at London Weekend TV. Buck's is said to be the model for the Drones Club and Frank Muir certainly has the manner of a character created by P. G. Wodehouse. He was very affable: we settled to meet for lunch and he agreed to read the Prologue for the pantomime. It's all going well. Just a pity I have to wait until 1970 for anything to *happen*.

---

* William Gaskill (b. 1930), theatre director; founder director of the National Theatre at the Old Vic, 1963; artistic director of the Royal Court Theatre, 1965–72.

Wednesday, 10 July 1968

Last night, the Royal Tournament at Earl's Court with Ma and Ben and Jen – rather fun and quite like old times. Tomorrow, Pa's 58th birthday and we are going to *Hadrian the Seventh* at the Mermaid – much acclaimed. Tonight, however, the play was not so memorable. I met Michèle at Charing Cross at 6.10 p.m. *Wonderful* to be with her again. (She seemed happy, too.) On to the Fortune Theatre where Bob Kidd was waiting and gave us our tickets for the first night of *Summer* – we had a £4 box all to ourselves! Paul McCartney was there, and smaller than I'd expected. He doesn't seem to know that it's all over with Jane . . . I said nothing, of course. We had champagne with Jane afterwards, with her brother and parents, etc. The performances are much improved, but it will still flop, I fear.

Sunday, 14 July 1968

Michèle is so beautiful. And *I* am now 'trendy' – wearing the new jacket we bought for me yesterday at Harrods. I rather like it! (And I have taken my trousers and suits to the tailors for tapering. She is changing me, the funny girl.) Last night we went to *Elvira Madigan* at the Academy cinema – beautiful, but perhaps not so beautiful as we had been led to believe. Today we walked around the West End and down Whitehall. We supped at the Royal Festival Hall and then walked along the Embankment to Charing Cross. I saw her off on the 10.10 p.m. train to Ashford. She parted with a striking remark: wouldn't I like *anyone* as much as her? She said it's just the idea of being in love that I find exciting – *who* it is hardly matters.

Tuesday, 30 July 1968

11.00 a.m. Went to interview Iain Macleod at the House of Commons. His office is a shoe-box tucked away somewhere in the roof of the building. He talked about the need for consensus – staying in the middle ground and taking the majority of people with you – and the frustrations of power. Governments can only do so much and what they try to do takes so long to take effect. He was impressive, clear-headed, but much shorter and more physically disabled than I had expected.[*]

Met David Kremer for lunch (he's on the OUDS committee and being very helpful) and picked up the set designs for *Cinderella* from Kathy Henderson (she's sweet and mild – so are her sets, alas).

Cultural happenings. Apple, the Beatles' shop, with the psychedelic murals, is closing. Because it's fifty yards from home, next door to the Baker Street Classic,

---

[*] The combination of a 1940 war wound to his thigh and the spinal condition, ankylosing spondylitis, left him in pain and with a limp for most of his adult life.

I visited it on a number of occasions, but there was never anything there that I wanted to buy. I suppose there was never anything anybody else wanted to buy, hence its closure after just six months. And, tonight, I sat down to watch the opening of Thames TV, but the screen was blank: industrial dispute – no programmes.

Wednesday, 31 July 1968

Meet Michèle at Charing Cross and go with her to King's Arms by Royal Court for lunch with Jane and Bob – both of them philosophical about *Summer* closing. He was firing on all cylinders, while she was a bit flat and limp – though she phoned later to say she's found a flat in Paddington Street, so soon we'll be neighbours.

With M to the Matisse exhibition on the South Bank and then to meet up with Pat Curran from Queen's who is directing *Twelfth Night*. I told him I'd like a part in the play. He said, would I have time? Aren't I directing a play for OUDS next term, *and* being Secretary of the Union, *and* writing columns for *Isis*, etc.? I pressed him. (If Michèle is playing Viola I need to be in his production!) He said he'd really finished casting. I told him I was happy to be an attendant lord. He said, would I consider playing the Sea Captain? It's a small part, but the Sea Captain has a scene with Viola, so I said, Yes!

Saturday, 3 August 1968

A good day. At noon, Ginny married Alan Allkins. She looked lovely and he grows on one. The service was long, but quite pleasant. The reception was long, but, I think, a success. As long as the parents enjoyed it, all's well.

Afterwards, Pa had organised a dinner party for twelve at the Savoy. The food was good, the dancing fun and Harry Worth provided a splendid cabaret. ('I nearly missed the show tonight. I got to the Underground and saw this sign: "Dogs must be carried on the escalators." Took me forty minutes to find one . . .') The day was a success – a proper wedding at St Marylebone (where Elizabeth Barrett married Robert Browning), a proper reception (at The Holme in Regent's Park), all done *comme il faut*. It went so well that one could almost forget the expense. (Pa is eaten up with money worries. He earns around £5,000 which sounds good – but with the rent for the flat and Ben's school fees and my Oxford fees and holidays and all the rest, it isn't quite enough. I am hoping I can make a contribution to the domestic budget soon. When I start the 'Luke Jarvis' column on *Honey*, I am going to get 45 guineas a month. And Gillian [Cooke, the editor] wants me to write a feature every other month as well. The column won't be easy. 'Luke Jarvis' is a swinging sixties young man about town – and I am not entirely sure that's me!)

Saturday, 17 August 1968

One of the most perfect days I can remember. Michèle is so beautiful. Met her, as usual, at Charing Cross, came back to 5H, babysat Polly [Hester's baby daughter], went to see *The Real Inspector Hound* at the Criterion – delightful: very funny. (Love and laughter – who could ask for anything more?)

We supped at the Greek restaurant in Marylebone High Street: taramasalata, lamb kebab, salad, Othello wine, Greek coffee, Turkish delight (with nuts in). We fell into conversation with a sad, thin ex-military man at the next table. He told us about his unhappy love life and how he was reading Lawrence Durrell's novel, *Tunc*. (I shall buy it for Michèle.)

Saw M off from Charing Cross – very content: none of that tension and anxiety that so often comes with railway platform goodbyes. Am going to bed determined to get the *Honey* article on 'Sex and the Single Boy' cracked by this time tomorrow. It can and will be done.

Saturday, 24 August 1968

The papers are full of the Soviet invasion of Czechoslovakia. Troops and tanks from the USSR and four other Eastern bloc countries have moved into the country to stop the reformers and crush 'the Prague Spring'. Alexander Dubček [the Czech Prime Minister] has been arrested and dozens have been killed. I am due to fly to Moscow next week.* Should I still go? Pa suggested I telephone Sir William [Hayter, the Warden of New College and former British Ambassador to Moscow] and take his advice. I did. He said he was sure I would be safe in Moscow. He said I should go. I will.

In Prague, it's hell – horrific pictures of ordinary men and women in the street attempting to defy the tanks. In London, it's heaven. I met Michèle at Charing Cross, as ever, and we went to Carnaby Street. It was fairly hilarious: the 'heart' of Swinging London is full of Americans!

We saw John Schlesinger's film *Darling* at the Baker Street Classic. Strong, stark, sexy – Julie Christie is beautiful. (Tomorrow we are going to *The Graduate*.) Met up with Clive Syddall for tea at the ABC, Baker Street. Nice man:

---

* Having spent his 'gap year' travelling in the USA, GB now wanted to visit the USSR. The visit was to be both a holiday and an opportunity, he hoped, to learn something about the Soviet prison system.

he suggests that I should do a TV show at lunchtime or even at breakfast time on a Sunday – it's never been done in this country. (Would anybody watch?) On to Tooting to Hester's party. Rather a quaint and tame affair: unmarried mothers, a lesbian or two and other drab folk. (Of course, had the evening been filmed by John Schlesinger it would probably have won several awards!)

Pa collected us and brought us home. M is staying in the little room off the kitchen. (I have bought her *Tunc* and the poems of John Donne as bedside reading. She is a perfect creature – blemish free.)

Thursday, 29 August 1968

With Pa to lunch at New Scotland Yard with Pa's friend, Bob Mark, Deputy Commissioner.* He's affable and straightforward, though I was surprised (shocked?) by how much wine was drunk. The tour of the Black Museum was fun: some wonderful stuff on The Brides in the Bath Murders and Dr Crippen.

Hubert Humphrey is to be the Democrats' presidential candidate. It's all over for Senators McCarthy and McGovern.

Friday, 6 September 1968

Full moon. With M to London [from Ashford]. I love her. She is flawless.

To dentist. All fine, as usual.

To BBC in Portland Place to meet Pa's friend from Oxford, Christopher Serpell, BBC Diplomatic Correspondent – quiet, cool, helpful. He gave me several useful Moscow addresses.

About to lunch at 5H with M when Jen and her new fiancé, Peter Woolfenden arrived. Conversation constrained as a consequence so we went off for a Chinese. Then on to Selfridges where we bought M a bag. Then back to 5H, then on by taxi to the University of London Collegiate Theatre to see the National Youth Theatre *Richard II* with Simon Cadell as York. On with Simon to the Baker Street Classic Late Show. Lots of laughs with Simon. We laughed at the rest of the audience as much as anything else. We like laughing at the world! (And I like loving Michèle. She is perfection.)

Monday, 9 September 1968

Rise at 8.00 a.m. To Cromwell Road Air Terminal. Brief haircut. To London Airport – breakfast. Make phone calls – Robert Kidd, Fred Burnley, Michèle.

---

* Sir Robert Mark (b.1917), former Chief Constable of Leicester; Metropolitan Police Commissioner, 1972–7.

Get carried away talking to Michèle, so miss BEA flight to Moscow! With some difficulty, arrange new route. Lunch and then leave at 14.05, on Austrian Airlines, for Vienna. Change at Vienna. There was brilliant sunshine as the door of the plane opened: as I stepped onto the tarmac the rain fell – not just dribs and drabs: a torrent. I was drenched, soaked to the skin.

Still damp, flew on Aeroflot from Vienna to Moscow. Moscow airport deserted and cheerless: no advertisements of course, just plain grey walls and a single palm tree. The whole place was dead. I went to the desk marked 'Hotels' to sort out accommodation and was told to wait. An hour later, I made a second enquiry at the same desk but from someone different. 'Did they tell you to wait?' Yes. 'Then wait.'

After more than two hours I was told there would be a room for me at the Hotel Bucharest. Took a taxi. The driver (who spoke some English) drove along a broad and empty motorway at 120 kph even though the signs said 40. The roadside was littered with broken-down and abandoned vehicles. The driver talked happily about the cold weather and Bobby Charlton (he kept repeating the words 'Bobby Charlton'), but when I asked him about the invasion of Czechoslovakia he went silent for several minutes – until we got near the hotel when he started to say 'Bobby Charlton' once more.

The hotel has the feel of an ornate Victorian public convenience: my room is bare but quite adequate. There is no soap and no plug to the basin, but I was warned to expect that.

Tuesday, 10 September 1968

Change money. Collect breakfast vouchers. Have breakfast – hard-boiled egg and tea.

Walk through Moscow. At Gum, the department store, everyone is eating ice cream, even though the temperature here is below 40 degrees [Fahrenheit]. Go past the Tomb of the Unknown Soldier. At 12 noon there were thirty fresh wreaths on display – by nightfall (when I passed it once more) more than seventy. Went into the Kremlin, past the Lenin Library, down Kalinin Street to No. 14. Quickly attended to: Mr Rozànov agrees to introduce me to 'leading criminologists'.

On the way back I was approached by two 16-year-old boys, both called Sacha. They spoke quite good English. They said they wanted to buy my shoes. I talked to them for two hours, bought them coffee, walked through the city with them and arranged a further meeting. I asked them how they knew so much about life in the West. They said via the BBC and foreign papers: one had a 1964 copy of *Newsweek*, the other a 1961 copy of *Time*. They wanted to talk about pop music: Sacha (with the moustache) plays drums; Sacha (with the 18-year-old girlfriend, Marina) plays guitar. They admire the Beatles, Rolling Stones, Animals. They knew all the Beatles' names and wanted to talk about John Lennon and Yoko Ono!

I am in my room. I have just received a mystery phone call. The telephone rang: I answered: silence.

Wednesday, 11 September 1968

I toured the Kremlin with an enchanting guide. The other tourists were Americans who bent over backwards not to make trouble. 'It is sensible not to allow us to take pictures here. Who would? If you take pictures you don't look properly.' There was plenty to look at – the cathedrals are of great beauty, the armoury chamber is magnificent. We were shown the building where Podgorny and Kosygin [two of the Soviet leaders] work, but nobody asked our guide any difficult questions. We stuck strictly to history: Peter the Great was seven foot tall and made his own gumboots. He knew seventeen trades and was the most modest Tsar. We saw the joint throne of Ivan and Peter, with the hole in the back where their sister sat prompting them with answers. Ambassadors were amazed at the wisdom of their answers . . .

At 4.00 p.m., as arranged, I met the two Sachas on the bridge. Marina was there too: an attractive 18, heavily made-up, wearing a short skirt and smart clothes. They told me they wanted me to buy a handbag for her at the foreign currency shop in the Hotel Rossya. They gave me ten francs, a dollar bill and assorted English and US coins, but when we got to the hotel they said we were being followed and should walk on. They then admitted that, in the past, both of them had been caught and imprisoned. They showed me the labels in their clothes: their jackets were made in North Korea, but their shoes came from Sweden and Switzerland.

Marina wants to leave Russia, for the US – not another Socialist country. The only way to do it is by marrying an American. She has been going out with an Italian for two months. She thinks he is 25 and unmarried, but she isn't sure because she speaks no Italian and he speaks no Russian. He comes from Milano and works at the Embassy. They meet four times a week for an hour. The Sachas are both members of the Youth Party. Marina isn't. She doesn't like politics. 'The Czech invasion is bad. But America is the same. Vietnam is bad.' Jack London is her favourite writer and Clark Gable, Robert Taylor and Vivien Leigh her favourite film stars.

Two more mystery phone calls tonight.

Oxford

Thursday, 12 September 1968

I queued to visit the Lenin Mausoleum. It is really more of a shrine than a mausoleum – and quite tastefully done. Lenin himself looks like a faded waxwork. (Perhaps he is? Perhaps this is just for show.) There is a fast track for tourists and important visitors: I filed past the glass-covered open casket with members of the Soviet Olympic team! The people in the 'people's queue' seemed real, not rent-a-queue. The American behind me opined: 'If Jesus Christ were embalmed in Jerusalem the crowds would be like this.'

The shops here are extraordinary. They have cash registers, but they don't use them. They do their calculations with an abacus and simply use the till as a cash box.

After queuing for several *hours* and being sent from one building to another to a third I succeeded in buying tickets for the Bolshoi *Swan Lake* at the Palace of Congresses.

The phone in my room has been cut off and there is a large lady dressed all in black sitting on an upright chair in the corridor immediately outside my bedroom. I said goodnight to her, but she didn't respond. I am going to bed now. I have done too much walking: my bones ache and I am very tired. I shall write up my notes on my meeting with the criminologists tomorrow – though I am not sure if there is much point. The Soviet prisons are apparently wonderfully uncrowded, crime is falling rapidly and ninety per cent of all crimes are solved. 'In our country, crime will be completely abolished and all reasons for crime wiped out. That moment will come. Everyday experience proves it.'

Friday, 13 September 1968

Lunch with Adam Kellett-Long, slight, young, seemingly shy chief of the Reuters desk here, at his flat in the 'Foreign Correspondents' Ghetto'. The flat is nice. He says that if ever he wants any improvements all he has to do is say so out loud and prompt action follows: he is permanently bugged. All the foreign correspondents are – and the diplomats – and the visitors. He told me the story of the correspondent who arrived in Moscow and, searching for the bugging devices, unscrewed every nut and bolt in his hotel bedroom – including the twelve sinister bolts set in a circle immediately under his bed. As he finished his task, the whole building shook as, on the floor below him, the ballroom chandelier crashed to the ground.

Adam said his only real sources of information are the newspapers. You can get nothing worth having out of the Government and you can't trust anyone you meet. He says the KGB are both a nuisance and a nonsense. We were joined by

Bob Evans of CBS and a large man from the *Toronto Star* who is convinced that the USSR is about to invade Yugoslavia. Adam smiled. 'If they are, we'll be the last to know.'

Wednesday, 18 September 1968

I am on the train going to Ashford to see Michèle. The train is delayed and rerouted because of the flooding – the worst flooding to hit south-east England since 1953. I am sorting through the post. It now comes in two 'classes': first class, 5d, delivered overnight; second class, 4d, takes a little longer.

John Betjeman* has written from 43 Cloth Fair, EC1. He has been away in the Isle of Wight making a film about Tennyson. He can't write the Prologue for the pantomime: 'I find writing to order in verse, a most awful sweat.' He suggests I approach Nevill Coghill:† 'He knows the Playhouse, he knows the undergraduates, and he has the sparkle and fun, which years of self-pity have washed off, yours sincerely, John Betjeman.'

Saturday, 28 September 1968

A bad day. With Barnabus and Caroline Bennitt (she is now definitely going to play Cinderella: she will be fine: she is blonde and slim and she can sing!) I went back to Bedales to be the Saturday evening 'entertainment' – talking about my experiences in America and Russia, etc. I shouldn't have done it, a) because of my rule, 'Never look back', and b) because I got it all wrong and got a very mixed reception as a consequence, some of it friendly, some of it quite hostile. What I did simply fell between two stools: it was neither funny enough to be wholly entertaining, nor serious enough to be of substance. There is a lesson here: people need to know what you are giving them. I feel quite dejected. (I saw Sally briefly: she is not very attractive.)

And speaking of mixed receptions, I should report that yesterday was the day when theatre censorship in England came to an end. The Lord Chamberlain has been licensing plays since 1737. No more. And to mark the new freedom, the cast of the musical *Hair* danced naked on the stage of the Shaftesbury Theatre last night. Mr Tynan will have been delighted. (The cast of *Cinderella* will be keeping their clothes on.)

---

* John Betjeman (1906–84). He was knighted in 1969 and appointed Poet Laureate in 1972.
† Nevill Coghill (1899–1980), Fellow of Exeter College and Merton Professor of English Literature at Oxford, 1957–66; best known for his modern English version of Chaucer's *Canterbury Tales*.

Oxford

Tuesday, 1 October 1968

Thanks to Clive Syddall's mother, Joanne, I went to Whitechapel in the East End today, to Toynbee Hall, and met Jack Profumo. Toynbee Hall was established in the 1880s as a 'settlement house': it's a place that helps all sorts – drunks, down and outs, the homeless, ex-offenders. And government ministers brought low by scandal! This is where Mr Profumo does his 'good works' and I have to say he bowled me over. He is utterly charming – perhaps the most charming man I have met (and that includes James Robertson Justice and the Aga Khan). He has boundless energy and infectious enthusiasm. He really believes in the work they are doing at Toynbee Hall: he is there every day, with his sleeves rolled up, getting on with it. What was especially impressive was the way he was himself – he didn't try to be one of the lads. He was natural, easy, unselfconscious and, he said, 'happier than I have ever been'.

Wednesday, 9 October 1968

My first piece in *Cherwell* [the Oxford student newspaper] – a nice spread. Thanks to Denis Matyjaszek, I'm to have a weekly column. Nice spread in *Oxford Tory* too – the Macleod interview. And *Student* [Richard Branson's magazine] has arrived: my US article looks the business. And R. Branson is still keen for me to do things with him. All's well. The *Cinderella* read-through was satisfactory. Ian Small [one of the Ugly Sisters] is brilliant. Michael Coveney [choreographer] is skipping about like a pixie on Benzedrine – he's invaluable. We will have problems with the set: Kathy [the designer] has her charming ideas and Robin [the stage manager] says they can't be achieved. The pair are irreconcilable. My attempts at negotiation are going nowhere. It's worse than Wilson v. Smith on board HMS *Fearless*.[*] Lunch with Diana Quick. She's fun. *Twelfth Night* rehearsals not so much fun. Rather heavy-going, in fact. But at least they enable me to see Michèle.

Thursday, 17 October 1968

Went to Oxford Station to collect Lord Chalfont[†] for the first debate of term. Quite a charmer – and quite a gossip. Not a good word to say about Robert Maxwell who has just launched a £26 million bid for the *News of the World*.

---

[*] Aboard HMS *Fearless* off Gibraltar, the Prime Minister, Harold Wilson, was hoping to negotiate a settlement on the future of Rhodesia with Ian Smith, the rebel Rhodesian leader.
[†] Alun Gwynne-Jones (b.1919), Baron Chalfont from 1964, Minister of State at the Foreign Office, 1964–70.

According to Chalfont, Maxwell is not to be trusted ('the bouncing Czech') and is generally regarded as a bumptious parvenu at Westminster. 'He's a joke, but not a nice one. And he's a bully.'

The debate was dull. I think Ian Glick is going to be a dull President. David Walter will be a worthy Treasurer. It will be left to the Librarian (Edwina Currie) and Secretary (yours truly) to liven things up.

Sunday, 3 November 1968

Agony with M because I couldn't get her to leave Richard Savage's ghastly party. It was three hours of hell. I hate parties anyway, and this was a party full of uninteresting people all having a 'great time' (i.e. smoking and drinking). M wouldn't come away. It ended when Pat Curran arrived and we went off with him to the cinema. Saw 2001 – A Space Odyssey – pretentious SF movie.

Tuesday, 5 November 1968

Richard Nixon beats Humphrey for the presidency of the United States – and my old friend (well, I met him once briefly in Baltimore!), Spiro T. Agnew, becomes Vice President. LBJ ordered an unconditional end to the bombing of North Vietnam at the weekend, but it didn't swing it for Humphrey. Nixon's comeback is extraordinary. There is a lesson here and it's to do with staying power.

My good news is that Nevill Coghill's Prologue is delightful. He sent a lovely letter which I have copied to Pa: 'How well I remember your father's *admirable* performance in my first-production-ever! He was most moving. I hope his genius has descended on you in full measure.'* The Prologue is witty and apt and on the first night I am proud to say it will be performed by Sir Michael Redgrave. Why? Because I wrote to him! I found his address in *Who's Who*. I wrote to him at length, telling him that his Uncle Vanya was, for me, the performance of my lifetime. Forty-eight hours later, I received this telegram: 'WHAT FUN. ACCEPT WITH GREAT PLEASURE. REDGRAVE.'

Monday, 11 November 1968

The good news: a nice picture of Cinders and the Fairy Queen in today's *Daily Mail*.

The bad news: a very slow and rather dismal dress rehearsal.

---

* In 1929, at Exeter College, GB's father played Manoa in Nevill Coghill's outdoor production of Milton's *Samson Agonistes*.

It's 2.00 a.m. and I am too weary to write more tonight. Except this: I found a note waiting for me when I got back to my room just now – from Xan:

The very best of luck.
You always have it, because you deserve it.

Tuesday, 12 November 1968

The opening of *Cinderella* at the Oxford Playhouse – a good show: lively, funny, well received. We are playing to full houses all week.

Sir Michael Redgrave read Coghill's Prologue beautifully. He was quite nervous in the wings. I steadied him with a libation (or two) of port. He thought his voice might go. As we stood together at the side of the stage, he seemed nervous and distracted. 'I'm not sure I can do this,' he murmured. As I gave him his cue to go on, for a moment I thought he was going to back away. 'No,' he whispered, 'no, I can't do it.' I urged him on – and on he went – his shoulders straightening as he moved from the darkness of the wings into the spotlight. He held the audience in the palm of his hand.

Afterwards, Diana [Quick] and the OUDS Committee hosted a dinner for us upstairs at the Elizabeth. Sir Michael was completely delightful. 'Now I can say I've done pantomime! I was asked to play Abanazar at the Palladium once, but I declined.' He talked about his favourite actresses: his daughter, Vanessa, and Edith Evans. Acting with Dame Edith, he said, was 'like being in your mother's arms – you are totally safe.' Edith Evans told him, 'You don't start acting until you stop trying to act. You won't leave the ground until you don't have to think about it.' He said that when he played Orlando to Edith Evans's Rosalind, 'For the first time in my life I felt free!'

It would have been a perfect evening except for the *vicious* phone call from Barnabus and Caroline Bennitt. Barny telephoned me at the restaurant – I was called from the table by one of the waiters – and spat vitriol. 'Why were the cast not invited to the dinner?' was the essence of his message. I said the dinner had been organised by Diana and the OUDS Committee. He said that I shouldn't have gone because the cast weren't asked. I said there were forty in the cast and eight at the dinner – 'Be reasonable.' He was not ready to be reasonable. He was very nasty.

Never mind. Overall it's been good. I'm fairly happy with the production. We've got lighting problems, but nothing that can't be sorted. Tomorrow is another day. On we go.

Thursday, 14 November 1968

Unbelievably unkind *Times* review. Equally nice review in the *Oxford Mail*. 'Treat those two impostors . . .'

James Robertson Justice read the Prologue last night – wonderfully. He had come all the way down from Spinningdale, Sutherland, to do it. I went to find him in his room at the Randolph and when I knocked on the door he simply said, 'Come!' He was lying sprawled out, stark naked on the bed, like a beached whale, a silver hip flask nestling in the undergrowth of his hairy chest. I helped him to dress, realising as I did so that he was probably the first grown man I have seen naked. He is wholly engaging – he told me he speaks twenty languages, but it didn't seem like boasting – and, of course, the audience loved him. He knows all they want is Sir Lancelot Spratt* come to life and he is happy to oblige.

The cast supper after the show was v jolly. Dandini (Chris McAll) and Amanda Warren (my favourite Fairy) were especially sweet. No one seemed distressed about the Elizabeth dinner – apart from Barny and Caroline. It seems that it wasn't the fact that the *cast* hadn't been invited, but that the *leading lady* hadn't been invited . . . Anyway, I tried to pour oil on troubled water. I did not stay late because I have quite a lot on: two essays, one article for *Honey* (due on Monday), article for *Illustrated London News* (on *Cinderella*), *Isis* column, *Cherwell* column, *Twelfth Night* rehearsals and tonight I am due to be in two places almost at once – at 7.45 p.m. I am on the stage of the Oxford Playhouse reading the Prologue to *Cinderella*; and at 8.15 p.m. I am on parade at the Union in my white tie and tails reading out the Minutes (I've written them in verse). Happily my evening dress will look fine for the Prologue and so long as the curtain goes up on time, and I don't trip over running from A to B, I should be able to manage the two without anyone being any the wiser.

Saturday, 16 November 1968

Cinderella at 5.00 and 8.15. Whole tribe down. Pa brought a coach-load from the office. M perfect. I'm exhausted, with a pain right across my chest.

Frank Muir performed the Prologue – complete delight. The audience *love* him. Afterwards we had dinner at the Sorbonne – downstairs, in the informal bit. It was a very happy evening. We talked about Jimmy Edwards and *Take It From Here*.† I told Frank how, as a little boy living in Earl's Court, I used to listen to the

---

* The character of the overbearing surgeon played by James Robertson Justice in *Doctor in the House* and its five sequels.

† BBC Radio series, 1948–60, scripted by Frank Muir and Denis Norden, and starring Jimmy Edwards, Dick Bentley, Joy Nichols and, later, June Whitfield.

programme in bed, under the blankets, on my tiny crystal set. With Polly (his wife) shaking her head (but smiling), he kindly acted out some of my favourite moments from *The Glums:*

'Oh, Ron beloved . . .'

'Yes, Eth . . .'

'Have you got anything on your mind?'

'No, Eth . . .'

Monday, 18 November 1968

First night of *Twelfth Night.* Michèle was wonderful – she really was. We cannot say the same of the Sea Captain! This morning, my back went again – I was bent double. 'What country, friends, is this?' 'France, lady, and here is Quasimodo to show you around Notre Dame!' At the dress rehearsal I had managed all the lines, but to make assurance doubly sure for the opening performance I had them written out on the capacious sleeves of my sea captain's shirt – hidden from the audience but within my eye-line . . . In the event, of course, my sea captain's cloak (made of rough brown blankets) obscured them and the long and the short of it is that I left out half my main speech and made a nonsense of the scene!

M was not amused, but she has coped. She is coping less well with the fact that on Thursday night I'm not going to be in the play at all. Because I've got to be at the Union, Pat [Curran, the director] is going to play the part. He knows the lines, of course!

Incidentally, it's gone midnight. I'm in my room, and I have just been through the lines again and I know them *perfectly.* But my back is no better. I'm truly bent double. I can't even stand up enough to see my face in the mirror above the wash-basin. I am going to bed now. Goodnight.

Wednesday, 27 November 1968

I have decided to stand for the presidency of the Union. This may be a mistake. David Walter, my main rival, thinks it is! He says it's a 'moral issue'! I have only been here a year. It's too soon. It's unfair. I should give others a chance. Is he right? Robert Jackson, Caroline Harvey,[*] Leofranc Holford-Strevens, etc., are all urging me on – so, anyway, I'm giving it a go. We'll see. It's in the hands of the gods.[†] I don't think Edwina stands much of a chance and I have the endorse-

---

[*] Caroline Harvey (b.1946), later married Robert Jackson; Conservative MEP since 1984.
[†] In the 1960s no campaigning for Union posts was allowed or undertaken. Contemporary students find this hard to believe, but it's true!

ment of *Isis*. Peter Adamson has written half a page on the subject: 'Brandreth, not so much a pansy, more a self-raising flower, is far and away the most exciting candidate.' Very generous, under the circumstances.

I'm off to London to appear on *Late Night Line-Up* on BBC2 TV (Denis Tuohy, Joan Bakewell & Co.). I am being interviewed about prisons and the value of creative work (poetry, painting etc.) to prisoners. And I have just heard that Mr Profumo is kindly arranging for me to visit Grendon Prison where they are doing pioneering therapeutic work with the inmates. All good.

Saturday, 30 November 1968

I lost the Union presidency to David Walter – by four votes.

I was disappointed, but not as much as others seemed to be. Ma and Pa had come down, bringing a bottle of champagne with them. When I didn't win, they took the champagne home – unopened. Michèle was shocked: she felt they should have cracked open the champagne all the same. I didn't. Either you win or you lose. If you win, you celebrate. If you lose, you move on. I'm moving on. I may try again, but I won't rush it. The truth is: Michaelmas term is the only term worth having – that's when the Freshers arrive and you get full houses. I'm for full houses!

Lots of kind letters of commiseration. From Caroline Harvey: 'I suppose nothing that I can say will dull the utter ghastliness of last night. I am extremely sorry, for your sake and the Union's, that you did not get the Presidency and that we are condemned to another term of gnome-dom.' From Leofranc – in Latin. From Pa – he has written out Kipling's 'If' for me! And from the conquering gnome himself [David Walter]: 'How does one offer one's condolences without seeming to gloat?' Actually, it's a nice note. He's a nice man – not very exciting, that's all. (And, of course, that may be what the people want!) He ends his letter: 'One final thing. You rightly saw through my attempts to persuade you it was a moral issue to stand or not to stand. Of course it wasn't, but that was the only line of argument I could think of. All the best.'

Last night I had dinner with Robert Jackson at All Souls. It was a most civilised way to end the day. I like the company of clever people. (In fact, I only want the company of people who are clever, funny or beautiful!) I met the celebrated Warden Sparrow.* He was gently waspish, but very charming. (Evidently, he likes young men. And old wine.) He was happy to talk about his famous rivalry with A. L. Rowse and acknowledged the authenticity of the great exchange

---

* John Sparrow (1906–92), Warden of All Souls College, 1952–77. He defeated the Cornish historian and Shakespeare scholar, A. L. Rowse (1903–97), for the post.

between them. One evening at high table Rowse reprimanded Sparrow for his disdain of Rowse's work: 'You never read any of my books, Warden. Do you know *Tudor Cornwall*?' Without pause, indicating the fellow academic sitting opposite Rowse, Sparrow replied: 'Do you know Stuart Hampshire?'

Sunday, 8 December 1968

Essay on Beaumarchais in the morning. With M watch *Pride and Prejudice* on TV at Tony Holden's in the afternoon. (*P & P** still my favourite film. And Tony Holden† one of my favourite people – except he smokes and drinks all the time.) Evening, sup at Chinese with M. We have been together six months. She is *so* beautiful.

Tomorrow, early start – to Southampton. We are taking *Cinderella* to the Nuffield Theatre for a week.

Thursday, 12 December 1968

Past thirty-six hours, not good. *Cinderella* opening in Southampton on Tuesday night: so-so. Poor house, cast a mite sloppy and glum. Trains back to Oxford yesterday morning. Lunch with David Walter at Trinity. Fine. Talk on Oxford for ATV Midlands – recorded at Union. Fine. Anchovy toast in Union bar. Excellent! M at New College – perfect. We went on to the cinema to see *Dracula* – quite fun, though M found it frightening and hid under the seat. Then to six-month anniversary dinner at the Elizabeth. Horrible. We shouldn't have gone. I began to feel ill during the film, but struggled on. By the time we got to the restaurant I felt really ghastly. We were shown to our table, upstairs in the middle of the room, and the waiter, unfurling my napkin to place it across my lap, pressed his hand firmly into my groin and groped me. I said nothing. We ordered. I had never been to the Elizabeth on my own before. It is supposed to be Oxford's best – but I hadn't realised the prices would be so terrifying. We had the *Carré d'agneau dauphinoise* for two – thirty shillings! Anyway, the room was hot, the waiter was ghastly, I was ill, M was grumpy – so, eventually, before puddings, we aborted the dinner. The bill still came to just over £5. £5 for one meal! And a ghastly meal. Never again.

This morning Michèle was still browned off with me – irritated and *bored*. I'm obsessed with myself, apparently. (I suppose I am. Look at this now. But aren't we all?) It was a bit better by the time we parted. I gave her some earrings. I am

---

* The 1940 Hollywood version, with Greer Garson and Laurence Olivier.
† Tony Holden (b.1947), an undergraduate at Merton College, had become editor of *Isis*; later, journalist, biographer and poker player.

on the train going back to Southampton. Business has picked up, it seems. And so has the show.

Thursday, 19 December 1968

Hugh Thomas is now one of our best friends. We know he is a fine actor because in *Twelfth Night* he made the part of Fabian *interesting* – amusing, even. (Not something that's been done since 1602, I imagine.) We know he is a good friend because today he invited us to join him as his only guests at the opening of Lindsay Anderson's film *If . . .* It was a star-studded occasion – John Osborne, Jill Bennett, Daniel Massey, Albert Finney etc. – and a strong film, a mixture of fact and fantasy, an indictment of the English public school system and a call to arms for our times: 'Violence and revolution are the only pure acts!'

Hugh plays one of the prefects (Denson) and is excellent. He said the film was being made during *les événements* in Paris in May. I said I was there and Michèle said, 'Yes, in a taxi. You let everything pass you by.' Her line is that I'm existing in the 1960s, but living in the 1930s. She thinks that I don't see/understand/notice what is happening around us. I think she's wrong. I do see what's happening, but I'm not sure that much of it is that significant (e.g. the students rioting in Paris) or interesting. I marched against Vietnam because there was a point to it, but I'm not for revolution for revolution's sake. I am in favour of equality between the sexes, homosexual law reform, sex before marriage in a loving relationship – specific goals, not general dancing around naked in the park high on marijuana! I am not interested in 'free love': I'm interested in *her*. I don't drink or smoke because I can see the damage they both do. I don't want to take drugs, partly, yes, because it is against the law (and I'm a goodie-goodie), but also because I want to stay in control. I don't want to 'drop out' or 'hang loose'. I want to work.

Hugh was very nervous. He smoked endlessly. He is a very conceited fellow (like I was not so long ago perhaps) but he is funny and clever and I like him. And the evening was 'an event' – and we were there!

Saturday, 28 December 1968

The *Apollo 8* spacecraft has returned to earth, having taken some truly amazing photographs of the moon. Here in London we have had a very happy evening. We went to the Baker Street Classic and saw Jack Lemmon and Tony Curtis in *The Great Race* – incredibly funny. Tomorrow I am taking Michèle to Paris, by train and plane – her first flight, her Christmas present. I love her.

Name Dropping

January 1969 – January 1970

Thursday, 30 January 1969

The post includes another effusive letter from Sir Gerald Nabarro MP who is happy for me to interview him and encloses 'for preliminary reading a miscellany of photocopies of recent contributions to the press and speech extracts'. Not so ready to be interviewed is Yehudi Menuhin, back from India last night, off to Berlin this morning. He does, however, have an important message he would like to share. It is this:

> More than anywhere else the University must be an institution of integration and 'whole food' is inseparable from the whole man.

That's it.

Saturday, 1 February 1969

I spent the afternoon with Bruce Forsyth. Interviewed him for an hour and watched his pantomime, *Babes in the Wood*, at the New Theatre. The panto is very weak – and he knows it. 'God, it's thin stuff, but it's only eight weeks and the money's not bad. I don't really like pantomime. It's *audiences* I like. I like to work 'em and win 'em.' He is 40 and the ultimate 'pro'. He sees himself as an all-round entertainer – not a comic with a mission or philosophy like Tony Hancock or Frankie Howerd. '*Thinking* about it only gets you depressed,' he says. 'I just do it and then have a round of golf.' He appeared absolutely sure of himself, completely contented and wholly unprofound. He likes being famous: 'Going on holiday abroad can be a bit of a shock – nobody knows who you are.' And his advice to anyone going into the business? 'Remember, only half the people will ever like you. Don't let the other half get you down – the bastards!' He was quite funny, in a mirthless sort of way. But history should know this: on a cold Saturday afternoon in a far-from-full barn of a theatre in a really tatty hand-me-down panto, Bruce Forsyth gives his all. He comes onto that stage like a whirlwind and for three hours he does not let go. He's a trouper with star quality.

Thursday, 6 February 1969

Generous letter from Garth Lean (leading light of the Moral Rearmament movement and Geoff's dad) following the 'Isis Idol' interview Tony Holden did with
me:

> You are refreshingly honest. My only anxiety for you is not that you should
> have too much ambition, but too little – for I believe you can, if you are
> willing, do a great deal for the world, far more than perhaps you think.

I am sorry to report that I let the world down badly tonight. Among the guests
at the Union for the debate on morality was Dominic Behan, Irish song-writer
and Republican, younger brother of the more-famous-Brendan and son (so he
told me) of one of the leading IRA men responsible for killing any number of
British soldiers during the Irish 'war of independence'. Because I wanted to talk
to him about his brother, I was asked to look after him. I failed – to put it mildly.
The man is mad, bad and very dangerous to know. When he arrived he was
already wild with drink and I simply found him impossible to control. He ranted,
he rambled, he lurched around the President's office, alternately breaking into
song and demanding more drink. He asked me to show him where the lavatories
were. I said I'd take him down to them. He stumbled down the stairs from the
President's office and – on the landing – proceeded to undo his flies and produce
his member for me to admire! 'I'm bursting!' he declared and then turning
towards the wall walked quite sedately down the corridor peeing profusely
against the wall as he went. 'Don't!' I bleated. 'That's William Morris wallpaper!
It's original!' 'Fuck William Morris!' he cried, warming to his task and spraying
the precious wall with ever greater gusto. 'He was a Socialist!' I called out. 'Fuck
Socialism!' he declared, turning to me triumphantly and shaking the final drips in
my direction. What a nightmare. The historic wallpaper is seriously damaged.

Wednesday, 19 February 1969

Last night, an interminable OUDS *Romeo and Juliet* at the Playhouse. (What
happened to the promised 'two hours traffic of our stage'?) This morning, train
to London. Eye test at 11.30 a.m. Lunch at 5H – what do I want for my 21st? Since
I drink so much coffee, I suggested an electric percolator or Cona machine or
some such, but on reflection I'm thinking that may be too extravagant. Money is
very tight at the moment. (Poor Pa.)

4.45 p.m. Tea at the House of Commons with Sir Gerald Nabarro, Conservative
MP for South Worcestershire. The Palace of Westminster is a wonderful build-

ing; the tea was excellent; Sir Gerald is utterly preposterous. He is 55, 5 ft 5 ins tall and appears on television more than any other MP. With his mutton-chop whiskers, his five cars numbered NAB1 to NAB5, he is a self-created Commons 'character', Westminster's Mr Toad. His views are appalling. Famously, on *Any Questions?* he asked, 'How would you feel if your daughter wanted to marry a big buck nigger with the prospect of coffee-coloured grandchildren?' He said to me today, 'I am not willing to be told by law that I must love my coloured neighbour or otherwise I shall be fined or sent to prison.' Naturally, he can't abide 'revolting students' – especially those currently on strike at the LSE. 'I expect undergraduates to behave like gentlemen, not undisciplined hooligans.' Essentially, it's all down to 'a decline in moral standards' and there are only three remedies: bring back the noose, the lash and National Service!

He was ludicrous, but I liked him. And he seemed to like me. He has gone out of his way to give me a mass of background material, cuttings, cartoons, photographs. He has even volunteered to let me have the services of his researcher to help draft the article. He is publicity mad.

Thursday, 20 February 1969

This is my week for parliamentary 'characters'. Yesterday, bold Sir Gerald – today, the dashing Jeremy Thorpe, MP for North Devon. At the Union tonight, the 39-year-old leader of the Liberal Party literally leapt over one bench and then another, as he bounded towards me. He greeted me as though I was the most important and exciting person he had ever met. He has a foxy look and a glint in his eye and huge energy. I was charmed and impressed – but not inspired. He reminded me a little of Norman St John Stevas. I didn't entirely trust him; and he didn't entirely trust me.

Friday, 28 February 1969

Not my finest hour. I was at St Anne's, with Michèle, lying on her bed, feeling sick. At 5.00 p.m. I was due in the Red Room at New College to be in the line-up for the sherry party to meet the Rt Hon. Edward Heath, MP, Leader of Her Majesty's Loyal Opposition and my hero. At 4.30 p.m. I said to M, 'I'm not well enough, I can't face it.' At 4.45 p.m. I changed my mind and decided that it was important to go. I ran all the way. I burst through the door of the Red Room and joined the end of the line just as the great man was being brought down it. As he shook my hand and heaved his shoulders, I heaved mine and threw up all over his brown suede shoes. Yes, I met the Leader of the Conservative Party and literally vomited as I did so.

I made my excuses and left. I ran straight back to Michèle and, bizarrely, felt much, much better. It's now 1.00 a.m. and I feel utterly fine. Tonight we are going to *What the Butler Saw*, the Joe Orton farce, at the New Theatre, with Sir Ralph Richardson and I'm really looking forward to it.

Monday, 3 March 1969

The sun is shining. This is the beginning of what is going to be a good week. I have decided to go for Librarian at the Union. That way, I can have a go at the Presidency next term and get it for Michaelmas – which will be ideal. Tonight I'm going to the Moulin Rouge to see a Czech film, *Disappearing Trains*. Tomorrow I am going to London to address the Fabians on the subject of prisons and prison art. Right now I'm off to my tutorial with Alex de Jonge. I will read my essay on Marivaux and he will talk about Baudelaire – and hunting! And possibly the Russian Revolution. And Gérard de Nerval. He is young and wild – and actually quite wonderful. We will sit in his room, with the sun pouring in, drinking sherry at eleven in the morning, discussing life and love and art and poetry. This is what being at Oxford in the week that I turn 21 should be about!

Sunday, 9 March 1969

I am now 21 years of age. I am not amused, but there's nothing to be done about it, so there we are. The day itself went well. It began nicely with my letter appearing in *The Times* – a clarion call for equality in the home! We then had a family outing to the Theatre Royal, Drury Lane, to see *Mame* with Ginger Rogers. It's not a great show (only one hit song) and Miss Rogers, alas, now has the look of a very mature Sugar Plum Fairy. Her 'dancing' involved her standing a little unsteadily centre stage, with her right arm raised high and her left foot gently tapping the floor just about in time to the music. It was good to have seen her in the flesh, and of course we cheered dutifully, but it wasn't memorable. *Top Hat* was a long time ago.

Post-*Mame* we made our way to the Singing Chef in Connaught Street where a feast was served: *Anniversaire de Gyles: Alpes Maritimes*. I had the *Pâté de foie de volaille*, then the *Oeufs mimosa*,. followed by the *Gigot rôti à l'amiral* with *Ris au saffron* and *Ratatouille niçoise*. There was salad, cheese and a *pièce monteé* (meringue and cream and chocolate mousse) to accompany the ritual singing. It was fine. It was fun. Michèle had volunteered to do something at the flat, but Ma was keen to go out so we did. I was very conscious of the cost. So was Pa. As I type this, I am looking at the menu that everybody signed last night and I see that Pa has signed it: 'Charles (Poor Papa!)'

The parents gave me £21 and I received assorted gifts of a guinea, and two 21/- book tokens – all very welcome. Also, from Joint Services Liaison Organisation, Villa Spiritus, Bonn, a letter from my godfather, John Paice:

> Some vague non-conformist strain in my background urges me to take a 'high moral ground' with the young, but I know so much about your parents, your environment, your interests and the demands of the world in which you will I hope live for at least another seventy years that I can only say I wish you a sense of *vocation* and *purpose* in what you do. It is probably too much to hope for happiness – at least for long periods.
>
> I've experienced no little pride in being your godfather – not just because you get your name in the papers – but just because I see you as the product of so much love and sacrifice and warmth (as well as the inheritor of so many gifts) that I have every reason to know pride – in what you've already accomplished and in what lies ahead.

PS: Golda Meir, a widow aged 70, has become Prime Minister of Israel.

Tuesday, 18 March 1969

In the *Daily Mail* this morning there is a delightful photograph of me and Michèle sipping champagne on board a private aeroplane. The headline reads: 'A Party in the Sky for Michèle'. The story reveals that yesterday was Michèle's 22nd birthday and because she had never been on a plane before. I hired one at £12 10s for the hour and took her for a birthday spin, 'putting a bottle of champagne aboard'. Her reaction: 'I'm afraid I felt rather queasy.'

Now the truth: Michèle's birthday was last week, not yesterday, and, of course, she has been on a plane before – with me at Christmas. I didn't hire this plane or pay for the champagne: John Knoote, the *Daily Mail* photographer, did. We cooked up the story between us. And the aeroplane never left the ground: we just took the photo and scarpered. Thus, it seems, are picture stories 'created' for the *Daily Mail*.

Saturday, 22 March 1969

In Gibraltar, John Lennon has married Yoko Ono. The happy couple are now enjoying a week-long 'bed-in' for peace in the presidential suite of the Hilton Hotel, Amsterdam. Here in London we've had nuptials of our own. Jennifer Brandreth has married Peter Woolfenden at St Marylebone Parish Church. The bride wore black-rimmed spectacles and a pale grey dress. (For some reason, she felt white was inappropriate.) Michèle came to London for the occasion, but did not attend the ceremony because she had to lend her black cape to Hester who, otherwise, would have had no outer garment to wear! Anyway, it all passed off smoothly enough and the reception at the flat was informal and jolly. Pa was in especially buoyant mood, explaining as he uncorked the sparkling wine that a bottle should open like a woman, 'with a sigh and not a pop'. (Unlike Pa to be vulgar. History please note: I have never, ever heard him use bad language. I have perhaps heard him say 'bloody' once – but nothing else.)

Peter was a bit vague and vacant through it all – like the dormouse but with his head still *in* the teapot – but there were no scenes and a very jolly musical send-off, orchestrated by Peter's composer/conductor brother Guy and featuring a range of medieval instruments. The honeymoon will be spent abroad.

Pa spent most of the day saying, 'Two down, one to go!' – which is ridiculous because Hester is not going to get married. She is a lesbian and Pa and Ma's attempts to find a husband through the personal column of the *New Statesman* etc. have all ended in tears. The last gentleman she went out with was an Egyptian widower, a doctor, I think. When, after taking her for a meal, the poor man made to place his hand upon hers (in a perfectly gentlemanly manner) she ran screaming out of the Lyons Corner House into the Strand!

M and I had a Chinese this evening. She's gone back to Oxford. I'm just in from taking her to Paddington. I don't mind Marvin Gaye's 'Heard It Through the Grapevine', but in fact I'm listening to Flanagan and Allen (which I prefer) and I'm about to sort through a mountain of correspondence. Sir Gerald Nabarro would like *twelve* copies of *Isis*. He wants to give our interview greater exposure and likes my idea of a sequel: 'I would certainly be most happy to cooperate with you in this important matter.'

Monday, 28 April 1969

This morning I tape-recorded a long conversation with Hester about her work at the Springfield Hospital, Tooting. The reality of life inside Britain's mental hospitals is harsh – and unseen. We are not interested. We do not want to know.

Hes has a ward with fifty beds. There are four nurses and a sister. There simply aren't the staff to do the job properly: 'Sometimes I have lifted bodily a patient into bed when I've known I should have waited for another nurse so that we could have lifted her in a more dignified way; but you just haven't got the time. Our old patients hate having baths. They struggle and scream and hit and spit and scratch. There are always supposed to be two nurses in the bathroom, but it can't always be done. And then this business of one flannel, one towel, per patient. You've got fifty patients and you want to make them nice for visiting, what do you do? You take a trolley in. Well, you're not going to take one with fifty flannels and fifty towels to wash their faces, no. And their hands might well be dirty, because senile patients have dirty habits, so you'll be wiping one person's shitty hands with the towel you go on to the next person and wipe their face with it. On this ward for fifty patients if you get six visitors you're lucky. Obviously the patients have been there a long time, twenty-five to thirty-five years some of them, and they don't have anyone. What an existence. Twenty-five years gazing out onto the cemetery. The ward's only outlook is over the cemetery.'

There are 1,400 beds in the hospital and, at night, just one doctor on duty between six in the evening and nine the next day. I am going to write all this up – and think about it, too. What's to be done?

This afternoon I joined Ma and Pa at the Old Bailey. Fred, Ma's lifelong friend from school, is up on embezzlement charges! 'He's a professional man – he comes from a highly respectable family,' Pa chortled. 'When his brother – the doctor – was imprisoned in the fifties it was only for interfering with his patients. Nothing serious.'

I'm now back in Oxford. Union Standing Committee at 5.00 p.m. Supper at the Hong Kong with M. *Le Misanthrope* rehearsal at 8.00 p.m. (Acting in French is not easy, but it's quite fun and it *feels* different. I am giving my character an absurdly long nail for his elegant little finger. I am making it out of a drinking straw. Olivier would approve, even if J.-L. Barrault might not.)

Tuesday, 6 May 1969

I took the 8.46 a.m. train to Robertsbridge. Malcolm Muggeridge[*] met me at the station and drove me to his cottage. He does indeed look like a wizened tortoise, but his movements are spry and his incisive way with words completely compelling. He has no time for the young today, 'trying so hard to be non-conformists, in their clothes and their behaviour, they are in a way the greatest conformists there have ever been'. He is alarmed by what he calls 'the over-screwing, over-orgasming' he sees all around: 'The Iron Curtain countries have not fallen into this particular softness. They've adopted a sort of puritanical ethic, for no *good* reason, but they have, and I think this may be a decisive factor in our future.'

Despite having made a fortune lecturing and broadcasting in the US, he has nothing good to say about Americans. 'Anybody who is on top is odious.' And all men in power are brutal: 'I'm afraid men are fated to be ruled by shits.' Are

---

[*] Malcolm Muggeridge (1903–90), writer, broadcaster, and later, in 1982, Catholic convert.

there no nice leaders? I asked. 'It's very difficult to think of one. There are a few who have been sympathetic. Lincoln, for example; but the test for him would have come after the Civil War and the more one looks into him the more one sees that he was a colossal opportunist, who didn't really care about the slaves as such; he cared about the Union.'

We sat talking at his wooden kitchen table. His wife, Kitty (who went to Bedales and whose aunt was Beatrice Webb, I think), said very little, but kept us supplied with herbal tea and served nut rissoles and a cut-up tomato for lunch. They are both vegetarians. After lunch, Malcolm proposed a drive and a walk and we clambered up hill and down dale, with him talking all the while, until we came to the cottage of Leonard Woolf.* 'He's one of my oldest friends. He's frail now and deeply pessimistic, of course. He must be. He has no faith. Nevertheless, he is a great friend of mine. I like him very much. You will too.' I did, of course. I was honoured to be there. The old gentleman reminded me of Mr Badley. As we came away, Malcolm said, 'Now you can say that you've shaken the hand that held the hand that wrote *The Waves*. Much good will it do you!'

He drove me back to the station, still talking. He wished me well at Oxford, but made it clear that he regards higher education as mostly a waste of time. 'Education has become an ersatz religion. People have been encouraged to believe in it as a panacea, even as an enlightenment in itself. Some of the most stupid people one has ever met have been highly educated. I mean, you see this man who can speak three languages and you think he must be able to tell me something, but you could speak ten languages and still be the most utter bloody fool who ever lived, couldn't you? You'd be a fool in ten languages instead of one.'

I liked him a lot.

Monday, 12 May 1969

I went to the BBC today in Portland Place to give my talk on women's rights on *Woman's Hour*. This came about as a result of my birthday letter to *The Times* about equality at home – men doing the chores as well as women etc. The producer (Jocelyn Ryder-Smith) seemed vastly intrigued that a young man should be ready to help with the ironing.

I arrived promptly at 11.30 a.m. as requested. Alarmingly, it then took thirty minutes (and more) for me to reach the studio. I had to be 'escorted' – all visitors

---

* Leonard Woolf (1880–1969), writer, publisher, widower of Virginia Woolf. He died three months after this, on 14 August 1969.

are – and my escort was an elderly commissionaire with the face of Charles Laughton and the gait of Richard III. This old boy moved incredibly slowly, dragging his lame foot behind him, sighing with every step, and losing his way at every turn – though he claimed to have been working at the BBC since before the war.

When eventually I reached the *Woman's Hour* suite, half a dozen female heads turned in my direction accusingly. 'We were expecting you at eleven-thirty.' I can't say the atmosphere thawed much. After the rehearsal – it is a 'live' broadcast, but everything is scripted, including the interviews: nothing is left to chance – we adjourned to a room adjacent to the studio for lunch – a formal affair, with waitress service and a strict seating plan. It was like eating at high table in a women's college, with Marjorie Anderson* presiding as the Warden. She was at all times gracious, but nevertheless *terrifying*.

The broadcast, when it happened, was fine. My throat went dry as I read out my piece, but I got through it – and Jocelyn Ryder-Smith said we should meet up to discuss doing more. I am to receive a fee of £10 plus £3 travelling expenses.

Thursday, 15 May 1969

A girl from the Central Office of Information brought a Yugoslav film crew to my room to record an 'informal conversation with English students' about the modern British attitude to marriage. This is 'Swinging England' and, apparently, we are in the vanguard of a sexual revolution that's set to sweep the world! I arranged for Michèle and Mark Hofman to be the other 'students' on parade. I think we were fairly honest. We said that life is full of contradictions: most boys want to marry a virgin, but don't necessarily expect to get married as virgins themselves! We said that, yes, nowadays some young people feel that 'sex before marriage' is acceptable so long as it is in a loving relationship, but that a lot of young people – probably a majority of girls and a large minority of boys – still believe you should not 'go the whole way' outside marriage. Yes, more and more girls are going on the Pill, but, no, young people in Britain do not believe in 'free love'. That's entirely newspaper talk. In fact, we said, it's the newspapers and TV people like you, who seem obsessed with sex. We are just getting on with our lives.

Wednesday, 11 June 1969

Another day, another party. Last night, Tony Holden. (We left quite early. Michèle said people were smoking drugs. I said I didn't think so. She says I am

---

* Marjorie Anderson (1913–99) was the presenter of *Woman's Hour* from 1958 until her retirement in 1972.

very naïve!) Tonight, Mark Hofman's party in Worcester Gardens – no drugs, plenty of Pimm's, the lake looking wonderful and the guests all dressed as Oxford's idea of how hippies should dress: basically quite conventional, except for the odd flowing scarf and beaded headband. In the appearance stakes, Duncan Fallowell took the honours, stalking across the lawn, dressed as a cross between Lord Byron and Oscar Wilde, and *wearing make-up*! (DF is at Magdalen and I think occupies OW's old rooms: the great man's ghost casts a long shadow.)

Tomorrow is the day that does me or undoes me quite. It's the Presidential Debate. The motion: 'That the British Press is both vulgar and dishonest.' I am *opposing* the motion, so the odds are stacked against me. My opponent in the presidential election is the Treasurer, the Reverend Robert Hood. He is tall, dark and handsome: charming, courteous, credible – and black. The odds are definitely stacked against me! However, being a graduate and a clergyman may count against him. We shall see.

Friday, 13 June 1969

Friday the thirteenth, a long, auspicious day. I didn't hang around the Union. I stayed away deliberately. I tried to work – on a French prose, on Rimbaud, on Molière. At six o'clock I went over to Christ Church for William Waldegrave's party – all very civilised. William belongs to the non-braying school of Old Etonian: he really *is* a gentleman. He has the brains, the looks, the ambition – but does he have the 'bite' to get to the top? We shall see.

At seven, I went to All Souls to dine with Robert Jackson. Warden Sparrow obliged me with some more of his verses[*] and, over the port and dessert, showed me the memoirs of Charles Osman who became a Fellow in the 1880s and left a memorable account of the fellowship examination. In the History paper, Osman was able to 'ramble around all manner of topics' – the Greek conception of the state, the social conditions of medieval Scotland, the claim of Napoleon to be the successor of Charlemagne, the history of the Crusades and so forth. The account concluded: 'There remained the paper of translation from five languages, ancient and modern, where I found four of them easy enough.'

After dinner, Robert came to the Union with me for the announcement of the election result. It was clear-cut. I won by a handsome margin. Yes, I am President of the Oxford Union.

---

[*] GB's favourite is entitled 'Growing Old': 'I'm accustomed to my deafness / To my dentures I'm resigned / I can cope with my bifocals, / But – oh dear! – I miss my mind.'

But what is odd is this: I have achieved exactly what I wanted and still I am not satisfied. Almost as I heard the result, in the very moment of elation, I felt a sense of emptiness, almost a pang of disappointment. Even as I heard of my triumph I thought and felt: 'So what? That's done. What's next?' I have everything and it's never enough.

I didn't linger in the Union bar. I took in the applause, commiserated with the Reverend Hood, did my best to look self-deprecating and skedaddled. I ran to St Anne's and there (believe it or not) I managed to spoil everything. I was over-emotional, melodramatic, self-indulgent and ridiculous. 'Boring' is the word Michèle used. As a consequence, instead of enjoying what should have been one of the happiest nights of my life, I had a miserable night. I am an idiot.

I am writing this on Saturday morning. I got up early, went out first thing and bought some carnations and took them over to Michèle before breakfast. I am now going off to the Union.

Wednesday, 18 June 1969

Monsieur Pompidou is the new President of France[*] and I am the new President of the Oxford Union. I have had lots and lots of lovely messages, telegrams, cards, letters. I have acknowledged them all. I have also coped with the backwash from the 'hoax' which turned out not to be as ghastly as I feared. Someone (I really have no idea who) sent out invitations in my name to a celebratory party in my room. I only discovered what was afoot when I got messages from John Sparrow (Warden of All Souls) and Maurice Bowra (Master of Wadham) expressing their regret that they could not come! I had no idea who had been invited. I had no idea what to do. In the event, I called the secretaries of various other heads of colleges and explained that I had been the victim of a practical joke. Everyone was very understanding and some expressed regret that they had not been asked because had they been they would have come. Lady Hayter sent me a note: 'Perhaps your practical joker was arranging a celebration party for you. I wonder if you chose the expensive way and had it, or what happened. I do hope practical jokes aren't coming into fashion again. They have been rare since my parents' generation. At least I think so.'

In his letter Pa says that Kenneth Tynan had similar problems in his day. Apparently Tynan, when attacked by hearties, would fall to the ground, rolling about, crying out, 'My hip, my hip!'

---

[*] On 28 April 1969, President de Gaulle held a referendum on constitutional reform, lost and resigned. On 15 June, Georges Pompidou was elected as his successor.

Apart from Pa's, my favourite note is the one from Michael Beloff at Trinity: 'Congratulations on your election to the Presidency – a revaluation of the currency. If anyone can turn the Union's *danse macabre* into a frug, you can.'

Tuesday, 24 June 1969

I am going to London to record a *Woman's Hour* discussion on the 'generation gap'. I am then returning to Oxford for the Queen's College Ball. I am then accompanying Michèle to Bournemouth. (Degree done, she has hopes for a job in TV – and we have irons in the fire! – but for now she is going to work for an electronics company called CETA Electronics, doing public relations etc. They make boards for circuit testing – whatever that may be!)

Judy Garland has committed suicide. She was 47 but looked much older. The Reverend Peter Delaney (of course) was first on the scene. Having married Gin last year and Jen this, he married Miss Garland to her fifth and final husband in between. On Sunday, when the news broke, he rushed round to Miss Garland's Marylebone apartment to administer the last rites. It is all very sad: apparently she took the stem of a rose and tried to swallow it so that the thorns would destroy her throat. (For me, *Meet Me at St Louis* is even more wonderful than *The Wizard of Oz*.)

Tuesday, 1 July 1969

I am going back to Bournemouth to see M on Thursday – via Southampton where I am talking to students at Southampton University. Today I am back in Oxford, at the Union, enjoying the office that goes with my 'office'. They say that, until you become prime minister, you will not have another room as fine as this to work in. I can believe it. The room is at the top of the building, large, light, spacious, gracious, wood-panelled, lined with books. I am sitting at my desk (with two telephones) despatching letters and telegrams around the world! I am inviting everyone to the Union, from the Duke of Edinburgh to Eldridge Cleaver, from the Archbishop of Canterbury to Fanny Cradock. I am hopeful that some of them will say Yes!

Later

Prince Charles was invested as Prince of Wales at Caernarvon Castle today. I watched some of it on the Union's brand-new colour TV. It wasn't very interesting. The Queen wore a hat like a spaceman's helmet; Lord Snowdon came dressed as Buttons; Prince Charles *is* Big Ears. It was all a bit contrived and passionless.

Sunday, 6 July 1969

Via Bournemouth and Southampton, in filthy weather, I made the long journey to Petersfield to attend my old French teacher George Smith's 'gala lunch' in his room at Bedales. I went because he asked me (which was kind of him) and because Diane Cilento* and Edna O'Brien† were the guests of honour. I shouldn't have bothered. Because of the trains, I arrived late. Because of the rain, I arrived wet. Because George was nervous, there was an unreal, awkward atmosphere in the air. I was seated at the wrong end of the table – not that the conversation amounted to much. Miss Cilento was not as beautiful as I had hoped and not at all gossipy. We wanted to hear about 'life with Sean Connery', but I don't think she referred to the great man once! And as for Miss O'Brien . . . she is so Irish, so gentle and fey and pixie-like that you do want to give her a good kick up the backside. When I told her that *Girl with Green Eyes* was our best-selling novel when I ran the Paperback Bookshop at Bedales, she simply closed her eyes and stroked my hand. I did not remind her of the first time we had met – when she came to look round the school as a prospective parent and I was appointed to escort her. We reached B Dorm and there, on the far side of the room, was a boy (I think it was Nick Wates) – he was naked, except for a strategically placed guitar. Instead of sparing the poor chap's blushes and retreating, Miss O'Brien stood transfixed. 'Is there a more beautiful sight on God's earth than that – a pure, hairless boy, with soft brown skin, on the very edge of manhood . . .'

I got back to Westbourne to find that poor Michèle had been turned out of her flat. The landlady discovered that M had had a 'visitor who stayed overnight' (me!) and was not having 'that sort of thing' in her respectable residence. (How she discovered we do not know: we were so careful: I sneaked in, I crept around the room on all fours until it was time to draw the curtains.) Anyway, M was instructed to pack her bags and get out – there and then. We found refuge (in separate rooms) at Mrs Smith's B&B.

Monday, 21 July 1969

'That's one small step for a man, one giant leap for mankind.' Today Neil Armstrong became the first man to walk on the moon. And I saw it happen! I wouldn't have done. I was fast asleep, but at about 3.00 a.m. Pa – in dressing gown and pyjamas – came into my room and woke me and said, 'You have to

* Diane Cilento (b.1933), Australian actress, married to Sean Connery, 1962–73.
† Edna O'Brien (b.1930), Irish writer.

watch this.' I am glad I did. The picture was fairly faint and fuzzy, but we saw it as it happened – Armstrong, the commander of *Apollo 11*, climbing down the ladder and stepping off the Eagle onto the moon's surface. It was 3.56 a.m., London time.

Thursday, 24 July 1969

Beverley Nichols[*] was President of the Oxford Union exactly fifty years ago. I have invited him back to speak in a special debate to mark the anniversary. Today he invited me to lunch. It was memorable. He is delightful, about seventy, a little stooped, but vigorous and full of charm. He met me at the railway station and drove me to his house – a beautiful eighteenth-century 'cottage' overlooking Ham Common, near Richmond in Surrey. He and his 'friend', Cyril Butcher, had prepared lunch themselves and it was delicious – quite perfect in fact: prawn mousse, cheese soufflé, cucumber salad, chilled Sancerre. Cyril fussed and served and cleared, but did very little of the talking. Beverley chattered all the time, but it was wonderful stuff. He has known everyone – from Churchill and Edward VIII to Nellie Melba and Noël Coward. He had extraordinary stories to tell of Somerset Maugham's cruelty to his wife, Syrie. 'He should never have married. His marriage brought out the viciousness that lurks just beneath the surface in so many men.' Beverley said his own father had been a cruel man – an alcoholic like Maugham. 'My father tried to destroy my mother – and me – and I tried to murder him. Yes, I deliberately set out to kill my own father – with a garden roller, as it happens. I regret to say I failed.'

I have some notoriety in Oxford now, but in his day at Oxford Beverley was *famous*. He was President of the Union and editor of *Isis* when these things meant something. His first novel was published when he was 21; his first volume of autobiography appeared when he was 25. It was called *Twenty-Five*. Of course, today he is best known for his sentimental newspaper columns (he *hates* being confused with Godfrey Winn)[†], his love of cats and his skill as a gardener. He showed me his latest book on flower arranging (it includes a striking arrangement featuring a whole red cabbage as the centrepiece!) and, after lunch, took me on a tour of the garden – his pride and joy. Now and then, he allows gardening ladies to come on a visit – and sets them a challenge. After the tour, he offers them tea. When they have had tea, if they ask to powder their noses he directs them to the loo, where

[*] John Beverley Nichols (1898–1983), writer.
[†] Godfrey Winn (1906–71), writer. For many years Winn and Nichols had rival weekly columns in Britain's two most popular women's magazines, *Woman* and *Woman's Own*.

they find that he has placed an exquisite arrangement of miniature roses inside the lavatory bowl . . .

More later. I am now off to Michael Coveney's 21st birthday dinner.

Monday, 15 September 1969

Lunch with Peter Morley at L'Escargot in Greek Street. I had vichyssoise and duck (£2) and a wonderful invitation – to host my own show for ITV this Christmas: a look-back at the 1960s, a ninety-minute review of the decade, a mixture of archive film and intelligent 'chat'. Peter produced the Mountbatten TV series and clearly knows his stuff. He's very serious, but I liked him. I think we'll get on well.

My programme for the Union is shaping up (slowly but surely) and today I sent off one final batch of invitations. I have a bulging file of interesting letters from people who *can't* make it: C. P. Snow, Brigid Brophy, Reginald Maudling, the Prime Minister, the Archbishop of Canterbury, Ken Dodd, J. K. Galbraith, Marghanita Laski, R. A. Butler, Hattie Jacques, Enoch Powell, James Mason, Peter Ustinov, Christiaan Barnard, Sir Oswald Mosley, John Lennon, Montgomery of Alamein etc. – scores of them! (At least I can now boast an impressive autograph collection. And some funny letters: 'Dear Gyles, I grow old: I grow old. And apart from wearing the bottom of my trousers rolled I have given up Union speaking. Yours, Iain Macleod.') Also lots of telegrams. This just in from Washington DC:

DEAR BRANDRETH I REMEMBER HOW MUCH BOBS VISIT MEANT TO HIM AND WOULD ENJOY A VISIT TO OXFORD UNION SOMETIME STOP THIS IS A PARTICULARLY BUSY TIME IN CONGRESS BUT I HOPE TO COME ANOTHER TIME = TED KENNEDY USS

A nice letter, too, from Eldridge Cleaver, Minister of Information, Black Panther Party:

I would be more than happy to accept your invitation to speak next term. I accept. But before I come, I must have a guarantee from your government that I will not be turned over to the agents of Warden Richard Nixon. Without that guarantee, I'm afraid that I will not be able to visit your country. I have always wanted to explore England because it is the origin of much of the shit, many of the problems, that we all have to deal with these days.

He gives me the details of his attorney in San Francisco and ends the letter, 'All power to the People! Eldridge' – signing his name in exactly the same coloured turquoise ink as Mr Harkness used to use at Betteshanger.

Anyway, though plenty can't come, plenty can – and some good names. I'm especially pleased about Fanny Cradock. She is bringing Johnnie!* We have started quite a correspondence, but I have to keep her address top secret: 'You may or may not know that my husband and I were blown up and burnt some time ago and have been compelled to move to the above address as our quacks have insisted on our having privacy at home if we are to continue with our work which we love. Because of this I would be grateful if you would not pass on our address or telephone number to *anyone*.'

Sunday, 12 October 1969

On the Shankhill Road, Belfast, British troops are firing tear-gas at stone-throwing mobs. It isn't much more peaceful here in the President's office of the Oxford Union. I have received the following letter from Fanny Cradock:

> I have just received on my return to England a cutting from *The Times* dated 7th October 1969 under the heading 'Union upswing' which includes the statement that you are 'trying to knock some life into the old place'; that you are 'turning the debating hall into a theatre' and that you think you will 'probably upset a few of the old guard'. The tailpiece of this report is as follows: 'two debates will be broadcast and the traditional humorous debate, with Fanny Cradock, televised in colour and played in by the Yarnton Silver Band'.
>
> My dear Mr Brandreth, you have told me none of this, you have asked me to speak for or against what I and everyone with whom I have discussed this regards as an extremely serious motion, 'England is a seven-stone weakling and proud of the fact' and with the best will in the world I flatly refuse to play horse to your Godiva. Rightly or wrongly I do not regard myself as a comic and I am appalled at the prospect of being played in by anybody's silver band.

The long and the short of it is that she is threatening to withdraw. I have written to her at length – essentially telling her that she is wonderful, that I am a fool, and that, come what may, I need her here on 4th December! (I also have Barry Humphries and John Wells in the line-up, but she is my star turn.)

---

* Fanny (1909–94) and Johnnie (1904–87) Craddock, popular TV chef and oenophile husband.

Name Dropping

Up early to send thank-you notes etc. re last night [the first debate of the Michaelmas term], then on, at 10.30 a.m., for my first tutorial with the great Richard Cobb, Fellow of Balliol and, apparently, the *world* authority on the French Revolution.[*] His claim to fame is looking at history from the people's perspective – not viewing it from the top down (from state papers etc.) but from the bottom up (the testimony of peasants etc.). Having been told how fortunate I am to have Cobb as my tutor, I turned up in good time, in good order and oddly nervous.

I found his staircase. I climbed the stairs. I stood on the landing outside his room and checked my watch. Just as the Balliol clock struck the half-hour I raised my hand to knock on the door – and then I heard him, inside the room. He was bellowing at the top of his voice: 'What the bloody hell have you done with it? Damn and blast your eyes! Where the hell is it?' I stepped back, not sure what to do. The shouting got fiercer: 'You are so bloody – bloody – *bloody* stupid!' His rage was mounting. 'For Christ's sake, where have you put it? God, how I despise you!' He paused. 'And where the hell's my pupil?'

I knocked on the door. Suddenly I heard a crash. It sounded as though he had heaved a great pile of books onto the floor. Then the voice rose to a great crescendo of fury: 'Where the fuck is he?'

I knocked again. 'Come!' he called. I turned the handle, pushed open the door and found him standing in the middle of his study, pale-faced, wild-eyed, hair all dishevelled, books and papers scattered pell-mell on the floor around him. He appeared to be alone. There was a door beyond him that led, presumably, to his bedroom. Had the other pupil taken refuge in there?

'Ah, yes, good . . .' he mumbled, beckoning me into the room. 'You must be, er . . .'

'Brandreth, yes. Am I disturbing you?'

'No, no. Find a seat. Move those books. I was expecting you. You're late.'

'I'm sorry,' I faltered. 'I thought you had someone with you.'

'No, no. I was talking to myself. I couldn't find a document I needed. Now what did you say your name was?'

'Brandreth.'

'Oh, yes,' he smiled. 'The "television star". Shall we have a glass of wine?'

He drank copiously – at ten-thirty in the morning! We got on famously and I don't think he is going to expect too much from me this term.

[*] Richard Cobb (1917–96), author of *Les armées révolutionnaires* and later Professor of Modern History at Oxford.

Saturday, 18 October 1969

Letter from Pa. He came on Thursday night, but I couldn't see him because of all the guests, etc. He is full of Pa-like congratulations: 'The way you handled the entire proceedings was perfect – all the right mixture of authority and tolerance, with shafts of wit and good humour. (And your tails looked fine too.)' But the real reason for his writing is this: 'Your wretched fees. The bank will not play, but since the fees are in *advance* it is possible the Bursar will allow deferred payment. I have had to do this in the past with school fees.' Poor Pa. He has more than £500 in outstanding bills and doesn't know which way to turn: 'I am so sorry to involve you in what for me has been a lifetime of money anxieties.'

I will go to see the Bursar. I have money coming in from *Honey* (£47 5s od for each Luke Jarvis), £100 for the piece I have done for Michael Wynne-Jones at the *Mirror* magazine and between now and Christmas I should get a total of £875 from London Weekend TV for *Child of the Sixties*. It will be fine.

Wednesday, 22 October 1969

I now have a literary agent. Her name is Irene Josephy. She wrote to me out of the blue, having read about me in *The Times*. She represents Patrick Campbell, Adrian Mitchell, Paul Foot, Nicholas Tomalin, among others, and will take ten per cent of any earnings that come through her. I met her today for the first time. She is quite eccentric, but very nice. She has steel-grey hair which she claims never to wash: its natural oils keep it clean, she says. She would like to represent me because I am a fellow Piscean and she senses that, though I will have problems with my feet all my life (!), I have high prospects. She gave me lunch at the Gay Hussar in Greek Street. It's her favourite haunt and the favourite haunt, too, of the left-wing establishment. While we were there Michael Foot and Tom Driberg walked through the restaurant on their way to one of the private dining rooms upstairs. We sat at a tiny table on creaking, rather uncomfortable old red velvet-covered chairs. The owner, Victor, is Hungarian and told us what to eat: cold cherry soup, roast duck and stuffed cabbage – it was delicious. While I was there I felt (as I often feel nowadays) that I was no longer me, but a character in somebody else's film.

I handled my first 50 New Pence coin today. It is seven-sided and is being introduced to replace the ten shilling note.

Thursday, 23 October 1969

Another good night at the Union. A packed house. Electric atmosphere. Interesting debate: 'That pop and culture will never meet.' This was Michèle's idea – get away from fuddy-duddy politicians, do something a bit more 'modern'. My line-up included Edward Lucie-Smith, poet and critic; Tony Palmer, film director and pop columnist; Emperor Rosko, disc jockey (Michèle's choice); and Sandy Wilson, creator of *The Boy Friend* (my choice!) – he seemed really nervous and genuinely thrilled with the note that I passed to him after his speech. Jimmy Young failed to show (as he warned me he might) but my surprise star substitute did indeed prove to be the star of the evening – Si-i-i-i-i-imon Dee!* He was wonderful – tall, skinny, blond floppy hair, charming and classy and wildly over-the-top, *exactly* what we wanted. He arrived in an E-type Jaguar (of course) and when I went to collect him from his room at the Randolph I found him drinking champagne with a beautiful actress/model, Joanna Lumley.† (She is very lovely: I glimpsed her in her crisp white bra and panties.) They were both delightful, full of fun, crazy but intelligent, and they seemed to love the evening, especially when I took them on the tour of the Union – they were very taken with the pre-Raphaelite murals and chased one another around the gallery of the Library.

All in all, a big success. I think even the old guard were won over. Next week we return to business as usual: the No Confidence debate – Shirley Williams, Robert Maxwell, Nigel Lawson, Gerald Kaufman & Co.

Monday, 3 November 1969

Yesterday afternoon I took Sir Michael Redgrave into the deserted Union chamber. He needed to test the acoustic. He stood on the dais at one end of the hall and I sat at the back while – to me and for me – he recited 'To be or not to be . . .' It felt strange and wonderful to have one of the great Hamlets of our time giving me a personal performance.

In the evening, to a good crowd, Sir Michael gave his readings from Hans Andersen. They worked well. He is lovely – though so nervous, so tentative, so unsure of himself before he goes on. Once he's centre-stage he's fine, but in the wings he is shaking like a leaf. Afterwards, we went to the Cantina di Capri for supper and he relaxed completely. He *blossomed* in his shy way. People nearby murmured 'film star' and I think he liked being recognised. He found it reassuring. His voice is amazing – there's a lilt and a rasp to it that makes everything he says sound haunting and poetic. With his fish he ordered spinach, '*en branches* not

---

* Simon Dee, real name Cyril Nicholas Henty-Dodd (1935–2009), pirate radio disc jockey and chat show host, hugely, if briefly, famous, with an audience of 18 million for his *Dee Time* TV series.
† Joanna Lumley (b.1947), actress, writer, broadcaster.

à la crème'. The waiter looked at him with tears in his eyes! Sir Michael rewarded him with a two-shilling tip. (He told me that, every day, his secretary puts out a stack of florins on the hall table by the front door. When he goes out he takes the florins with him and distributes them to all and sundry – the taxi driver, the hotel porter, the stage doorkeeper. 'It smoothes the path,' he explained. 'When you're a "film star" that's what they expect.')

Later

I have just been presiding at the Union Standing Committee meeting. Stephen Milligan* is a most excellent Secretary – intelligent, good-humoured, gets on with it. Actually, it's a good team, no prima donnas – Julian Radcliffe, Anthony Speaight, Libby Purves†, all solid chaps. (We cannot say that it is the beautiful girls who are drawn to the Union. 'Nor yet the handsome men . . .' I can hear Michèle muttering. And she is right. The Union Harry is not a prepossessing specimen – though Speaight has fine red hair. He is the nephew of Robert Speaight, the actor, and his father is the world authority on toy theatres. We can see why I like him!)

And we can see why I like Fanny Cradock. She has received my missive. She is coming on 4th December, after all. She writes: 'I read your letter. I read it to the family. There was a chorus of "you can't refuse anybody who writes to you like that." We were all immensely touched and having mentally decided you were marvellous I have got to tell you so.'

Nice letter, too, from Sandy Wilson – pleased with my compliments, happy with the response he got on the night, but 'rather shocked by the nature of the debate, and by what I can only call the degradation of the Union for the purposes of Show Biz. But perhaps that is just another symptom of the current obsession with Success at any Price.'

Tomorrow I am telephoning assorted newspapers for the photocall for this year's 'Zuleika Dobson'. I have chosen Caroline van den Bosch, 21, daughter of the Belgian Ambassador. She is blonde and leggy and seems happy to oblige!

Friday, 14 November 1969

The Beverley Nichols night went well. He said to me afterwards, 'I had forgotten what it was like to play the Union. It is a subtler instrument than you might imag-

---

* Stephen Milligan (1948–94), Secretary and later President of the Oxford Union; Conservative MP for Eastleigh, 1992–4.
† Libby Purves OBE (b.1950), journalist and broadcaster; Secretary of the Oxford Union when GB was President.

ine.' He played it with extraordinary delicacy: he was nostalgic and reflective and yet he held them completely. He disarmed them with understated charm. (There is a lesson here!) And for those requiring something more robust, we had Lord Boothby!* He did not disappoint – either in debate (he growled and gurgled and the crowd cheered) or before and afterwards when he staggered about, wheezing, drinking, smoking, like an ancient debauchee enjoying one last night out on the town. He arrived with his young Maltese bride on his arm and I was grateful for her presence: he needed looking after. I felt he might well die during the course of the evening. Beverley had told me extraordinary stories about him – scandals involving gangsters, mistresses in high places, love children, blackmail and worse – but said, 'Don't believe a word of it, Bob's a dear, an absolute dear.'

Thursday, 20 November 1969

I went to see the Bursar this morning and explained the desperate position to him. He was sympathetic, but said there was really no question of us phasing payment over a period of time. I have written to Pa. What I save from my London Weekend fee, I will use for my day-to-day expenses between now and June – food, fares, clothes, etc. I am not going to be able to earn much from January because I will be studying for Finals. If Pa can find a way of raising a loan to cover the fees, I should at least be able to pay the interest for him. I will also make what other gestures I can – e.g. paying the next quarter's phone bill. I wish I could wave a magic wand and solve it, but I can't.

Tuesday, 25 November 1969

Amusing letter from John Wells:

> *20 Cadogan Gardens, London SW3*
> *24th Nov.*

Dear Gyles,

I must say the line-up for the debate sounds emetic.

Do for God's sake get someone to replace B. Humphries as soon as you can, because you won't get the telegram to say he's fallen off the Post Office

---

* Robert Boothby (1900–86), Conservative MP, 1924–58. Queen Elizabeth the Queen Mother described him as 'a bounder but not a cad'. He was bisexual, twice-married, the lover of Harold Macmillan's wife, Dorothy; reputedly the lover of the gangster, Ronald Kray, and the father of several illegitimate children.

Tower and fractured every bone in his body until some time on the evening of the debate.

FANNY CRADOCK!!!!

See you on the 4th.

Regards,

J. Wells

Meeting with Iain Macleod. Peter Morley and I went to see him at his flat at Grosvenor House. It is where he lives during the week when Parliament is sitting. He likes it because of the swimming pool – he needs to swim for his health. He was even more bent and gnome-like than when I last met him. He is going to be one of the panel of four 'commentators' on my end-of-the-decade TV show – alongside Michael Foot, Fred Friendly (of CBS News)[*] and Lady Longford.[†] Peter Morley wanted to take him through our plans for the programme – year by year. But Mr Macleod said there was 'no need for that'. I think he had a game of Bridge he was anxious to get to. He said the only problem he could foresee with the programme was that he and Michael Foot would probably agree on most things!

Wednesday, 26 November 1969

I am in my final year at Oxford, but I seem to spend most of my time commuting to London! Happily, Mr Cobb, my History tutor, has now decided to join me on these excursions and gives me my French Revolution tutorials on the train. We do our work in the Buffet Car so that he can have a beaker (or two) of wine while we work. If we have to change at Reading, we look in at the platform buffet to find another beaker (or two) of wine there!

Today I was in London to take lunch at the celebrated *Punch* table,[‡] courtesy of the editor (William Davis) who spoke at the Union on 6 November. He was very friendly – everybody was very friendly: Basil Boothroyd, Miles Kington, Alan Coren: there were about sixteen of us in all – but there was something 'forced' about the occasion. I kept very quiet and listened to the others all being rather self-consciously 'witty'. Wm Davis has asked me to write a piece for them.

[*] Fred W. Friendly (1915–98), celebrated American newsman and former president of CBS News.

[†] Elizabeth Pakenham, Countess of Longford (1906–2002); née Harman; biographer and historian.

[‡] From 1841 to 1992, *Punch* was Britain's best-known humorous magazine. Long-serving contributors were given the honour of carving their initials on the magazine's dining table.

I will try, but the truth is that, for me, *Punch* isn't a magazine you *read*: it's one where you look at the cartoons!

Wednesday, 3 December 1969

Letter from John Wells: 'I am extremely sorry to do that with which I find fault in others . . .' He is in Scotland writing a script with John Fortune and is pulling out of tomorrow night's Farewell debate. He says would I apologise to Barry Humphries on his behalf and suggests I try Richard Ingrams (GER 4017) 'as long as you don't tell him who he's replacing' or William Rushton (KNI 1913).

In fact, I am relatively calm because I anticipated something like this and have already persuaded Robert Morley to step into the breach.

Later

Telegram received this afternoon:

> IT IS WITH GREAT REGRET THAT MR BARRY HUMPHRIES FEELS IT HIS DUTY TO ADVISE THE PRESIDENT OF THE OXFORD FLAMING UNION THAT HE IS BLOODY SORRY THAT HE FINDS IT IMPOSSIBLE TO CARRY OUT THE BONZER HONOUR CONFERRED UPON HIM OF BEING REQUESTED TO ADDRESS THE UNION STOP THE INCONVENIENCE PLACED UPON HIM BY THE BRITISH BROADCASTING CORPORATION AT THIS PARTICULAR TIME FORCES HIM TO SHOOT THROUGH STOP AND IF YOUSE DON'T LIKE IT YOUSE CAN STICK YOUR NOSE UP A DEAD BEARS STOP LETTER FOLLOWS = BARRY HUMPHRIES

Thursday, 4 December 1969

She has no eyebrows! Fanny Cradock has drawn-on eyebrows, orange lipstick *around* her lips and a voice like a foghorn – but I love her and so did the Union. She was a triumph and is now my best friend. Johnnie was with her – and wearing his monocle. He didn't say much, but he kept an eye on her at all times. She was quite nervous beforehand, but once she stood up and heard the crowd she was away – and brilliant. Only Robert Morley could have followed her – and he did, with considerable style. It was a very funny, very happy evening. (Even my speech went well!) After we had paraded in, I had to get the Yarnton Silver Band to play an encore while I rushed out again to go to the loo!! It was a night to remember in every way. The Cradocks have a huge Rolls-Royce and flair to match. Goodnight.

Friday, 5 December 1969

The BBC broadcast *Any Questions?* 'live' from the Union tonight. (I asked them to come. They said 'Yes'. It's the only way.) It was a good end to a good term. During the broadcast, on air, Norman St John Stevas MP said several amusing and nice things about me! Afterwards, in his cups, he took me to one side and said, 'Gyles, you are far too amusing for your own good. Take care.' Somebody had told him we had had too many 'funny debates' this term. I said, 'Not so,' and told him about the prisons debate with Lord Longford, the Lord Chancellor's visit, the Biafra exhibition, etc., etc. He replied, 'Yes, but they'll only remember the *clowning*.' He said, 'You should use me as a dreadful warning. Because I try to be amusing, I'm dismissed as a dilettante and a lightweight. I'd like to drop Bagehot on their toes.'*

Monday, 15 December 1969

I went out to the London Weekend studios at Wembley today to rehearse the programme with the Autocue. The whole script is typed out in large letters on an endless scroll of paper and a lady then turns a handle to roll out the script while you read it. The rolling script is positioned just underneath the TV camera and the trick is to be reading the script *and* looking into the eye of the lens at the same time. Not easy.

'I am a child of the sixties. I was eleven when this decade began. 1960 was the year of the Sharpeville shootings – Helen Shapiro – and the election of President Kennedy . . .' I think it reads quite well and I am trying to memorise it so that I don't have to rely on the Autocue machine. Sometimes they break down, the paper scroll gets stuck, etc. We are covering the decade in five chunks – two years at a time – and I think we have got plenty of variety in the news clips we are showing, everything from the Aberfan disaster to Tommy Steele's wedding. The real challenge will be to keep the chat with the guests stimulating and *to time*. Peter M[orley] is obsessed with the timings. Throughout the proceedings there will be a floor manager standing to the right of my camera giving me signals.

Tuesday, 23 December 1969

Michèle and I went to the Dower House, Grove Mill Lane, near Watford, Herts, for Fanny and Johnnie Cradock's Christmas party. It was our first 'showbusiness party': everyone was there – even Lionel Blair. (Joke of the night: 'Yes it's Fanny

---

* St John Stevas, a former academic and future Cabinet Minister, was editing a fifteen-volume edition of the works of Walter Bagehot, the Victorian constitutional lawyer.

and Lionel – Butch Casserole and the One Dance Kid'.)* The champagne flowed, Fanny's buffet was amazing (she is a *very* good cook), everyone was friendly (I think I prefer the 'showbusiness set' to the *Punch* crowd) and at eleven o'clock she clapped her hands and announced that it was 'cabaret time'. Turning to Nicholas Parsons, who was standing right beside her, she announced: 'Nicholas will now entertain you!' He did – with a very funny routine involving a lot of Scottish gobbledygook. He said afterwards that he had *no idea* that Fanny was going to ask him to perform. She is a little bit mad, but she couldn't have been more generous and we were very happy to be there. When people asked me what I was doing, I mentioned the programme on ITV on Saturday night, but I did try to do it as casually as possible, with a nonchalant shrug of the shoulders.

Thursday, 1 January 1970

The dust is settling, the fan mail is sorted, the press cuttings are pasted in. My favourite is Monday's *Daily Sketch*. The headline reads: 'Suddenly, a new Frost is born . . .' And alongside a photo of me (taken in the schoolroom at 5H) a full-page story: 'Success to Gyles Brandreth means being Gyles Brandreth. Which means that overnight fame is unlikely to turn the head of this cool, self-assured young man. Gyles is the 21-year-old student who appeared on a London Weekend Television look-back programme on Saturday and was told afterwards: "You can write your own ticket in TV now."'

Lots of letters – from Grandpa and Auntie Edith, from Penny Wilson's parents (of all people, after all this time), from Cordelia Fraser (*laughing* at another headline: 'Child of the Sixties – Heart-throb of the Seventies'), from HEG [Harold Gardiner], etc., etc. I have sent thank-you notes to all of them. I have *not* written to all the strangers – some really strange people were watching, including Glenda Spooner, Chairman of the Ponies of Britain, who asks: 'Do you mean to say that you will not object to or deplore it if one day there is a coloured majority in this country?'†

One of the most unlikely letters came from Dennis Lipton, associate director

---

* *Butch Cassidy and the Sundance Kid*, starring Paul Newman and Robert Redford, was the highest-grossing film of 1969.
† Also watching was Richard Crossman (1907–74), MP and Secretary of State for Health and Social Security in 1969. On 31 December, he recorded in his diary: 'This Christmas and New Year there have been a whole series of television programmes looking back not only on 1969 but at the whole decade. I saw one which had the President of the Oxford Union, a young Tory, handsome, good-looking, waving his delicate fingers about as he sat on a dais and put questions – this is the strange thing – to Michael Foot, Elizabeth

of Crawfords Advertising: 'No doubt you are being inundated with offers and I do not suppose you have even considered doing any commercials. However, we are responsible for advertising *milk* – and we are looking for someone really outstanding and new to Television to act as presenter, or almost a host, in a new and exciting series of commercials we are planning and you could well fill the bill.'

I am having lunch with Mr Lipton in High Holborn in an hour's time. 'Gyles Brandreth – the new face of milk!' Who knows what excitements the New Year will bring?

Longford, Iain Macleod and Alf Friendly. The idea was to see the 1960s through the eyes of a child of the decade, someone who had grown up in the age of television. This young man had no ideas or ideals. He just shared the general disillusionment and all his illustrations of the decade were public occasions in the newsreels, Vietnam, the murder of Jack Kennedy, the murder of Robert Kennedy, of Martin Luther King, everything that obviously illustrated the 1960s as a period of degeneration, decline, disappointment, lack of hope, deflation. This young man didn't stand for anything. Michael struggled with him from his elderly position. Elizabeth, in her own Catholic style, stood for something, and even Iain Macleod did but it was an extremely depressing programme. Not only were they being cross-examined by this young pup, but they fawned on him, all saying, "It's you that matters, your ideals, your beliefs." '

Fingers Crossed

January – December 1970

Wednesday, 7 January 1970

Last night was Twelfth Night and we had the usual family ritual: unwrapping one
last Christmas present before taking down all the decorations. It was cosy –
except Ma isn't feeling very well (it isn't Asian flu!)* and Pa is worried about
money. We were festive all the same.

Today, a letter from Fanny Cradock. 'Gyles dear,' she begins, 'this is a
difficult letter because I want to talk to you properly':

> We watched your television debut, of course. We were staying at Gravetye
> and we canvassed opinions afterwards. This is what I want to talk to you
> about. Of course, it was a *tour de force* and you are ever so slightly preco-
> cious to have subdued that awful Michael Foot, who almost behaved like a
> civilised human being. Of course, you are what we call in typically slovenly
> manner 'a natural' . . . but you are using your hands too much even so – try
> sitting on them – not putting them in your trouser pockets which can be
> misconstrued.
>
> Concentrate on your flair for changing voice levels; it is enormously
> effective but capable of getting 'mannered' if you do not train yourself to
> become conscious of it without getting self-conscious.
>
> Come to supper soon. We can for once guarantee you will enjoy yourself
> because we shall talk incessantly about YOU.

Sunday, 25 January 1970

Calls/proposals/articles: 1. *Spectator*; 2. *Punch*; 3. *Honey*; 4. *Vogue*; 5. *Sun*; 6.
Mirror Magazine; 7. ATV; 8. STV; 9. Ray Colley (BBC Manchester); 10.
Woman's Hour; 11. Book; 12. Irene Josephy.

Academic priorities: this week, essays for Alex de Jonge (New College),
Richard Cobb (Balliol), Theodore Zeldin (St Anthony's); Balzac, Racine

---

* In Britain, the previous week more than 4,000 deaths from Asian flu were reported.

(*Andromaque*), Robespierre. My priority this term must be the academic work. It *must* be. I have so much to catch up on. So much.

Lovely letter from Mr Stocks. He must be in his nineties now. He still hopes that I am 'the hardest worker in the world and therefore really happy – you will recall this old school theme of mine!' I do. He goes on:

> Have you yet discovered and absorbed the great Teilhard de Chardin? If not, start on him, because he is a really wonderful inspiration: after studying *The Phenomenon of Man* I felt that I was quite different, much calmer and more balanced, and the feeling has lasted.

He feels pretty sure that I am 'or will be' a Teilhardian. I must explore. But not today. Today a French Prose requires my attention. Now. *Now.*

Thursday, 29 January 1970

Mick Jagger has been presented with a £200 fine for possession of cannabis. I have been presented with a bill for £65 3s 1d for last term's presidential entertainment at the Union – 'inclusive of sherry, dinner and supper'. Jagger can afford to pay his fine. I'm not sure about my bill . . . I entertained 28 guests, it seems, who don't count as 'official' guests and I have to cover their costs. Heigh-ho. (Money does not interest me, but I know it's important. When I was Hugh Anderson's guest at the Cambridge Union and met Neil Shand (scriptwriter to David Frost, Spike Milligan & Co.) Shand said to me: 'You've got to decide – are you going to be a £5,000-a-year man or a £10,000-a-year man? You can get to £5,000 a year and have a good life. Aim for £10,000 and it will kill you.' Pa earns around £5,000 as a successful London solicitor – it's a lot, but it isn't quite enough.)

Tutorials with Zeldin and Cobb today – both a little mad, but I like that.

Saturday, 7 February 1970

Not my day.

Letter from Crawfords Advertising:

> Advertising is a very fickle business and we have in fact decided to abandon altogether the idea of a 'Presenter' show for milk. It's a pity, but there it is.

At 12 noon I went over to the Warden's lodging to have drinks with Harold Macmillan. As I arrived, Sir William said, 'He's curled up by the fire. Go and keep him company.' I found the former Prime Minister seated in a large armchair, with his back to the room. His eyes were closed and his hands were resting on his cane between his knees. I sat at his feet for three-quarters of an hour, making occasional small-talk. The great man dozed throughout.

Friday, 13 February 1970

Yesterday, I cancelled my Zeldin tutorial and went to London to meet Robin Denniston, editorial director at the publishers, Hodder & Stoughton, in Bedford Square. He sent me a telegram last term asking me if I wanted to write a book. I have just telephoned Irene [Josephy, literary agent] and the deal is agreed. Hodders are buying my book: *Created in Captivity*, a study of prison life and the effect of creative work on the rehabilitation of offenders. I wanted to sign my first book deal while I was still 21 – and I have!

The papers have been full of pieces about Bertrand Russell.* I liked this line of his: 'Men who are unhappy, like men who sleep badly, are always proud of the fact.'

Today I am happy. And this weekend I will be happier still. I am joining Michèle for Valentine's Day in Ashford. We are having a celebratory dinner at the George Hotel.

Friday, 10 April 1970

At lunch-time, in Eastbourne, I became the youngest person ever to address the Institute of Public Relations Annual Conference. My theme: 'The Generation Gap'. My fee: £15 plus £6 expenses. It was fine, except I don't think I gave them enough of what they hoped for – stuff about 'pot' and 'protest' and girls on The Pill. Of course, that's part of the picture, but only a part. On the whole it's a pretty innocent world out there: Andy Williams, Mary Hopkin and Dana are top of the pops and the best-selling book this year is the New English Bible. (A million copies sold on publication day last month and 20,000 a week still flying out of the shops.)

That said, tonight Michèle and I witnessed theatre history of a sort: the first attempt to *sing* the F-word on the West End stage. We went to *Mandrake* at the Criterion Theatre. It is a musical inspired by Machiavelli's *Mandragola* and it's a collector's item it's so atrocious. Roy Kinnear sets the tone when he comes on stage with a beer bottle significantly positioned in his codpiece, and the first-half closer has the hero singing, full-blast:

> And guess what luck!
> Yes: guess what luck!

* The philosopher Earl Russell OM FRS (1872–1970) had died on 2 February.

Tonight I'm having
My first f—

. . . and the curtain falls.

Monday, 27 April 1970

Today, at Broadcasting House, over lunch, to amuse the extraordinarily prim and proper ladies at *Woman's Hour*, I attempted my impression of Lee Marvin talk-singing 'Wandrin' Star'. It left the earnest blue-stockings suitably bemused, but I think Michèle would have been impressed. She'd have considered it a move in the right direction, just a touch more 'contemporary' than my impression of Noël Coward. (M would prefer me to be offering impressions of Simon & Garfunkel singing 'Bridge over Troubled Water'. Quite right. That's where the real money is.) Anyway, today, for £8 I gave a talk on *Woman's Hour* about the horrors of examinations and, off-air, the talk around the table was of Tony Curtis being fined £50 for possessing cannabis. I have never taken cannabis (I wouldn't know how), but because I am 22 and at Oxford they all look at me as if I am the expert on all things permissive. The 'permissive society' is the phrase of the hour. That's all anyone's talking about. (I feel another *Woman's Hour* talk coming on . . .)

From Broadcasting House to White City and BBC Television Centre and, at 6.00 p.m., my meeting with Paul Fox, Controller, BBC1. He is a force to reckon with in the land and he knows it. He was fairly genial but quite grand. He is a large man, with a large office, and a large retinue of secretaries and assistants. He is treated like a god and has a touch of the Buddha about his appearance. I tried not to burble too much, but I don't think I succeeded. He said I should go to see Aubrey Singer, Head of Features, Television, and Christopher Brasher, Head of General Features, Television. I asked him what was the difference between Features and General Features? He laughed: 'I'm not sure. This is the BBC!' Will this lead to anything? I wonder. He looked at me as if I was a slightly exotic creature somewhat alien to his world. He said, more than once, 'You are a very strong taste, you know – a very strong taste.'

Thursday, 4 June 1970

I begin my Finals today. I am as ready as I ever will be. I have been rising at six and revising, revising, *revising*. I know what we need to achieve: comprehensive and thoughtful answers to the questions being asked plus that little extra something . . . We shall see.

Later

It was History I. It was okay. Oddly, the formality of it all really helps. At Bedales, you wore what you wanted for exams. Here we wear subfusc: dark suit, white shirt, white tie, gown, mortar board. Everyone looks the same: there are no distractions. And the concentration in the room is intense. I was nervous (hands sweating) until I turned over the paper and read the questions and took out my pen and started. Then it had its own momentum.

Lots of cards from family arrived today. One from Ma (on behalf of brother Ben): a drawing (by her) of a Schulz *Peanuts* character at his desk at school with his hand up: 'Happiness is knowing the answers.'

Monday, 8 June 1970

E. M. Forster died yesterday, aged 91. Michèle collected her degree on Saturday – our second anniversary. The general election is happening on Thursday 18 June with Harold Wilson set fair to win. No other news because I am in the midst of my Finals. 'France 1870–1914' begins in half an hour. Wish me luck. Thank you.

Thursday, 18 June 1970

All done. My last exam – French Prose – completed this morning. Not wonderful, but I hope adequate. And at least I completed all the papers! There were some who simply turned up, turned over the paper and sat gazing at it for three hours without lifting a pen. When it was over, the High was awash with revelling undergraduates breaking open bottles of champagne. I didn't linger. I ran back to my room, changed, picked up my briefcase and ran on to the station. I am now on the train to London a) to get my hair cut with Michael at Crimpers in Baker Street and b) to vote for Quintin Hogg in St Marylebone – my first vote in a general election. As Mr Hogg reminds us in his election leaflet, 'Your vote is a responsibility as well as a right.' His leaflet is a model of its kind: clear, personal, to the point – and with a message from his wife on the back.

When I have voted I am coming straight back to Oxford to be on parade at the Union to take part in the BBC's Election Programme Outside Broadcast.

Friday, 19 June 1970

Hair done, vote cast, I got back to Oxford in time to take part in the BBC OB from the Union garden and join in the revels. Much mockery from Alex de Jonge and Anthony Palliser[*] (both in their cups!) about my travelling to London to get my hair done. I did not reveal to them that I was returning to London again to be on stand-by this morning to be interviewed by Robin Day in the Election Studio at Television Centre. Jack Straw (President of the National Union of Students)[†] and I were the chosen representatives of British youth – him for Labour, me for the Conservatives. He is much more overtly political and serious – and made great play of knowing Wilson and all the senior Labour people – but we got on well enough.

The whole BBC circus was extraordinary – the chaotic comings and goings and the sense of bewilderment/hysteria that the result was not what they had expected or planned for. They were all set for a Labour victory and, suddenly, had to change tack. Interesting to note how well the politicians got on with one another (regardless of party), how wary they were of the BBC people, and how pleased with himself Robin Day is. It really is Mr Toad in a bow tie.

Later

The result: Conservatives, 330 seats; Labour, 287; Liberals, 6; Others, 7. Mr Heath is promising 'strong and honest government'. Jack Straw's chums are now asking themselves what went wrong and my friend, Iain Macleod, is set to become Chancellor of the Exchequer.

I am rather pleased that my Oxford career should come to an end on the very day of the general election. It's been a good three years, but I am ready to move on. Clearly, the country is ready to move on, too. I have taken the last exam I will ever take. I have been having dreams – nightmares, really – about Finals. Now they can stop. And I can start earning my living in earnest. For my contribution to the general election programme I am getting £35 plus £6 expenses (train fare and overnight).

Final thought, re Jack Straw. Which of us will become Home Secretary first?

Tuesday, 30 June 1970

I am not sure what to make of these BBC types and I am not sure what they are making of me. They take themselves so seriously and, when they talk about it, their world, which should be exciting, seems incredibly dull. I had lunch with

[*] Anthony Palliser (b.1949), a contemporary of GB at New College, Oxford; Paris-based artist, son of Sir Michael Palliser, diplomat, and grandson of Paul-Henri Spaak, Prime Minister of Belgium and one of the founders of modern Europe.
[†] Jack Straw (b.1946), Labour MP for Blackburn from 1979; Home Secretary, 1997–2001; Foreign Secretary, 2001–06.

Chris Brasher at the Trattoo, 2 Abingdon Road, just off Kensington High Street. (Lunch is clearly an important part of these chaps' lives: Mr Brasher appeared to know everybody at every other table.) It was a good lunch – especially the avocado and prawns – and a trendy setting – like eating in a garden hothouse – but our conversation was pretty desultory. I had come to talk about 'features', but Mr B. clearly only lives for sport! He is an Olympic athlete – he paced Roger Bannister at Oxford in 1954 when Bannister ran the first four-minute mile – but he does not have the look of a Greek god (he is bespectacled and balding) and spent most of our meal trying to interest me in the joys of a new kind of cross-country running, invented in Norway and known as *orientation*.* I liked him, but I'm not sure that I belong in his world.

I know for certain that I do not belong in the world of Lawrence Wade. He is the oh-boy-do-we-take-ourselves-seriously producer of *Tomorrow's World* and today, in Room 4060 at Television Centre, he graciously gave me fifteen minutes of his time. As I sat down, he took off his watch and explained to me that it was 'the latest thing' – a watch with a timing device. Our interview was timed for fifteen minutes. He said that the alarm would therefore go off after thirteen minutes. It did. And when it did, as it did, he got up and moved me towards the door. We shook hands, knowing we would never meet again.

Saturday, 11 July 1970

Pa's 60th birthday. A good day. The sun shone. In the afternoon we went to a matinee of the National Theatre's *Merchant of Venice*: the Jonathan Miller production, in a Victorian setting, with Joan Plowright, totally credible and compelling as Portia and Olivier, looking like Disraeli played by Henry Irving, as Shylock. It fulfilled all my expectations – including his much-talked-about off-stage cry of anguish. When Shylock has lost his daughter and his ducats, he wails. Olivier read about the way trappers in the arctic set about catching baby seals. They throw salt onto the ice. The baby seals lick the salt and, as they do so, their tongues stick fast to the ice. They're caught. The trappers then come and claim them. For Shylock's wail of anguish, Olivier tried to recreate the cry made by the seal as its tongue is ripped from the ice.

We went down the road to the Parioli for the birthday meal. Pa, Ma, children and spouses. Quite jolly – though Peter [Jennifer's husband] lay down on the banquette and went to sleep (or affected to). I booked the table and did a special

---

* Better known as 'orienteering'. Brasher (1928–2003) pioneered the sport in the UK and, later, co-founded the London Marathon.

menu: *Stracciatella à la Charlie, Poulet à la Princesse Alice, Sorbet Tooting*, etc. We raised our glasses to dear old Pa. I think (hope) he had a happy time.

Tuesday, 21 July 1970

Iain Macleod has died. He was 56. He had a heart attack at 11 Downing Street last night. This is devastating news at all sorts of levels.

He incurred a spinal injury during the war and it led to arthritis. When we were doing the programme just before Christmas, he told us he needed a swivel chair because he couldn't turn his head and shoulders. He was quite tetchy. When Elizabeth Longford asked, 'Are you in pain?' he snapped, 'I am always in pain.' That evening he only came to life when talking about his time as Secretary of State for the Colonies – that was the work he was most proud of, 'my one achievement'. When the recording was finished, he disappeared without saying goodbye. He wrote later to apologise for his rudeness, explaining that he had been in considerable pain.

Wednesday, 22 July 1970

A colleague's account of Iain Macleod at Cabinet meetings: 'When he had a point to make he made it with brevity, relevance and force. If he had nothing new to contribute, he did not speak unless invited to do so.'

That's the way to do it.

And I hope, too, that one day I will have the wherewithal to do my Christmas shopping the Macleod way. He told me that he had followed the same routine all his adult life – certainly since the end of the war. On the last weekday before Christmas, he would get his chauffeur to drop him at one end of the Burlington Arcade. He would then proceed through the arcade, walking down the left-hand side, choosing his presents. Half an hour later, loaded with gifts, he would emerge at the other end of the arcade where his chauffeur would by now be waiting. Did he ever look into the shops on the right-hand side of the arcade? 'Never. I am a creature of habit.' (I realise now that he could look comfortably to the left, but not to the right.)

The *Evening Standard* says Anthony Barber will be the new Chancellor.[*] I am currently getting the first edition of the *Standard* on a daily basis. Michèle and I are going to get a flat. I'd be inclined to get something around here – Baker Street, Marylebone, St John's Wood – but M says we can't afford it. Her plan is that we

[*] He was, on 25 July. Anthony Barber (1920–2005), Chancellor of the Exchequer, 1970–74.

rent somewhere for £10 per week and save so that we can then *buy* somewhere. Pa and Ma have always rented. M's parents have always bought. Anyway, I am looking for flats every day, but by the time I telephone they have *always* already gone.

Monday, 27 July 1970

I might have gone to the Round House in North London tonight to see Kenneth Tynan's erotic revue *Oh! Calcutta!* As it happens, I am quite happy not to be going: it has had mixed notices, to put it mildly. I love Robert Helpmann's line: 'The trouble with nude dancing is that not everything stops when the music stops.'

Instead I have come to Canterbury Cathedral. I am making a film for Southern TV marking the nine hundredth anniversary of the murder of Thomas à Becket and, this afternoon, in the crypt of the cathedral, on the very spot where Becket was martyred, I interviewed his successor, Michael Ramsey, 100th Archbishop of Canterbury.* We got on really well. He is a delightful man, all eyebrows and twinkle – and all the right ideas, on homosexuality, on developing relations with other churches, on the war in Vietnam etc. I was told he was going to be very awkward and inarticulate. In the event, he was inspiring. 'We need saints. We need men who are true to their beliefs, who do not swerve or waver. In a complicated world, we need the simplicity of unwavering faith, complete honesty and goodness without compromise. Becket gives us that.'

Tuesday, 1 September 1970

The Feast of Saint Giles and I have moved to my new address: 11 The Close, Muswell Avenue, London N10. It's a 1930s block and looks as if it might be more at home on the front at Sandwich than tucked away in a back street in north London, but (except for the fact that it's a hike to Highgate tube) I really like it. I have signed a two-year lease at a rent of £461 per annum, inclusive of rates and water rates. I have also paid the outgoing tenant £250 for fixtures and fittings, curtains, carpets, three-piece suite, gas fridge, gas cooker, wardrobe, chest of drawers etc. The removal men struggled to get the upright piano up the two flights of stone stairs, but otherwise all went well. No breakages. And we have already discovered some of the local delights – a nice kebab restaurant and a useful Launderette. Also, Barny [Kremer] has offered to come and help paint both the sitting room and the second bedroom, which is going to be my study.

The parents don't know where they are moving to yet.

* Michael Ramsey (1904–88), Archbishop of Canterbury, 1961–74.

Monday, 21 September 1970

When I was President of the Oxford Union, Hugh Anderson was President of the Cambridge Union. We were friends; we were the same age; he was a really nice person; and now he is dead. It was some form of cancer. I have just come back from his memorial service at All Souls', Langham Place. The church was packed. Harold Wilson was there. Trevor Huddleston gave the address. Canon Perfect led the prayers.

Canon Perfect is Pa's age, perhaps a little older. Pa and Canon Perfect were at school together. Pa *loathed* him at school because Perfect was exactly that: perfect. At least he was perfect as far as the masters were concerned: he bullied the other boys. All my life I have been hearing about this ghastly prig of a schoolboy and I turn up at my friend's memorial service and there he is leading the prayers! I hadn't realised that Hugh went to St Lawrence College, Ramsgate, too.

It was a moving and an amazing occasion. At 21, Hugh's impact was enormous – he was destined to go a long way. He was a Christian socialist and during the service we were invited to 'view his premature death from the Christian perspective, by which alone it can make sense'. I fear the truth is: it doesn't make any sense at all.

It was interesting to see H. Wilson at close quarters – small and hunched. Mary Wilson has a collection of her poetry being published today. Mr Wilson had just come from her first 'signing session'.

Saturday, 3 October 1970

I am in Wells, at the Red Lion Hotel, making my film about the life of Wells Cathedral for BBC2. Letter arrived from Pa this morning. Ma's 'dizzy spells' are still unexplained, but he reports a 'highly satisfactory' two-hour consultation with a GP in Harley Street. (How much did that cost?) 'Nerves' are ruled out; also low blood pressure. No 'heart' trouble. Most likely cause is the ears, so the next step is an aurist followed by a neurologist. And on the weight problem, the enemy is fluids. Ma is to cut it down to no more than four cups a day.

They leave 5H on 14 October: 'a sad occasion – we've been happy here.'* Pa is hoping to sell bits and pieces of surplus furniture to the new tenants. He says, 'even £10 will be acceptable.' They are going to take a room at the West London

---

* By running a Montessori nursery school at 5H Portman Mansions, GB's parents had broken the terms on the lease of the flat; also, now that GB and his sisters had left home, they were hoping to find a smaller and less expensive flat.

Hotel in Bayswater on a week-by-week basis until they can find somewhere affordable to move next. It's not good. Pa says: 'We miss you *very much* and hope that on your return we may see more of you.'

Monday, 9 November 1970

General de Gaulle died today. It is the end of an era. He was a giant. (And, yes, he *almost* shook my hand.)[*]

Went to 2 Mansfield Street to the launch of Sir Robert Mayer's book, *My Life and Music*.[†] Sir Robert spent a lot of time holding Michèle's hand. He didn't quite chase her round the room (he is 91) but he was certainly very attentive! (And he knew what he was up to: he kept a sharp eye open for Lady Mayer who stalked nearby.) In his speech he reminded us that, in 1923, when he founded his children's concerts he insisted that the children pay for their tickets – even if it was only a penny. 'Never give people something for nothing: they won't value it.' As we left, he kissed Michèle with considerable gallantry and shook me firmly by the hand. He is a remarkable old boy. 'You are now shaking the hand that shook the hand of Johannes Brahms,' he said. 'I thought you'd like that.'

Saturday, 28 November 1970

I am writing this in my bedroom at the Montrose Hotel, Dublin. I am here because tonight I was a guest on *The Late Late Show* hosted by Gay Byrne.[‡] Mr Byrne is the most famous man in Ireland – by a margin. (Here he is more famous than the Pope. Truly.) He is also very charming and leprechaun-like and appears quite unspoilt by his incredible success. Everybody in Ireland watches his programme – which goes on for several hours and rambles across a wide variety of topics, none of which seemed particularly exciting to me.

My excitement of the evening was meeting Sinead Cusack, actress daughter of the great Cyril Cusack. We became immediate friends: we are exactly the same age, born two weeks apart.[§] We exchanged phone numbers at once and talked simultaneously, nose to nose, non-stop. Our hands kept touching. She is not

---

[*] In 1960 President de Gaulle had paid a state visit to Britain, during which he addressed Members of Parliament in Westminster Hall and visited the French Lycée in South Kensington. GB was one of the pupils lined up for presentation to the President, but when he passed down the line, he patted or shook hands with every child but one – GB.
[†] Robert Mayer KCVO (1879–1985), businessman and founder of the Youth and Music children's concerts.
[‡] Gabriel Byrne (b.1934) hosted *The Late Late Show* from 1962 to 1999.
[§] In fact, Sinead Cusack was born on 18 February 1948.

conventionally beautiful, but she is incredibly attractive – and funny and intelligent. And she liked me. For an hour or so, at the party after the show, we had a really lovely time together – and then . . . And then I introduced her to George Best!!* Why did I do it? She had told me she wasn't interested in football! I believed her. George is fine, of course, but he's not that articulate and he's not that funny and he's not that good-looking. He's rather awkward and scruffy, in fact. But he is George Best. Anyway, she went off with him. And here I am, alone, in room 23 at the Montrose Hotel. Goodnight.

Saturday, 12 December 1970

This morning I woke up and looked out of my bedroom window onto a wonderful sun-filled view of the bay of Haifa. I am in Israel.

Yesterday, with Michèle and Mark Hofman, I took the 10.00 a.m. El Al flight from London, via Rome, to Lod. (The El Al security is impressive.) At Lod we were met by May Hofman and her beau (Arthur Dahl) and driven to Haifa and the handsome Hofman house on the hillside. Mark and May's parents are lovely people and leading figures in the world of the Baha'i Faith. Mrs Hofman, tall and wiry (a former US Olympic swimmer), seems to be the intellectual one and the driving force, but it is Mr Hofman, naturally, being the man, who is the revered member of the Baha'i International House of Justice – the council of nine wise men who run the religion. (They claim ten million adherents in 200 countries around the world.) Mr H. is very sweet and has been most welcoming. (I say that: in fact, as we arrived he retreated to his room to 'do his exercises'. Mrs H. explained that he likes his snoozes.)

Last night we went to a gathering of assorted luminaries in the Baha'i world – if not people who knew Baha'u'llah personally (the founder of the faith died in 1892), certainly folk who had known Abdul Baha and Shoghi Effendi, his son and grandson. Everyone had that slightly wide-eyed seraphic look with which the Almighty blesses the faithful, but they were a friendly crowd and didn't over-proselytise. I scored by having been to Wilmette and seen the Baha'i Temple there. (I have observed that just one nugget of insider knowledge can get you a long way in life.)

Today we are going to the shrine to the Bab (he is the Baha'i equivalent of John the Baptist) and then on to Elijah's tomb on Mount Carmel. Tomorrow, we are taking the early train to Jerusalem and then going on to Bethlehem. We are covering the faith waterfront.

* George Best (1946–2005). In 1970 he was at the height of his footballing fame.

M is in a separate room, because Bahai's do not approve of sex outside marriage. Homosexuality is taboo. Gambling is out. *Gossip* is forbidden. The faith's principal thrust is a belief in peace, internationalism and world government – the unity of God and the unity of mankind. They have been severely persecuted, especially in Persia, where Baha'u'llah was born.

Thursday, 17 December 1970

This has been one of the happiest days of my life.

We began the day in Jaffa. In brilliant sunshine, through a wonderful warm breeze, we drove to Mount Tabor, the Mount of the Transfiguration. Mark is a fearless driver: if he sees a track marked 'No Entry: Not Cleared for Mines', he charges straight down it. He roared up Mount Tabor. We took the *eighteen* hairpin bends at such a lick I had no time to scream. (And the drive was preferable to the alternative: 4,000 rocky steps carved into the hillside.)

At the summit we were shown round the fine Romanesque basilica by an American monk and then given the most perfect four-course lunch in the Franciscan hospice. The pasta dish – spaghetti with tomato sauce and herbs, that's all it was – was perhaps the most delicious thing I have ever eaten. (And the Tabor table wine wasn't bad.) As we ate, Father Augustine – head of a community of five monks and three nuns – played the organ for us and sang. He told us it was the Feast of St Lazarus. It was the setting – and the food – and the weather – but chiefly, I think, the personality of Father Augustine that made the day so special. He was a good man and we felt better for our brief time in his company.

We drove on to Galilee and walked by the Sea of Galilee at the Ein Gev kibbutz. It was quite perfect.

And tonight we played cards – my first, proper game of Bridge. Who could ask for anything more?

Friday, 18 December 1970

It has been a memorable seven days: the train to Jerusalem packed with soldiers – old Jerusalem itself – the dusty streets of Bethlehem crowded with donkeys laden with petrol cans – the Church of the Nativity – the old prison at Acre – Armageddon – the Negev desert – Galilee . . . If I had to pick a second highlight (yesterday on Mount Tabor will remain unmatched) I might choose the Persian lunch we had today. David and Marion Hofman drove us to the Shrine of Baha'u'llah outside Acre. We toured the immaculately kept gardens and the house and the shrine. In the shrine, boldly but when the Hofmans could not see me, I looked on the image of the prophet. It is not forbidden to do so, but nor is it encouraged. Baha'u'llah means 'Glory of God' and everything about him is to be treated with reverence and discretion: he is God's ultimate messenger, after all. There are only two photographs of him in existence and they are not generally displayed – but one of them was here and I looked upon it. I mean no disrespect, but with his straggly beard and piercing eyes, he looks very like Rasputin.

After the tour of the shrine we had a delicious Persian lunch with the caretakers of the House of Abu where Baha'u'llah lived for two years. We were treated with such respect: travelling with Mr Hofman is like travelling with the Pope. Our hosts wouldn't touch their food until we had eaten ours – and had second helpings. And when Michèle, to be polite, admired our hostess's necklace, it was immediately removed and presented to her. (I believe this was the late Queen Mary's philosophy, too.)

After lunch, we played Backgammon.

Tomorrow, Caesarea, then Tel Aviv, Beer Sheba and Eilat. I have written a piece for *The Spectator* ('Christmas in Bethlehem') and have an excellent souvenir bought at the Good Shepherd General Store: a small linen sachet filled (so it says on the label) with 'The Earth Christ Trod – Inspected for Authenticity by Catholic Personnel'.

Thursday, 31 December 1970

Time for my end-of-year review. It is six months since I left Oxford. What has been achieved?

Prisons: Some worthwhile visits: HM Prison Bristol, HM Prison Grendon, Lowdham Grange Borstal, HM Prison Liverpool, HM Prison Holloway. No easy answers. Indeed, whatever the conditions of the prison, the level of recidivism remains much the same. Horrific conditions aren't a deterrent: most prisoners are 'present-dwellers': when they commit an offence they are not thinking about the possible outcome. Good conditions are more civilised, but don't, of themselves, improve the inmates' chances. Only education and training for work and life can do that. Some of this I can cover in my book – when I start it!

Television: The Becket film was fine. The Wells Cathedral film was dull. *Brandreth in Orbit*, the optimistic producer's preferred title for our series, will not materialise. I have had meetings galore – Robin Scott (né Scutt, Controller, BBC2), Edward Barnes and Monica Sims (Children's Department – boy, do we take ourselves seriously!), Chris Brasher (more lunches) . . . All talk, leading to *more* talk. My best idea for the Features Department – *That's Life*, a kind of popular newspaper on TV— seems to have gone away. They paid me £50 for it. I don't really mind. I'm not that interested.*

Radio: I like Tony Whitby, Controller, Radio 4. I think that meeting *will* lead somewhere. I like Con Mahoney, Head of Light Entertainment, Radio. He's straightforward: a bluff naval man with a shiny face to match the highly polished brass buttons on his blazer (I don't think the war has stopped for him yet). I like his no-nonsense approach and I like the people I bump into in his office – e.g. Ted Ray and Arthur Askey. (They are funny off-stage as well as on: the performance never stops.) I like the producer he has given me, Peter Titheradge – full of old-world courtesy AND the son of the great Madge Titheradge. (She was a great beauty, a famous Peter Pan – and a childhood friend of Noël Coward.)

Writing: £15 for the *Spectator* Bethlehem piece. £26 5s 0d for the *Punch* piece. *Vogue*: £25. *Guardian*: £18 for Prison Art, £20 for the Canterbury Festival. It adds up. I had lunch with Lynn Barber from *Penthouse*. (A disappointing experience given the nature of the magazine: she was completely unsexy and made sex seem completely unsexy. But she has £20 to offer me for an article so I'm going to give it a go.) And Irene [Josephy] has some pieces lined up for me in the *Observer* magazine and I am meeting Brian Redhead to talk about a possible weekly column for the *Manchester Evening News*. All okay, but nothing startling.

Archway Productions: Our brochure looks good. We have the possibility of a production. Fingers crossed.†

Colin Smythe Ltd:‡ I am grateful for the £78. 7s 4d per month and they are an interesting double act, though there is something odd/uncomfortable about their world. Colin is in love with all things Celtic (I think he really does believe in fairies): they are both obsessed with the paranormal: and Peter . . . well, he's a rum one, for sure. The chivalric orders of the Catholic Church are his chief delight (alongside his friendship with the papal nuncio, Archbishop Cardinale) and

---

* *That's Life*, hosted by Esther Rantzen, was eventually launched on BBC1 in 1973 and ran until 1994.

† With three people he had met at Oxford (Graham Baker, Joy Masefield and Colin Sanders), GB had formed a company to present *son et lumière* productions: sound and light shows telling the story of historic buildings.

‡ A small publishing house based in Gerrards Cross for which GB worked part-time. The firm, specialising in Anglo-Irish letters, was founded in 1967 by Colin Smythe (later Terry Pratchett's literary agent) with Peter Bander (1930–2004), teacher, author and authority on orders relating to the Catholic Church. Sir Robert Mayer was the company's chairman.

there's a glint in his eye and a wobble to his lip that aren't altogether reassuring. When he and I had dinner at Trattoo, he brought the subject back to corporal punishment again and again and *again*. Nominally it was a straightforward conversation about education and discipline, but as he described the swish of the cane on the boys' bare buttocks, little dribbles of saliva appeared at either edge of his mouth and he shifted his knee towards mine. Each to his own, I say, but physical violence – whatever the motive – is of no interest to me. None whatsoever. And the way he sits with that huge Irish wolfhound of theirs in his lap – it isn't an Irish wolfhound, I know: whatever it is, it's a dog as big as a donkey . . .

Anyway, that's 1970 done and dusted. It's been fine. The flat here is a success. (Even Barny's purple sitting-room wall is a success.) We *like* Muswell Hill (I thought I'd never live anywhere but Baker Street!) and we love the Side Saddle (we eat there night after night). And Michèle is lovely. And Israel was memorable. Everything is good . . . And yet . . . I need to do more and better – much better. (Will that always be my cry?)

The Alien Porn

January – December 1971

Wednesday, 20 January 1971

Took M to Euston.*

11.30 a.m. Meeting at the House of Commons with Sir Clive Bossom MP.† An amiable buffer (Major Sir Clive, 2nd Baronet) best known for his name. On hearing it, Churchill is said to have harrumphed: 'Bossom? Bossom? Neither one thing nor t' other.' We were seeing Sir Clive because he has had a wonderful idea: during the summer recess open the historic Westminster Hall to the public and tell its incredible story by means of an Archway Productions *son et lumière*. We stood with him, alone in the middle of the vast Hall – when it was built, in 1097, it was the largest enclosed space in Europe – on the spot where Thomas More and Guy Fawkes and Charles I were tried, where George IV held his coronation banquet and Churchill lay in state – gazing up at the famous hammerbeam ceiling and marvelling at the potential. It is a matchless setting and the story we could tell – from the eleventh century to the present day – is England's story. It could be fabulous. We could certainly do it, but will the 'Commons authorities' let it happen?

Thursday, 21 January 1971

A curious evening. A séance at the home of Colin Smythe and Peter Bander in Gerrards Cross. We heard the dead speak – through the good offices of Peter's friend, Dr Konstantin Raudive, a Latvian who contacts the departed by means of recording their 'voices' on tape. The session was conducted like a scientific experiment: there were parapsychologists there, but also independent engineers from Belling & Lee Ltd who assured us that the equipment hadn't been tampered

---

* Michèle, now 23, had left the electronics company in Bournemouth and found success as a television presenter, first with the BBC in Bristol (where she was a presenter on the children's science programme, *Tom Tom*), then with the BBC in Manchester where she worked as a continuity announcer and newsreader.

† Sir Clive Bossom Bt (b.1918), Conservative MP for Leominster, 1959–74.

with and that the tapes were virgin tapes fresh from the factory. To cut to the chase, after a lot of mumbo-jumbo and hours of waiting, we *did* discern distinct voices through the crackle and hiss of the tapes when they were slowly played back to us and heavily amplified. Most of it was in Latvian, but I did hear a voice sounding uncannily like Winston Churchill. It declared that it *was* Winston Churchill. Dr Raudive interpreted what Churchill said thus: 'Mark you, make believe, my dear, yes.' Once we had heard the recording played back a number of times I realised that what the voice was saying was a phrase from 'Land of Hope and Glory': 'Make thee mightier yet.' Peter Bander was literally salivating as we listened to the recordings: his lips were dribbling. I wasn't sure what to make of it.*

Monday, 8 March 1971

My 23rd birthday.

9.00 a.m.	Hair at Crimpers in Baker Street.
11.00 a.m.	Brigadier Short at the House of Commons to discuss *son et lumière*.
1.00 p.m.	Meet Mike Palmer (from Oxford *Isis* days), Leicester Square tube.
3.00 p.m.	Meet Reg Davis-Poynter† in Berwick Street. He is starting a new publishing imprint and I am going to edit a series of playscripts for him – starting with editions of *Cinderella* and *Aladdin* by H. J. Byron.
4.00 p.m.	Irene [Josephy] at her office in Craven Street. She sits at a tiny desk in the corner of her vast, empty room: bare floorboards, bare walls, manuscripts in piles on the floor around her. All day long she sits there, sipping at a glass of gin and water, taking calls, making calls, doing deals. The deal for my column on the *Manchester Evening News* is done: £54 per month, starting next month.
6.00 p.m.	Join the parents in their room at the West London Hotel, Bayswater. It's a big room, but a bit bleak. Ben [now 12]

---

* GB still has a copy of the recording and still does not know what to make of it. For a fuller account of Dr Raudive's experiments with recording the voices of the dead, see *Carry on Talking* by Peter Bander, 1972.

† Reg Davis-Poynter (1924–2004), influential post-war publisher whose authors included Michael Foot and Colin MacInnes.

sleeps on a put-you-up bed behind a makeshift curtain in the corner. We went for a festive meal in Queensway.

Wednesday, 11 March 1971

I am on the train returning to London from Manchester. My meeting with Brian Redhead [editor of the *Manchester Evening News*] went well. He was very fatherly (they all are – it's rather irritating) and seemed to know quite a bit about me. He told me his real passion is contraception – we need much more of it, apparently, and Redhead's at the ready – and his one remaining ambition is to become editor of the *Guardian*. He is a bit 'chippy' and self-consciously 'northern' (he was quite disconcerted when I told him Grandpa lives in Accrington and Pa was born in Cheshire), but I liked him and I want to do this well.

As I write (5.30 p.m.) I am featuring on *PM* on Radio 4. I have launched the National Scrabble Championships! I put an advertisement in the Personal Column of *The Times* inviting anyone who wanted to take part to write to me at 11 The Close, N10. Hundreds have! The official public relations people for Scrabble have also been in touch asking me what I think I'm up to. I have *not* replied saying 'doing your job for you' because the truth is I now realise that I am going to need their help to make it all happen!

Harold Lloyd has died.* Of those silent American comedy performers, he was the only one who really made me laugh. I could do with an evening of Harold Lloyd. Instead, I am going to the cinema with Simon Cadell. He has chosen *Assault* for our mutual entertainment. It is an X-rated film about sex, rape and violence. Simon is partial to that kind of thing.

Sunday, 18 April 1971

Charing Cross: 10.40 a.m. train to Etchingham. Cyril Fletcher† met me at the station and drove me to his magnificent house, Summerhill Park, Old Heathfield, an *exact* reproduction of the Queen Anne house in which he last lived. He is very droll and very nice and besotted with his wife, Betty Astell – who is sweet, twittering and bird-like. Their mutual devotion is touching to see: they married in 1941 and go back to St Martin-in-the-Fields each year to renew their vows. Betty was an actress, a pioneer in television (she appeared on John Logie Baird's original thirty-line TV),

* Harold Lloyd Sr (1893–1971) died on 8 March. Best remembered for the sequence in *Safety Last*, 1923, where he hangs from a clock high above the street.
† Cyril Fletcher (1913–2005), comedian, married to Betty Astell (1912–2005), English actress. GB met him first when they recorded the pilot programme for GB's first radio series, *A Rhyme in Time*.

a film star in the thirties, she danced with the Prince of Wales ('He was a terrible drinker, my dear, and a very poor dancer – whatever they tell you') and now she dances attendance on Cyril. Cyril was a TV pioneer too. He appeared on the first BBC television broadcasts from Alexandra Palace in 1938: 'Reciting Odd Odes wearing bright yellow face make-up so that my ugly mug would show up on the flickering screen.' (It's because of his Odd Odes that Cyril is to be one of the team captains in the *Rhyme in Time* panel game I've devised for Radio 4. If it happens.)*

The other lunch guest was George Rylands,† known as 'Dadie', Cambridge don, Shakespeare scholar, merry sprite. He knew Virginia Woolf, he devised John Gielgud's *Ages of Man*, he directed his *Hamlet* in 1945, he is the mainstay of the Arts Theatre, Cambridge, where Cyril and Betty have been putting on pantos for years. It was my kind of lunch – full of funny stories.

Dadie gave us the *definitive* Gielgud 'gaffe' story. John G. was taken to lunch at The Ivy by Edward Knoblock, a minor playwright noted for his dullness. A familiar figure brushed past their table and Gielgud remarked, 'There goes the second biggest bore in London.' 'Who is the first?' asked his host. 'Why, Eddie Knoblock, of course . . . Oh, I don't mean you, Eddie, the *other* Eddie Knoblock!'

Wednesday, 28 April 1971

Lunch with Simon Dee. He is quite mad. He did not stop talking. 'Do I have things up my sleeve? Yes. And under my pillow. Also in my study, lying around my flat, gathering dust in a couple of spare rooms and permanently circling in my mind. Ideas for films and television, radio and advertising, series for children and for adults. Formats for radio stations. Poetry, both obvious and obtuse. Short stories and long stories. And even longer stories. And, of course, the book.' He accepts that his career as a television interviewer is over. 'Everyone knows I should have a show and everybody knows I want a show and everybody knows I can do a show and everybody knows I haven't got a show. Obviously something is wrong, but let us leave that to the historians. At the moment there are far more important things to be done for the race and the planet. Perhaps with your help, Gyles, I can find a way.' We talked about outer space, inner peace, sex, drugs, Women's Lib ('Up with Women's Lib!'), hot pants ('Down with hot

---

* It did. Produced by Simon Brett, the other panellists were Graeme Garden, Caryl Brahms and June Whitfield.
† George Rylands CBE CH (1902–99), Fellow of King's College, Cambridge, from 1927.

pants!') – it was all crazy. And rather uncomfortable. He kept getting louder and louder until everyone in the restaurant was listening. We went to the Barracuda in Baker Street and had the works – lobster, champagne, brandy. And I paid! He has nothing. He used to earn £1,000 a week. He claims to be the first man on British TV to earn as much. Now all that's left is the flat in Drayton Gardens, the double-double bed, and Bunny [his wife]. 'Peace, Gyles. Peace, man. PEACE.'

Friday, 7 May 1971

At 12 noon I presented myself at the Dorchester Hotel in Park Lane for the Associated Speakers' Annual Conference. Cyril Fletcher owns the agency (formerly The Maurice Frost Lecture Agency) and I am now the youngest speaker on their books. It was a very strange occasion – a cattle market really. I arrived with the Duke of Bedford and Ben Lyon. (Bebe Daniels died six weeks ago: this was his first public outing since.)* We – 'the speakers', whether world-famous or quite unknown – were given name badges (colour-coded according to booking price: mine was red, I'm thirty guineas) and instructed (firmly) not to talk to one another but to mingle with 'the bookers', scores of stout ladies in flowery hats, the chairmen and secretaries of the nation's assorted literary societies and ladies' luncheon clubs. 'Who are you? What do you talk about? You're very young – I hope you don't expect to travel first class?'

At one o'clock luncheon was served. We speakers sat on a raised top table facing the bookers. I was seated between Polly Elwes,† who was sweet, friendly and chatty, and Godfrey Winn, who was less so. Throughout lunch I was fixated by his hairpiece: it was lightly attached to the front of his head and the room was very hot and he seemed very nervous – he was due to speak first after lunch – and, as the meal proceeded, the glue from the wig trickled over the poor fellow's forehead and down onto his cheeks. He is homosexual (obviously) but he spoke of not being married as though it was something that hadn't quite happened yet and was about to – the moment the right gal came along. When he got up to address the room I noticed two things: how nervous he was (his hands trembled without ceasing) and how much the ladies loved him. Famously Lord Beaverbrook said, 'Godfrey Winn shakes hands with people's hearts.' How does he do it? It is partly because he speaks very simply and he *dares* to be sentimental.

* Ben Lyon (1901–79) and Bebe Daniels (1901–71) were an American-born British-based husband-and-wife acting team famous for the radio and TV situation comedy, *Life with the Lyons*.
† Mary 'Polly' Elwes (1928–87), television presenter.

Thursday, 13 May 1971

Telephone call from Lord Longford. He is setting up an independent commission of inquiry to look at the whole question of pornography. Is there a problem? If there is, what can be done about it? 'It's a high-powered group. We've got two bishops, an archbishop, a High Court judge and Malcolm Muggeridge. But we need some young blood. I thought of you and Cliff Richard.* What do you say?' I said yes.

Tuesday, 25 May 1971

To the Institute of Advanced Legal Studies, 25 Russell Square, where the Pornography Commission gathers for the first time. I sit with Cliff who is dressed in the most gorgeous nut-brown chamois-leather suit, with silken shirt and scarves to match. He must be ten years older than me, but he looks so young and so, so wholesome. And, of course, he's goody-two-shoes nice.

The room is crowded: mostly distinguished old buffers, clerics, lawyers, retired civil servants, one or two senior journalists (I recognised Peregrine Worsthorne)†, a couple of token women (middle-aged doctors, with heavy specs and low-slung bosoms: Cliff is the prettiest thing here by far). We sat at long tables set in a square, pencils and paper to hand, earnest and eager, and at 4.30 sharp Lord L. called us to order and welcomed us to 'the crusade'. (Crusade? I thought this was supposed to be an independent open-minded inquiry.) He told us he had worked with the late Lord Beveridge on the famous Beveridge Report that, thirty years ago, had formed the basis of the welfare state. He hoped, he prayed, that our work would prove as significant.

After the rallying cry and roll-call, we discussed aims and methods. It was all rather humdrum and platitudinous. I think I was expecting something more sparky from this gathering of the great and the good. Cliff and I kept stumm. Lord L. did most of the talking. He is 65 and as nutty as a fruitcake, but the mad professor look and the fumbly-bumbly way of speaking make him oddly endearing. And because he's been around forever, he knows everybody. He was a minister under Attlee and Wilson, but he started out as a Tory. When we were chatting over the pre-meeting cup of tea, he told me about his first encounter with Stanley Baldwin. In the early thirties Frank ('You must call me Frank') was a Conservative Party researcher and found himself at a country house-party where

---

* Sir Cliff Richard (b. Harry Webb, 1940); a Christian activist and a major pop star since 1958.
† Sir Peregrine Worsthorne (b.1923), journalist, then editor of the *Sunday Telegraph*.

Baldwin was guest of honour. After lunch, the Prime Minister invited young Frank to join him for a stroll. The conversation didn't exactly flow, but eventually Frank thought of something intelligent to ask the great man. 'Tell me, Prime Minister, who would you say has most influenced your political ideas?'

After an interminable pause, Baldwin replied, 'Sir Henry Maine.'

'And what did he say?'

'That whereas Rousseau argued all human progress was from contract to status, the real movement was from status to contract.' Baldwin halted in his tracks. His face darkened. 'Or was it the other way around?'

Tuesday, 1 June 1971

Bank Holiday weekend. We went to Accrington and visited Grandpa and Auntie Edith: they are very sweet and old and the house really does smell of lavender. We stayed in Burnley, at the Rosehill House Hotel – yes, Burnley is in the *Good Food Guide*! And we ended up here in Manchester, where, last night, I sat with Michèle in the tiny, self-operating studio at the BBC and watched her present BBC1 in the North-West for the penultimate time. It's not been much fun for her: when she's on the late shift, she sleeps on a camp bed in the ladies' loo, unless the star presenter needs it for one of his assignations. (He has different girls, daily.) The atmosphere is pretty sleazy, but at least M can say she was the first woman to read the News on BBC TV. Of course, it is only the local News.* As the news editor explained to her: 'We can't have a woman reading the proper News. People wouldn't take it seriously. People wouldn't believe it.'

I'm still in Manchester. I'm in my dressing room writing this between recordings of *Call My Bluff*.† Frank Muir is lovely, but he does bang on a bit. He has just been boasting about being made president of his local rifle club. *Sotto voce*, Patrick Campbell murmured: 'Small bore, I suppose.' God, Robert Robinson is smug. Much mockery of my involvement in Lord Longford's porn inquiry. Understandable, I suppose. Julian Orchard‡ is the other guest: a wonderful lugubrious face, like Fernandel's, and a lovely self-deprecating manner. He is naturally funny. I'm not. I *try* to be funny. Doesn't work.

* Angela Rippon (b.1944), became the BBC's first female newsreader on national television in 1974.
† US-originated television panel game that ran on BBC2, 1965–88, with Robert Robinson as chairman and Frank Muir and Patrick Campbell as team captains.
‡ Julian Orchard (1930–79), English comedy actor.

Tuesday, 8 June 1971

First gathering of the Porn Commission TV Sub-committee. I put on my new flared turquoise trousers, but, sure enough, Cliff quite outdazzles me in a sumptuous plum velvet outfit, complete with medallions and silver and gold chains. His skin is pretty peachy too. The meeting is chaired by Malcolm Muggeridge, broadcaster and sage. Looking like an ancient dandified turtle, he gets away with not knowing who anybody is by calling everybody 'Dear boy'. He introduces me to Peregrine Worsthorne: 'Dear boy, you must meet this dear boy.' I get the impression from Perry that, once upon a time, Malcolm was a bit of goer, a proper red-blooded ladies' man, but now that his libido has collapsed he's discovered the joys of chastity and vegetarianism.

Malcolm opened the meeting by reading out to us the BBC's original statement of intent, inscribed on the wall at the entrance to Broadcasting House: 'This temple of the arts and muses is dedicated to Almighty God by the first governors in the year 1931 . . . It is their prayer that good seed sown may bring forth a good harvest, that all things hostile to peace or purity may be banished from this house, and that the people, inclining their ears to whatsoever things are beautiful and honest and of good report, may tread the paths of wisdom and righteousness.'

We all agreed that, sadly, things ain't what they used to be – and Cliff declared that some of the dancing on *Top of the Pops* is undoubtedly designed to titillate – but, hand on heart, we couldn't say there was anything approaching what you'd call pornography to be seen on British TV. 'Mark my words,' said Malcolm, narrowing his eyes and smacking his lips, 'the rot's set in. If we don't do something now, within a generation nudity and profanity on the box will be commonplace, and rampant homosexuality will be offered to us by way of entertainment.'

Tuesday, 15 June 1971

Lunch at the Garrick Club with Lord Longford and the *Evening Standard* film critic, Alexander Walker. Lord L. was particularly mellow, fresh from yesterday's trip to Windsor where he was installed as a Knight of the Garter. He is devoted to the Queen: 'She is wonderful, beautiful and very funny. People don't realise how amusing she can be.'

I suddenly heard myself asking, 'Do you think the Queen enjoys sex?' Frank wasn't the least abashed. 'Of course she does,' he enthused, raising his glass of Beaune to her, 'She's a healthy Christian woman. And she enjoys riding, as I do. She isn't a puritan, you know. And nor am I. People expect me to be teetotal, but

I'm not. I love wine. And I enjoy sex greatly. After all, I've had eight children. I swim in the nude, regularly. There's nothing nicer. I doubt that the Queen swims in the nude. Prince Philip might. They've got a pool at Buckingham Palace, you know.'

Alexander Walker, his Cannes tan very much in evidence, then brought us back to earth with a crisp analysis of the current cinema scene. Forget what it says in the papers, old-fashioned romance is not making a comeback: ever more explicit sex and violence are on their way. Lord L. sighed, 'This is bad news, Gyles. You and I are going to have to go and see some of it.'

There was a fourth man at the table, David Reed. I am not sure who he was. He didn't say anything. He just sat there, rather limply. I think Lord L. called him his 'adviser on social affairs'.

Wednesday, 23 June 1971

Took a cab from Muswell Hill to the BBC Playhouse at Charing Cross to join Cyril Fletcher who was doing a guest spot on a rather drab new radio quiz. We went round the corner to the Sherlock Holmes pub afterwards for a snack. Cyril told me the tale of his first West End cabaret engagement, at the Ritz in the 1930s, and how Godfrey Winn – who died on Sunday – talked loudly to Dorothy Dickson throughout it. We were joined by Alastair Scott-Johnson (radio producer, whose name I feel I've known all my life) and Richard Murdoch. A lot of reminiscing ensued. Murdoch's doing a summer season at Bournemouth. (Cyril said later that he thought it was sad that Murdoch felt he had to do summer season still. 'He doesn't need the attention. He must need the money.' Or perhaps he just likes to work?) William Rushton was there, too – fat and funny.

Cyril then drove me to Old Heathfield. He wants to do a one-man show, in the tradition of Emlyn Williams's show about Dickens. I have suggested Lewis Carroll and we're working on it. Betty was there to greet us, with Jilly, their daughter – now recovered from the depression following her divorce. Jilly is a magician. Her 'act' – equipment and secrets – cost £400. I am hoping she will saw me in half. (I have always wanted to be sawn in half. I would be a magician myself if I had the patience to do the homework.)

We walked around the garden, worked and then had dinner – a well-risen cheese soufflé, chicken with banana, strawberries. The three Fletchers jabbered away as we ate – all theatre stories. Several of the stories were *exactly* the ones I had heard when I was last here – word for word the same.

Thursday, 24 June 1971

To the BBC, Portland Place, for the press conference to launch the summer season. Peter Titheradge has had to pull out of producing my series because he has cancer. Clearly I overdid my sympathy note. He wrote back saying, 'Give me a chance – I'm not dead yet!' Simon Brett has taken over and seems very pleasant. Smiles a good deal, while not giving a lot away. (Why can't I manage that?) He met me in reception and took me up. It was all rather grand. I moved straight over to Cyril for security. He was wearing his wig and kept reminding everybody of the fact. He introduced me to Kenneth More and Liza Goddard and we chatted. Kenneth More told us about his technique for finding out the names of people whose name he should know but has forgotten. He says, 'It's on the tip of my tongue now, come on, what's your name?' The other party replies, 'Michael' and More comes back, 'No, no, not your Christian name – I know that. What's your surname?' He gave up the technique when he met up with an old RAF chum whose surname was John. (Clearly these theatrical types repeat the same stories *shamelessly*.)

We trooped up to the roof garden to have our photographs taken and I was much chuffed to be included in the 'star' line-up: Kenneth More, Liza Goddard, Kenneth Williams (who was genuinely funny in his outrageous way), Liz Gebhart (whose dark glasses I accidentally walked off with) and Nicholas Parsons (who began a gag that died but he carried on with it laboriously nonetheless.)

Tonight we gave a dinner party. M did a lovely meal: vichyssoise, chicken casserole, strawberries. Plenty of wine and Simon Cadell brought some champagne. Darling M was anxious about her soup – quite unnecessarily. The guests were the right mix: Simon C, Simon Dee and wife Bunny (she was feeling queasy and burped incredibly), Kirsty McLeod (M's friend from Oxford), Derek and Pam Willoughby (our new medical friends, encountered at the next table at the Side Saddle). The two Simons were excellent and kept the table on a roar. We played charades and other games and are off to bed with a bit of a glow of satisfaction.

Sunday, 27 June 1971

Last night we did some Porn Commission fieldwork in Soho. There are around thirty specialist shops within 'the square mile of depravity' (as Lord L. likes to call it): we looked in on three. Our fellow customers really were wearing shabby fawn-coloured raincoats. At the last shop, the largest, we spoke to the manager.

We told him that we were doing research work for Lord Longford. He chuckled: 'That's what they all say nowadays.' He was very friendly and open about his business – and it's a good business. He sells around five hundred magazines, books and pictures a week and takes in about £2,000. His rent and rates cost £100 and his wages bill comes to nearly £200. We asked to see the most *unusual* sample of his wares and he produced a magazine called *Amigo*, a glossy publication designed for foot fetishists. It contained thirty close-up photographs (with accompanying toe-by-toe, step-by-instep descriptions) of naked feet. We were not aroused.

A more innocent day today. Earlier this year, I dreamed up the idea of the National Scrabble Championships and this morning early, before eight, I set off for the Grand Finals in the Ballroom at Grosvenor House, Park Lane. Plenty of press, some excitement, not too many squabbles. I hosted the event and presented the prizes with old Mr Spear (chairman of J. W. Spear & Sons) who is funding the event. I think we'll do it again next year.

Scrabble done, we went to Watford to dine with the Cradocks. Feeling in need of post-Scrabble fortification, we stopped off for tea and toast at a local hostelry. A mistake. As we arrived at the Dower House, huge dishes of strawberries and thick yellow cream were served and Johnnie emerged from the cellar bearing a magnum of 1949 champagne. Then we moved to the dining room to eat: caviare in sour cream, quails' eggs, lamb sweetbreads in cream with raw broad beans, followed by the richest chocolate cake in the history of the world – all washed down with a '52 red Burgundy and a white whose origin I didn't catch. Johnnie explained that, with a good wine, however much you drink, you don't get a hangover.

The other guests were Admiral Ross and Lady Calley. Fanny announced that we were her four closest friends. (I don't think any of us has met her more than half a dozen times.) It was a very cosy, happy evening. Johnnie beamed benevolently as Fanny prattled on – tales of her three husbands ('*Husbands*, mark you – I marry my men!'), her first child ('I was just fifteen, my dear – that's all. I knew *nothing* of the world!'), her second husband ('A disciple of the Marquis de Sade! And we all know what that involves – don't we, Admiral?'). She is outrageous ('A woman had a child at seventy-two – it is a *fact*, medical history says so') but completely endearing.

Tomorrow I am lunching with Simon Dee – outrageous, but less endearing. He wants to discuss the publication of his poetry. It's drivel, with a Christian twist. Can you imagine anything worse?

Wednesday, 30 June 1971

11.30 a.m. At the Royal Court Theatre, Sloane Square, I meet Athol Fugard, South African playwright – gentle, warm, generous. I tell him I want his play for the Davis-Poynter playlist.

1.00 p.m. Lunch with Stephen Milligan at *The Economist*, 25 St James's Street. We discuss Britain's negotiations to enter the European Economic Community. Stephen says that Geoffrey Rippon (our chief negotiator) says 'we're almost there'. Our subscription will be around £100 million a year. 'Well worth it,' says Stephen, who loves being 'in the know'. He expects to be prime minister one day. Perhaps he will be. Wanting is the first step to getting, as we know.

3.30 p.m. Meeting with Reg Davis-Poynter. I feel with him (as I often do) that I don't do myself justice. Irritating.

5.00 p.m. Tea at the Charing Cross Hotel with a girl who interviews me for the *Radio Times*.

6.00 p.m. Drinks at Eve Arnold's flat in Mount Street with Francis, her son [GB's friend from Bedales] – still a rather ludicrous 'hip' figure, now plans to be a doctor.

7.00 p.m. Rendezvous with Lord Longford in the Ladies' Annexe of the Athenaeum Club. We are having supper with a couple of girls before going on to a dirty movie. 'I've brought the tickets,' says Lord L., positively trembling with nervous excitement. I say, 'And I've brought the raincoats.' He doesn't get the joke. 'What are we going to see?' I ask. '*Catch-22*,' he says. *Catch-22*? Ye gods! I try to explain to him that, whatever it is, *Catch-22* isn't pornography. It's a serious film based on a tremendous novel. Frank won't be deflected – 'I've been told it's quite disgusting' – so he takes his young lady (a trainee publisher, I think) to *Catch-22* and I take mine (a student nurse) to a double bill at a tiny cinema at the top end of Piccadilly: *Anybody's Body* and *Collective Marriage*. Naturally, my nurse had seen it all before, but (let's face it) I hadn't, and (Frank, forgive me!) I rather enjoyed it.

Thursday, 1 July 1971

I am on my way to the Broadway Hotel, Letchworth, to address the Letchworth Women's Luncheon Club – in place of Godfrey Winn.

When Paddy Davis (from the Associated Speakers' office) telephoned them to offer them me instead of Godfrey Winn, the club secretary responded: 'I'm sure Mr Brandreth is very good, but, really, we do want Mr Winn.'

'I'm afraid you can't have Mr Winn. Sadly, Mr Winn is dead.'

'But we've booked Mr Winn.'

'He's died, I'm afraid. Of a heart attack. On his tennis court.'

'But we have a *contract* with Mr Winn.'

'Nevertheless,' persisted Paddy, 'he's dead.'

'You don't seem to understand. We *must* have Mr Winn. There's no alternative. *We've had the menus printed.'*

Saturday, 17 July 1971

Philip Hodson* has sent me a letter from an elderly friend of his. The letter is addressed to me and Philip wants me to take it seriously because he believes that the Pornography Commission is 'no joke, but potentially very damaging'. This is what the man says:

> I am one of those who have suffered from the suppression of pornographic information. What the prude calls pornography is an essential element in the mental and emotional diet of the growing young. Recently I saw my first 'blue' film. I found myself wishing I had seen it some fifty years earlier. You people on Lord Longford's team are so arrogant. To say that, because you yourself don't feel you want it, somebody else must be denied it, is a curiously perverse form of argument. I don't at the moment wish to visit America, therefore I demand that all transatlantic transport facilities must be removed. The argument is obviously absurd. Where is the harm in pornography? I can vouch for its value. It relieves tension and anxiety and takes away a life-long sense of shame. Can you show me the damage it does?

Well, can we?

Thursday, 22 July 1971

Frank Longford tells me that today is the Feast of St Mary Magdalene. He also tells me that one of his daughters (Antonia,† I think) has invented a new dinner-party game. The idea is that for the length of the soup course all the guests must converse in words of one syllable; with the next course they are allowed two, and so it goes on through the meal, until you get to the brandy and liqueurs by which time antidisestablishmentarianism is the one topic on everybody's lips.

---

* Philip Hodson (b.1946), friend of GB at Oxford, psychotherapist, journalist and broadcaster specialising in sex and relationships.

† Lady Antonia Fraser CBE (b.1932), biographer; married, first, to Hugh Fraser MP; second, to Harold Pinter, playwright.

The meeting itself was useless. No Cliff, which was a bore because I'd splashed out on a special silver-buckled belt for the occasion. Instead I sat next to a charming, rather pretty peeress called Lady Masham. She is confined to a wheelchair and told me to watch what the men did the moment the meeting came to an end. I did and every man jack of them – except for Lord Longford – darted for the door without offering to help get her up the stairs. She told me that coming to London by train she has to travel in the goods van, even on a first-class ticket. We should be campaigning about that, shouldn't we? Instead, the meeting deliberated for ninety minutes and concluded that *Catch-22*, if not pornographic, is certainly obscene.

Friday, 30 July 1971

Last night we went to the Mermaid Theatre for the first night of *The Old Boys* by William Trevor. As we arrived we greeted the diminutive Caryl Brahms (small in stature though broad of beam) and bought her a brandy. She was reviewing the play for the *Guardian* and was worrying about how she was going to get it written in time and then about how she was going to telephone it in to the paper. She is an odd creature. Michèle said, 'Where on earth does she come from?' She doesn't, that's the point. She's an ancient goblin who has turned up from nowhere, but she has her own peculiar genius. (Michèle says I must read *A Bullet in the Ballet* and *No Bed for Bacon*, the books she wrote with S. J. Simon.)[*]

The Old Boys is a fine play (we are going to publish it in our playscript series), but the evening was a sad one. Michael Redgrave, dear, great man, stumbled through his part, forgetting so many of his lines that the whole audience was on edge from start to finish. It was agony to watch. He was prompted through a hearing aid – ingenious as he was supposed to be playing an old boy, but disastrous because we heard the prompts before Sir Michael did. In the interval, William Trevor told us the hearing aid was vital: he couldn't have gone on at all without it. In the second act he had one strong moment, but at the curtain call you knew that he knew what we knew: that we'd been witnessing the end of a wonderful career. It was heart-breaking. His nerve has gone and the bottle has taken hold.

Reg Davis-Poynter was there – with his assistant . . . Or is she his mistress? We never see his wife: she stays down in Chichester. He was being paternal as usual, reproving me (as I reprove myself) for having got involved in the Longford

---

[*] Caryl Brahms (b. Doris Abrahams, 1901–82) wrote seven humorous novels with S. J. Simon and later collaborated extensively with Ned Sherrin.

porn probe. 'It's interesting,' I protest. 'It's wrong,' says Reg. 'You are a writer and a publisher. You should stand up for freedom of expression.'

Sunday, 8 August 1971

We are in Bristol at the end of our long weekend. The culinary highlight was dinner at Floyd's. The social highlight today's curious encounter at the Grand Spa Hotel. We came for lunch – we had the set meal – all went well – and then, as the coffee was being served, the waiter pressed his hand on my shoulder . . . I looked up and I recognised him at once – a boy I had been at Betteshanger with. 'You don't remember me, do you?' he said. 'Of course, I do, George. How are you? What are you doing here? I didn't notice you.' 'Of course you didn't. I'm your waiter.' 'Sit down!' I said. 'I can't sit down. I'm your waiter.'

Half an hour later we met him at the side of the hotel, by the staff entrance. He took us to his flat and told us his story. He had wanted to be an airline pilot. He had come to Bristol to train, but his eyesight wasn't good enough. Then his life changed. He went to the ballet and fell in love with one of the dancers. He wrote to her. He met her. Nothing happened because she was already married. He became obsessed. He followed her everywhere. He stood outside her house waiting to see her. He travelled round the country watching her every performance. When she went to South Africa, he went too. Eventually, because of her complaints, he withdrew. He came back to Bristol, alone. He found work as a waiter. He has no idea what the future holds.

We got to his tiny flat and, as we came through the door, our jaws dropped. From floor to ceiling, every inch of wall space – in the hall, in the bed-sitting room, in the bathroom – is covered in photographs of his ballerina – hundreds of photographs: everywhere you look, you see this beautiful girl. He, of course, looks like a scarecrow in a hand-me-down suit: horn-rimmed specs, beaky nose, round shoulders.

We ended the day at the Purdown Mental Hospital Open Day. When M was living in Bristol, she used to come and visit. The sun was shining and the gardens full of patients wandering about – old men and women, shuffling simpletons, who have lived here all their lives; children with Down's syndrome; young men and women muttering to themselves and twitching uncontrollably. We did our best to mix and mingle.

Tuesday, 24 August 1971

I have come to Copenhagen with the Earl of Longford, KG, PC, to reap the alien porn. This is Sin City, advertised as 'the most permissive place on earth' and we're here till Thursday. There are six of us from the Commission and an accompanying posse of at least two dozen newshounds. I have not known a charabanc outing like it. On the plane (the 4.50 p.m. from Heathrow) I sat next to Lord L. From take-off to landing he read the Bible (Book of Proverbs), and didn't lift his eyes from the page once. 'I am preparing myself for the ordeal we are going to have to face.'

We arrived early evening and, over dinner at the hotel, were briefed by a British embassy official on where to find Denmark's hottest sex clubs. 'You seem remarkably well informed,' said Frank, brow furrowed. 'We try to be of service,' said the diplomat, with a smile. After we'd eaten, Frank gave us each £10 spending money. 'That should be more than enough,' said our man from the Embassy. 'You can usually get live sex for around a fiver.' We decided to hunt in pairs and agreed to meet back at the hotel at midnight to compare notes.

I teamed up with Sue Pegden (21-year-old social psychologist and one of the Commission's official researchers) and Lord Longford went off with Dr Christine Saville (wise old bird and prison psychiatrist). Chaperoned by the *Daily Mirror* and the *News of the World*, Sue and I wandered somewhat sheepishly in and out of assorted sex shops and eventually ended up at the Private Club where (for £7) we had ringside seats. Stark naked hostesses offered us plastic beakers of beer and, frankly, anything else we wanted. The man from the *News of the World* couldn't resist a quick fumble and as a consequence one naked girl removed his spectacles and made them disappear about her person. When eventually they were returned, he was too self-conscious to wear them and so missed the rest of the performance. Sue and I missed quite a bit of it too. The press presence was inhibiting. During the most lurid moments, we simply grinned inanely at each other or gazed steadfastly at our knees.

When we got back to the hotel, Frank was looking positively wild-eyed. 'I feel exhausted, disgusted and degraded.' He had had a night to remember. The first club he had been to was 'small, crowded, no more than fifty in the audience'. When Frank arrived, he found a fat middle-aged man on stage with his trousers round his ankles being attended to by a naked dancer equipped with a battery-operated vibrator. To put it delicately, the girl was not getting much change from the fat man. Frank gazed on the scene aghast and then the penny dropped. The fat man was not part of the act: he was a visiting tourist. This was a club where audience participation was the order of the day. Hastily, Lord L. got to his feet and, dragging Dr Saville with him, made for the exit as discreetly as he could. Unfortunately, the manager caught sight of him and, taking him for a disappointed customer, chased after him, 'But, sir, don't go, you haven't seen any intercourse yet. The intercourse here is excellent. I assure you it's next on the programme.'

Frank fled into the street. 'I wanted to come straight home, but, in fairness to Christine, I felt we should give another club a chance. It was even worse than the first. We were placed in the front row and, almost as soon as we arrived, a naked girl approached me with a whip. She used the whip to caress the top of my head and then looped it round my neck. She vibrated me for seconds that seemed like minutes. The next thing I knew she was sitting on my neighbour's lap caressing him indescribably. I realised what was about to happen. I could sense whose lap she was going to be landing on next. I had to get out, and I did. Don't think me faint-hearted, Gyles. I had seen enough for science and more than enough for enjoyment.'

Wednesday, 25 August 1971

Copenhagen. A day of meetings. At the Ministry of Justice officials explain to us that Danish society now 'takes sex in its stride' and the essence of the law here is that anything goes, so long as you keep it out of the reach of children and don't impose it on the general public by littering the streets with it. They maintain that decriminalising porn has drastically reduced domestic consumption and coincided with a substantial drop in sex crimes.

This afternoon we met Jens Theander, 27, the man they call 'the pornographer royal'. For a moment, I think Lord L. thought he might have been by appointment to the King and Queen. He isn't. He is simply the biggest noise in the Danish porn trade, a big teddy bear of a man, twinkly and fun, difficult to resist. Lord L. took him in his arms and embraced him warmly. (Frank is marvellous the way he lives his philosophy of loving the sinner while hating the sin.) Jens told us his business would collapse if countries like Germany, Japan and Britain didn't maintain strict censorship. The bulk of his business is exporting. Having almost won us over to his side, he then undid all the good he'd done by giving us a flavour of his merchandise. It was appalling. 'Surely, you don't use children?' asked Frank, voicing the general disgust. 'Of course not, Sir Longford. It is against the law. These are midgets.'

The bestiality is gross, too. We were shown photographs of women sucking the penises of pigs, dogs and bulls. When I suggested that this was degrading for both the women and the animals, our host said, smiling, 'Not at all. The animals love it and the girls are all volunteers.' Peregrine Worsthorne stood gazing up at a gigantic poster of a naked young woman standing on a step-ladder in between the legs of a giraffe. '*Fellatio* with a *giraffe*? Now I've seen everything.'

Thursday, 26 August 1971

Last night we took in a blue movie. It could not have been more explicit. In the front row Lord L. and Peregrine Worsthorne perched on tubular chairs, eyes popping as they studied outsize genitalia thrusting to and fro on a scratchy screen. Quite soon, and quite loudly, they began to tell one another how desperately boring it was. 'Let's go,' said Perry. 'I can't,' said Frank, 'I walked out of the live show last night, I've got to sit this one out. You go first.' 'No, you're the leader,' hissed Perry. 'You must leave first.' In the end, a compromise was reached: we endured five minutes' more thrusting and then all left together.

Today Lord L. and I had lunch in the Tivoli Gardens with one of the press retinue. Frank pretends to be wary of the press, but, in truth, he can't get enough of them. This trip to Denmark has turned us all into ludicrous figures of fun, but he doesn't seem to mind. He loves the publicity. He told me a taxi driver had dropped him off the other day and said, 'I can never remember your other name. I know you're Lord Porn, of course, but your other name escapes me.'

He's even ready to admit that my favourite 'Longford story' may be true. In it, he is walking up Piccadilly and passes Hatchard's bookshop. He looks into the window for a moment and then, suddenly, storms inside demanding to see the manager. 'Where's my new book? It's only just out. Why isn't it on display?' 'I'm so sorry, Lord Longford,' mumbles the manager, 'I didn't know about it. What's it called?' '*Humility*, and you should have it in the window.'

He may be a vain old goat, but he's good company, patently sincere and his eccentricity is genuine. When we got up from lunch, he inadvertently put on my jacket, so I put on his. He really didn't notice. He walked back to the hotel wearing a jacket whose sleeves only reached his elbows.

Friday, 27 August 1971

Our BEA Trident brought us safely back to Heathrow at 6.50 last night. As soon as we reached the customs hall Lord L. accosted a young man in uniform and thrust a thick blue folder into his hands. 'I want you to examine these magazines. Carefully. You may have heard of me. I am the Earl of Longford. I was a member of the last Government. I have just returned from a fact-finding mission to Copenhagen . . .' The young man leafed through the sordid material, nodding appreciatively. At this point Lord L. realised he was not addressing a customs officer, but a courier for American Express. Eventually, Heathrow's Chief Customs Officer appeared and, having secured Frank's assurance that the magazines would remain in his 'personal control', allowed us back into the country.

It's been a funny few days. Frank is disappointed that the rest of us haven't been as horrified by what we have seen as he has been. He believes sex outside marriage is sinful and pornography is the devil's work. It's as simple as that. 'Sex should be something beautiful. What we've seen isn't beautiful. It's revolting. It is total degradation. Every instinct in me tells me that it ought not to be allowed.'

On the flight back I asked him, 'Are you sorry we came?'

'No, it has been necessary, dreadful but essential. Of course, I would rather have gone to Rome with Mary [Whitehouse].* You know she flew to Rome yesterday. She's gone to see the Pope. She wants to show him *The Little Red School Book*. I said to her, "Mary, you are off to Heaven, while I am going to Hell." That's where we've been, Gyles. You do realise that, don't you? I have taken you on an excursion to Hell. Will you ever forgive me?'

Later

Will Lord Longford ever forgive me? The press coverage of our trip is completely out of hand. 'LONGFORD PORN TEAM SPLIT' is the front-page lead in the *Daily Mirror* ('Britain's Biggest Daily Sale'). According to the *Mirror* (and most of the other papers too) 'a furious row' has blown up between Lord L. and 'the younger members of his team' – i.e. Sue Pegden and me. Sue is quoted as saying, 'Some of us feel that we can no longer accept Lord Longford's rigid attitude to pornography' – an unfortunate turn of phrase, but there you go. I'm quoted as saying that some of what we saw was an aphrodisiac; Sue is quoted as saying that some of it was 'beautiful'.

What the pressmen really wanted, of course, was to catch me and 'pretty Sue Pegden, 21' in each other's arms. At the hotel in Copenhagen, our bedrooms were on the same floor. The newspaper photographers took it in turn to hide in the corridor through the night in the hope of catching one or other of us indulging in a bit of corridor creeping. They were to be disappointed. But Fleet Street doesn't give up that easily and, lo, this Friday morning, who do we find adorning the front page of the *Sun*? My darling Michèle. There is a huge picture of her (she looks lovely) alongside the ludicrous headline: 'My Life with the Porno Rebel'.

Michèle Brown, girl in the life of Gyles Brandreth, rebel of Britain's 'Porn Squad', talked last night of their life together.

* Mary Whitehouse CBE (1910–2001), teacher-turned-'Clean Up TV' campaigner and articulate champion of traditional Christian values.

The interview is a complete farce and the quotes are all inaccurate (they've even got our ages wrong), but what can you do? I had breakfast with Nick Tomalin* (*Sunday Times*) at his house in Gloucester Crescent. He commiserated. He says the only thing to do when approached for an interview in such circumstances is to say, 'Yes, I'll talk to you if you quote my statement in full. This is my statement: "Bugger off!"'

Friday, 3 September 1971

There is clearly something in the air. I went to see Mary Kenny at the *Evening Standard* and found her wearing a see-through blouse with nothing underneath. Every time she moved in her swivel chair her breasts wobbled. She moved a lot. It was quite disconcerting. Lunch with Peter Meyer was disconcerting, too. I like him: he is a wood importer and translator of Feydeau farces. We are going to publish some of his translations in our playscript series and he keeps taking me to the Savile Club to discuss the finer details. He wines me and dines me and then, before we adjourn for coffee, he rests his hand on mine – just a little too long for comfort . . . I then mention Michèle, he then mentions his wife, and we move through to the drawing room where, invariably, Robert Robinson is holding court.

Did my ninth radio interview of the week tonight. (The porn charabanc outing has certainly proved profitable.) This was *Look Who's Talking*, the Nicholas Parsons 'chat show' for the BBC, and my fellow guest was the great Paul Raymond† – roguish smile, tanned leathery face, hair like silver candyfloss. I liked him. He claims his business isn't pornography: it's erotic entertainment. After the recording, he said, 'Shall we have a glass of champagne?' He drove me to the Whitehall Theatre (in his very comfortable Rolls-Royce – my first ride in a Rolls-Royce and I had Paul Raymond at the wheel!) and there, at the back of the stalls, champagne saucers in hand, we stood and watched the second half of his show, *Pajama Tops*. 'Look,' he said proudly, pointing at the leading lady, 'small titties. This is *family* entertainment.'

As I left, he gave me a copy of his magazine, *Men Only*. Michèle has been reading me choice extracts. This is Fiona Richmond's 'European Report' on one of her continental conquests:

* Nicholas Tomalin (1931–73), journalist, later killed in the Golan Heights while covering the Yom Kippur War.
† Paul Raymond (b. Geoffrey Quinn, 1925–2008), publisher of men's magazines and promoter of sex shows, with considerable property interests, principally in Soho.

And as for his sword: *terrifioso*! Pale-coloured pure Toledo steel. Maybe not the largest but certainly the straightest I had ever seen.

Thursday, 16 September 1971

The Out of Town Luncheon Club, Leicester. The ladies all wear hats and when I tell them that a hat really finishes off an outfit I can actually hear them purring.

Back to Bush House to do a World Service broadcast for a pink-cheeked, silver-haired producer named Francis Crowdy. Very fruity, very nice. I was there to talk about pornography (what else?) with George Melly, writer and jazz singer. Melly, looking like (if only marginally more alive than) Nikita Krushchev,* was very funny and kept teasing Crowdy, saying, 'Now it's *buggery* you want us to discuss, isn't it? "Buggery – the next ten years". I've got a lot to say on this.'

Francis reminded us that our target listener was 'a serious engineering student in Zagreb' and, when it came to the recording, of course, Melly behaved beautifully, and talked so reasonably, and in a wonderfully rich and mellow voice, chuckling delightfully at his own jokes. I really liked him. (I am going to get one of his records.)

This evening we went to the Kensington Odeon: *Sunday Bloody Sunday*, directed (beautifully) by John Schlesinger. About a young man (Murray Head) who has affairs with an older doctor (Peter Finch) and a young woman (Glenda Jackson). According to George Melly, Ian Bannen was cast in the Peter Finch part, but couldn't cope with the idea of kissing another man on screen and dropped out. (Interestingly, there was an uncomfortable feeling in the auditorium when the male kissing started. I felt it too – and I've seen *everything*. You can see things on your own and it's fine: it's when you are seeing it with others that you feel embarrassed.)

Monday, 20 September 1971

Tonight, at the Salisbury Arts Theatre, I attended the world premiere of *Lewis Carroll Through the Looking-Glass*, devised by me, directed by me, performed by Cyril Fletcher. Oh dear.

The idea is fine: we meet Charles Dodgson in his rooms at Christ Church, Oxford. He is an insomniac. In Act One, he is pottering about his room, preparing for bed and trying to get to sleep. He tells us about his world as he does so. In Act Two, he is in bed working at his Nyctograph (the device he invented for

---

* Krushchev, the former Soviet leader, had died the week before, on 11 September 1971. George Melly (1926–2007) was then film and TV critic for the *Observer*.

writing in the dark), falling asleep and dreaming – in his dreams he (and we) meet some of the amazing characters Lewis Carroll has created. The set is fine: it looks like an Oxford room. The costume is fine – especially the wig. The problem, let's face it, is the performance – or, rather, the performer.

Because I had been in Bristol in the morning I only got to the theatre in time to wish Cyril luck and take my place at the back of the stalls. At 7.15 p.m. the theatre was full – and expectant. The house lights dimmed and we all settled back, awaiting the strains of Liszt that I'd chosen to ease us back to Oxford in the 1860s . . . Instead, we got the oompapah of the March of the Gladiators (Cyril's 'signature' tune) and when the tabs should have gone up to reveal Lewis Carroll in his room at Christ Church, we got a furious rustling of the curtains followed by the appearance of Mr Fletcher, in dinner jacket and toupee, gurning gleefully, striding onto the stage and launching into twenty minutes of his vaudeville routine! Essentially, he had lost his nerve. He said to me afterwards, 'I thought I ought to warm them up.' In fact, he simply confused them.

Eventually he got round to the play – but it was a sorry affair. It was fairly obvious that he didn't believe in it – he kept *winking* at the audience! It was even more obvious that he didn't know any of the lines: all around the stage, onto assorted props and various bits of the scenery, he had pasted, pinned up, half-hidden the entire script. Pretending not to, he *read* virtually every word.

Friday, 1 October 1971

Meeting with Douglas Muggeridge, Controller Radio 1 and 2, at Broadcasting House, to discuss my future. Meeting with Cyril Fletcher to discuss his. (Actually, a good meeting: Cyril is going to learn the lines and make a fist of it in time for our opening at the Arts Theatre, Ipswich.) Meeting with Philip Hodson to discuss sex – and so earnestly. ('Erectile dysfunction, Gyles – we *must* talk about it more.') Meeting with George Gale to discuss pieces for *The Spectator*. He is now the editor and very friendly. He communicates by means of grunt and growl; he likes a liquid lunch. When I met him, at 5.45 p.m. in his office in Gower Street, he was just back from it. He went to sit down at his desk and, with some ceremony, sat down immediately alongside his empty chair. He collapsed straight onto the floor, but didn't appear to notice that he had done so. Patrick Cosgrave (deputy editor) carried on chatting as if nothing had happened.

Friday, 22 October 1971

Generous letter from Frank Longford. At the Porn Committee meetings now, the others look at me warily – but not Frank. He really does have a loving disposition. In Denmark, when there were no cameras present, he embraced one of the models we met, hugging her close to him, putting his arms right around her: she was stark naked, amply bosomed and with an extraordinary amount of pubic hair, but Frank seemed truly not to notice. In his letter, knowing of my 'deep interest in prisoners', he promises to copy me in on his 'very moving and remarkable correspondence' with Ian Brady.[*] 'It does *not* deal with pornography on which I fear he takes a view similar to that of John Mortimer, QC.'

After yesterday's triumph at the Washington Tea Club, County Durham (I am doing three or four of these ladies' groups a month now: at £26.77 a time, net, it adds up), I travelled down to Shipston-on-Stour for a less successful engagement. For £30.60 (net) I made my debut on *Any Questions?* I was okay, but I made a basic mistake: when I had nothing to say I said so! The others all had plenty to say on everything – they seemed so certain of their opinions. My problem is that I see several sides to every issue. The most memorable part of the evening was returning to London in the chauffeur-driven limousine belonging to Vic Feather, general secretary of the TUC. He sat in the back of the car, with a rug across his knees, a cigar in one hand and a glass in the other – and put the world to rights. I was much amused that the champion of the workers, no-nonsense Yorkshireman, shop steward, and leader of Britain's trade union movement, should travel in such style. All he needs is a peerage and then he'll be Lord Feather, a proper Restoration fop![†]

Monday, 20 December 1971

Godfrey Winn was the highest-paid journalist of his time. For more than a generation he was the star columnist in *Woman*, Britain's best-selling women's magazine. Now he is gone, who is to replace him? For months the search has been on. Who is there possibly who can step into the shoes of this lamented Fleet Street legend? Could it be? Yes it could. I had a meeting with the editor this morning and I've a feeling she's made up her mind. This could change my life.

---

[*] Ian Brady (b.1938) was convicted with his lover, Myra Hindley, of a series of child murders committed on Saddleworth Moor in Lancashire between 1963 and 1965. Lord Longford, a prison visitor over many years, took a special interest in both murderers.
[†] Victor Feather (1908–76) became Baron Feather of Bradford in 1974. He was general secretary of the TUC, 1969–73, and led the opposition to the Heath Government's Industrial Relations Act 1971.

PART THREE
Husband and Father

'The Man You'll Want to Know'

January – December 1972

Sunday, 9 January 1972

It is 8.00 a.m. on Sunday 9th January, 1972, the first Sunday after Epiphany. It is a cold morning, and dark. I am sitting at my desk in my study at 11 The Close, Muswell Avenue, N10. To the left of my typewriter stand my framed portraits of Lenin and Noël Coward, and my Mr Punch toby jug containing my pencils and pens and the large pair of scissors that belonged to Granny Addison. To my right is a plate of Marmite toast and a mug of tea.

Michèle is asleep in our bedroom next door. We had a late night, made later by discovering a *mouse* scuttling across the bedroom floor. It took an hour to corner the creature and another half to catch it. (Where are the Brandreth family Have-a-Heart animal traps when you need them?) Eventually, we secured the mouse between an upturned colander and a baking tray and, at around 3.00 a.m., I padded down to the front garden to release it to the world. Perhaps the mouse was a sign? Perhaps it's time to move on?

It is. And we are. That's the week's big news. On Monday we secured our first mortgage: £12,900 from the Guardian Building Society 'to assist you in defraying the purchase price of 170 Clarence Gate Gardens, London NW1'. The loan will cost us £91.40 a month for the next twenty years. We exchanged contracts on the flat on Wednesday morning. The deed is done. I am excited.

There was more news yesterday. I have been fired from Lord Longford's study group. My teasing (though accurate) account of our proceedings has appeared in the January issue of *Nova* and given offence.[*] The magazine's cover carries a photograph of a masked girl in suspenders, bullwhip in hand. The piece

---

[*] *Nova* was a ground-breaking magazine of its day, 1965–75. The then editor was Gillian Cooke, formerly of *Honey*. The caricatured model of Lord Longford was made by Roger Law, who, in the 1980s, with Peter Fluck, created the puppets for *Spitting Image*.

is illustrated with a sculpted model of Lord Longford with his head in the form of a phallus. My article is innocent enough (I reckon), but I can understand Lord L. taking a different view. He has written in the tone I would have expected: 'I am sorry that it should have ended in this way . . . I wish you all success and happiness in other fields.' Yesterday's post brought a letter from Malcolm Muggeridge that was less obliging: 'The ethical implications of what you have done, I leave to your conscience . . . May I add, on a personal note, that when you first came to see me as the editor of an undergraduate journal I formed a high opinion of your gifts and qualities. Indeed, on the strength of this impression, I recommended you in various quarters. It therefore saddened me to see your undoubted talent put to so poor a purpose as this very trivial, and I fear rather squalid, *Nova* piece.'

I have replied to both letters – carefully: standing my ground on the content of the piece, but apologising, sincerely, for any offence given. The truth is, I'm glad to be free of the Committee, but I *do* have regrets. I don't like upsetting people. And I'll miss Cliff!

This morning we're off to St Marylebone Parish Church for the christening of Ginny and Alan's baby: Catherine Emma. First a bath and another slice of Marmite toast.

Saturday, 22 January 1972

This is an historic day. The Prime Minister, Edward Heath, has signed the Treaty of Brussels. After a decade of difficult negotiations, Britain, Ireland, Denmark and Norway have now joined the European Economic Community, enlarging it from six nations to ten. The Common Market is now larger than the United States of America and accounts for more than forty per cent of world trade.

Elsewhere, things don't look so good. Ulster is in turmoil. Bangladesh is in crisis. In Rhodesia, Ian Smith has arrested the former Prime Minister, Garfield Todd. And where am I on this momentous day? As it happens, on the train to Cheltenham. I am on my way to the Everyman Theatre to see Cyril Fletcher in *Mother Goose*.

Friday, 28 January 1972

Today we left 11 The Close and moved to 170 Clarence Gate Gardens, London NW1. I love the address. I love the flat. We are on the lower ground floor: the kitchen opens onto a back yard that leads to Siddons Lane – named after Mrs Siddons, who lived nearby. In the yard we have our own shed and from the shed you can see the Abbey National building – set on the site of 221b Baker Street. Yes, this is the place to be. Edgar Wallace lived around the corner. So did Frank

Richards – and George and Weedon Grossmith, authors of Pa's favourite book, *The Diary of a Nobody*. According to Mr Verian, the friendly Irish head porter, T. S. Eliot lived in this block – possibly in this very flat!

It all bodes well and it all looks good. It's a Victorian block so the ceilings are high and there is period cornice work, etc. The wooden parquet floor gleams. We have three big rooms at the front: our drawing room, bedroom and study and, on the other side of the long corridor, a loo, bathroom, a bedroom, the dining room and kitchen – and the kitchen is big enough to eat in. We are going to be happy here.

Friday, 4 February 1972

Interesting letter from Dr Schindler, the Viennese psychoanalyst who lived next door to us at Portman Mansions. He has read my *Nova* piece and sent me his lecture on 'Eros and Thanatos, Constructive and Destructive phenomena of art in the service of escape'. Plato tells us that 'love is a longing to belong to each other mutually' and Freud teaches that love is nostalgia (*Heimweh*) – meaning a longing for home, essentially the warmth and beauty of the mother's womb. The essence of Dr Schindler's message seems to be: the properly erotic (sensual beauty, the nude in art) can offer comfort and escape, while the pornographic (harsh, crude, depersonalised) does damage. He wants to give us supper to tell us more. I like him, but his accent makes him so difficult to understand. (Of course, that won't bother his patients. They do all the talking.)

Second lunch with Wilbur Stark, film producer.* He thinks I should be writing scripts for him. We met in a hotel opposite 25 Welbeck Street. After lunch, he invited me to join him for his afternoon casting session. He is looking for girls for *Looking for Love*. They need to be versatile as they are expected to play two or three different characters in the same film. 'We give them wigs to disguise them – pubic wigs. The audience isn't looking at their faces.'

Saturday, 5 February 1972

Last night, supper at the Parioli and then *A New Leaf*, a wonderful film written by, directed by and starring Elaine May. Utterly enchanting. Walter Matthau brilliant. Amusing as I find Mr Stark, *this* is the kind of movie I want to make. Tonight we are going to see Jane Fonda in *Klute* at the Cinecenta and, before that, it's a matinee at the Globe: David Storey's play about a northern rugby club, *The Changing Room*. There is male nudity. At the early performances, apparently,

---

* Wilbur Stark (1912–95), American-born film producer, director, writer, whose credits included *Vampire Circus*, *The Love Box* and *The Stud*. Father of the actress, Koo Stark.

there was anxiety on stage. When the actors started to take off their kit, from out front came repeated sharp, clicking sounds, as though rifles were being cocked in the circle and the back of the stalls. The stage manager was sent to investigate. It turned out the noise was the sound of binoculars hitting spectacles all around the auditorium. Noël Coward went to see the play and was bitterly disappointed: 'I don't need to spend £3.50 just to see three acorns and a chipolata.'

Did I report that Michèle has passed her driving test at the first attempt? If I didn't, I should.

Wednesday, 16 February 1972

It's Ash Wednesday and the lights are going out all over the land – literally. The miners' pay dispute means a shortage of coal; a shortage of coal means a lack of electricity. Today we are getting nine hours of blackout and, apparently, there's more and worse to come.

That said, the trains were running so I made my way to Petts Wood to offer the Bromley Ladies' Luncheon Club 'America & Russia – an entertaining romp across two continents'. They appeared amused. *I'm* amused because today's post includes a funny letter from our new friend, Monja Danischewsky.* He is pleased that I'm enjoying his autobiography, *White Russian, Red Face*:

> Who knows – I might join Agatha Christie and Harold Nicolson as another author you're never not reading. By the way, the use of the double negative is Hungarian . . . My partner, Henry Cornelius, worked for Alexander Korda as a cutter, and he once angered Alex by coming into his office without knocking. 'Please don't come in,' Alex said, 'until I don't tell you not to don't come. Now go.'

Wednesday, 8 March 1972

My 24th birthday and my birthday present has to be the finished copies of my first book. It looks good; it feels good; it *smells* good. Yes, I have opened it and breathed in the smell of the pages – and I've removed the dust jacket to run my fingers down the spine. I am very happy to have it and happy to have done it and only sorry that it isn't better done – better *written* I mean, better thought through. And, if I'm honest, while I'm excited and delighted, there is also a sense of anticlimax: *Created in Captivity*, my first book, well, there you are. What now?

---

* Monja Danischewsky (1911–94), Russian-born producer and writer, whose films included *Whisky Galore!* and *Topkapi*. His daughter, Sophie, was a friend of GB at Bedales.

The day's gone well. Hair at Crimpers at 9.45 a.m. (They serve you coffee with your haircut: I like that.) Interview with the *Marylebone Mercury* at 11.30 a.m. (This was the first of the book interviews: Gordon Clough for *PM* next, then Richard Baker for *Start the Week*, then Alan Hargreaves for Thames TV *Today*.) Birthday lunch with the parents at 164 Chiltern Court.* (They are settling in well. Hughie Green† lives in the flat next door and lets brother Ben play with his train set. Actually, I don't believe he lets him *play* with it: I think he allows him to stand there admiring it while Hughie does the playing.) 3.00 p.m. train to Liverpool Lime Street. I am judging the Inter-Varsities Debating Contest and then speaking at the dinner. I like the idea of working on my birthday. I like the idea of spending the night in the city from which my forebears set out to make their fortunes.

Tuesday, 14 March 1972

Michèle's 25th birthday and, at twelve noon, the press preview and opening of my *Created in Captivity* prisoners' art exhibition at the Foyle's Gallery in Charing Cross Road. The exhibits are striking – paintings, drawings, sculptures I've gathered from prisons in the UK and around the world. John and Valerie Profumo came. He was dapper and charming: she was gracious and looked chic in a pale blue coat and matching helmet-style hat. (She wears very white, powdery make-up: it's almost as if she had dipped her face in a bag of flour.) It was very good of them to come. I had asked him to open the exhibition, but he said he couldn't: 'I avoid all publicity and will until the day I die.'

I'm pleased with the way the whole thing looks. Foyle's is impossible, as we know – the staff are paid nothing and don't speak English, the stock is vast but all over the place, to buy a book involves three separate and fairly incomprehensible transactions – but *this* has been well-organised. It's come about simply because I wrote to Christina Foyle suggesting the idea. She didn't reply, but a little man called Ben Perrick did. He took me to lunch at the Gay Hussar (he seems to dine there every day: they keep a personal bottle of sherry for him) and said the space was mine – and so it is, until April 1st.

After the opening, I was taken for a celebratory lunch in Greek Street by James Hale and Lyn Godser from Hodder. James (son of Lionel) is

---

* GB's father, having reorganised his finances by deferring his retirement until his 70th birthday in June 1980, was now renting a three-bedroomed flat in the block above Baker Street Underground station.

† Hughie Green (1920–97), TV host, best known for *Double Your Money* and *Opportunity Knocks*.

charming,* and full of bounce, but I'm not sure what my prospects with Hodder are. The book is getting really good reviews in all the right places (*Times*, *Telegraph*, etc.), but, of course, it isn't selling. Why would it? It's a book about prison art! I should have thought about that.

Monday, 27 March 1972

Jimmy Savile† is an odd one. I spent the evening with him, recording *Savile's Travels* from County Hall. It was like being with the Mad Hatter. He didn't stop talking, but none of it quite made sense. He's weird, but I think he means well. The same cannot be said for Sir Bernard Miles,‡ another oddball but, after today, rather less to my liking.

At three o'clock this afternoon we had the read-through of the script for the *son et lumière* we are presenting at Temple Newsam House on behalf of Leeds City Council. The recording is on Wednesday. Joy Masefield (who I pretend is some sort of cousin of the late Poet Laureate though she isn't) has written the script and it's rather good. The 'narrator' is a working man who sees the story unfold across a thousand years – he's peasant, farmhand, foot soldier, builder and, eventually, ends up as janitor in the Temple Newsam House of today. The people in Leeds were very anxious that we have a theatrical knight in our cast – they wanted a 'name' and a title. Given the yokel nature of our narrator, I thought Sir Bernard Miles was the perfect choice.

I called his agent. I booked him. I sent him the script. And today he turned up for the read-through. He was late and inscrutable. He arrived in a shabby fawn raincoat, wearing a hat and thick glasses. I greeted him effusively. He said not a word. M made him tea. He took his place in the drawing room, joining the circle of other actors waiting to start. He didn't greet them. When people said hello he barely grunted. He sat, slumped in his seat, still in his raincoat. By now, it was 3.30. I said, 'Shall we begin?'

At this point, Sir Bernard leant down towards his briefcase and pulled a large envelope from it. It was the script, apparently unopened. He peered at it. 'Is this it?' he muttered. He flicked through the pages. 'You speak first, Sir Bernard,' I said, a little too brightly. 'Do I?' he growled. He turned to the opening page and pulled the script right up to his eyes. In a voice that was barely audible, he mumbled the words

* James Hale (1946–2003), publisher and literary agent, was GB's editor at Hodder & Stoughton and the son of the once-celebrated broadcaster and writer, Lionel Hale.
† Sir Jimmy Savile (b.1926), disc jockey, TV host and charity fund-raiser.
‡ Sir Bernard Miles (1907–91), later Baron Miles of Blackfriars, actor, producer, founder of the Mermaid Theatre.

on the page. The other poor actors had no idea what to do. Peter Clay and Peter Howell (bless them) played it for all it was worth, but the stronger they were the quieter Sir Bernard became. We struggled on for half an hour or more and then, suddenly, he lowered his script and looked at me. 'We need to speak,' he grunted.

The rest of the company broke for tea and Joy and I led Sir Bernard down the corridor to the study. At last the man was galvanised. 'I wanted to do this,' he announced, 'but I shouldn't have. The script's no good.' Poor bird-like Joy blanched and began to twitter nervously. 'It could be good, but have I got time to work on it? The man is a real man – a man of the soil, a man of the earth – he's seen war, he's known death. I could rewrite this, but have I got the time? And, of course, I'd need a fee.' He looked around the study and sniffed the air. 'I'd better be going.' He waved the script under our noses contemptuously. 'There's no point you going on with this. You'll have to change the recording date. You've got to get this right. I can work on it. I can't do it as it stands.' And that was that. He made no excuses. He simply left, without saying goodbye to anyone. Through the window we saw his feet trudging by.

He gave me his number: 248 3129. I'm going to call him first thing. We can't have him rewriting the script. He's a walking nightmare.

Later

All sorted. I spoke with Sir Bernard who told me he was already 'working away' at the script and would have it 'shipshape' in a week. I told him that, sadly, we would have to proceed without him. He told me I was a fool. 'Nevertheless . . .' I said. He put the phone down.

And here is the news. I have reshuffled the cast. Christopher Hancock is now the narrator, but Leeds City Council will not be disappointed. We have a 'name': Cyril Fletcher is playing the Prince Regent. We have a 'knight': Sir Michael Redgrave (lovely man) will make a cameo appearance as Lord Darnley. (Up yours, Sir Bernard!)

Tuesday, 9 May 1972

Rogation Day, according to my diary. (What is Rogation Day?)* The Paris long weekend has gone well. Anthony Palliser's exhibition was wonderful. He is a real artist – and a good friend. And a great story-teller. He gave a touching account of his father being in attendance when Sir Winston Churchill went to have lunch

---

* In the Christian Church, one of three special days for fasting and prayer leading up to Ascension Day.

with Somerset Maugham in the south of France. The two giants met and sat face to face across the luncheon table, rattling their spoons in their dishes, both completely gaga.

Last night we went to the Crazy Horse Saloon and the Lido in search of glamour and excitement – and left before ordering the ludicrously priced champagne. It was awkward to leave, but I'm glad we did. The shows had a certain soulless style and feathers galore, but no feeling, no fun, no *joie de vivre*. We compared them to our last major theatrical treat: Donald Sinden in *London Assurance* – it's the toast of the town because he is outrageous, hilarious, over-the-top but, somehow, completely human, completely real. Our other bit of Paris culture: *Tout Va Bien*, the new Jean-Luc Godard film, with Jane Fonda. Complete tosh.

Thursday, 25 May 1972

At the Hodder authors' gathering, at eleven in the morning, I stood in a corner of the room, drinking champagne with Robin Maugham.[*] I liked him at once. And he liked me. He was flattering and flirtatious and *louche* in an appropriately literary way. He spoke about his uncle – 'the monster' – and talked very freely about the goings-on among the boys (and masters) at his prep school. He talked deliberately about naked bodies and rough hands on pale skin – not, I think, to shock me, but possibly to test the ground. He says he wants to 'escape from the shadows' – from the shadow of his father, the former Lord Chancellor, from the shadow of 'shame' that being homosexual still involves – but I rather think he enjoys the feeling of still living his life in a sort of twilight zone. He told me he had just turned fifty-six, but he seemed older: his hands shook, he has a drinker's face. I was pleased to meet him: I felt I was being dipped into a more dangerous and exciting world.

Friday, 16 June 1972

Leeds. The Griffin Hotel. (Note to self: stay somewhere else next time. Anywhere else.)

The East Blows Cold, the Archway Productions *son et lumière* at Temple Newsam House, opened tonight. The truth is: it's a bit of a disaster. The one thing we got right is the title: it's blowing frigging cold up here! The building is dull; the lighting is unadventurous; the script is plodding; the performances are fine, but *we can't hear*

---

[*] Robin Maugham, 2nd Viscount Maugham (1916–81), author, best known for his first novel, *The Servant*; son of the celebrated lawyer, Frederic Maugham, and nephew of Somerset Maugham.

them! It isn't just the wind: we have a corrugated iron roof over the seating and the rumble of the rain makes it impossible to hear the soundtrack however high Colin[*] ratchets up the volume. The shows run until 16 September – but in Leeds in August you can expect ferocious weather. We can look forward to the regular clatter of hailstones on the roof, apparently.

The parents have driven up for the show, bless them. We are all going back together tomorrow. Joy seems to think it's fine. It's adequate, I suppose, but I'm disappointed.

Saturday, 15 July 1972

I couldn't bring myself to write about this yesterday. Now I think I can. Last night was probably the worst night of my professional life so far. It was horrible.

I had been badgering Dabber 'Mr Showbusiness' Davis[†] to get me a cabaret booking. He did – here, at the Clockhouse Hotel, Chideock, Dorset. 'They'll love you, Gyles – your sort of crowd.' No fee, but two nights at a beautiful hotel, all found. We came down by train yesterday morning, Dabber regaling me all the way with tales from his days working with Bob Monkhouse and Denis Goodwin. In Plymouth, we stopped off at the ITV station where I was interviewed for *Westward Diary* and stood on my head on air – 'a first for Westward', they told me. We came to the hotel. They showed us our bedrooms, chintzy and charming; they showed us the dining room and the tiny stage at one end of it where I was to perform. I was to be 'top of the bill', following on from a local act, a much-loved Chideock favourite known as 'Fred the Spoons'. He plays the spoons while singing Dorset folk songs.

To cut to the chase: I spent the evening in my room, with my stomach churning. I had prepared an 'act', but I had not performed it out loud before. At around 9.30 p.m. I went down to the dining room. Fred the Spoons was on – and wowing them. With each succeeding number they loved him more. And when he reached his finale – during which he played empty Coca-Cola bottles – they simply went wild. When he'd finished, he introduced me. I went on – in silence, to silence. Or rather, to the sound of cutlery on china and the murmur of conversation. The diners looked up at me briefly and then turned back to their plates and carried on

* Colin Sanders CBE (1947–98), inventor and entrepreneur, founder of Archway Productions with GB and Joy Masefield.

† Anthony 'Dabber' Davis (b.1927), variety agent and partner in Associated Speakers. He had cut his teeth working in the office of the comedy scriptwriters Bob Monkhouse and Denis Goodwin.

eating. My throat was dry, my heart was thumping. I stood on the tiny stage gazing out at the sea of heads bent over their dinners and began my act. To say that I 'died' would be an exaggeration since I made no impact whatsoever. The business of the dining room continued as though I was not there. I was terrible, of course – I lost my nerve, I lost my way, I gabbled my way through my material. When I got to the end I stood on my head – yes, I stood on my head on a tiny dais in the corner of this cramped and crowded dining room and NOBODY NOTICED. Waitresses passed in front of me, customers paid their bills and went on their way. I left the stage in silence.

I came off the stage and walked straight into the bar. Dabber was standing at the far end of it talking to the barman. He failed to look my way. He didn't even say goodnight.

I had a miserable night. I did not sleep. I simply went over the disaster again and again. And the only reason I am recording this now is because twenty-four hours have passed and tonight – well, *tonight*, I *triumphed*. Perhaps that's an exaggeration: tonight I survived, I even did quite well. It was down to Fred the Spoons. As he got to his finale and began playing the Coca-Cola bottles, one of them cracked. I was standing watching and I could see blood streaming from his fingers. I had heard that it was his birthday, so as he stopped mid-number to put down his broken bottles and examine his bleeding fingers, I leapt onto the dais and asked the audience to give him a cheer. I then led them in a rousing chorus of 'Happy Birthday!' and, on the crest of the wave of applause for Fred, launched into my act and swept on and on *and on* until I threw myself onto my head and, upside down, watched them clap and cheer.

I bowed and waved and walked off to find Dabber in the bar, waiting for me with an open bottle of champagne. That's showbusiness.

Tuesday, 18 July 1972

Reginald Maudling, the Home Secretary, has resigned, caught up in the Poulson bankruptcy and corruption scandal.* Gyles Brandreth, would-be Home Secretary, has had lunch with Barbie Buss, editor of *Woman* magazine, plus entourage, at The Ivy. They fêted me royally. I am their new 'star'. I'm getting £65 a week. I have to give up writing for anyone else – *Woman's Own, Daily Mail, Observer,* etc. I have to clear any radio and TV I do if the magazine's name is likely to be

---

* Reginald Maudling (1917–79), Conservative MP, Chancellor of the Exchequer and Home Secretary. He had been a non-executive director of one of the companies of John Poulson, an architect who routinely used bribery to secure local government contracts.

mentioned. They are taking it all very seriously. Glasses were raised: my fingers were crossed.

Tea with Barny. It was fine, but we are not friends in the way we were. Apart from Simon [Cadell], I don't see anyone from school any more.

Monday, 14 August 1972

Yesterday we had a very civilised lunch with Lady Dowding* at her home in Tunbridge Wells. She is a vegetarian and the food was really tasty – especially the avocado mousse. She has her own cook. As M said: we could all be vegetarians if we had our own cook.

Tonight we had a really uncivilised meal at the Savoy. We went to see Simon [Cadell] in *Lloyd George Knew My Father*. The play (by William Douglas-Home) is pretty flimsy, but Peggy Ashcroft and Ralph Richardson are strong and Simon and his now-girlfriend, Suzan Farmer, excellent as the juveniles. We booked a table in the Savoy Grill for 10.30 p.m. and arrived on time. It seems we outstayed our welcome. Dishes were being cleared while I was still on my main course; we were asked to choose our liqueurs mid-meal; we weren't offered a choice of desserts from the menu, just given a cursory glance of what was left on the trolley. By 11.40 p.m. they had removed the silver toothpick holder and replaced the silver ashtrays with saucers. By midnight, they were whisking tablecloths off the tables around us, lowering the lights and starting the hoovering. I asked our waiter to call the manager. He shouted at me from across the room, 'Get the manager yourself!' A nasty experience for which we were expected to pay £28.26. I am planning to cancel the cheque.†

Monday, 11 September 1972

We took Michael Redgrave to lunch at the Empress in Berkeley Street today. He arrived promptly and looked well: pink-cheeked and baby-faced. He walked in a little slowly, but he seemed fine. He said he was enjoying *A Voyage Round My Father*. He said if we come we mustn't tell him we are out front. It will make him too nervous. He had told the management that he would only do it if he could open in it without a press night. The audience arrived expecting to see Alec

---

* Muriel, Lady Dowding (1908–93), widow of Air Marshal Hugh Dowding, hero of the Battle of Britain, and founder of Beauty Without Cruelty, cosmetics created without animal-testing. Michèle had interviewed her on *Good Afternoon*, one of the new daytime television programmes she was then co-presenting.

† He did. The ensuing correspondence with the Savoy's solicitors continued until October.

Guinness and found Michael instead. He has a horror of first nights and openings now. 'My nerve has gone,' he said, smiling sweetly, 'and my memory isn't too good either. Let's not talk about *The Old Boys*.' We didn't. We talked about *The Go-Between* and *The Browning Version* and how he had hated the opening season at the National and his ambivalence towards Olivier and, then, all of a sudden, in the middle of the main course, his head fell forward. I thought he was going to collapse into his food. He looked up very slowly and his eyes were half-closed and the colour had drained from his face. He whispered, 'I am so sorry. I don't feel very well. This keeps happening.' I helped him to the street and found him a taxi. He had two-shilling pieces to give everyone as we passed. I put him into the cab and waved him on his way. He peered out of the window and waved back. He looked quite frightened.

Tuesday, 12 September 1972

My first weekly column appears in *Woman* today. I am on the front page: 'INTRODUCING GYLES BRANDRETH THE MAN YOU'LL WANT TO KNOW'. I come with '2 BIG TYPHOO TEABAGS – FREE' and 'HOW TO GET A NEW HAIRDO WITHOUT LEAVING HOME'. The introductory spread is impressive: a full-page photograph (a good one) beneath the headline: 'This is Gyles Brandreth. He's 24 years old. He's got a keen eye for all that's amusing or touching, lovable or deplorable. Modern as tomorrow he still has a lot of time for yesterday.'

My first piece is on 'The Most Romantic Person I Know' – a lady who has been confined to bed for nine years but still lives for romance. (*Woman* found her for me.) Next week I'm looking at modern ways to make a date.

Last night I took the overnight sleeper to Plymouth. I am here recording *Open House* at Westward, edited and presented by Angela Rippon. She is alarmingly fierce with everybody, except me. We do the programmes 'as live', but in the middle of one of my pieces today I 'dried'. I just came to a standstill. It was half-way through the recording. We had to stop the tape, roll back and start the *entire programme* all over again. She took it incredibly well.

Tonight I was going to watch TV, but I have seen enough of the Olympics.* Mark Spitz is amazing, but he leaves me cold. Olga Korbut is charming, but she reminds me of Kim, the girl I rescued from the waves in California – and that was then and this is now. So instead I'm going to the pictures, to see *Young Winston*.

* The US swimmer, Mark Spitz, and the USSR gymnast, Olga Korbut, had emerged as the stars of the Munich Olympic Games which had just ended.

Simon [Cadell] was up for it, and got so close, but his lopsided smile did for him, and it went to Simon Ward.

Tomorrow, more *Open House* then back to London. Pa, Hes and her girlfriend Su are coming round. Right now, I am sitting in my room at the Continental Hotel with *Woman* magazine's Evelyn Home for company. A reader writes: 'How can I tell whether my husband's behaviour is just antisocial or whether he is suffering from mental illness? He refuses to see a doctor but his appearance seems to have altered slightly; when we married I noticed he had a nervous tic. I am middle-aged with two children over ten.' Evelyn suggests the reader goes to see the doctor without him. Will that help?

Sunday, 17 September 1972

We went to lunch with Michael Redgrave at 35 Lower Belgrave Street. He's only recently moved, but he's very pleased with it. He has posters of past productions lining the walls and showed us all the boxes containing old programmes and press cuttings – all carefully sorted and filed by Joan Hirst, the invaluable secretary he inherited from Noël Coward. He welcomed us with his usual shy smile and seemed fine – until he was showing us around the upstairs and suddenly stumbled in the bedroom and had to sit at the top of the stairs, holding on to the banister. 'I don't know what is happening to me,' he said. He is obviously frightened. It is something more than the drink.

Brian Desmond Hurst made up the party. He is an Irish film director, friend of Robin Maugham, full of good stories. He and I kept the show going, while M and Michael looked on. Michael talks very affectionately of Rachel [Kempson] (Lady Redgrave), but we never see her. She is in the country when he is in town. The meal was served by a batty housekeeper who wore an outsize wig at a funny angle. It was a memorable occasion, but a bit like being in a Pirandello play.

We are just in from supper with Simon at Odin's – our new favourite restaurant. We love the paintings (wonderful paintings), we love the crisp white tablecloths and the big chairs with arms, I love the mushroom pâté *en brioche*. We all rounded off the meal with *crème de menthe frappé* and persuaded the waiter to let us have straws! Simon told us plenty of Ralph Richardson stories. During matinees, Sir Ralph manages to shave fifteen minutes off the performance playing time. Does he speak very fast? No, he simply cuts out great chunks of the play. 'I don't think anybody notices, do you, cocky?'

Monday, 18 September 1972

M and I went with Pa by train to Bournemouth and then on to Poole, to 50 Parkstone Road, to say goodbye to his family home. Auntie Helen died on 8th June and the house is going to be sold. All Pa said was, 'It's the end of an era.' He did not talk about Auntie Helen or his parents. He doesn't. Because they died around the time I was born (when *did* they die? 1950? 1952? I don't actually know). I have no sense of them at all. If I saw a picture of them, I wouldn't recognise them. My grandfather (was his name Henry? Yes) was a solicitor. Like Pa he had been a barrister (up in Liverpool), but he came south and became a solicitor because the living was more secure. (I say that: I have no idea. I know he was a solicitor, and senior partner with a firm in Bournemouth, but I have no idea what led him there.) My grandmother (I don't know her name: isn't that extraordinary?) was a housewife and a keen anti-vivisectionist. Auntie Helen, the spinster daughter who gave up her life to looking after her elderly parents and who I never saw without a cigarette in her hand, took on her mother's commitment to animal welfare. I think she was treasurer of the local RSPCA. I liked Auntie Helen, but I didn't really know her. I remember the tortoise she kept in the garden when I was a child and, last year, I had coffee with her at Bobby's [the department store in Bournemouth], but who she was (her hopes and fears) I couldn't tell you. She was quite small and spindly, with short grey hair and spectacles, and not so much shy as *restrained*, contained, quite formal. When we had coffee I could not believe how thin and elderly she had become. She died of cancer, having been blown over by a gust of wind in the street. She was 65.

We looked round the house. Everything had been packed up. We were the last visitors, so everything anyone wanted had already gone. I think Auntie Hope and family have taken the best pictures and pieces (I imagine Auntie Helen bequeathed them to them) – Pa didn't seem to want anything at all. He said at Chiltern Court there isn't room. We took the three remaining paintings (including one of Dr Brandreth, the Pill man, and one of Prince, my great-grandfather's Newfoundland dog, on the beach in North Wales) and the dining-room table. Auntie Helen simply kept it in a corner with a cloth over it: it's some wonderful Canadian wood and, with all eight leaves added, makes a table that can seat twenty-four. Pa remembered being made to dance on it as a child.

Tonight, on the box, there was a *Panorama* profile of Lord Longford. I featured.

Wednesday, 20 September 1972

Publication of the Longford Report. There's nothing in it – nothing of substance, really not. At 7.45 a.m. I was interviewed by Robert Robinson on *Today*. I was okay, but encapsulating what you want to say in three minutes is a lot more difficult than it sounds. And Mr Robinson does descend on one from such a height.

At their press conference I was knocked by Muggeridge (with lip-smacking relish) and Lord L. shook his head when my name was mentioned and said I was very young. I was out all day so I managed to avoid most of the press calls. I have agreed to go to Bristol in the morning to be interviewed by Jan Leeming for *Women Only*, Harlech TV. £15 fee + £7.60 for the train.

At 5.30 p.m. I went to Hanover Square for my first meeting as a member of the Advisory Council of BBC Radio London. I was flattered into this because the appointment is made by the Minister for Posts and Telecommunications and I thought it would look good on my CV. It seems it's a pretty pointless talking shop. The other members appear to be people who do nothing in their lives but go to meetings like this. Extraordinary.

Friday, 29 September 1972

It is Michaelmas Day and the Feast of St Michael and All Angels and I want to be writing my diary properly, but I can't because time is against me. I must do the draft of the *Woman* phobias piece today and tonight we are going to *A Voyage Round My Father* at the Haymarket. This means that my account of the 'encounters of the week' is going to have to wait. Chief among them: the gentle, pretty, slightly fey let's-speak-quite-softly Duchess of Kent at the NACRO reception on Monday night;* the almost-as-fey ballet dancer John Gilpin at Westward TV on Wednesday – he sat on a swivel stool and said, 'My legs have given up on me. I've got to start acting again, but people think of me as a dancer. The public will only accept you as one thing: change tack and it confuses them. If I can't get any work I'll just have to go somewhere and die!';† Anne Wood, editor of *Books for Your Children* (we travelled up from Plymouth together – she could get on your nerves, but I liked her: I liked her awareness of her own worth and the way she

---

* GB was actively involved in the National Association for the Care and Resettlement of Offenders and a friend of its then director, Jimmy Gordon; HRH The Duchess of Kent (b.1933), attended a reception for NACRO at Whitehall Palace on 25 September.
† John Gilpin (1930–83), leading dancer with the London Festival Ballet. He died of a heart attack in Monte Carlo six weeks after his second wedding.

knows it all!);* lunch yesterday with Jack de Manio – he drank and he drank and he drank: and he had already been drinking when we met. He was fruity and funny. He's deaf but denies it. He spent the whole of lunch berating the BBC, while ordering more wine at the Corporation's expense.

Thursday, *19 October 1972*

Dr Kissinger is holding peace talks in Paris and telling us that a settlement in Vietnam is within reach. Cyril Fletcher is recording *Alice Through the Looking-Glass* (the Brandreth version) at Thames TV. And GDB is on his way to Beaconsfield to give a lunch-time lecture, followed by another, in Bury St Edmunds, tonight. That's £50 today for speaking, plus the *Alice* fee, plus a flurry of cheques this morning, including £270 from *Woman*, £20 from Cyril for the Lewis Carroll show and £90 from Westward for *Open House*. Plus a jolly letter from Angela Rippon – which is a bit of a relief because yesterday morning, when we were recording the final show in the series, she was in one of her 'frightening' moods. The floor manager got the countdown wrong at the end of the programme and didn't give Angela enough time to do a proper sign-off. The moment we finished, face like thunder, she flung her clipboard across the studio at him and screamed that the end-of-series party was cancelled. We all went our several ways in silence.

Friday, *20 October 1972*

For one of my *Woman* pieces, I am having my fortune told, my personality tested, my bumps felt. Today, after lunch with Graeme Levin,† I made my way to 100 Marylebone High Street and climbed the stairs to meet a palmist who calls herself 'Estelle'. I rang the bell and waited. I rang again. The door opened, just a crack and slowly. Around the latch I suddenly saw a tiny, wizened, black hand. I stepped back and, as the door fell open, a monkey, in a little red jacket, swung into view. This was Estelle's 'assistant'. While she made tea, he leapt about the room, swinging from bookcase to table to sideboard. I didn't much like him and I wasn't impressed by Estelle's 'predictions' either – long life and happiness was what she promised, with the possibility of some heartache along the way.

I am much more impressed with the insights on offer from Jeanne Heal,

---

* Anne Wood CBE (b.1937), went on to become a television producer, creating, first, *Puzzle Party* with GB, and later, and more notably, *The Teletubbies* and *In the Night Garden*.

† The founder of *Games & Puzzles* magazine. GB was a consultant editor and regular contributor.

sometime TV presenter and producer, now leading graphologist. Anonymously, I sent her a page of my handwriting and I have just now opened her rather startling report:

> This huge and very individual writing is the expression of an independent and somewhat explosive personality. It shows the writer has a high IQ and considerable imagination, very good muscular coordination (a games player/dancer) and considerable aesthetic appreciation.
>
> There is a very strong sexual drive. This, in fact, dominates the handwriting.
>
> However although there is tremendous strain, and considerable demand for expression in the areas dealing with imagination and sex, these are regulated by a decidedly conventional attitude to daily life.

Let's take the muscular coordination and sex drive with a pinch of salt and focus on this. Here I do think Miss Heal is spot-on:

> He requires elbow room, and he wants prestige. Inclined to be egocentric, his attitude appears to be that if society does not suit him, he will change society. However, under the aggression he really dislikes friction, and is receptive, and far more sensitive and friendly than he allows acquaintances to realise. As a result, he tends to keep himself a little apart, avoids close friendships, and is definitely not a man for communal life. He has no need whatsoever for the support of a 'gang', because he has his own philosophy for life.

There are three pages of more of this. It's certainly one for the archives. Given that she's never met me, and doesn't know me from Adam, I'm impressed.

Thursday, 2 November 1972

Today is the official publication day of *Brandreth's Party Games*.[*] I love the cover design. I love the orange end-papers. I love the look and feel of the book.

This afternoon I went out to Enfield, to the Spear's Games factory, to see Mr Richard Spear. He is very old, very blind and very nice. He held my sample board for the *Alice in Wonderland* game right up to his eyes, so that the board actually touched his nose – and pronounced himself satisfied. He is a remarkable man: his office is completely uncluttered. He and the factory manager and the

---

[*] GB's second book and the first of four published by Geoffrey Strachan at Eyre Methuen. The others: *Brandreth's Bedroom Book*, 1973; *I Scream for Ice Cream: Pearls from the Pantomime*, 1974; *Yarooh! A Feast of Frank Richards*, 1976.

sales director, George Hanna, run this huge multi-million-pound business between them. They sell *Scrabble* and *Tell Me!* and all the rest all over the world – and it is just the three of them running the show. There are twelve of us on the Advisory Council for Radio London and all we do is talk. There are just three of them running Spear's Games and you will find their products in homes across the planet. And now, they are going to manufacture my game. I am very happy.[*]

This evening Mark Boxer[†] came to draw my 'caricature'. He is tall and smooth, friendly, comfortable in himself, comfortable with his place in the world – he is completely an 'insider' in the London of the seventies in a way in which I don't think I'll ever be. I met him first with Eve Arnold when he was editing the *Sunday Times* colour supplement. I remember him telling a joke about Christ on the cross – 'What a way to spend Easter!' Eve Arnold reproved him for telling the story in front of Ham and me, so he made it worse by giving a different punchline – something about Jesus having his legs crossed because he was desperate for the loo. It was shocking. I was shocked. I didn't like him then. But I liked him a lot today. He, more than anyone I know, represents the metropolitan man of our time.

He'd come to draw me because I'm being profiled in the *New Statesman* in a series called 'Figures of Our Time'. 'What's it going to say?' I wondered out loud. 'Nothing nice,' he replied. 'With these things, that's rather the point.'

Monday, 6 November 1972

Today, on behalf of the publishers, Hodder & Stoughton, disguised as Charles Schulz's creation Snoopy, I appeared at a press conference at the Playboy Club in Park Lane to launch Snoopy's first foray into fiction, *It Was a Dark and Stormy Night*. The costume is outstanding, hot to wear, but satisfying because it does look good. The hound's head is huge – so big I discovered I couldn't get into a London taxi wearing it. When I'm in the outfit, I see the world through a gauze in the dog's mouth.

Have I already explained the background to this? In case not, this is it in a nutshell. I sold my second book to Eyre Methuen, overlooking the fact that there was an option clause in my contract with Hodder obliging me to give Hodder

---

[*] For J. W. Spear & Sons GB also created *The Treasure Island Game* and *The Teddy Bear Games Box*. As well as originating and hosting the annual National Scrabble Championships, GB became a non-executive director of the company and remained involved until its acquisition by the American toy giant Mattel, in 1994.

[†] Mark Boxer (1931–88), first editor of the *Sunday Times Magazine*, later editor of the *Tatler*; as 'Marc', caricaturist and pocket cartoonist.

'first refusal' on whatever I came up with next. Robin Denniston [editorial director at Hodder] summoned me to his office and tore me off a strip. He told me that *Created in Captivity* would lose them money, but a Christmas stocking-filler like my *Party Games* book might not. What was I proposing to do about it? I asked him what Hodder's Christmas list looked like – and he mentioned the Snoopy novel. I said, 'I have an idea! Bring Snoopy over from America and send him on an author tour. I'll play Snoopy for you.' He said, 'You're on.' And I was. And I am. Today was the day of Snoopy's 'arrival'. At the press conference (hosted by Clement Freud, connoisseur of dog food and director of the Playboy Club) we pretended I'd just come in from the airport. It all went wonderfully well. Loads of press and no awkward questions. The only person who seemed discomfited was Clement Freud. He's an odd fellow: his smile is completely cold. There is an edge of sarcasm in everything he says. The photographers didn't want him in any of the pictures. 'Just Snoopy, if you don't mind, Mr Freud?' Even though I could only glimpse him through the gauze darkly, I could see that he was not amused.

Wednesday, 8 November 1972

It is ludicrous, but wonderful. Snoopy is a smash hit wherever we go. The coverage has been extraordinary – front-page pictures, TV News, the works. We are selling three hundred plus copies at every signing – the 'signature' is in fact a paw print. Whenever I'm near the public I stay in full costume: if I need to take off the head for a breather I disappear to a storeroom. At the Midland Hotel, where we stayed last night, they wouldn't let me into the French restaurant. 'Don't you serve dogs?' I demanded. 'It's not that, sir,' said the maitre d' smoothly. 'It's just that you're not wearing a tie.'

We watched the US election coverage on TV in my room: a landslide for Nixon – he secured 47 million votes to George McGovern's 29. Nixon is promising 'peace with honour' in Vietnam and launching a fresh bombing attack to 'coax' Hanoi towards a ceasefire. At home, Mr Heath is also set on draconian measures. Since the CBI and the TUC can't agree on a voluntary pay agreement, the Government is imposing a statutory wages and prices freeze – initially for three months, but it could be for longer.

Later

Holdsworth Hall and Kendal Milne, Manchester, this morning. A bus nearly drove onto the pavement at the sight of me prancing down the street. (No injuries.) Birmingham this afternoon. At Hudson's bookshop we bumped into Jilly

Cooper[*] who went wild with excitement, gurgling and purring: 'I love dogs. I love Snoopy. What a beautiful wet nose!' (We sold many more books than Miss Cooper, too.) Cardiff next, then Bournemouth and Southampton. It's a funny way to earn a living.

Saturday, 11 November 1972

The *New Statesman* profile could be worse. It's the usual guff, cobbled together from old cuttings. There is one sentence that stings: 'As a writer he was always repetitive (as a penologist he is rotten), but his *Woman* column is very dreary stuff indeed.' Too true for comfort, but as Noël Coward would say, 'Rise above it, dear boy, *rise above it!*' I shall. I have.

Lunch at the Verbanella, supper at the Campana, and in between a wonderful film about a race for the US Senate: *The Candidate* with Robert Redford.

Thursday, 16 November 1972

Another day, another luncheon club: more ladies in flowery flower-pot hats and glasses like Mrs Whitehouse. (Views like Mrs Whitehouse, too.) Today it's the East Lancs Ladies. I am on the train to Preston and reading a kind letter from Fanny Cradock:

> You may or may not know I am in fact a witch, hopefully a white one, but just occasionally my witchlike and 'insatiable curiosity' impels me to have a little private peek forward. This, my latest peek, tells me that for some time to come you will emulate that famous character who jumped on his horse and galloped away in all directions! Curiously enough I did exactly the same thing and long before anyone else arrived at the same conclusion I had decided that *my* alleged early promise was not going to justify itself. You will do the same thing at some future stage which will be a much sillier exercise than it was for me because, if I live long enough, I know I shall say I knew you were front-line material when I heard you delivering a speech standing on your head! Try everything that opportunity puts on your way. Enjoy it to the full and you will find none of it will be wasted and they will all come together in some form of outstanding success, which I would not want to know now and should not tell you if I did because it would damage the pattern.
>
> Now tell me I am a silly old bag and I shall not blame you – but remember.

[*] Jilly Cooper OBE (b.1937), columnist and author.

GB, Esther Rantzen and
Roy Hudd at the publication
party for *Discovering
Pantomime*, GB's eighth
book, November 1973

GB disguised as Snoopy, warming up the
crowd for Eric Thompson, the man behind
The Magic Roundabout (and Emma's dad),
14 April 1973

GB, children's author

GB, official European Monopoly champion, coming third in the World Monopoly Championship, New York, 23 November 1974

GB after breaking the world record for the longest ever after-dinner speech, 17 May 1976

Anna Gael, Viscount Weymouth, Doris Hare, Sheila Scott, Patricia Hayes, Juno Alexander, Andrew Lloyd Webber outside the London Palladium for the 'People for Europe' reception, 20 May 1975

GB and Bonnie Langford in the *Puzzle Party* Christmas Special, 1977

Kenneth Williams congratulating GB on his final attempt at the longest ever after-dinner speech, 4 April 1982

TV-am's second birthday, 1985. Above the Rat, David Frost, to the left of the Rat, Nick Owen, to the right of the Rat, Anne Diamond and GB

The *Countdown* final, October 1986. From left to right: GB, Bill Tidy, Carol Vorderman, Richard Whiteley, Kathy Hytner and the winner Harvey Freeman

Saving the Oxford Playhouse – the May Day gala, 1983: Dame Peggy Ashcroft,
Dame Flora Robson, Ronnie Barker and Dame Hilda Bracket

Sir John Gielgud celebrating his eightieth birthday, 13 April 1984: 'Gyles – you've
thought of everything'

Friends in jumpers . . . Simon Cadell

Christopher Biggins

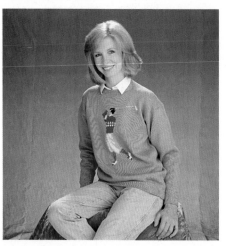

Jane Asher

Joanna Lumley

Martin Jarvis and Rosalind Ayres

Roddy Llewellyn

John Inman

Richard Briers

Anneka Rice

Floella Benjamin

and George Hostler, who designed them

At one point GB had more than 1,000

And the family wore them, too . . . Michèle, Oscar the cat, Benet, Aphra, GB and Saethryd

'Most kids model themselves on James Dean . . . our Kevin chose Gyles Brandreth!'

Cartoon by Tom Johnston, *Evening Standard*, 1986

Now We Are Sixty. Christopher Robin Milne, GB and the musical director, Stefan Bednarczyk, July 1986

Saturday, 25 November 1972

Last night, at the White Elephant on the River, I found myself washing my hands in the basin next to Peter Sellers. This morning I find myself on the 10.04 from St Pancras on my way to Leicester to spend a day dressed as Snoopy. Fee: £30. I am having to tread carefully as Snoopy nowadays. Charles Schulz got wind that we had launched Snoopy in England at the Playboy Club. As a born-again Christian, he did not approve. Now my proposed itinerary has to be approved by him personally in California in advance before I go anywhere.

I think Mr Schulz would at least approve of my reading matter this morning: *Woman* magazine. We are celebrating the Queen's silver wedding anniversary with a World Exclusive trumpeted on the front page: 'The Queen's Private Silver – for the first time in colour'. Yes, the first-ever colour photographs of the silver teapot given to the Queen on her wedding day by the people of Aberdeenshire. There's more: an eight-page pull-out Royal Anniversary Song Book, 'your keepsake that recalls 25 years of happiness'. And for Petula Clark and her baby: 'We design his layette – knitting patterns inside'. And my column? It's up against stiff competition – tucked away between two huge full-colour ads: 'How to keep him satisfied . . . American Long Grain Rice is *tasty* rice . . .' and 'She said: I'D LOVE A BABYCHAM' – but can I say something? It's not bad. The theme is 'Things I can't resist' and, for what it's worth, I think it reads pretty well.

Wednesday, 6 December 1972

Value Added Tax is being introduced in the UK on 1 April 1973. Last night, Mr Crumlish from Customs & Excise came to call. I liked his name and his helpful manner. In surprisingly straightforward terms, he explained to me how I have got to keep my books after 1 April and provide him with quarterly returns.

This morning, I began the day in the sub-basement of Broadcasting House with The Settlers. We were recording songs for my *Pop into Panto* radio programme. I liked Cindy [Kent, the lead singer], even though she wasn't wearing one of her trademark miniskirts. This afternoon, I took tea with Earl Grosvenor[*] at 53 Davies Street, Mayfair. When he turns 21 on 22 December he is going to inherit *millions*. He was pleasant enough, while giving nothing away. He left Harrow without a single O Level. Perhaps he thought he wouldn't need them! (Now, why didn't I ask him that? I've a feeling I was nauseatingly sycophantic.)

---

[*] Gerald Grosvenor, 6th Duke of Westminster KG (b.1951), now reckoned to be worth £7 billion, making him the wealthiest British-born UK citizen.

He looked utterly exhausted. The one weakness he admitted to was a fondness for fast cars – motorway madness in the middle of the night. I had no sense of being with someone 'special' – he has no plans to use his vast wealth to any particular 'purpose'.

This evening, the Mumtaz – our new 'favourite' restaurant, Indian food in the grand manner. Tomorrow, Burnley and the delights of the Nelson Dinner Club. Treat of the week: *Behind the Fridge* with Dudley Moore and Peter Cook at the Cambridge Theatre. I can see them doing a sketch in which Mr Crumlish from Customs & Excise calls on Earl Grosvenor, the richest young man in the land.

Saturday, 9 December 1972

Letter from Barbara Buss, editor of *Woman*:

> It is very sad for me to have to write this letter, but I am afraid I have decided to discontinue your column in *Woman*, the last one to appear in the March 17th 1973 issue of the magazine.

She says lots of nice things about my efforts and professionalism, but the nub of the matter is this: 'Your writing has not developed the qualities I feel necessary to promote a personality who, in the readers' eyes, has a voice that speaks for, and to them all.'

I am disappointed (I'll miss the money!), but I know she is right. Godfrey Winn *did* shake hands with the readers' hearts. I don't.

We're going off for a consolation lunch at Mumtaz. Chicken Mughlai here I come.

Sunday, 31 December 1972

The news out there: 10,000 killed in the Nicaraguan earthquake on Christmas Day; President Harry S. Truman is dead; President Richard M. Nixon has halted the bombing offensive against Hanoi. The news in here (David Schuchat's apartment on Connecticut Avenue, Washington DC): after a good week, ranging from the Library of Congress to *The Sunshine Boys* on Broadway, we are seeing the New Year in with champagne, caviare and beans on toast, while watching TV! Our maxim for 1973: 'Onward! Upward! The best is yet to be!'

If I May Say So, a Perfect Wedding
January – December 1973

Monday, 22 January 1973

I have had to abandon my scrapbooks. My cutting and pasting days are over. I am still keeping everything – letters, programmes, articles, clippings – but now all I have time to do is put them in a box for the relevant year. I am just putting 1972 away and I have come across this – *Cosmopolitan* magazine's list of 'Britain's most eligible bachelors' . . .

Gyles Brandreth, writer and panellist
David Broome, show jumper
Robert Carrier, gourmet
Tom Courtenay, actor
Georgie Fame, singer
Michael Fish, fashion designer
Benny Hill, comedian
John Hurt, actor
Simon Jenkins, journalist
Eddie Kulukundis, wealthy impresario
Ian McKellen, actor
Brian Patten, poet
Ned Sherrin, scriptwriter
Dave Cash, disc jockey
Jack Wild, actor
Oliver Reed, actor
Earl of Lichfield, photographer
Peter Wyngarde, actor
John Peel, disc jockey
John Bentley, multimillionaire tycoon
Karl Green, a Herman's Hermit

Cosmo asked us each to define what we'd look for in a wife. I specified a non-smoker who is 'kind and jokey'. Georgie Fame was more direct: 'Nice legs and big bristols'. Ditto Oliver Reed: 'She must have good knockers. I hate the bull-dyke Women's Lib type of bird.' Clearly, Ian McKellen is rather more of a gentleman: 'I'll know my ideal women when I meet her. An aristocrat without a title.'

I'm lunching with Irene [Josephy] at Rules in Maiden Lane. I'm seeing the accountants in Jermyn Street at 4.00 p.m. I'm meeting up with Michèle for tea at Fortnum's at 5.00 p.m. I am not entirely sure my darling fully appreciates that she is living with one of England's most eligible bachelors.

Wednesday, 24 January 1973

Lyndon Johnson has died (aged 64, of a heart attack, at home in Texas) and, in Paris, at the peace talks, they have agreed a ceasefire in Vietnam that looks set to be the real thing. I'm on a train bound for Yeovil, looking at my column in *Woman* (one of the final few) and thinking it isn't that bad. It's about the way to a man's heart and it was fun to do. I phoned up Percy Edwards[*] and spoke to his wife. She turned away from the telephone and *tweeted* a summons to her husband. He told me that when he first met his wife it was her hands – small, neat, delicate – that captured his heart. Anona Winn[†] told me that you win a man through his *ears*. Tell him the things he wants to hear about himself. 'Men are only interested in food when they are bored.' Mrs Shilling,[‡] our neighbour in Clarence Gate Gardens (who travels to Ascot in her Rolls with her hat at her side while her husband follows in the Ford Cortina behind), opted for *constancy*. My friend the Dean of St Paul's[§] said, 'Fastidiousness in a woman goes straight to my heart – fastidiousness in appearance and habits and values.' My favourite answer came from Jack Warner:[¶] 'I've been happily married for forty-three years and I know the way to a man's heart,' he said. 'But it's a secret and it's far too good to give away.'

Wednesday, 14 March 1973

M's 26th birthday. She isn't here. She has flown to Scotland for *High Street*, the new 'daytime' programme for housewives. I spent the afternoon in Oxford Street,

[*] Percy Edwards MBE (1908–96), ornithologist and animal impersonator.
[†] Anona Winn MBE (1904–94), Australian-born actress and broadcaster.
[‡] Gertrude Shilling (1910–99), notorious for the huge hats she wore to Ascot.
[§] The Very Rev. Martin Sullivan, New Zealander who was Dean of St Paul's, 1967–78.
[¶] Jack Warner OBE (1895–1981), actor best known for playing PC George Dixon in *The Blue Lamp*, 1949, and on TV in *Dixon of Dock Green*, 1955–76.

at Preview II, doing the first of the recordings for our new *son et lumière*: the story of Royal Greenwich. Today's guest star was Sir Alec Guinness,[*] who had said yes, then no, then yes again. He was courteous, but inscrutable – except that he made it clear he did not require my direction! I wanted him to end his big speech with a dying fall, but he just wouldn't. 'To do it that way is a little obvious, don't you think? I always try to end a sentence on an upward inflection. It leaves the listener expecting something more – keeps them on the edge of their seats, so to speak.'

I'm aiming for an early night, going to bed with Virginia Woolf. (The two-volume Quentin Bell biography of VW is my birthday present for M.) Up early so that I can give my all to the Buxton Ladies' Luncheon Club. I'm back at Euston at 6.54 p.m. We're meeting up in Flood Street at 7.30 p.m. for one of our Bridge evenings with Francis Crowdy. He is lovely: he mixes the very best gin and tonic, tells tales of Milos Forman, and teaches us Bridge in a really civilised way. 'There's many a man walking barefoot along the Embankment tonight because he failed to draw out all the trumps . . .'

Monday, 26 March 1973

It's just gone six o'clock. An hour ago, on the radio, I heard that Noël Coward has died. He was 73. I went out straightaway and bought a copy of the *Evening Standard*. It's the lead story. I am glad about that – he was a great man, a major playwright (whatever they say), an extraordinary performer (I can do *Noël Coward in Las Vegas* by heart) and, by every account, a really nice, generous human being. I try to follow his assorted maxims, especially 'Keep coming out of a different hole' and 'Read all the notices, but only remember the good ones'. He was very funny. 'One day I will retire from public life.' How will we know when that day has come? 'You may follow my coffin.'

We are going to *Il Trovatore* at the Coliseum in a minute. I'm really sorry it's not *Private Lives*.

Saturday, 14 April 1973

A roller-coaster week of glamour (Solihull, Coventry, Blackpool, Altrincham) came to a heady climax today in Leicester where Snoopy led the Knight Children's Book Promotion through the streets of Leicester.

This morning, at the offices of Brockhampton Press, I went in to the ladies' lavatories to change. (If I have a choice, I always choose the ladies': it's bound to be cleaner and there is usually more space.) Because it was a Saturday and the

---

[*] Sir Alec Guinness CH (1914–2000), English actor and film star.

offices were closed I assumed I would be alone. Unfortunately, one of the cubicles was occupied. I was just putting on Snoopy's gigantic head, when the cubicle opened and out popped a startled lady – she squawked loudly when she saw the six-foot dog and then shrieked in alarm when I yanked off my head to apologise. She was an unlikely sight herself: spindly, bespectacled and dressed in an Akela's uniform. Her name is Jane Osborn: she is the children's book editor here and, as the day wore on, we found we got on famously. She wants me to write a book for her. It seems I am to be a children's author.*

Friday, 4 May 1973

Last night we went to *Cage*, a dark (and ludicrous) play about imprisonment at the Open Space. I was reviewing it immediately afterwards for *Kaleidoscope* at 10.30 p.m. on Radio 4. It was a desultory experience, made memorable by Milton Shulman who was there to review it for the *Evening Standard*. The play involved a ghastly moment of 'audience participation'. One of the actors approached Shulman and put a long and penetrating question to him. Shulman looked up, shrugged his shoulders and replied: 'No speaka da English!'

I am writing this on the train coming back from Oxford where I have had contrasting meetings with two strong-willed beaky-nosed ladies of riper years. First, at the Randolph, with Joy Masefield. She is very irritating, limited in her vision and set in her ways. But also a fundamentally good soul. She knows I am ambitious for Archway Productions and accepts that she is holding us back because, for her, *son et lumière* is a hobby. She will bow out after Greenwich if that is what we want. That is what *I* want, but since the whole thing is her baby it's difficult. I want to get rid of her, but I lack the courage to do the deed.

My next meeting was with Elizabeth Sweeting, administrator, Oxford Playhouse. The Playhouse will be fifty in October. Would I like to produce an all-star Golden Gala to mark the occasion? I said yes. And – still more exciting – the Arts Council has decided that it has come to the end of the road with Frank Hauser and Meadow Players.† It's all very hush-hush – they don't know it yet –

---

* GB wrote *The Knight Book of Party Games* for Jane Osborn, followed by a further twenty Knight Books. This chance meeting changed his life: as a result of it, through the 1970s and 1980s GB was a prolific children's author, creating dozens of fun and games books for 7-to-11-year-olds and, later, stories for small children and fiction for young readers.

† Frank Hauser (b.1922), theatre director and founder of Meadow Players, the resident company at the Oxford Playhouse, 1957–73. Judi Dench, Leo McKern and Alan Badel were among those who appeared with the company.

future plans are still in the melting pot, etc., etc. – but, in the event that there is a gap at the Playhouse, might I be interested in the possibility of presenting a season of plays myself? My mind is now racing. I'd have to find the money, too – there's the rub. But it could be wonderful.

Wednesday, 9 May 1973

Yesterday we recorded Edward Woodward's contribution to our *son et lumière*. (He is playing General Wolfe.) Today Rachel Kempson* joined our line-up of leading ladies – now including Peggy Ashcroft, Claire Bloom and Rita Tushingham. Before the recording M and I took her to lunch at L'Escargot Bienvenu in Greek Street: we ate downstairs on the right, vichyssoise and turbot with hollandaise sauce – excellent. She is lovely: clearly Lynn is the apple of her eye (Lynn is sane, conventional, conservative) while Michael is devoted to Vanessa and Corin. Rachel worries that their devotion to their politics gets in the way of their duty to their art.

Tonight we saw Lynn on screen – she has a cameo in *Everything You Always Wanted to Know About Sex*, the very funny Woody Allen film. He is very funny. Still my favourite: 'I can't listen to that much Wagner. I start getting the urge to conquer Poland.'

Monday, 14 May 1973

Recorded a World Service pilot for Francis Crowdy at lunchtime and met Marghanita Laski.† I told her that *Little Boy Lost* had been one of my favourite books when I was a child and the compliment was clearly of no interest to her. I loved her coolness, her clarity of thought, the economy and precision with which she expressed herself. While I waffle, she speaks concisely and to the point. She knows what she wants to say. What I liked about my time with her was that, with her, I felt I raised my game. (Normally, when I admire someone, to some extent I *desire* them too. I didn't desire ML (!!) but I did admire her. Or, perhaps, desire was involved – and I desired her mind?)

This afternoon M was on *Good Afternoon* (Thames). This evening we are going to the Royal Ballet at the London Coliseum. We are having a ballet splurge: *Romeo and Juliet* tonight, *Anastasia* on Friday, a triple bill next Monday. (I share my birthday with Lynn Seymour and Lynn Redgrave. Different years, of course.)

---

* Rachel Kempson (1910–2003), actress, wife of Sir Michael Redgrave and mother of the actors Vanessa, Corin and Lynn Redgrave.
† Marghanita Laski (1915–88), novelist, essayist, broadcaster, atheist and active supporter of the Campaign for Nuclear Disarmament.

Wednesday, 23 May 1973

Auntie Hope has died. I did not know her well: she was a lady exactly like the ladies I meet at the Ladies' Luncheon Clubs I address. She did not approve of Michèle and me 'living in sin'. She wore a blue or purple rinse in her hair and her proudest moment was asking a question on *Gardeners' Question Time*. She was a fine gardener (with a handsome pergola) and I know Pa loved her very much. He will be very sad. He has now lost all his immediate family. He says he has eight years to go. He will die at 71. He knows it because when he was a boy he went to a fortune teller in Margate and she told him so. (I think he believes it. He claims that all her other prophecies came true.)

Ma and Pa did their best for Auntie Hope. She had cancer though nobody was allowed to tell her. Last year Ma and Pa went on a pilgrimage to Lourdes and, in the hope of a miracle cure, brought back some holy water for Auntie Hope from the shrine of Saint Bernadette. When they got back, they didn't know how to administer the holy water without giving the game away – then Pa had a bright idea. One day, when visiting Auntie Hope in Mill Hill, he used the water when he made her a cup of coffee. Nevertheless she died. A few days ago, he raised the matter with the vicar. 'There doesn't seem to have been a miracle,' said Pa, sadly. 'Of course not,' replied the vicar. 'You *boiled* the holy water. You boiled the goodness out of it.'

Thursday, 24 May 1973

On the back page of *The Times* today, in the Personal Columns, the announcement of the death of Auntie Hope. On the front page, the announcement of the resignation of Lord Lambton[*] and the headline: 'Call-girl dossier names two other ministers'.[†] We don't yet know who they are, but the story has all the makings of a juicy saga that's set to run and run. Lambton, Under-Secretary of State for Defence, looking louche behind dark glasses, admits using cannabis and call-girls, but denies a heroin addiction and any threat to national security. It seems the husband of one of his playmates took secret photographs of the minister *in flagrante* and tried to flog them to Fleet Street for £30,000. 'I have no excuses,' says Lambton, 'I behaved with credulous stupidity.' His statement is open, direct

---

[*] Antony Lambton (1922–2006), known by his courtesy title as son of the Earl of Durham, Conservative MP for Berwick-on-Tweed, 1951–73.
[†] In fact, no other ministers were named and the subsequent inquiry into the affair concluded that the security risks posed by Lambton's behaviour were 'negligible'.

and rather impressive: 'This is the sordid story,' he says. It certainly is – which is why we can't get enough of it!

The real scandal of the day seems to have been caused by my friend Peregrine Worsthorne, silver-haired smoothie and editor of the *Sunday Telegraph*, who when asked on *Nationwide* last night how he thought the nation would react to top people going with call-girls replied: 'I don't think they give a fuck.' The BBC has been apologising for the incident ever since.

Meanwhile, also on the front page: 'Nixon admissions fail to convince critics the whole story is out' – the Watergate saga is also set to run and run. And 'Mr Heath: "Excesses" of capitalism condemned.' The Prime Minister believes that greed is bad and we should turn our back on the unacceptable and unpleasant face of capitalism. What *is* the world coming to?

Re Lambton: lovely pocket cartoon by Marc: the front door of Toynbee Hall, with a notice saying 'Vacancy filled'.

News just in: Earl Jellicoe, Lord Privy Seal and Leader of the Lords, has also resigned.* And we're off to *The Cherry Orchard* at the National. Bah. Tonight's a night for watching the News. Chekhov will have nothing on this.

Friday, 1 June 1973

Son et lumière recording with Sir John Clements (who is playing John Flamsteed) and Sir John Gielgud (who is playing our narrator, 'Time') – both very friendly. When the photographer said, 'Look this way, Sir John,' John C. said 'Which Sir John do you mean?' while John G. fluted, 'He means me, I fear! I take a poor photograph.' It was intriguing to watch the way in which Clements's body language showed unspoken deference to Gielgud – and the way in which Gielgud accepted it. We are blessed to have actors of this calibre reading our script – they are making Joy's joyless and rather predictable prose sound wonderfully rich. As Simon Cadell says: 'It's the old story – fat actors saving a thin script.'

Friday, 8 June 1973

At 11.45 this morning, at St Marylebone Register Office, Marylebone Road, London NW1, Mr G. D. Brandreth and Miss M. K. K. Brown were married. Our

---

* It transpired that George, 2nd Earl Jellicoe KBE, DSO, MC (1918–2007), was caught up in the affair incidentally. Norma Levy, the prostitute associate of Lord Lambton, had connections with Jellicoe House in St Pancras and the coincidence of the name prompted the press to make inquiries about Earl Jellicoe. As he had also, but separately, had associations with call-girls he volunteered his resignation.

two witnesses were Simon Cadell, actor, and Michèle's friend, Veronica Hodges, secretary. It was, if I may say so, a perfect wedding.

We told no one – except Simon and Veronica, of course, and Philip Ingram who came to take the photographs. I didn't even make a note of it in my appointments diary. I simply circled the date. On 8 May I gave the required 'notice' and made a down-payment of £1. We paid the balance of £2 today. On Monday we went to Hampstead to get a ring and were somewhat thrown on entering the jeweller's shop to find we were being served by Donald Sinden's son, Mark. I don't think he will tell anyone, and if he does and the secret's out, so be it. We were going to telephone our parents from Rome tonight, but, in the end, we didn't. We were too tired. We will let them know in due course, but the point is: we didn't get married for them. We got married for *us*. And we got married today because it is exactly five years since we met. And we got married at St Marylebone because we live across the road – less than a minute away – and because this is where – and how – Ma and Pa got married on 15 March 1937. (They forgot to bring witnesses and, so the legend goes, went out into the street to find some.)

I wore my light grey suit with the dark grey stripe. M wore a black outfit with little pink flowers on it. Veronica wore a hat. (Well, it was a wedding – someone had to.) We were both nervous. I dropped the ring. The sun shone. We went on to The Empress for lunch. We sat right in the centre of the dining room. It was exactly right: champagne cocktails, salmon roulade, beef Wellington. (John Le Mesurier at the adjoining table.) Simon took us on to Heathrow. We caught the 17.35 to Rome. I am writing this in the Hotel Napoleon, Piazza Vittoria Emanuele. It is my first diary entry as a married man. Do I feel subtly different? I think the answer is 'yes'.

Sunday, 10 June 1973

This morning we walked to the Vatican. We saw the Pope. He was very small and up on his balcony, but he was there and we saw him. We feel our marriage has been blessed.

Tuesday, 10 July 1973

I am writing this over coffee and a sandwich in the first-floor lounge at the Charing Cross Hotel. I have just come from a meeting with Jeffrey Archer MP.[*]

---

[*] Jeffrey Archer, Lord Archer of Weston-super-Mare (b.1940), Conservative MP for Louth 1969–74; best-selling author from 1976; later, deputy chairman of the Conservative Party; imprisoned for perjury and perverting the course of justice, 2001–03.

I need to raise money for my Oxford Theatre Festival. I need £40,000. I have been going through *Who's Who* from A to Z looking for people who might like to invest. I thought Jeffrey could be one of them. We have a connection – Betteshanger. When Jeffrey was 22 and teaching PE at Dover College he came over to Betteshanger to help coach athletics. Mr Burton says that Jeffrey is the best athletics coach he has ever known.

Anyway, I wrote. Jeffrey replied. And the money may be mine! I saw him in his swish office at the top end of Whitehall. The building is called Arrow House, appropriately enough. He was full of beans and bounce – and a fair bit of bluster and bombast too. He has a picture of himself and the Beatles on the wall. Secretaries were stuffing envelopes – hundreds of them. 'I keep in touch with the constituency, Gyles. It's essential.' Clearly he expects to be Prime Minister one day. 'When you are ready to become an MP, Gyles, let me know. I'll get you sorted.' He saw me into the street and gave me all his telephone numbers and told me I could call him any time – 'day or night, night or day – *any time*. I never sleep.' He liked my ideas – he'd read my prospectus – and he says he will find the money for the festival if I can get Celia Johnson to appear. 'She's my favourite actress. She's our finest actress. She should be a Dame. I must speak to Ted [Heath] about that. Get Celia for me and you've got your money, Gyles.'*

Friday, 13 July 1973

Letter from Jeffrey in response to mine:

> At this stage I think it would be unwise to have 'Arrow Enterprises present . . .' as I would have no hesitation in falling out if I thought the plays or the casts were not of the right calibre, and at that point of time it would be embarrassing for us both.
>
> Cunning blighter – you have already put the price up to £45,000, so I am bringing it back down to £40,000.

And he's enclosed a 'To Whom It May Concern' letter indicating his general backing. I am grateful. I notice that his telegraphic address is 'Bullseye London SW1'.

It is one o'clock and I am about to watch my beautiful wife on ITV. She is a guest on *Cuckoo in the Nest* – programme recorded in Cardiff on the night before our wedding. (Jeffrey's wife, Mary, was also at St Anne's.)

---

* Dame Celia Johnson (1908–82), actress best remembered for her role in the film *Brief Encounter*, eventually received her DBE in 1981.

Tuesday, 17 July 1973

Our *son et lumière* opened in Greenwich last night. It runs until 22 September. It's fine. The essential problem is Joy: she is very literal: she won't let us light anything unless it was actually *there*, built and standing, at that point in the story which – since her stories are always written chronologically and start in the dark ages – means that we spend the first thirty minutes of the show gazing at a dimly-lit tree stump and a small bush. That said, our star voices sounded good and the roof stayed on. (No corrugated iron this year: tarpaulin. The wind threatened to yank it from its moorings, but didn't.) Assorted luminaries and cast members came: the Duke of Bedford, Sheridan Morley, Cyril [Fletcher], the beautiful Stacey Tendeter.* (She is very beautiful. Is she the most beautiful girl in the world today? Could be. She is represented by John Cadell who a) has supplied all our non-star cast, and b) when I had supper chez Cadell the other night, suggested that *Daphne Laureola* by James Bridie might be a good play for Celia Johnson. I have her address – thank you, *Who's Who* – and shall write to her tomorrow. Not today. Today I am going to Cardiff to record *Cuckoo in the Nest*.)

News from the world: President Nixon installed listening devices in the White House. If he *was* involved in the Watergate 'cover-up' it seems we shall find out.

Saturday, 25 August 1973

This time next week we shall be setting off for three weeks on the island of Elba. We have rented a one-room house on the beach, to read, relax, get away from it all. Despite useful telegraphic exchanges with His Excellency the Governor, our expedition to St Helena is not going to materialise in the near future. Boats only reach St Helena every six weeks. To get to Elba takes a matter of hours: we fly to Pisa and take the ferry.

Today, I am in Southampton, with Hughie Green, the Napoleon of entertainment, recording *Opportunity Knocks* to be broadcast this Monday night on ITV. Mr Green is an odd mix, managing to be both twinkly and terrifying at the same time. I am here to appear on the talent show – Britain's most popular TV programme, according to Mr Green – as 'sponsor' of one of this week's contestants: Jilly Fletcher, daughter of Cyril. Jilly is giving us her 'comedy-magic' – she can't win, she won't win, she knows that – but it's a big audience and a chance for her to be seen and (who knows?) 'discovered'. All I have to do is sit with Hughie watching Jilly and say how wonderful I think she is. I'm doing it because Cyril

---

* Stacey Tendeter (1949–2008), film actress, best known for her role in François Truffaut's 1971 film *Anne and Muriel*, later known as *Two English Girls*.

asked me. Because of Cyril, Hughie is being very friendly towards us, but towards everyone else his behaviour is quite alarming. When the cameras are on, he's all smiles – forced smiles, like Olivier as Archie Rice. The moment they're off, he looks like thunder. He doesn't raise his voice: he doesn't need to: he is in complete command. I get the impression that everyone here admires his skill (he does what he does flawlessly) but nobody really likes him and most people keep as far from him as possible because they are *petrified*. At all times, he appears physically isolated. He approaches people: nobody approaches him.

Tuesday, 2 October 1973

Lunch at the Gay Hussar with Anthony Blond, publisher, ex-New College man, conscientious objector, self-aware charmer (I liked him), knows everyone in literary London, great admirer of Irene [Josephy]. He has offered to pay me £5 a week for a year to write a novel for him. He says that he has started off a lot of young authors in this way. Will I be one of them?*

Saturday, 6 October 1973

The autumn sun shone this morning as I walked through the backstreets of Kensington and Chelsea. I felt pleasantly nostalgic: these were the Victorian streets I used to walk round, hour after hour, with Ben in his pushchair, when he was one or two and I was eleven or twelve. What I remember most vividly about those walks is that on them I thought intensely – passionately – about whoever I was in love with at the time – but now, incredibly, I can't remember who on earth it might have been!

I walked from South Ken tube, through Onslow Square, where Mr Cash [the art master from Bedales] drew my picture, past the dentist, along Sydney Street, across the King's Road and into Oakley Street – where we once lived. (I don't remember much about it, except that the hallway was always dark and there was a large oil painting on the landing: it was a sombre portrait of a man and I was always scared when I ran past it.) Today I was visiting 15 Oakley Street to have lunch with Richard Goolden.† He is old, small, bent, gnome-like and completely delightful. He was in the original Oxford Playhouse company in 1923 and, with John Moffatt

---

* Anthony Blond (1928–2008), London publisher from 1952, whose authors included Simon Raven. GB did not take up his offer and Michèle regards this meeting as one of several 'missed opportunities' in GB's life. 'In 1973, Gyles was busy running the National Scrabble Championships, founding the British Pantomime Association, dressing up as Snoopy, inventing games and puzzles, when he could have been writing his first novel . . .'
† Richard Goolden (1895–1981), actor.

(who was an Ugly Sister at the Playhouse with Tony Hancock in the 1940s), is going to be one of the compères for our Golden Gala. His great claim to fame, of course, is being Mole in *Wind in the Willows* in the original production in 1929 – and ever since. He is doing it again this Christmas. He *is* Mole. He chattered away merrily about Oxford in the twenties and A. A. Milne and life in the trenches during the First World War. He was in charge of the latrines! He scurried about the house – it's his family house, left to him by his mother – and, when I told him how much I liked our chicken soup, ran off to the kitchen and returned triumphantly waving the empty Swiss Knorr soup packet at me! Later he took me into the kitchen and showed me his collection of empty Swiss Knorr soup packets – hundreds of them. He does not throw anything away. He took me upstairs to the top room in the house – bare floorboards with old suitcases and cardboard boxes all over the place – and showed me the shelves where he has kept every bank statement and cheque book stub that he has had since he first opened a bank account in 1914!

Monday, 8 October 1973

Broadcasting history was made today and, happily, I was a small part of it. The BBC monopoly of the airwaves has ended and commercial radio has arrived on-shore in the UK for the first time. The London Broadcasting Company is the station that will provide a 24-hour news service for the capital. Because no one is sure whether or not listeners will cope with the commercials, I have been engaged to provide brainteasers for the all-important driving-home programme. The idea is that I set a puzzle just before each commercial break – and give the answer immediately the advertisement is over.

Tonight went well, a real sense of adventure at the beginning of a new enterprise. The studios are in Gough Square, opposite Dr Johnson's house, off Fleet Street. They haven't finished building them yet: there were no doors to the studio itself so, during the broadcast, a secretary stood in the corridor, by the open doorway, going 'Sshh' when anyone came by.

Wednesday, 17 October 1973

Yesterday, Blackpool. Tomorrow, Oswestry. Today, in our living room, Dame Flora Robson,[*] Jane Asher and Marius Goring[†] rehearsed the scene we are

---

[*] Dame Flora Robson (1902–84), English actress of Scottish descent who was in the original Oxford Playhouse company in 1923 and made her first film, *Catherine the Great*, in 1934.

[†] Marius Goring CBE (1912–98), English actor particularly associated with the film *The Red Shoes*, 1948, and the TV series *The Expert*, 1968–76.

going to be doing from *The Importance* at the Gala on Sunday. It was Dame Flora's idea and a wonderful one – she is so real as Miss Prism, it is very poignant. I cast Jane and Marius as Cecily and Dr Chasuble – they're perfect. It's a perfect scene with some of my favourite lines: 'The chapter on the Fall of the Rupee you may omit. It is somewhat too sensational.' Michèle did us salmon quiche and salad for lunch. Dame Flora talked about her window boxes. Jane talked about her cookery. Marius talked about Marius. Michèle said: 'Men – they're all the same!'

Monday, 22 October 1973

I am on the train to Tadworth to address the South Headlands Group of WIs. As I go, I can report on last night's Golden Gala. It was all I could have hoped for – and more. Valentine Dyall* risked outstaying his welcome and was a touch too self-referential ('The man in black is now the man in the red . . .'), but everyone else was spot-on, especially Celia Johnson (the audience *loved* her: Jeffrey is right), Janet Suzman† (v strong – and nice) and Fenella Fielding‡ (outrageous) who ended Act One by bursting through an eight-foot-high photograph of herself and singing a fabulous near-the-knuckle number with Sapphic references to Vita Sackville-West and Violet Trefusis that worked a treat.

Micheál MacLiammóir§ was completely extraordinary and unreal. I went over to collect him from his room in the Randolph and he treated me as though I'd been working for him all my life. 'Ah, dear boy, there you are. Now . . .' I helped him to tighten his truss. He looks like an ageing Pierrot on steroids. In broad daylight he wears full make-up, powdered face, mascara, lipstick – and an improbable wig that is too small for his domed head. For his fifteen-minute scene, he had insisted on bringing his own carpet with him from Dublin – he needed it, he said, so that he could find his way around the stage. He did a sequence from *The Importance of Being Oscar*: his evocation of Wilde is a wonder to behold.

---

* Valentine Dyall (1908–85), English character actor, best remembered as 'The Man in Black', the narrator of the BBC radio series, *Appointment with Fear*.

† Janet Suzman (b.1939), South African actress and director, married to the director Trevor Nunn, 1969–86.

‡ Fenella Fielding (b. Feldman, 1934, or possibly 1927), versatile British actress whose work includes Shakespeare and Ibsen, but best known for appearances in the *Carry On* and *Doctor* films of the 1960s.

§ Micheál MacLiammóir (b. Alfred Willmore, 1899–1978), English-born Irish actor, director, writer; with his partner, Hilton Edwards, he founded the Gate Theatre in Dublin in 1928.

Afterwards, in the wings, he was shaking with nervous energy, sweating profusely, but so happy that it had gone so well.

Act Two opened with John Gould at the piano. Nobody knew who he was but he threatened to steal the show. And he might have done had it not been for Sir John Gielgud . . . He had told me he would do a bit from *Richard II*. I told him he didn't need to come to the run-through, but he turned up at the beginning of the afternoon, in a chamois leather jacket with a Paisley handkerchief tied round his neck and sat in the third row of the stalls, gazing up at the stage expectantly, apparently spellbound. I offered him tea. 'No, no – I want to see my colleagues. That's why I've come. They're all so good. Even Marius is doing well.'

He closed the show with Richard II. I watched him do it twice: once in the run-through and then in the evening. Each time it was precisely the same – every inflection – and each time, at exactly the same moment, tears began to trickle down his cheeks.

Wednesday, 14 November 1973

A dilemma for the newspapers today – do we go for drama or romance? The *Daily Mail* offers a compromise. On the left-hand side of the front page, the headline: 'HEATH'S MOMENT OF TRUTH':

> Faced with the blackest situation since he took office, the Prime Minister yesterday dug in for a bitter economic and industrial siege.
>
> It was a day of drama and shocks. On top of the fuel crisis, and the miners' and power engineers' threat to the whole anti-inflationary policy, came the news of the most disastrous trade figures in our history.
>
> Ministers were left in a mood for belligerent defensive action. Even a winter general election on the issue 'Who rules the country – the unions or the Government?' is being discussed.

On the right-hand side we have a fabulous photograph by Norman Parkinson of Princess Anne and Captain Mark Phillips – 'On the morning of their wedding: the souvenir picture that spells out the happy days ahead.'

And inside the paper details of the 'minute-by-minute' TV coverage. On BBC:

7.30 a.m.	Fyfe Robertson with news, views, horoscopes.
8.00 a.m.	Alastair Burnet and Valerie Singleton discuss the day.
9.00 a.m.	Pete Murray on the royal route; Cliff Michelmore in Great Somerford, plus Bob Wellings.

11.00 a.m.   The Queen and Royal Family leave the Palace. Reporter, Michèle Brown.

And I've just been watching my girl outside Buckingham Palace. This is the royal event of the year and my wife is the reporter of the day – younger, prettier, more professional than all the rest! (And I'm not just saying that in case you try to take a sneak peek in here. I mean it.)

I have also now seen Princess Anne. She doesn't look quite as lovely as Norman Parkinson's pictures make her out to be, but I have to say, the dress is simple and striking, and she does look good.

Friday, 30 November 1973

The country is stumbling into darkness – no coal, no oil, no sign of when or how it's going to end – and yours truly is shambling back to London after thirty-six hours on the road touting my wares. Today it was Birmingham. I've been a guest on *Pebble Mill at One*, talking with Arthur Negus[*] (professional old darling) about my *Discovering Pantomime* book. Afterwards, in the green room, I had a jolly sandwich lunch with Mr and Mrs Charlie Williams. Charlie (the star guest on the show) must be Britain's first First Division black comedian.[†] He's huge – making a fortune, millions, I imagine. He's very charming – very Yorkshire, everyone's 'Me old flower' – very self-deprecating, apparently amazed by his own good fortune ('I'm just a poor booger from Barnsley') and he plays on his colour with almost every gag. 'Eh, if you don't shut up I'll move in next door' – he said that three times to various people this morning. He does all the 'Paki' and 'coon' jokes you get from Bernard Manning & Co., but because of his colour they are somehow acceptable. Also, he's *likeable*. You can't not warm to him.

Yesterday, I was not far from Williams country, in Bradford, for the *Yorkshire Post* Literary Luncheon – me, Denis Norden, Leslie Thomas, Jilly Cooper, and the entire Monty Python team. Too many, too much, we were still at it at 5.00 p.m.! The Pythons were the stars, but where Charlie Williams would have given the crowd an old-fashioned 'turn', their contribution was a bit rambling and ramshackle. They are friendly – except for Graham Chapman (oddity) and Terry

---

[*] Arthur Negus OBE (1903–85) became a popular broadcaster in his sixties after a lifetime in the antiques trade.
[†] Charlie Williams MBE (1927–2006) became famous because of the ITV series, *The Comedians*. He was mixed-race (his father came from Barbados) and, before turning to comedy in working men's clubs, was one of the country's first black professional footballers, playing for Doncaster Rovers.

Gilliam (loner). Michael Palin, Terry Jones, Eric Idle, normal and straightforward. I liked John Cleese: he passed a note along the table to me when I sat down. It said simply, 'Nice speech.'

Jilly Cooper didn't speak, but crinkled up her nose when she was introduced and shook her head like a Labrador puppy. Everybody loved her. Denis Norden was impeccable: laconic delivery, arched eyebrow and a very nice man. I spent a lot of time talking to Leslie Thomas. He has sold a million copies of *The Virgin Soldiers* in Britain alone. He talked much about himself and his achievements – but the audience was happy. They knew where they were with him. With the Pythons they weren't entirely sure. Eric Idle said, 'John [Cleese] is normally very dull but can be interesting on Mondays between 5.30 and 6.00 p.m. and on the first Thursday of every month.' The ladies of Bradford in their petalled cloche hats were not sure whether this was a joke or not.

Monday, 17 December 1973

News from the world: according to our beleaguered Chancellor of the Exchequer [Anthony Barber] the nation is facing 'the gravest situation by far since the end of the Second World War'. In an emergency Budget he is cutting public expenditure by hundreds of millions and because of the shortage of coal (thank you miners) and the price of oil (thank you Sheikh Yamani) electricity consumption for business is being reduced to three days a week. After Christmas, television is going to be obliged to shut down at 10.30 p.m. The lights are going out all over the land . . .

News from the home front: we are buying in candles and taking refuge with an assortment of mad ladies – e.g. Sunday night supper with our new friend, the solo aviatrix, Sheila Scott.[*] She flies around the world in her tiny aeroplane, breaks another amazing record (she has more than a hundred to her credit), and then sits alone in her flat at Marble Arch. Her best friend is her mascot 'Bucktooth' – and now us. Her achievement is colossal and her stories of flying over the Pole without sleep simply amazing (she does sleep – she catnaps, alone, at the controls, mid-air), but, essentially, she is barking mad. Her company is interesting, but exhausting. Ditto, Fenella Fielding. Just in from drinks with her in Connaught Place. She is lovely: that husky, purring voice is for real – but she is unreal. Fun, clever, funny (it's *Carry On Screaming* sprung to life), but ultimately wearing.

---

[*] Sheila Scott (1927–88). In 1971, as part of a 34,000-mile flight, 'the world and a half', she became the first person to fly over the North Pole in a light aircraft.

If I May Say So, a Perfect Wedding

Friday, 21 December 1973

I envy people who don't feel the need to hide their vices. At ten in the morning Jack de Manio takes me to a pub behind Broadcasting House. It is closed – except to him. He knocks on the door and is admitted. The landlord serves us whatever we want. There is no charge: we are the landlord's guests so it's quite within the law. Jack drinks shamelessly all day long. (It will kill him, of course, but he seems reconciled to that.) Paddy Campbell is completely unselfconscious about his drinking, too. And, at 12 noon today, I had coffee with Bob Monkhouse at his house in Loudon Road, St John's Wood. Before I left I asked to go to the bathroom. He said, 'Go downstairs – it's more fun.' And it was: the bathroom walls are covered with huge, amazing, larger-than-life full-colour photographs of naked girls with huge, amazing . . . Well, you get the drift. But what impressed me is the fact that Bob – at home, with wife and family – should be so at ease with himself and the world that he can have these incredibly sexy pictures on open display.

It's been a long day, but a good one.

8.30 a.m.	With David Jessel at LBC previewing the station's festive fare. Michèle and I are hosting (and making) the Christmas Day programme for LBC – three hours of it. (I like the idea of working on Christmas Day. I like the idea of working when others are not – getting ahead of the game.)
11.00 a.m.	Went on to record Paddy Campbell stuttering charmingly in Eaton Square.
12.00	Record Bob Monkhouse on Christmas cracker gags in St John's Wood.
3.00 p.m.	To Barnet to be met at the station by Barbara Cartland's white Rolls-Royce.* Miss Cartland is a joy: pale gold hair like spun candyfloss, white powdered face, jet-black eyelashes the size of tarantulas and a dress of flowing pink tulle. She did look like a very old version of the Sugar Plum Fairy – but what a pro. She greeted me at the front door and led me straight through to her drawing room, asking at once about William [Lewisham, her grandson] and whether I am taking the right vitamin pills. 'Have you tried my Brain Pills? And the right honey – the right honey is *so* important.' She sat herself down in what she called her 'interview chair' and I perched on a stool at her feet. As I pushed

* Dame Barbara Cartland (1901–2000), pioneer woman glider, journalist, prolific novelist, and champion of the St John Ambulance Brigade, romance and 'health foods'.

293

the microphone towards her, she leant over the arm of the chair and flicked a switch. Suddenly she was suffused in a warm glow of pink light. On the floor around her chair were a series of theatrical lamps tilted towards her. 'It's only radio, I'm afraid, Miss Cartland,' I said, awed. 'I know, my dear, but it's a performance nonetheless and I owe it to my public to always look my best.'

She talked a lot of twaddle – at great speed – all about the joys of virginity and the number of proposals she had had before she was twenty-one and the ten novels she has written this year (or was it since breakfast?) – but it flowed effortlessly (it'll barely need editing) and I am very grateful. I am grateful, too, for the pot of honey, the tubs of vitamins and the autographed first edition of *Men Are Wonderful* – wrapped in pink wrapping paper, signed in pink ink. She promised to name one of her heroes after me – 'Sir Gyles has a ring to it' – and told me I would go far. 'You have good manners. Good manners are absolutely essential to success. All the great men of history have had perfect manners. And I can tell you something else, young man. Good manners are a sure way to a gal's heart. Mark my words, courtesy conquers everything.'

Saturday, 29 December 1973

Yesterday we went to the matinee of *Peter Pan* at the London Coliseum. Outside of Shakespeare and *Uncle Vanya* and *The Importance*, it's probably my favourite play. Maggie Smith as Peter was good. Dave Allen, as Mr Darling and Captain Hook, was not. We couldn't hear him. The Coliseum is a vast space: he was lost in it. And he is an outstanding Irish raconteur and this is a piece that requires an outstanding English actor. I loved it all the same. When I was a child and used to see it every year at the Scala, when we got to the bit where Peter asks us to help save Tinkerbell, instead of clapping our hands, we lit matches and cigarette lighters. It was magical: all over the theatre tiny flickers of firelight. (My favourite *Peter Pan* story is the Hermione Gingold* one. She is seated in the fourth row of the stalls. Peter Pan calls out: 'Do you believe in fairies?' Gingold in a stage whisper: 'Believe in them, darling? I *know* most of them.')

Supper at home last night for M's parents and brother Simon, plus Ma and Pa, Polly, Jen, Peter, Sarah and Lizzie. All quite jolly. At 11.15 p.m. the last of my panto talks on Radio 4 ('The truth about Robinson Crusoe'). Today, at 5.00 p.m., we are going to see *Toad of Toad Hall* with Richard Goolden giving us his Mole. 'And next year,' asks Michèle, 'are there plans for us to move beyond your childhood?'

* Hermione Gingold (1897–1987), English actress known for her sharp-tongued, eccentric persona.

Dramatic Moments

January 1974 – December 1976

Monday, 14 January 1974

Oxford Theatre Festival update. Rita Tushingham has definitely agreed to play Saint Joan, but today she cancelled our meeting scheduled for 11.00 a.m. at the Holiday Inn, Heathrow. I am not unduly worried. She is a film star: these things we must accept.* I have written to Jonathan Miller asking him to direct it. I have written to Richard Briers asking him to play John Worthing in *The Importance of Being Earnest*, to Celia Johnson asking her to play Lady Kitty in *Daphne Laureola*, to Alan Badel asking him to play the title role in Dürrenmatt's *Romulus the Great*, to Alastair Sim asking him to consider a James Bridie revival (John Cadell's idea – play the Scottish card) and to Ian Carmichael asking him to consider a stage version of *Lord Arthur Savile's Crime*. If you don't ask you won't get.

Michèle began her six -week stint on *Monday Monday* on BBC1 this afternoon at 2.40. She triumphed. We celebrated at the Greek place on Baker Street. Taramasalata, lamb kebabs and a bottle of Othello. Most excellent.

Tuesday, 15 January 1974

Well, they can always say No – and some of them do. I have now written to Richard Chamberlain asking him if he'd like to do John Worthing in *The Importance* and Dunois in *Saint Joan*. (A little touch of Dr Kildare could be just what the box office needs.) I have also written to Derek Nimmo and Dora Bryan suggesting they might consider *A Spot of Bother*, the Vernon Sylvaine farce. I've written to Arthur Lowe suggesting he play Watney in that *and* Toby Belch in *Twelfth Night*. (Cyril could be Malvolio?)

We shall not be asking Frankie Howerd to essay his Feste – or anything else. (Actually, we might if we get desperate!) We went to the Palladium tonight to see

---

* Rita Tushingham (b.1940) enjoyed huge success with a series of films in the 1960s, including *A Taste of Honey*, *Girl with Green Eyes*, *The Knack* and *Doctor Zhivago*.

Babes in the Wood. F. Howerd sleep-walked through it. The audience wasn't much amused. M was positively angry. 'It's so lazy, so insulting to the audience.' We were in the circle: he barely looked up once.

Wednesday, 16 January 1974

I have written to Sir John Clements suggesting he play the Inquisitor in *Saint Joan* and Clive Champion-Cheney in Somerset Maugham's *The Circle*.

I am just in from an evening in Pimlico with Sara Morrison, vice chairman of the Conservative Party. I was there at the suggestion of William Waldegrave. It was a gathering of 'bright young people'. We sat on sofas, on the arms of chairs, on the thick pile carpet, while Mrs Morrison and William talked in hushed tones of the challenge to the nation of the three-day week and whispered to us that an election could come 'any minute now'. We must be ready and when the moment comes we must spread out across the land to give support in marginal seats where, apparently, all the so-called 'activists' are infirm and their associations moribund. It is through galvanising 'the youth vote' that we will win the election. It was exciting to be there, but I don't think I endeared myself by saying, repeatedly, 'This sounds wonderful, but what's the actual *plan*?'

Sunday, 20 January 1974

We are off to Joy Adamson's in a minute for an evening of Bridge. (I am *living* for the first gin and tonic.) I am a walking zombie. I began yesterday in Coventry with Simon [Cadell]. We saw the Belgrade's *Babes in the Wood* (gentle) and the Coventry Theatre's *Dick Whittington* with Dick Emery (robust!) – Mr Emery was very friendly afterwards, in his dressing gown in his dressing room, fruity, flirtatious and funny – and kindly obliged with a telephone interview from the stage door at 10.30 p.m. We came back from Coventry and went straight to LBC where I was doing the overnight shift: hosting *Nightline* from 10.00 p.m. to 6.00 a.m. – eight hours of talking, just me and my guests and, once they'd gone home, the listeners – a truly bizarre collection of the sad and the insomniac. One fellow (apparently a regular) called in from his bath: he's an elderly queen who calls himself 'Charles'; he is useful because he does fill the time quite entertainingly, but the trick is to get him off the line before he tells you precisely what he's doing with his rubber duck. The studio guests were Richard Briers (v engaging) and Max Wall – wholly eccentric: bent shoulders, wild eyes, lugubrious drawl. He ranged from the monosyllabic to the manic, for a while saying nothing in response to my questions, then suddenly pacing the studio with his trademark funny gait, announcing that he was a descendant of the Great Wall of China.

Tuesday, 22 January 1974

I have spoken – at length – with Sir John Clements. He is going to direct *Saint Joan*. I have agreed that he can have four weeks' rehearsal, a fee of £500 and £50 per week expenses. (I have *not* told him that Jeffrey has not yet confirmed the money – and won't until we have all the plays in place – but at this stage in the game I don't have much/any alternative.) Ian Carmichael isn't interested in *Lord Arthur Savile's Crime*, but has come up with his own suggestion: a Benn Levy farce called *Springtime for Henry*. On the phone his agent said, 'I haven't heard of you. Who are you?' I have sent her my CV and the Festival 'prospectus'. I imagine we'll get more of this.

Tonight we're going to the panto at the Players' [Theatre], under the arches at Charing Cross, as guests of Michael King. He is a very sweet man, an octoroon: his father was a half-Jamaican barrister, a 'character' around the Inns of Court in the 1930s, which is how Pa met him. (Or did Ma meet him first, when she was reading Law at London University? Why do I know none of this?) Michael is an odd, solitary figure, who is only properly happy at the Players', or with Ma and Pa – or with fat ladies. 'I have a weakness for the fuller figure,' he says, closing his eyes and tilting his head to one side.

Tuesday, 29 January 1974

Saint Joan is confirmed, starring Rita Tushingham, directed by John Clements. *Springtime for Henry* is confirmed, starring Ian Carmichael, directed by me. I have written to Michelle Dotrice asking her to play the girl. The challenge now is to clinch Celia Johnson. I am hopeful. I have spoken with Alastair Sim and he has promised to hail Miss Johnson when he sees her on his afternoon stroll – they are neighbours, apparently. He is the great Bridie buff and he is going to tell Miss Johnson that Edith Evans, who originally played the part, while excellent, was wholly miscast and that it is only 'dear Celia' who can realise the role as it should be realised! (The games we play.) I have written to Jeffrey with an update.

I am now on my way to lunch with Irene [Josephy] at La Bussola, then on to meet Una Hamilton-Wright at the Grosvenor Hotel, Victoria. She is the niece of Frank Richards, the creator of Billy Bunter and the most prolific published author in history. I am hoping to do a book about him.

Tuesday, 5 February 1974

A good day: £965.27 in royalties from the *Alice in Wonderland Game*. (The world mocks while I clean up.) As I came through the door from Cleethorpes

(£34.65), the telephone was ringing. A tinkly, distant voice (it might have been the Queen's) enquired: 'Is that Mr Brandreth? Celia Fleming here.' For a moment, I wondered who it was – then the penny dropped: it was Celia Johnson.* 'Yes, I'd love to do your Festival, Mr Brandreth. Oxford's just down the road. But I don't think *Daphne Laureola* really works any more, do you? Of course, Edith carried it off, but Edith can carry off anything, don't you find?' I am now sending her *The Circle* – even though I've already offered *The Circle* to Rachel Kempson and Lynn Redgrave. It's a tightrope.

Thursday, 7 February 1974

The general election has been called – and Jeffrey has been in touch to say that he can't think or talk about the Festival until after polling day – 28 February. This is to be the shortest election in forty years – Harold Wilson is accusing Mr Heath of 'making a run for it'. The Prime Minister is saying the miners are out to challenge our democratic way of life. 'Who runs Britain?' And who pays for the Oxford Theatre Festival?? I am off to address the Southsea Ladies (£44).

Tuesday, 26 February 1974

A fatuous day on the campaign trail. Was there any point to it? With Tim Rice† I was due to lead Sara Morrison's shock troops in an assault on Norwich and Cambridge universities. I got to Liverpool Street as agreed at 8.30 a.m.: Tim failed to show. I got to Cambridge and found the 'troops', a sorry bunch of chinless wonders. There was a minibus which ferried us here and there. We handed out some leaflets; we knocked on a few doors; we encountered a few students, who were either completely uninterested or positively hostile. At the University of East Anglia I attempted to say a few words on behalf of Dr Tom Stuttaford, the Conservative candidate. Nobody was listening.

Thursday, 28 February 1974

1. Finish writing *The Knight Book of Christmas Fun* – my third children's book.
2. Drinks with Rita Tushingham and her agent. She is charming, earnest, and *very* excited about playing Saint Joan. The deal is done. And Eric

---

* From 1935 until his death in 1971, she was married to the explorer and writer Peter Fleming, brother of Ian Fleming. They lived at Merrimoles House, Nettlebed, in Oxfordshire.
† Sir Tim Rice (b.1944), lyricist.

Thompson[*] is now set to direct *Springtime for Henry*. I plan to direct *The Circle*. It's Maugham's centenary. I have written to Hayley Mills asking her to play the girl. All we need now is Celia Johnson. And Jeffrey's money.

3. Am writing this at the parents', about to watch the election results on TV. We look set to win, but it's going to be a close thing.

Friday, 1 March 1974

A nail-biting night. Labour have 301 seats; we have 297. Mr Heath is not letting go. He has been to the Palace and told the Queen that he is hoping to form a coalition with the Liberals. Jeremy Thorpe, in his porkpie bookmaker's trilby, and suspect coat with the velvet collar, is jumping all over the place in a state of high excitement. He has 14 seats at his disposal and is key to the whole thing. If he does a deal, he will expect to be Home Secretary and will want some promise on electoral reform. (If we *had* managed to get out the student vote, perhaps none of this would have been necessary. The truth is: the contribution of Sara Morrison's 'young guard' was *nil*.)

Wednesday, 6 March 1974

Harold Wilson is Prime Minister. Heath couldn't clinch the deal. Wilson is set to govern without a majority in Parliament and was quite funny when asked what he had to say: 'All I can say is my prayers'. James Callaghan is Foreign Secretary, Denis Healey is Chancellor. The miners are cock-a-hoop. All their demands have been met and the strikes are over. 'Who governs Britain?' Not you, Ted.

And who pays for the Oxford Theatre Festival, now just four months away? I have written to Jeffrey Archer, congratulating him on his re-election and saying we must now meet. I am going to phone his secretary and fix a date. I have also had a wild idea: Micheál MacLiammóir as Lord Porteous in *The Circle*. I have written to him. And Margaret Leighton. On we go.

And I have started on the pantomime book. And I should report on our funny supper with Dabber and Paddy Davis out in Hayes. Paddy was a nurse and has a raft of outrageous tales to tell of her time on the Accident and Emergency admissions wards – principally stories of men arriving in the middle of the night with

---

[*] Eric Thompson (1929–82), actor and narrator and writer of the English scripts for the children's TV programme *The Magic Roundabout*, had recently become a sought-after theatre director. The father of Emma and Sophie Thompson, he died of a heart attack, aged 53.

unlikely objects trapped up their backside. Imagine Paddy's gentle Irish brogue: 'There was a milk bottle up the backside most nights – and not always with the neck-end in first!'

Tuesday, 19 March 1974

I had a meeting with Jeffrey Archer in his office at 27 Whitehall this morning. He was as bouncy as ever, but he wouldn't commit. He said he wasn't retreating, but I could see that he was. When I told him that I had secured Celia Johnson, he closed his eyes: 'Lovely actress, lovely actress. She's the best we have.' When he opened them, he jumped to his feet, reminded me that he'd increased his majority when all about were losing theirs and ushered me to the door. 'It's all very exciting. Keep me posted. Keep in touch. I'm your man.' But clearly he isn't. Something has changed. He denied it, but something's up. Perhaps he doesn't have the money after all.[*]

Consolation lunch with M at Mumtaz. Chicken Mughlai, my favourite.

Friday, 22 March 1974

Princess Anne has escaped being kidnapped in the Mall and I may have escaped the humiliation of having a theatre festival but no money with which to put it on. Laurie Evans (agent to all the greats: Olivier, Gielgud, Richardson, etc.) telephoned to say, 'Who are you?' It seems everyone wants Celia Johnson to appear in a play, but the only person she has said yes to is me. Ray Cooney wants to invest in her next play. Will I go and see him?[†]

I went this morning. He has cramped offices high up in a block of flats next to the Garrick Theatre on the Charing Cross Road. He is small and slight and amusing, sprite-like – famous, of course, for his farces, but now a West End producer with aspirations to go legit. He would love to present Miss Johnson and Ian Carmichael in the West End and likes the idea of staging Bernard Shaw's *Saint Joan* with Rita Tushingham. I will produce the plays in Oxford: he will take them into town. We will share the proceeds. We've a way to go yet, but this could be the answer to my prayers.

---

[*] He didn't. Unbeknown to GB at the time, on 11 March Archer had been issued with a High Court writ demanding repayment of a £172,000 loan with interest. Archer was on the brink of bankruptcy proceedings brought about by his investment in a company called Aquablast. The embarrassment caused him to step down as an MP later in the year.

[†] Ray Cooney OBE (b.1932), actor and playwright, author of *Run for Your Wife* and seventeen other farces.

Wednesday, 3 April 1974

The Sting has won seven Oscars. I loved it: I'm not surprised. Glenda Jackson gets an Oscar too, for *A Touch of Class*. Georges Pompidou has died. It's all happening. This morning I went to Ray Cooney's office and met his 'men of business': John Lesley, a rough diamond with a drinker's face, and Noel Davis, a camp actor with a beard, a mince and a very funny line in stories. Over lunch in the coffee place near the office, when I said how happy I was that Ray [Cooney] is funding the Festival, Noel Davis said, 'You know the two greatest lies in the world, don't you? "I won't come in your mouth" and "The cheque is in the post"!' The idea is that Noel is to be Ray's man on the Festival team, working alongside me and reporting back to Ray via John Lesley.

Friday, 5 April 1974

Ray Cooney has just signed – the deal is done – and now Celia Johnson is going wobbly! Having said No then Yes to *Daphne Laureola*, she's now said No again. She telephoned yesterday. 'Celia Fleming here.' She seemed to be calling from the garden – I could hear birds in the background. I pictured her with a trug over her arm and the gardening gloves and the secateurs in the hand that wasn't hold-ing the phone. 'I'm frightfully sorry, Mr Brandreth, but I don't think it'll do.'

My mouth was already dry. 'What won't do?'

'The play. It really won't do. I read it again last night. It's so dated. I'm sure Edith was marvellous, but Edith's Edith. It just won't do.'

'But—'

'I *am* sorry.' A lawnmower had started up. I could barely hear her. 'The trouble is no one's writing my kind of play any more. Why can't people write like Noël and Terry nowadays? Willie's the only one who comes anywhere near. I am so – *very* – sorry. Do read the play again. I'm sure you'll agree.'

She hung up. *At once* I telephoned William Douglas-Home. He has a bottom drawer stuffed with plays. He said he's got 'just the thing for Celia'. It's called *In the Red* – about the travails of a bank manager and his stockbroker-belt wife. I asked him to send it to her at Merrimoles directly.

Tuesday, 9 April 1974

Celia Johnson loves *In the Red*! I have written to John Clements asking him to play the bank manager.

More encouraging news. Sir Ralph Richardson is interested in the possibility of joining our season! Patrick Garland has found a play for him – 'a new play, a ver' strange play, deah boy, ver' curious.' It's about a missionary – Sir Ralph – and all the other characters are animals. Sir Ralph thinks Anna Massey would make a ver' clever giraffe. Heigh-ho cocky. Ray [Cooney] *loves* the idea of presenting Celia and Sir Ralph. On we go.

Thursday, 18 April 1974

Up to Moat Lodge, Nan Clark's Lane, NW7, to meet Ian Carmichael. He *is* Bertie Wooster.* Sunshine in the morning room: coffee, biscuits, happy chat about who else he wants in the play, sets, lighting, the challenges of 'high comedy' – 'not exactly farce, you see, old bean, so it can be a mite tricky, eh what?' – then he drove me in his 'Roller, don't-yer-know' to the Underground.

Lunch at Baker Street with Noel Davis. Crisis. John Clements said No to *The Bank Manager* – Wm Douglas-Home's new title for his play. (He always has success with plays containing the word 'The' in the title – *The Reluctant Debutante*, *The Secretary Bird*, etc.) At Celia's suggestion, I dropped it off on Michael Hordern – reminding him that I'd been in *Twelfth Night* at Bedales with his daughter, Joanna. This was a mistake. He *hated* my Malvolio. Having read the play, he telephoned Celia to tell her that not only was he not going to do the play, but on no account must she do it either. 'It's a dreadful play. Crude and obvious. Complete rubbish.' Celia telephoned me from the garden: 'I am so – *very* – sorry.'

Sunday, 28 April 1974

My second ludicrous weekend at Butlin's in Minehead playing Snoopy. The place is hateful – like a prisoner-of-war camp. In fact, I think it *was* a prisoner-of-war camp. The food is dire, the chalets made of cardboard, the water from the taps runs slow, tepid and light brown. The children are truly ghastly: they run up to Snoopy, shouting abuse, kicking the costume, yanking the tail. Never again.

Yesterday, before I came down to this hellhole, I met up with Ray Cooney first thing. *Springtime for Henry* is looking good: Ian Carmichael and Barbara Murray, both top notch. *Saint Joan* is looking classy: Rita Tushingham is a film star and perfect casting; John Standing as the Dauphin and James Villiers as Warwick, Noel Willman, Charles Lloyd Pack, Charles Dance – a fine cast. Our problem is the third play. We are dependent on Sir Ralph. He doesn't want to do *The Missionary*. 'I know Anna Massey would be the best giraffe since Johnnie G. did André Obey's *Noah* before the war, but I just can't see little Anna Calder-

---

* Ian Carmichael (b.1920) appeared in numerous films in the 1950s and 1960s, before the success of *The World of Wooster* on BBC TV.

Marshall as the leopard, can you?' We are now trying to tempt him with a play about Goya. There is a problem: it is a modern piece about the Spanish artist at the end of his life and when the great man goes blind the audience is invited to shut their eyes to fully share the sensation. 'Won't they miss the best of my performance?' enquires Sir Ralph, not unreasonably.

Peter Coe (the purveyor of Goya and celebrated as the original director of *Oliver!*) has come up with another idea: *The Trials of Oscar Wilde*, a courtroom drama based entirely on the original transcripts. Suggestion from Noel Davis: 'Celia can drag up and play Oscar.'

Wednesday, 5 June 1974

I am in Grimsby. I have had no sleep. Rather, I have had what sleep you get when you leave King's Cross at 1.15 in the morning and reach Grimsby at 5.50 a.m. I am to give my all (what little's left of it) to the Grimsby Luncheon Club at noon. Right now, over tea and biscuits, at the Humber Royal Hotel, I am going to try to catch up with the diary. I should have come up here last night. I didn't because Noel lured me into joining him for a night of consolation and alcohol at Macready's Club – with Jimmy Villiers, Ronnie Fraser and other inebriated thesps. We – Noel and I – have had a difficult few days, to put it mildly. Let me try to tell the whole story as succinctly as I can.

Less than a week ago, Rita Tushingham's agent called. 'I am afraid Miss Tushingham will have to pull out.' 'But she can't.' 'But she must – she's got a film to make in Israel.' 'But she can't – she's got a play to appear in in Oxford.' 'I am sorry. You'll have to release her. It's a big movie.' 'Saint Joan is a big part.' 'You are paying her £50 a week. The film is worth thousands. If need be, she'll buy her way out of the play – but I'm sure that won't be necessary.'

I didn't know what to say. I was so angry, so distressed. Noel scrawled offensive remarks all over her photograph in *Spotlight*. (The word 'cunt', actually.) 'We will never, ever, ever, *ever* use that cow again,' I bawled. 'Until we need her,' said Noel.

We reported the bad news to Ray – with M's suggestion for a replacement, not a star, but a fine actress: Frances de la Tour (client of Simon [Cadell]'s father, available, interested). 'Good God,' spluttered Ray. 'No, no, no. I'm not risking thousands putting on George Bernard Shaw's *Saint Joan* with Frances de la Number Three Tour. I want a name, a *canopy* name.' We trawled *Spotlight*. Eileen Atkins, not available. Diana Rigg, not available. Maggie Smith, not available. Anna Massey.

'We're looking for a martyr, not a giraffe.'

'She's good.'

'Not that good.'

Janet Suzman, not available. Susan Hampshire, not available. Jane Asher, not available. Billie Whitelaw . . . Billie Whitelaw! How about Billie Whitelaw?

I called Miss Whitelaw's agent. I called Miss Whitelaw. She wasn't sure. She was flattered, but uncertain. Wasn't she too old?[*] I told her that Sir John wanted her above all others. (Truth is I hadn't yet told Sir John about the bitch Tushingham's flight to Israel. I wanted to sort it first.) Anyway, she asked for time. She had been planning to use the summer to get her teeth fixed, but she was certainly interested. Could she sleep on it? In her sleep, she must have heard voices. They told her to say Yes. She called me with the good news on Saturday night. I called Sir John at breakfast-time on Sunday.

'Sir John, I have bad news and good news. The bad news is that we've lost Rita Tushingham. The good ne— '

'Get on a train at once,' he barked. 'At once. Bring *Spotlight*. We'll sort it out today.'

'But Sir John— '

'At once!'

I caught the ten o'clock train from Victoria. I reached Marine Parade at 11.30 a.m. I found the Clements flat: 4 Rufford Court – not spacious, musty, heavily hung with theatrical memorabilia. Sir John was in fighting form. He showed me his collection of swordsticks and ushered me onto the balcony overlooking the seafront. He left me there, alone, with his sweet, frail wife, who struggled, slowly and painfully, to tell me that she had been something of a star herself before she had had her stroke. 'I know,' I said stupidly. 'I loved *Genevieve*.' As I said it I remembered that *Genevieve* was Kay Kendall. This was Kay Hammond – *Blithe Spirit*. Sir John returned with goblets of gin and tonic and regaled me with the crisis that befell him when Danny Kaye pulled out of his promised appearance at Chichester. 'We did *Italian Straw Hat* instead – worked a treat.'

He would not let me break the news to him. 'Lunch first,' he insisted, 'then work.'

Lunch was served in a small alcove off the drawing room and brought in by an elderly servant in an improbable wig – was it the same lady who waits at table in the Redgrave household? She was summoned from the kitchen by means of an electric bell positioned discreetly by Miss Hammond's place at table. Unfortunately, while the bell made a dreadful racket all over the flat, the servant

---

[*] She turned 42 that week. Stage and film actress, particularly associated with Samuel Beckett, she had recently appeared in Alfred Hitchcock's film, *Frenzy*.

in the kitchen appeared not to hear it and Sir John had to go and fetch her between courses.

When coffee was served, I broke my good news. 'I've secured Billie Whitelaw.'

Sir John's jaw fell. 'But you can't have.'

'I have.'

'No, no, no. You haven't.' He was wild-eyed, incandescent.

'I have.'

'But you *cannot* have recast the title part without consulting the director. If you have, I resign.'

To cut to the chase, he did not resign. He would not budge on Billie Whitelaw – he knows her, he likes her, he respects her, but in a month of Sundays she cannot (in his view) play Saint Joan. I returned to London and, on Monday morning, broke the news to Miss Whitelaw's agent. She told me that, in her long career, she had never known anything like it and that she, personally, would see to it that I never, ever, worked in the theatre again. I was an 'utter disgrace' and if Miss Whitelaw were now to have a breakdown – which was entirely possible – the responsibility would be mine. I did not have the courage to telephone Miss Whitelaw, but I wrote her an abject (and heartfelt) letter of apology.

We have now cast Julia Foster – Sir John's idea. Ray is happy. She is a film star (well, she was in *Alfie*) and, more to the point, she has had a West End triumph in *Lulu* so she counts as a 'canopy name'.

Saturday, 8 June 1974

Our first wedding anniversary. We are at the Grand Hotel, Brighton. Last night we went back to the Empress with Simon and Veronica [the witnesses at GB's marriage] and recreated our wedding 'breakfast' of a year ago. Today we came here by train. M is having a bath and Noel has just telephoned, 'Room Service is bringing up the champagne. Good news!' It's the best.

Background. Eight days ago, Friday 31 May, after *Romeo and Juliet* at the Redgrave Theatre, Farnham, we stayed overnight with William and Rachel Douglas-Home at East Meon. We arrived late. No sign of Rachel. William offered us bread and cheese and shambled about the kitchen, affecting to be totally lost. He attempted to slice the bread using the blunt edge of the knife. M saw through the ploy, but took over all the same. While she fixed the snack, William took me to his study. Together, bleakly, we contemplated his desk, piled high with heavily thumbed old scripts: his unperformed works. 'Nothing here for Celia, alas.' We munched our bread and cheese, drained our glasses and went up to bed. As his bedside reading, William took up with him a book he had just started – a biography of Sybil Hathaway, the Dame of Sark, a gallant lady who, throughout the Second World War and the German occupation of her island, remained defiant and heart-warmingly British.

At breakfast, he said to us, 'There might be something in this.' Five days later – by the end of Wednesday – he had finished the first draft. Celia Johnson got it last night. She has read it. Noel has spoken to her. It's a definite Yes!

Sunday, 23 June 1974

Who needs sleep? Over the past six days, in total I have not slept for more than sixteen hours. Tuesday morning I recorded *Jack de Manio Precisely* (it's an afternoon programme, but we have to do it in the morning or the star would not be 'capable') and then started a forty-hour non-stop stint sorting all the OTF [Oxford Theatre Festival] print and publicity – including a return trip to the printer in Bournemouth. On Thursday night I slept. On Friday night, after we went with Simon [Cadell] to see Roy Dotrice in *Brief Lives* at the Mayfair (wonderful), I slept again, but on Saturday, after Uncle Wilfrid and Cousin Beryl's wedding at Southwark Cathedral, we went to Oxford for the Trinity Ball and were up until dawn. No sleep at all. I am now back in London, woozily writing this as I preside over the fourth National Scrabble Championship, sitting alongside my friend, Dr Bob Burchfield, New Zealand editor of the Oxford English Dictionary.* Dr Burchfield looks a lot more bleary-eyed than I do. And he has red scratch-marks all over his face. I asked him what they were. He said, 'My wife did that. I am afraid we have been fighting. We fight a lot.'

And how will the marriage go between Uncle Wilfrid and Cousin Beryl? Auntie Hope died a year and a month ago. There was much behind-the-hand muttering at the reception about Uncle Wilfrid marrying again so soon – *and* marrying Beryl, Auntie Hope's cousin and best friend . . . Pa provoked nervous laughter from the crowd with his toast: 'Let us raise our glasses to Wilfrid and Beryl and the triumph of experience over Hope . . .'

Wednesday, 17 July 1974

The IRA mainland bombings are getting worse. On 17 June, Westminster Hall. Today, 17 July, the Tower of London – one killed, dozens injured. We are carrying on regardless.

---

* Robert Burchfield CBE (1923–2004), New Zealand-born lexicographer and editor of the Supplement to the *Oxford English Dictionary*, 1957–86.

Noel was peeved about our five nights away in Cumberland, so I played down the delights of the near-perfect Sharrow Bay Hotel and gave over the whole day to catching up on everything with him. He has been casting the part of the Native in *The Little Hut*.[*] This has involved inviting every good-looking black actor in London to come to our flat and take his clothes off – with Noel insisting: 'Trousers and all: this is a loin-cloth part.' Apparently, Mrs Shilling, among others, has been walking up and down the pavement outside trying to get a discreet butcher's.

At six, we left M with Oscar, Neville and Rosie[†] and went on the razzle, first to Macready's, then to Le Jardin des Gourmets, then on to Gerry's Club. We drank, we ate, Noel told stories, we drank some more. He is amazing: his fund of material is limitless. Mostly filthy or theatrical – but not always. He has a lot of royal stories – e.g. Queen Mary during the war meeting a small boy who'd been bombed out of his home. 'Where do you live normally?' asked the Queen. 'Back 'a Selfgridges,' answered the urchin, 'what about you, missus?' Queen Mary, then resident at Marlborough House, replied, 'Back 'a Fortnum's.'

Tuesday, 6 August 1974

The Oxford Theatre Festival (my baby) opened tonight: five plays plus Sundays (Bernard Miles, Paul Scofield, Larry Adler, etc.). The theatre was packed. The advance is healthy. The opening show – *Springtime for Henry* – is a huge success. It is wonderful to watch Ian Carmichael in action: it all looks effortless, natural, easy, spontaneous. In fact, it is meticulously crafted: he reproduces the same movements, inflections, gestures every time – fine-tuning them until he achieves the laugh he's after. Tonight, just before the final curtain, he tilted his hat forward – he said it would signal to the audience that the show was over and they could applaud. It did. And they cheered!

Afterwards we all went out to the cottage Barbara Murray is renting for a party. Only Cheryl Kennedy didn't stay – she is racing back each night to the arms of Tom Courtenay. Ian C. (as happy as Larry) drove me to the party in the Roller – he was pleasantly squiffy. Later, he drove me back – he was completely sozzled. I am writing this in my room at the Randolph. I am happy to report: we have a hit.

---

[*] With the withdrawal of Sir Ralph Richardson, André Roussin's desert island comedy, *The Little Hut*, starring Geraldine McEwan and Gerald Harper, had replaced *The Missionary* as the fifth play in the Oxford Theatre Festival season.

[†] Three kittens that GB and Michèle had acquired from Ikarus, the restaurant in Baker Street.

Friday, 9 August 1974

Richard Nixon has resigned as President of the United States. Gerald Ford has succeeeded him. In Oxford, these events have gone virtually unnoticed. In the neverland of theatre where I now dwell outside considerations matter not a jot. I recall Beverley Nichols telling me a story about John Gielgud in 1940. It was at the time of Britain's darkest hour, when the nation faced the very real threat of a German invasion. Nichols and Gielgud were fellow guests at a country house-party. On the Sunday morning, Beverley got up early to go and buy the news-papers, only to find that Gielgud had forestalled him and was already sitting in the drawing room surrounded by the newspapers of the day, their front-page headlines double-decked with tidings of disaster. In the middle of the morass of newsprint sat Gielgud, ashen-faced. 'What on earth has happened?' demanded Nichols, anxiously. 'The worst!' wailed Gielgud, shaking his head in despair, 'the very worst – Edith has had the most dreadful notices.'

Friday, 23 August 1974

Sir John [Clements] is both charming and a nightmare. Every evening is now the same. We have dinner with him, during which, with a face like thunder, he tears us off a strip (*everything* is wrong – especially the costumes, especially the set) and then, wreathed in smiles, he regales us with his favourite anecdotes. After dinner we meet up with Julia [Foster] in the Randolph and sit around in a circle worrying about the play. Sir John and Julia sit side by side holding hands. She then goes off to bed. I walk her to the lift while she tells me that Sir John is sweet but, as a director, *no help at all*. I return to Sir John who tells me that Julia is sweet but, as an actress, *no good at all*. Tonight he was at his worst. We must have drunk two bottles of port between us. He is determined to postpone the opening night: it was Tuesday: I have agreed to make it Thursday. He says we may not even be able to open then. 'She can't do it – and the set's not built yet.' He is right on both counts.

   At 4.00 a.m. we all stumbled off to bed. At 9.30 a.m. Sir John rang Noel's bed-room. 'Is that Noel Davis?' he growled. 'Why the hell aren't you down here?'

   'Is that you, Sir John? Where are you? In the foyer?'

   'No, you fool. I'm in the *fucking* theatre where I *belong*.'

Sunday, 25 August 1974

Thursday night, it was 4.00 a.m. Friday night, it was 2.00 a.m. Last night, it was 6.00 a.m. I blame Simon Cadell. He is here – and he encouraged him. First he got

Sir John to take us right through the production [of *Saint Joan*], scene by scene, with Sir John telling us what's wrong with who and why, and Simon throwing in his two cents' worth, and then, at around 3.00 a.m., he got Sir John to start showing us card tricks. He is a brilliant magician – brilliant.

Michèle is here. She is pregnant (only just: it's our secret) but nonetheless has spent the day and half the night sizing the set.

Wednesday, 28 August 1974

First night of *The Trials of Oscar Wilde*. Tom Baker[*] is quite mad: an eccentric, a loner (he travels without luggage, except for a toothbrush), he looks like Harpo Marx, but he has a wonderful voice and the play works – almost. Nigel Stock is excellent. Supper with Ray and Noel at the Saraceno. Ray is frustrated: Ian Carmichael doesn't want to take *Springtime* into town and won't be persuaded. He says the play isn't 'robust' enough. Ray doesn't think tonight's piece has transfer potential without a 'star' and he's dreading tomorrow's opening of *Saint Joan*. Aren't we all?

Friday, 30 August 1974

It wasn't bad. It *sounded* good. It was intelligently spoken. The set is a disaster – dreary, amateur. The costumes have the feel of *1066 and All That*. But, for me, the real horror of tonight was that, during the interval, the management of the New Theatre insisted on showing advertisements on the safety curtain – including one that featured James Villiers, our Earl of Warwick, as a silly-ass chinless-wonder advertising Benson & Hedges cigarettes. Oh God.

Julia acquitted herself well. John Standing is a perfect Dauphin. Villiers strong. On radio, we'd win awards. Anyway, we opened. It's done. And the company party is done too. All very jolly – all very drunken. At about three, when everyone had gone to bed (including Sir J. Clements), I was left with a trio of sozzled actors: J. Standing, J. Villiers and Villiers's friend, Ronnie Fraser, who had come up from London for the first night. Fraser passed out on the sofa and then, somehow, Standing and Villiers started talking about money and discovered that one of them was getting £35 a week and the other was getting £40, when I had told everybody that everybody was getting exactly the same! Villiers got a serviette and scrawled on it: 'I, Gyles Brandreth, bastard producer of the Oxford Theatre Festival, hereby agree to pay J. Villiers, actor, £40 per week' and, together with Standing, chased me round and round and round the lounge of the Randolph until I signed.

---

[*] Tom Baker (b.1934) played Wilde. This was after he had played Rasputin in the film *Nicholas and Alexandra*, 1971, but just before his success as Dr Who, 1974–81.

I am returning to London this weekend to write *The Knight Book of Easter Fun*.

Wednesday, 18 September 1974

Last night, at the New Theatre, the opening of *The Little Hut*. Tonight, at the Playhouse, the opening of *The Dame of Sark*.

The roller-coaster of *The Little Hut* continued to the last. Having lost our director,* last night our leading man decided to lose his nerve. Gerald Harper sat whimpering in his dressing room, telling me it was all too much, he wasn't ready, he wasn't up to it, he couldn't go on. I did my best to bolster him, telling him how wonderful he was, how the audience would warm to him because his personality is so warm etc. (all tosh, of course) – and then, fifteen minutes before curtain up, Noel came in, told him to pull himself together and, as he went on whimpering, slapped him across the face. 'If you don't go out there and give the performance of a lifetime, you'll never work again.'

Gerald went out – and did his best. He's fine. He's just not in the same league as Geraldine [McEwan] and [James] Villiers, that's all. And no one is in the same league as Celia Johnson. She is extraordinary: she appears to do absolutely nothing, but when she comes on something magical somehow happens. She is so touching in this. When I visit her in her dressing room, she is always sitting quietly at the dressing table playing patience. She has very few visitors. I have noticed that the stars have the fewest visitors: people are nervous about knocking on their doors.

Noel does a very funny impression of Celia playing *Saint Joan* in her clipped Home Counties tones: 'Taxi! I need to go to Rouen, stopping off, if you don't mind awfully, at Peter Jones.'

Sunday, 13 October 1974

Dust has now settled on the general election. Labour 319. Conservatives 276. Liberals 13. Nationalists etc. 27. Labour has an overall majority of three. Harold Wilson carries on.

So it seems does Simon [Cadell]. We had dinner at A L'Ecu de France. Simon revealed that he had sex with a girl in the lavatory on the train. (Why is my life so tame?! The big excitement for me: tomorrow sees the publication of *Games for Trains, Planes and Wet Days*. Amazingly, there's no mention of sex in the lavatory.)

---

* Philip Dudley, the original director, had lost the confidence of the cast and been replaced by Hugh Cruttwell, Geraldine McEwan's husband and head of the Royal Academy of Dramatic Art.

Dramatic Moments

Thursday, 17 October 1974

A crowded forty-eight hours.

Yesterday. At 12 noon: in the Cinderella bar at the London Palladium, the launch party for *I Scream for Ice Cream*, my illustrated history of panto. A good line-up: Richard Goolden, Gordon and Bunny Jay (seasoned panto double act), Claude Zola (*the* pantomime cat – from a distinguished family of panto 'animals'), Pat Kirkwood (*the* post-war principal boy) plus husband, Hubert Gregg; Richard Hearne (Mr Pastry); Danny La Rue (who pointed out that the picture we have in the book is him in 'cabaret' drag, not as a panto dame); Cyril Fletcher plus Jilly. All jolly. I am pleased that I shall be able to tell my grandchildren: 'I once had lunch with Mr Pastry.' ('Who is Mr Pastry, Grandpa?')

7.00 p.m. First night of *The Little Hut* at the Duke of York's. The moment when the hatchet is thrown across the stage went horribly wrong – the dagger popped out of the tree a good ten seconds before it was supposed to, with the sound effect following behind, pointlessly, *incomprehensibly* as far as the audience was concerned. Agony, but, overall, it was fine. Gerald kept his nerve and Geraldine and James were stylish and funny. The notices are not bad, so fingers crossed. Afterwards we went for supper *chez* Bumble Dawson:* me and M, Noël and Margaret Rawlings, Geraldine and Hugh Cruttwell. Bumble is so-called because she does look like a bumblebee and dresses like one – and has dressed every leading lady you can think of. They all love her because she makes them look divine and feel comfortable and because she is a comfort to be with. (She admitted finding Marilyn Monroe a challenge: on *The Prince and the Showgirl* she was obliged to make Marilyn tops for her frocks in *triplicate* because MM kept spilling food down them.) Noel was very funny – and very wicked about Gerald. Geraldine screwed up her face and made lots of little squeals of delight. All jolly.

And today all jolly too. Lunch with Noel at Sheekey's – making plans for next year's Festival! Radio London at the Motor Show this afternoon – usual burbling. 7.00 p.m. The first night of *The Dame of Sark* at Wyndham's. Celia, playing patience at her dressing table, seemed nervous – which I have never seen before. On stage, she was flawless. She will only do three months: Ray already has Anna Neagle in mind as her replacement. One of our actors, anticipating a long-run, has had the cupboard in his dressing room equipped with a built-in armchair – somewhere comfortable for his mistress to sit when his wife is visiting him.

---

* Beatrice Dawson (1908–76), award-winning theatre and film costume designer.

Afterwards, William Douglas-Home hosted a splendid post-show party at the Travellers' Club. Very jolly, once more. *The Dame of Sark* is certainly a hit. I am now a West End producer: I have two shows running, with my name on the posters to prove it. It's good; I'm happy; I'm pleased; I'm grateful. And yet . . .

Heigh-ho. Goodnight.

Sunday, 27 October 1974

Last night, overnight with David and Anne Mayer in Manchester and with them to *The Marriage of Figaro* at the Liverpool Royal Court. Open squabbling in the car as we drove from Manchester to Liverpool: their marriage won't last.[*] I like David Mayer III: he is an American academic and the world authority on Victorian pantomime. Mander and Mitchenson[†] always refer to him as David Mayer the Turd. I like them too: a couple of queens (one tall, with bouffant hair and a way of walking with a swagger; the other bent, wiry, with a boxer's face and a syphilitic nose): they speak simultaneously, finishing each other's sentences: no one knows which is which, but we are grateful to them because theirs in the best theatre collection in the world and they know their stuff.

Today I took a taxi from Altrincham to Accrington and had tea and played whist with Aunt Edith and Grandpa and caught the 6.12 back to Euston where Jeffrey Archer was waiting to greet me at the ticket barrier. How are the mighty fallen! The former member for Louth was making his debut at LBC at 10.00 p.m. – the overnight shift: I've been there, done that. Jeffrey wanted me on hand as guest, guide and mentor. I was happy to oblige. He did okay, though he was very nervous and compensated by being alternately loud and bombastic – and sometimes both. At almost every commercial break he called Mary to ask her what she thought. He told her how good he thought he was and then asked her if she agreed!

Wednesday, 30 October 1974

Lunch with Pa at Rules. Good, but a mite strained. We are neither of us easy at being 'intimate'.

---

[*] It didn't.

[†] Raymond Mander and Joe Mitchenson met in the 1930s and together formed the finest collection of British theatrical memorabilia in private hands. Professor David Mayer, a leading authority on Victorian theatre, was then teaching at Manchester University. GB met Mayer, Mander and Mitchenson while doing research for his books about pantomime.

Tea with M and her wayward pupil, Sally Ann Lasson. She is only fourteen, but M says it will all end in tears.[*]

Supper at the Mumtaz: sorted our Christmas card list.

Thursday, 21 November 1974

On Monday I got a telephone call. 'Is that Charles Brandreth?'

'Gyles Brandreth – yes.'

'Brian Cartmell 'ere – pooblic relations, Blackpool. Do yer play Monopoly, lad?'

'Well, actually, Scrabble is more my game.'

'There is a fee involved. £100.'

'Monopoly? My *favourite* game. I owe my life to Monopoly!'[†]

'Good. Could you be free to play in a match on Friday?'

'Er, yes.'

'Good. We'll send you the tickets.'

'No need. I'll get a ticket at the station and you can pay me when I send in my invoice.'

'There's no "station" involved, lad. The game is in New York.'

And so it came to pass . . . I have just checked in at the St Regis Hotel in the heart of Manhattan. I am here for the weekend pretending to be the European Monopoly Champion! Tomorrow morning I shall be playing a demonstration game in the window of Dunhill's on Fifth Avenue. Tomorrow evening I am competing in the World Monopoly Championships. I am here because the US organisers of the event are not too happy about the 'media appeal' of the American competitors and have decided to import a European 'champion' to liven things up. It's a strange life I'm leading.

---

[*] Sally Ann Lasson (b.1959), cartoonist and writer, later had an affair with Earl Spencer and married Simon Kelner, editor of *The Independent*. Enjoying TV presenting less and less, Michèle had started tutorial teaching from home and writing non-fiction books.

[†] GB's parents met, in London, shortly before Christmas 1936. At Selfridges Charles Brandreth had bought one of the first sets of Monopoly to be sold in the UK. He took it back to his digs in Gower Street and enquired of the landlady if she knew anyone who might like to play the game with him. He was introduced to a fellow resident, a lady recently arrived from Canada with her daughter, Alice Addison, a law student at London University. They played Monopoly and, within a matter of weeks, Charles and Alice, without telling their parents, were married at Marylebone Town Hall.

Saturday, 23 November 1974

I got through to the Final – without cheating. They offered me a secret stash of Monopoly money to hide about my person. I refused. I played fair! And I came third!! I did a lot of playing to the cameras – asking for cups of English tea, saying 'Cheerio-pip-pip' and enquiring why the game was set in Atlantic City rather than good old London Town. I amused the organisers and infuriated my fellow competitors. When he won, the victor retreated to his room and said he wouldn't emerge until his mother was flown in from Ohio. He was overwhelmed by it all. He declared, in all seriousness, 'This thing's too big for me.'

Wednesday, 4 December 1974

7.00 a.m. LBC AM programme promoting my *Knight Book of Christmas Fun*.

2.00 p.m. *Macbeth* at Stratford with Nicol Williamson in the title role. It was a schools matinee. We were surrounded by ghastly schoolchildren, fidgeting, chattering, making nuisances of themselves. Fifteen minutes into the performance, Nicol Williamson had had enough. Halfway through a speech, he grabbed the wooden stool on which he had been resting his foot and with terrifying violence flung it the length of the stage. He turned on the audience. 'Shut up! Shut up the lot of you! I have come to Stratford earning nothing a week to play Shakespeare when I could be in Hollywood making films and earning a fortune. There are people here today who have paid for their seats. And you kids had better shut up and let them hear the play. And if you won't shut up, get up and go now. *Now!*'

Nobody moved. You could have heard a pin drop. He began the speech again and the play proceeded without further interruption.

Wednesday, 25 December 1974

New York, Boston, Salem, Washington DC, Atlanta, New Orleans. Christmas Eve on the *Mark Twain*, cruising along the Mississippi River. Christmas Day at the Hotel Pontchartrain. We have just had Roast Tom Turkey and all the trimmings, followed by the Pontchartrain speciality: Mile High Ice Cream Pie. If you finish your portion you get another one free. In the history of the hotel, no one has ever managed to finish a portion.

We watched *Star!* on TV – Julie Andrews as Gertrude Lawrence (oh dear), Daniel Massey as Noël Coward ('Dear boy, you have me saying too many "dear boys", dear boy.' NC) It wasn't very good.

Dramatic Moments

I begin 1975 in Williamsburg, Virginia, USA. This is colonial America preserved in aspic: Disneyland for grown-ups with an historical bent. We saw in the New Year over champagne cocktails at the Williamsburg Inn. This morning we are going to tour the old Governor's Palace and gardens. For my appointments diary this year I will be using The Williamsburg Almanack. It is a handsome volume, beautifully designed, and has useful quotations on every page. It opens with this:

> Let the world slide, let the world go;
> A fig for care, and a fig for woe!
> If I can't pay, why I can owe,
> And death makes equal the high and low.

Monday, 6 January 1975

I am writing this on the Pan Am flight to London. We began the day in our room at the Waldorf-Astoria – breakfast brought to us on a wobbly trolley: scrambled eggs, crispy bacon, toasted English muffins (you can't get them in England, but I love them here), and on TV, at 7.00 a.m., the first broadcast of *AM America*. (I like to be in at the start of things.)

We have seen some good things while we've been here: the CBS tribute to Jack Benny,* *The Sunshine Boys* on Broadway, the film of *The Front Page*, Jim Dale in *Scapino*. It's all been good: I am reading *The House of the Seven Gables* by Nathaniel Hawthorne, bought by me on 12 December at the House of the Seven Gables, Salem, Mass. We have been away a while. It will be good to get home. There is much to be done: books to write, games to invent, speeches to make. I start again within thirty-six hours: the Huddersfield Wednesday Club, to be closely followed by the Uttoxeter Ladies' Lifeboat Guild.† On today's page in my Williamsburg Almanack I read this, from J. K. Galbraith: 'Wealth is not without its advantages and the case to the contrary, although it has often been made, has never proved widely persuasive.'

---

* Jack Benny (b. Benjamin Kubelsky, 1894–1974), comedian (and a particular hero of GB) had died on 26 December.
† Throughout the 1970s and 1980s, GB earned the bulk of his living making speeches (hundreds of them), inventing games (for J. W. Spear & Sons and, later, Waddingtons) and writing books. He wrote more than one hundred assorted fun and games books for children and about three dozen non-fiction books for adults, on games and puzzles, words and language, and popular entertainment.

We need the money! Two months from now we will be parents! There are bootees to be bought!!

Wednesday, 5 February 1975

It's all over for Ted Heath. The poor man (my sometime hero!) has been trounced in the first round of the ballot for the leadership of the Conservative Party: 119 for Mr Heath, 130 for Mrs Thatcher. It's not over yet: William Whitelaw, Geoffrey Howe and others now join the fray. But, for what it's worth, when the dust has settled, I think we'll find that Mrs Thatcher's our man. (And, who knows, we may meet her on one our Bridge evenings in Flood Street.)*

Women are on the march – but not everywhere. I am writing this in the train coming back from Accrington. Pa and I have just been attending Grandpa's funeral – and in the north of England in 1975 women still do not go to funerals. It's men's work.

Ma didn't come, even though Grandpa was her father. Auntie Edith, who lived with Grandpa and has looked after him since 1947 when he came back from India, didn't come. While we men trooped to the church, she stayed in Harcourt Road, preparing the tea and sandwiches for the modest wake that took place after the funeral. It was all very low-key: a handful of mourners. But in the church, sitting right at the back, there *were* two women, in raincoats and hats. They didn't know Grandpa. They are simply funeral 'regulars'. The vicar said to Pa, 'It's only women who do this.' Interesting: only men go train-spotting and only women go 'collecting' funerals.

Tuesday, 11 February 1975

I marked Shrove Tuesday by tossing the world's tiniest pancake 'live' on the *Today* programme. Conservative Members of Parliament marked it by electing Margaret Thatcher as the first female leader of a British political party. She walked it: 146 for M. Thatcher; 79 for W. Whitelaw (who shed tears as he promised to unite behind her); 20 for the rest. History is made.

I am spending the morning sorting the VAT and accounts. Next stop: lunch with Richard Carswell, European Movement, 1a Whitehall Place.

---

*Margaret Thatcher (b.1925); Baroness Thatcher of Kesteven LG OM FRS; Conservative MP for Finchley, 1959–92; Prime Minister, 1979–90. Mrs Thatcher, her husband Denis and their twin children, Mark and Carol, then lived in Flood Street, Chelsea, neighbours of GB's Bridge mentor, Francis Crowdy.

Friday, 7 March 1975

Michèle has gone into the Middlesex Hospital to have the baby and I am here, at home, alone, and anxious. I pray it will all be all right. I love her very much. I have remembered to flea-powder the cats. Tomorrow is my twenty-seventh birthday. I shall read *Vanity Fair* (now my favourite book: arguably the best novel ever written by an Englishman) and go to bed.

Friday, 14 March 1975

Benet was born last night at 8.50 p.m. It has been a nightmare, but it's over now and I think he's fine. He's in an incubator – he has jaundice – but all seems okay. Yesterday was the worst day of my life. When I got to the hospital M was already in labour. The consultant was there. He took me out and walked me down the corridor and sat next to me on an empty bed. Very quietly (he has glasses and looks like an accountant), he said it was serious, but that it should be all right, but you never knew. He would probably need to give M an anaesthetic. He couldn't predict the outcome or how long it would take. I was numb – terrified. My poor, darling girl lying there and there was nothing I could do. He told me to go away – 'don't go far'. For several hours, I walked around the streets of Marylebone, just walked and walked, my stomach churning. Each time I went back there was no news. And then, it was all over – and all was well. Our boy had been born: my girl was alive and recovering. I found her lying in the bed, knees akimbo, being stitched up by what appeared to be a couple of students! She has been so brave. I am so happy. And our little mite, yellowish and still attached to tubes, is going to be fine, too.

M was exhausted. I left her and walked back to Baker Street. I called in on the parents and broke the news. I phoned M's parents. I lay on Ma and Pa's bed and Pa made a sandwich while I gave them a blow-by-blow account of it all. I got home around midnight.

It's M's birthday. I have sent her two telegrams – one wishing Benet a happy birthday for yesterday – one wishing her a happy birthday for today. I am going in to see them now. I am a father. How does it feel? Good. Very, very good. Welcome to the world, Master B.!

Tuesday, 18 March 1975

On the back page of today's *Times*:

> On 13th March at the Middlesex Hospital, London, W1, to Michèle Brown, wife of Gyles Brandreth – a son (Benet Xan).

On the front page: Mr Wedgwood Benn, Secretary of State for Industry, is widening the scope of the Government's plans to nationalise the shipbuilding and aircraft industries; Mr Callaghan, the Foreign and Commonwealth Secretary, says the Cabinet is likely to recommend a 'Yes' vote in the referendum on the renegotiated terms of our membership of the European Economic Community; and in Ireland Protestants and Catholics have spent the night killing one another. Inside there is a photograph of the Queen meeting Barbra Streisand at last night's Royal Film Performance of *Funny Lady* and I even get a mention in the *Times* Diary, a small item about Scrabble.

M and Benet are set to come home on Thursday. We are ready and waiting – cot in place, pram in hallway, nappies folded, Johnson's baby powder, Vaseline, etc., by the changing mat.

The good thing about the announcement in *The Times* is that it lets people know we are married. Some, like Cyril Fletcher, have been saying, pulling pained but friendly faces, 'How different you would feel if you were married,' not realising that we already were. Everyone seems to find Benet's names a challenge. We love them. Benet was M's choice. (At first I was backing Max.) Benet suits him perfectly. I have registered the birth. We are not planning a christening. (The family is coping.)

Thursday, 27 March 1975

I am now, officially, director of the European Movement's 'People for Europe' campaign. Getting this far has not been easy, simply because the 'Britain in Europe' organisation is being run by a load of anxious old buffers who are terri-fied that anyone will do anything risky or interesting. My 'Wombles for Europe' idea has been vetoed (of course), ditto 'Odd Odes for Europe', but the introduc-tory press release (bland as it is) has been approved by Sir Con & Co.[*] and has gone out from Europe House today:

> 'The People for Europe campaign,' says Brandreth, 'won't be involving professional politicians at all. It won't involve heavyweight industrialists or earnest trade union officials either. It will involve all kinds of other people – many of them very famous, lots of them very young – and its object will be to present an exciting, comprehensible and credible picture of the advantages of Britain's continuing membership of the EEC.'

* Sir Con O'Neill (1912–88) was director of the Britain in Europe campaign; he had been the diplomat leading Britain's negotiations to join the EEC.

Our aim is to produce a Layman's Guide to Europe and telephone information centres in the UK's ten largest cities. I am running it from home, though they are letting me have a corner of a desk at 'Europe House' – so called: actually cramped, over-crowded open-plan desks at the back of the National Liberal Club behind Charing Cross Station.

I have bought Easter eggs. In his powder-blue perambulator, M and I will be taking our son to feed the ducks in Regent's Park before taking part in his first Brandreth family traditional Easter egg hunt. (Yes, he is only two weeks old today, but he is *very* advanced.)

Sunday, 11 May 1975

Anxious letter from Archy Kirkwood, 'Youth Coordinator', Britain in Europe.[*] He is fretting about our press conference – and our finances. These people don't have enough to do! The truth is, we have done well. All the people I have recruited have donated £5 to the cause and we have quality names: Peter Ustinov, Richard Briers, Paul Eddington (everyone is loving *The Good Life*: the European life will be even better!), David Bailey, Michael York, Antoinette Sibley, Katie Boyle, Robert Powell, J. B. Priestley, etc. – £380 to date, with Henry Moore and Dirk Bogarde coming in with £10 apiece and Frederick Forsyth stumping up £20. The press conference is scheduled for Thursday and we're going ahead with it, regardless of wee Archy. I am now off to the Polygon Hotel, Southampton, to chair the Wessex Youth for Europe Rally. John Selwyn Gummer[†] is giving me a lift. He looks like a carrot, but he knows his stuff.

Tuesday, 20 May 1975

Our People for Europe press reception at the London Palladium went well. I think. Slightly motley turn-out: Nicholas Parsons, Viscount Weymouth, Lord Montagu of Beaulieu, Tom Hustler, Sheila Scott . . . Christopher Hitchens (representing the *New Statesman*) stood at the bar in a combat jacket, drinking, smoking and raising a cynical brow above a very watery and bloodshot eye. (I think he is completely ridiculous; he thinks I am completely ridiculous; but we have Oxford in common and we like one another.) The photographers took our two actresses, Doris Hare and Patricia Hayes, into the street outside the theatre and got the game old birds to do high-kicks by a 'one-way' road sign, with a bemused

---

[*] Archy Kirkwood (b.1946), Baron Kirkwood of Kirkhope, Liberal Democrat MP, 1983–2005.
[†] John Selwyn Gummer (b.1939), Conservative MP, 1970–74, 1979–.

Andrew Lloyd Webber looking on. He was our 'star attraction', but he lacks 'star personality': he can barely string a sentence together. He wore an open-necked floral shirt under a crumpled old sports jacket. Grubby trousers, belt with a huge buckle and terrible posture. (Cry from Michèle in background: 'You're not one to talk!')

Friday, 6 June 1975

The referendum result: an overwhelming victory! Twenty-six million went to the polls. 67.2 per cent voted Yes. 32.8 per cent voted No. We stay in Europe. It's the right result – and we played our part.

Now back to normality. (Well, perhaps not quite normality. I met Hugh Thomas for lunch. He is now wearing a toupee. As he greeted me, outside Leicester Square tube station, he lifted it as though it were a hat. He did the same as he said goodbye. And then I met Ronnie Barker* who showed me his collection of saucy seaside postcards – but I don't think he collects them because he finds them amusing: I think he finds them positively *exciting*. Very strange.)

Wednesday, 2 July 1975

Lunch with Simon [Cadell] and Sir John Clements at Stone's Chop House. He seemed older, wearier. He wouldn't have even one glass of wine. 'I never touch a drop before a performance. It's my one rule.' Simon (who is appearing with him in *The Case in Question* at the Haymarket – a C. P. Snow drama, but not his strongest) told his story about how Sir Ralph manages to shave twenty minutes off a matinee. Sir John shook his head. 'Always give your best performance – always. There may be someone out there who is seeing you for the very first time. You must give them your best.' I like him. I told him we hoped to do another Festival next year – funding permitting. (I did not tell him that [the Oxford Playhouse administrator] Elizabeth Sweeting is a difficult old cow and that nothing is certain.) He suggested *Arms and the Man* as a possible Shaw. (I don't think we will be asking him to be the director. Nor Julia Foster to star. Cry from Noël : 'Unless we need them!')

Saturday, 11 October 1975

'Gyles Brandreth is the sort of person that a breakfast cereal company would give their right arm for. He's bursting with vigour, fizzing with happiness, sizzling with vim, and *Cosmopolitan* magazine once picked him as one of England's most

---

* Ronnie Barker OBE (1929–2005), actor and comedian. *The Two Ronnies* ran on BBC Television from 1970 to 1987.

eligible bachelors, though he was actually married at the time.' Lynda Lee-Potter's interview has appeared in the *Mail*. We get a full page, with a charming picture of M and me – with me holding Benet and giving him his bottle. Lynda was lovely: gentle, funny, quirky – and that's what the piece is, too. It's generous and amusing – but rather ghastly, too. Embarrassing. All that boasting – talking too much, trying to get everything in, trying to be agreeable and ending up sounding egregious. Saying I'm the happiest person in the world – possibly true, but I know it just annoys people.

On the reverse side of the piece about us, it's 'Margaret the magnificent!' 'My vision for Britain.' 'Mrs Thatcher began her historic speech to the Tory conference with a furious onslaught on the Labour Party.' This is her first Party Conference as leader and she's wowed 'em.

Monday, 13 October 1975

Our dinner party for ten last night went well. Guests were due at 7.30 p.m. At 8.30 p.m. everyone had arrived, except Francis and Mary Crowdy. Francis phoned to apologise. They'd been held up: they were on their way. They arrived around nine. We had a jolly time. They went off with the rest around midnight. Francis has just phoned, full of apology and regret at their rudeness in arriving so late – 'frightfully bad manners'. 'It was just that, as we were getting ready to go, standing in the hallway at Flood Street, Mary told me that she's leaving me – for the au pair.' And still they came to dinner! I believe it's called 'breeding'.

Monday, 1 March 1976

I think I have found a new play for this year's Oxford Theatre Festival. It's not completely 'new': it was commissioned by the Royal Court a couple of years ago and they've sat on it. I think it's wonderful: wordy, witty, intelligent, emotionally gripping. It's called *Dear Daddy*, it's by Denis Cannan,[*] it's about an acerbic literary man in crisis and his relationship with his wives and children, and I want us to do it. It's a modern Chekhov with the verbal flair of John Osborne – yes, it's that good. And when I read it in bed (have I ever reported that I always sleep on the right side of the bed?), I said 'Yes!' out loud and I gave it to Michèle and she said yes – and Noel said yes. And today I went down to Chichester to meet Alan Badel[†] to talk to him about it and he said no. He could have said no on the

---

[*] Denis Cannan (b.1919), screenwriter and playwright best known for *Captain Carvallo*, produced by Laurence Olivier in 1950.
[†] Alan Badel (1923–82), distinguished English actor.

telephone, but he thought it more courteous to drag us down to Chichester so that he could say no in person!

Actually, I liked him. He is small and serious and a wonderful actor – intelligent, interesting, with a unique voice and that something 'extra' that makes him both watchable and a star. But he seems to have reached the age and stage they seem to reach (cf. Ian Carmichael) when they prefer to *talk* about plays and projects than actually take them on.

Sunday, 14 March 1976

Michèle's birthday dinner at the Ritz. Is it the prettiest room in London? Probably. Is it the best food in London? Probably not. Is it the most expensive? Certainly. We went with Simon [Cadell] and he suggested that, as a starter, caviare might be rather fun. 'It's a special occasion.' I opted for the smoked salmon (£2): M and Simon went for the caviare (£35!). It was brought on a clanking trolley and served like a holy sacrament. Simon scoffed his in a matter of moments. M managed to linger over hers a little longer – but when the trolley came rumbling past again, Simon called out 'Waiter!' and, turning to M, said 'I think we could manage another portion each, darling – don't you?' They did. (I paid. It was ludicrously expensive, but, unusually for M, she did not resent the extravagance.)

Wednesday, 17 March 1976

Harold Wilson has resigned. No one seems to know why. *I* know why. We are fellow Pisceans. Last week, he celebrated his 60th birthday. I imagine, years ago, he promised himself that he would hang up his boots at 60.[*]

I am on the train to Oxford, going to see Barry Sheppard, La Sweeting's successor at the Playhouse. He is a funny-looking creature.

Tuesday, 30 March 1976

Goodbye 170 Clarence Gate Gardens, NW1. Hello, 1 Campden Hill Gardens, W8. We (and the Guardian Building Society) are now in proud possession of a fine, late-Victorian five-storey freehold family house in Kensington. Pickfords ran the removal well. Everything is chaos here, but it's going to be good. The vendors took the *doorknobs* – from every decent door in the house. And they walked off with light fittings they were supposed to leave. We are getting them

---

[*] GB's speculation turned out to be partly correct. Harold Wilson was also concerned that his mental powers were no longer as acute as they had been.

back – and, eventually, it will all be wonderful. Lower ground floor: big family kitchen at the front, playroom opening onto the garden at the back, utility rooms; ground floor: proper drawing room (fine fireplace) at back, large dining room at front into which the Monkey[*] is putting a wall of hand-crafted bookshelves. First floor: main bedroom, dressing room, bathroom, second bedroom which I am going to use as my study. Second floor: interconnecting children's rooms, bathroom, laundry room, etc. Then up a tiny flight of stairs to the two rooms in the attic – for the nanny. It is all very Mr and Mrs Darling – and from Benet's bedroom you get a fine view right up the street to the church at the top of Campden Hill.

We have stretched ourselves to capacity – and beyond. We are selling Goodwood Court;[†] Irene [Josephy] has advanced me £2,000;[‡] and I have squeezed every penny I legitimately can out of Simon Clarke Productions.[§] When we were looking for our first place five years ago, everything that we saw then and *wanted* was just one step higher up the ladder than we could afford. Same again. We are living beyond our means – but, with a bit of luck, our means will catch up! And this is a house for life.

Tuesday, 6 April 1976

James Callaghan has 'kissed hands' with Her Majesty and is now the nation's new Prime Minister. In the final ballot of Labour MPs, he secured 176 votes to my friend Michael Foot's 137. Callaghan is 64. Harold Wilson is enjoying saying to the world that he decided to step aside to make way for an older man.

I began the day at Goodwood Court supervising the Pickfords' removal of all our stuff from the flat. I decided to leave the doorknobs! I am sorry we have to sell our 'investment', but I am not sorry to bid farewell to our ghastly tenant, 'Prince Ali'. He has not been a good advertisement for the Arab world: he took the flat so that he could have unspecified 'treatment' in Harley Street. He is gross – and graceless. When he arrived he *demanded* that I do his shopping, walking *backwards* in front of him through the grocery department at Selfridges, pulling the

---

[*] Mike Elles was both a carpenter and an actor. He had played 'The Monkey' in GB's production of *The Little Hut* in 1974.

[†] A small flat in Devonshire Street, W1, that GB and his wife had bought two years before as an investment.

[‡] GB quickly earned back this advance, but remained a client of Irene Josephy for longer than he wanted to because of a sense of indebtedness to her.

[§] Simon Clarke Productions had taken over from Ray Cooney as the financial backer of the Oxford Theatre Festival.

trolley and placing his selected items in the basket. He expected us to be at his constant beck and call. The kitchen floor is thick with grease and food droppings. The state of the bathroom is unspeakable. I left poor Mrs Recouso cleaning up. (History needs to know: she is wonderful.)

I have just returned from meeting the gang at Action Research for the Crippled Child. They have had a novel idea: get 100 'personalities' to break 100 records from the *Guinness Book of Records*, raising £1,000 in sponsorship each time. I am to make an an attempt on the world record for the longest after-dinner speech. The current holder is a Victorian clergyman, the Rev. Henry Whitehead. He spoke at the Rainbow Tavern, Fleet Street, in January 1874, without pause or notes, for just on three hours. Beat that. (I will.)

Friday, 9 April 1976

What a difference twenty-four hours makes. Yesterday at noon I was dressed as a dinosaur at the Magpie Toyshop in Dartford. Today, dressed in the light grey suit in which I got married, I had lunch at the Ritz with Denis Cannan and Nigel Patrick.* 'Paddy' Patrick (as we are to call him) is going to be our leading man. Of course, because he is a director and producer as well as an actor, he is already wanting to 'manage' the entire enterprise. We'll cope. (Denis said to me afterwards: 'Remember, Larry [Olivier] produced my first play. I am used to the ways of charming monsters.')

We sat at one of the window tables overlooking the park. Reginald Maudling was at the next table – fast asleep. He looked very fat and old. And rumour is rife about the leader of the Liberal Party.† Did he or didn't he have an affair with a male model? Did he or didn't he threaten to kill the said male model if ever he spoke of it? 'Always believe the worst of people,' said Denis. 'Then you won't be disappointed.'

Monday, 17 May 1976

On Saturday, John Selwyn Gummer, prospective Tory candidate for the Eye Division, Suffolk, broke the longest after-dinner speaking record, speaking for four hours, one minute and fifty seconds. At the Mayfair Hotel, London, this evening I established a new world record when I talked non-stop for four hours

---

* Nigel Patrick, born Nigel Wemyss (1913–81), distinguished English film and stage actor.
† Jeremy Thorpe, denying the rumours, resigned as Leader of the Liberal Party on 9 May. He claimed he was the victim of 'a sustained Press witch hunt' and was particularly embarrassed by the publication of a note he had sent to the male model, Norman Scott, that read: 'Bunnies can and will go to Paris.'

nineteen minutes and thirty-four seconds. Those in attendance included Bob Burchfield (official adjudicator), Cyril Fletcher, Nicholas Parsons, Gayle Hunnicutt, Simon Williams and sixty others – good supportive friends, Kirsty [McLeod], David Graham, Noel [Davis], Ma and Pa. Simon Williams sent an amusing good luck telegram: 'FROM THE TALLEST ACTOR TO THE LONGEST SPEAKER'. I am hopeful that with sponsorship and donations – Yehudi Menuhin and Elizabeth Beresford each sent £10, ditto Bob Monkhouse; Irene Josephy sent £100! – we shall comfortably exceed our target and that the record will stand long enough for me to feature in the *GBR*.* I am just looking down the list of donors again. Terry Jones, Janet Suzman, Sinead Cusack, William Franklyn and the Marquess of Londonderry each sent £10. Bernard Miles sent £2. Nicholas Parsons gave £1.

Friday, 11 June 1976

I returned from Chicago and the American Booksellers' Association and went straight to Sheekey's for a catch-up lunch with Noel. Over Dover sole (off the bone), new potatoes and spinach (*en branches* not *à la crème*!) we 'reviewed the situation'. ('Re-view-*ing* the si-tu-a-*shon*' is Noel's theme song. He sings it every morning as he arrives at our office: we are now in a small room – once a bedroom – on the top floor of the National Liberal Club in Whitehall Place. There is a cracked wash-basin in the corner – cracked, according to Noel, by Maggie Courtenay trying to pee in it.† I usually get to the office before Noel, but I know when he's on his way because, as he gets to the top of the stairs, before he starts singing, he hisses in a huge stage whisper, 'Bunnies can and will go to Paris!' Last time, when we ran the Festival from Clarence Gate Gardens, he arrived singing, to music from *Carmen*: 'Mrs Recouso polishing the door / dropping the dishes / scrubbing the floor . . .')

The Festival news is all good: Sinead Cusack, John Stride, Peter Egan, Barbara Murray, Nigel Stock, all confirmed for *Arms and the Man*. And the Shaw Estate (difficult buggers) are graciously allowing us to use two sets rather than three. Best news is that Patrick Magee will direct *Waiting for Godot* – the first major revival since the original and now to be directed by an inner member of the Beckett circle.‡ I like Pat. He is impenetrably Irish, profoundly genial and

---

* He did. See *Guinness Book of Records*, 1977 edn, p. 231.

† Margaret Courtenay (1923–96) was an amply proportioned leading character actress.

‡ Patrick Magee (1922–82), Northern Irish actor, particularly associated with Beckett and Pinter. Beckett wrote *Krapp's Last Tape* for his voice.

permanently sloshed. (And he is like Sam – as we now call the Master. We know that what he is saying is funny and intelligent even though we don't really understand a word of it.)

Saturday, 19 June 1976

We said goodbye to Lope on Wednesday and today we went to Braintree for her wedding.* It has been a brilliant summer: scorching hot, blue skies and dazzling sunshine – until today. On the day darling Lope got married (to Charles Norris, nice accountant), the skies darkened, the heavens opened and the rain came torrenting down. I think she was sorry to leave us. I know we are sorry to lose her. As she got into the car to 'go away', Benet [now fifteen months] tried frantically to cling on to her – and she wanted to hold on to him, too. Lope (looking like Lettice Leaf, the greenest girl in the school, with her moon-like face and gold-rimmed granny glasses) has been part of us. (The jury is still out on her successor, 'Lumpen Lara'.)

Monday, 5 July 1976

The United States of America has been running riot celebrating the nation's bicentennial. There has been much dancing in the streets. There has been dancing, too, in the bar of the Irish Club, Eaton Square, SW1, where we are having the *Arms and the Man* rehearsals – partly because we went to see the first 'run' this morning and it's looking good, but chiefly because Noel was having his first 'open drink' in days. He is just back from his visit with Robert Shaw† at his castle in Ireland and, because Shaw is off the booze, the rest of the house-party was expected to be teetotal also. Noel was severely reprimanded when caught climbing the stairs to his bedroom, bottles clanking beneath his raincoat. Noel knows Shaw and the bottle's a serious issue – Shaw's father was an alcoholic who committed suicide when Robert was 12. Noel loves him, but he loved Mary Ure more. She was an alcoholic, too. Noel was with her on the night she died. She took an overdose after the opening of her play [*The Exorcism*] – Noel: 'You might have expected her to kill herself *after* the notices appeared, darling, but she did it *before*!' He was called back to the house by the police to identify the body. Noel

---

* Penelope Webb had been Benet Brandreth's nanny since shortly after his birth in March 1975.

† Robert Shaw (1927–78), English stage and film actor, especially remembered for *The Sting*, 1973, and *Jaws*, 1975. Mary Ure (1933–75), Scottish actress, was the second of his three wives, 1963–75. She was first married, 1957–63, to the playwright John Osborne in whose *Look Back in Anger* she starred in London and on Broadway, 1957/58.

blames John Osborne – such a monstrous first husband, she was driven to drink.

Monday, 2 August 1976

Michael Winner is a monster, an arrogant nobody.* But Noel regarded him as a 'catch' so we booked him for the second of our Festival Sunday Nights – and that's when the trouble started. The fuss, the bother, the phone calls from assistants with preposterous demands – e.g. on the stage Mr Winner will require a side table, a large ashtray and a new box of long Swan Vesta matches: the match heads must be checked and *must all be in the box pointing in the same direction.* We billed the evening as 'A Man and his Movies' – the most spectacular film clips from 'the most amusing young man in a profession of awful people' (*Sunday Times* – quote supplied by Winner!) . . . He came (in powder-blue Roller) with dark glasses and cigar: I introduced him, from the stage: he did his stuff. He was not very funny and the films are self-evidently not very good. That said, the small audience who turned out for him seemed happy enough.

That was last night. This morning was altogether more civilised. We gathered for the first *Dear Daddy* rehearsal. And because Paddy Patrick is a gent of the old school, instinctively it was all done as these things always were – i.e. the Company Manager and Co. were on parade at 9.45 a.m., laying out scripts, making coffee; the junior members of the cast arrived at 10.00 a.m.; the principals were in position at 10.15 a.m.; Mr Patrick arrived in a suit – always a suit for the first rehearsal – at 10.25 a.m. and, on the dot, at 10.30 a.m. Miss Phyllis Calvert† walked through the door: summer frock, summer coat, summer hat – always a hat for the first rehearsal. We call them 'Mr Patrick' and 'Miss Calvert' unless invited to do otherwise.

Wednesday, 11 August 1976

We live in Campden Hill Gardens, within five minutes of Notting Hill where, last night, the carnival ended in a race riot – bricks thrown, windows smashed, shops looted: 350 police injured, many with stab wounds. It all passed us by, partly because the 'trouble', apparently, never moves south of Holland Park Avenue, but chiefly because we were seventy miles away, having dinner at the Elizabeth here in Oxford. We had dinner there again tonight – celebrating the

---

* Michael Winner (b.1935), film director and producer, then best known for *Hannibal Brooks*, 1969, and *Death Wish*, 1974.
† Phyllis Calvert (b. Phyllis Bickle, 1915–2002), English leading lady, appeared in more than forty films from 1940.

first night *triumph* of *Dear Daddy*. It was the 'civic night', with the Town Hall reception, and all went well except that Noel was truly miffed that I failed to introduce him properly to the Lord Mayor. He (Noel) made a terrible scene in the Playhouse foyer – screaming that he did all the work while I took all the credit. M asked how much he had drunk so far today and I did the calculation – we meet at the Mitre for Irish coffee at 10.00 a.m., then it's Bloody Mary bracers at the Randolph at 11.00, followed by a gin before lunch, wine with it and brandy (doubles) as the *digestif*. However, no champagne was taken before six! Anyway, we made it up later over the Château Latour (truly!) at the Elizabeth. The truth is: we are a very good double act and we both know it.

Friday, 3 September 1976

Francis Crowdy's 60th birthday. It isn't Flood Street, Chelsea, and the wing of a stately home in Hampshire any more: it's a compact ground-floor flat off Earl's Court. But it's Harcourt Terrace and beautifully 'finished' (a startling thick pile carpet – buttercup yellow) and a good time was had by all. A slightly too good time was had by Francis. When Robin Maugham had proposed the toast, Francis, leaning up against the wall, slurred a sentimental response, closed his eyes and slid slowly to the ground. We made our excuses and left.

PS: It rained today. This is *news* simply because this has been England's hottest summer for a century. And still we're managing to fill the Playhouse! (Noel and I stood together watching the audience come out last night: an ugly lot, unprepossessing, unappealing, *uninteresting*. We reflected on the fact that we have been *killing* ourselves to put on a season of plays for people we wouldn't normally want to spend two minutes with. Strange. Noel says he knows leading actors who, at the end of a performance, while seemingly beaming gratefully at the audience, shout 'Fuck you!' at them through clenched teeth every time the curtain falls.)

Monday, 6 September 1976

Last night, in Oxford, old Emlyn Williams[*] (now in his seventies) evoked the young Dylan Thomas for us. He was spellbinding: he simply stood centre stage for two hours and talked – he used only his hands, his voice and his eyes and somehow convinced us we were with a boy in Swansea fifty years ago. It was totally compelling. And he is very charming and flirtatious and young at heart. (Lots of 'You must come to Dovehouse Street, Gyles'!) Tonight, in London, we went to the National Theatre (the least user-friendly building in the history of architecture – give the

---

[*] George Emlyn Williams CBE (1905–87), Welsh actor and playwright.

man a knighthood!)* and saw the new John Osborne play, *Watch It Come Down*. Watch us walk out. We did. We left at the interval – some went earlier. I have never done that in the theatre before. M said we should do it more often. The piece is pretentious tosh.

Friday, 10 September 1976

Chairman Mao has died and we are going to *Plunder* (the Ben Travers farce) at the new National Theatre. Good news/bad news: Good – *Dear Daddy* is transferring to the Ambassadors', opening on 20 October. Bad – the Shaw Estate are bastards. Having told us that we could do *Arms and the Man* in Oxford with just two sets, they now tell us we can't *tour* because our production only has two sets – we have to have the third act set in the drawing room as specified by Shaw. We can't afford to build a new set and re-rehearse, so the tour (plus possible transfer) won't happen now – and the Shaw Estate will lose a hefty chunk of royalties. Fuck 'em! as Noel would say. They are idiots – who gives a monkey's where the third act is set? Anyway, at least we have one West End transfer – and everything else has been good. Nice piece in the *Oxford Mail* about our 'fringe'. Last time we 'discovered' Hinge & Bracket: this time we've scored with Chris Langham† and (Noel's choice!) *Mr X* from Gay Sweatshop.

Monday, 13 September 1976

Last night was the last Sunday night of the Festival: Michael Redgrave with his Hans Andersen readings. The week before, Emlyn, aged 71, swept all before him. Last night, poor Michael, aged 68, struggled to hold the attention of the crowd. I met him at the station and took him to the Randolph. He stood alone on the railway platform, looking bewildered, his fawn raincoat flapping in the wind, clutching a little, battered overnight case that, when he opened it at the hotel, contained nothing but some bottles of pills and his shaving kit – no pyjamas, no change of clothes. He's a stricken giant, stooped, anxious, going on because he has to (he needs the money) and because acting is what he does – it's what he is. His hands shake all the time now: it's not just the drink. Something is wrong with him. He's having tests at the Hospital for Nervous Diseases. He said there is a brain operation that he may have to have. The idea terrifies him. The idea of

---

* The National Theatre building on the South Bank was completed in 1976 and the architect, Denys Lasdun (1914–2001), was indeed knighted and later awarded the CH.
† Chris Langham (b.1949), actor and comedian, later imprisoned for downloading indecent internet images of children, 2007.

performing last night terrified him, too. In the wings, he said he couldn't do it – but, when the time came, he did. He shuffled onto the stage. He sat to read the stories – he sat awkwardly – and he kept getting the pages muddled up. At one point, several sheets slipped from his folder onto the floor. He bent forward to retrieve them, but they were out of his reach. He leant towards them, slowly, painfully. I was at the back of the stalls and thinking I had better go and rescue him when someone in the front row got up, collected the fallen pages and handed them back to him. The stories – translated by one of Michael's old teachers from Clifton – have great charm and his voice (with that heart-rending rasp) is still unique, but the power has gone and with it the authority. He can no longer command the house. The audience stayed with him out of respect and affection: they could see he was not well. The evening was sad, but not disastrous. Afterwards, he gave me one of his sweetest smiles: he felt it had gone rather well.

Noel wouldn't join us for dinner. 'I can't face it. He's a sad old bugger, but he's your sad old bugger, not mine!' (Noel has discovered a 'secret floor' at the Randolph: it's the floor above the top floor: it's where the waiters live. I think Noel is spending some of his nights up there!) I took Michael to the Elizabeth. Simon Cadell came too, as planned. We did most of the talking: Michael sat between us, blinking at us, but smiling. I think he had a happy evening. I hope so. He has been a very great man and I feel the privilege of knowing him.

Lunch today with another great man: Lord Hailsham – a year older than Sir Michael, but 'a different gether altothing' as Noel likes to say. (Noel says this is an expression used by Princess Margaret. How does he know?) N was v excited about Lord H. and had gone to a lot of trouble with the lunch – smoked salmon, lamb cutlets, cheese and salad, fruit and ice cream. Lord H. was giving one of our Festival Lunchtime Lectures. The lunch was really a bonus for Noel. (Because N is an actor he isn't star-struck about other actors: Hailsham was a star from a different constellation and Noel was in awe.) And his lordship was on song. He is very brilliant and very funny. He rattled through a raft of F. E. Smith[*] stories – several of them new to me, e.g. at an election meeting FE suggested to a heckler that he might like to take his cap off before asking his question:

Heckler: I'll take my boots off if you like.
FE (*sighing*): Ah, I knew you'd come here to be unpleasant.

You still can't beat the best:

---

[*] F. E. Smith (1872–1930), 1st Earl of Birkenhead, lawyer, Conservative MP, and one of Lord Hailsham's predecessors as Lord Chancellor, 1919–22.

Judge: I have read your case, Mr Smith, and I am no wiser now than I was when I started.

FE: Possibly not, my lord, but far better informed.

Lord Hailsham, accepting a third libation of port from Noel, told us: 'It was the drink that killed him.'

Thursday, 7 October 1976

We got back from our week in Athens at lunch-time. We have made a decision. Tomorrow, I am firing the nanny. She has been a disaster from the start: fat, ugly, spotty, lumpen, lazy, *stupid*. She has no redeeming features. I do not want Benet spending any more time in her company. She was awful in Athens – lazing by the poolside, rubbing oil onto her hideous body when she should have been about her duties, and muttering and sighing whenever she was asked to do the slightest thing. 'It is supposed to be a holiday for me, too, isn't it?' she bleated. 'No, you fat bitch,' I wanted to say – but didn't. Anyway, the plan is that I tell her tomorrow and she goes at once, with three months' notice, cash in hand. (I am dreading it. I hate firing people.)

Not a good day. The Bank of England has put up interest rates from thirteen to *fifteen* per cent. Our National Westminster overdraft already costs a fortune. It's a nightmare.

Tuesday, 2 November 1976

It's all happening. 1. Nina Tishlakis has arrived as our new nanny. She's not a fat, lumpen girl: she is a petite lady of riper years and Greek extraction. She is a widow, about fifty, highly experienced, very enthusiastic – she looks the business. She has her own uniform. Fingers crossed.

2. I have been the support act to Bernard Manning!* Yes, last night, I took my cabaret act to the Piper Club in Preston – and survived. I shared a dressing room with a pair of topless go-go dancers (should that be a quartet?) and 'the stripper' – a rough-looking lady of about forty who put one foot on a chair and shoved her naked rear-end out towards me while giving me a Pritt Stick. 'Rub it on me arse, darling,' she ordered. 'I'm going to glue on me sequins – gives the arse a bit of sparkle, covers up the crepey bits.' I did as I was told.

The club room was long and narrow, so you had to perform like an umpire at Wimbledon, turning your head from side to side. The go-go girls went on first,

* Bernard Manning (1930–2007), Manchester-born comic and club owner who came to prominence in the TV series, *The Comedians*.

each favouring one end of the room. I followed: I managed *just*. The trick (should I ever do this again) is to be on the attack without rushing: keep it strong, but take your time. I gabbled too much at the beginning and my throat was so dry – but it was fine and given that I was completely clean and inoffensive it went down remarkably well. While I was on, someone shouted, in broad Lancashire, 'What are yer drinking, lad?' I said, in broad South Kensington, 'Mine's a gin and tonic, thanks' – and when I came off there were a dozen of them lined up for me. I suppose they took sympathy. I drank them all. (Actually, I must stop drinking gin. I'm getting fat.)

When I sat down, Bernard Manning rolled on. He came on *from the street*. He travels the circuit in his white Rolls-Royce. He gets to the club and waits outside in the Roller till he's on – then he walks in, picking up the mic as he comes through the door. He launches straight into the act – it's filthy and racist from the word go. But also undeniably funny. He did forty minutes – relentless, non-stop, sweating profusely throughout. At the end, all the lads cheered – including the two Asians. I had a drink with Bernard – 'You're a fucking cunt, Gyles, but I like you. We must work together more often – you make me look good' – and then he stepped back into the Roller and set off for his next gig. He did three last night – and it was a *Monday*.

3. Jimmy Carter, from the peanut state of Georgia, is the new President of the United States. He got almost forty million votes to Gerald Ford's thirty-nine.

Sunday, 7 November 1976

Fund-raising evening for Action Research at the Athenaeum Hotel, Piccadilly. We played a game called *Petropolis – Monopoly* with oil. The company: Clement Freud (with son, Dom), Nicholas Parsons, Simon Williams (& Belinda), John Stride (& April), John Dunn[*] (& Margaret), Sinead Cusack (& Jeremy Irons)[†]. All relatively jolly, except that Clement was determined to win at all costs – and did. I told Sinead that Jeremy is a distinct improvement on George Best. She did not seem to want to be reminded of Mr Best. Simon Williams and John Dunn are not just incredibly tall: they are incredibly nice – good fun and easy company. It's worth noting, because it cannot be said of everybody.

---

[*] John Dunn (1934–2004), broadcaster; in GB's view, the best radio interviewer in the business; he stood 6 ft 7 ins.
[†] Jeremy Irons (b.1948), stage and film actor; a contemporary of Simon Cadell at the Bristol Old Vic Theatre School, he married, as his second wife, Sinead Cusack in 1978.

Friday, 3 December 1976

Ludicrous scenes on Thames TV tonight. Bill Grundy out of control with the Sex Pistols. He tried to be amusing while they abused him. Several 'shits', a couple of 'fucks' and a 'fucking' were aired – there will be howls of protest.* Poor old Grundy: he bleated facetiously while the 'punks' (clearly out of their minds on something) jeered at him contemptuously. It was a broadcaster's nightmare.

We have nightmares of our own at Campden Hill Gardens. The noise from our neighbours continues – horrible loud music played by the young Mexicans on the ground floor. Mrs Windeler [the landlord] affects to be sympathetic, but the Mexicans don't give a damn. They go quiet for a day or two and then it starts again. M is reduced to tears. The apprehension is as bad as the noise itself. We are desperate and looking at sound-proofing (incredibly expensive and not necessarily effective) and possible legal action (ditto).

We are also considering legal action against Simon Clarke Productions. We are not getting our agreed cut from the West End run of *Dear Daddy*. We can't even get hold of the figures. We are due five per cent of the gross box office takings. (They wanted to give us a share of the *profits*, but Michèle said, 'There won't be any *profits* – there never are. *Profits* can be made to disappear. You must go for the *gross*.' We did.) The play is a hit: we are due thousands. Noel is frantic for the money. He has no work. We need the money, too. The only answer may be a High Court action, but the solicitors advise us not to *threaten* action unless we are ready to take it. And running a High Court action, according to Jim Phillips [the solicitor], is costly 'in terms of time and money and spirit'. Is it worth it?

Monday, 6 December 1976

We went to Stratford by train. It takes an age. (Why isn't there a proper train service to Stratford? It must be one of the country's leading tourist destinations.) On the Underground we saw one of my posters,† but when we got to Paddington, I resisted the temptation to visit W. H. Smith and ask for a copy of *A Royal Scrapbook*. Have I already written about this? The book – a gentle royal spoof to mark the Silver Jubilee: the Queen's own scrapbook recovered from the dustbins in Buckingham Palace Mews: *My Twenty-Five Years on the Throne*: photos of HM

---

* There were. Bill Grundy (1923–93), the presenter of Thames TV's *Today* programme, was suspended for two weeks and, eight weeks later, the show was cancelled.
† GB had persuaded a group of his publishers to club together to fund an advertising campaign to promote eight of his books. The poster carried the headline 'Gyles Brandreth is perfect' with, beneath it, 'At least in book form he is.'

and family with balloons and commentary by me – has been banned by Hatchard's because they are royal warrant holders. W. H. Smith will stock it, but only supply it from beneath the counter!! I have pressed Michael Joseph [the publishers] to have some fun with this, but they won't. They don't want to upset W. H. Smith – or Her Majesty. The book can't sell, because no one is selling it.

Heigh-ho. At least the Silver Jubilee diaries are doing well. And we may have the rights to produce the *Action Man* Annual. And I have plans to buy Hamleys of Regent Street . . .*

Much Ado was marvellous – Judi Dench and Donald Sinden as Beatrice and Benedick definitive, both hilarious and deeply touching. There is always a moment towards the end of a Shakespeare play when I want to cry. Always. It is part of the magic of Shakespeare. It's why I want to die having just seen a Shakespeare play. (M has not said this, but I can hear her saying it: 'Yes, dear, it's called catharsis.')

---

* The acquisition of Hamleys toy shop did not materialise, but this marked the beginning of a publishing and editorial services business through which GB and Michèle created greetings cards, diaries, calendars, annuals, books and boxed games over the next thirty years.

Being a Father Isn't Bad

January 1977 – December 1978

Tuesday, 11 January 1977

Went to Bush House for a World Service discussion on the monarchy. The Queen's Silver Jubilee falls on 6 February. There will be much rejoicing. Is it justified? Of course it is – but we took thirty minutes to say so, with a lot of pompous huffing and puffing as we did. The others on parade were John Grigg,[*] the man who disclaimed his peerage and caused a national sensation in 1957 when he called the Queen's way of speaking 'a pain in the neck', and Anthony Howard,[†] editor of the *New Statesman* and general rent-a-smug-opinion. (It's funny: not so long ago, someone like Anthony Howard was a hero to me – a journalist of note, a voice in the land. Now, he's just another middle-aged man with dandruff and a high opinion of himself. He really *does* think he's rather special. He has a harelip and teeth like broken tombstones, poor fellow, so perhaps he's compensating. Grigg turned out to be quite jolly.)

Thursday, 3 February 1977

Last night, at 11.57 p.m., at the Middlesex Hospital, London W1, Saethryd Charity Brandreth was born. Mother and baby both doing well. I like to think the date –2.2.77 – is auspicious. The arrival was swift. We had supper (chicken roasted by M), we collapsed in front of the box and then, halfway through a programme on Marie Stopes (yes!), M said, 'I think this is it. I think you'd better call a cab.'

This morning I have been phoning round the good news. Everyone is nonplussed by the name. I now rattle off the explanation – 'Saint Saethryd was the

---

[*] John Grigg (1924–2001), 2nd Baron Altrincham, 1955–63. In a widely criticised article in 1957 he wrote of the Queen: 'Like her mother, she appears to be unable to string even a few sentences together without a written text . . . The personality conveyed by the utterances which are put into her mouth is that of a priggish schoolgirl, captain of the hockey team, a prefect, and a recent candidate for Confirmation.'

[†] Anthony Howard CBE (b.1934), journalist.

daughter of King Anna, the King of the East Angles in the late 600s. Michèle found the name in the Venerable Bede's History of the Church in England' – and add that she can always call herself Charity if she's unhappy with Saethryd. Noel said: 'Let's hope the poor child doesn't have a lisp.'

I had an amusing exchange with Simon Cadell:

SC: Why *such* an extraordinary name?
GB: Because she's such an extraordinary girl.
SC: Already?
GB: Always!

I love my daughter's name. I love my daughter!

Saturday, 5 February 1977

Saethryd's birth is announced in *The Times* today. It has a supplement celebrating the Queen's Silver Jubilee, but other than that I cannot pretend it is a very exciting edition of the paper. On the front page: 'Rhodesia will contain rising guerrilla tide,' says Ian Smith. 'Two held after bomb cache find' – Irish terrorist bombs found in Liverpool. (The *London* bomb scares are over: they have opened up the postbox in our street again and restaurants like Odin's and Walton's – two of our regulars – no longer have sandbags outside. We feel safe on Campden Hill.)* This is interesting: 'Reprieved murderess to be White House nanny'.

A convicted black murderess, who is an old friend of President Carter's family, was reprieved today in order to take up a post as a child's nursemaid at the White House.

Getting good staff isn't easy! Nina, our nanny, has no criminal record, so far as we know – though she has known sadness. She doesn't speak of it, but I think she had a son who was killed in a road accident when he was a little boy, twenty years ago. Today, she is very gay – very excited about the new baby – anxious too: she is scurrying about the house, checking and double-checking that everything is where it should be. I am going out now, a) to get a present for Benet (so

---

* Fifteen months before, there had been a spate of Provisional IRA bombings in Central London. The targets had included fashionable restaurants and the homes of prominent figures such as Edward Heath. Ross McWhirter, co-founder of the *Guinness Book of Records*, was murdered on 27 November 1975, a month after a car bomb exploded in Campden Hill Square, outside the home of the Conservative MP, Sir Hugh Fraser, and his wife, Lord Longford's daughter, the writer, Lady Antonia Fraser.

his nose is not put out of joint by the new arrival, b) to go to the Middlesex to collect my darling wife and daughter.

(Have I ever recorded one of my favourite Monja Danischewsky lines? The Famous Last Words of the Fatted Calf: 'I hear the young master has returned.')

Later

Well, no fatted calf, but I did do M cheese on toast + tomato ketchup and a salad. It's what she wanted. She is exhausted. She is in bed, asleep now – and looking very lovely in her full, white Victorian-style nightgown. (I like having a beautiful wife.) And I love having a beautiful daughter! Except, of course, the whole thing of the broken nights is suddenly coming back to me: the horror of the 2.00 a.m. feed! M will breastfeed her at first, but my turn will come – sitting up in bed, with an aching back, completely shattered, holding the bottle at the correct angle so that the water goes down (mustn't get any air in it!) . . . Of course, it's worth it, but it's wearying, too. (I say that having children is 'the most beautiful thing that has ever happened to me' and it's true and I mean it – but, at the same time, there's a part of me that isn't really interested at all.)

Anyway, all's well. Benet is happy. Nina is the business. M and Saethryd are fast asleep. I'm here, tapping away as usual. I watched some TV while they slept – but, of course, there was nothing on. Saturday night: *Jim'll Fix It*, *Dr Who*, *Mike Yarwood*, *Starsky and Hutch*, *Match of the Day*. I like Mike Yarwood, but the rest of it is not for me. And on ITV? Larry Grayson then *Hawaii Five-O*. No, thank you. I watched Peter Hall with Christopher Isherwood on *Aquarius* and then caught a bit of Peter Ustinov on *Parkinson*. Quite droll – but essentially a waste of space, time and energy! I should have been writing a sonnet in honour of my daughter.

Tuesday, 15 February 1977

An amusing letter from Mr Miller [the bank manager]. Well, not altogether amusing – he wants the overdraft reduced. He is hearing 'somewhat rude noises from further up the line'. But he is charming about Saethryd – he loves her 'charming names':

> You may be interested to know that in the Bank we have an account called 'Sundry Creditor Balances', or S.C.B. for short, into which we put any bits and bobs of money which cannot be immediately applied, and it is delight- ful to know that you have given your daughter such an encouraging start, and even in infancy have guided her feet into the right paths, by giving her similar initials, so encouraging her to think *black* instead of red!

Last night we went to the National Book League 'Bookrest' dinner and auction – perhaps not an ideal Valentine's Night treat. Talked with Jilly Cooper (all dotty dizziness, but fun), Katharine Whitehorn* (sane, sensible, amused), Lord Longford (full of forgiveness, full of love and nutty as a fruitcake) and John Braine† (full of his own dourness).

Tuesday, 8 March 1977

My 29th birthday. I had supper with M and the parents at the Mumtaz and launched my first High Court action. We are pursuing Simon Clarke Productions for the thousands owed to us. I discovered *Dear Daddy*. I made it happen. Noel and I cast it, produced it and presented it. It's a hit. It's the Play of the Year! But we have not received a penny of the royalties due to us. We will have justice! We will have our money! (Our counsel says we should certainly get justice. He thinks we'll win the case, but he has his doubts as to whether there will be any money to be had once we do.) I am sorry it has come to this – especially because it means that, at the moment, we are prevented from visiting the Ambassadors', seeing the cast, etc. And if we pursue the action – which we will – Simon Clarke is threatening to close the show. That's not a happy prospect for the company – we hear that Phyllis Calvert is calling me all sorts of ugly names – but what choice do we have? Clarke is vermin and I look forward to seeing him, and his midget girlfriend, in court. Right will prevail!

Sunday, 13 March 1977

Benet's 2nd birthday. We had a very jolly party in his honour: Charlie Allkins, Natasha and Harriet Browne, Harry Moore-Gwyn, Sam Holden, Charlotte Festing, Katie Scarfe.‡ Balloons, games, sandwiches, jellies, and a chocolate birthday cake in the shape of a hedgehog. M's birthday tomorrow – the Big T. We are taking a gang to the Caprice and I have organised souvenir matches, menus and huge T-shaped chocolates for the occasion. Simon Cadell and

---

* Katharine Whitehorn (b.1928), columnist and author.

† John Braine (1922–86), English author, best remembered for his first novel, *Room at the Top*, 1957.

‡ The children of GB's sister, Virginia, and her husband, Alan Allkins; of Desmond Browne (libel barrister, now QC and head of the Bar Council) and his wife, Jennifer; of David and Alison Moore-Gwyn (now deputy chairman of Sotheby's and director of the National Playing Fields Association); of Tony and Amanda Holden (journalist and opera librettist); of Andrew Festing (portrait painter) and his wife, Virginia; of Jane Asher and her cartoonist husband, Gerald Scarfe.

Christopher Biggins[*] will be proposing the toasts. Noel will *not* be telling the story that 'closed the old Caprice' – we don't think Mrs Festing could cope. (It's the one where the old Jewish lady has returned from her husband's funeral. In the kitchen, she lights the stove and gets out her favourite frying pan. Into it goes a knob of butter, a chopped onion, a diced tomato, and assorted seasonings. When it's sizzling nicely, she opens her handbag and pulls out a small parcel, wrapped in old newspaper. She undoes the packet and from it takes her late husband's withered shwong. She tosses it lightly into the frying pan and turns it gently with a wooden spoon. She explains to her old friend, Myra, who is looking on aghast: 'All his life I had to eat it his way. Today I'm eating it my way.')

Tuesday is the parents' 40th wedding anniversary. We are taking them to the Inn on the Park.

Tuesday, 29 March 1977

I am writing this on the train, travelling back from Norwich where we have now recorded eight programmes in our series *Chatterbox*. My companions are our amiable host, Chris Kelly,[†] and the jolly farmer, Ted Moult.[‡] It is Budget Day. The star attraction has been Leo Abse – a good man.[§] The main feature has been a reduction in basic rate income tax from 35p to 33p, conditional on the trades unions committing to pay claim restraint. The truth is the Government is in free fall: the unions are running amok, inflation is rife (up 69.5 per cent in just three years!) and the Government is hanging on in there only thanks to being shored up by David Steel and his motley band of Liberals.[¶] It can only end in tears.

Monday, 11 April 1977

I should be returning from Venice right now. Instead – thanks to the British Airways strike and the consequent cancellation of our planned Easter in *La*

---

[*] Christopher Biggins (b.1948), actor.

[†] Chris Kelly (b.1940), TV presenter, writer and producer. He was the host of *Chatterbox*, a children's public speaking contest, on which GB and the speech teacher, Betty Mulcahy, were the regular judges.

[‡] Ted Moult (1926–86), Derbyshire farmer and radio and television personality; the first guest in 'Dictionary Corner' on *Countdown*, 1982, he shot himself in 1986 after a period of depression.

[§] Leo Abse (1917–2008), Labour MP, 1958–87, noted for his dandified dress on Budget Day and for promoting the decriminalisation of homosexuality and the liberalising of divorce laws.

[¶] To survive a 'No Confidence' vote the week before, the Labour Prime Minister, James Callaghan, had formed an alliance with the Liberal Party in Parliament, the 'Lib-Lab Pact'.

Serenissima – I am just in from Cheyne Walk and Katie Scarfe's third birthday party. While the kiddies played, I talked with David Hemmings,* who is amusing and amazing and lovely with other people's children as well as his own. He does wonderful close-up magic. Chatting, I mentioned that on Friday – Good Friday – we had been to see Bruce Forsyth at the Palladium. 'Crucifying, I imagine,' said Gerry Scarfe, chuckling. 'No,' I said, 'in his way, he's a genius.' 'I agree,' said Hemmings. 'At the end of the show, when you thought it was all over, did he send the orchestra home and just sit on his own at the piano and do another half-hour?' 'Yes,' I said. Hemmings laughed. 'I thought he might. It's an old trick. It saves money on Musicians' Union overtime *and* makes the audience feel they're getting something extra and unplanned. These old troupers know what they're doing, don't they?'

Friday, 29 April 1977

Good news: I did the Tyne Tees *Puzzle Party* pilot yesterday. I think it's going to happen. Anne Wood is a clucking mother hen, and completely new to television, and can rub everybody up the wrong way, but, somehow, she's making it happen.

More good news: I joined Pa at El Vino's at lunch-time to celebrate the publication of his book on Parking Law. He is so happy to have it in print at last and I am so happy for him. I *think* he enjoyed the party, but I couldn't be sure. He has been a lawyer working in this part of London for forty years. He *knows* El Vino's – and yet I could see he wasn't wholly at ease there. His book is *definitive* (foreword by Sir Robert Mark etc.) – and yet he was self-deprecating about it. Why are we all so insecure all the time? Why do our stomachs never stop churning?

Mine is churning this afternoon for two reasons: I attended the meeting of the creditors of Simon Clarke Productions Ltd. They are collapsing the company to avoid paying us. They are bastards. I wish them dead. (In the end, I will surely get my way.) I have had the estimate from Roof and Lining Construction Ltd for the sound proofing to the party walls at home: £927. Ditto our bastard neighbours.

On a lighter note, I have just sent a letter to *The Times* complaining about the sight-lines and acoustics at the National Theatre. We went to *Volpone* on Wednesday (not marvellous) but that wasn't my point. My point was that, even with Gielgud and Scofield in the cast and booming, and us at the end of the front row of the circle leaning forward, frequently we simply couldn't *hear*. And it's the costliest theatre in the history of the world!

---

* David Hemmings (1941–2003), actor, writer, director, artist, best remembered for starring in *Blow-Up*, 1966, and *The Charge of the Light Brigade*, 1968.

Being a Father Isn't Bad

Tuesday, 3 May 1977

I have learnt much about life this past twenty-four hours.

1. There are bastards out there. I spent yesterday on the telephone to the National Westminster Bank, Customs & Excise and the Inland Revenue. As creditors of Simon Clarke Productions 'in liquidation', they get their money before we get ours. I don't know why, but that's the way it is. Worse: we have discovered that a new company, Simon Clarke Presentations, has been set up and is acquiring the assets of Simon Clarke Productions. We are going to win our case in court – with judgment and costs in our favour – and still not get a penny. It makes you sick. (Noel is truly desperate.)

2. Love is cruel – and a man will say anything so as not to lose the girl. Michèle's friend came round last night with 'The Man' (we have sworn not to speak his name), her lover (the MP and ex-Minister). She is besotted with him and he is frantic not to lose her. He says he will leave his wife and marry her. He came round to say it at our house, he claimed, so that her friends could witness him making the declaration. The pair of them stayed the night. He's just gone off to the House of Commons. M says he will never leave his wife. 'They don't.' (How does she know?)

3. However much you have, you never have quite enough. I am working like a demon. I've just finished the *Pears Quiz Book*. Today I start on *The Big Book of Secrets*. Next week I begin my biography of Dan Leno. I work every hour there is, but still, steadily, the overdraft grows. It's a bugger. ('But I note that you're still planning a few nights next week at the Manor House Hotel, Castle Combe . . .' Yes, well . . .)

Friday, 27 May 1977

All good. Tasty supper at the Greek place. Cuttings in from the National Scrabble Championships – best coverage to date. For the London Final at the Connaught Rooms, I wore my new 'Gyles Brandreth Loves Scrabble' jumper – a bright yellow machine-knitted jumper emblazoned with a complete Scrabble board.* Lots of pics. We are on the trawl for nursery schools. I try to impress the heads by suggesting that I knew Maria Montessori personally, but the truth is we've no idea what we're looking for. A good *atmosphere*, I suppose. And a teacher you feel is intelligent and alive and kind?

* This was the first of GB's novelty jumpers. Over the next thirteen years they became his 'trademark'.

I'm just in from Ewell, where the atmosphere was *musty*. I took tea with Herbert and Audrey Leno, the son and granddaughter of the great Dan Leno, 'the funniest man on earth'.[*] Dan, the King's Jester, the champion clog dancer of the world, the greatest panto dame of them all – the six-mile route of his funeral was lined with crowds, twenty deep. He was the greatest star of his age, yet who has heard of him now? The Lenos were welcoming and helpful, but they don't have much material to give me and they may have a slightly inflated view of the great man's standing nowadays. (To put it mildly.)

Friday, 24 June 1977

A horrid experience. I went to Hamish Hamilton [publishers of the Dan Leno book] to have lunch with my editor, John Henderson. I went up to his office first to show him some of the pictures. I was sitting opposite him at his desk when his telephone rang. He picked it up and I heard the voice on the line ask, 'Is the appalling Gyles Brandreth with you yet?'

I'm going to Glasgow now for the Knight Children's Book Week. H. E. Todd[†] will be there. He is a shoe salesman turned children's author, the creator of Bobby Brewster and the best story-teller I know. He can take a room of a hundred noisy, fidgety kids and keep them spellbound for an hour. I like him and he likes me. (Some people do.)

Tuesday, 16 August 1977

'The King is dead.' Elvis Presley has died, at Graceland, his mansion in Memphis, Tennessee. He was 42. It is not clear whether it was drink, drugs, tranquillisers, or what, but it's a sad end to a life that, in its way, shook the world. Literally. Dan Leno died at 43. These stars that shine so bright do burn out. I imagine Showaddywaddy and the Sex Pistols will now take a back seat to make way for an Elvis revival.[‡] I was never a fan – I never bought a record – but I could see he had star quality, and then some. And I never met him! I met Johnny Rotten in the lobby of the Midland Hotel, Manchester. 'Oh, Mr Rotten,' I cooed, 'what an honour to meet you.' 'Fuck off, fuckface,' he replied.

The deal is done with Collins Diaries. The contract is signed and I have a feeling

---

[*] Dan Leno (b. George Galvin, 1860–1904), English music-hall entertainer and pantomime star. See GB's *Dan Leno, The Funniest Man on Earth*, 1977.
[†] H. E. Todd (*c.*1910–88), English children's author.
[‡] They did. An estimated twenty million Elvis records were sold worldwide on the day following his death and his recording of 'Way Down' moved to Number One in the UK charts.

that with these people the royalties *will* be paid.[*] I start work on the 1979 range next week: they are 'sold in' by the reps in January!

Odd how being a parent of young children changes your life completely. M is insisting I take Sundays off – making me mark DO [Day Off] in my appointments book. And the social highlight of our week? Clare Sainsbury's third birthday party on Saturday.

Saturday, 17 September 1977

Maria Callas has died. Aged 53, of a heart attack, in Paris. Who's next?[†] I'm not feeling too good myself.

The morning post has brought another communication from Cotton Gumersall & Palmer, solicitors, on behalf of the unhappy Herbert Leno. In my book I say that the great Dan died aged 43 of drink and exhaustion, shut up in an asylum suffering from what his death certificate described as 'general paralysis of the insane' – a phrase commonly used at the time to suggest syphilis. His son will have none of it and accuses me of recklessly 'rushing into print'. But all the evidence is in my favour. The solicitors say I am a novice biographer (true) and that if my book is published (which it will be) they will be writing letters of protest to *The Times*, *Daily Telegraph* and *Observer* so that the family's denials can be heard and 'truth will out'. Good. I think we could use the publicity! That said, I am sorry to have distressed the old boy. I believe I'm telling the truth – and it *was* a long time ago: seventy-five years – but it's his dad. I do see that. (Life would be a lot easier if one could just go somewhere and lie quietly in a hole.)

Humphrey Humphreys, our 'gentleman gardener' is here, doing three hours a week at £3 an hour. He is so grand it's very funny.

Tomorrow is a Day Off. The highlight? Natasha Browne's third birthday party at 3.45 p.m.

Tuesday, 4 October 1977

We went to see Rachel Kempson in *The Old Country* by Alan Bennett. Alec Guinness, the star, is so good at making the ordinary sound elliptical and intriguing. We went round afterwards and had to wait for Sir John and Lady Mills (all

---

[*] They were. They still are. GB created a wide range of calendars and diaries for Collins; more than thirty years later, Collins Debden still publish two of them: the International Management Diary and the Academic Year Diary.
[†] Bing Crosby died on 14 October, followed by the playwright Terence Rattigan on 30 November and Charlie Chaplin on 25 December.

twinkle and charm) to depart before we could open our bag of swag. We were taking Rachel her £1,000 in cash. This is the agreed fee for the Food from France poster campaign: 'The Redgraves love French cheese' / 'The Denis Nordens love French cheese' / 'The Patrick Campbells love French cheese'. I set it up and my reward is £1,000 too, plus a wheel of Brie and two Camemberts per month for six months.

Rachel was anxious to have the loot in used notes. They are strapped for cash: the taxman is on their heels: they keep moving to smaller and smaller houses. Michael is away in Canada doing his 'Shakespeare readings'. 'I think he's fine,' she said, blithely. They are locked into one another, but I am not sure how close they really are. M said: 'Messy lives these actors lead.'

Monday, 10 October 1977

Because I was working yesterday, M has obliged me to take the Day Off today. We are going to Harrods to buy crockery and find wallpaper for the hallway.

Yesterday was good. Bonnie Langford* came round to rehearse. She is the 'guest star' on the *Puzzle Party* Christmas Special we're recording on Wednesday. She is just thirteen and an absolute poppet. I love her. I *like* her. I respect her. She works so hard and she knows what she's doing. She came with her parents: her father (Donald) takes it as it comes, smiles gently and says not a lot; her mother (Babette) is the driving force. Bonnie is her mother's creature, but she's also her own girl. She asserts her independence without being disloyal. She knows what people say about her. She made her Drury Lane debut aged seven in the musical version of *Gone with the Wind*. Famously, Noël Coward was there on the opening night when one of the live horses disgraced itself on stage. He remarked, 'If they had shoved the child's head up the horse's arse they could have solved two problems at once' – except that I don't think he did. I'm not even sure he was there. Bonnie says he *was* there and what he said was: 'Two things should have been cut: the second act and that child's throat.' But I happen to know that Coward used that line way before *Gone with the Wind*. Indeed, I have proof, which I produced for Bonnie. In *The Wit of Noël Coward*, on page fifteen, the exact story appears, word for word, except it's told by Griffith Jones about a play he was in with an insufferable 14-year-old infant prodigy. The book was published in 1968, three years before *Gone with the Wind*. I showed it to Bonnie. I don't think she wanted to believe it.

* Bonnie Langford (b.1964), English dancer, singer and actress.

Being a Father Isn't Bad

The New Year plan was clear. Weight bad (11 stone exactly), overdraft horrendous, action required. And then tonight we had Hes over for her birthday meal: ate too much, drank too much and ended up paying £280 for a pony for Benet! He's called Tonka. Hes will look after him and we'll take Benet over to Tooting for rides. Every child should have a pony . . .

Sunday, 22 January 1978

M's father arrived with Our First Car – a third-hand Hillman Hunter with amazing deep purple go-faster stripes. M drives like a dream, of course. Now I have to learn. (What happened to my plan always to have a chauffeur?)

I'm writing this in my room at the Midland Hotel, Manchester. I've just had dinner with Derek Nimmo[*] and Neil Shand, star and writer of *Just a Nimmo*, Derek's TV chat show. Derek is so convivial, such a happy *bon viveur* – and he knows his stuff. The Château Batailley 1961 really *was* outstanding. I'm not sure where he gets his plummy voice and dandified manner from. He hails from Liverpool and lived in a caravan till about ten minutes ago. And I think his turned-up silly-ass nose is the result of a nose-job that went wrong. But he's fun. The theme of the show was after-dinner speaking. 'The best kind of evening,' said Derek, 'is the one you spend eating with beautiful people, drinking with beautiful people, and sleeping . . . with a clear conscience.' Neil Shand's theme was the nightmare of working in New York for David Frost. He ended up going crazy and flinging a TV set out of his hotel window onto the Manhattan street below. Frost was on the box at the time. 'If anyone had been killed,' said Neil, 'it would have been Frost that killed them.'

Tuesday, 31 January 1978

At 10.30 this morning, in the Companies Court, before Mr Justice Slade, we TRIUMPHED. We secured everything we asked for: every penny of royalties due to us and every penny of costs. Simon Clarke and his dwarf girlfriend sat on the other side of the court, routed. We didn't look at them and they didn't look at us. I had to leave at lunch-time to come to Cardiff. M went back in to hear the full judgment. She called me with the details. It's possible of course that we'll not see a penny of the money[†] – they can just say the cupboard is bare or leave the

---

[*] Derek Nimmo (1930–99), English actor, producer and raconteur.
[†] They didn't.

country – but the the point is: we won. Justice has been done. Right has prevailed. Victory this day. Fuck you, Simon Clarke.

And while we're on the subject, I have just left Molly Parkin* in the bar offering to 'have it off' with whoever's in the mood. She is blind drunk, boasting of having pleasured an entire Welsh rugby team and assuring any who care to listen that the night is young and she's 'well up for it'. She was in my room half an hour ago, just before I began writing this, literally crawling about on the floor.

I'm at the Beverley Hotel, Cardiff. We've been recording *Cuckoo in the Nest* at HTV. Neither is to be especially recommended. But I'm completely happy. We had our day in court – and we won! M and I are celebrating tomorrow with lunch at Quaglino's. I'm then going on to meet Mr Park at John, Bell & Croydon in Wigmore Street to have my 'tubing' fixed.

Tuesday, 14 February 1978

Last night, at 6.30 p.m., I arrived at the Hyde Park Hotel to make my second attempt on the world record for the longest-ever after-dinner speech. I first got into the *Guinness Book of Records* in 1976 when I spoke for 4 hours 19 minutes and 34 seconds. In 1977, Nicholas Parsons established a new record by speaking for 7 hours 8 minutes and 3 seconds. Last night, again to raise funds for Action Research for the Crippled Child, we had a play-off: Nicholas and I, in adjacent rooms in the same hotel, vying to see which of us could speak the longer.

My real anxiety had been the matter of going to the loo. I was confident I could talk through the night, but could I survive the night without needing a pee? That was my dilemma – resolved by Action Research who sent me to John, Bell & Croyden to be fitted with a surgical appliance. As JB&C's kindly Mr Park explained, when he produced the extraordinary contraption, 'This isn't just for the incontinent. This is used by generals and field marshals on parade grounds when taking the salute. Wear this and you can stand out in the freezing cold for hours without having to worry about a thing. The Duke of Edinburgh has one. They're invaluable.' Essentially, the device is a lengthy piece of rubber tubing that you attach to your member and then strap to your leg. It has a four pint capacity and a 'no spillage' guarantee.

All strapped up, ready and willing, a little after 7.30 p.m., Nicholas and I shook hands, smiled for the cameras, bowed to the toastmasters and adjudicators, and moved into our separate dining rooms. We were out of earshot of one another, but the audience could mingle between the rooms. I had a good and sup-

* Molly Parkin (b. Molly Thomas, 1932), Welsh painter, journalist and author.

portive crowd – Pa, Noel Davis plus Margaret Rawlings, Simon Cadell, Tim Smith,* the Saatchis,† Derek Nimmo, Sally Ann Lasson, etc. It began well. It continued well. My voice held. I paced it nicely. At about two in the morning I began to feel the need for the loo. I began to think, 'When am I going to do this? What will it feel like? How much is four pints?' The more I thought about it, the more eager I was to pee and the more inhibited I became. The problem, I think, was knowing that I would be peeing *in front of people*. Of course, they wouldn't be able to *see* what was happening, but would they be able to *tell*? And would there be a noise – a terrible swooshing?! I thought I'd 'go for it' at the end of a story, on the punchline – letting it happen 'masked' by laughter or applause . . . Anyway, the moment came. I finished the story: there was laughter, a smattering of applause and I said to myself, 'Now – *now*, Gyles – *now*! Let it flow.' Then I looked down and suddenly saw it – a long, thin sausage-skin of pale white rubber tubing snaking its way from my left trouser-leg and slowly moving across the floor. My contraption had shifted its moorings and come adrift. At once (and, oddly, without difficulty) I put the notion of peeing right behind me and forged on with the speech. (Interestingly, it's now twelve hours later: I am writing this at 2.00 p.m. and *still* I haven't been for a pee. Perhaps I never will again?)

But the pee that didn't come in the night was not the worst of it. The worst of it was this. At about 6.00 a.m. one of the Action Research people passed me a note asking, 'How are you doing? Are you ready to stop?' I read it out loud and declared I was just warming up. Another note came, then another. Apparently, Nicholas was still going strong and so was I. The organisers had therefore decided we should both stop, simultaneously, at seven o'clock and share the new world record: eleven hours. I thought, 'Fuck that.' I said, 'No, thank you. I'm here to win. I carry on.' Another note came, 'We are worried about Nicholas's heart. We're a health charity. At 7.00 a.m. you must both stop.'

And we did. At 7.00 a.m. they forced each of us to stop. The toastmaster got up and said, 'It's over.' I was very, *very* angry. I don't know how Nicholas felt (I didn't ask), but I was incensed. It was a challenge. It was a duel. And, suddenly, out of the blue, for no good reason, the frigging organisers had decided it was to

---

* Tim Smith (b.1947), a contemporary and friend of GB at Oxford; he later became a Conservative MP, falling from grace and leaving politics in 1997 in the 'cash-for-questions' affair (see pages 576–8).
† Maurice Saatchi (b.1946), now Baron Saatchi of Staplefield, Baghdad-born co-founder of the advertising agency, Saatchi & Saatchi, and his first wife, Gillian Osband (b.1948), then one of GB's children's book publishers.

be a draw. I'm afraid I did not behave graciously or well. I gathered up my notes, collected my coat and went. I did not say goodbye to anyone.

I am still angry now. Of course, it's only a stupid little competition to raise money for charity. I know it's not important, but I am angry. I am going to have to share a world record with Nicholas Parsons. Of course I'm effing angry.

Thursday, 23 February 1978

I began the day in Wellington, having done my best to wow them at the Wrekin Ladies' Circle dinner last night. (I may have succeeded. A charming lady, mid-thirties, very pretty, only a touch overweight, told me her husband was away if I felt like a nightcap.) I reached Euston at 10.15 a.m. and went straight to Capital Radio to do a children's books interview with jolly Maggie Norden (Denis's daughter. I think we call girls 'jolly' when they're nice but we don't fancy them.) On to lunch at Ruggantino's in Romilly Street with Peter Lavery from Hamlyn Paperbacks and his new side-kick, Gail Rebuck.* (Should that be 'jolly Gail Rebuck'? She is *almost* fanciable. Long hair, broad mouth, poor skin, but lots of energy – and energy is fanciable. I imagine she'll have poor Peter out of there in no time. She eats men like him for breakfast.) We talked about the books we're going to do with famous names attached – the cartoon books, the crosswords, the wine guide with Derek Nimmo etc. I'm hopeful. Then on to Eric Marriott at Pelham Books. We talked about Clare Francis.† I had met her, hadn't I? Yes, I said, with you – several times. 'Isn't she lovely?' he asked. 'Yes,' I said, 'very.' 'Don't you think she's really lovely?' he repeated. 'Yes, Eric, she's lovely.' 'I love her like a daughter,' he sighed, 'like a daughter.' 'Yes, Eric.'

Monday, 13 March 1978

It's a horrible world out there. Arab terrorists have just killed forty Israelis who were sitting in a bus on a hillside – we visited the very spot when we were there. In Rawalpindi (where Ma was born) they look as if they are readying themselves to hang their former Prime Minister, Mr Bhutto. In Northern Ireland, according to M's friend, Robert, who is in the army there, the violence is endemic: fourteen killed in a restaurant the other day.

Out there, it's horrible. But in here, where I am, in London W8, it's all rather

---

* Dame Gail Rebuck (b.1952), English publisher, now chairman and chief executive of Random House UK, and married to Philip Gould, Baron Gould of Brookwood.
† Clare Francis MBE (b.1946), lone yachtswoman whose sailing books were published by Eric Marriott; later, best-selling novelist.

cosy. Benet's 3rd birthday party went with a swing (Smartie Artie delivered the goods); tomorrow I'm taking M (in a new outfit) to lunch at Ma Cuisine in Walton Street followed by *Bedroom Farce* at the National; and, today, I'm just in from coffee with Penelope Keith[*] – 'Call me Penny, everybody does.' She is such a decent sort and completely and utterly and exactly like Margot in *The Good Life*. I sat there, being docile like Jerry, while she gave me coffee and agreed to front one of our cartoon books.

Tuesday, 4 April 1978

This morning I travelled up on the train from Cardiff with Lord George-Brown. Our former Foreign Secretary clearly had no recollection of the drunken stupor he was in last night. He recalled having a drink with me in my room, but not crawling around my bed on all fours. What was interesting was that though he drank copiously, I don't think he drank much more than I did, but the effect on him was extraordinary. He is aware that he has 'a problem'. He told me a story of being at the United Nations in New York and having to give a speech after lunch. He'd had a glass or two, but thought he was fine – and he *was* fine until just before he rose to speak when he reached forward and picked out a grape from the arrangement of fruit that was the dining-table centrepiece. He popped the grape in his mouth and bit into it. It was made of wax. He struggled to speak as he chewed on the wax grape, but the words came out all wrong. 'They thought I was drunk, of course, but I wasn't.' And he wasn't drunk either on the night President Kennedy died when he appeared on TV in what appeared to be a state of alcoholic confusion. 'I was *emotional*. Of course I was. Jack Kennedy was my friend.'

Boldly, I asked him for the truth about the famous story of him, at an official reception at the British Embassy in Lima, approaching a vision in scarlet as the band struck up and requesting the honour of the next dance, only for the vision to turn to him and say, 'Mr Brown, I will not dance with you for three reasons. One, you are drunk. Two, this is the national anthem of Peru. And, three, I am the Cardinal Archbishop of Montevideo.' He denied it absolutely, said he'd never been to South America, but was almost sorry there was nothing in it because it's such a good story. I like him.

This afternoon, at 2.00 p.m., at Atlantic House, Holborn Viaduct, I attended the Official Receiver's creditors' meeting re Simon Clarke. We won the case, but we'll not get a penny. There's nothing there. But we have Equity on our side, as

---

[*] Penelope Keith CBE (b.1940), English actress, still best remembered as Margot Leadbetter in *The Good Life*, 1975–8.

well. S. Clarke will not work as a producer in this country again. (And I have a feeling he may die young. M's friend, Veronica, tells the story of seeing S. Clarke's father swimming out to a boat she was on in the Mediterranean holding a tray of drinks aloft as he swam. Halfway there, he had a stroke, sank and died. As Noel likes to say: 'God is not mocked.')

Happier news: 1. Simon [Cadell] has a new girlfriend: Stephanie Turner.* She has a pointy nose and comes from Bradford, but, even so, we like her. 2. We are about to take Benet on his first ride on Tonka – at long last. 3. I am getting to grips with the 1975/76 income tax – at long last (sort of).

Sunday, 30 April 1978

My son has ridden *alone* on his pony for the first time. Benet on Tonka was a lovely sight to see. Being a father isn't bad. And we had a McDonald's picnic afterwards. (Whatever they say, I love a quarter-pounder with cheese and I adore the fries.)

Mrs Power, my new part-time secretary, is a huge success. She is small, trim, spruce – a neat little body, who lives in Shepherd's Bush with her husband and two boys and comes to me to collect tapes, takes them away and brings back the work, all done up in a folder. It's my kind of relationship: we barely need to meet.

Went for a drink with James Michie† at 84 Eaton Terrace. He is a poet, translator and editor whose authors include Sylvia Plath, Anthony Burgess, Alexander Solzhenitsyn, and now me. I am doing a book about *darts* for him. I know nothing about darts, so it's a bit of a trial. He is hugely amiable, tells funny stories about W. H. Auden, loves my children's names (he has a son called Drogo), but – my dear! – his home is a *pigsty*. He led me down into the basement, clambering over manuscripts piled higgledy-piggledy on the stairs (charming) into a dark and dusty kitchen where there was nowhere to sit and the sink was piled high with a month's supply of filthy pots and pans (not charming). He gave me a glass of wine and I tried to drink it without letting my lips touch the edge of the glass.

Tuesday, 23 May 1978

I am in my room at the Beverley Hotel, Cardiff. The light from the single bulb in the ceiling is so dim I can barely see to write. I am just in from supper with Lady

---

* Stephanie Turner (b.1944), English actress, best known as the lead in the television drama series *Juliet Bravo*, 1980–83.
† James Michie (1927–2007), English poet, translator of classic poetry and idiosyncratic publisher, then working at the Bodley Head.

Isobel Barnett* and Wynford Vaughan-Thomas.† Isobel and I get on so well: she is one of my favourite people. We are always, instantly, at ease with one another. (That is so rare a thing for me that I even forgive her her non-stop smoking.) Vaughan-Thomas is a wiry Welsh windbag, but good value. He told a story tonight that he swears is true. As a young reporter for the BBC, in the late 1930s, he was sent to interview the former Prime Minister, David Lloyd George. He arrived at the great man's hotel and was sent up to his room. He knocked. 'Come!' commanded Lloyd George. Vaughan-Thomas entered and found the old goat sitting up in bed, naked, with a couple of tarts either side of him, breasts exposed. Lloyd George was utterly unabashed and recorded the interview where he was, how he was. Vaughan Thomas hurried back to the BBC with his recording equipment and told his editor what had happened. 'Just give me the tape, boy,' he ordered, 'and keep quiet about the rest.'

Tuesday, 4 July 1978

I am just in from my first driving lesson. It is a nightmare, but I must and will do it. My instructor has already suggested I simply learn to drive an 'automatic'. I have said no: I am going the whole hog, however long it takes. He thinks it may take some years.

Yesterday, we went to Norland Place School‡ again. It is the school for Benet. We have seen several: it's another nightmare! How do you choose? We were seriously tempted by Hill House, but the self-consciously eccentric headmaster is a touch elderly now and the uniform is ludicrous and it's a bit too far to get to . . . but Norland Place is perfect: sane, down the road and the Lost Boys went there! Who could ask for anything more? Only problem: no room. We should have put Benet down the minute he was born. (Seriously.) We didn't and consequently he's way, way down the waiting list. I did my best to flutter my eyelids at Mrs Garnsey, headmistress. She said there was very little hope. I said, 'Never mind, I'll keep badgering you.' She said, 'You do that, Mr Brandreth. Keep badgering.'

So I did. Yesterday afternoon I went to the Harrods toy department and, at

---

* Lady Isobel Barnett (1918–80), Scottish-born doctor and JP, who became a well-known radio and television personality in the 1950s; she committed suicide shortly after being caught shoplifting from her village store.
† Wynford Vaughan-Thomas CBE (1908–87), Welsh broadcaster, most celebrated as a BBC wartime correspondent.
‡ Norland Place School in Holland Park Avenue, W8, was founded in 1876; the Llewelyn Davies boys, favourites of J. M. Barrie, and the inspiration for *Peter Pan*, were pupils there.

vast expense, bought a huge, soft, cuddly toy *badger*. I delivered it to the school in person. The school secretary has just called. Benet starts in September. Yes!

Tuesday, 18 July 1978

This morning at 5.00 a.m. M said, 'I've got to go.' I phoned for a taxi. (This is our third child: I'll be driving by the time we have our sixth: I know I will.) We raced to the Middlesex and at 11.05 a.m. our lovely, little baby girl – Aphra Kendal Alice Brandreth – was born. I nearly fainted. When Benet was born it was all so serious, I was kept out of the room. When Saethryd arrived, I was there and almost useful – well, I kept saying 'Keep breathing!' But this morning, I was overcome. Seeing M in such pain – all the sweating and pushing. A nurse wheeled me into an adjacent room to recover. I was back for the birth – the arrival of our little scrap, covered in blood and squawking. She's here and she's healthy and all's well with the world.

Aphra is named in honour of Mrs Aphra Behn – the first woman to earn her living as a writer.[*] And M's mother – Kendal. And Ma – Alice. We want happiness all round.

I am keeping today's newspaper to put in a time capsule for my girl – though I can't pretend today is a hot day for news. The headlines: 'W Germany and Japan agree to boost economic expansion'. 'Police get rises of up to 45%'. 'Mrs Thatcher urges ending aid to Russia unless behaviour improves'. She is doing well and, on the inside pages, there is plenty of speculation about the election and the prospects for Thatcher v. Callaghan.

'Today's birthdays' lists no one I've heard of (Sir Ivo Stourton? Sir John Partridge? Sir Robert Steed?), but on the front page there's this: 'Nelson Mandela is 60'. The 'undisputed leader of South Africa's blacks who wish to free themselves from white domination' is serving a life sentence on Robben Island and, apparently, ten thousand birthday cards have been sent to him from the UK.

Monday, 24 July 1978

Start the Week: Desmond Wilcox, Sheridan Morley, Kenneth Robinson, Barry Norman, Diana Quick, me. Driving lesson: we're getting there. Bodley Head proofs: done. Mrs Power: useful session. Family: all's well. Benet back from his weekend away with the parents in Broadstairs and happy. Nina enveloping

---

[*] Aphra Behn (1640–89), English dramatist, poet, novelist, spy. According to Virginia Woolf, 'All women together, ought to let flowers fall upon the grave of Aphra Behn . . . for it was she who earned them the right to speak their minds.'

Saethryd in love. Aphra is lovely and the nights are fine – early days. But the news of the hour is this: Mrs Windeler is going to agree to sell us the house next door! Numbers 1 and 2 will then make one huge, detached whole and we will no longer have noisy neighbours. But can we afford it? Or must we move to a detached house elsewhere? At least now we have an option. Hooray.

Sunday, 27 August 1978

Today we took Benet by Underground to Tooting to ride Tonka. It was his first Underground trip. He took it entirely in his stride. (I love the London Underground. It is, I suppose, where I have spent much of my life. I remember, revising for A Levels, spending days going round and round on the Circle Line, reading and rereading my notes, and getting off at Paddington every time I reached it to reward myself with a cup of tea.) Tonka is looking well and, according to Hester, Benet is a natural rider with a good 'seat'.

The sun is shining. I love London in August – when everyone is away, just as I love working when everyone is on holiday. But M says, 'Why aren't we in Italy? That's where the sensible people all are.' Certainly, today, that's where the action is. In Turin, the shroud displaying Christ's features has just gone on display for the first time in forty-five years. In Rome, they have just elected a new pope: John Paul I. Apparently, he was swiftly chosen – God was in the mood to be decisive. There is plenty about it in today's paper, but nothing about the ritual that intrigues me. As I understand it, since the unfortunate election of Pope Joan (*c.*850), to ensure that no further female impostor slips through the net, every newly elected pope is required to sit on a raised ringed stool, robed but *sans* underwear, while cardinals pass beneath him, gazing upwards, each one declaring, '*Testiculos habet et bene pendentes.*' I hope it's true.

Thursday, 21 September 1978

I am in bed with gastroenteritis. I am never ill, but today I am. It struck at 2.00 a.m. I feel like death and I fly to New York on Saturday. I have been getting up at 5.00 a.m to finish the Words book. I have been having daily driving lessons. We had the excitement of Benet's first full day at school – he looked so grown-up in his slightly-too-large school uniform. I took a photo of him on the doorstep, looking very serious, holding his satchel and lunchbox. Yesterday was too much: up at five, finish Words, lunch with Gail Rebuck (jabber-jabber), interview with *Nursery World* (jabber-jabber), photograph for *Over 21* (grin-grin) – then collapse. I will be fine, but I feel grim. I am reading *The Last Chronicle of Barset* for comfort.

Friday, 22 September 1978

This afternoon packing my case for the flight to America tomorrow, I dug out my passport and, to my horror, discovered that it had expired. By Underground and on foot – running all the way – I reached St James's Park station at 4.27 p.m. and the Passport Office at Petty France at 4.29. As I reached the doors they were being closed. 'Sorry, sir, we're closed now until Monday.' 'But I need my passport renewed.' 'Sorry, sir.' 'But I must have my passport renewed, I *must*.' 'Sorry, sir. We're closed.' Suddenly, exhausted and overwhelmed, I burst into tears. 'I need my passport. I must go to New York tomorrow. My mother has died.' Within forty minutes, I had the new passport in my hand. I perjured myself: on the form they gave me I declared my mother's date and place of death as 21 September 1978, Brooklyn, New York. To secure my American visa, at 6.00 p.m. I repeated the whole exercise (tears and all) at the US Embassy in Grosvenor Square. (May God and my mother forgive me. If she dies tonight, I shall feel guilty indeed.)[*]

Saturday, 30 September 1978

I am writing this at JFK Airport, waiting to board BA Flight 176, scheduled to depart at 22.00. When I get home I shall speak of the trip as a triumph, but in truth it's been pretty much a disaster. Why did I come? To promote *The Great Big Funny Book* – my first children's book to be published in the US. What did I expect? To be the star guest on *The Dick Cavett Show* and wow the nation, I suppose. In fact, the highlights of my tour were as follows:

1. Guesting on the Joey Adams radio show. Mr Adams is very old and very famous and, apparently, very funny. Certainly, he thought so. My book of jokes was a splendid opportunity for him to retell many of his. In the ten minutes I was on air, I reckon he spoke for eight. At least I was broadcasting from 1500 Broadway.

2. For *The Harry Schneebaum Hour*, I made the pilgrimage to I know-not-where. I got into a cab and gave the driver the address. Forty minutes later I arrived, somewhere north of Central Park. I found where I was going – a dilapidated apartment block. A decrepit hall porter directed me to the eighteenth floor. I found the apartment. On the front door, which was ajar, was a piece of paper bearing the words: 'The Harry Schneebaum Hour – Come Right In'. I entered a cavernous, dimly lit room. There was very little furniture, but in the far corner an elderly

---

[*] At the time of going to press, GB's mother is 95, alive and living in Kew.

man wearing earphones was seated at a table fiddling with spools of tape and an antiquated tape recorder. 'I'm Harry Schneebaum,' he called out, croakily. 'Welcome to the show!' It turns out that he makes a bi-monthly tape of interviews with authors and sends them personally by post to three radio stations in the Midwest who transmit them in the middle of the night.

3. And, today, my one and only TV show. Okay, it was a morning show on a channel no one appears to have heard of, but at least it was television – if a long way out of town. The taxi took an hour and the welcome was disappointing. At reception, they had no idea who I was or why I'd come. Eventually, someone emerged from the back and said, 'Oh, sorry! You're here – but we cancelled you. We called your publicist. You're cancelled. Haven't you heard? The Pope has died.'* Suddenly, I heard myself saying, 'I know. That's why I've come. I was in Rome recently and I met him.' The guy went berserk. 'You met the Pope?' Within the hour I was on air – with a nun, an academic and the Cardinal Archbishop of New York. They did all the talking. I was just brought in at the end. I told my story – ridiculous, absurd, every word of it a fabrication – and as the host leant towards me, clearly urging me to finish, I rounded off my hysterical spiel with this: 'Pope John Paul was a lovely man, a happy man. He had laughter in his soul. The world saw that. And I have a feeling that when he gets to Heaven he will be going straight to the celestial bookstore and ordering this –' and here I held my tome up to the camera – '*The Great Big Funny Book* by Gyles Brandreth.'

Friday, 20 October 1978

Horrible experience. I spoke at a lunch at the Savoy and I misjudged it. The event: a celebration of fifty years of women's suffrage, sponsored by the Publicity Club of London and *Cosmopolitan* magazine. I tried to be funny. I *was* funny. I talked about the emancipation of women and then teased *Cosmo* for its obsession with sex, men and the way we look now. The audience across the room laughed heartily. The ladies at the top table did not. Oonagh McDonald (Labour MP) scowled; Deirdre McSharry (*Cosmo* editor-in-chief) wept; Anna Raeburn

---

* The papacy of Albino Luciani, 1912–78, lasted only thirty-three days. He was famous for the delight he showed on his election and was immediately nicknamed, '*Il Papa del sorriso*' ('the smiling Pope'). Controversy still surrounds the cause of his death, given officially at the time as a heart attack.

('advice' columnist) spoke after me and tore me to shreds. As I left, no one said goodbye. I tried to apologise to D. McSharry but she turned her head away. Raeburn snarled. I have just been walking round Holland Park with M to try to get over it, but my stomach is still churning. M says there is a lesson here: they are paying you so don't try to be clever, just give them what they want. She is right and I will. I know it is the secret: listen carefully to your audience and then play them back to themselves.

Tomorrow I go to Birmingham to do one of my stints for West Midlands Gas – rather more my cup of tea.

Sunday, 5 November 1978

We have to make a decision. We know we need a detached house. We cannot live with neighbours ever again. Even if they are quiet, there is now always a sense of apprehension: when will the noise start? We have a choice: we can either buy the house next door, joining up the gardens, and knocking through on some of the floors or we can buy a detached house. We have now seen several: 11 St Mary Abbot's Place ('a country house in Kensington'), 13 Dawson Place (my favourite, I think), 80 Addison Road (but it's a sixty-year lease), etc. We are just in from viewing something in Abbotsbury Road, priced at £395,000, *worth* £195,000 max. That's the horror of it: the prices. The world is going to rack and ruin – inflation, strikes, national collapse – but the housing market doesn't seem to have got the message. What do we do? We can't sit put.

Later

Happy lunch at McDonald's followed by unhappy trawl through the whole of central, west and south London in search of frigging fireworks. None to be found. Not one. Well, a wretched Catherine wheel, two Roman fountains and a packet of sparklers. M: 'I did ask you to get the fireworks a week ago. I did *ask* you. Do I have to do *everything*?'

Sunday, 17 December 1978

St James, Barbados, West Indies

I should report that it is perfect here. Others may prefer Sandy Lane, but we are very content with the Miramar Beach Hotel. This is our kind of luxury: intense, but not excessive. And they make the children very welcome. Nina is a bit of a wet blanket and doesn't like the sun or the food and won't let the natives launder her uniform – but we are not going to allow the *nanny* to spoil our fun. And she has her uses. And she does her job.

Being a Father Isn't Bad

I am sitting in the shade, on the quiet side of the bar by the pool, with a pre-prandial rum punch at my side. (It does grow on you.) M is with Benet. Nina is with Saethryd. Aphra is fast asleep, we hope. I have just finished the *Sunday Advocate-News*. It seems the island has been threatened with invasion by international bandits. We hadn't noticed: we have not emerged from the hotel compound. And the Prime Minister (Mr Tom Adams) assures us that he will not 'bend to blackmail' and is ready to 'repel boarders' – so that's all right then.

I have to say everything here is very much all right: the brilliant sunshine, the dazzling sea, the friendly staff, the fabulous food. Some of our fellow guests leave a *touch* to be desired – but I suppose East London jewel thieves do have to go *somewhere* for their holidays. (Seriously, some of the folk here do look pretty sinister – and the vulgarity quotient is pretty high. There is a lady in the pool at this moment who keeps telling anyone who will listen that she is a close personal friend of the Governor of St Lucia '– and the Governess, of course.') However, Mr Diefenbaker, lately Prime Minister of Canada, is also a fellow guest and very amiable. I sent Benet and Saethryd past his deckchair to trip over his feet to effect an introduction. I can now say that I have shaken the hand that shook the hand that wrote *The Thirty-Nine Steps*.*

* John Diefenbaker CH (1895–1979) was Canada's 13th Prime Minister, 1957–63. John Buchan, 1st Baron Tweedsmuir CH (1875–1940), author of *The Thirty-Nine Steps*, was Governor General of Canada, 1935–40.

My Life with the Stars

January 1979 – December 1980

Monday, 1 January 1979

The flight back from Barbados was a nightmare. Three weeks in heaven followed by thirteen hours of hell. The plane was packed and late and Nina sulked from Kingston to Heathrow, deliberately breaking her glasses mid-flight so that we might focus on her (and pity her) the more. (The day will come when we don't need a live-in nanny. I look forward to it. Not that we want to dance naked in the hallway, but it would be nice to feel that we could.) We saw in the New Year stuffed in a taxi travelling from the airport to Campden Hill. We got the children sorted and into bed. We collapsed and slept the sweetest sleep we've known in years – until the doorbell went at 7.00 a.m. It was the car to take me to *Start the Week*, a 'New Year Special', live from the Savoy Hotel. M was appalled. 'Why? Why? Why did you say you'd do it?'

Because I thought it would be fun to start the New Year at the Savoy on national radio with Richard Baker & Co. And it was. The usual crowd (Kenneth Robinson, Sheridan Morley, Esther Rantzen, Mavis Nicholson, Lance Percival) with special guests: Bernard Miles (harrumphing like an old turnip) and Elaine Stritch, fizzing with energy and Noël Coward stories. Miss Stritch *lives* at the Savoy. Perhaps that's the way ahead?

Coward attended the first night of *Titus Andronicus* at Stratford in 1955, with Olivier in the title role and Vivien Leigh as Lavinia. At the climax of the play, Lavinia enters, having been cruelly ravished, her hands cut off and her tongue cut out so she cannot name her attackers. She comes on, holding a stick between her wrists to scrawl the names of her assailants in the sand. Unfortunately, as she enters, the stick slips and clatters noisily onto the stage. After the performance, Noël sweeps into Vivien's dressing room, finger wagging: 'Tut-tut, butter-stumps!'

Sunday, 21 January 1979

Domestic news: we are going to have to send Tonka to 'The Home of Rest'. According to the vet, 'the radiographs show the presence of sidebone formation in both forefeet'. Her London days are over: no more hard surfaces, a little light hacking at best. Hes is offering to find a replacement for her, but we can't afford two ponies: we can't really afford one.

Evening with Noel. We picked him up at John Schlesinger's house where he is now lodger and friend-in-residence. (There is no physical relationship: John has a boyfriend.* Noel is simply there to keep an eye on the house when John is away and to be funny when he isn't. Besides, Noel claims to have the lowest libido in London.) We had a White Lady at the Royal Garden Hotel and then went to Nick's, Lord Avon's, restaurant. His lordship† was at the door to greet us: tall, willowy, handsome, charming and – according to Noel – 'queer as a coot'. Noel says Nick is the sort of person who gives 'buggery a good name' – unlike the late Lord Bradwell‡ who, in Churchill's phrase, 'gave buggery a bad name'. The world now knows that Driberg got up to unspeakable things with complete strangers in public lavatories, but you didn't need to *know* it to *sense* it. Noel introduced me to him in Oxford one Sunday morning at the Randolph (Driberg was on his way to Mass, needless to say) and the old boy reeked of depravity. Lord Avon, by contrast, who is also (according to Noel), 'not averse to a bit of rough', comes across as a really sweet and wholesome man.

Noel was on song and told the story of the elderly queen in rep who was appalled to learn that there wasn't to be a part for him in the forthcoming production of *King Lear*. The young director tried to explain that there simply wasn't a role in the piece that would suit his style and temperament, his limp wrist and mincing gait. 'But there is, there is!' screeched the old poof, flourishing his copy of the New Arden Shakespeare in front of the director triumphantly. 'Look at the list of characters. What does it say at the bottom? "A *camp* near Dover!"'

Friday, 9 February 1979

The country is grinding to a halt, but we are carrying on – regardless. Things are truly terrible out there. In Liverpool (land of my forefathers), the municipal

---

* John Schlesinger (1926–2003), Oscar-winning film director, had a partner for more than thirty years, photographer Michael Childers.
† Nicholas Eden, 2nd Earl of Avon (1930–85), younger son of the former Prime Minister, Anthony Eden; restaurateur, Conservative politician, Government Whip and junior minister, 1980–85, until his death from AIDS.
‡ Tom Driberg, Baron Bradwell (1905–76), Labour MP and Chairman of the Labour Party, his confessional autobiography, *Ruling Passions*, was published posthumously, 1977.

grave-diggers have at last called off their strike. The dead can again be buried, but the streets are still piled high with uncollected rubbish. The strikes and, even more so, the 'working to rule' and other forms of 'industrial action', are affecting everything – schools, hospitals, prisons, petrol stations, supermarkets: they can't get the supplies to the shops. It's grim, but on Campden Hill we're rising above it. We have just bought ourselves an Elizabethan four-poster bed. £3,000 (ridiculous, I know) but wonderful.

This morning Paul Callan from the *Daily Mirror* came to interview me. He looks like a junior version of Mr Toad, but he was amiable and I tried not to be too garrulous. (It's difficult, they come to interview you, so you talk. You talk, so they say you say too much. You can't win.) Anyway, I think we got on well. He has a child at Norland Place, too, which helps.

For our Collins *VVIP Diary* Anthony Burgess sent me an amusing Thought for Saint Valentine's Day: 'Laugh and the world laughs with you. Snore and you sleep alone.'

Thursday, 22 February 1979

It was ridiculous and painful, but it's done. I have fired Nina. The relief is immense. I didn't 'fire' her. I simply said, 'It isn't working any more.' And that's the truth. She is fine with one small baby to love – she was perfect with Saethryd. She adored her. She loved her to bits. She bought her a little coat from Harrods; she let her sleep in her bedroom; she spoiled her – but always in a loving way. She couldn't cope with the new baby. It was too much for her. And we had had enough. It was ridiculous. M sat up the road, hiding in the car at the top of Campden Hill, while I went back to the house and found Nina in the kitchen and did the deed. We both burst into tears and I hugged her and she said she'd go at once. M has taken the children to Hythe to her parents for the weekend. Anyway, it's done. The 'burden' of Nina has gone. She had many strengths, but she wasn't right for us. And now she's gone, what on earth will we talk about? All we have done for months is discuss 'the problem of Nina'!

Friday, 23 February 1979

Horrible. The Paul Callan piece has appeared in the *Daily Mirror* – a full page and it is vile: 'Paul Callan meets the wonder author, lecturer and former Monopoly champion – THE BIGGEST HEAD IN TOWN – that's Gentleman Gyles of the Smug Squad'. It's a horrible, *horrible* piece. I am very unhappy. (The photograph is grotesque too.)

Later

I had a call at about 12 noon from Paul Callan. My stomach churned as soon as I heard his voice. I stood up at the desk. (I always stand up during difficult calls.) He was very fruity. 'Hello, old chap. Sorry about the piece. You know how it is. We have to spice these things up a bit – make them readable. Anyway, I'm calling to apologise. Keith Waterhouse is standing at my elbow. He suggested I call you because I'd told him I liked you and he said, "Well, it doesn't sound like it from the piece, so give him a call now to explain." So that's what I'm doing. No hard feelings, eh?' I mumbled something like, 'Of course, not.' 'Let's have lunch,' he said. We won't.

Monday, 5 March 1979

Day at the desk. I completed *Famous Last Words* and *The Z to A of Total Nonsense* and sent them both off to the US publishers (Sterling). The latter I've had illustrated by Lucy, 18-year-old daughter of my *Start the Week* friend, Kenneth Robinson. He is obsessed with his girl, completely: she is the love of his life: he thinks, breathes, talks only of Lucy. She finds it quite oppressive.

Went tonight to the Vaudeville to see Margaret Rawlings in her one-woman show about the Empress Eugénie. Most entertaining, but, inexplicably, no mention of the Brandreths, Deans, Daubeneys or even George R. Sims.* Performance only marred by Miss Rawlings's slightly shaky acquaintanceship with her lines.

Now I'm off to bed with spiritual thoughts in mind. Tomorrow I start preparing thirteen 'epilogues' for Anglia TV.

Thursday, 29 March 1979

An historic twenty-four hours. Last night, at 10.20 p.m., the Government fell – the first government to be brought down by a No Confidence motion in fifty years. The Government was defeated by just one vote. Chaotic scenes in the Commons, apparently. Neil Kinnock and friends started singing The Red Flag. Mrs Thatcher, trembling with contained excitement, demanded a dissolution – and got one. Mr Callaghan: 'Now that the House has declared itself, we shall take our case to the country.' The election is expected on 3 May. I am not standing. I don't have a seat. Does that matter? Not really. I have time on my side.

---

* GB's father (Charles Daubeney Brandreth) was the son of Annie Hope Dean whose first cousin was George R. Sims, journalist, playwright, author of the ballad, *Christmas Day in the Workhouse*, and great-grandson of Elizabeth Montijo, daughter of Count Jose de Montijo and first cousin of Eugénie de Montijo (1826–1920), wife of Napoleon III and last Empress Consort of the French (1853–71). In exile, she lived in Chislehurst, Kent, a place of pilgrimage for several generations of the Brandreth family.

And I have cause for celebration. At 2.00 p.m. this afternoon, in Mill Hill, I took my driving test. I cannot tell you how many lessons I have taken (dozens, scores, I confess it), but I can report that I passed first time. (Yes, the man testing me told me he had bought one of my books for his children, but he only told me when the test was over.)

I am now on the 4.50 p.m. to Nottingham. Another day, another speech, another dollar.

Friday, 6 April 1979

I am in Broadway in the Cotswolds, in a beautiful room in a beautiful hotel, having just come from a memorable dinner. My hosts were the security company Group 4. I spoke after dinner, along with Jorgen Philip Sorensen (the chairman of the company, Swedish, cool, early forties, frighteningly focused), Sir Eric St John (Police Commissioner) and a strange American who sat on my right at dinner, saying very little and drinking quite a lot. I chatted away, while he drank steadily looking into the middle distance. Just before the speeches, I said to him, 'Why are you here? What's your claim to fame?' He looked at me and raised an eyebrow. 'My claim to fame? Walking on the moon, I suppose.'

After we'd both spoken, we talked. He is called David Scott: he was the seventh person to walk on the moon and the first to drive there. He described himself as 'a disgraced astronaut – though I did nothing wrong'. He told a complicated story of taking a cache of postage stamps with him on his lunar mission and then, when he was up there, producing his John Bull printing set and franking them 'The Moon'! The plan was to bring the stamps back, keep some and sell some to benefit the families of the *Apollo XV* crew's children – he was the Mission Commander. 'We weren't well paid as astronauts. I just got my US Air Force basic.'* When the crew returned to earth, the stamps were discovered by NASA and confiscated. Scott and his men – though they had done nothing illegal – were put out to grass. He is full of resentment. He told me how he had seen President Nixon presenting a piece of moon rock to the Pope, but that neither he nor any of his colleagues was allowed any souvenir of their lunar expeditions.

Saturday, 5 May 1979

I am on the train going to Birmingham for the Midlands Finals of the National Scrabble Championships. It is the end of an historic week. It began with the completion of our purchase of the house next door: we are now the proud owners of

---

* One of the stamps – there were 398 in all – was sold at auction in 2008 for $18,000.

Numbers 1 and 2 Campden Hill Gardens. It ended with the election of Britain's first woman Prime Minister. I have the front page of today's paper in front of me:

- 'MRS THATCHER IN NO. 10 – Heath in running as Foreign Secretary'. She has a majority of 43, enough to see her through five years and enough, I'd have thought, for her not to include Heath in her team if she doesn't want to. 'I feel a sense of change and an aura of calm,' she announced from the steps of Downing Street. 'The dignity of office began to work from that moment', according to the *Telegraph*!!
- 'CALLAGHAN GENEROUS IN DEFEAT'. He was. I watched him on the box. He said it was 'a tremendous moment in our country's history' to have our first female Prime Minister. He is right.
- 'THORPE UNBOWED'. Jeremy 'Bunnies' Thorpe was trounced in North Devon. What happens to him now is anybody's guess. (Noel is very clear on the subject. 'Buggery? He virtually *invented* it! That poor Marion Harewood.')*

Thursday, 7 June 1979

Today are the first elections in Britain for the European Assembly. I shall be going to vote in a moment. First I shall try to encapsulate yesterday. I am having to record the events of 6 June on the morning after the night before for reasons that will become apparent.

I began the day at Simpson's in Piccadilly having my beard shaved off. The beard was not a success: I shan't try one again. At lunch-time I performed to the American Petroleum Wives' Club at Quaglino's. It went well: my kind of crowd. At 5.00 p.m. we took Aphra to the doctor: tonsillitis. At 8.00 p.m. M and I were due at the Garrick Club to join Noel [Davis] and his new friend Martin for dinner. Noel is a newly elected Garrick member: this was his first time 'entertaining' there. It was an important occasion. At the last minute, M decided she couldn't go. Aphra was fine, but she didn't feel she could leave her with the babysitter. I went alone.

As I climbed the Garrick stairs and reached the hallway, I heard Noel's voice. He was in the dining room, giving instructions to the waitress. He wanted the table setting 'just so'. I found him and broke the news: Michèle can't make it. He

---

* In 1973, Thorpe had married the concert pianist, Marion Stein (b.1926), formerly the wife of the 7th Earl of Harewood, following the death of his first wife in a car crash.

coped well, shrugged his shoulders and instructed the waitress to reset the table. 'Where's Martin?' I asked. 'Parking the car.'

We went upstairs to the bar and quickly worked our way through a bottle of champagne. Noel was fidgety, not as funny as usual, and kept looking out of the window anxiously onto Garrick Street. We embarked on a second bottle of champagne. There was no sign of Martin. At nine-thirty, the head waiter appeared to press us to take our table for dinner. We did as we were told. Conversation was desultory, but the drinking was steady. Noel had ordered some fine wines: a Petit Chablis to get us started followed by an outstanding Chambolle-Musigny. At about 10.40 p.m., as we were silently draining our glasses, Martin suddenly appeared. Noel barely acknowledged the boy as he sat down our table. Instead, Noel managed to catch the eye of Laurence Olivier – yes, Olivier, looking quite shrunken and frail, was sitting at the head of the communal club table in the centre of the room. Noel nodded to his lordship – and then blew him a kiss. Olivier smiled sweetly and raised his hand to catch the kiss. He clasped it between his palms and brought it briefly to his mouth. He opened his hands and, gently, blew the kiss back to Noel.

'A glass of port, I think, don't you?' said Noel. We got to our feet: Noel led the way, taking my arm, ignoring Martin entirely. He signed the bill and took me into the hallway. We found our place in the snug beneath the stairs. We sat side by side on the leather sofa, drinking port, while Martin stood silently looking on. Noel was now back on song, but performing entirely for my benefit. As we sat there, we watched the passing scene – familiar faces came and went: Noel addressed warm words to them all. Martin he continued to ignore. At one stage, he pottered off to find a club servant to recharge our glasses while I went to the loo. As I returned, Noel caught me by the sleeve and pulled me across the hallway. Advancing towards us were two familiar figures in evening dress: Sir Richard Attenborough and Earl Mountbatten of Burma. 'Yes,' breathed Noel happily. 'The two Dickies together at last.'* He pulled me across the great men's path and effected an elaborate introduction. 'May I present Mr Gyles Brandreth who has contributed so much to charity in this country?' The two Dickies shook my hand and moved on. Noel was suddenly elated. 'We're going dancing,' he announced. And, together, we tripped down the stairs of the Garrick Club,

---

* Both Sir Richard Attenborough (b.1923), actor and film director, later Baron Attenborough, and Earl Mountbatten of Burma KG OM (1900–79) were known as 'Dickie' to family and friends – odd in the case of Mountbatten, whose Christian names were Louis Francis Albert Victor Nicholas.

where, as we reached the street, a huge limousine appeared. As we reached the bottom step, the doors of the limousine swung open and out of the car stepped Yul Brynner. At once, without a moment's hesitation, Noel fell to his knees on the pavement, yanking me down with him, offered a deep salaam and cried, 'Welcome to England, O King of Siam.'

We ended the evening in a nightclub called Heaven. It is under the arches at Charing Cross, opposite the Players' Theatre. The boy waiters wore make-up, silk shorts, roller-skates – and nothing else. Eventually – I don't quite know when – I found a taxi and came home. I had the hiccups. I climbed the stairs and fell onto the bed fully clothed. I did not sleep well. I have no idea what happened to Martin.

Tuesday, 12 June 1979

John Wayne has died, aged 72. Pa says he will die at 71. He says it because that's what a fortune teller told him, years ago, on the front at Margate. I wish she hadn't. These things can become self-fulfilling prophecies. I am now giving the parents £100 per month. Hope it helps.

Later

We had a very jolly dinner with George and Sophie Brown tonight. It was the usual stuff – 'Wilson was a schemer, Mary Wilson is lovely, the Kennedys were my friends, I should have been Prime Minister, we all know that,' from George; 'Oh, George, do shut up,' from Sophie. It was the usual stuff, except that George was on the wagon, and wouldn't be put off his stride. 'I'm not the only one who says I should have been Prime Minister,' he insisted. 'That's what the *people* think. Remember the other night, at that dinner at the Garrick, when a complete stranger came up to me and said, out of the blue, "You are the best Prime Minister we never had."' Sophie scoffed: 'The man was drunk, George. And so was his friend. I saw them both in the street afterwards, sprawled out on the pavement – completely drunk, the pair of them.' It was me and Noel, but clearly she had no idea and, of course, I said nothing.

Their daughter Pat was there: it was a cosy evening. George wasn't drinking, but he made sure everybody else was, trundling round the sitting room, serving champagne or gin and tonic from a little drinks trolley. (It amuses me how *bourgeois* are the lives of my Socialist friends.)

I'm doing a book on great oratory with George: we are calling it *The Voice of History*. Of those he's heard, he ranks Churchill and Aneurin Bevan as the most formidable. Macmillan, he says, was a complete phoney, 'all histrionics and ham acting'. He says the single most brilliant speaker of his lifetime was Professor Harold Laski[*] who broke all the rules of public speaking, delivering every address as a lecture, with the minimum of movement, one hand fixed on his lapel, the other locked in his jacket pocket, the voice grating, almost monotonous, but the content, logic, wit and presentation, overwhelming. (Laski sounds to me to be in the same tradition as Enoch Powell.)

I showed George something intriguing I'd come across – *The Times* correspondent's reaction to Abraham Lincoln's great Gettysburg Address:

> The ceremony was rendered ludicrous by some of the sallies of that poor President Lincoln . . . Anything more dull and commonplace it wouldn't be easy to imagine.

(I don't think journalists realise how much they are despised – and not just by politicians.)

'Fourscore and seven years ago our fathers brought forth upon this continent a new nation . . .' It's matchless – but, intriguingly, even Lincoln was disappointed at the time. His immediate verdict: 'That speech fell on the audience like a wet blanket. I am distressed about it. I ought to have prepared it with more care.'

Wednesday, 20 June 1979

A happy day, sunny and busy. We have acquired rights in Popeye, Flash Gordon and Felix the Cat. I spent the morning devising interesting ways in which to exploit them – puzzle books, diaries and so on. I then went off to the the *Evening Standard* lunch at the Hyde Park Hotel. This was the hotel where, as a child, with Pa, I saw Randolph Churchill climbing up the steps. Well, today, I sat with another of the Churchill offspring – Mary Soames.[†] She was charming and very happy to talk about her parents. Her father was clearly her great hero: even when he was an old man she loved to sit and listen to him talk. He hated having to go to bed. After dinner, he would sit at the dining-room table late into the evening, lighting another cigar, demanding another brandy and telling another story from his long and incredible life. Mary would sit enraptured. Her mother would look reprovingly at the clock and say, 'Winston, it's

---

[*] Harold Laski (1893–1950), Professor of Political Science at the London School of Economics, chairman of the Labour Party, 1945–6.

[†] Mary Soames, Baroness Soames LG DBE (b.1922), youngest daughter of Winston Churchill (1874–1965) and his wife Clementine (1885–1977); married to Christopher Soames, Baron Soames GCMG, GCVO, CH, CBE (1920–87).

gone midnight.' Churchill would then eye the clock himself and rumble: 'Command the moment to remain.' Mary told me that her mother had owned a marble cast of her father's hand, made after his death. His hand was quite small and delicate – surprisingly so. She said that her mother cherished the cast – 'it meant that she could go on holding his hand even after he had gone.'

Also at our table: Christopher Soames, genial, large, jowels wobbling; and Victor Matthews and Jocelyn Stevens, chief executive and managing director of the *Standard* and *Express*.[*] These two, one rough, one smooth, were wonderful to watch. Their self-confidence – the sense that they owned all they surveyed, that they were masters of everything (especially things the rest of us knew nothing of) – was breathtaking.

Thought for the day, sent to me by Emlyn Williams: 'I seem to spend many of my days, and most of my evenings, avoiding the temptation to take Saki's perilous advice: "The art of social behaviour is to know exactly where to stop . . . and to go a bit further." It's not always easy!'

Monday, 9 July 1979

Lunch with Kenneth Williams at Pomme d'Amour. He is so funny – if not totally easy. He arrived, all demure and buttoned up, keeping himself to himself, hiding under a hat so as not to be recognised; then, over lunch, he began telling stories so loudly that no one in the restaurant (or possibly within one mile of the restaurant!) could have had any doubt as to who was there. He has agreed to do the book. He loves my title [*Acid Drops*]. He thinks it is entirely right for him. It is.[†] And it'll be fun to do. I like him – despite the non-stop smoking. He is obsessed with his health (his bowels mostly) and money (his lack of it; and the amount of tax he has to pay on the little he does earn; the maximum he got for any of the *Carry On* films was £5,000). He has a small cast of characters who people his stories: 'Baxter'

---

[*] Lord Matthews (1919–95) was chairman of Fleet Holdings, owners of the Express group of newspapers; Sir Jocelyn Stevens CVO (b.1932) had owned *Queen* magazine before joining the Express Group as managing director.

[†] *Acid Drops*, a collection of caustic humour, became a Number One best-seller. Kenneth Williams's diary entry for 9 July 1979 reads: 'Went to see Gyles Brandreth and he told me about the idea of the book of "acid drops" which he would collate & have me sponsor: the foreword which they want from me can be done with tape recording & I don't have to write a spiel. I found him very engaging & because of this I became more and more forthcoming & was eventually talking in terms of the confessional: "My sexual indulgence is all masturbatory . . ." etc. He said he would arrange for the publishers (Dent) to pay for my endorsement of the book over 3 years.'

(Stanley Baxter), 'Gordon' (Gordon Jackson) and 'Mags' (Maggie Smith). He doesn't explain who these people are. He just launches into a story and expects you to catch up. I can't believe there is a funnier anecdotalist in the land.

Nina [the former nanny] is coming to tea. We're slightly dreading it, but we know it's the right thing to do.

Monday, 27 August 1979

We returned today from Corfu to the news of the murder of Lord Mountbatten.[*] Horrible. Corfu was wonderful. We will do it again. I thought four weeks would be too long, but it worked, got better and better. Somerset Maugham, C. P. Snow, Anthony Trollope and W. M. Thackeray were our good companions. I am bronzed, Michèle is beautiful, the children are content. The post awaiting us is horrendous – so much to be dealt with and too few cheques. The sun in Corfu was dazzling. Here it's sunny and our house is lovely, but it all feels a bit cramped and dark after our island idyll. And the news from Ireland is truly terrible.

Monday, 10 September 1979

An amusing lunch with the engaging Dr Magnus Pyke.[†] I went to his house in St Peter's Square, W2: it is airy and full of clocks. He was reading *Pride and Prejudice*. He rereads Jane Austen every year. 'I've reached that age.' He told me not to worry about insomnia. 'You won't die of it. People don't. If you can't sleep, get up and do something. You'll fall asleep eventually.' We went round the corner for an Indian meal. In the street, as we walked, he waved his arms about exactly as he does on television – but, possibly, a little more ostentatiously. I think he likes to be recognised. M asks: why doesn't he get his teeth fixed?

Wednesday, 26 September 1979

I went by train to Poole, to the Arts Centre, to see Kenneth [Williams] in *The Undertaking*, a lugubrious, wordy, and largely unintelligible play by Trevor

---

[*] Mountbatten was murdered by the IRA while on holiday at his summer home in County Sligo. Also killed in the bomb attack were his grandson Nicholas, 14, and a young boatman, 17.
[†] Dr Magnus Pyke (1908–92), nutritionist, scientist and one of many television and media personalities with whom GB created books over the next ten years. Others included Richard Briers, Michael Caine, Henry Cooper, Charlie Drake, Larry Grayson, Frankie Howerd, John Inman, Spike Milligan, Dudley Moore, Patrick Moore, Derek Nimmo, Leonard Rossiter, Ned Sherrin, Donald Sinden, Tommy Steele, Richard Whiteley, Barbara Windsor and Mike Yarwood.

Baxter. It's set in a morgue and the atmosphere, on stage and in the auditorium, is appropriately funereal. Kenneth can't decide whether it's a profound work of genius or a load of old cobblers. His performance is very mannered: cheeks sucked in, buttocks held tight, paragraphs spat out like machine-gun fire with an incredibly elongated vowel thrown in every now and then for no good reason. The audience, hoping for *Carry On Hearse*, is sorely disappointed. Kenneth seems resigned to the play being a failure. 'All I do now is flops.' His mood-swings are quite exhausting. Tomorrow I am seeing Barbara Windsor.* (Kenneth loves Barbara and Barbara loves Kennie. 'I love him to bits.') The joy with Barbara is that she is always the same: jolly. And she sees the best in everyone. We were driving back together from Norwich once and we came into London through the East End and we passed *The Blind Beggar*, the Kray twins' pub. 'They wasn't bad boys, Gyles. Not really. They loved their mum.' 'But weren't they murderers, Barbara? Didn't they kill people?' 'You'd have been quite safe with them, darlin'. They only ever killed their own.'

Wednesday, 3 October 1979

I have come to Yorkshire where the Yorkshire Police have just a launched a £1 million campaign to find the 'Yorkshire Ripper'.† He claimed his tenth victim here in Bradford a month ago. At lunch, the Archbishop of York (Stuart Blanch: doesn't give a lot away) said a prayer for the victims. After lunch, I made them laugh, but James Herriot‡ it was who made them smile. He made them feel good about themselves. There is a lesson here. I didn't find him that interesting or remarkable, but the audience *loved* him. There are just some folk who are loved. The last of these literary lunches I did was with David Attenborough: they love him too (warm to him and respect him) – in a way they never will his brother Richard, for example. Interesting.

Wednesday, 10 October 1979

Reginald Bosanquet has resigned from ITN.§ The drink has finally got to him. We shall all miss the slurring and the skew-whiff toupee. Coffee with Leonard

---

* Barbara Windsor (b. Barbara Deeks, 1937), English actress, best known for her roles in the *Carry On* films and, later, the TV series *EastEnders*.

† Eventually identified as Peter Sutcliffe (b.1945) and convicted of murdering thirteen women and assaulting others; currently serving a life sentence at Broadmoor Hospital.

‡ James Herriot, pen name of James Alfred Wight OBE (1916–95), Yorkshire vet and best-selling author of *All Creatures Great and Small* and several sequels.

§ Reginald Bosanquet (1932–84), journalist, best known as a newsreader for ITN.

Rossiter[*] at his little house in Billing Road, SW10. He crackles with tension: his nervous energy is alarming. We are going to do a book with him on sarcasm. All he has to do is appear on the cover and cash the cheque. I think he's happy about that. I left him preparing for a game of squash. I would not have wanted to be his opponent. Spent the rest of the day with Kenneth [Williams] working on *Acid Drops*. Clive[†] has prepared a load of raw material and Kenneth and I are going through it, quote by quote, Kenneth retelling the stories in his own words and adding some extras along the way. One he came up with that I hadn't heard before. Bernard Shaw and a fellow music critic at a concert. The friend says of the string quartet: 'These four have been playing together for twelve years.' Shaw: 'Surely we have been here longer than that.'

Kenneth smoked a complete packet of cigarettes and then went out to buy some more. And he doesn't want to have lunch – and when I do, he gets ratty and says, 'Don't you want to work then?'

Sunday, 28 October 1979

A quite wonderful evening followed by a quite ghastly morning. Last night we went to the Peter Shaffer play, *Amadeus*, at the National Theatre. It is as good as everybody says: intelligent, moving, beautifully staged by Peter Hall. This morning I have been taking part in a ludicrous football match organised by Jonathan Routh[‡] to promote his book of Queen Victoria paintings. He had 'personalities' (vaguely known/barely known suckers like me) and friends of his dressed as Queen Victoria and in a corner of Hyde Park we kicked a football about for the benefit of a very small band of press photographers. I took Benet and kept him on my shoulders throughout the game – for comfort and security. Why did I go? People think I'm garrulous, but I'm not. I don't like parties. I like going to the theatre to see an intelligent play and then having supper *à deux* with my wife. As a child, from one of my favourite books, *The Faber Book of Comic Verse*, I learnt this poem.[§] I never understood it properly until today.

> I wish I loved the Human Race;
> I wish I loved its silly face;

[*] Leonard Rossiter (1926–84), English actor, best remembered for his leading roles in the television series, *Rising Damp* (1974–75) and *The Fall and Rise of Reginald Perrin* (1976–79).
[†] Clive Dickinson (b.1953), writer and editor, worked with GB and Michèle on almost all their projects from this period onwards.
[‡] Jonathan Routh (1927–2008), TV presenter, author, artist, best remembered as the prankster from *Candid Camera* on ITV, 1960–67.
[§] By Sir Walter Raleigh (1861–1922).

I wish I liked the way it walks;
I wish I liked the way it talks;
And when I'm introduced to one,
I wish I thought 'What Jolly Fun!'

Thursday, 1 November 1979

The Old House, Wickham, Hants

The Government has announced £3,500 million in spending cuts and increased prescription charges. Our new Prime Minister [Mrs Thatcher] means business.

And we mean to come here again and to keep up our practice of taking just two glasses of champagne before dinner. (We got the idea from C. P. Snow.) Last night, when we were having dinner, Mr Skipwith [the proprietor of The Old House Hotel] came to our table and said, 'There's a young gentleman to see you.' Benet had come downstairs, starkers, and presented himself at reception. This is a lovely hotel: the Skipwiths are lovely people: and the *pommes dauphinoise* are a reason for living. Another reason for living – last night, after our picnic in the New Forest, we took the children to Salisbury and parked in the cathedral close. They were exhausted and lay, higgledy-piggledy, fast asleep on the back seat, but we were wide awake and saw the sun setting on the honey-coloured stone of Salisbury Cathedral. I don't believe I have ever seen anything more beautiful.

Tuesday, 6 November 1979

The advent of Margaret Thatcher has been wonderful for everyone, whether they realise it or not. Except for one man – and he voted for her. I had lunch today with Mike Yarwood.[*] He is very sweet, but shy and rather dull, and he has a problem. He can't do Mrs Thatcher. His Heath, his Wilson, his Denis Healey – all masterly, but all now yesterday's men. He is really concerned that Mrs T.'s success will be his undoing. I tried to persuade him to do some of his 'characters' for me at lunch, because, sorry to say, when he's himself it's as if no one's there.

Tuesday, 1 January 1980

Welcome to 1980. A new year and a new resolve. We are going to get on top of our mountain of mortgages and start making some serious sums. We have a raft

---

[*] Mike Yarwood (b.1941), impressionist, whose TV career spanned 1966–87 and whose shows in the 1970s were among the most popular on television.

of good books planned for a widening range of publishers. In the next seven days I am having lunches with Anthony Cheetham (he's planning to start his own business and needs product), Tony Lacey (Puffin), Sally Floyer (Beaver), Nigel Hollis (Hutchinson, son of the spy – but was he? wasn't he? even the son doesn't know!)* – the aim is to sell at least a book a week. Plus the diaries, calendars, games, etc. Currently I have around a hundred ideas on my list. I will be writing less and 'packaging' more. Onward!

Domestic start to the New Year. Yesterday, we took a party of children to *Sooty* at the Mayfair. (Sooty still works for me! Though Sweep is the star. Can't stand Soo.) We've just driven Catherine and Charlie [GB's niece and nephew] back to St Albans. We are now going to the BBC to watch Simon [Cadell] recording his *Hi-de-Hi* pilot. He plays a reluctant holiday camp manager. It's set in the 1950s. He says it's very funny. We shall see.†

Alan Whicker sent me this little bit of wisdom with which to start the New Year: 'Judge a man by the way he treats someone of no use to him.'

Friday, 18 January 1980

Recruiting new writers: Martin Bergman and Rory McGrath came round. Ex-Cambridge Footlights, not a load-of-laughs on the face of it, but we'll see. (I need someone to write *The Irish Kama Sutra*.) Recruiting new talent: I went over to 17 Balmuir Gardens, SW15, to see Patrick Fyffe (aka Dame Hilda Bracket). He has permed curly blond hair and a very sweet way with him. He lives the life of Dame Hilda B. (lives it completely: his sitting room is all antimacassars and Edwardian *bric-à-brac*) and wants to write her 'autobiography'. When he's being Patrick there is something a touch pathetic about him; when he switches into Dame Hilda he acquires a personality, he becomes funny and fun.

Friday, 25 January 1980

A long day in Strackton Tressle [the imaginary village where Dame Hilda Bracket and Dr Evadne Hinge had their home] followed by an even longer evening at *The Undertaking*. It has opened at the Fortune, but it can't last. Drinks afterwards with the producer, Bill Kenwright (amiable), the author, Trevor Baxter (fruity), the star, Kenneth [Williams] (morose), the leading lady, Miriam

---

* Sir Roger Hollis (1905–73), Director General of MI5, 1956–65; there was speculation, never wholly resolved, that he might have been a double agent.
† *Hi-de-Hi!*, created by Jimmy Perry and David Croft, ran from 1980 to 1988. Simon Cadell later married David Croft's daughter, Beckie.

Karlin (just normal – gosh, I like that. She knows it's rubbish, but hopes it works because she could use the money. It's a long time since *The Rag Trade*.)*

Tuesday, 5 February 1980

A ridiculous day. I arrived at the office (the ground floor of the house next door) to find Leo (our new bookkeeper) already there, on all fours, awash, mopping up a lake of water around her. Last night, she worked late and left the taps running in the bath. The bathroom on the ground floor contains a bath. We have covered it with a board and use it for the coffee things – but the bath still works. Leo, bless her, is a Buddhist and she likes to have the sound of running water in the background while she prays. Yesterday, she was here alone. I was with Kenneth all afternoon and then went straight off to supper with Jonathan Cecil. Leo finished work, then got out her prayer mat and bells and turned on the bath taps. When she had finished her spiritual endeavours, she was on such a high that she set off home without remembering to turn off the taps. The carpet in the bathroom, hallway and front office look ruined. Bah.

I am just in from lunch with Hayley Mills at Sambuca. It really was ridiculous. *I* really was ridiculous. I told her how I had loved her since I was eleven. She smiled. We held hands. It was absurd – at every level. I said all these ridiculous things to her, while at the same time thinking, suddenly, how old she looked (I suppose she is 33, but her skin has not weathered well) – and how I'm not really sure I like her at all. She has ludicrous views about life and love and Hare Krishna. Oh dear, oh dear. Embarrassing.

We were having supper with Chris Biggins, but he has just phoned to cancel. Tomorrow I'm off to Norwich at dawn to record some 'epilogues' for Anglia, then on to Nottingham to see Simon in *Private Lives*.

Wednesday, 19 March 1980

I spent the morning with Larry Grayson.† We travelled in his chauffeur-driven white Rolls-Royce to the photographer to get the pictures taken for the book. Larry was . . . well, he was happy as Larry. He always is. Kenneth is demanding. Patrick Fyffe is needy. But Larry is just grateful. He sat in the back of his car, a cashmere rug across his knees, simply beaming. 'Isn't the snow lovely? Isn't life

---

* Miriam Karlin (b.1925) had starred in the hugely popular situation comedy, *The Rag Trade*, 1961–3 and 1977–8.
† Larry Grayson (b.William White, 1923–95), English comedian, best remembered for hosting *The Generation Game*, 1978–81.

grand? Aren't you a pretty boy, Gyles? Pity about the wife and kiddies.' He is so thrilled with his sudden, late-life success. 'What a surprise! What a gay day!' His act is limited, but his charm is infinite.

And he is entirely at ease with his homosexuality. I don't think much 'happens', but I doubt that it bothers him. Kenneth, on the other hand, talks about his non-existent sex-life all the time. The last time anything *happened* in that department, so he says, was after the war, in Ceylon, with a young Sikh: 'It was only fumbling, just the Barclays Bank.' Kenneth is tortured: guilt, desire, disgust – they're all there, bubbling away. Patrick Fyffe is not so tortured, but he is unhappy. He is not brooding about sex, I don't think: he is hungry for love. He wants a companion. He wants to be a good man's wife. And the photographer has love, but won't admit it. He has a boyfriend, but we never see him. He was there this morning (I'm sure), but locked away, hidden in the bedroom, with the key turned. Yes, the photographer's boyfriend was literally locked in the closet while Larry Grayson was camping it up in the front room. *What* a gay day!

Sunday, 20 April 1980

Sunday morning at the end of our week in Wickham. It's been a good week. The children have loved the picnics under 'our tree' in the New Forest, by Beaulieu. We have loved our dinners here: last night, *L'avocat Fermont* (avocado with poached egg and sauce béarnaise, served hot), followed by *Blanquette de veau Alsacienne*. Glorious desserts. Wonderful pudding wines. Bill to match: £651.94 for the week.

Today we are lunching with Desmond and Jennifer Browne at Stansted House, home of the Earls of Bessborough, kin of Desmond's of some kind. We have been before: his aunt (?) lives in a wing where it's dark and dusty and rather draughty and there's newspaper covering the lino on the kitchen floor. (These aristos all live like this. Their cuffs are always frayed.) At 1 and 2 Campden Hill Gardens, where the completely middle-class Brandreths live, we will be returning tonight to find the new playroom completed. The new hall carpet arrives on Thursday.

As I write, I am sitting on our hotel bed with a coffee and the papers. News of the week: the Union flag has been lowered in Africa for the last time. Our colonial age is past. Rhodesia is now Zimbabwe and the new Prime Minister, Robert Mugabe, is looking for reconciliation between black and white: 'If yesterday you hated me, today you cannot avoid the love that binds you to me and me to you.' If the photographs are anything to go by, the outgoing Prime Minister, Ian Smith, has his doubts about this.

My Life with the Stars

Monday, 5 May 1980

In Zaire, nine worshippers have been trampled to death trying to catch a glimpse of the Pope. In London, W1, I have been on *Start the Week* interviewing Gerald Campion, the actor who played Billy Bunter. He still looks and sounds exactly like Bunter.* Michael Palin was also on the programme. He is doing a kind of Greyfriars spoof called *Ripping Yarns*. We all agreed that anyone who could create Bunter *and* translate the complete works of Gilbert and Sullivan into Latin has to be classed a genius of some sort, but we couldn't quite put our collective finger on what it is about the world of Greyfriars that remains so compelling. I got home full of all this and Michèle said, 'Can we move on from your childhood, please?'

Later

The Iranian Embassy siege is over. The SAS have stormed the building – in spectacular style. Nineteen hostages rescued in an operation that lasted eleven minutes. We drove past – it's only five minutes from here. The front of the building is blackened: there are cordons, armoured cars, police everywhere. As we drove by, M mused: 'The SAS – I think that's what we call *real* men. Now, Gyles, do tell me some more about Billy Bunter.'

Wednesday, 14 May 1980

My back has gone, but I am struggling on. (M says: 'Isn't this where I came in?' She is right. I think the last time I had it this bad was 1968. When I do too much, the back goes. That's it. The trouble is: there is much to be done!) Lunch with Gail Rebuck (worthwhile: we have ten projects with her and more in the pipeline) and then tea with Julian Slade. The creator of *Salad Days* lives in the basement of a beautiful house in Priory Walk. His mother lives upstairs. (What is it about these middle-aged homosexuals and their mothers? Kenneth has his mother, Louie, living in the flat next door. He finds her increasingly tiresome, but he can't keep away from her. He goes to have supper with her every evening. He hates watching the TV programmes she wants to watch, but he can't keep away.) Julian is very sweet and very sentimental. My 'beauty and charm' overwhelmed him: he cried several times during our time together! But he loves the idea of the A. A. Milne musical and we are going to give it a go. This is not a play about

---

* Gerald Campion (1921–2002), actor, restaurateur, founder of Gerry's Club, played Billy Bunter on television, 1953–61.

Winnie-the-Pooh. This is a play about Alan Milne, writer, husband, father, a man all his life trapped by his own creation.

Today is the TUC's 'Day of Action'. It has not taken the nation by storm. Mrs Thatcher is our captain now. The world has moved on and Michèle and I are off to the Pomme d'Amour for a light supper.

Wednesday, 28 May 1980

Lunch with Anna Ford* at Odin's. Absurd. I wanted to get there first so that I would already be seated and she wouldn't see me bent double. Unfortunately, we arrived at the same time. I hoped to be taken for an English Robert Redford. In the event, I escorted her to our table looking like a disabled Quasimodo. And she is so beautiful – *so* beautiful. I did not seduce her, nor even, I think, amuse her very much. She is a cool customer and quite conscious of her own worth.

We are going to Wickham for half-term. I have just phoned the agents for the Playhouse Theatre.† I am going to see it next week for the second time. I want to buy it and develop it, using it as a conference centre by day and as the home of the London Repertory Company by night. We shall see.

Saturday, 28 June 1980

Sweeney Todd at Drury Lane. Well, the audience loved it. The house was packed and they roared. Certainly the refrain is haunting – 'Attend – the tale – of Sweeney Todd – the demon barber of – (long pause) – Fleet Street!' – but all the bloody Grand Guignol and strangulated shout-singing didn't do it for us. Simon [Cadell] and Stephanie [Turner] enjoyed it more, but not much. We all loved meeting up with Biggins and Peter Polycarpou at Joe Allen's afterwards. Now, *that* was fun.

Lots of important things to report, but I am too squiffy now (it's one in the morning – M's in the bathroom) and tomorrow I am working on our plan to develop Peter Rabbit – take him beyond the Beatrix Potter books, while remaining true to the Potter values. M mocks my obsession with things childish, but it's making us the loot. (Also, loan arrangement with County Bank progressing.) Unemployment in the UK now highest since the war, but here on Campden Hill we are *busy* and thankful for it. Goodnight.

* Anna Ford (b.1943), English broadcaster, best known as a newsreader from 1978 onwards.
† The Playhouse Theatre in Northumberland Avenue, adjacent to Charing Cross Station, built in 1882, rebuilt in 1907, had a distinguished history up until the Second World War. From 1951 to 1976 it was used for BBC radio broadcasts.

Thursday, 3 July 1980

This morning, Leonard Rossiter – in cracking form. Lots of nervous energy, but plenty of good humour too. (He lunged at the girls in the taxi, but took it well when rebuffed. He was in high spirits.) This afternoon, *Woman's Hour* recording with Les Dawson:* what makes a joke funny? He had no idea, but he made me laugh a lot. 'I had ambitions to be a sex maniac, but I failed the practical.' 'The mother-in-law thinks I'm effeminate. Of course, beside her, I am.' This evening, Anthony Palliser's private view at 62 Pimlico Road, followed by supper chez Charles Low in Warwick Square. Alex de Jonge, still wild and wonderful; Lizzie Spender, beautiful and distant; Maurice Macmillan, skin like pale parchment, hands that shake. Anthony's paintings are wonderful. He has done well to stick to his last.

Saturday, 12 July 1980

Last night, Pa's 70th birthday dinner at the Reform Club, a black-tie, gentlemen-only affair, given by Amery-Parkes & Co. to mark both Pa's birthday and his retirement from the firm after forty-five years' association. It was well done – melon *frappé*, *Saumon fumé*, *Entrecôte grillée Tyrolienne*, *Mela stregata*; Mâcon Lugny; Château Cissac; brandy; port. A High Court judge I had never heard of led the toasts and did it well. Pa responded, amusingly, with the right mix of self-deprecation and accepting the evening as nothing less than his due. I think he enjoyed it: he never looks totally at ease with his colleagues, which is odd since he is so much more interesting, high-powered and distinguished than any of them. I tried to keep quiet in my corner.

Tonight we are at the Ye Olde Bell at Hurley. Ma and Pa first came here together in the spring of 1937. We have brought them back for the night as Pa's birthday treat. It has been a total success: both of them really happy. I am so glad. Pa means the world to me. (I hope he knows. I think he does.)

Friday, 25 July 1980

News from the world: Peter Sellers has died, aged 54; Ronald Reagan has been chosen as the Republican Party's presidential candidate, aged 69; Steve Ovett, Sebastian Coe, Duncan Goodhew are wowing them at the Moscow Olympics. I am just in from tea with Tommy Steele, a wonderfully gifted performer, but a rather opaque personality. I went with Simon to see his 'show' at the Prince of Wales Theatre: we were impressed by his skill, but underwhelmed by the

---

* Les Dawson (1931–93), English comedian.

experience. He does a routine involving the audience, where there is the possibility of a member of the audience winning a bottle of champagne. TS contrives to 'forget' to present the prize – and then, at the curtain call, remembers. It was neatly done, but we noticed that the 'bottle' of champagne was actually a *quarter* bottle. That's what the performance was too: wonderfully thought through, but ultimately without generosity, without real heart.

Friday, 5 September 1980

I am on the 6.20 train from Blackpool to Euston. I have spent the day with John Inman.* He does what he does very well – but that's all he does. His range is nil! But he is sweet and enthusiastic and so long as you stick entirely to stories from the golden age of variety, all's well. We minced together along the front: almost every passer-by cried 'I'm free!' John *loves* Blackpool. In theory, I love it, too. I love the piers, the front, the Tower, the shows . . . and yet, though it will have cost ten times as much, I am very happy that we rented Kinopiastes House [in Corfu] again this August. I *say* I love Blackpool, but I don't really. Not the way John does. (Tommy Trinder once told me that the best smell in the world to him was the smell of a pantomime matinee: 'oranges and wee-wee'.)

Thursday, 11 September 1980

Lunch with Michael Redgrave. I picked him up on the corner of Elizabeth Street at 12.45, as arranged. He is 72, but seems so much older. He is very frail. We went to Odin's. I think he took some pleasure in ordering his meal, but when it came he only toyed with it. His fork rattled on the plate. Getting the wine glass to his mouth required both hands. I told him Monja Danischewsky's joke (borrowed, I think, from James Thurber): 'Forgive me if I fall over. I've got Parkinson's disease. I'm hoping he's got mine.' He laughed, but said, 'I've got something else as well.' He didn't seem to know what it was. He talked of going to New York next month to have an operation: 'They bore a hole right into your brain – through your skull.' He doesn't think he can face it. I asked about the Redgrave Theatre in Farnham. I told him that we'd been on Monday and seen Rowan Atkinson there. I tried to remember some of the jokes, but I struggled, really, to keep the conversation going. He wants to work again. Last year he appeared at the National, in Simon Gray's play, *Close of Play*. He was on

---

* John Inman (1935–2007), English comic actor, best known for his role as Mr Humphries in the long-running situation comedy, *Are You Being Served?*, in which his catchphrase was 'I'm free!'

stage throughout, silent, alternately dozing and observing the scene. He loved it. 'But that sort of role doesn't come along very often,' he smiled. I took him home after lunch. The outing had exhausted him. In the taxi, he started talking about Edith Evans again, how much he had loved her, how he had slept with her on the night Vanessa was born . . . I took him to Ebury Mews. He seems to be living in a single room in a converted coach-house. It was quite ramshackle, suitcases open on the floor, bed unmade. I left him standing in the doorway. He waved me off, smiling his sweet smile. He was still waving when I reached the corner.

Sunday, 28 September 1980

Cyril Connolly is right. The pram in the hallway really is the enemy of promise. It certainly makes keeping a daily journal something of a challenge. I have to take my children off to the Zoo, *now* – which means that I have about thirty seconds in which to report on twenty hours of the *Ring* cycle. We completed the marathon at Covent Garden last night. It was an experience. I stayed awake throughout. I listened carefully. I was intrigued. I was mostly held. I was never moved. We went the night before to see Donald Sinden's Othello – not quite right, too fruity (of course), too blacked up (inevitable – it doesn't work any more), but, even so, I was moved again and again. Words touch me in a way music never has. (Excepting Cole Porter and Charles Trenet. Strange how potent cheap music is. Deep down I'm shallow &c.)

I was also in Covent Garden yesterday with Kenneth [Williams] – promoting *Acid Drops*. He is very funny. He signs a book, leering up at the member of the public who is buying it, and telling them what pleasure it is to present it to them and what a privilege it is to meet them – and the moment they turn their back he pulls a face at them and mutters, 'Cunt!'

I am being called. I must go. But, yes, I think Diana Spencer will marry the Prince of Wales. She looks charming.[*]

Saturday, 4 October 1980

This has been a really happy evening. Supper in the kitchen: M, me, Noel, John Schlesinger, Kenneth Williams. We had arranged it because John hadn't seen Kenneth for years – they were good friends in their army days and in London in the fifties, but John got tired of Kenneth's tantrums and screaming and

[*] Paparazzi pictures of Lady Diana Spencer (1961–97) had begun to appear in national newspapers, following her visit to the Prince of Wales and his parents at Balmoral.

self-indulgence. Anyway, tonight Kenneth was on best behaviour and it was just lovely to watch and listen – stories of their time together in Singapore in 1947, with Stanley Baxter and Peter Nichols, the stuff of Peter Nichols's play *Privates on Parade*, in fact. After supper, we watched Kenneth on *Parkinson* – he began saying 'Aren't I awful? Don't I look terrible? Look at her, falling down the stairs!' (He tripped as he made his entrance on the show.) But as we reassured him – he was truly brilliant on the programme – and the studio audience response got ever more rapturous he began to change his tune: 'Yes, it's getting better. That's a good story. Got the tag just right on that one, didn't I? I suppose I do look a bit of a dish.' He was completely endearing and it was touching to see him and Schlesinger embrace when it was time to leave.

Wednesday, 8 October 1980

Jimmy Edwards[*] met me at Haywards Heath. He was in rollicking form. I jumped in the car and off we sped. He drove hard and fast, handlebar moustaches bristling, stories of the war and the Windmill and *Take It From Here* and *Whack-O!* all tumbling out. We stopped off at a pub en route – 'for a refresher': a pint of beer and a large vodka. We got to Riven Oak, his shambling cottage in Fletching, Uckfield, and he proposed a 'libation' before lunch. He opened a carton of orange juice and a bottle of champagne and poured them both into a large glass jug. 'This is mimosa, not Buck's Fizz,' he explained, handing me a pewter pint pot of the stuff and smacking his lips. Mimosa quaffed, we moved to the kitchen, where I sat on the banquette in the corner while he gave himself a gin and tonic and set about preparing lunch: two huge steaks which spat fat and caught fire (repeatedly) as he poked and turned them under the grill. He served them with salad (lettuce and a cut-up tomato) and two bottles of claret. After lunch, he went off to find the brandy, telling me, as he went, about his pride and joy: his Swedish hot tub, newly installed. When he returned, he was stark naked. 'Are you going to join me?' he asked. I declined. He slapped his huge belly with both hands, went away and got dressed again.

We spent the afternoon in the sitting room, going through his ideas for his book. Once we'd finished the brandy, he served us tall glasses of lager. 'We're working – we'd better not drink,' he said. At six o'clock he drove me back to the station. He appeared no worse for wear.

---

* Jimmy Edwards (b. James O'Neill, 1920–88) served in the RAF during the Second World War and was awarded the DFC; in 1946, he appeared at the Windmill Theatre and quickly became a radio and television star as a comedian, actor and raconteur.

Monday, 20 October 1980

Horrible news. My friend, Lady Isobel Barnett, has committed suicide. On Friday she was convicted of shoplifting at Leicester Crown Court – fined £75 for stealing a tin of tuna and a pot of cream valued at 87p. It seems she could not face the humiliation. She got into the bath and pulled a lighted electric fire in after her. I liked her so much. She was so nice to me. I cannot express my sadness properly. She was 62.

Tuesday, 28 October 1980

My life with the stars. They are all very different – they have in common self-obsession, but it manifests itself in different ways. Who have I seen today?

1. Richard Briers, actor[*] – normal, nice, self-deprecating but always aware of his own worth.
2. Rita Hunter, opera singer[†] – huge: a vast woman (she needs two seats on the aeroplane; to get into her dressing room at the Coliseum she has to turn sideways), obsessed with her health, but doesn't see her amazing bulk as a problem at all.
3. Henry Cooper, boxer[‡] – I went out to see him in Hendon, taking cash: I found him a little frightening – not menacing – he was perfectly friendly, but his world is not my world. He has a cabinet in his hallway stacked with his trophies.
4. Jonquil Antony – she doesn't really count. She's not a star. She is the creator of *Mrs Dale's Diary* – she wrote the first script in 1948, the year that I was born. She went on writing it until 1963. For a generation, *Mrs Dale's Diary* was an essential part of the British way of life – and now Jonquil Antony lives alone in a council flat off Russell Square. She is lonely and forgotten. She told me she hopes she is dying. Her sight has gone and she can no longer read.[§]

* Richard Briers CBE (b.1934), English actor whose first television success was *Marriage Lines*, 1961–6, but who is still best remembered for *The Good Life*, 1975–8.
† Rita Hunter CBE (1933–2001), celebrated Wagnerian soprano, especially noted for her Brünnhilde for the English National Opera.
‡ Henry Cooper OBE (b.1934) was the British, European and Commonwealth heavyweight boxing champion in 1970 and the only British boxer to win three Lonsdale Belts outright.
§ Jonquil Antony (1911–80) wrote more than four thousand scripts for the BBC. GB went to see her with a view to reissuing some of her novelisations of *Mrs Dale's Diary*. She died five weeks later, on 6 December.

5. And Ken Dodd.* Tonight we went to see him at the London Palladium. The man is simply a genius. Yes, he went on and on and on – but we kept laughing. We didn't want it to stop. 'I haven't spoken to the wife's mother for eighteen months – I didn't like to interrupt her.' How tickled we were.

Tuesday, 9 December 1980

John Lennon has been shot dead in New York. He was coming home to his apartment in the Dakota Building late last night when a young man simply walked up to him and shot him five times at point blank range. He must have died instantly. The world is reeling.

I am reeling, too – but for a slightly different reason. I have had a curious afternoon. I had lunch with Frankie Howerd. At one o'clock I went to find him in his house in Edwardes Square – it's a cold house, sparsely furnished, antiseptic. I always feel his boyfriend is lurking, hidden in a backroom, when I am there. As I arrive, I hear a distant door being quietly closed. We went round the corner to eat, to Al Gallo d'Oro in Kensington High Street – Frank's local. He was at his most morose: self-pity is Frank's long suit. He had some wine, but not a lot. It didn't cheer him. He feels his career is going nowhere. I imagine he has felt that since it started. When we'd eaten, I said, 'We must work.' 'We can't go home,' he said, terrified that I was about to suggest it. 'We'll go to my agent's office. We'll work there.'

We took a taxi to Mayfair. The taxi driver was excited to have Frank as a passenger. 'I suppose you want me to say "Titter ye not!" Well, I won't.' At the office, I followed Frank up the wide wooden staircase as he called down to the receptionist, 'This young man and I have a great deal of work to do. We do not wish to be disturbed. Is that understood, Madam?'

On the first floor, Frank showed me into a spacious panelled room that appeared to be more of a drawing room than an office. He gestured towards a leather sofa in the middle of the room. As I went towards it, I heard him locking the door. I turned. He was putting the key into his pocket. 'We don't want intruders.'

I sat on the sofa and opened my briefcase. I pulled out the manuscript we were supposed to be working on. 'Never mind that,' he said, lolloping slowly towards the sofa. 'I need to take the weight off my leg.' He began to ease himself onto the sofa next to me, but halfway down, suddenly, his face contorted, he clutched his thigh and began to yelp with pain. 'No, no,' he whimpered.

'What is it?'

* Ken Dodd (b.1927), Liverpool-born comedian and singer.

'It's my groin! No, ooh, ah, ow . . .' he grimaced. Clutching himself, he struggled to his feet and limped back across the room to the large partners' desk by the window. He opened a drawer and produced a jar of ointment. 'This is what we need,' he muttered. He then staggered slowly back towards me, thrust the jar of ointment into my hands, undid his belt, pushed down his trousers, lowered his underpants and collapsed in a heap at my side.

He closed his eyes and murmured, 'You know what to do.'

'I don't.' I blanched.

'You do.'

'I don't.'

'Apply the ointment,' he barked. 'Rub it in.'

'Where?'

He thrust his exposed crotch towards me and hissed, '*There!*'

'Where?' I gulped, not believing what was happening.

'There!' he repeated. 'Haven't you seen one before? It's perfectly harmless. Treat it like a muscle.'

I did not know what to say or do. I couldn't make my excuses and leave because the door was locked and the key was in Frank's trouser pocket and his trousers were round his ankles on the floor. I got up and walked to the window and stood there staring out.

Gradually, I heard Frank getting to his feet and pulling up his trousers. Muttering, he returned to the desk and put the ointment away. 'I'm just going to wash,' he said. He unlocked the door and left me. I stood gazing out of the window until he returned. He came back, bright and breezy, as if nothing had happened. 'Now, let's get down to it, young man. There's work to be done. No more dawdling.'

We did the work and shared a taxi back to Kensington. I dropped him off at the corner of Edwardes Square. As he got out of the cab, I hugged him. Odd as this may seem, I felt somehow that I had let him down. 'You won't tell Dennis,[*] will you?' he pleaded, looking at me pathetically. 'Promise?'

'Promise,' I said.

Thursday, 25 December 1980

The parents are in California: Jen & family were in North London (North London is a foreign country to me: *Guardian* readers live there): Gin & Co.

---

[*] Dennis Heymer (1929–2009), Frankie Howerd's partner and personal manager for more than thirty years.

were in St Albans: so we had a motley crew here today for Christmas lunch. Hes and Polly, Peggy Lynch and Patrick Fyffe. Peggy and Patrick got on famously. Peggy is a maiden lady of 66. She is severely hard of hearing. Her speech is distorted, but her heart is true. We had her because she and her mother have come to us ever since I can remember. (Mrs Lynch had a little wispy beard: why did her daughter never do anything about it? Pa used to tease her terribly – shocking her when he carved the turkey by offering her 'breast' – rolling the word around in his mouth – when what she had distinctly asked for was 'white meat'.) Peggy hadn't heard of Hinge & Bracket and when Patrick tried to explain to her that what he did for a living was dress up as a 66-year-old maiden lady who looked a little like her she was completely bemused. 'I don't hear very well, dear,' she said.

They've gone now. Patrick did stay and stay. (He does. At the first night of H & B at the Globe, when we went to Langan's he kept us there until gone three.) I am tired. Being a father is very exhausting, especially at Christmas. I was up at five, remember, creeping about the house, putting pillow cases packed with presents by the beds of all the children. It should be a pleasure. And it is. But it's also rather nerve-racking. You don't want them to wake up and catch you 'at it'. Anyway, it's all done now and I think the children had a happy time. I always prefer Boxing Day.

PART FOUR
Under the Jumper

All Human Life is Here

January 1981 – January 1983

Wednesday, 7 January 1981

Just in from dinner at John Schlesinger's. It was the rematch of our happy kitchen supper with John and Noel and Kenneth – except that tonight wasn't happy at all. It didn't work, partly because it was grander and less cosy, but chiefly because Kenneth was impossible. The problem: Kenneth was not the star attraction. Alan Bennett* was also of the party and he was so droll, so gently wicked, so comfortably amusing that he quite stole the show. As the evening wore on, Kenneth got louder, queenier, ever more outrageous. John won't want to see him again. Pity.

Wednesday, 28 January 1981

New York

In London they are 'breaking the mould'. Shirley Williams, Roy Jenkins, David Owen and Bill Rodgers are leaving the Labour Party to form a 'Council for Social Democracy' – whatever that may be.† And Rupert Murdoch is buying *The Times*. The times they are a-changing indeed. Here in New York, too. I am writing this in Rockefeller Plaza, where I am having a celebratory coffee. (This is what I like best in all the world: having a cup of coffee on my own, surrounded by strangers, in an interesting place.) I have just come from a meeting with Dan Perkes at Associated Press Newsfeatures. I have agreed to write a weekly column on words and language to be syndicated across the US to whichever newspapers are inclined to take it. If enough do, I shall make serious money. Art Buchwald is a rich man.‡ Last night I went (alone) to *Barnum* at the St James Theatre. Jim

---

* Alan Bennett (b.1934), Yorkshire-born playwright and actor; he was then working with John Schlesinger on the script of *An Englishman Abroad*.

† 'The Gang of Four' formed the Social Democratic Party in the summer of 1981 and the party contested seats in the 1983 and 1987 general elections before merging with the Liberal Party in 1988 to form the Liberal Democrats.

‡ Art Buchwald's humorous column was syndicated in more than 550 newspapers; GB's *Alphabet Soup* column appeared in about fifty, but ran successfully for several years.

Dale is a joy and the show an inspiration. I think P. T. Barnum knew my great-great-grandfather, Dr Brandreth, the Pill king. I must follow their entrepreneurial example: ideas – energy – action – follow-through. When I return to London, I am going to raise my game. Tonight I'm going to *Ain't Misbehavin'*.

Saturday, 7 February 1981

I spent the day working on the Snap, Crackle and Pop games I am creating for Kellogg's new-look packs of Rice Krispies. (Mock not. Someone's got to do it and it turns out to be me. The fruits of my endeavour will give pleasure to millions.) I spent the evening in Row C of the stalls at the Wimbledon Theatre watching a theatrical farrago called *Big Bad Mouse*. It's a farce by Philip King in which Eric Sykes and Jimmy Edwards have been touring for years. They've done two long stints with it in the West End and taken it all over the world. It's a ropey piece made bearable by the way the two old rascals use it as a springboard for anarchic improvisation. Essentially, they send up the play and play to the crowd – Jim even plays his trombone in it, for no good reason. He also has pint pots strategically placed all over the stage so that he can take a swig whenever he needs one (which is often). Afterwards, in his dressing room, I noticed that he has a milkman's crate for his vodka, so he can carry six bottles around with him at the same time. At the Italian restaurant where we went to eat, I sat next to him and watched the pulse in his temple throb as the waiter took an eternity to bring us the wine. I thought Jim would explode with desperation. Once the drink was with us, he was fine, almost mellow. He had a young man called Philip with him. As Barbara Windsor puts it so well: 'Funny to think Jim's tommy-two-ways, innit?'

Thursday, 12 February 1981

The world is awash with alcohol. Lunch in Cambridge with Melvyn Bragg.[*] He is intelligent, smooth, charming, gracious. He drinks a bottle of red wine and he is *still* intelligent, smooth, charming, gracious. (That said, it seems no one rates his novels. No one reads them either. Perhaps that's why he drinks – to deaden the pain? 'Everyone says I'm intelligent, smooth, charming, gracious, with amazing hair – but all I want them to do is rate my novels!') Went to see Irene [Josephy] at St Thomas's Hospital. She is not well. The drip-drip-drip of gin is taking its toll. 'We'll soon be back at Muriel's,' she said. The last time we were

---

[*] Melvyn Bragg (b.1939), Baron Bragg of Wigton, author, broadcaster, producer/presenter of *The South Bank Show* on ITV since 1978.

there both Dan Farson and Francis Bacon fell off their stools.* It's gone midnight. We are just in from Alex and Katy de Jonge's party in Harley Gardens. Alex drank so much that eventually he simply slid to the floor. When I went to the Gaudy with him at New College, coming out of Hall after dinner, he fell forward and rolled down the long flight of stone steps, from the top step to the bottom, sixty steps or more, and steep. At the bottom he got up and strode off across the Quad as though nothing had happened.

Saturday, 14 March 1981

M's birthday. Hayward Gallery for the Edward Hopper exhibition. Soothing. National Theatre for lunch. Not bad. 7.45 p.m. *Present Laughter* at the Vaudeville. It's not an easy play: a lot of wit, not much heart. Drink afterwards with Donald Sinden (who was fruity and brilliant) and Julian Fellowes who plays the young playwright, Roland Maule. (He was good, but not extraordinary. When I saw it with Nigel Patrick in the Garry Essendine part, Richard Briers played Roland Maule and he was extraordinary: hilariously nervous and manic.) I had not seen Julian since we shared a bath in Wetherby Place.† He is very jolly and I like that. We had dinner at Langan's Brasserie. £75.05 including service. (And think how shocked I was thirteen years ago when dinner at the Elizabeth came to £5.)

Donald Sinden didn't believe it, but it's true. On Monday we went to the Haymarket to see Maggie Smith in *Virginia*, the Edna O'Brien play based on the writings of Virginia and Leonard Woolf. We sat in front of an American couple who were disappointed to find there were no songs. They had come to *Virginia* thinking it was a sequel to *Oklahoma!*

Thursday, 19 March 1981

I like leading a double life: I like the mixture of the serious and the slight. For example, this morning I had coffee with John Wain‡ and we talked about Thom Gunn and Philip Larkin, then I had lunch with John Inman and we talked about *Pajama Tops* and Mollie Sugden. Tonight, we are going to the Quintavalles, where (no doubt) we shall talk of Catholicism and the ethics of reproduction. It

---

* The Colony Room in Dean Street, Soho, founded by Muriel Belcher in 1948, was a small drinking club that opened for business at 3.00 p.m. each day and was a favourite haunt of GB's literary agent, Irene Josephy. Dan Farson, writer, was another of her clients. Francis Bacon, artist, was a founder member of the club.
† Julian Fellowes (b.1949), actor and, later, screenwriter; in the early 1950s GB's parents lived in the basement of the Fellowes' house in Wetherby Place, London SW7.
‡ John Wain (1925–94), poet and critic.

will be earnest, but interesting – and leavened (balanced and made bearable) by our glorious high camp outing on Monday with Chris Biggins and Duggie Squires to see Rita Moreno at the Talk of the Town.* I do prefer the company of people with better minds than mine, but I like all the frou-frou nonsense, too. Actually what I think I like is the *best* of everything, whatever it is. Rita Moreno is an all-singing-all-dancing fag-hag, but she's an Oscar winner, too.

Friday, 3 April 1981

In Washington DC, President Reagan, 70, has survived the attempt to shoot him. A bullet hit him in the lung, three inches from his heart. In hospital, as he was being given an anaesthetic, he said to the surgeons: 'I hope you guys are Republicans.' In London, Asians and skinheads are rioting in the streets of Southall. I am sitting here waiting for Simon and Stephanie to come for supper. I had lunch today at the National Playing Fields Association in Ovington Square. Josephine Seccombe has moved there from Action Research and wants me to help with the fund-raising. I said 'yes' for three reasons: 1) she asked; 2) when I was a child Ma always used to use the NPFA diary, so somehow (quite irrationally) I feel committed to the cause; 3) the Duke of Edinburgh is the president and apparently quite actively involved. M says I might get to meet him and I'd like that.

Tomorrow I am going to Norwich, to Anglia, to record thirteen epilogues on the trot.†

Thursday, 23 April 1981

Last night, with Simon we went to the Palladium to see 'Mr Jim Bailey' (female impersonator) and Mike Yarwood (general impersonator) – both good, both skilful, both a bit soulless. We telephoned Mike later. We didn't go round. He's just a bit dull, that's all. Tonight, we went to Chelwood House, Gloucester Square, for supper with the Porters. Leslie is the NPFA Appeals Chairman, thoroughly nice: diminutive, 60, bumbly, affable. He is also the chairman of Tesco, but, frankly, would he be were he not married to the founder's daughter? I think not. He doesn't seem that bright, and he enjoys a drink, whereas Shirley (daugh-

---

* Josephine Quintavalle, a fellow parent at Norland Place School, later founded Comment on Reproductive Ethics; Rita Moreno, who won an Oscar for her performance in *West Side Story*, was appearing in cabaret at the Talk of the Town nightclub in Leicester Square.

† GB recorded two series of 'readings with a spiritual dimension' for the religious affairs department at Anglia TV.

ter of Jack Cohen) is as sharp as a knife.* Lady Cohen was also on parade. She told me about the early days. Jack (Jacob) really did start with just one market stall in Hackney in 1919. He used his demob money to buy surplus NAAFI stock and sell it at a profit. He was 21. By the time he was 40 he had opened a hundred Tesco stores. How did he manage it? 'He was honest and he wasn't greedy and he gave his customers what they wanted before they knew they wanted it. And he never stopped working. Never. Hard work. It's the only way.' She looked towards Leslie and sighed a little.

Wednesday, 29 April 1981

We went to Liberace's Gala Night at the Palladium. He was wholly preposterous. He is not handsome: he is 60† and looks like an outsize doll made up to look like Liberace. His piano playing is good, but not unique. His patter is amusing, but quite predictable ('You remember that bank I cried all the way to? Well, I bought it.') His costumes are sumptuous, but essentially gaudy. Only his jewellery feels authentic. It sparkles – it dazzles. He sparkles, he dazzles, non-stop, from the moment he is swept on in a diamond-encrusted limousine, to the grand finale when waltzing waters and indoor fireworks explode around him. Why does it work so well? Why is this man still the highest-paid entertainer in the world? Jack Tinker‡ was there with Biggins (of course) – both squealing with delight, but they couldn't answer the question either.

Had lunch with Patrick Moore§ at the Mikonos in Frith Street. He got through two bottles of Othello red and gabbled away nineteen to the dozen – about astronomy, music (he has composed a symphony for orchestra and xylophone), cricket and Mrs Thatcher. (Mrs T. hasn't gone far enough for Patrick. Genghis Khan is the man for him.) I observed that whatever he says he never smiles. 'I am glad you noticed,' he said. 'It's a policy of mine – never be seen smiling. If you do, the public don't take you seriously.' He said I must send Benet down to his house in Sussex one weekend. He will let him use his telescope.

---

* Dame Shirley Porter (b.1930) became a Conservative Westminster City Councillor in 1974 and was leader of the Council from 1983 to 1991, when she received a DBE. She retired to Israel in 1993 following the so-called 'homes for votes' scandal. Her father, Jack Cohen (1898–1979), was knighted in 1969, and her husband, Leslie Porter, in 1983 for his work for the National Playing Fields Association.
† He was almost 62. Wladziu Valentino Liberace (1919–87) was certainly the highest-paid live performer at the height of his success in the 1950s and 1960s.
‡ Jack Tinker (1938–96); from 1972, *Daily Mail* theatre critic.
§ Sir Patrick Moore (b.1923), amateur astronomer, writer, presenter of *The Sky at Night* on BBC Television since 1957.

Tuesday, 5 May 1981

Germaine Greer[*] arrived at the office at 2.30 p.m. as planned. She was wild and strident and determined to shock. The book we are doing with her is about fertility, but for some reason Germaine is determined that the cover should feature a close-up photograph of female pubic hair – preferably her own, or if we think it'll be too grey, grizzled and unappealing, then she will consider a model's pubes, 'a fine full bush, something you can grab hold of'.

Tonight we went to *The Duchess of Malfi* at the Round House. When it was over, Michèle said: 'Never again. I have been to my last Jacobean revenge tragedy. *The Duchess of Malfi*, *The White Devil* – I don't need them. I don't like them. I don't want them. No more. That's that, thank you very much.' I know what she means.

Thursday, 7 May 1981

Went to the Poetry Society in Earl's Court for the evening to celebrate *Everyman's Book of Nonsense* and *Everyman's Book of English Verse*. The idea was an hour of drinks followed by an hour of readings, to be introduced by me. During the drinks I was stuck in a corner with John Heath-Stubbs[†] (why do blind people smell?) but I couldn't concentrate on anything he was saying because our star attraction (Spike Milligan,[‡] my responsibility: I said I'd get him there) had phoned at the last minute to say he couldn't make it after all. The man is impossible: self-indulgent and not that funny even at his funniest. Anyway, I rejigged the running order and, at around eight o'clock, the readings began. Truth to tell, it was all a bit flat until we got to what was to have been the 'Spike Milligan moment' – at which point there was a sudden banging from a cupboard in the corner. Yes, you guessed: the cupboard burst open and Spike appeared. He had been there all along. He was very funny and I forgave him everything.

Tuesday, 12 May 1981

At 5.00 p.m. I took Maurice Saatchi and Martin Sorrell round the Playhouse. My scheme remains the same – by night I run the theatre: by day they run the confer-

---

[*] Germaine Greer (b.1939), Australian-born writer and academic, best known as the author of *The Female Eunuch*, 1970.
[†] John Heath-Stubbs OBE (1918–2006), English poet, afflicted by blindness from the 1960s.
[‡] Terence 'Spike' Milligan KBE (1918–2002), Anglo-Irish comedian, writer, poet, playwright, musician, best remembered as the co-creator of *The Goons* on radio.

ence centre – but our problem is that the 'mystery owner' won't come out of hiding to engage in a useful conversation. The agent says he wants £400,000 and no questions asked. But Maurice and Martin have plenty of questions – sensible ones. They are shrewd guys: I like them very much. And I like their style: clear, direct, dynamic. We shall see.[*]

At 8.00 p.m. we went to *Cats* at the New London Theatre. It's done wonderfully well, but it left me cold. There's no story and no sense of engagement. Bonnie [Langford] gives her all (and some) – Wayne Sleep,[†] Elaine Paige,[‡] they all do. But essentially it's simply Eliot's verses set to music and staged *con brio*. Fine, but so what? My problem is probably that I know the poems too well: Andrew Lloyd Webber's 'Macavity' isn't *my* 'Macavity' – and I'm not sure that Eliot's verses as *lyrics* really work. The best song by a long way is 'Memory' – and it's written by Trevor Nunn.

Thursday, 14 May 1981

Pope John Paul II has survived an assassination attempt. We had a late night with Simon [Cadell]. We went to Le Détour. He arrived late and without Stephanie. They are splitting up. It wasn't 'going anywhere'; he felt closed in; he had to get out. He has. At the beginning of the evening he was very twitchy. By bedtime, he admitted feeling mightily relieved. The deed is done.

The parents have returned from the US. We went to find them at their hotel in Lancaster Gate. Pa looks terrible – gaunt and yellow. He is in great pain. He could barely walk down the corridor. We drove him out to Totteridge to see Dr Simmons, Ma's osteopath. The parents trust 'Simmy'. He is obviously a good and caring man. He looked at Pa's X-ray – taken in America – and told him to go and see his GP as soon as possible. Pa doesn't have a GP so M is going to take him to the Middlesex tomorrow. On the way back from Totteridge, he sat in the front of the car, his eyes screwed up, groaning whenever the car slowed or accelerated. Every sudden movement hurt him. At one point, he asked M to pull over and said, 'You will look after Ma, won't you?'

[*] The Playhouse was sold elsewhere, as was the Fortune Theatre which GB, Maurice Saatchi and Martin Sorrell also looked at acquiring at that summer. Martin Sorrell (b. 1945), was then finance director of Saatchi & Saatchi; he founded WPP, now the world's largest advertising group, in 1986 and was knighted in 2000.
[†] Wayne Sleep OBE (b.1948), British dancer, formerly a principal with the Royal Ballet.
[‡] Elaine Paige OBE (b.1948), British singer and actress, especially remembered as Eva Peron in *Evita*, 1978–80.

Saturday, 16 May 1981

In Northern Ireland everything is out of control. In my little life, I think everything is a bit out of control as well. I spent the night sleeping at King's Cross
Station. Absurd, but last night I was addressing the Southend-on-Sea Law
Society and my train back didn't get in to Liverpool Street until 11.55 p.m., so, by
minutes, I missed the Scottish sleeper and had to sit at King's Cross for four hours
waiting for the next train. I am on it now, aching and unhappy, on my way to
Edinburgh for the NSC [National Scrabble Championships] Scottish Finals. (It's
all ridiculous, I know.) M took Pa to the Middlesex as planned. They admitted
him at once. No one can understand why the American doctors didn't tell him
how ill he is. The Middlesex are going to do tests next week. He is on painkillers
now and much more comfortable. It's obviously very serious (*very* serious), but
Ma seems to think all will be well.

Saturday, 30 May 1981

A roller-coaster of a day. We went to *Nicholas Nickleby* at the Aldwych. It was
overwhelmingly wonderful – brilliantly adapted, staged and played. Flawless.
And very moving. Towards the end I began to cry, tears just tumbled down my
face in the darkness. It was the play – and Pa. I know he is dying and it is so sad.
Ma cannot accept it – will not accept it. At the Middlesex, when we had our
'family conference' with the consultant, she sat bolt upright on her chair and told
him, 'He cannot be allowed to die. You must cure him. You must.' I am so
unhappy.

But our evening was very jolly. We had champagne cocktails at the Royal
Garden Hotel and dinner round the corner at Maggie Jones. We are going to Part
II of *N. Nickleby* on Wednesday.

Saturday, 6 June 1981

For some, the excitement of the week has been Shergar winning the Epsom
Derby by the widest margin on record. We watched it on the box and it was
exciting, but not *that* exciting. We didn't place a bet. We never do. For us, the
excitement of the week was Part II of *Nicholas Nickleby* – just matchless – and
might have been the Robert Maxwell party at Headington Hill Hall today. We
intended to go. We dressed for the party. We drove to Oxford. And then we
chickened out. There were picket lines at the gates. M said, 'I don't want to cross
picket lines to have lunch' – so we drove on to the Sorbonne [restaurant in
Oxford]. It might have been quite jolly, but M's back has gone. We ordered some

food. It came. But M couldn't sit to eat it. She tried standing at the table to eat, but it was ridiculous. We paid the bill and abandoned ship. The truth is: we're both in a bad way.

Wednesday, 24 June 1981

Hinge & Bracket are appearing at the Theatre Royal, Northampton. I have spent the day with them in a bedroom at the Saxon Motor Inn working on the first episode of *Dear Ladies*. It's exhausting stuff. How it works: we agree on a basic story outline, then Patrick [Fyffe] (Dame Hilda) improvises the whole thing, playing all the parts, while I scribble notes and Peter Ridsdale-Scott (producer) sits on the sideline squealing with delight. When we're done, George [Logan] (Dr Hinge) sniffs, shakes his head and says, 'It isn't very funny, is it?' Then we start all over again. We have scheduled two days for outlining each script. The idea is that I'll then take the notes away and turn them into a proper script. Hope it works.

Wednesday, 8 July 1981

Sports update. Ian Botham has quit as England cricket captain and I have taken part in the Norland Place School Sports Day. Benet did well, but for some reason I was determined to do better. When it came to the fathers' race, I almost killed myself. There were younger fathers there – most with gym shoes, one with spikes – and *still* I thought I might win. And if I hadn't skidded as I neared the tape, I might have done. Absurd.

As I write, there is rioting in Liverpool [in the Toxteth area] and, in Belfast, a fifth IRA hunger striker has died, so there will be more rioting there too. But we're just in from *Private Lives* in Richmond, with Simon as Elyot and Joanna Lumley as Amanda. Same country, different worlds.

Saturday, 11 July 1981

Pa's 71st birthday. After eight weeks and five sessions of radiotherapy, he is out of the Middlesex and back at 164 [Chiltern Court]. We have moved his bed into the sitting room and he is quite cosy. He is on four-hourly doses of Nepenthe, which keeps the pain under control but leaves him, he says, feeling permanently 'fuzzy'. His mood is relatively mellow – he is on Valium to help with that – and he talks optimistically about the future. His feet are horribly swollen. Gin cut his toenails for him. He liked that. He liked seeing everybody, though he tires easily. He is still preoccupied with his money worries, sending letters to his partners, the DHSS in Newcastle about his pension, the doctors in the US about outstanding medical bills, etc. Ma is coping. He won't hear a word said against her. They both talk about what they are going to do when he has 'shaken off this wretched thing'.

Friday, 17 July 1981

Yesterday: morning with Germaine Greer – she is good value, stimulating company and completely ridiculous: for the original feminist she is hilariously man-mad. Children's end-of-term treat: the Royal Tournament – still exactly the same after all these years. Today: lunch with the bank manager (I am blessed in Eric Miller: a decent man who seems to accept that it will all come right in the end); Richard Goolden's memorial service at Chelsea Old Church – John Gielgud read the lesson, Harold Hobson gave the address: a touching occasion in a beautiful setting and truly celebratory because Richard was so delightful and had led such a long life; evening: Alec McCowen's solo recital of St Mark's Gospel at the Globe – extraordinary. Extraordinary as a feat of memory – he just comes onto the stage, puts a closed copy of the New Testament on the edge of the table 'just in case', turns to the audience and speaks. It's mesmerising and profoundly moving, and, at the end of it, you begin to understand why Christianity is still with us after two thousand years.

Wednesday, 29 July 1981

We watched the Royal Wedding: Lady Diana Spencer married Prince Charles at St Paul's Cathedral – or did she marry his father? When making her vows she got the Prince's Christian names muddled up: 'I take thee, Philip . . .' No other glitches.

We are now packed and off to Corfu – a different villa and, because of Pa, just two weeks away. I am taking Daphne du Maurier, C. P. Snow, J. I. M. Stewart and Anthony Trollope for company.

Friday, 11 September 1981

Pa moved into the hospice of St John and St Elizabeth on Tuesday. I went today and met with Dr Halbert. He said – in hushed tones: in the hospice everyone speaks in 'hushed tones' – that they are doing their best to 'control' Pa's pain: that's all they really can do. Pa is very weak, gaunt and weary, and the hospice – though light and airy, with kindly, caring staff – is essentially grim. Of course it is. It is full of dying people – and some of them are very young. It's heartbreaking. I left Pa to go to a meeting to discuss the new Tony Tiger promotion for Kellogg's Frosties. And now I'm off to St Thomas's where I am addressing the Hospital Caterers' Association annual dinner.

Tuesday, 15 September 1981

Cabinet reshuffle. Mrs Thatcher is purging her government: three 'wets' are out, with more to follow if they don't toe the line. Jim Prior goes to Northern Ireland, to be replaced by Norman Tebbit.* Cecil Parkinson† is the new Party Chairman.

I spent the day in Manchester, talking *Dear Ladies* and *The Railway Carriage Game* with Peter Ridsdale-Scott [the producer of both series]. When I got back I went straight to the Royal Albert Hall and arrived in time to wander in (unhindered) for the finale of Dame Edna. She is glorious. I caught a gladiolus, found M and went on to the party at John Schlesinger's. Wandered about being genial with the stars, but essentially all I am thinking about is Pa. M has been wonderful, driving Ma in to see him every day. He is very weak. We have decided to cancel our trip to Venice.

Monday, 2 November 1981

I travelled down to the Penguin sales conference at the Saunton Sands Hotel, near Barnstaple, with Roald Dahl.‡ He was not easy company. I think perhaps he likes to give off an air of menace. He sat, curled up, scowling in the corner of our railway compartment. He didn't read. He seemed to want to talk, but his conversation was awkward, random. He did tell me his idea for the perfect murder. The victim is bludgeoned to death with a frozen leg of lamb. The murderer then cooks the lamb and serves it to the police when they come calling – so getting rid of the evidence by having the detective eat it. He has a wonderful imagination (clearly), but a somewhat alarming manner. (It's just occurred to me: perhaps he is quite ill? He is the same sort of age as Pa and has a similar gaunt look.)

Thursday, 12 November 1981

Went to Manchester to be a guest on *The Russell Harty Show.*§ Russell is a generous and nice man. He knows he's too intelligent to be doing this sort of TV, but

---

* Norman Tebbit (b.1931), Conservative MP, 1970–92, Cabinet Minister, 1981–7, later Lord Tebbit CH.
† Cecil Parkinson (b.1931), Conservative MP, 1970–92, Cabinet Minister, 1981–3, 1987–90; later Lord Parkinson.
‡ Roald Dahl (1916–90), British-Norwegian author, best known for his children's books and short stories. He died nine years after this, in November 1990, aged 74, of a rare blood disease, myelodysplastic anaemia.
§ Frederic Russell Harty (1934–88), Lancashire-born teacher-turned-television presenter.

he still wants to do it – he wants to be famous and funny and loved. Before we went on, he stood in the wings and, as the theme music for the show began to play, he started to dance on the spot like a mad thing – working himself into a frenzy for his entrance. (No wonder he always looks sweaty on screen.) The other guests were John Inman – who did a clever routine about being a shop-window mannequin – and The Tweets who sang the utterly ludicrous 'Birdie Song'. As we all danced around the studio inanely – doing the Birdie Song 'movements' – and the credits rolled, Russell whispered in my ear, 'Is this why we went to Oxford, Gyles?' And he got a First.

Wednesday, 2 December 1981

Went to the BBC Paris Studio in Lower Regent Street at lunch-time to record two editions of *Just a Minute*. Nicholas Parsons said the only reason they hadn't asked me before is that I sound too like Derek Nimmo and they didn't want to 'confuse the listeners'. The truth is I was only there because Kenneth badgered them on my behalf. He is a good friend – and a good son. He arrived for the recording with his mother in tow – he calls her Louie – and installed her in her 'usual seat' in the third row. The other panellists were Peter Jones (wonderfully droll) and Sheila Hancock (sharp and good at the game). Kenneth stole the show (of course) but I acquitted myself reasonably. Indeed, I won the first game, though I know that's not the point. Being funny is the point. (People don't necessarily like you if you win.)

Wednesday, 16 December 1981

Last night, Francis Crowdy came over for supper. We watched the penultimate episode of *Brideshead Revisited* – it has been so wonderful: there will be a yawning gap in our lives when it ends – and then played Bridge. A perfect evening. (There is nothing like a game of Bridge and an ice-cold gin and tonic for shutting out all the worries of the world.) And now – 6.00 p.m., Wednesday – I am writing this on the train from Newton Abbot, returning home at the end of a memorable day.

This morning, as planned, M collected the parents and took them to Waterloo to catch the 11.48 train for the Isle of Wight. A wheelchair etc. had been arranged for Pa. They are going to Osborne House for a Christmas break at the army officers' convalescent home. It's the ideal solution. They will both benefit from a change of scene, they will both love the Queen Victoria connections, and it's clear from talking to the Osborne House people on the phone that they'll be completely on top of the situation with Pa's medication.

By complete coincidence I discovered today that among the army officers who convalesced at Osborne House during the First World War were Robert Graves and A. A. Milne. I have spent the day with A. A. Milne's only child. Christopher Robin* is 61 now, spindly, slightly bent, with owlish glasses and a charming, mischievous glint in his eye. I travelled down to Devon to meet him with Julian Slade. We came to talk about our play about his father. We arrived expecting to find him painfully shy, diffident and reluctant to talk about either Winnie-the-Pooh or his parents. Not so. His manner is gentle, but he was completely forthcoming. 'We must talk about Pooh,' he said straightaway. 'It's been something of a love-hate relationship down the years, but it's all right now. Believe it or not, I can now look at those four books without flinching. I'm quite fond of them really.'

Those four books – the two Pooh books and the two collections of nursery verses: 70,000 words in all – were published between 1924 and 1928 and have dominated Christopher's whole life. Until he was eight or nine, he said, he quite liked being famous. It was only when he went to boarding school, to Stowe, that the teasing from other boys began to get him down. In his dormitory they played the record of Vespers – 'Little boy kneels at the foot of his bed . . .' – and goaded him with it until he took the record 'and broke it into a hundred pieces and scattered it in a distant field'. After the war, he accused his father of 'building a reputation by standing on a young boy's shoulders'.

As a small boy the love of Christopher's life was his nanny [Olive Rand]. She was the centre of his universe – 'apart from her fortnight's holiday every September, for eight years we were not out of each other's sight for more than a few hours at a time.' He was closest to his father during his adolescence, when Nanny was no longer there. What did they do together, father and son? '*The Times* crossword, algebra and Euclid. We looked for birds' nests, we played cricket, we caught things in the stream.' But when Christopher went to Cambridge they began to drift apart. It was after the war, when Christopher was in his mid-twenties, that his resentment of his father came to a head. 'Six years in the Army don't qualify a man for employment and being a sentimental storybook hero doesn't help either.'

In 1948, Christopher married his first cousin, Lesley. He says the marriage 'saved' him – but it distanced him further from his parents. Lesley's father and Christopher's mother had not spoken to one another for thirty years. After A. A. Milne's death in 1956, Christopher's mother lived on for fifteen years. In all that

* Christopher Robin Milne (1920–96), bookseller and author.

time he saw her only once. His mother was the one area he didn't talk about. He implied that she was 'flighty', that he had been no more than 'a part-time hobby' for her, but he did not really explain his resentment of her. I suppose he had a choice: to love his mother or his wife and he chose his wife.

The love of his life now seems to be his daughter, Clare. She has cerebral palsy. She has to be looked after all the time. When he was first married, he was fiercely independent. The idea of taking money from his 'fictional namesake' was anathema to him. 'In the end, I had to accept it, for Clare's sake.' He told us that his chief delight in life – greater than the satisfaction he has derived from book-selling or writing or from his lifelong love of studying insects and caterpillars and weeds – has been using his hands to adapt and make everyday things for Clare: a chair, a tricycle, an unbreakable plate, a special fork and spoon. He has this fantasy that one day they will launch into business together: 'C. R. Milne & Daughter – Makers of Furniture for the Disabled'.

We are reaching Paddington. The snow has cleared. I must stop. I can at least tell my children that today I shook the hand that held the paw of Winnie-the-Pooh.

Friday, 8 January 1982

The parents were due back from the Isle of Wight today, but they didn't make it: the island was snowed in. I made it to Beoty's in St Martin's Lane for lunch with Kenneth Macmillan. I want to create a ballet – the equivalent of Britten's *Young Person's Guide to the Orchestra* for dance. I think he took to the idea. We are going to do a book as well. We got on easily. He was comfortable to be with.*

The same, alas, cannot always be said of Julian Slade! I love him. He loves me. But, at times, like this afternoon, it really is a struggle. Is it drink or drugs or a combination of the two? He potters about his basement flat, stumbling over the *bric-à-brac*, confused, somnolent, absurdly sentimental. We can spend two hours 'working', getting nowhere. The real problem: the man who created *Salad Days* can't come up with fresh tunes any more: the best he has managed for our show are ones that he has unearthed from his bottom drawer. His bathroom is filthy and that's depressing too.

Tonight we went to *The Mitford Girls* at the Globe. Stylish and fun.

---

* Sir Kenneth Macmillan (1929–92), ballet dancer and choreographer. Neither ballet nor book materialised.

Monday, 11 January 1982

I like the company of Anthony Burgess.* He is amusing, intelligent and fearless. He doesn't give a damn. On *Start the Week* this morning he caused huge alarm by referring to a fellow writer as someone who writes to be read by readers who like to hold their books with just one hand. It took a moment for the import of his suggestion to sink it, but as it did you could see the flurrying and scurrying behind the studio glass. Flushed and flustered, Peter Estall [the producer] crept in, took Burgess out, and while Richard Baker did his best to interview Miss United Kingdom, we watched Estall and Burgess in the control room gesticulating at each other wildly. Chuckling, puffing on his cheroot, Burgess returned to the studio and made a retraction. 'If what I said had any implication that the fellow is a pornographer, I apologise. That's not what I meant at all.'

I walked from Broadcasting House to Baker Street, via Marylebone High Street – one of my favourite walks. Coffee with the parents. Pa in bed, but relatively mellow. He likes the district nurses. He likes being back home.

Wednesday, 17 February 1982

Jolly supper with our photographer friend Francis Loney and his photographer friend, Beverley Goodway – the man who takes all the Page 3 photographs for the *Sun*. He seemed so wholesome: glasses, bow tie, nice wife. Essentially it's the same picture every day: the shorter girls (around 5' 3") work best – nice and compact. That's all he does: goes into the office, gets a different girl to strip off and snaps her. A career for our times.†

Saturday, 6 March 1982

Went to Sunningdale in Berkshire to see Diana Dors.‡ She is going to be a guest in the *Memories* series I am doing for HTV. I felt like a walk-on character in a not-very-good made-for-TV American movie: it was one of those open-plan houses, made for stars to wander round rather than families to live in. She

---

* Anthony Burgess (b. John Burgess Wilson, 1917–93), author, composer and critic, best known for *A Clockwork Orange*, 1962.

† Beverley Goodway (b.1944) retired in 2003, after thirty-three years of taking Page 3 photographs.

‡ Diana Dors, born Diana Fluck (1931–84), actress and, in the 1950s, 'blonde bombshell' British film star in the Marilyn Monroe/Brigitte Bardot tradition. Her third husband, actor Alan Lake (1940–84), committed suicide, shooting himself five months after Diana Dors's death from cancer. Other guests in the *Memories* series included Windsor Davies (b.1930), Welsh actor known for his role in *It Ain't Half Hot, Mum*, 1974–81.

wasn't there when I arrived, but the front door was open and her husband – Alan Lake – was swimming in the indoor pool. He didn't offer a greeting: he just carried on doing his lengths. I wandered about the potted palms and marbled-topped tables until Diana appeared. She did not look good. 'I am over-weight and underemployed,' she said. I know from Noel, who was involved in one of the tours she did with Mr Lake, that she has been in a bad way recently: drinking too much and brawling – hand-to-hand fighting with her husband. Born Diana Fluck, she told me there was no truth in my favourite story – the one about the vicar in her hometown of Swindon who welcomed her back to open the church fête and was so nervous about getting her name right he announced her as 'Miss Diana Clunt'. She said, 'What *is* true is that when I started they used to put your name up in lights outside the cinema and they were worried about what might happen in my case if one of the lights blew . . .' She made her first film in 1947, before I was born. She is a fine actress, according to Noel (among others), but now she's having to do comic turns in the likes of *Confessions of a Taxi Driver*. When we do the programme she doesn't want to talk about the Krays or Ruth Ellis or her 'problems'. 'We'll just chat and have a few laughs, won't we?' she said, somewhat bleakly. I imagine what we get will depend entirely on her mood on the day. (I think these pre-meetings are a waste of time. I saw Windsor Davies on Wednesday. He was drunk when I met him and blind drunk when I left. Today Miss Dors didn't really want to tell me a thing – and what she did say I could hardly hear for the noise of water gushing into her swimming pool.)

Wednesday, 10 March 1982

Went to see Elizabeth Taylor in *Little Foxes* at the Victoria Palace. At least she appeared – albeit in a wheelchair. She has damaged her ankle but 'the show goes on'. The piece is dated and so, alas, is Miss Taylor. I know she has lovely eyes, and, yes, for a few years, long ago, she was a great beauty, but (off-screen anyway) she has no 'presence'. She is overweight and underwhelming. She was there, she knew the lines and we applauded the glamour of her fame, but as an 'event' it was a dud. Nothing happened.

Sunday, 4 April 1982

At around 9.00 p.m. last night, at the Embassy Hotel on the Bayswater Road, as they were clearing away dinner, I got to my feet and began to speak. At around 9.30 a.m. this morning, as they were clearing away breakfast, I sat down again. I spoke non-stop for twelve-and-a-half hours. Once more, and this time without having to share it with Master Parsons, I hold the record for making the world's longest-ever after-dinner speech.

I made the speech in aid of the National Playing Fields Association: we should raise a few thousand. I was sponsored by Cockburn's Port: I appeared to drink an entire bottle during the course of the marathon. (In fact, before I started, I substituted Ribena for the port: the audience was in awe of my capacity.) I spoke with a few notes, but no script. I did the speech as an A to Z of life, giving myself around half an hour with each letter of the alphabet. The audience (bless them) stayed awake throughout. Andrew Festing* (bless him) came and sketched the proceedings with a view to painting a commemorative picture of the event. Kenneth Williams (bless him) turned up at the finish to say a few words and wrap it up. It worked well and I quite enjoyed it – I was amused by the challenge – but through the night, as I spoke, as the stories tumbled out, I found my mind reverting to two things: Pa and the Argentinian invasion of the Falkland Islands. I did not refer to either – but I kept thinking of both. I pictured Pa lying all alone in his bed at the Middlesex. I know he is dying and there is nothing to be done. And I . thought about the Falklands crisis – and how there is a real world out there, a world in which I should be playing a part.† Instead, I'm busy with this sort of footling nonsense.

Anyway, it's done now. It was fun. It was in a good cause. Move on. (But, first, supper with M at the Mumtaz. Chicken Mughlai and a bottle of Chablis, I think, don't you?)

Sunday, 16 May 1982

I am writing this in the departure lounge at Edinburgh Airport on my way back to London from the Scottish Finals of the National Scrabble Championships. It's been an odd day. Breakfast at the Mount Royal Hotel was memorable because the head waiter was more manic than Manuel and Basil Fawlty combined. After breakfast we watched the Moderator of the Church of Scotland's procession at St

* Andrew Festing (b.1941), son of Field Marshal Sir Francis Festing; soldier, director of Sotheby's and, from 1980, portrait painter; later president of the Royal Society of Portrait Painters.
† On 3 April, the day of GB's speech, Parliament had been recalled for its first Saturday sitting since the Suez Crisis of 1956. Argentina invaded and captured the Falkland Islands on 2 April, overwhelming the single company of Royal Marines guarding the islands' capital, Port Stanley. A British Task Force was despatched to recapture the islands on 5 April and the mission was accomplished by 14 June, with some 255 British lives lost in the action and around 670 Argentinian.

Giles, looked in at the National Portrait Gallery (one of my favourite galleries in all the world) and then ran riot in a second-hand bookshop and bought all twenty-three volumes of the *Complete Works of Thackeray* – the Smith, Elder edition, 1869. I am thrilled to have it. Then we had lunch at the George Hotel and found the current 'Mr Universe' (truly) sitting at the table next to ours. Here I have just seen Matthew Evans from Faber, who turns out to be a member of the Franco-British Council – whatever that may be. They have come to Edinburgh for a 'jolly'. All this is going on while at the bottom of the world our men are fighting to retrieve the Falklands. We are doing the right thing and Mrs Thatcher's leadership is inspirational. (I say that, but it may not be the general view. I have just been speaking with a Frenchman who wanted to take me to task over the sinking of the *Belgrano* and the *Sun*'s gung-ho 'Gotcha!' headline. I simply said, 'War is a nasty business and perhaps it's understandable that a popular British paper should take a populist patriotic line.')[*]

Saturday, *12 June 1982*

We went to Robert Maxwell's party at Headington Hill Hall. As we lined up along the pathway to get in, assorted Maxwell children popped out from behind the bushes to greet us: 'I'm Ian Maxwell, Robert Maxwell's son, welcome to Headington Hill Hall,' 'I'm Kevin Maxwell, Robert Maxwell's son, welcome to Headington Hill Hall.' Inside the grounds, the great man wandered among us so that we might touch his garb. I noticed he was personally amplified this year: he had a microphone around his neck and there were speakers in each marquee. He adjusted his own volume, depending on whether he wished to be heard simply by those around him or the general crowd. We spent most of our time with Donald Sinden and Cliff Michelmore. The general consensus is that, with the Falklands conflict, Mrs Thatcher has shown her mettle. Don says there will be statues raised to her in the fullness of time – and he is ready to subscribe to the first of them.

Thursday, *17 June 1982*

The last of the *Memories* series – April Ashley, born George Jamieson in Liverpool in 1935,[†] sex-change pioneer who had his dangly bits lopped off in

---

[*] The sinking of the *Belgrano*, with the loss of 362 men, was controversial. The *Sun* had reported the news on 4 May under the headline, 'GOTCHA!': 'The Navy had the Argies on their knees last night . . . WALLOP: they torpedoed the 14,000-ton Argentina cruiser the *General Belgrano* and left it a useless wreck.'

[†] *April Ashley's Odyssey*, written by GB's Oxford contemporary, Duncan Fallowell, was published in 1982.

Casablanca in 1960 and lives to tell the tale. And tells it well. It was a good show – probably the best, though Miss Ashley was a touch pie-eyed by the end of it. (She had spent the previous evening cruising round Cardiff looking for 'her lost youth'. I know because I found her at the hotel having a set-to with the taxi driver who had driven her. He wanted paying, so I paid him and packed Miss A. off to bed.) I like her – she is fun, glamorous, 'feminine', but entirely in a drag-queen way. I like her, but I couldn't fancy her. As I was saying goodbye to everyone today, I told Julie, one of the backing singers, that I had fancied *her* since Programme One. She said, 'Why didn't you say so? Why are you telling me now when you're going? We could have had an affair. I'd have loved that. Wouldn't that have been fun?' I think she meant it.

Monday, 21 June 1982

Went to Edenhall to see Pa.[*] He is bad again. In pain, very weak, very quiet. He is depressed. He does not want to die. In the eight weeks that he has been here, three other men have died in beds near to his. Of course, it's depressing. Of course, the patients don't form relationships with one another: they dare not. They lie there, staring into space, surrounded by other people, but essentially alone. They have come here to die: this is the anteroom to death. As Ma says, above the doorway they should put a sign: 'Abandon hope all ye who enter here.' Edwin, the man in the bed next to Pa, was here for two years before he died last week. How many deaths did Edwin witness during those two years?

Tonight we went to the Coliseum to see Rudolf Nureyev in *Homage to Diaghilev*. He is not so sprightly as he was, and not *subtle*, but there's certainly a presence: you know he's there. Then Ikarus for supper. (Taramasalata and lamb kebab.)

Wednesday, 30 June 1982

Pa died at 6.30 this morning.

Thursday, 1 July 1982

Pa was alone when he died. That doesn't matter. He knew that we all loved him. So much.

I got there by 10.00 a.m. They gave me all his possessions in a large black plastic bag – a bin-liner. There wasn't much: a suit, a shirt, his prayer book, his

---

[*] GB's father had been admitted to the Marie Curie Edenhall Hospice in Lyndhurst Gardens, NW3, on 26 April 1982.

glasses, his wedding ring – his teeth! Ma wants me to wear his wedding ring, but I won't. I'm not one for rings. We took Ma out for a drive to Beaconsfield last night. She's bearing up. It's all a bit strange.

I have kept busy and that's helped. My first port of call was Camden Registry Office, opposite Euston Station. They were very friendly. I have the death certificate. Cause of death: 'ıa. Carcinomatosis; ıb. Malignant primary hepatoma of liver.' I have been on to Kenyon's – I did not ask for family terms, though I know Pa would have wanted me to!* I have been on to Frank Coventry [the rector of St Marylebone Parish Church] about the funeral. It's going to be on Monday at 11.00 a.m. We are arranging refreshments in the Browning Room – tea, coffee, squash, white wine, sandwiches, quiches, simple but something for those who have braved the elements and defied the train strike to get there. I have done the announcement for *The Times* and *Telegraph*. I have sent an obituary to *The Times*. I have written to Ben in America. I have set the wheels in motion for Ma to get the death grant, widow's pension, etc. Pa's will, made in 1939, is very simple – everything goes to Ma. But he has left nothing. He had nothing left – less than £2,000. We'll pay for the funeral. I'd like to.

Friday, 2 July 1982

I took Ma this morning to the Chapel of Rest at Kenyon's in Westbourne Grove to see Pa for the last time. It was an interesting experience. And useful. I was apprehensive, but I need not have been. The undertakers were very friendly, easy, not unctuous. They took us down to the basement and let us into a small room, like a doctor's surgery. Pa's body was laid out in an open coffin. It was him and yet it wasn't. It was like a waxwork and, like a waxwork, it didn't quite ring true. We stood by the coffin for a minute or two, in silence. Ma stroked his hair very gently and said, 'Goodbye, hon. I love you.' And then we left. It was easy really because he wasn't there.

Monday, 19 July 1982

Of all the letters about Pa, I think the best was the simplest – the card from Kenneth [Williams] with the quotation from Nietzsche: 'To endure is all.' I have now completed all the replies to the letters of condolence.

Jolly lunch today with Joanna Lumley at Pomme d'Amour. I gave her a good idea for a book: she should write a range of interesting letters to a range of inter-

---

* GB's father had cousins who belonged to the Kenyon family, founders of one of the country's best-known firms of undertakers.

esting people – politicians, churchmen, actors, thinkers, campaigners, travellers, etc. Some would write back, some wouldn't, but the correspondence (especially if her letters are intelligent and discursive, as they would be) could have the makings of a Christmas best-seller. We are making good progress with Kenneth's new book [*Back Drops*]. Geoff Atkinson is working wonders with *The Alternative SDP Manifesto*.* And I'm having fun with Ned.† Two new ones on me: 1) Sylvia Miles, American actress, distraught after the collapse of her latest affair with a homosexual, is drowning her sorrows in Joe Allen's in New York. A large, witty, black waiter asks her if she'd like some coffee. She would. How would she like it? Miss Miles eyes the waiter up and down and drawls, 'Like my men!' The waiter's voice goes up a register: 'Oh, Miss Miles! We don't serve no gay coffee here!' 2) An F. E. Smith story I'd not heard before. The Labour MP J. H. Thomas arrived at the House of Commons and asked FE the way to the lavatory. 'Simple,' said FE. 'Along the corridor, first left. You'll see a door marked "Gentlemen", but don't let that deter you.' Smith and Thomas became friends. When Thomas said he had 'one 'ell of an 'eadache', FE prescribed 'a couple of aspirates'.

1.00–6.30 p.m. Aphra's 4th birthday party.

Friday, 15 October 1982

Woozy and irritable this morning.

Woozy because of a late night at the Caprice. We took Stephanie Turner and Ginny Festing. As we arrived we encountered Jack Tinker, smaller and sweeter than ever, sitting alone because his guest, the astrologer Patric Walker, had been held up by unforeseen circumstances. Other sightings: Jill Bennett,‡ drunk, having grapes fed to her by a young Adonis and, at the next table, David Hicks,§ sober, having what appeared to be sour grapes fed to him by a different Adonis. Steph – so much more buoyant and comfortable since she and Simon split up – remarked how odd 'fame' is. Why did we all recognise David Hicks? Steph's third series of *Juliet Bravo* ends in a few weeks and she has decided to do no more.

---

* Geoffrey Atkinson (b.1958), comedy writer and producer, now best known as the producer of *Bremner, Bird and Fortune*.
† Edward 'Ned' Sherrin CBE (1931–2007), producer, director, author, raconteur. The book was *Cutting Edge: Ned Sherrin's Anthology of Wit*, 1984.
‡ Jill Bennett (1931–90), actress, married to the playwrights Willis Hall and John Osborne.
§ David Hicks (1929–98), interior decorator and designer, married to Pamela, younger daughter of Lord Mountbatten.

She is recognised by all and sundry in the street today, but won't be in eighteen months. Ginny won't ever be recognised in the streets, but doesn't want to be. She is defiantly a housewife and intends to remain one. She is very much 'to her own self true' and I envy that.

Had I the courage of my convictions I'd be less irritable right now because I would not have gone for a swimming lesson this morning, nor every morning for the past fortnight. I never enjoyed it and, once or twice, I loathed it. M can't understand that I don't like it and I feel bad because I know my attitude spoils it for her. After the swim, breakfast is served and I sit with my two fellow pupils being 'a bloke'. They are pleasant-enough solicitors knocking forty and happiest when exchanging smutty prep school banter. Perhaps I should have tried telling them my favourite Jill Bennett story? When she was very young she had an affair with a much older actor, Godfrey Tearle – and someone said, 'I never really understood what Godfrey got out of his relationship with Jill Bennett until I saw her eating corn on the cob at the Caprice!'

Friday, 22 October 1982

I am on the flight from Glasgow at the end of my week-long promotional tour for *Great Theatrical Disasters*. Memorable moments have been few. On the flight to Edinburgh I travelled alongside a 60-year-old businessman who was handcuffed to a policeman and spent the entire flight protesting that Gestapo tactics had come to Britain. In Liverpool, in the black cab taking me to the hotel, as I got out to pay, I discovered a half-caste prostitute crouching in the luggage compartment at the front of the taxi. The driver offered her to me at 'a special rate'. In Edinburgh I had a happy drink with Johnny Shand Kydd, the young and very sweet stepbrother to the Princess of Wales. The downside of the week has been my 'minder', Nina Martyn, 27, not totally unprepossessing but totally naïve. She wears a mask of make-up that ends abruptly at her jaw, bites her fingernails to the quick and eats Danish pastries with her mouth open. Her boyfriend is called Tom and is the son of Ted Moult. I wish I had been able to do the tour without her. All she has done is double the cost and leave me out of sorts. She has had one moment of glory, however. In Wolverhampton, at Radio Stoke, I was telling the wife of a Canadian psychologist (who was in the studio flogging his *Psychology of the Unborn Child*) what a bore it was being 'looked after' by Nina because I was obliged to carry her enormous suitcases. Nina interjected: 'And it's a bore for me because I have to carry his enormous ego.'

Thursday, 4 November 1982

New York

The Waldorf-Astoria is as good as ever. The lobby is one of my favourite places in the world. The visit is going well: I think deals will be done. And so far we have been off-Broadway to *Little Shop of Horrors* and very much on Broadway to *Dream Girls*. The New York audiences appear enormously naïve and *roar* at anything at all showy or vaguely risqué. There is tremendous innocence here and not a very keen sense of what I call the 'amusing'.

Tuesday, 16 November 1982

North British Hotel, Glasgow

Well, here I am – but God knows why! It's only 10.45 p.m. and I have abandoned an alcoholic Scottish television producer in the bar to take sanctuary in my sordid little room. There is 'Gaelic' music playing in the background. However, tawdry as it is (and it is the end of the world) it is the ultimate in *luxe* by comparison with the Midland in Manchester last night, where I arrived late, and after a fairly self-indulgent dinner with Peter Ridsdale-Scott – scrambled eggs and poached salmon, partridge and a cheeky French waiter – I checked in and rolled up to my room at midnight to find it filthy: fag ends all over the place, dirty coffee cups, used towels, grubby carpet. This morning, after an uneatable breakfast – for which they attempted to charge me twice – I checked out, getting £15 knocked off the bill and being handed a bottle of whisky as I departed. This I refused rather grandly, declaring that they would be better advised to use their resources to raise their standards – only to discover on arrival here that the whisky wasn't a gesture of goodwill towards an unhappy patron, but a ludicrous promotion. This hotel – the North British – is also owned by British Transport Hotels and when I arrived I was greeted with a sign advertising 'An Irresistible Offer from an Incomparable Hotel – spend a night at the Midland Manchester and leave with a bottle of Haig whisky.' It is all a far cry from the Waldorf-Astoria.

Thursday, 18 November 1982

I have just come from a reception at Buckingham Palace. It was an event for NPFA to mark the success of the Christopher Leaver Mayoral Appeal.[*] The 'climax' of the reception was the unveiling of Andrew Festing's painting of my attempt on the world record for the longest after-dinner speech. I was first to

[*] Sir Christopher Leaver, the Lord Mayor of London in 1981, had designated NPFA as one of the charities to benefit from his year of office.

arrive because I brought the painting with me. In the main entrance hall I was greeted by a posse of flunkies – 'pages', the gay young men who do the work round here. Squealing with excitement, they took the painting and the easel from me and bore it up to the Music Room. I followed, spotting a gap between Rembrandts in the long gallery where the picture would have fitted in nicely.

In the Music Room, though strictly against the rules, one of the pages volunteered to photograph me with the painting, centre stage. Another went off to find a sheet with which to cover it up. 'You can't unveil it unless you veil it first.' Between 3.00 and 3.30 p.m. the guests arrived. Everyone is always mellow at a Palace party. On the dot of 3.30 p.m., Prince Philip marched in. He looked tanned, fit, ready to begin. 'Shall we get on with it?' he asked. We did. Christopher Leaver said a few words and set the scene. Prince Philip replied – at first confusing NPFA with the Central Council for Physical Recreation, then mistaking Leslie Porter for his father-in-law. Repeatedly he turned to Leslie, saying, 'We owe a great deal to you, Mr Cohen. Thank you. I think a round of applause for Mr Cohen is due, don't you? Well done, Mr Cohen.' Finally, we unveiled the painting. HRH gazed at it suitably bemused. Amused too: he kept the banter going. (It's what he does.) He was particularly pleased when he discovered the painting was by Field Marshal Festing's boy. 'Good man, Festing.' And he wants an answer to everything. 'Where are you going to hang it?' 'I don't know, sir.' 'Well, you must know.' 'I don't know.' 'How about the Garrick Club? They might take it. That's it – the Garrick.'

Friday, 26 November 1982

I set off at the crack of dawn to get to Leeds by 10.00 a.m. to be a guest on the revamped version of the ill-fated Channel 4's much-abused very first show: *Countdown.** What a farce. In the event, on arrival I found I wasn't needed till two, the producer was drunk and we probably wouldn't be able to record the shows anyway because of an impending industrial dispute. It really was a shambles – not helped, of course, by the fact that I hadn't seen the programme so didn't actually know what anyone was talking about.

As the morning wore on, I began to understand what was afoot. I wasn't there

---

* *Countdown*, a words and numbers TV game, originated in France, and was brought to Yorkshire Television, initially as a local programme, *Calendar Countdown*, presented by the local News presenter, Yorkshire-born Richard Whiteley OBE (1943–2005). On 2 November 1982, as *Countdown*, with Richard Whiteley as host, Cathy Hytner putting up the letters, Carol Vorderman looking after the numbers and Ted Moult at the dictionary, it became the first programme to be broadcast on Britain's fourth TV channel, Channel 4.

to take part in *Countdown* as a guest: I was there to make a *pilot* of a children's version of the programme: *Junior Countdown*. Eventually, we got round to it, but it too was a shambles: I had no briefing, no rehearsal of any kind, and an unusable script on an unreadable autocue. Ted Moult was the guest and he bumbled on amiably as I busked away for all I was worth – which seemed to delight/amaze everybody.

The moment it was over I fled the studio, raced to the station and jumped aboard the 4.45 p.m. train with seconds to spare. I travelled back to London sitting opposite Lord Harewood, whose snore is a collector's item. I reached King's Cross at 7.18 p.m., raced to the Middlesex Hospital, changed in the catering manager's office and performed in the Sisters' Dining Room to the Junior Doctors' Mess. The Professor of Surgery looked just like Bruce Forsyth, but wasn't as funny. Nor, unfortunately, was I.

All in all, an annoying day.

Wednesday, 1 December 1982

An Audience with Kenneth Williams at London Weekend. We were part of the set-up audience who were fed questions to ask 'on the spur of the moment'. Before the show, I felt incredibly anxious for him – my stomach really churned. But he triumphed. It was a bravura performance – very funny and very likeable. Afterwards, at the party, Mary Whitehouse descended on me like a long-lost sister and for a split second I thought (I really thought) it was Dame Edna. I like Mary, but, let's face it, she's a bore: relentless, insensitive, well-intentioned, sometimes right, but a person 'to be avoided' because she does go on so. Once we'd shaken her loose, we were picked up by Cecil Korer, now head of entertainment at Channel 4. He was sweet and Monsieur Hulot-like and we sat with him and Ned Sherrin (in bull-queen mode) and a boy of Ned's. Peter Nichols was pissed (it can't be post-*Poppy* euphoria);[*] Joan Sims appeared to be making a guest appearance from another planet (is she dying?);[†] Bernard Bresslaw[‡] was amiable (the last time we were together was at the Cambridge Union. His son is

---

[*] Peter Nichols (b.1927), playwright; as an authority on pantomime, GB had been peripherally involved in Peter Nichols's 'pantomime' play about the Opium Wars which had just opened in a Royal Shakespeare Company production at the Barbican.

[†] Joan Sims (1930–2001), actress, best remembered for her appearances in the *Carry On* films.

[‡] Bernard Bresslaw (1934–93), English actor, also remembered for his contribution to the *Carry On* films.

at Cambridge now and he's so proud.) Gordon Jackson* was twinkly and, from the members of the public, received by far the warmest welcome of any of the celebrities. We took Ted Moult home. His wife's in hospital having a hysterectomy – 'after seven children she deserves a break,' says Ted. He's as bluff-and-hail-fellow about her and her condition as he is about the 'rubbish' he does and the double-glazing ads. 'She's married to me,' he said, 'no wonder the poor woman drinks.'

Saturday, 4 December 1982

Our last morning in Wickham. This is our now-traditional three-day pre-Christmas shopping break. We shop by day (Winchester/Chichester/Salisbury) and then, while Michèle has her bath, I wrap. Over one hundred items so far, including stocking-fillers. Work done, we descend for our two glasses of champagne and a delicious dinner. (Last night, snails *en croûte* with Pernod sauce were the dish of the day.) The news of the day is that we have spies for neighbours – Russian agents have been discovered living in our street. 'The Sputniks of Campden Hill' is the headline in the *Daily Mail*. M now claims she knew something was up. There have been 'GPO workmen' sitting in tents digging up the roadway for weeks.

Saturday, 18 December 1982

Home at last. I am exhausted. Last night was not a triumph. Billy Connolly† and I were the guest speakers at a charity dinner at the Dorchester. It was a recording industry event and our contributions were greeted with jeers, boos, catcalls and an avalanche of flung mince-pies. (Some were given added velocity by having coins pushed into them.) The only consolation was that the Big Yin fared no better than I did. The day itself was fine: I scooted up to Leeds to be the dictionary guest on *Countdown*. I recorded four programmes and they are going to make me a regular. It's been a week of scooting up north: once to Leeds, twice to Manchester, once to Newcastle-upon-Tyne – and a foray to Cardiff, too. Such is the lot of the second-division author and minor TV celebrity. But there have been compensations: useful fees and memorable encounters. In Manchester I did a late-night programme about panto with Freddie 'Mr Parrot Face' Davies‡ and

---

* Gordon Jackson (1923–90), Scottish actor, best remembered as Hudson, the butler, in *Upstairs, Downstairs*; Jackson and his wife Rona were probably Kenneth Williams's closest family friends.
† Billy Connolly CBE (b.1942), Scottish comedian.
‡ Freddie Davies (b.1937), English comedian.

Les Dawson – the former sweet (he came dressed like an accountant from Bromley in a three-piece suit and a homburg hat), the latter (looking like a very stout pig) so pissed he could barely stand and wheezing so badly he could barely be understood. (He smoked an entire pack of cigarettes in the hour I was with him.) The programme was memorable entirely because Les (who loves to remind you that he's no fool) was so bitterly morose he reduced the poor presenter almost to tears. For the entire thirty minutes (it was a live broadcast), she shook like a leaf.

Saturday, 1 January 1983

Happy New Year! I feel it's going to be a good one. 1982 had lots of jolly moments, but over it all lay the sadness of Pa's death on 30 June. 'Dear, sweet, loveable Pa.' Ma is desolate and with cause. It's been a year of family deaths – Pa, Nana Allkins,* Connie Purcell,† and, just before Christmas, alone and senile, in Accrington, poor old Auntie Edith.

And it's been a week of farewells. We said goodbye to Ma: she has gone to California with Jen. We said goodbye to our bank manager in Oxford: after forty-three years with the bank, at 60 he's out. That's that. (He has been good to us: he has been an ally and friend.) We gave a 'Contact the Elderly' tea party – and some of them we won't see again. (One lady is 100.) Truth is: we could do with a few months free of the old, the infirm, the desperate and the dull. We could do with a break from family, M's and mine. (That said, Hes is coming over on Monday to celebrate her 41st birthday. Her latest job (part-time): running the mobile coffee bar on Wandsworth Common. All human life is here.)

My Christmas highlights were a lovely stocking from Michèle and the realisation that I love her very much. We also went to see an almost successful *Peter Pan* at the Barbican, attended John Schlesinger's party (where M asked Richard Gere to repeat his name *twice*, and Frederick Raphael and Philip Roth decided that no independently wealthy man had ever written a major novel), and I did a quirky broadcast on Radio 2 at midnight with Larry Grayson who was pissed as a newt but sweet as ever. (The new boy in his life was very sweet, too.)

Yes. We've been busy and it's all been fine. And we went to the Norland Place nativity play in which Saethryd read a piece beautifully and made me glad to be alive and oh-so-proud to be a father.

---

* GB's sister Virginia's mother-in-law.
† An old family friend who traditionally spent Christmas with the Brandreths.

'Roland Rat is Helping Hugely'

January 1983 – December 1985

Thursday, 6 January 1983
Twelfth Night

12 noon. Caryl Brahms's memorial service at St Paul's, Covent Garden. A long life (Caryl was 84) and a celebration to match. Dorothy Tutin conquered the foul acoustics and stole the show. Ned, as widower-cum-compère, presented a sort of Side by Side by Brahms with an all-star cast (and congregation). Felicity Kendal was inaudible, Penny Keith not much better. Robert Meadmore, David Kernan and Cleo Laine sang vigorously and were ushered in and out by a galaxy of refined rough trade. Caryl would have loved it. I'd wanted to wear the tie she gave me, but realised I couldn't because I'd changed it. The man in the shop knew it had been 'a present from Miss Brahms – all her friends come back to change the ties she gives them.'

After the service I raced to Sotheby's to meet Andrew Festing. He took me to Boodles for lunch and regaled me with stories of his eccentric family – the military Mitfords. He is a delightful chap, completely decent, and happy because he has decided to take the plunge: give up Sotheby's (he's the head of English pictures) and become a portrait painter full-time. He knows that's what he wants to do with his life and he's going to do it. (What do I want to do with my life? This year, I want to make money. I *need* to make money. I will make money!)

Sunday, 9 January 1983

Tonight: two very jolly editions of *Just a Minute* with Kenneth at his sweetest. Last night: a very jolly evening with Patrick Fyffe at his new home in Putney (he has turned it into a Victorian gem). The principal guest was the head of the Royal Military School of Music who gloried in the name of Colonel Beat. He joined the Army as a drummer boy and worked his way up to the rank of colonel in the Scots Guards. His 'lady wife', with a few glasses of 'bubbly' inside her, was fairly unstoppable – as was Mrs Fyffe, Patrick's mother, now 81, who sang for us. *In extenso*. I enjoyed her croaking. Michèle cringed. Tomorrow night: I'm at the Penta Hotel,

414

Heathrow, addressing a gathering of computer salesmen: £300 is £300. Tuesday: I go to Leeds for three days to record a dozen *Countdowns* at £600 per day. Onward!

Thursday, 20 January 1983

It's just after one in the morning and I'm in the *grand luxe* of my suite at the Carlton in Bournemouth, feeling wide awake and somewhat disconcerted. I've been performing to the top management of Truman's the brewers and I gave them my usual – which was enjoyed by all, except for one: a David Gilbert-Smith, an ex-SAS Edward de Bono lookalike who runs something glorying in the name of the Leadership Trust, a sort of outward bound course for executives. Inevitably, he was a butt for some of my sallies, but while my other 'victims' at least appeared to be amused he fumed, and when I went to say goodnight was unbelievably, alarmingly, abusive. He was quite frightening. I have locked the door to my room and (absurd, I know) pushed the sofa up against it. I pity the poor Truman executives who are about to go on his five-day course.*

Tommy Trinder† followed me and upset nobody – except possibly the waiters. He did an hour and was ready to do more. He's a teetotaller, an old school comic with a well-turned tale to tell about everybody from Vesta Tilley to Jack Benny. It was like being taken back to a vintage night on the halls. 'I'm so old my father was a Bow Street runner. My mother was a Bond Street walker, but that's another story . . .'

Tuesday, 1 February 1983

The advantage of not drinking (I am taking my new year resolution into February) is that, while others stumble to their beds semi-comatose, I'm sitting here, bright-eyed, at work on my diary. I'm at the Gosforth Park Hotel, Newcastle-upon-Tyne. It's twenty past midnight and I am happy to report that tonight I secured a sustained standing ovation. (Yes, sometimes they do like me.) The flight up here (to the Thistle Hotel Management Conference) was alarming: gales are sweeping the country. I am a coward, I own it, and my life is rather tame. I don't take risks. Gossiping with Patrick and George (Bracket & Hinge – series two progresses) it's interesting how unhibited others are ready to be. We

* Major David Gilbert-Scott MC (1931–2003) founded the Leadership Trust in Ross-on-Wye in 1975. During his stewardship, more than 20,000 executives took part in his courses.

† Tommy Trinder CBE (1909–89), London-born comedian with a huge following between the 1930s and 1960s, remembered for his porkpie hat and catchphrase, 'You lucky people.'

started with stories of Leonard Sachs[*] positively haunting the Gents at Whiteleys in search of excitement, moved on to sightings of Victoria Wood and Julie Walters as happy as larks in the Ladies in Manchester, and ended up with Patrick's recollection of the amusing party where everyone stripped off, got tied up and sprayed with shaving cream. The lives some folks lead . . .

PS: Not all are living dangerously. Wearing a seat belt in the front of your car is compulsory from today. (Actually, it's now tomorrow. This PS is coming from the departure lounge at Newcastle Airport. I'm on my way home for Saethryd's 6th birthday party. She will be wearing her new gown. I was up at dawn and caught the first few minutes of the second morning of TV-am: Robert Key looking distinctly bleary-eyed as he read us the News at 6.00 a.m.)[†]

Friday, 11 February 1983

News:

Professional. I spent the morning at Hampton Court talking mazes. I am going to do a book of 'classic mazes', but I also have plans to design an original maze myself.

Domestic. Tomorrow Benet takes his entrance exams for both Westminster Under School *and* Colet Court. They do them on the same day deliberately to discourage you from trying both. I am sick with nerves. Ludicrous, I know.

National. A civil servant by the name of Dennis Nielsen has been charged with multiple male murder. (It's not always funny when they strip you naked and tie you up.) He was caught because heads, hands, and great chunks of flesh had blocked the drains at the house where he lived. I imagine Lord Longford is already on his way to see him.[‡]

Friday, 18 February 1983

My brilliant boy sailed into both Colet Court *and* Westminster Under School. The apprehension seems ridiculous now, but in the run-up to the exams and on

---

[*] Leonard Sachs (1909–90), British actor, founder of the Players' Theatre music hall, chairman of *The Good Old Days*, 1953–83. Though married to the actress Eleanor Summerfield, he had a reputation for 'cottaging'.

[†] Robert Key, Anna Ford, David Frost, Michael Parkinson and Angela Rippon were the so-called 'Famous Five' presenters who launched Britain's first commercial breakfast TV station on 1 February 1983; this was five months earlier than planned and two weeks after the BBC had launched their own daybreak programme, *Breakfast Time.*

[‡] He was. Dennis Andrew Nielsen (b.1945), known to have killed at least fifteen men and boys between 1975 and 1983, was sentenced to life imprisonment at the Old Bailey in November 1983.

the day itself it was real enough. Only four of Benet's classmates got in to CC; eleven got in to WUS. (The competition for these London day school places is terrifying.) We've settled on Colet Court a) because he preferred the feel of the place on the day, b) because it has the reputation of being more challenging, c) because Mrs Garnsey (Benet's headmistress) and Miss Hutchings (Benet's teacher) felt that the larger school, the more robust environment and the academic sweating would all be good for him, and d) because the facilities are so much better and the location so much more convenient. I don't know why I was quite so anxious for him, but I was. He has asked for lunch at the Ritz as his reward. (He is 7.) We shall be happy to indulge him. As I write, we are indulging ourselves with a post-exam weekend in Wickham. I am stepping off the wagon to allow myself a celebratory glass of champagne. (Two actually. And then, I think, some Chablis with dinner.)

Tuesday, 22 February 1983

I am sitting in my dressing room at London Weekend Television having – of course – been called hours too early for a panel game called *To Tell the Truth*. Who else is here? My friend Denise Coffey (I love her);[*] the bonhomous Jeremy Beadle (warm heart, withered hand);[†] Nigel Rees (whom the make-up lady persisted in calling Roger);[‡] Libby Purves (whom I haven't seen in twelve years: she is mountainous now, with breasts like giant marrows; she has just become editor of *The Tatler*); and Patrick Stoddart (yes, it's very much a second eleven affair). Oh, and one other big lady: Claire Rayner.[§] She *is* enormous. As Paddy Davis pointed out on the phone this morning: what a cheek she has advising others on how to lead normal, happy lives when she – and her offspring – look like overblown hippos. Claire does not draw breath, nor does Jeremy – that's why I'm hiding in my dressing room rather than tucking into the sandwiches in hospitality. (People think I talk all the time, but I don't. Do I?)

Tomorrow, incidentally, is the 350th anniversary of the birth of Samuel Pepys.

[*] GB and the actress Denise Coffey (b.1936) had plans to write a play together.
[†] Jeremy Beadle MBE (1948–2008), writer and broadcaster, had stunted growth in his right hand due to Poland syndrome.
[‡] Nigel Rees (b.1944), author and broadcaster, friend of GB, not to be confused with Roger Rees (also b.1944), actor who had recently won Tony and Olivier awards for his performance in the title role of the *Life and Adventures of Nicholas Nickleby*.
[§] Claire Rayner OBE (b.1931), nurse-turned-broadcaster and agony aunt.

Tuesday, 1 March 1983

Lovely evening. Noel's 56th birthday dinner at the Garrick. He told three stories I'd not heard him tell before and John [Schlesinger] flushed with giggles as he described the Queen draping his CBE around his neck and saying, 'I'm afraid we aren't quite straight, are we?' The highlight of the evening was meeting Vincent Price. He was completely charming – possibly the most charming man I have ever met. (And, bizarrely, he shares a birthday with both Christopher Lee and Peter Cushing. Weird or what?)*

Wednesday, 23 March 1983

A Yorkshire week. We spent the weekend in York, buying lots of second-hand books, a couple of mirrors and several cream teas. The highlight was mattins at the Minster where we spotted George Morpeth,† seated completely alone in the family pew, taking snuff during the sermon and twitching at irregular intervals in the true tradition of the chinless upper-class twit. It was good to see him. He was sweet if odd and, alarmingly, appears to be in command of a battalion.

I'm now in Leeds, with Kenneth [Williams] for company. We are supposed to be recording *Countdown*, but we aren't because there's a strike. It's pretty much a shambles here. The producer (John Meade) is a nightmare – principally because he's a drunk and out of control. (He also visits prostitutes. He is quite proud of this. In Leeds, he says, you're spoilt for choice. 'Quality totty.') I get on with him well enough, but he and Kenneth have fallen out. At the end of the day, John wants to go to the bar and drink and he wants Kenneth to join him. Kenneth won't. Kenneth thinks this will cost him his place in Dictionary Corner. He may be right. Anyway, as there was no *Countdown* and we didn't fancy an afternoon in the bar or the brothel we went to the Odeon and saw *The Verdict*. Every time Paul Newman appeared, Kenneth murmured, 'Isn't she a dish?'

Thursday, 21 April 1983

I am on the island of Jersey where *everybody* has to have a title. I have spent the evening hobnobbing with His Excellency the Lieutenant Governor General, Sir Peter Whiteley GCB OBE (my kind of civilised soldier – and he gave a very witty speech), the Bailiff (who looks like Lloyd George but thinks like Genghis

---

* Vincent Price (1911–93) and Christopher Lee CBE (b.1922) were born on 27 May. Peter Cushing (1913–94), also a Hammer horror film star, gave his birthday as 26 May.
† George, 13th Earl of Carlisle (b.1949); Oxford contemporary of GB and, later, major in the Prince of Wales Royal Armoured Corps.

Anne Diamond as Queen Victoria and Noel Davis as Edward VII at the opening of *Royal Britain*, 9 August 1988

GB as Baron Hardup with the Ugly Sisters in *Cinderella*, Christmas 1989

GB and Prince Philip

GB and the Princess Royal

GB and the Queen

GB and Prince Edward

Prince Philip with Tommy Trinder,
20 December 1983

Michèle and Princess Alexandra,
17 December 1984

GB with Keith Barron, Kenneth
Connor, Suzanne Danielle, *Jack and
the Beanstalk*, Richmond Theatre,
17 December 1984

At Guildhall, for the 40th anniversary of the Queen's accession – the 'Annus Horribilis' speech, 24 November 1992

GB and Prince Charles share a joke, 17 October 1995

Michèle, Lord Strathclyde (minister of tourism), Lord Bradford, GB and the court jester, preparing to lose several millions, 27 September 1989

GB, daughters and mother at the Teddy Bear Museum, 1989

GB and son in 1985 after Benet had won the three flying ducks at a fairground rifle range. They had gone unclaimed since 1956

Exploring Iceland's flora and fauna with Michèle, July 1985

Exploring art outdoors with Patty and John Bratby, 1985

Simon and Beckie Cadell at Le Manoir aux Quat'Saisons on the day they got engaged, 1985

GB and three ladies, 19 April 1986. From left to right: Jancis Robinson, Prue Leith, Delia Smith

2-30 a.m. CHESHIRE EDITION

DAILY POST

Friday, March 15, 1991   Britain's fastest-growing regional daily newspaper   Price 24p

QUALITY 24p AND VALUE

EXCLUSIVE CHESTER SURVEY — Page 3

Major braced for revolt as he ditches poll tax

By David Rose
Political Correspondent

JOHN Major finally killed off the poll tax last night and told Michael Heseltine to press ahead with plans for a property tax that would be fair to all.

Just four months after ditching Margaret Thatcher the Tories new leadership decided her vote losing legacy had to go as well.

But, with up to 60 Tory MPs threatening to rebel, the new tax will be a compromise aimed at uniting the Party and winning back vital local support to pave the way for a general election.

The new tax will, like the old rates, be levied on property. But to ensure that as many people as possible pay the key element of the poll tax the property tax will vary according to the number of working adults living in the home.

People on their own will pay less than families. Couples, too, will face lower bills than those with grown up children. The plan will be to set a standard tax – and then allow people on their own and others who qualify to claim discounts.

And the Government is prepared to spend millions of pounds more to check soaring poll tax bills over the two years it will take to sweep away the poll tax and replace it with the property tax. As well as preparing the massive legislation that will have to be approved by both the Commons and the Lords, the switch will mean an enormous upheaval in town and country halls up and down the country.

Mr Heseltine will announce the outline of the new tax next Thursday after it has been approved by the Cabinet.

Mrs Thatcher claimed the Community Charge would ● Continued on Page 2

TV STAR THE TORY CHOICE

CONSERVATIVES last night chose a TV personality as their candidate for Chester. – as an exclusive Daily Post poll predicted they were set to lose the seat.

Gyles Brandreth, 43, known to millions of breakfast viewers as 'the man in the jumpers' was chosen to fight Sir Peter Morrison's constituency.

Mr Brandreth said: "People feel they know me, and it makes it easier for them to talk to me. I hadn't stood for office before but I am a seasoned campaigner for the Conservative Party. My experience in politics began when I was president of Oxford Union during my student days.

The Daily Post survey suggests that electors are set to follow the Ribble by-election

□ Jackie Lait

– but poll warns of shock in Chester

By Eileen Nederlof and Sarah Batley

lead by switching from the Tories to the Liberal Democrats. In Chester it would allow a Labour victory.

The poll shows that, since 1987, the Tory share of the vote has slumped from 45 pc to 40 pc, just four points higher than Labour. During the same period the Liberal share has risen from 19 pc to 24 pc.

And nearly nine out of ten voters told independent researchers that the single main issue facing the Tories before the next election was

the poll tax, which Prime Minister John Major last night dramatically rejected.

Sir Peter Morrison, formerly Margaret Thatcher's parliamentary private secretary, quit in January and intends to concentrate on his career in business.

In the June 1987 election, Sir Peter had a majority of 4,550 over Labour's David Robinson. The Daily Post poll shows that Sir Peter's majority would be slashed by at least 2,500 votes.

Liberal Democrat candidate Andrew Stunnell, who this time will be standing in Stockport, polled 10,282.

Chester Conservative Association executive committee put 78 pc of their votes behind Mr Brandreth, leaving the other two candidates Nicholas Bourne and Jackie Lait far behind.

Mr Brandreth is director of a chain of wool shops, the nearest of which is in Crewe. And although he was born in West Germany in a British forces hospital, he says his family has been in Chester for generations.

Constituency chairman Jim Cooper said he was proud of the overwhelming majority vote for Mr Brandreth. "It very rarely happens that they could not get down to his knowledge of politics and his presentation of that knowledge – and of course his obvious affinity for people."

Mr Brandreth's nomination will now be rubber stamped at tonight's general meeting of the Chester Conservative constituency.

Survey details - Page 3

□ Gyles Brandreth – the party favourite

Norma Major and Michèle inspecting the bites, 31 March 1992

GB and Douglas Hurd, looking for swans, 22 February 1992

John Major on the campaign trail in Chester, 31 March 1992. 'Look towards the balcony now, see the camera, now wave.'

Candidate and Wife: the campaign photograph

We had our reservations . . . GB with
Sir Peter Morrison, 1992

We had none . . . GB with
Sebastian Coe, 1992

We were drawn together . . .
GB and Glenda Jackson in *The
Times*, 25 March 1993

WESTMINSTER
UNDERSCHOOL
New Pupils
← THIS WAY

Class war: Gyles Brandreth and Glenda Jackson start their political careers

Khan), the Attorney General (to whom I warmed because he was so enthusiastic about my speech, but whose chambers I didn't visit this afternoon having been warned of his penchant for pressing guests to accept four o'clock champagne cocktails) and assorted Constables, Senators, Deputies and Poohbahs of every hue. Frank Walker, my genial host, owns the local paper and was instrumental in making the NPFA Superkid Contest a real triumph on the island. He took me to a lovely restaurant for lunch – fine fresh seafood and a view of France and the islet where the notorious 'Jersey Beast' exiled himself until he had established his innocence.* The one downside of the day was meeting a garrulous Guernseyman who pushed his face into mine and spat as he spoke. (I find I get a lot of this in the life I lead.)

Friday, 29 April 1983

This morning I was asked to join TV-am as one of its 'resident characters'. The poor beleaguered station has 300,000 viewers and poor prospects – largely due to the BBC getting in first and cornering the very limited market for breakfast television with their early-morning version of *Nationwide*. The BBC is crowing over its triumph. We've been scripting *Dear Ladies* at Lime Grove, where champagne breakfasts are the order of the day. The BBC is spending money it cannot spare on a service it does not need. (Incidentally, *Dear Ladies* is now No. 3 in the BBC2 ratings with an audience of five million plus.) Of course, Peter Jay's earnest 'mission to explain' can't be helping TV-am much either.†

I have also just had a call from a West German newspaper asking for my views on the so-called 'Hitler Diaries', brought to light this week by the hapless Hugh

* Edward Paisnel, known as 'the Jersey Beast', was sentenced to thirty years imprisonment for paedophile and other offences committed in the 1960s. For eleven years he stalked the island, in grotesque disguises, preying on women and children. He died in 1994, but was known to have visited the children's home where, in 2008, human bones were allegedly discovered. Frank Walker was the first Chief Minister of Jersey, 2005–08, and criticised in some quarters for his handling of the investigation into the allegations of child abuse on the island. His approach was vindicated by events.
† Peter Jay (b.1937), economist, journalist, former UK Ambassador to the US and founding chairman of TV-am, was ousted from the company and replaced by Jonathan Aitken MP and his cousin, Tim Aitken. Of the 'Famous Five' presenters, all but David Frost departed. Nick Owen, the sports presenter, became the station's weekday host, alongside Anne Diamond. Greg Dyke was brought in from London Weekend to run the station along more popular lines and introduced 'characters' such as GB and the celebrated puppet, Roland Rat.

Trevor-Roper,[*] who rushed in declaring them genuine when perhaps he should have thought twice. Since my history at Oxford didn't really extend much beyond the French Revolution, I couldn't be of much help – and I didn't want to be flippant because Hitler isn't funny.

M and I are off now to take Benet for his celebratory lunch at the Ritz.

Monday, 2 May 1983

I must not do this again, but, now it's over, I am glad that I did it. That's what I always say and it's always true. Last night I produced the May Day Gala to mark the 60th birthday of the Oxford Playhouse. Organising it, making it *happen*, took weeks, months – letters, phone calls, meetings – and I don't have the time. These things are luxuries I can't afford. (Or, rather, in this instance, have only been able to afford thanks to receiving some £30,000 in unlooked-for royalties in the past eight weeks.) Anyway, it went wonderfully well and this morning I'm feeling very mellow. There were hiccups – fairly dire lighting that only came together at the end, occasional glimpses of stagehands, the tabs going out prematurely, the band a bit slow off the mark – but the overall feel was good and the audience *roared*. The Denisons,[†] celebrating their 44th wedding anniversary, were thirty-four years too old to do Bernard Shaw's *Village Wooing*, but it didn't matter. Ned [Sherrin] fluffed his lines, Edward Fox fluffed his lines, Dame Peggy [Ashcroft] fluffed her lines – but it didn't matter. I had qualms about the amateurs, but even they worked. The scene-stealers: Ronnie Barker (who got wonderfully pissed afterwards and wallowed in contented nostalgia), Michael Hordern (who used his pauses to quite dazzling effect – and got fairly pissed as well), The Great Soprendo (sweet Geoff Durham, ably assisted by Shirley Williams), Janet Suzman (I love her: she squeezed so much juice out of a ninety-second D. H. Lawrence poem), Stefan Bednarczyk (young, gifted, and very funny at the piano), and Hinge and Bracket (who *made* the finale: Patrick peaked at exactly the right moment.) It all went according to plan . . . even the 'Dame Flora moment' worked.

Flora Robson was in the first production at the original Oxford Playhouse back in 1923 – *Heartbreak House*. She spoke the very first words: 'God bless us!' I wrote to her asking her to come and speak the words again. I didn't want to over-tax her: she is 81. She wrote back saying she would delighted to come and open

---

[*] Hugh Trevor-Roper (1914–2003), Baron Dacre of Glanton, Regius Professor of Modern History at Oxford University (1957–80), was a director of *The Times* newspaper group and authenticated hoax 'Hitler Diaries' prior to their serialisation.
[†] Michael Denison CBE (1915–98) and his wife, Dulcie Gray CBE (b.1919), actors.

my Christmas Fair! Then she wrote again saying, on second thoughts, she couldn't make it. Finally, she wrote a third time to say 'Oxford is very special' and, 'If you still want me, I will certainly come and open your fête'. She came and sat in the middle of the stalls and, on cue, when introduced by Dame Peggy from the stage, rose and turned to face the audience and gave a wonderfully gracious regal wave. I am not sure that she knew who she was or where she was or why, but we were thrilled to have her.

Wednesday, 4 May 1983

I am in Leeds recording the semi-finals of *Countdown*. Kenneth [Williams] and I are doing alternate shows. I have just left Kenneth in make-up having his nasal hair trimmed. 'With nostrils that flare in the way mine do, nasal hygiene is of the utmost importance. No one likes gazing up a hairy hooter.'

I am needing a lot of make-up today. I had three hours' sleep. M and I were up till 2.30 a.m. at the Rank party following the royal premiere of *Educating Rita* – in aid of NPFA, Prince Philip in attendance. We arrived at the cinema in good time only to find there were no drinks to be had in the 'royal enclosure'. There was also tension in the air because Sandy* had brought his paramour, Susan, who was furious to see herself described on the list as 'Mrs Gilmour' which she isn't because Sandy hasn't got around to his divorce yet . . . 'I've had four years of "promises, promises",' she announced angrily to anyone who would listen . . . The tension worsened when Sandy realised that because she isn't his wife she couldn't be presented to HRH: only *spouses* can be presented. She hovered fuming, while M and the other legitimate wives had their moment of glory with HRH. I have to say he does this sort of thing very well. He arrived smiling, he pumped our hands, he did his stuff. I think he even enjoyed the film. He should have done: lovely script, lovely performances. We sat immediately behind the author, Willy Russell, who smoked nervously throughout.

The party afterwards was at the Royal Garden – de luxe and de-lightful. Julie Walters was easy and likeable (and told me that her £750 dress had been *loaned* to her for the night by the *Daily Mail*), Lewis Gilbert red-eyed and elated (though it was not a major piece of direction I told him it was his finest hour), Maureen Lipman angular and humorous (her performance didn't quite come off), but the funniest/happiest sight of all was Michael Williams and Judi Dench skipping about the dance floor like a couple of demented gnomes. (Joe Loss and his band

---

* Alexander 'Sandy' Gilmour CVO (1931–2009), stockbroker, then chairman of the National Playing Fields Association.

pumped it out with tireless, almost touching enthusiasm. He must be 106,[*] but he worked so hard and so well. We bebopped with the stars and loved it. Poor Sandy and Sue didn't. For some reason their invitation to the party hadn't come through. Sue was not amused.)

Wednesday, 11 May 1983

Mrs Thatcher has called a general election for Thursday 9 June. The Labour Party, to make assurance of defeat doubly sure, have today published their manifesto. It promises unilateral disarmament and immediate withdrawal from the EEC. Michael Foot is a brilliant man, but not a prime minister in waiting.

Am I an MP in waiting? Would I like to have spent my evening at the House of Commons or as I did – dining at Carrier's with Simon [Cadell] and Joanna [Lumley]? We went to see them in *Noël and Gertie* at the King's Head: Simon is spot-on, Jo is lovely, the evening was fun. (Simon revealed to us that he *never* wears underpants. We were all quite shocked.)

Friday, 20 May 1983

John Bratby RA, ARCA, RBA, FIAL, FRSA[†] is a wonderful artist and a crafty old man. I received a letter from him – on spectacular notepaper, designed like a sunflower – and this is what he said:

> *Dear Mr Brandreth*
>
> *Would you come to Hastings for four hours, or less, to let me paint you as we talk, with something to eat from my wife, Patti, on the side. No commercial considerations at all.*
>
> *Let me elaborate.*
>
> *I believe the Individual is an endangered species with the advance of the collectivist state and the rapid materialisation of Orwell's 1984; and for years I've been painting individuals from life . . .*

He then lists a range of his favourite sitters – from the Queen Mother to Paul McCartney – and concludes:

> I'd very much like to meet you and paint you.

---

[*] He was 73: Joshua 'Joe' Loss (1909–90) founded his orchestra in the 1930s and was for many years a favourite with the royal family.

[†] John Bratby (1928–92), artist, founder of the 'kitchen sink' school of painting in the 1950s, so-called after one of his paintings, *The Kitchen Sink*.

It's irresistible, isn't it? I imagine he leafs through *Who's Who* (and the *TV Times*) and sends off exactly the same letter to one and all. Vanity being what it is, we all succumb. We go, we're painted and then we think – why not? – I'll buy the picture after all . . .

Well, today was the day I went to the Bratbys' glorious address – The Cupola and Tower of the Winds, Belmont Toad, Hastings – and had my portrait painted by the great man. He looks exactly like Raymond Briggs's Father Christmas, but a touch more dissolute and dishevelled. Patti, his wife, is wonderfully blowsy, with hair dyed as black as her black leather trouser suit – which she wears, she told me, to 'excite' her husband. They met through the Lonely Hearts column in *Time Out*. We didn't talk much as he painted, and Patti stayed out of the way, down the corridor, in the kitchen. He works at huge speed, piling the paint onto the canvas with a knife. He gives it his all: the intensity is palpable. Every forty minutes or so, he'd sigh and stop and mop his brow and sip his coffee and call out to his wife, 'Patti! Patti! Blue paper! Blue paper!' Patti would then come scurrying down the corridor and into the room, holding a piece of blue notepaper and a pencil. For a second she'd study the work in progress and then write something on the paper and give it to him, retreating at once without saying a word. This happened four or five times. Towards the end of the session, when John went out to the loo, I got up from my chair and went over to look at the blue papers which were now scattered on the floor around the canvas. The messages were all in the same vein: 'I love you!', 'This is your best work', 'Wonderful!', 'Keep going. I love you!'

I didn't buy my painting. It didn't interest me. Instead, for £200, I bought John's portrait of Cyril Fletcher: he has caught him completely, even if the paint he has used is entirely yellow and green! I also liked his full-length portrait of Kenneth [Williams]. And I love his sunflower pictures. And his Venetian paintings – not the ones of Patti showing us her all (and some), the ones of the Grand Canal.

Monday, 6 June 1983

Last night we went to see Liza Minnelli strut her stuff. She was good – very good – but she wasn't her mother and that's really what all the screaming queens around us wanted her to be. We went with Simon and his new girl (Beckie Croft, daughter of the producer of *Hi-de-Hi*) and Christopher Cazenove. He was rather touching about the end of his marriage: 'I didn't want to give up on it, I really didn't.'[*]

---

[*] Christopher Cazenove (b.1943), actor; he married actress Angharad Rees in 1973: they separated in 1983, but were reconciled and remained married until 1994.

Everywhere I turn marriage is in free fall. Andrew Lloyd Webber has found himself a younger model. So has Trevor Nunn. (That is madness: Janet Suzman is divine.) I have just been doing *Tell the Truth* with Graeme Garden, recently remarried after a mid-life crisis, money worries and the demise of *The Goodies*, and a journalist, whose husband appears to be having *his* mid-life crisis, manifesting itself in a penchant for 20-year-olds, and little Jack Tinker, who has been married (with children) but is manifestly gay. Hang on in there, Gyles. At least till Wednesday.

Wednesday, 8 June 1983

Our 10th wedding anniversary began with me giving M breakfast in bed before shooting off to Broadcasting House for *Midweek* where I met David Frost who is celebrating ten weeks of matrimony. (Lynne Frederick didn't last long. His new wife is Lady Carina Fitzalan-Howard, daughter of the Duke of Norfolk. David will enjoy the monogrammed slippers.) He greeted me as he always does: 'Gyles, a *joy* – an absolute *joy*.' He is nice to everyone he meets and he has the gift of being able to make disappointment and failure disappear simply by ignoring them. On the programme, David talked about money, I talked about sex and Stefan [Bednarczyk] sang a so-so song about the election. (No one is really interested in the election. We know she's going to win!)[*]

I took M for lunch at the Caprice where I spent the first half-hour of the meal on the telephone trying to alert Gabrielle (the new au pair) to the fact that there was a saucepan of mince cooking in the kitchen while she was getting sunstroke in the garden! Eventually, I got hold of Francis Loney's studio across the street from us and his receptionist very sweetly went over and hollered to Gabby over the garden wall.

This evening we took all three children (plus tanned au pair) to Fu Tong in Kensington High Street and had a family celebration of ten amazing years. I often think of Sloan Wilson's line: 'A happy marriage is an unearned miracle.'

Monday, 13 June 1983

I am writing this on the little island of Torcello at the northern end of the Venetian lagoon. I am having coffee. I have just had a perfect lunch – salad and pasta and

---

[*] She did, handsomely. Mrs Thatcher became the first Prime Minister in more than thirty years to be re-elected after a full term in office. The Conservatives secured an overall majority in the House of Commons of 144, the biggest since Labour's landslide victory of 1945.

lobster and a local white wine – with a perfect wife in a perfect setting. (With Sydney Poitier sitting at the next table. And, at the table beyond, a pregnant Joanna Hordern: I have not seen her since I was Malvolio to her Olivia exactly twenty years ago.) This is the happiest holiday I have known. The flight, the water-taxi to the Accademia (Simon was right: damn the expense – when you arrive in Venice you *must* arrive by water), the hotel itself . . . it's all been perfect.*

Monday, 20 June 1983

We went to the Renaissance Bal Masqué at Sutton Place, in aid of Action Research. We went appropriately dressed in Renaissance garb and felt horribly conspicuous as we drove along the motorway. We felt even more wretched as we turned in to the drive and realised, looking into the others cars, that we were the only people who had come in costume! M hated her frock – hired from the Oxford Playhouse and looking as if it had been made from a pair of old hotel curtains – and I cut a truly pathetic figure in my ludicrous doublet and hose. We'd been briefed that our host, one Roger Chubb, curator of Sutton Place, would be coming as Henry VIII. He was dressed in a drab DJ. We found drinks and stood alone, feeling ridiculous and miserable. And then the guests of honour arrived: Prince and Princess Michael of Kent stepped out of their limousine cos-tumed in immaculate sixteenth-century attire! Roger Chubb came scuttling over to ask me to give up my outfit for him to wear. I declined politely. The moment Prince Michael saw me, he said: 'Thank God someone else is wearing the gear.'

From then on, all was well. I was MC, did my stuff and it worked out fine – even though I brought the entire gathering to their collective feet because I thought Princess Michael was leading the top table out of the dining hall when in fact she was simply setting off for the loo. On the stairs, going to the loo myself, I encountered a woman in a truly beautiful ball gown. It was so beautiful, I stopped her and said, 'I've never seen a lovelier dress. Never. Who designed it?' 'I did,' she said. 'Aren't you clever,' I cooed. When she had trotted away, M told me who she was: Elizabeth Emanuel.†

Sunday, 3 July 1983

Lunch at Les Quat' Saisons – perfect. Evening performance of *Henry VIII* – strong production, forget the notices. (Who do these critics think they are?)

---

* The reader will be spared GB's 10,000-word account of the delights of Venice.
† Elizabeth Weiner (b.1953) with her husband David Emanuel (b.1952) created the wedding dress for Diana, Princess of Wales.

Night at the Stratford Hilton – excellent wide bed, firm and really comfortable, good breakfast. Coffee just now at the Arden, meet up with Sheila Hancock and her husband, John Thaw – he is a powerful Wolsey: Wolsey as a man of power – and Richard Griffiths (much maligned as Henry VIII). He's a real sweetie. M says the fat are so jovial because their nerve ends are less exposed.

Wednesday, 13 July 1983

I'm sitting at the National Theatre, on the South Bank, having a cup of tea in a heat-wave waiting to go to London Weekend Television at 4.00 p.m. to record a couple of *Babbles* – more nonsense for Channel 4. The day began with my debut at TV-am. An astrologer, a graphologist and a metal-feeler all gave character analyses of me and seemed to be spot-on – at least spot-on if I see myself as a jolly extrovert who has known suffering, can be secretive and is ambitious and good fun. Actually, we had fun on the show. Nick Owen is especially good: relaxed, easy and witty. I'm ready to do more.

Lunch with Elizabeth Roy [children's publisher at Hodder & Stoughton]: I'm going to do more with her, too. I like writing children's books: I like the market: I like the revenue. She told me Alan Gordon Walker is dying of Hodgkin's disease, but carrying on as MD. It's grim out there. M's friend is in the Middlesex with a brain tumour – or is she simply stressed? And does Stefan have a heart condition? Is his pins and needles really MS or simply paranoia?*

Louis Blom-Cooper† was on TV-am because tonight is the vote on the reintroduction of the death penalty. It won't happen. It mustn't.

Later

It didn't. The hangers lost decisively. And the *Babbles* weren't bad. The cast included Sheila Hancock (chirpy with a touch of chippy), Melvyn Bragg (*still* looking divine), Angela Douglas (actress widow of Kenneth More), Peter Purves (relic of the golden age of *Blue Peter*), Bernard Falk (who smoked and drank with demonic determination) and Claire Rayner (still me-me-me, but she's big-hearted too). On the way to make-up, I met Bruce Forsyth in the lift, with his new wife – Wilnelia, Puerto Rican, age 24, formerly Miss World and we can see why. 'You're looking very cheery,' said Bruce. 'Well, why not?' I replied. 'I'm here for the evening, making two shows and earning £400. What's not to smile

---

* Twenty-six years on, happily, all three are still living.
† Sir Louis Blom-Cooper QC (b.1926), lawyer and campaigner, had been chairman of the BBC Radio London Advisory Council when GB was a member.

about?' Bruce grinned: 'I'm here for the evening,' he said, 'making two shows and earning £8,000. Nice to see you.' Didn't he do well?

Thursday, 21 July 1983

The trouble with this journal nowadays is time – finding it. I'm just listing the people I've bumped into because I don't seen to be able to find the tranquil hours I need to record more than headings and headlines. (Speaking of which: peerages for Harold Wilson and Jo Grimond were announced today.) I suppose it's par-enthood: the pram in the hallway etc. Even now, as I write this, I know I shouldn't be here: I should be out in the garden reading the girls a story. (They sound very jolly through the window, but do I give them enough time? I hope so. I want to.)

Yesterday was Aphra's Sports Day – a gently chaotic event, at which I won the fathers' race and Aphra won one of hers and came second in another. We sat on the grass and picnicked with Piers Paul Read* and family. PPR is *un homme très serieux*, who takes himself *au serieux* also – though judging from the first half of *A Married Man* which we watched on the box on Sunday night his way with words and *aperçus* are locked between the mundane and the banal. (I'm probably missing something.) Have I reported that, on his last day at Norland Place, Benet won the form English prize? And on Tuesday he scored twenty-six runs at Lord's. (He is doing a two-day cricket summer school. It's been a triumph.)

We went to *As You Like It* in Regent's Park. David William gave a definitive Jacques. And this morning I met up with Greg Dyke at TV-am. He has asked me to host Saturday mornings. Will I? Won't I? Probably not. We are booked to spend August in Corfu. M puts up with quite a lot as it is.†

Thursday, 6 October 1983

This is extraordinary. Last night I was speaking at a dinner at Grosvenor House. It was a big affair, a thousand there and alongside me on the top table was the keynote speaker, Cecil Parkinson MP, Secretary of State for Trade and Industry. He was the best of company, easy and engaging, though he did disappear a couple of times during dinner to make calls and he asked me to excuse him if he had to shoot off the moment I'd spoken. Anyway, he spoke – and spoke well: he's

* Piers Paul Read (b.1941), Catholic writer; his novel, *A Married Man*, was published in 1979.
† GB went with his family to Corfu and Chris Tarrant OBE (b.1946) hosted Saturday mornings at TV-am. In September GB became a TV-am regular, presenting a video report and the viewers' letters, from 1983 to 1990.

on top of his brief – and then I spoke and then off he went, apologising again for slipping away before the party ended. He had a late-night meeting he had to go to. I came home to M, singing his praises. And now, this morning, I am gobsmacked.

Overnight, the same Cecil Parkinson has confessed to having an affair with his secretary. Sara Keays is expecting his baby in January. He had once promised to marry her, but he has now changed his mind. It seems that the calls he was making during dinner last night were to Mrs Thatcher at No. 10. He issued a statement at 11.45 p.m. – an hour after he left Grosvenor House – acknowledging the affair and saying, while he will make financial provision for Miss Keays and the baby, he is going to stay with his wife. He is the coolest customer I have ever encountered. I defy anyone who was at Grosvenor House last night to have had an inkling of the troubles that were overwhelming the man. Amazing.

Saturday, 15 October 1983

We recorded two episodes of *Funny Peculiar** last night and, in the green room, inevitably, talked of Cecil Parkinson. (No one is talking of anything else.) Freddie Trueman[†] said, 'It's the word "abortion" the pooblic don't like. The fact that he wanted the lass to have an abortion. That's what's done for him. Pooblic won't stand for it.' Stirling Moss[‡] was more sympathetic. 'He won the election for Mrs Thatcher, but this is all anyone will remember. The public can only see you in one way. "Who do you think you are? Stirling Moss?" I get it every day of my life – every day. Nothing else.' Richard Briers chipped in: 'Yes, and I'm doomed to be the fellow from *The Good Life* until the day I die.' Alan Jay Lerner[§] had the last word: 'Well, I'd have married her.' 'Oh, yes,' giggled Liz Robertson, Alan's *eighth* wife, 'My husband only sleeps with women if he's ready to marry them.'

More talk of Cecil tonight. Ned Sherrin, Noel Davis, Christopher Biggins, Stephanie Turner came to supper. Ned said: 'Stick to buggery, that's my advice.' We all laughed, but Ned appeared in earnest. 'Women like a bit of buggery and you don't run the risk of an unwanted baby.' Stephanie said, 'I'm sorry for the poor baby. And Mrs Parkinson.' Biggins said, 'I'm sorry for Mrs T.' M said: 'Men, they're all the same!' (That's what she always says.)

---

* A BBC Radio 4 panel game that GB devised and hosted.
† Fred Trueman OBE (1931–2006), Yorkshireman and cricketer.
‡ Sir Stirling Moss OBE (b.1929), racing driver.
§ Alan Jay Lerner (1918–86), American lyricist whose many hit musicals included *My Fair Lady* and *Gigi*. Liz Robertson (b.1954), actress, appeared in *My Fair Lady* in the West End and became his eighth and final wife.

Noel had a new joke: 'What's the question all gay Christians are asking? Was Jesus divine – or merely gorgeous?'

Monday, 17 October 1983

Cecil Parkinson has resigned from the Cabinet. The papers are full of pictures of him and Mrs P. and two of their daughters (plus Oliver the dog) outside the family home, showing solidarity, smiling bravely. Mrs Thatcher, it seems, has known all about it for months. She urged Cecil to abandon Sara and stick with his wife. She would have liked him to stay in the Cabinet (he'd have been Foreign Secretary if it hadn't been for this) but Miss Keays and her father have fanned the flames of adverse publicity and it's just gotten too hot ('Parkinson's a cad – he promised to marry my daughter and he's gone back on his word. And he was ready to have my grandchild aborted. Is that the sort of fella we want in the Government? I think not.') Anyway, it's over. Parkinson has gone, replaced by Norman Tebbit, described in *The Times* this morning as 'the most outspoken and most agile Conservative hawk'. He certainly looks like a nasty piece of work.

Sunday, 30 October 1983

This week: *Woman's Hour, Countdown*, TV-am, *Funny Peculiar*. And my 'celebrity encounters': Jonathan King (he's an odd one), Irma Kurtz (oh no!), Charlotte Bingham and Terence Brady (nice), June Whitfield (lovely), Brian Johnston (as good as you get), Tony Blackburn (better than they say), David Hamilton (ditto), Valerie Singleton, Magnus Pyke, Roy Kinnear, Nerys Hughes, Lord Oaksey, Fiona Richmond, Robert Dougall, Martin Jarvis, Nigel Havers, Ned Sherrin, Richard Whiteley . . . these are the middle-England middle-brow 'personalities' of our time (and several of them are my good friends – not Fiona, though I have seen more of her than of most),[*] but it's life at the shallow end of the pool, I know that. I'm happy with it most of the time, but then I come up against a piece of work like *An Englishman Abroad* and think 'Why aren't I doing *that*?'[†]

And, tonight, why wasn't I presenting Jean-Louis Barrault[‡] at the Barbican?

---

[*] Fiona Richmond (b. Julia Harrison, 1945), a clergyman's daughter who became famous as a nude model, actress and purveyor of soft pornography. She was the long-term girlfriend of Paul Raymond.

[†] That week GB attended the BAFTA screening of *An Englishman Abroad*, written by Alan Bennett, directed by John Schlesinger, cast by Noel Davis and starring Alan Bates and Coral Browne.

[‡] Jean-Louis Barrault (1910–94), France's leading actor-director, who first became internationally known through Marcel Carné's 1945 film, *Les Enfants du Paradis*.

France's greatest actor – France's Olivier – came to the London home of the Royal Shakespeare Company and was put through an evening of humiliation. It was truly horrible. He had been booked (by our friend Patricia MacNaughton) to present an evening entitled *Le Langage du Corps*. We had booked not knowing quite what to expect, but excited at the prospect of simply seeing the great man. In the event, *Le Langage du Corps* turned out to be a lecture in French on the history of mime – and the audience didn't like it. They were wanting a *show*. They felt they'd paid for a show. They were going to have a show! As the hapless Barrault stood at his lectern chuntering on in French about the importance of the actor's body, the bulk of his audience was getting restless. At first they fidgeted, then they coughed, then they began to leave, some of them barracking as they went. 'Boring!' shouted one man. 'We can't understand you!' Eventually, poor Barrault, getting the message, left the stage, mumbling, *'Je suis désolé, messieurs-dames, désolé.'* The audience was now divided: half were angry (those that spoke no French), the other half (us) appalled that this great Frenchman was being treated in such a way. We sat, confused, not knowing what was going to happen next. Trevor Nunn was there, sitting on his hands. He is the director of the RSC. He should have been on stage apologising for the fiasco. Patricia MacNaughton was there, slumped in her seat. She speaks French. She could have been on stage, translating. In the event, someone emerged from the wings to tell us that Monsieur Barrault was greatly distressed by the mis-understanding. He had come to deliver a lecture in French. Clearly the audience was expecting something different. There would now be a short intermission. Those who wished to leave could do so. Monsieur Barrault would then resume his lecture for those that wished to hear him. We stayed and were rewarded. Poor Barrault, having lost confidence in his written lecture, returned to the stage and, apologising further in halting English, said he would now do his best to entertain us with a piece of mime. And then the 73-year-old literally *threw himself* into a fran-tic recreation of the celebrated sequence from *Les Enfants du Paradis* (made when he was 24!) where the mime impersonates a horse. He snorted, he whinnied, he ran in circles around the stage, he pawed the ground, he threw his head in the air – it was wonderful to watch in its way, but agony, also. He should never have been put in such a position. Those responsible should be deeply ashamed.

Tuesday, 1 November 1983

TV-am. Breakfast with Peter Bull.* He is very engaging. He believes (really believes) in astrology, teddy bears and not working in months that don't contain

---

* Peter Bull (1912–84), character actor, author, arctophile.

the letter R. That's when he abandons the King's Road and makes for Lesbos. ('I don't look like a natural Lesbian, do I? But I have residency, you know.') After the show, Tim Aitken addressed a staff meeting. Unlike Jonathan, he is short and ugly. No one likes him, but everyone accepts that the Aitkens have brought in new money* and more focused management. With them, and the Greg Dyke touch, we may survive. Audience figures have moved from 100,000 to near one million. Our rodent superstar, Roland Rat, is helping hugely. The rat is genuinely funny (works for adults as well as kids) and David Claridge (his creator, operator, voice and Svengali) and I have become good friends. He is coming to supper (David, not the rat).

Tuesday, 8 November 1983

TV-am. Coffee with Andrew Lloyd Webber – he is a funny-looking creature. He says we should write a musical together – 'something funny'. We'll see. I haven't yet finished the one I'm writing with Julian Slade. On to a 'sitting' with Andrew Festing.† I find these sessions up in his garret off Holland Park Road very soothing. We talked about fairy painters in general – and Richard Dadd in particular. (The story of Dadd, madman, murderer, incarcerated in Bedlam and Broadmoor . . . is there a musical in that? Not many laughs, but lots of fairies. That's a start.) According to Festing, most of Dadd's pictures were painted during his incarceration and many disappeared, pilfered by the asylum attendants. Apparently, they turn up now and again. I shall keep an eye out.‡

Thursday, 8 December 1983

Too much happening, can't quite keep track. The past twenty-four hours: yesterday – lunch at the RAC with Greg Smith (producer of the *Confessions of* . . . films,

---

* Tim Aitken (b. 1944), grandson of the celebrated newspaper magnate, Lord Beaverbrook (1879–1964), and Jonathan Aitken (b.1942) were cousins. It later transpired that the Aitkens' £3 million controlling stake in TV-am came from Arab sources. Jonathan Aitken disguised this at the time as it could have invited a block on the purchase by the Independent Broadcasting Authority. When the truth came out, Anna Ford threw a glass of wine over Aitken who apologised for his 'lack of candour' and resigned from the TV-am board.

† Andrew Festing was painting a portrait of the Brandreth family to mark GB and Michèle's 10th wedding anniversary.

‡ In fact, a watercolour by Richard Dadd (1817–86) turned up on the TV programme *Antiques Roadshow* in 1987 and later fetched £100,000 at auction. Dadd's most celebrated work, *The Fairy Feller's Master-Stroke*, inspired a song by the rock band Queen and Angela Carter wrote a play based on his life, *Come unto these Yellow Sands*.

looks like a cross between Danny Kaye and Jon Pertwee) and Laurie Mansfield (agent to the stars – well, Charlie Drake and Mike Yarwood and me): they want to recreate *Billy Bunter* on TV. Will I write the script? Yes! (Yes, but I already have the situation comedy series I'm supposed to be writing with Denise Coffey, *and* the one with Ned Sherrin *and* the one with Geoff Atkinson *and* the one with Hinge & Bracket!) 4.00 p.m.: the Boilerhouse Project at the V & A. Interesting. 7.30 p.m.: Ray Cooney's farce, *Run for Your Wife*. Irresistibly funny. You cannot not laugh – and, as Ray says, you have to play what's written: do as you're told, nothing besides: add anything extra (mugging to the crowds) and it doesn't work. Supper afterwards with Ray and Linda at Winston's. Good people. Turned out to be their twenty-first wedding anniversary. Sleep. Wake. Breakfast with children. (Remember their names – just.) Desk – stuff for Kellogg's, Collins, Mirror Books, on it goes. Meeting with Kevin Roast to discuss *Vintage Quiz*.* We agree that we like Patrick McNee (a touch of class), and we love Derek Nimmo (he brings his own footman to the studio – truly: a fellow in knee britches comes to the green room after the show and serves Derek proper wine in a proper silver goblet while the rest of us are quaffing warm white from paper cups) and we have to go on with Lord Montagu of Beaulieu, even though he has a very limp wrist and no charisma on the screen, because the show was his idea and he does provide the vintage vehicles. On to London Weekend where my afternoon encounters include Ken Dodd, Roy Kinnear and James Stewart.† Mr Stewart is immensely tall and effortlessly charming. Because he is a major film star, he is like royalty: nobody is quite normal with him. He stands physically apart from the rest of us. We talk to him as though he is talking to us from the silver screen. He has that quality that Barbara Cartland says is the prerequisite of all charmers: impeccable manners. And then I had a cup of tea with Lulu.‡ I love her. We held hands and she seemed happy with that. (Some have fantasies about having an affair with Princess Diana. I'd rather have Lulu.) And where am I now? Well, it's midnight and I am just in from a long evening at the Café Royal. This is where Oscar

---

* A nostalgia quiz with questions devised by GB, with the actors Derek Nimmo and Patrick McNee (b.1922), as team captains and Lord Montagu of Beaulieu, founder of the National Motor Museum, as the adjudicator. Lord Montagu was imprisoned for homosexual offences in 1954.

† James Stewart (1908–97), American actor and film star, whose screen credits included *Mr Smith Goes to Washington*, *The Philadelphia Story*, *It's a Wonderful Life* and *Rear Window*.

‡ Lulu (b. Marie Lawrie, 1948), Scottish pop singer and actress who first came to fame in 1964 with 'Shout!'

Wilde entertained Lord Alfred Douglas. After dinner, I did my best to entertain a rowdy crowd of beery businessmen. It was not easy. After I had spoken I had to stay for the main event: a charity boxing bout. I imagine Oscar would have enjoyed that. Goodnight.

Tuesday, 20 December 1983

A day with Prince Philip. At 10.30 a.m. HRH chaired the Special General Meeting of NPFA. We are changing the rules and some of the old guard don't like it. If Sandy [Gilmour], our chairman, had chaired the meeting it would have been a disaster. Sandy, sweet as he is, says all the wrong things and rubs everyone up the wrong way. He also gets into the most hopeless muddle. HRH, by contrast, is cool, calm, collected, crisp but not brusque, and *good-humoured* from start to finish. Of course, it helps that he is who he is – but this bunch would have cut up rough with Queen Victoria. HRH deflected all hostility with easy charm, let the opponents have their say and called for each vote at the exact moment when he knew he'd win it. It was a master-class in how to handle a difficult meeting. He said beforehand, 'What *precisely* are our objectives?' We told him. He said afterwards, 'Mission accomplished?' and smiled. He was pleased with his morning's work.

He was back on parade this evening for our Royal Pantomime Performance: *Aladdin* at the Shaftesbury. I lined up the family – all the children, plus Hester. He does the small-talk and the hand-shaking incredibly well – and with a will, which is extraordinary given that he's been doing it, week in, week out, since 1947. He seemed genuinely to enjoy the show (especially Tommy Trinder) but, rather disconcertingly, kept chatting and commenting on it throughout. During the interval, we stood alone in a little corridor behind the royal box and had a gin and tonic. His equerry stood *cave* outside the Gents. Standing next to HRH at the urinals was disconcerting. Inhibiting. (Absurd, I know, but there it is.)

At the end of the performance, I took him backstage to meet the cast – another line-up, another row of hands to shake, another bout of banter followed by slightly forced laughter. But it could not have gone better and HRH could not have delivered more.

Towards the end of the performance, at the back of the circle, M noticed a tall, dark-haired woman slip into the auditorium and stand with her back against the wall. She was in an evening dress, late thirties, very English, very chic. M said, 'I imagine she's having a late supper with HRH, don't you think?' I wonder. (And, if so, why not?)

Monday, 6 February 1984

I am in Switzerland, at the Grand Hotel Victoria-Jungfrau, Interlaken, having breakfast in my room. It is a beautiful day. The night was pretty horrendous. The delegates to the pharmaceuticals conference are a lively crowd. On arrival one of them threw himself, headlong and fully clothed, into the swimming pool. The pool was empty. He survived, but only just. And last night, at the dinner, I survived, but only just. I was seated next to the managing director's wife. She was unhappy and tipsy, a lethal combination. She told me all her secrets and they were grim. After dinner, the chairman got to his feet and introduced me. I got to mine to begin my talk. But, as I began to get up, my drunken companion gripped my arm and said, 'What are you doing? Where are you going?' 'I am going to give my speech now,' I whispered. 'No,' she said, 'you're talking to me.' As I attempted to stand and address the room, the poor lady clung on to my arm, pulling me back towards her. 'Talk to me,' she pleaded, 'don't go.' I did my best to pacify her and turned to address the room. But she wouldn't stop. She didn't stop – until one of the directors (not her husband) came over and escorted her out of the room. Difficult to get many laughs under the circumstances. And the acoustic was terrible.

Wednesday, 15 February 1984

We had the press launch for *Ultraquiz*** on board *The Princess on the Thames*. (Whose idea was that? We were stuck on the wretched boat from Charing Cross to Greenwich and back. No escape.) It was an all-star line-up: David Frost, Barney Colehan, yours truly and the correspondent from *Titbits*. It's all right for David: he is going to get £5,000 a programme and first-class travel. 'Give him the money, Barney!' 'A *joy*, Gyles, an absolute *joy*.'

Thursday, 16 February 1984

Lunch at the RAC with Greg Smith and Laurie Mansfield. We fine-tuned our pitch for the *Billy Bunter* presentation. Laurie to set out the background – the place of Bunter in our cultural heritage, his appeal to different generations, how he can work for today's kids *and* their grandparents. Greg to explain the integrity of our enterprise – this is not sitcom: this is a classic serial with comedy: this is the

---

* A summertime ITV quiz show, hosted by David Frost, with games devised by GB and Barney Colehan (1914–91), veteran producer responsible for *Have a Go!* with Wilfred Pickles on the wireless (the origin of the catchphrase, 'Give 'em the money, Barney!') and *The Good Old Days* and *It's a Knockout* on television.

Sunday tea-time slot: in principle, John Gielgud has agreed to play the headmaster. Finally, I act out 'edited highlights' of the pilot episode I've scripted.

All good. All excellent. We're excited. We're confident. And then we get to the meeting and walk into the room and there she is – the lady to whom we are pitching: Anna Home,* ITV children's commissioner, the fattest woman you have ever seen. She *is* Bessie Bunter. The joke's on us: she can't see anything in our idea that's remotely interesting or amusing.

Tuesday, 28 February 1984

I have just had a cup of tea with Ted Heath. The way he cannot contain his vitriol against Mrs Thatcher is actually comical. He *loathes* her and assumes others must loathe her, too. I tried to steer him onto other territory – e.g. Broadstairs – but he kept coming back to 'that woman'. She is 'ruining the country'. I didn't like to tell him, but most people I meet think she's *making* it.

Last night, we went to see Simon in the stage version of *Hi-de-Hi* at the Victoria Palace. Quite fun, I thought. M thought it was *dire*. Jolly supper afterwards at his flat with Chris Cazenove. He cooked. He's far too nice (and handsome) to be living alone. I was saying how nice David Frost is. Chris said, 'Yes, well, um . . . you know his live-in girlfriend only heard about David's engagement when she read about it in the papers.' Cue Michèle: 'Men – they're all the same.'

I am at TV-am, about to go upstairs to try and get my money. Not being paid: that's the one disadvantage of working here!

Thursday, 15 March 1984

Yesterday, we marked M's birthday by buying a Romney at Sotheby's (the process of bidding is exquisite agony), going to *Pack of Lies* at the Lyric and having supper at the Caprice. Today, I worked on *Great Sexual Disasters* all day and then drove to Birmingham for the *Birmingham Post* Literary Dinner. I arrived just in time for the main course. I am glad I didn't miss it: Patrick Moore, playing the mad scientist, the Earl of Bradford† playing the lord who is one of us (and is), and Germaine Greer. I was pleased to see her: she makes me laugh a lot. Not so the good burghers of Birmingham who looked wanly into their

---

* Anna Home OBE (b.1938), award-winning television producer and head of BBC Children's Programmes, working for ITV in 1984, but mainly associated with BBC programmes from *Jackanory* to *The Teletubbies*.
† Richard Bridgeman, 7th Earl of Bradford (b.1947).

coffee cups as Germaine told them about the merits of masturbation and the futility of 'squirting the jam into the doughnut'. I followed GG and, given her performance, it wasn't very difficult . . . We sat next to one another at the signing session and while my book (*The Complete Public Speaker*) sold out, Germaine sold three of hers. But seeing her made me feel warm and amused by life in all the best ways.

Wednesday, 28 March 1984

They were all there: The Queen Mother, Princess Olga of Yugoslavia, Princess Asfa-Wossen Asserate of Ethiopia, Countess Mountbatten of Burma, John Gielgud, John Mills, Yehudi Menuhin, Joan Collins and me. Westminster Abbey was packed for the unveiling of the memorial stone to Noël Coward. The inscription: his name, his dates and 'A talent to amuse'. I was glad to be there – everyone was there – but the truth is, though it had everything – John G. fluting, Dickie Attenborough weeping, the Ambrosia Singers giving us songs from the shows – it didn't quite come off. The Abbey echoed: it felt a bit soulless. We didn't sense the Master was there.

That said, it was an event: Danny La Rue, Peter O'Toole and Tommy Steele side by side in front of me. And now, back to reality: *Crack It!*,* *Dear Ladies* and a speech at the Crest Hotel, Coventry. (Did Coward do much of this?)

Wednesday, 11 April 1984

Breakfast with Duncan Goodhew,† lunch with Jeffrey Archer. I took Jeffrey a copy of my Gielgud book.‡ He took me to the Caprice: he is always generous, always gregarious, always good value – but his boasting and exaggerating are completely out of control. Whatever the deal on his latest book, he adds an extra million. He can't help himself. His PA (and girlfriend) Andrina picked us up after lunch and kindly dropped me off at Bush House. She has the boyish-girl look: she's very playful. I quite fancy her myself. (How does Jeffrey get away with it? What does Mary think?)

---

* A monthly puzzle magazine created by GB for Robert Maxwell's Mirror Group, the first in a series of puzzle magazines created by GB and his company.
† Duncan Goodhew MBE (b.1957), swimmer, Olympic gold medallist in 1980, one of a number of sporting personalities who helped GB with his work at the National Playing Fields Association.
‡ *John Gielgud: A Celebration*, the first of two books GB wrote about the actor; this one was published to mark his 80th birthday.

'Roland Rat is Helping Hugely'

The party at the Old Vic for Sir John Gielgud's 80th birthday (my idea) followed by lunch at the National Theatre (Michèle's idea). It all went wonderfully well, thanks entirely to Sir John who gave unstintingly of himself from the moment he arrived (driven up from the country by the local taxi firm) to the moment he left, loaded down with cards, telegrams, presents, three red roses from Glenda Jackson, an orchid from Edward Fox. I knew the day couldn't fail as a 'media event' – I was putting him on the stage of the Old Vic where he first appeared in 1921 and doing this the day *before* his birthday to catch tomorrow's papers: we've made all the TV channels tonight – but I wanted it to succeed as a party for Sir John as well. I think it did. The cake ceremony worked a treat. Stefan arrived in the nick of time to play the piano and, on cue, Christopher Reeve[*] brought on the cake with the eighty candles. 'Oh, Gyles,' cooed Sir John, '*Superman!* You really have thought of everything.' He gave an enchanting impromptu speech – fluent, witty, elegant, generous – and the cream of the acting profession stood in the stalls gazing up at him, tears in their eyes. Christopher Reeve had been nervous about carrying on the cake – didn't want to seem to be the pushy American movie star. He told me that he had met Sir John before – in a corridor at Pinewood. Sir John had asked him was he was doing there. Christopher was dressed in his full Superman costume at the time.

Everyone had a Gielgud story to tell. Sir John still does *The Times* crossword every day. A fellow actor peered over his shoulder, amazed at the speed with which he had just finished it. 'Sir John,' he enquired, looking intently at the completed crossword grid. 'Fourteen across – what on earth is "DIDDYBUMS"?' 'I don't know,' replied Sir John airily, 'but it does fit frightfully well.' He rattled off story after story himself. My favourite – Sir Frank Benson at the opening of the Open Air Theatre in Regent's Park: 'Ladies and gentlemen, you'll be pleased to know that all the sods in this theatre come from Stratford-upon-Avon.'

At the lunch at the National we had M and Noel, John Stride, Ros and Martin Jarvis, Edward Fox (who flirted, for no good reason and quite eccentrically, with Mrs Robert Hardy), Trevor Howard (looking very old and lived-in: I imagine not long for this world),[†] the clearly long-suffering but very sweet Helen Cherry, Constance Cummings (who is lovely), Michael Denison, Lindsay Anderson and

---

[*] Christopher Reeve (1952–2002), American actor, best known for playing Superman in four films, 1978–87.

[†] Trevor Howard (b. Trevor Howard-Smith, 1913), film actor, died at the beginning of January 1988; he had been married to the actress Helen Cherry (1915–2001) since 1944.

Emlyn Williams. (I don't wish to sound like Jeffrey, but Emlyn really should have a knighthood – even if his real love in life now is scatological talk about the size of Napoleon's penis.)

Noel's Gielgud story. Assorted actors are saying where they would most like to be in the world at that very minute – some choose Hollywood, others go for Havana, Hawaii and the south of France. 'And, you, Sir John, where would you most like to be at this very minute?' 'At this very minute? At this *very* minute? Under a big black man, going "Woosh! Woosh!"'

Tuesday, 1 May 1984

Breakfast with Peter Ustinov. Lunch with the Duke of Westminster. Supper with Simon [Cadell] in Birmingham – where I am now, staying at the Plough and Harrow. I came up to see Simon's Hamlet at the Birmingham Rep – it's wonderful. Not a cry of 'Hi-de-Hamlet!' from the stalls – complete concentration from a full house and a great ovation at the end, richly deserved. My friend can do it.

Thursday, 3 May 1984

Went to one of Jeffrey's regular all-male lunches in the penthouse-with-Picassos overlooking the Thames. (It's a fabulous flat on the south side of the river, with a wonderful view of the Palace of Westminster.) The cast included Denis Healey, Norman Lamont, Derek Jameson, Lou Kirby, Alec McCowen, with Arthur Hailey (blockbuster novelist) as guest of honour. It was very jolly (and generous) but wholly unreal: rather like parties at Robert Maxwell or Fanny Cradock. Whenever the host is out of the room, the guests talk about him – not as a proper friend, but as a kind of oddball curiosity.

Thursday, 17 May 1984

Kenneth [Williams] came to supper last night and was at his most mellow. He told us he had befriended a couple of Swedish boys and paid for them to stay in a hotel and then given them money to get to Paris. 'Nothing happened,' he insisted. (I believe him. He's not Ned [Sherrin]. Ned told me he goes out on the town 'looking for a bit of rough' – and he eschews 'protection': 'You don't go to a party in a raincoat.' 'What about AIDS?' I asked him. 'If I get it, I get it.' 'And then,' said Michèle, to me later, not to Ned, 'he spreads it to others, selfish bugger.') Kenneth told a funny story of the night he spent in some minor stately home where his host introduced himself to Kenneth's bedroom and was proposing to climb into bed with Kenneth until Kenneth protested, 'Oh, no, you can't. I'm a Methodist.'

I am just in from the NPFA SGM & AGM. The newly created Council was elected and I came top of the poll. Prince Philip presided, without much relish. He likes it when there's a problem to solve: once it's all sorted it's just routine. Afterwards, over tea, HRH introduced me to a distinguished, Indian-looking gentleman wearing a bright summer suit and an overblown rose in his button-hole. 'This is the President of Pakistan,' he said and wandered away. I struggled to find small-talk. None too soon, HRH came back. 'How are you two getting on?' he asked. I was still struggling. HRH listened for a moment to whatever I was saying and then interrupted: 'He's the President of the Pakistan Playing Fields Association, you idiot. He is not General Zia. Does he look like General Zia? Good God, man, do you know anything?'

Saturday, 9 June 1984

The miners are revolting. Their leader has been arrested. Their strike is doomed. It's grim at the pithead.[*] Here in the south of France on the other hand . . .

We are so lucky – and we know it. We are just in from dinner at the Voile d'Or. Simon and I had the *menu gourmande* – seven courses, four wines, brandy and liqueurs to follow. The weather has not picked up: M and I huddled in our overcoats on the Paloma beach as Simon braved the waves. Today, Cap Ferrat. Tomorrow, Cap d'Antibes. We are pretending to be Rex Harrison and David Niven.

Tuesday, 17 July 1984

Supergirl at breakfast, Russell Harty at lunch, Lew Grade at cocktails. I liked Helen Slater:[†] she is very pretty and very normal. (I am intrigued by how small so many film stars turn out to be and how their faces, up close, appear relatively uninteresting. John Schlesinger says they are nothing without the camera: only a screen test can tell you what you need to know.) I like Russell Harty – but the risks he takes for love! (He belongs to the Ned school of having it all and hoping for the best. But the AIDS virus is deadly. It is now taking people we know.) I think Lew Grade[‡] is truly ridiculous! We went to Chuck Ashman's party for the

* The twelve-week-old national miners' strike had become violent. Arthur Scargill, president of the National Union of Mineworkers, had been arrested after rioting at the Orgreave coking plant in South Yorkshire.
† Helen Slater (b.1963), American actress, made her film debut in *Supergirl*, 1984.
‡ Lew Grade (b. Lev Winogradsky, 1906–98), later Baron Grade of Elstree, Ukrainian-born impresario and television producer, creator of ATV. In GB's view, his finest achievement was producing *The Muppets*.

Aaron Spellings* – 'She's a diamond millionairess, you know.' I saw Lord Grade standing alone, chewing his cigar, looking like a beached whale. I brought him into our little group because he looked a bit pathetic on his own. He preened himself and embarked at once on a self-regarding tale of triumph and then, suddenly, out of the corner of his eye, caught sight of someone of significance and *pounced*! It was wonderful to see his piranha technique at work.

Went on to *Wild Honey* at the National – Chekhov adapted by Michael Frayn: funny, touching, nicely done. Had a drink in the interval with Robin Chichester-Clark† and Caroline, his much younger second wife. (We like her.) Marvelled (again) at the ho-ho vacuity of most politicians.

Sunday, 19 August 1984

Civilised party at John Schlesinger's in Victoria Road. (John takes cocaine in California, but not apparently in London.) Noel had covered his face in Man Tan and looked rather jaundiced in consequence. Also present: Alan Bates, embracing middle-age with enthusiasm; Tom Courtenay, still giving us the North Country diffidence; Alan Bennett, the dormouse brings his head out of the teapot for the evening and is truly very droll; John Standing. I asked after his stepfather: Sir John [Clements] is still in Brighton, but not working, lonely, unhappy and (at least to his stepson) 'a bit of a bore'.

Today we went to Lamport Hall, Northants, family seat of the Ishams – motto: 'I show, I sham not'. We went with Sir Ian Isham, Bart, a shy, mild, stick-insect of a man, about 60, lives in Croydon. At the Society of Authors Centenary Dinner I saw his name on the guest list and went and introduced myself. Sir Ian inherited his title from his father's cousin, Sir Gyles Isham, 1903–76. I don't know for sure, but I think I'm Gyles-with-a-y because of him. Pa and Ma always said I was Gyles-with-a-y because it was a family name, a tradition going back to the time of Gyles Daubeney, cup-bearer to Henry VII (or some such) – but when I went to Westminster Abbey to inspect the Daubeney tomb it's clearly Giles-with-an-i and always was. But when Pa went up to Oxford at the end of the 1920s, Gyles Isham's name was folkloric – he was the golden boy of the age:

---

* Aaron Spelling (1923–2006), Dallas-born American TV producer, associated with *Charlie's Angels, Dynasty, Starsky and Hutch* and many hit series besides; married Candy Gene as his second wife, 1965.

† Sir Robert 'Robin' Chichester-Clark (b.1928), MP for Londonderry, 1955–74, the only Northern Ireland MP to be a government minister since 1920; brother of James Chichester-Clark, Prime Minister of Northern Ireland, 1969–71, and Penelope Hobhouse, gardener.

President of the Union, editor of *Isis*, President of the OUDS *and* the under-graduate Hamlet of his generation. I think I am named after him. For a while, in the thirties, he was a leading actor, until he was eclipsed by Gielgud and Olivier. After the war, he abandoned the stage, went to Lamport and played the squire. He became the local MP, but made no mark. He was also, I imagine, gay – from the photographs, he has the bull-queen look.

Anyway, today, Sir Ian took us to Lamport. He inherited the title, not the house – that belongs to a trust. We had to line up and pay to get in. (Yes, that's what it's come to!) It's a fine building, dating from 1560, 1730 frontage, the usual Lelys – but it's in the middle of nowhere. You wouldn't want it. After the tour, proprietori-ally conducted by Ian, somewhat to the irritation of the resident curator, we went into the garden and watched the local amateurs present *A Midsummer Night's Dream* – it was really enjoyable, lumpen Hippolyta and all. Revels ended, we fin-ished up at the church – where, as Patron, Sir Ian still holds sway – and toured the graveyard. It felt quite odd to see my own first name engraved on a tombstone.

Thursday, 23 August 1984

Thirteen TV programmes in forty-eight hours: two stints at TV-am and eleven episodes of *Countdown*. Plus *Tell the Truth*, *Babble*, *Star Choice* and now *The Railway Carriage Game*. And a new jumper for each occasion – all supplied by the excellent George Hostler, head of design at Leicester Polytechnic and knitwear purveyor to yours truly, Princess Diana and Elton John. I send him my 'idea' by post and he sends me the jumper by return – by rail: I pick them up at the back of King's Cross Station. (I even have a black one for when the Queen Mother dies. True. And I got George to do a mini-one for David Frost's first-born, Miles. *Ultraquiz* has worked, sort of. David is extraordinary: fuelled entirely by white wine and finger food. He is a greedy eater, furiously pushing the food into his face with greasy fingers, but a great pro. During the countdown to the show, he counts himself in – out loud: 'Seven, six, five, four, three, two, one – *I'm on!*')

We've had treats in recent days – Antony Sher's *Richard III*: exciting; Natalia Makarova in *On Your Toes*: less so – and took ourselves to Raymond Blanc's new Quat' Saisons: perfect food in a picture-book manor house – but I've been doing sixteen-hour days, relentlessly. Business is good: diaries, calendars, books; Dent are offering £15,000 for Kenneth's autobiography and £12,500 for the Donald Sinden theatrical anecdotes; and I'm hopeful we will be renewing the *Crack It!* contract at £49,500 p.a. But I'm weary and therefore happy that relief is at hand. Tomorrow we set off for Italy: Sorrento, Positano, Amalfi, Ravello, Pompeii, Herculaneum, Caserta, Capri. All this and *He Knew He Was Right*.

Tuesday, 23 October 1984

It's six minutes past midnight on Tuesday 23 October 1984 and I'm sitting in bed in Leeds (at the Queen's Hotel), having put aside Arnold Bennett's *Journals* for a moment to pursue my own.

In the world at large, an amiable, ageing President Reagan looks set for a second term having survived last night's TV debate with a lacklustre Fritz Mondale, an indomitable Margaret Thatcher carries on regardless having survived last week's IRA bomb attack in Brighton, and the newspaper headlines are dominated by the miners' strike now in its thirty-second week. Richard Whiteley was in the Grand Hotel – in the lobby, still drinking – at 2.54 a.m. on 12 October when the IRA bomb exploded. He said it was chaos: dust and debris everywhere, cabinet ministers wandering, dazed, along the Brighton front in their pyjamas. He saw the firemen rescuing Norman Tebbit. Mrs Tebbit is badly injured. In all, four people were killed. Mrs T. escaped by chance – her bathroom was wrecked. Richard said she was completely incredible: when she emerged in the morning, absolutely calm, resolute but without a hint of hysteria. 'Life goes on. We go on.'

In the little world of GB, the news is less dramatic and more encouraging. Peter Ustinov likes the script of *The Old Boy* and may do it.* We may be buying a small house in Stratford-upon-Avon,† a stone's throw from the church where Shakespeare is buried: the auction is tomorrow. Book deals a-plenty are coming through and I am beginning, at last, to devolve some of the work onto Sandy and Clive.‡

We got back from Italy six weeks ago and we go again (to Venice for half-term) on Saturday. The gap has been filled with a merry mix of television, writing and train journeys. I'm here doing *Countdown.* Thirteen episodes – would have been nineteen, but when, very gently, I said I needed to check train times before committing myself, John Meade (producer) said 'Please yourself' and slammed the phone down. I am visiting him in hospital in Horsforth this afternoon. Whether it's his heart, his liver or a dose of the clap, I'm not sure. The first two episodes of *The Railway Carriage Game* went well: Lennie Bennett's mother died on the morning of the recording, but he soldiered on magnificently; Stan

---

* He didn't. The part in the pilot of the situation comedy by GB and Ned Sherrin about a retired prime minister was played Graham Crowden; the series did not materialise.
† They did.
‡ Sandy Ransford and Clive Dickinson, the two principal editors and writers then working for GB's editorial services company.

Boardman was loveable; John Inman very funny; Barbara Windsor turned up with a butch boyfriend twenty years her junior. (And why not? 'He can do it, Gyles. It's not a big one, but it does the business.' Followed by a waterfall of throaty gurgling laughter.) George Logan (Dr Hinge) has put on two stone since he gave up smoking. Lynda Bellingham's husband Nunzio is a nightmare (never easy marrying someone when you don't share the language). Katie Rabett (Prince Andrew's sometime fling) is a fun girl. Ditto Suzanne Danielle. (I like her. She likes me.) Bonnie Langford came to Biggins's house-warming with her *dad*. (I said she should marry Biggins. Bonnie Biggins is such a great name. She is 19 now – and very funny. 'I don't know about Lena Zavaroni and *I don't care!*')[*] On *All Star Secrets* I told my Russian lavatory story – for the last time. New material now required.

Other highlights: some progress on my scheme for the British Book Awards[†] . . . a return visit to the glorious RSC production of *A New Way to Pay Old Debts* . . . a roaring *Henry V* at Stratford . . . *Volpone* in the Pit (no more Ben Jonson: that must be a rule for life) . . . Leonard Rossiter in *Loot* at the Lyric: completely brilliant, but he was sweating profusely from start to finish: M said, 'He's desperately ill'[‡] . . . several sessions with Kenneth on his memoirs: he told me that his father took his own life, but he won't say so in the book; Kenneth says he has his own 'stash of poison' just in case . . . We had dinner with Simon Cadell at the Ritz (£340 – it's the price of caviare these days!) . . . We bought a new Mercedes . . . We went to Laurie Mansfield's tenth wedding anniversary bash: all the 'turns' were married to dancers or hairdressers: we counted eight chocolate-coloured Rollers in the drive . . . My sisters are high and low and in-between . . . Ma is going back to California . . . Brother Ben has written a woefully naïve letter from the States asking *me* to fix *his* divorce . . . I have finished my first novel for 9-year-olds: *The Ghost at Number Thirteen*. I want to do more proper writing. I met the very elderly Reverend Awdry at TV-am the other day – along with the amiable

[*] Lena Zavaroni (1963–99) was a singer and child star who died after a long and public battle with anorexia nervosa. She and Bonnie Langford met at the Italia Conti stage school and starred together on TV in their own show, *Lena and Bonnie*. Bonnie did, of course, care about Lena, but became fed up with being asked about her by journalists and the public.

[†] An idea first floated by GB in a speech to the Society of Bookmen the year before and then developed by him with Martyn Goff at the National Book League. They eventually emerged in 1990 as the British Book Awards, now known as 'the Nibbies'.

[‡] Leonard Rossiter died backstage at the Lyric Theatre on 5 October 1984, three weeks into the run.

Ringo Starr.* With *Thomas the Tank Engine* the Reverend Awdry has created a complete world: I envy that.

Okay, I'm going to sleep now. That's enough catching up for one evening. Goodnight.

Tuesday, 4 December 1984

Dinner for Bob Satterthwaite [retiring director of the National Playing Fields Association] at the Savoy. HRH [the Duke of Edinburgh] in happy form. Leslie Porter told a very rude story very well – about a lady and her chihuahua. She shaved the dog and was thrilled with the result. On Sunday, she cycled to church and told the vicar, 'I've shaved my chihuahua! I do want you to see.' 'I'd be delighted,' said the vicar, 'but doesn't it make riding your bicycle uncomfortable?' (It was the way he told it.) Sandy Gilmour then asked if he could tell a joke – adding, 'It's a bit racist.' Prince Philip leant across the table and said, not unkindly, 'Then don't tell it.' Sandy was going to plough on, but HRH raised a hand, 'No, Sandy. No.'

Monday, 17 December 1984

Jack and the Beanstalk: our Royal Pantomime Performance at the Richmond Theatre with HRH the Princess Alexandra.† She was lovely: chatty beforehand, chatty afterwards, chatty throughout the show. (I think they keep talking to make you feel it's going well.) HRH was lovely, but in the run-up to the evening, her lady-in-waiting (one Mona Mitchell) had been entirely ludicrous – obsessive about every tiny detail of royal protocol and adamant that no divorced person could possibly be presented to HRH. 'It simply isn't allowed. They shouldn't really be in the room. It could prove embarrassing for Her Royal Highness.' So po-faced was Miss Mitchell that I was tempted to greet the Princess with an entire line-up of divorcees all exposing themselves and shouting 'Fuck!' (I didn't. I simply left the name of the one divorced person on the Appeals Committee off the list we sent to Mona Mitchell, and then, on the night, slipped them into the line of those to be presented and kept my fingers crossed. In fairness to Miss Mitchell, she did introduce me to a gem of a euphemism. She required us to include a comfort stop for HRH in the minute-by-minute programme of the

* The Rev. Wilbert Awdry OBE (1911–97) began publishing *The Railway Series* in 1945; Ringo Starr (b. Richard Starkey, 1940) narrated the TV animations of *Thomas the Tank Engine* from 1984.
† HRH Princess Alexandra, The Hon. Mrs Angus Ogilvy (b.1936), granddaughter of George V.

evening. As a consequence I learnt that a royal pee-break is correctly described as 'Opportunity to tidy'.)

Wednesday, 16 January 1985

I went to support the Society of Authors Anti-VAT-on-Books rally at the Royal Overseas League. I wore my 'Don't Tax Reading' jumper. I wore it on TV-am this morning as well. We received several calls from people living in the town of Reading, claiming to be confused.

We also featured a new kind of car, the C5, invented by Sir Clive Sinclair.* It's a battery-operated tricycle really, dressed up as a tiny car. It's only thirty inches high and currently has a range of twenty miles. Before the end of the century, according to Sir Clive, the petrol engine will be a thing of the past. (The Brandreth Mercedes runs on diesel, I am proud to report, but the downside is it rumbles and splutters like a London taxicab and I have to go to the garage behind Paddington Station to get fuel.)

Our finances are up the spout. The overdraft situation is horrific and has just got infinitely worse. The pound is falling against the dollar. It now stands at a new low of $1.1105. Yes, I read economics at Oxford, but I can't pretend that I know what this means beyond the fact that, as a consequence of it, the Government has raised the base rate from 9.5 to 14 per cent. Given our indebtedness, this is seriously bad news.

Saturday, 2 February 1985

This is Saethryd's 8th birthday and this morning she made her television debut as a special guest on the Wide Awake Club at TV-am. I was launching the search for Britain's best-dressed garden gnome, with Saethryd at my side, sitting on a toadstool, holding a fishing rod, wearing her Brownie uniform and a gnome's red hat. We are now bracing ourselves for this evening's excitement: Saethryd's disco party, from 6.30 to 9.00 p.m.

Monday, 11 February 1985

This has been a memorable weekend: our first weekend at our new house in Stratford-upon-Avon. We love it. The children love it. They are still there. We tried to leave yesterday afternoon, but we were forced back by the snow. In the morning I drove around the backstreets of Stratford Old Town looking for

---

* Sir Clive Sinclair (b.1940), entrepreneur and inventor, pioneer of the electronic pocket calculator and mass-market home computers.

somewhere to buy bread and the papers and the car simply skidded from one side of the road to the other. At one point, very slowly, very gently, I collided with another car skidding towards me from the opposite direction. It turned out to be Chris Tarrant. He appears to have a house in Stratford, too. Anyway, M is driving back to London with the children when she can and I'm now on the train with my stomach churning. I am due at Stationers' Hall at 12.45 to address the IBM lunch. I set off at 7.00 a.m. I am going via Leamington Spa and Reading and I'm not going to make it. (No play, no pay.)

Tuesday, 26 February 1985

Yesterday I set off at the crack of dawn for a flight to Glasgow for the first in a series I am hosting for BBC Scotland: *Catchword*. I don't know why I agreed to do it: the people are sweet enough (I have fallen for Magnus Magnusson's daughter, Topsy), but it is all very second division, the money's derisory and it's in *Glasgow*! (M knows why I did it: vanity and an inability to say No.) The recording finished at 9.30 p.m. and the BBC said they'd have a taxi to take me to Leeds where I needed to wake up this morning for a batch of *Countdowns*. They promised me a taxi and a taxi is what I got – a superannuated London taxi that had done ten good years' service in the capital in the fifties, before doing another ten years in Manchester and then being put out to retire in Glasgow. I clambered in, I huddled in the back and we set off. It was the journey from hell. Over five long hours I was tossed and jolted from Glasgow to Leeds. The heater didn't work: I was frozen. Halfway across the Pennines, the taxi's lights went out. The fuses had blown. They went out not once, but four times. Using silver paper from a bar of chocolate the driver eventually managed to get one headlamp to produce a faint glow. I reached the dreary Queen's Hotel just after 3.00 a.m. I was so cold I slept in my overcoat.

Wednesday, 13 March 1985

Benet's birthday. 10 today. No celebrations at breakfast because he goes off to school first thing and, before dawn, I'm driven up to TV-am. At 8.45 a.m. I doffed my jumper, jumped in a cab and got to Broadcasting House in the nick of time to be the Birthday Guest on *Midweek*. (Other guests: an enchanting lighthouse keeper who looked *exactly* like Captain Birdseye and a couple of witches who seemed perfectly harmless.) At 10.00 a.m. I went on to TVS for the first of twelve days working on this year's *Ultraquiz*. I'm devising the games. It comes to £1,000 a day so I have to do it, but the enterprise is such rubbish that I really feel I am wasting my life in the process. Last year our hosts were David Frost and

Willie Rushton. This year: Stu Francis and Sarah Hollamby. (Indeed: *who?*) It's become a sort of *Seaside Special* with games and quizzes thrown in and the clichés that are bandied about at the meetings – 'he's a strong taste', 'we need a dance routine that's refreshing', 'we must work on a killer finish' – are too depressing for words. I am a little depressed. I read an interview in *The Times* with Bill Alexander, whose production of *Merry Wives* we're going to see in Stratford shortly. He said, in passing, that he could never, ever, *ever* take seriously an actor who appeared on *All Star Secrets*. That's sad. It means that people have to choose on which side of the intellectual fence they are to sit. I'd like to direct Shakespeare *and* appear on *All Star Secrets* – but the world won't have it: the world wants people in recognisable compartments.

M's birthday tomorrow. Michael Caine's too. And Albert Einstein's. Tom Stoppard sent me a verse in honour of the date:

> Einstein born
> Quite unprepared
> For E to equal
> MC squared

Friday, 22 March 1985

TV Scrabble and I outscored Clement Freud. Clement is eaten up by the need to win. He *has* to win, always . . . but he didn't. I did.

Now on my way to do another bit of nonsense: a kids' programme called *The Game*. Without thinking twice about it, the cheery host leers down at the little tots and asks, 'Are you ready to go on *The Game?*' – that's the catchphrase, believe it or not. *The Game* involves a computer – which, of course, slows everything down.

In Nottingham last night I addressed the Institute of Chartered Surveyors. I sat next to the Bishop of Derby who *read* Grace. He had it written on a little card: 'For what we are about to receive, may the Lord make us truly thankful.' He had the Lord's Prayer on a card, too. He keeps them like that, he said, 'just in case the mind goes blank'. On the other side I had the chairman of Derbyshire County Council, who came from Ireland to Derby in 1946 with absolutely nothing. He got a job sweeping the platforms at the railway station, but he was determined and ambitious so in time (and, of course) he became Mayor of Derby, a Freeman of the City and now chairman of the County Council. The Chief Constable couldn't attend: he's been suspended on full pay pending inquiries . . . The Chief Fire Officer couldn't make it: he's been fiddling the books . . .

Later

I have just read that Michael Redgrave has died. One of the obituaries quotes Kenneth Tynan on the gulf that exists between good and great performances and how the triumvirate of Olivier, Gielgud and Redgrave tackled it: 'Olivier pole-vaults in a single animal leap; Gielgud, seizing a parasol, crosses by tightrope; Redgrave alone must battle it out with the current.' He made his own life so much more difficult than he needed to. Rachel told M that when they got married Michael, who couldn't drive, insisted on being seen to drive away from the reception. Once they were out of sight, he let her take over the controls. He was vain, selfish, self-indulgent – and wonderful, too, both as a man and as an actor: honest, intelligent, fastidious, delightful. He was flawed (aren't we all?) but he was the first 'great man' to befriend me and I loved him.

Friday, 29 March 1985

David Frost is kindly pre-recording a contribution to the cabaret for the Sixties Ball. I went to see him. 'A *joy*, Gyles, a *joy*!' He told me that Diahann Carroll had given him a nice line to use when you go round to greet a chum in the dressing room after the show and really don't know what to say about the performance you've just seen. Pop your head around the door and cry: 'Boy! Were you on that stage!' David was on his way to Heathrow to negotiate an interview with Mikhail Gorbachev.* He asked me to pass him a loose-leaf folder from his desk. On the cover of the folder were written the words: 'David's airport quips'.

Lunch at White's Club with Sandy Gilmour. The taxi dropped me off at Boodle's next door. I said 'Gilmour' cheerily to the hall porter. He told me to wait in the bar. I waited for thirty minutes before realising I must be in the wrong place. Sandy's half-brother (Iain Gilmour) is a member of Boodle's. Sandy isn't. I hate these gentlemen's clubs. I hate the overcooked cabbage. I hate the way they won't have women in the building – except to wait at table. I hate the ludicrous way they refuse to put the club's name on the door.

Just in from the Regency Ball at Somerset House – overcrowded, uncomfortable, vaguely amusing if you like laughing at the ways of the world. (Not altogether funny, though. A former pupil of M's was there, a nice girl, but she couldn't wait to meet up with her 'pusher' – also at the party – and they both went off for a snort of cocaine.)

---

* Mikhail Gorbachev (b.1931), the only Soviet leader to have been born after the October 1917 Revolution, had become General Secretary of the Communist Party of the Soviet Union on 11 March 1985 and head of state in the USSR from 1988 until its collapse in 1991.

'Roland Rat is Helping Hugely'

'A Night in the Sixties.' Michèle has spent months organising this – months. And I think it's fair to say she had a triumph. A thousand people, Grosvenor House, thousands raised, Princess Anne as guest of honour. It was a ball to celebrate the sixtieth birthday of the National Playing Fields Association, hence the theme: the 1960s. M chose the 'acts': Ricky Valance, the Swinging Blue Jeans, Billy J. Kramer and the Dakotas. I invited assorted sixties luminaries . . . Harold Wilson proposed the Loyal Toast and, like the Bishop of Derby, wrote out every word on a piece of card beforehand. (There were only seven words: 'My lords, ladies and gentlemen: The Queen.' He wrote them out in a very neat hand. I've kept the card.)[*] He also made M laugh by spending all dinner talking about himself and regularly peppering his monologue with the immortal phrase, 'When I was Prime Minister . . .' Jeremy Thorpe was frail and old and appears to have Parkinson's disease . . . Ringo Starr coped well with Princess Anne's firm belief that he was a footballer – 'Do you still play?' 'Yes, Ma'am.' 'What do you do to keep in training?' 'Being a Beatle helps . . .' Still, she didn't get it. (She had had a long day. She came to us from a lunch with the police and she was off at the crack of dawn for her first taste of flat-racing as a jockey.) . . . Bobby Moore was not mistaken for not being a footballer . . . Michael Caine glowed as a film star should . . . Joanna Lumley came in a perfect sixties frock with perfect sixties make-up . . . Viscount Weymouth came dressed as a hippie (i.e. as per usual)[†] . . . Hinge and Bracket did the cabaret beautifully – they pretended it was an occasion for people *in* their sixties . . . Paul Jones bought a teddy bear Prince Philip had donated for £1,000 – it was auctioned by John Wells, hilarious in the guise of Denis Thatcher . . . I spent dinner rubbing knees with HRH, but only because the top table was tightly packed and her chair was immediately in front of the table leg so she had no choice but to sit with one knee one side and one the other. (And we had spent hours in the afternoon checking and rechecking the top table. We just never lifted the tablecloth.) She did her stuff impeccably, but she does not *give* a lot. When I said what fun it was to be sitting with her thigh to thigh, she arched her eyebrows, sipped at her Coca-Cola and asked about the challenges currently facing the NPFA.

---

[*] GB did not appreciate at the time (nor did the world at large) that Lord Wilson was already beginning to suffer from the early stages of Alzheimer's disease.

[†] Alexander Thynn (b.1932), styled Viscount Weymouth, 1946–92, now 7th Marquess of Bath; noted for the 'bohemian dress sense' he first adopted in Paris in the 1950s.

Saturday, 11 May 1985

Happy, memorable, unlikely – my night tonight at the Brighton Festival with A. L. Rowse. It was billed as 'The Dark Lady of the Sonnets – Who was She?' It was intended to be a contest between Rowse (advocating his much-vaunted candidate for the honour, Emilia Lanier) and Anthony Burgess (championing Lucy Morgan, also known as Lucy Negro because she was black). Burgess pulled out and, for reasons unknown, proposed me as his substitute. I am glad that he did. I have had a happy few days doing my homework. I won't rehearse my arguments here – how Lucy could have met both Shakespeare and Southampton at Gray's Inn; how there are puns and quibbles on Morgan in the Sonnets and (more convincingly) on Lucy/Lucia/Light; how the physical description can be read as pointing definitively to a negress. Suffice to say that, at the end of the debate, the audience were asked to consider their verdict and, two to one, they found in favour of wayward, wanton, witty Lucy Morgan!

Rowse was a delight – absurd, boastful, brooking no argument, but completely charming and disarming, too. And eager to declare, aged 81, that he has recently discovered his bisexuality. He was very taken with the actresses who portrayed the Dark Ladies for us (Nina Baden-Semper was perfect as my Lucy) – kept commending their Elizabethan posture and patting their knees. (Now I want to write a book about the Dark Lady. Rowse said, 'Please don't. I have written three. We don't need more.')

I have just turned on the television. A fire has been sweeping through Bradford City football ground. More than forty fans have died.

Saturday, 25 May 1985

We went to Longleat to have lunch with Alexander Weymouth. We went to 'his' part of the house. He and his father (Henry, 6th Marquess of Bath) appear not to be on speaking terms. 'My father was beastly to me when I was a child. A disciplinarian, totally unbending. He has never once said anything encouraging to me about my murals. He humiliated me by appointing my younger brother, Christopher, to run the house. The loss of face is intolerable. On the day my father dies, on the day I inherit Longleat, I shall tell Christopher to leave.'*

He took us on a tour to see his famous murals – he is especially proud of the bedroom where the walls are covered with scenes from the Kama Sutra: 'I painted them in '69, a fortuitous year given the subject matter.' He was very happy to talk about his 'wifelets'. Down the years they have come in all shapes and shades:

---

* And on the day his father died, 30 June 1992, he did exactly that.

black, brown, young, local, yokel. 'Yes, I like a Wessex farm girl, don't you?' They number more than fifty and he has executed three-dimensional portraits in sawdust and oils of every one of them. They are fixed to the walls on a spiral staircase, just off the kitchen, with the date he met each girl inscribed to the left of her face, and the date of painting to the right. 'You can tell which were my active years.'

He was anxious for us to know that Anna (his wife – not present: she is in Paris) knows all about his polygyny. ('A polygamist has more than one wife; a polygynist has more than one mate.') And he was keen too for us to appreciate that he approaches his romantic life as a gentleman. 'It's very rare that I've seduced anybody's wife,' he told me while holding Michèle's hand. 'And, if infidelity does occur, it should always be done tactfully, so that it doesn't offend anybody's pride. I don't want anyone to be hurt or lose face.'

We liked him a lot.

Sunday, 16 June 1985

We had a musical afternoon and tea. Vicky Locock, M's piano teacher, came with all her other pupils and they gave an informal concert in the drawing room. It was a lovely event.

Over tea, I said to Vicky Locock, 'It's amazing: you look exactly like Princess Anne.' She said, 'I know.' She turns out to be a descendant of Henry Locock, born 1867 and brought up as the son of Sir Charles Locock, gynaecologist to Queen Victoria, but long rumoured within the Locock family to be the illegitimate son of Queen Victoria's sixth child, Princess Louise. In 1870, Louise, said to be something of a 'goer', married the Marquess of Lorne, a noted homosexual. From 1880, Louise and her husband lived separate lives and Louise was the only one of Queen Victoria's children who *apparently* had no issue. There you have it: M's piano teacher is a Princess Anne lookalike because she is directly descended from one of Queen Victoria's bastard grandchildren.

Friday, 21 June 1985

Mellow evening. M cooked a beautiful meal. The dining room looked charming. Everyone was happy. Joanna [Lumley] was funny. Stefan [Bednarczyk] was funny. Roddy [Llewellyn]* was funny. And Kenneth was hilarious and on best

---

* Sir Roderic Llewellyn, 5th Bt (b.1947), gardener and broadcaster; best known for his eight-year relationship with Princess Margaret which began in 1973, when he was 25 and the Queen's sister was 43. He married Tania Soskin in 1981.

behaviour. He took a shine to Roddy.[*] We all took a shine to Roddy. (Didn't Princess Margaret do well?) It was a perfect evening, too, because there was just one conversation: the table stayed together from start to finish. I hate it when there are half a dozen conversations going on – I *always* feel I'm taking part in the wrong one. Tonight, it worked perfectly. The funny people were on song and M and I and Tania [Llewellyn] and Juliet [Mountcharles] were happy to be the audience. This is all we need: laughter and the love of friends.[†]

Wednesday, 31 July 1985

We are flying from Iceland to Greenland today to meet eskimos. This is the most wonderful holiday. It is light in the middle of the night; I have eaten reindeer; I have seen the original geyser; I have been pony trekking. (Yes, I squawked a bit, but I loved it.) Iceland claims the world's oldest parliament, the Althing, and the world's highest level of literacy. Television is banned on Thursday evenings to encourage reading.

Wednesday, 11 September 1985

This morning I met up with Adrian Gilpin at the Barbican. He thinks this could be the perfect location for our Royal Story.[‡] I still prefer the old Marylebone Grammar School (near Madame Tussaud's) or somewhere in Victoria (near Buckingham Palace), but this may be more realistic. We shall see.

---

[*] In his diary for the same date, Kenneth Williams wrote: 'To dinner with Gyles Brandreth, and Michèle. It was a big party! . . . Roddy told a story about a man going into the home of two spinsters to view a Ming vase & seeing a french letter lying on the piano stool. The old lady explained, "We found it lying in the grass on the common & it said *Place on organ to avoid infection* and we haven't got an organ so we put it on the piano & do you know we've neither of us had *any colds* this year!" He's one of the few people I've ever come across who knows how to tell a story.'

[†] A reference to GB's favourite lines from 'Dedicatory Ode' by Hilaire Belloc: 'From quiet homes and first beginning / Out to the undiscovered ends, / There's nothing worth the wear of winning, / But laughter and the love of friends.'

[‡] Earlier in 1985, GB conceived the idea for a permanent exhibition telling the story of British royalty, from the reign of King Edgar to the present day. He recruited Adrian Gilpin (a theatre producer) to manage the venture and a board that included Sir Leslie Porter, the Earl of Bradford, David Graham (Geneva-based banker and a friend of GB from university), Peter Slattery (Adrian Gilpin's father), and, later, Charles Fry. The exhibition, eventually called 'Royal Britain', opened at the Barbican in 1988 and closed two years later. Its creation and failure dominated GB's business life for five years and fills many hundreds of pages of GB's diary.

Lunch with Clement Freud. I met up with him at the Waldorf in the Aldwych where he had been addressing a conference. He insisted we take a taxi all the way to Chelsea to a favourite Chinese restaurant of his. We were the only customers. Throughout lunch he managed to be amusing and difficult at the same time. He makes sure you are always on edge. At the end of the meal he played an ingenious trick on me: a bet I didn't really understand, involving some complicated calculation relating to the bill and the size of the tip. Needless to say, I lost and had to pick up the tab. He's an odd fish: there are flashes of sweetness, but he is *terrifying* too. I wouldn't want to be Jill [Freud] for all the world.

And I wouldn't want to be Biddy Baxter[*] either. She is married to *Blue Peter*. She lives for *Blue Peter*. She *is Blue Peter*. I went to see her to discuss a fund-raising idea for NPFA. I don't think anything will come of it and I don't mind. In fact, I'm relieved. She takes herself and her programme so seriously we would undoubtedly have fallen out. *Blue Peter?* Who cares? It's only a frigging TV programme. (And I never watched it as a child. Too po-faced. I liked *Crackerjack*.)

Sunday, 6 October 1985

We have had riots in Toxteth and Peckham. I am going a little mad too.

> I burn my candle at both ends,
> It will not last the night.
> But ah, my foes, and oh, my friends,
> It gives a lovely light.

Countdown Series VIII (five shows per day); *Catchword* (Series II + Topsy: happy meals at the Ubiquitous Chip); TV-am at dawn (I love Twiggy at breakfast and Harry Secombe is as jolly as he seems; not so, Terry Scott); launch of *Record Breaker*;[†] Victorama under control – just; NPFA under control – just; but the days are long and the nights are late. Monday, Glasgow. Tuesday, first night of *Torch Song Trilogy*. Wednesday, Martini Terrace then the Caprice with Paul Jones and Fiona. Thursday, the Odontological Section of the Medical Institute in Birmingham (oh yes, it's all happening); Friday, Biggins and Vince and Gaye Brown at the Caprice. Yesterday, Newark at lunch-time for the North-East Ladies' Circle Rally, then the 4.48 to King's Cross and on to Waterloo to catch

---

[*] Joan 'Biddy' Baxter MBE (b.1933), producer and editor of the BBC children's programme *Blue Peter*, 1962–88.

[†] A magazine GB's company, Victorama, had created for Guinness Superlatives.

the 6.35 p.m. – but I missed it by ten seconds. I had to *drive* to Bournemouth for the British Telecom Mobile Phones sales conference. Heart pounding, I arrived just in time to give my speech and got home again just before 3.00 a.m. We are going for brunch at Tootsies, but it's all a bit much.

But one important thing to report. My friend Roland Rat wants to spread his wings/extend his claws: he is leaving TV-am and I have introduced him to my friend and agent, Laurie Mansfield, who, for a vast sum, is taking him to the BBC. My reward: a £5,000 'finder's fee'. My other reward is knowing David Claridge (the man with his hand up the rat's whatsit): odd, angular, wiry, with a whine in his voice, but intelligent – and committed. He came to supper (fresh from an international conference of puppeteers) and stood in the kitchen with his left forefinger pressed hard into the lower part of the palm of his right hand: 'The soul of the puppet, Gyles – it's here. It's right *here.*'

Wednesday, 16 October 1985

I began the day with Eamonn Andrews[*] and Pia Zadora[†] and ended it with Terry Jones,[‡] Brian Patten[§] and Michael Bond.[¶] Will any of us be joining the ranks of the great immortals? Will the Liverpool poets be remembered in a hundred years? Michael Bond might be. I've a feeling Paddington Bear could stand the test of time. And Miss Zadora? Who knows? Apparently *Santa Claus Conquers the Martians* is already a cult classic. (She and her bust are wholly improbable, but I liked her.) Michael Bond, of course, really wants to be remembered for his adult fiction featuring the gourmet detective, Monsieur Pamplemousse. And Pia wants to be known for her singing. And Terry Jones yearns to be recognised as a medievalist not a Python. No one is happy with what they've got! (Actually, Eamonn Andrews seemed contented enough.)

Tuesday, 5 November 1985

Back from half-term week in Crete, sorting through post. Alongside the usual (bank statements, bills, final demands – but, curiously, never that long-overdue

---

[*] Eamonn Andrews CBE (1922–87), television presenter especially associated with *What's My Line?*, *Crackerjack* and *This Is Your Life*.
[†] Pia Zadora (b.1954), American actress and singer named in the Golden Raspberry Awards as 'Worst New Star of the Decade, 1980–89'.
[‡] Terry Jones (b.1942), Welsh actor and author, best known as a member of Monty Python's Flying Circus.
[§] Brian Patten (b.1946), Liverpool poet.
[¶] Michael Bond OBE (b.1926), English author, creator of Paddington Bear.

cheque), some good letters from friends: Cyril [Fletcher], John Bratby, Kenneth [Williams], Joanna [Lumley], the Nimmos. I should be preparing myself for tomorrow's visit from Mr Greenwood of Customs & Excise to discuss the VAT ('Just a routine visit, sir – shouldn't take more than three hours'), but instead I am thinking about the way I keep – the way I *store* – the diary. At the moment, I keep the diary itself, the actual journal, on loose pages in a box-file, and everything else – letters, cards, invitations, menus, theatre programmes, newspapers, ephemera of all sorts – I just chuck into a large cardboard carton. I am now thinking that what I should really do is *integrate* the correspondence with the journal, literally interweave the letters with the diary. What's inspired this is this letter just here from Roddy Llewellyn. I sent him a copy of *Wit Knits* (my first book of knitting patterns – Roddy is one of the models, along with Joanna, Simon, Richard Briers, John Inman, Bonnie, Faith Brown, etc., etc.) and an invitation to come to the launch event in Covent Garden in November. This is his amusing reply:

31st October 1985

My dear Gyles,

Thank you so very much for the book & letter. Doesn't scrumptious Joanna positively ooze . . .

11 a.m. at the Jubilee Hall, Covent Garden, is inked in for the morning of Saturday, 30th November. No question of a pencilled entry. May I bring Tania? We love any excuse for a visit to Covent Garden whose recent metamorphosis can be paralleled to the Peacock butterfly any time. Do you agree?

I find it so difficult to decide what to wear at this time of year. A sweater is all very well in the morning on one's way to work, but one then has to pull it off during lunch. Then arrives that terribly difficult decision of whether to carry it or put it on again. I think a tie, coat and waistcoat is the answer as the peeling-off process is less exhausting.

I don't think I've ever quite recovered from a train journey I made with my father in the 50s in the 'Red Dragon', travelling from Newport to Paddington. We were travelling first class to start off with, but I was made to travel third from the Severn Tunnel junction onwards as I was wearing brown shoes. 'No one wears brown shoes in London,' he said sternly.

Forgive me for rambling on, but I well remember my mama telling me what fun it was going to Chelsea before the war – (my grandparents had a house in Grosvenor Square & she was never allowed out without hat, gloves and lady's maid) – as 'one actually saw people wearing sandals in London'.

What's Crete like?

Love,

Roddy

Isn't that charming? Crete was a bit dull, as we know. The hotel was the problem, not the island or the antiquities.

And, look, I've just opened this from Jane Asher. She is in the knitting book, too. And she and Jo are now rehearsing *Blithe Spirit* with Simon . . .

Of course SOME actresses who shall be nameless but who also appear in Blithe Spirit *make the front cover and about 125 pictures inside, and SOME of us only make one wistful little picture inside the book. The fact that this caused a huge rift at rehearsals and that the two leading ladies are no longer speaking to each other needn't worry you at all.*

She is funny. And lovely. (And, tell me, why do I fancy her in a way that I have never fancied Jo?) Back to the point at issue. Do I now start to include letters in the journal file?*

Saturday, 14 December 1985

Robert Graves has died and I never got to Majorca. The Nobel Prizes have been announced and I have been overlooked again. But, look on the bright side: this morning at TV-am I did my stuff as the Joke Correspondent on the Wide Awake Club and then, as NPFA Appeals Chairman, I masterminded the World's Biggest Cracker Chain Pull in Trafalgar Square. It was ridiculous, but rather fun.

Tuesday, 17 December 1985

I feared a complete fiasco. The truth is: this charity fund-raising is a nightmare. If you don't do it yourself, nothing happens. We had had a success with the Sixties Ball because M and her committee worked their socks off for *months on end*. It only happens with effort, attention to detail and follow-through. The Manchester committee were delighted at the prospect of having the NPFA Royal Panto Performance at the Palace Theatre, but what did they do to *sell* the event? Sod all. A week ago, when I called the committee chairman to ask how it was going (he didn't call me, please note), he said lamely, 'Not very well. I think we're

* He didn't.

going to have to cancel.' He'd sold about thirty seats – out of 2,000. I went berserk. We didn't cancel. We went through with it. He found an audience. How many of them paid, I don't know. But the event happened and it gave the illusion of success.

Princess Michael of Kent was our royal. She has had a rough year,[*] but she did her stuff for us like a pro. She had not been to a panto before. It was *Babes in the Wood*, starring Les Dawson, plus the Roly-Polys, a spangled line-up of buxom dancers of riper years. HRH had never seen anything like it. 'What is zis?' she kept repeating, wide-eyed with amazement. 'Is zis supposed to be funny? Are we meant to laugh at zese fat ladies? I do not understand.' Afterwards I presented the Princess to Les. She was at all times gracious, but, I think, rather revolted when she realised that Les was a man.

After HRH had gone, I found Les sitting alone on a stool in the downstairs theatre bar. I joined him for a drink. He liked the fact that Princess Michael had found the entertainment confusing. 'Nice lady,' he gurned, lugubriously, 'but foreign. You've got to be British to understand panto. It defines us. It's why we won the war, you know.'

---

[*] HRH Princess Michael of Kent (b. Baroness Marie Christine von Reibnitz, 1945); as her second husband, she married Prince Michael of Kent, grandson of George V, in 1978. In 1985 there had been press stories about her love-life and her father's wartime association with the Nazi Party. GB's archive includes the July 1985 cover of *Private Eye* featuring the Kents in the Royal Box at Wimbledon. 'Is it true about you having a lover?' someone asks. Princess Michael replies: 'Nein.' Prince Michael's speech bubble adds: 'Not that many surely?'

The World is Changing

February 1986 – December 1987

Thursday, 13 February 1986

Good news: Mrs Thatcher and President Mitterrand have signed a treaty to build a Channel Tunnel. It might actually happen – and within my lifetime. Bad news: the strike at *The Times* continues and is turning nasty. There are 5,000 pickets outside Murdoch's new printing works at Wapping and they're not happy. There will be blood on the pavement before it's over (the police are being heavy-handed), but we know who'll win. When I left Oxford, journalism was a closed shop: if I hadn't managed to join the NUJ I wouldn't have been able to work. It's different now. The world is changing. And there's no fighting change. Mrs T. and Rupert Murdoch are going to teach us that.* Our news: dinner with Pat and Derek Nimmo: Rearsby Sitwell, Antoinette Sibley, Denise, Lady Kilmarnock – black tie, a butler, a footman in gaiters (oh yes), the gentlemen lingering for port and cigars while the ladies sit around in the hostess's bedroom . . . all this in *Earl's Court*.

Monday, 24 February 1986

A fun lunch for ten in the boardroom at Sotheby's with the Moore-Gwyns, the Hoyer Millars, Sir Edward Tomkins, an aunt of David [Moore-Gwyn]'s who was Sir Somebody Somebody's housekeeper-turned-second-wife and a very spirited old bird named Lady Willoughby de Broke who owns the St Martin's Theatre (and much besides) and who has just, reluctantly, retired her servants – cook, lady's maid, butler, the lot – and moved to a flat on Campden Hill where she lives on Marks & Spencer meals which she shares with her friend the Queen Mother when HM comes round for a cosy supper. She was really *very* grand, in the nicest possible way, much grander in fact than the star turn, Angus Ogilvy,† who was

---

* They did. After a year, the strike at Rupert Murdoch's News International and Times Group newspapers ultimately collapsed and industrial relations within the printing industry, and beyond, were irrevocably changed.

† Sir Angus Ogilvy KCVO (1928–2004), businessman who married Princess Alexandra in 1963.

sweet and wonderfully unstuffy. *He* is trying to get rid of Princess Alexandra's lady's maid – who is 72 and desports herself like a grand duchess. In Australia she summoned the Governor General to complain about her quarters; in America she was indignant at the rank of escort provided for her at the opera – nothing below First Secretary will do . . . 'She is impossible.' According to Angus, the only one who is worse is the Queen's own Bobo MacDonald. He was delightfully indiscreet, chatty and charming, though he seemed only ninety per cent there. Of course, he drank everything in sight and smoked non-stop, which he admitted wasn't quite what you'd expect from the president of both ASH and the Imperial Cancer Research Fund.

Wednesday, 26 February 1986

7.30 a.m.   TV-am with Michael Barrymore[*] (zany, but dead behind the eyes: he offers hilarity without warmth) and Sigue Sigue Sputnik (I told them they were my kind of band).

9.00 a.m.   *Midweek.* I interviewed Kenneth [Williams] – he turned 60 on Saturday. The usual stories: the familiar voices. 'I've painted myself into a corner, haven't I? That's why I don't get any decent work any more. And you don't invite me round 'cos you hate my smoking. You *haaaaaate* it, don't you?'

11.00 a.m.   The Barbican Estate Office. Will we raise the necessary £3 million and launch our Royal Britain exhibition? Yes, I think perhaps we will.

1.00 p.m.   Lunch in Islington with Dan Crawford, founder of the King's Head pub theatre. Will we raise the necessary £30,000 and launch the Pocket Musical Season there? No, I think we won't.

3.30 p.m.   An hour back at the office: last rites for *Crack It!* and *Record Breaker*, but the *Trivial Pursuit* books are looking good.

5.00 p.m.   Gathering of the NPFA cabal at Sandy [Gilmour]'s flat to decide whether or not we are going fire the nice-but-ineffectual director. We think we will. We have to.

And another big decision looms. We are thinking of renting an office, selling these two houses [1 and 2 Campden Hill Gardens] and buying a single, detached house to live in. We are wasting space here and stacking up debt. Something's got to give.

[*] Michael Barrymore (b. Michael Parker, 1952), English comedian and TV game show host.

Friday, 7 March 1986

Simon Cadell and Rebecca Croft Sharland were married at Chelsea Town Hall at 10.00 a.m. today. We were the witnesses, along with Beckie's friend, Amanda Donohoe.* We all went together by car, Simon and I wise-cracking nervously en route. He was *very* nervous. Beckie is lovely. She is a professional model – but wholesome: girl-next-door and young mums are her speciality. Will it work? Who knows? Simon is my closest friend and has been for nearly twenty-five years, but we are English and male: these things we don't discuss. I don't know why he left Suzan or Steph and I don't know why he is marrying Beckie – except that she's lovely, and the baby is due in August! Over lunch at Le Manoir I learnt more about Amanda Donohoe's love-life in twenty minutes than I have learnt of Simon's in twenty years. Talk about about sex, drugs and rock 'n' roll. Girls, boys, Adam Ant – she's had 'em all, darling. She is slim, beautiful, fun, sexy, but, curiously, not nearly so *fanciable* as Beckie. I said how beautiful the bride looked. 'Oh, yeah,' giggled Amanda, 'fucking the bride on the wedding day – that's everyone's favourite fantasy. We could both get off on that one.'

Post-lunch, Simon returned to the theatre where, at the curtain call, Jo [Lumley] stepped forward and introduced the new groom to the house. They cheered him to the rafters.

Sunday, 9 March 1986

Simon and Beckie's wedding party at the White Elephant was ludicrously generous. (Thank you, Mr and Mrs Croft – they have the money and I like the way they spend it.) And it was fun. All actors – Cazenove, David Suchet,[†] the whole gang. Why do I prefer actors to rock stars? I had breakfast with Bill Wyman (Rolling Stone)[‡] and John Taylor (Duran Duran)[§] and there weren't a lot of *laughs*. Bill told me about his relentless sex-life and his 15-year-old Lolita girl-friend ('I look, I don't touch, mate') but he doesn't seem to be having much *fun*.

---

* Amanda Donohoe (b.1962), English actress who first came to prominence playing opposite Oliver Reed in *Castaway*, 1986.

† David Suchet (b.1946) actor, best known for playing Agatha Christie's Poirot since 1989.

‡ Bill Wyman (b. William Perks, 1936), bass guitarist with the Rolling Stones, 1962–92; in 1989, he married his young girlfriend, Mandy Smith, when she turned 18.

§ Nigel John Taylor (b.1960), bass guitarist with Duran Duran, one of the biggest groups of the 1980s.

Su Pollard* on the other hand . . . Actually, Su is not only a manic bundle of comic energy (and No. 7 in the charts this week), she is also a truly decent human being. We took M's mother to see *Me and My Girl* and, afterwards, Su treated her as if she'd been *her* mum. I love her.

Wednesday, 12 March 1986

At TV-am this morning I plonked myself down on the sofa next to a familiar figure. 'Call me Willy,' he said. 'Call me Gyles.' It was Willy Brandt,† former Chancellor of West Germany. He was very charming, if a little bemused. I was sorry I couldn't introduce him to Roland Rat. I offered him a wild and woolly David Bellamy‡ instead. I liked him. He is still Leader of the SDP [Social Democratic Party]. I asked him how he hoped to be remembered. He laughed, 'Not for the scandals.' He opted for his Ostpolitik and the Brandt Report. 'One day, eastern Europe and western Europe will come together again and I hope I will have helped to make that happen.' He believes the Brandt Report has changed the way the West thinks about the developing world. He likes to think Live Aid and all that is a direct consequence of his endeavours. I asked him to name his favourite British politician. He said, 'Ted Heath. A great man. A man of vision. A world figure who has never been understood properly in his own country.'

Thursday, 20 March 1986

Jeffrey [Archer] is riding high, loving life as Deputy Chairman.§ Over lunch he tells us (me, King Constantine,¶ Leon Brittan,** Geoffrey Rippon,†† Eddie Shah,‡‡

---

* Susan Pollard (b.1949), actress who came to prominence in *Hi-de-Hi*; she starred in *Me and My Girl* at the Adelphi in 1986 and reached No. 2 in the UK Singles Chart with her recording of 'Starting Together'.
† Willy Brandt (b. Herbert Frahm, 1913–92), Chancellor of West Germany, 1969–74.
‡ David Bellamy OBE (b.1933), academic, botanist, author and broadcaster.
§ Margaret Thatcher had appointed Archer Deputy Chairman of the Conservative Party in September 1985.
¶ Constantine II of Greece (b.1940), King of Greece 1964 until deposed in 1973 when he and his family moved to live in exile in London.
** Sir Leon Brittan (b.1939), Baron Brittan of Spennithorne since 2000; Conservative MP, 1974–88, and Cabinet Minister; later European Commissioner, 1989–99.
†† Geoffrey Rippon (1924–97), Baron Rippon of Hexham from 1997; Conservative MP, 1955–64, 1966–87, and Cabinet Minister.
‡‡ Eddie Shah (b.1944), businessman, founder of the *Today* newspaper in 1986.

Bryan Organ,[*] Gordon Reece,[†] Louis Kirby[‡]) that he and the PM are in constant touch. 'I think she needs me,' he says grandly, adding, with a mock-modest shrug, 'I hope I am of service.' Jeffrey implies that he and Mrs T. are on the phone to one another almost hourly and that he's in and out of Downing Street like a yoyo.

Over coffee, I get the impression from Denis Thatcher (also of the party) that the contacts are rather less frequent and the relationship a mite less intimate than Jeffrey suggests. Clearly the Thatchers like him, but they have the measure of the man. He's the court jester, not Cardinal Wolsey.

Tuesday, 29 April 1986

Royal news: King Constantine tells me that Sarah Ferguson[§] is 'a great girl', 'really lively' and 'the best thing to happen to the royal family in a long time'. The worst thing to happen to the royal family in a long time is no more. The Duchess of Windsor is dead. She was laid to rest alongside her late husband at Frogmore in Windsor today. The royals turned out in force for the funeral, but no one said a word. There was no address and no mention of her title or her life during the service. The Queen Mother was spared the burial: I imagine by then she was back at Royal Lodge, kicking up her heels and raising a glass.

It's 2.45 a.m. and I am just back from the Grand Hotel, Birmingham, where I have been joining assorted culinary saints – Delia Smith,[¶] Prue Leith,[**] Jancis Robinson,[††] game girls all – raising funds and awareness for 'Food Aid'. Thanks to St Bob we're all at it now.[‡‡] I like the ladies – Jancis knows about wine: Delia knows how to drink it – and I don't forget that it was Mr Delia Smith (Michael Wynne-Jones) who kindly sponsored me when I needed to join the NUJ. Next stop: the Imperial Hotel, Torquay, where I am addressing the sales force of the London

[*] Bryan Organ (b.1935), English portrait painter.
[†] Sir James Gordon Reece (1929–2001), journalist and media adviser to Mrs Thatcher in the 1970s and 1980s.
[‡] Louis Kirby (1928–2006), journalist, editor of the London *Evening Standard*, 1980–86.
[§] Sarah Ferguson (b.1959) became engaged to HRH Prince Andrew, Duke of York, the Queen's second son, in March 1986.
[¶] Delia Smith CBE (b.1941), English cook, cookery writer and TV presenter; she met her future husband, Michael Wynne-Jones, in 1969 when he was setting up the *Daily Mirror* magazine and looking for a cookery correspondent.
[**] Prudence Leith OBE (b.1939), English cook and restaurateur.
[††] Jancis Robinson OBE (b.1950), wine writer.
[‡‡] Robert Geldof KBE (b.1951), Irish singer-songwriter, produced the Band Aid record 'Do They Know It's Christmas?' as a fund-raiser for Ethiopia in 1984, and masterminded the Live Aid concerts in July 1985, raising many millions for famine relief.

Rubber Company. And *then* I am going to the London Palladium, to the Gay and Lesbian Benefit performance of *La Cage aux Folles*, freshly stocked, I imagine, with freebie prophylactics for all. (If it isn't 'Aid' it's AIDS: welcome to the 1980s.)

Tuesday, 6 May 1986

It is coming together at last and I am happy, relieved and pleased. I find that every-thing I *really* want I get – ultimately. Just have to keep at it, that's all. Anyway, the point is: my play about A. A. Milne, with music by Julian Slade, will have its pre-miere at the Arts Theatre, Cambridge on 22 July, as part of the Cambridge Festival. Guy Woolfenden[*] (my brother-in-law's brother) is the Festival director: the play will be directed by James Roose-Evans[†] – I like him, though I am wary of him still. He is a part-time clergyman (with a boyfriend) and a director with a fine track record (notably *84 Charing Cross Road*). The main thing is he understands what we are trying to achieve, he likes the piece (he really does) and he has had an idea of genius. So far we have not found a 'star' to play Milne. We had high hopes of Graham Chapman: he said yes, he said no, he said yes again, he disappeared. (He's mad, he's got AIDS, or both.)[‡] We haven't yet found our Milne, but we have found our Christopher Robin – it's a small part, he only comes on in Act Two – but he is a star: Aled Jones.[§] I went to meet him today at the Barbican. He is 15, but seems much younger – totally straightforward, really nice (normal) parents (Nest and Derek), very keen to give 'acting' a go. We mustn't oversell him because the part is small, but he is exactly what we need. So long as his voice doesn't break. (M has promised to go round between performances and adjust the rubber bands.)

Saturday, 24 May 1986

We went to see Peter Bowles[¶] in *The Entertainer*. He is a wonderful actor, but it's a thin play. Osborne doesn't stand the test of time. John Curry[**] is a wonderful ice

---

[*] Guy Woolfenden OBE (b.1937), composer, conductor, head of music at the Royal Shakespeare Company, 1963–98.

[†] James Roose-Evans (b.1927), theatre director, founder of the Hampstead Theatre Club; author of the *Odd & Elsewhere* children's books.

[‡] In fact, Graham Chapman (1941–89), one of the original Monty Python team, died of a rare form of spinal cancer.

[§] Aled Jones (b.1970), Welsh boy soprano, best known for singing 'Walking in the Air' which reached No. 5 in the UK charts in 1985.

[¶] Peter Bowles (b.1936), actor, soon to become friend and neighbour of GB.

[**] John Curry (1949–94), Olympic and World ice-skating champion, 1976, died of an AIDS-related heart attack.

skater I am sure (Olympic Gold: you can't argue with that) but he isn't an actor. He simply can't do it. He came to the house today to audition for us. He wants to play the part [of A. A. Milne] and James [Roose-Evans] wanted him to be good – wanted it badly. But Curry couldn't cut the mustard: he can't act at all and you can't ask him to be himself because whatever A. A. Milne was, he wasn't a limp-wristed flouncing queen. (Also, I didn't warm to Mr Curry at all. And we must warm to Milne.)

Wednesday, 11 June 1986

I keep bumping into Carol Thatcher[*] – literally. You meet the Prime Minister's daughter and she somehow manages to bash into you. Jolly-hockey-sticks gawky, that's her style. I love her: she's fun and manages the almost impossible – she is Maggie's daughter but she seems *normal*, she hasn't let it ruin her. She despises her brother, openly, but acknowledges that he is the apple of her mother's eye. Had lunch with Carol. Breakfast with Bernard Bresslaw[†] (so tall, so decent) and little Ernie Wise.[‡] Morecambe was funny-ish on his own, but not nearly as funny as he was with Ernie. It was a double act, but the world still treats Ernie as the poor relation. He knows it and resents it.

I think we have found our A. A. Milne. Ian Gelder, not a star, but he can do it. He looks exactly right. And Allan Corduner is going to be glorious.[§] It's shaping up. (This is what I like doing: building a company to make a play. Pity there's no money in it. Heigh ho.)

Saturday, 21 June 1986

We drove up to Leeds yesterday. M drove. She doesn't like me driving. (And she hates me squawking when she drives. I have tried to be good.) I wore my new summer suit, linen, the colour of pale sand – acquired at Selfridges on Thursday afternoon after my triumph in the Fathers' Relay. (Well, someone's got to drop the baton.) The sun shone and settled on Settle very beautifully.[¶] Russell Harty

---

[*] Carol Thatcher (b.1953), journalist daughter of Margaret and Denis Thatcher, and twin sister of Mark.

[†] Bernard Bresslaw stood 6 ft 7.5 ins in bare feet.

[‡] Ernest Wiseman OBE (1925–99) joined forces with Eric Bartholomew OBE, 1926–84, in 1941, and, as Morecambe and Wise, they became a much-loved British comedy institution.

[§] The eventual cast of *Now We Are Sixty* comprised Rosalind Ayres, Peter Bayliss, Allan Corduner, Sarah Crowden, Julian Firth, Ian Gelder and Aled Jones.

[¶] Settle in North Yorkshire, where Russell Harty had a cottage close to Giggleswick, one of England's oldest public schools.

hosted the loveliest drinks party in our honour: champagne, Pimm's, white wine and the kind of conversation I love – a mixture of nonsense and substance. We really did touch on Gracie Fields, Henry Fielding and the Field of the Cloth of Gold. We talked about Pa, too. And Nevill Coghill. Russell was at Exeter [College, Oxford] – got a First and it shows. When he taught at Giggleswick, Richard Whiteley was one of his pupils – and now Russell's in Dictionary Corner and Richard is hosting the show. But still Richard is in awe of his old teacher. Giggleswick is everything to Richard. 'I love the place. I love it more and more.' It's the chapel he loves most, he said. 'You feel quite close to God there, you really do.' Richard thought of becoming a clergyman. He still says his prayers, every night, in bed, before going to sleep. He is a sweet man. And we had a happy evening. After drinks we went on to supper at the Cock Revived. 'They named it for me,' said Russell. 'Alan Bennett disputes that,' said Richard.

This morning I did my stuff, officially opening the Study Centre at Catteral Hall, the Giggleswick prep school. I have my name on a plaque. I like that.

Friday, 27 June 1986

I've reached the end of the road with the temp.[*] Last night, she left a complete folder of correspondence on my desk for me to approve and sign. Every letter – every document – was gibberish: beautifully typed gobbledygook from start to finish. It isn't drink. It's drugs. I don't know what kind and I don't care. I have told her she has to go. She was tearful, but said she knew it was coming.

With Julian [Slade], it's drugs *and* drink. He's on prescription medicaments of every kind and he washes them down with alcohol. And when he's nervous he goes completely overboard. Today, in the garden, in the sunshine, we had the *Now We Are Sixty* company lunch: cast, choreographer, director, designer, lighting, stage management, the lot. It was a happy gathering – until we got to pudding. Julian started to smear the jelly and cream all over his face: he just dipped his hand in the bowl and slowly, grinning inanely, he smeared it all over himself. Heart-breaking.

Sunday, 29 June 1986

This morning we took the children to Barnes to see the house we think we are going to buy. The upside: it's detached, late Victorian, huge, with high ceilings, a good basement, a great garden and a swimming pool. The children loved the

---

[*] At this stage, as well as GB and Michèle, the Victorama team comprised a secretary, three editors and a book-keeper.

swimming pool. Of course. The vendor is Peter Marsh, advertising man.[*] He is selling his company and going abroad for a year to avoid tax. We found him floating in the middle of the pool, seated in an inflatable armchair, sporting a straw fedora, smoking a cigar and holding a drink in one hand and a portable telephone in the other. He is a ludicrous figure and he knows it – but it's what made him his fortune. He is the fellow who pitched for the British Rail account and when the executives arrived at his offices to meet him he wasn't there, the reception area was filthy and it took half an hour for Peter to appear. When he did, he said: 'Now, gentlemen, you know what it feels like to be a customer of British Rail.' I imagine he is a nightmare to live with. (He was married to Pat Phoenix, but not for long. His present wife looks pretty cowed.) There is an internal sound system that enables him to speak to any room in the house at will. There are security cameras everywhere – including one on the front doorstep so that, in the morning, in bed, he can see when the newspapers have arrived. We'll need to make superficial changes – we don't need a Victorian billiard room, nor the two walk-in safes for the solid gold dinner service, nor the enclosed 'run' in the garden for the Irish wolfhounds – but, fundamentally, it's got everything we want. Except . . . There is a downside: it's south of the river. M thinks I'm absurd. And I know I am, but I never thought I'd live south of the river. You don't. One doesn't. I have lived in London all my life. I know these things. One lives in Marylebone or Mayfair or Kensington. And that's that. Barnes is halfway to Southampton dammit – and on the Heathrow flight-path . . . but it's near St Paul's [School] which is good for Benet and Hammersmith is on the Piccadilly Line and it *is* a lovely house and I don't need to *tell* anyone we've moved . . .

Tuesday, 1 July 1986

Prince Philip came to Ovington Square today [the offices of the National Playing Fields Association]. We gave him a belated birthday present: three pairs of carriage-driving gloves – chosen by Sue, Sandy's wife-to-be. (She's pukka: she knows about these things.) HRH unwrapped the parcel and inspected his gift. The first pair of gloves were a light tan colour. He sniffed approvingly. The second pair were dark tan. He said, 'Thank you very much.' The third pair were a pale lilac colour. He held them up disdainfully between his thumb and forefinger and said, 'I think we'll give these to the Prince of Wales.'

[*] Peter Marsh (b.1931), co-founder of the Allen, Brady & Marsh advertising agency in 1966. He married Pat Phoenix (who later played Elsie Tanner in *Coronation Street*) when, briefly, he was an actor, but the marriage only lasted a year. He divorced his second wife shortly after selling his house to the Brandreths.

Wednesday, 2 July 1986

Breakfast at TV-am with Christiaan Barnard.* Yes, I have shaken the hand that conducted the world's first heart transplant. It is a shaky hand now and the poor man has arthritis. He seemed a touch 'on the edge'. He believes he may have found the elixir of youth – actually, a very expensive face cream. Judging by appearances, I don't think it's very effective.†

Dinner in the dining room: Leslie and Shirley Porter, Christopher and Helen Leaver, Prue Leith and Rayne [Kruger, her husband], Claire Palley‡ and Kenneth Williams. It went well, until Kenneth got totally carried away. He didn't quite drop his trousers to reveal the 'bum hanging down in pleats', but he certainly talked about it and he used the c-word to Dr Palley repeatedly. I couldn't contain him. M said, 'Never again.'

Thursday, 3 July 1986

Went with Sandy Gilmour [the chairman of NPFA] to see Sir John Harvey-Jones at ICI.§ It was a waste of time. Sir John saw us because he is a genial cove who is fond of Sandy. He chuntered amiably, screwed up his face and twitched his eyebrows, but couldn't really help us because it was clear that we didn't know exactly what we wanted.

Just in from the TV-am flotation drinks party. We know what we want: investors. And they'll be there. We are becoming a success. (Of course, it was much more fun when we had our backs against the wall.)

Monday, 7 July 1986

Yesterday we had all the NPFA staff and all the NPFA Appeals Committee over for lunch in the garden – about thirty in all, plus children. John Holborn [from NPFA] has just called. Everyone was ill afterwards. Everyone. 'I thought you'd want to know.' The curse of coronation chicken. This is so embarrassing I have to change the subject. Martina Navratilova and Boris Becker have each won their Finals at Wimbledon.

---

* Christiaan Barnard (1922–2001), South African cardiac surgeon who performed the world's first successful human-to-human heart transplant, 1967.

† It wasn't. He later publicly regretted his promotion of Glycel, a self-proclaimed 'anti-ageing' cream.

‡ Dr Claire Palley, Principal of St Anne's College, Oxford, 1984–91; Michèle was then editing the St Anne's alumni magazine, *The Ship*.

§ Sir John Harvey-Jones (1924–2008), chairman of ICI, 1982–7.

Wednesday, 16 July 1986

We celebrated Winnie-the-Pooh's 60th birthday at TV-am and I managed to get in plenty of plugs for *Now We Are Sixty*. We need them: we haven't sold out yet. Coffee with Richard Harris,[*] who is a (well-organised) shambles (he has been on the wagon three years now, but the two bottles of vodka a day have taken their toll). I like him – he plays the gentle Irish-eyes-are-smiling card to perfection, but his 'star quality', either on screen or off, I don't quite get. Also Suzi Quatro,[†] who managed to be fun and quite sexy at 7.30 in the morning. (Don't knock it: it's a skill.)

This morning I addressed the Jewish Blind Society (they could see: they were good-hearted female fund-raisers: Golders Green was empty on my account). This afternoon I went to a run-through of *NWAS*. We're getting there. This evening we had an NPFA Appeals Committee meeting. Raising money is *hell*. Then supper with the Shadbolts [members of the committee]. Nice people. We talked about Horatio Nelson.

I am v tired and a touch depressed. We have spent a lot of time wooing Lazard's.[‡] We are getting nowhere – though I am becoming familiar with the style of the modern merchant banker: smooth, skin too full, suits, braces, effortlessly superior, they patronise you with such ease and then go back to their rather ordinary homes in Stamford Brook. They operate in packs, never fewer than two, usually four or five, including a token female who makes notes in a large book. We don't talk their language, nor they ours.

Monday, 21 July 1986

The end of a long day. But good. Started on *Start the Week* with Aled [Jones]. He is a darling. So is Nest, his mum. Train with them to Cambridge. Arrived at 11.40 a.m. At 12 noon I was on air. From 12 to 2.00 p.m. every day for the next fortnight I am hosting the lunch-time show on BBC Radio Cambridgeshire – I am determined to sell every ticket for every performance of *Now We Are Sixty* at the Arts. They said it couldn't be done: it will be.[§]

This afternoon, photocall, TV call, tech. The set is simple, but it works. The show is simple, but it works. Aled's entrance in Act II is electric. James [Roose-

---

[*] Richard Harris (1930–2002), Irish actor, singer, film star.
[†] Suzi Quatro (b. Susan Quatrocchio, 1950), American singer-songwriter.
[‡] GB and Adrian Gilpin were still trying to raise investment for their 'Royal Britain' exhibition at the Barbican. Eventually, the money was raised through a Business Expansion Scheme fund promoted by Charles Fry of Johnson Fry.
[§] It was. At the end of the run, the manager gave GB a framed drawing of the Arts Theatre to mark the run's sell-out success.

Evans, the director] has Aled start the song ('Little boy kneels at the foot of the bed') off-stage, so as to kill the possibility of an entrance round. The boy looks perfect. And quite unselfconscious. Everyone is in love with him. Peter Bayliss[*] has Aled sitting on his knee whenever Aled will allow it – and because Aled is lovely (and sane and knows what's going on) he allows it quite a lot.

Wednesday, 23 July 1986

A long day. Up at dawn to TV-am for the special 'Andy & Fergie' show.[†] I did my stuff. Train to Cambridge. 12 noon, my two-hour radio stint: I did my stuff. Tonight: *Now We Are Sixty*: the Royal Wedding Gala – a piece of wedding cake for everyone and a speech from me. Yes, I did my stuff.

Also today: we exchanged contracts on the house in Castelnau. A new era awaits.

Thursday, 24 July 1986

Press Night. I couldn't bear to watch, so, once the house was in, I walked the streets of Cambridge for an hour. (They were deserted.) I got back to the theatre just before the interval and stood alone in the little corridor at the back of the stalls. Suddenly I heard a soft bang – the sound of a seat going up as someone was leaving. It was followed by another. Then another. My stomach lurched. The audience was leaving – one by one they were walking out of the show. My mouth went dry. My heart stopped. And then the penny dropped. The distant noise was the sound of a keg of beer being humped down the stairs to the bar. But that's how paranoid we poor authors can be . . .

I was going to stay with Jeffrey and Mary Archer this weekend at the Old Vicarage, Grantchester, but I have cancelled. I'm too jangly. (I can't relax. I don't relax. I get through life by working.)

Wednesday, 30 July 1986

6.00 a.m. car. Boy George[‡] at TV-am – common piggy-face beneath the make-up, but amusing, intelligent, gay and giggly. We liked one another.
10.35 a.m. from Liverpool Street, straight to the Spade & Becket for 'Smiles with Gyles' – I did my radio show as an OB today. Then Anglia TV filming at Trinity

---

* Peter Bayliss (1922–2002), tall, fruity-voiced English character actor.
† HRH Prince Andrew, created Duke of York on his wedding day, married Sarah Ferguson at Westminster Abbey on 23 July 1986. They were divorced on 30 May 1996.
‡ Boy George (b. George O'Dowd, 1961), English singer-songwriter; part of Culture Club in the early 1980s, he was beginning to enjoy a solo career in 1986.

College – I was so exhausted when I came to talk about A. A. Milne that I put up no defences, offered no artifice, and was really, *really* good.

3.00 p.m.   Garden House Hotel cast tea party – Martin Jarvis[*] came too. He has been very supportive.

6.00 p.m.   Cambridge Arts Club workshop: James Roose-Evans (in knee boots in July) and I did most of the talking: Julian [Slade] sat by, weeping quietly.

Good performance tonight. Cast supper at Charlie Chan's. We all talked about the show's 'future' knowing that, almost certainly, it has none. This is what we do. With every show there is always talk of 'a tour', 'a transfer', a cast album, a producer who wants to take it to Australia. Actors live on hope. I don't think the case for us is hopeless – but Aled's voice is on the brink of breaking and, without him, we have no star. And the piece needs a star. It isn't (I own it) *robust* enough without. Julian's music is too gentle. My words too whimsical. We've buckets of charm, but no cutting edge.

And the other thing we all do on nights like tonight is exchange phone numbers and promise to keep in touch. We know we won't, but we might and, in the moment, we mean to. We really do.

My favourite theatre story. The young actor, playing Hamlet for the first time, wrestling with the complexities of the role, seeks advice from one of the older members of the company. 'Excuse me, sir, but I have been wondering about Hamlet's relationship with Ophelia. Do you think Hamlet actually sleeps with Ophelia?' 'I don't know about the West End, laddie,' replies the old stager, 'but we always did on tour.'

In a small company, rehearsing together, playing together, living together, for a brief spell, we all fall in love. It's intense, ridiculous and transient. I love it.

Saturday, 9 August 1986

The girls have gone to Brownie camp. I have taken Neville [one of the Brandreth cats] to the vet. We are going to *A Room with a View*.

I spent the day yesterday with Imagination.[†] They are designing Royal Britain

---

[*] Martin Jarvis (b.1941), English actor, married to Rosalind Ayres (b.1946) who was the leading lady in *Now We Are Sixty*.

[†] Imagination, international design agency, initially specialising in trade exhibitions, founded by Gary Withers in 1978.

for us. I like the founder, Gary Withers, and he likes me. We amuse each other. And we can both talk the talk. Can we walk the walk, I wonder?

Sunday, 17 August 1986

Visit Patrick Cadell, age three days, at Queen Charlotte's. He looked like babies look. Beckie looked pink and happy. Simon came back with us for supper, unshaven, exhausted, but content, I think. He smoked several celebratory cigars and we wet the baby's head with a 1968 Moët. (You pronounce the 't'. Derek Nimmo told me so. The Moëts were Dutch, not French.)

Saturday, 27 September 1986

We completed on Castelnau yesterday. I was in Leeds for the final of *Countdown*, plus the extended celebrations of the 500th episode. We arrived at the house at lunch-time today to find the Marshes still moving out. It's our house, but they are still there! And walking off with things we think we now own – e.g. the kitchen table. M put a stop to it. And they *have* left us the doorknobs. And there's water in the swimming pool. (It's going to be fine.)

Saturday, 4 October 1986

I went to see Sir Leslie Porter, chairman of Tesco, at his office in Piccadilly. It was 9.30 in the morning. He seemed startled to see me and a bit anxious as I walked across the room to greet him. When I got to him, I realised why. On the screen on his desk he was watching a Mickey Mouse cartoon.

I am writing this on the train from Manchester. I have been at the Royal Exchange Theatre wearing my hat as a children's author. It went well. I met up with Michael Rosen (+ sons). At Oxford he was one of the golden boys, destined to be at least the new Wesker, if not the new Pinter . . . and now? Well, his children's books do very well. He has found his niche. (That's what the world wants you to do: find your niche and sit in it.)

Friday, 21 November 1986

I took Cyril Fletcher to TV-am. He'd so love a gardening slot. He is 73 and sprightly and says, when he is wearing his trilby at a jaunty angle, nobody notices his wall-eye. Andy Williams[*] is knocking 60, but does not look it. He is small, but perfectly formed and effortlessly charming. 'My kind of singing is coming back,' he said. 'As far as I am concerned, it never went away,' I replied. (Okay, pass the sickbag, Mabel.)

[*] Howard Andrew Williams (b.1927), American singer.

I am writing this at the Shakespeare Hotel, Stratford-upon-Avon. I stayed in our house here last night, but I am treating myself to a 'full English' before I go down the road at ten o'clock to visit the Chaucer Head Bookshop. We are thinking of buying it: we would retain a bookshop on the ground floor and add a family visitor attraction upstairs – either a Museum of the Miniature (doll's houses and all that's tiny) or a Teddy Bear Museum . . . It's an idea that's come to us because, at the moment, Stratford is all Shakespeare – it needs a *family* attraction.

Wednesday, 26 November 1986

If you want twenty-four hours that give you a fair impression of my life right now, here they are. Last night, the start of series 12 of *Countdown* followed by a long drive to London with the producer John Meade, who spent every minute of the journey telling me what a remarkable and undervalued talent he has. I agreed. TV-am this morning with David Essex (a star who isn't) and Petula Clark (ditto, I fear).* (Having just written that, I can hear M saying: 'They've both done rather better than you, though, haven't they?' And, yes, they have. But my point still stands.) Coffee with Paul Levinson at Prestwich Holdings to talk about my idea for a series of video quizzes which I shall host. I think he liked it and I think I liked him. He spent much of the meeting telling me I was 'driving my own taxi' and limiting my income potential as a consequence. I agreed (and I do). Race to Guildford to supervise the felling of Britain's Tallest Christmas Tree – wearing my Christmas tree jumper, of course. Race back to Leicester Square for Royal Britain board meeting and Imagination presentation. Dinner with M at the Caprice. (Where are my children? Where is the life of the mind? Well, you can't have everything all the time.)

Thursday, 18 December 1986

Lunch with Jeffrey [Archer] at the Caprice. His capacity to bounce back is extraordinary. He seems totally unaffected by the Monica Coghlan affair.† He's

---

* David Essex OBE (b. David Cook, 1947), English actor-singer, and Petula Clark CBE (b.1932), English singer.
† Allegations about Archer and a Rochdale-born Mayfair prostitute, Monica Coghlan (1951–2001), had appeared in the *News of the World* and *Daily Star* in October and forced Archer to resign as Deputy Chairman of the Conservative Party. On 24 October 1986, the *News of the World* filmed and audiotaped Michael Stacpoole, on behalf of Archer, giving Coghlan £2,000 in £50 notes on Platform 3 of London's Victoria Station to help her leave the country to avoid reporters. In 1987 Archer successfully sued the *Daily Star* over their allegation that he had had sex with Coghlan and won record damages of £500,000. It was his perjury in this case that led to his trial and imprisonment in 2001.

determined to get back into politics eventually, but meanwhile he is going to make 'a few more million' with his books. He is extraordinarily boastful when he doesn't need to be. He says he has made £12 million, when I know from his publishers it's £5 million at most. He has to exaggerate everything. Today he told me he had won the Somerset Maugham Award! It can't be true.

After lunch we walked up to Piccadilly and made a detour via the Ritz where he searched out the head waiter and ostentatiously pressed a £50 note into his hand. 'Merry Christmas,' said Jeffrey to the fawning maitre d'. 'That's the way to get the right table, Gyles.' I am sure it is.

He is both absurd and delightful. At lunch, I told him all about the Royal Britain venture. As we were passing through the lobby of the Ritz he stopped by one of the telephones and picked it up. 'I am just going to have a word with my financial adviser,' he said, a touch too loudly. When he got through he said simply, 'I have been having lunch with my friend Gyles Brandreth. He's been telling me about a Business Expansion Scheme of his – it's called Royal Britain. How much can I put in? £50,000? £30,000? £30,000 it is then.' He replaced the receiver and turned to me, beaming. 'There you are, Gyles. £30,000 for you. Merry Christmas.'

Sunday, 19 April 1987

It is Easter Sunday and I am writing this in the front room of our little house in Stratford-upon-Avon. From the room above me – the girls' bedroom – you can see the church where Shakespeare is buried. I like that a lot. What I don't like – but can do nothing about – is the fact that our car was broken into last night. We were the fools: we left a suitcase and my briefcase in full view on the back seat. The suitcase contained several of my jumpers and GB, the toy black cat that I use on TV-am. The briefcase contained my diary. The police say that they might turn up, dumped because they are of no value.

I had a pang about losing the diary – but it didn't last long. It's just the first three-and-a-half months of the year that have gone – thousands of words, hours of scribbling, but it doesn't matter, really. I know that. I had thought for a moment this morning of not mentioning the break-in, so that January to April 1987 could become the mysterious 'missing months', the only months in my life that have gone unrecorded. Where was he? What happened? What was going on? The truth is we know *exactly* what was going on. My life has a routine to it now – I write books, I publish books, I create games, I have projects, I go to NPFA, I run the National Scrabble Championships, I go to *Countdown*, I go to TV-am, I go to the theatre. I see everything. *Hyde Park* at the Swan last night,

Phantom of the Opera at Her Majesty's on Wednesday. (We came out whistling the chandelier. And then had supper at the Caprice.) Most weeks have their highs, their treats, their surprises – this week we took the children to the Beaconsfield model village: that was fun; and on Tuesday, at TV-am, courtesy of the *Daily Mail*, I was able to handle the Duchess of Windsor's jewellery; and, in the afternoon, at the Contact the Elderly charity tea at the Barbican, we hobnobbed with Princess Alexandra . . . It's all fine, it's all good (I am content), but it's quite predictable. I am not rocking the world. Three months of my life has gone missing – and even I don't care.

Wednesday, 22 April 1987

And to prove the point . . . yesterday I went to Leeds and recorded the first four episodes of *Countdown*, series 13. Richard Whiteley loves the show so much he hopes it lasts for ever. It probably will. And if it does, Richard will have spent his one life on earth simply sitting behind a desk growing fatter while repeating the words: 'And the *Countdown* clock starts now.'

This morning, tea and toast with Lulu. I fancy her and do nothing about it. Rest of the day, meetings about Royal Britain: we are going to make it happen. That'll be good. This evening: Barn Elms meeting at Castelnau Library. I am chairman of the Barn Elms Protection Association. Our aim: to safeguard the future of Barn Elms, the 100-acre site behind our house where Samuel Pepys once walked. Henry Fielding, too. The reservoirs on the site will soon be surplus to the requirements of Thames Water. What will happen to the land then? A housing estate? A shopping mall? It's a site of special scientific interest. We must protect it and will. This is Nimbyism, of course, but with a higher purpose.

Sunday, 3 May 1987

I became a godfather again today. My new godson is Benjamin Bridgeman, third offspring of the Earl and Countess of Bradford. The christening was nicely done and the lunch beforehand in the Orangery at Weston Park was very jolly. But I know already that I will be a useless godfather. I don't care. I'm not interested. I said yes because I was asked and couldn't say no. The baby is sweet: I was pleased to hold him in my arms. But I have no *feeling* for him. I realise I have very little feeling for anyone beyond M and the children. Last Sunday I was moved by seeing Aphra and Saethryd in the Brownie church parade. I am moved by my own children and by Shakespeare – and that's about it. (We went to *The Merchant* in Stratford last night. The 'In such a night as this' sequence at the beginning of Act V never fails to bring tears to my eyes. It is the loveliest poetry I know.)

Heigh ho. M will remember my godchildren's birthdays and buy them presents. I will make the right noises. The really good people in this world are the women who run the Brownies. Week in, week out, they do it. (Oh yes, I do lots of things for assorted charities, but it's not the same and I know it.)

Wednesday, 6 May 1987

David Rappaport at TV-am. We all pretended not to notice that he is a dwarf. On air, he was very jolly, saying how gratifying it is to be taken seriously as an actor. Off air, he was morose. In his heart he knows that when he works he is being engaged as a gifted freak.*

This morning: dentist – as ever, my teeth are in perfect nick. Sotheby's sale – bought a signed first edition of *Winnie-the-Pooh* for our Teddy Bear Museum. This afternoon: NPFA. This evening: dinner party – Jeffrey Archer, Alec McCowen, Clare Palley, Noel Davis, Robert and Elizabeth Burchfield. (Jeffrey was bombastic for the first half-hour, then calmed down and was delightful. Noel was surprised by how much he liked him.) A dinner party is a responsibility. Every time, at the beginning of the evening, before the guests arrive, when we are lighting the candles and feeling exhausted and worrying about the *placement*, we say, 'Never again.' And every time, when it's over, and it's been rather jolly, and we've heard stories we haven't heard before, and Noel has set the table on a roar, we think, 'Well, it wasn't too bad. Perhaps one more . . .'

Sunday, 31 May 1987

Went to the Laurence Olivier 80th Birthday Gala at the National Theatre. It never took off. The stars came out – Peggy Ashcroft, Albert Finney, Jeremy Irons, Antony Sher, etc., dozens of them – but they failed to shine. The only thing that lit up the night sky were the fireworks over the river once it was over. And Sir Laurence. He was there – plus Joanie and the children – sitting, rather awkwardly, to one side of the stage. We wanted him on it, of course. They should have let him stand centre stage in a spotlight. That's all we wanted. As it was, we cheered him where we found him – to the side, looking like a slightly bewildered old colonel, tiny eyes glinting behind heavy spectacles. We went on cheering: he went on waving. Nothing else about the evening was in the least bit memorable.

---

* David Rappaport (1951–90), English actor, 3 ft 11 ins tall, best remembered as the leader of the band of dwarves in the Terry Gilliam film *Time Bandits*, 1981; he committed suicide, shooting himself in the chest in California in May 1990.

Thursday, 11 June 1987

I had a cup of tea and scrambled eggs on toast with Placido Domingo* this morning. (That's the joy of TV-am: money before breakfast *and* breakfast.) Placido was very unstarry – sane, intelligent, unassuming. Now I'm off to vote. Jeremy Hanley† is the Conservative candidate here: a tall man, full of bounce and spirit. Peter Marsh introduced us and he is now a proper friend. He has my vote.

Friday, 12 June 1987

Mrs Thatcher is returned for a third 'historic' term. No Prime Minister has achieved this in more than a century, but no one is surprised. Even those who don't like her have to admire her. (That said, those that hate her truly despise her.) Anyway, the results:

Conservatives: 375 seats
Labour: 229
The 'Alliance' (SDP/Libs): 22 (hardly the breakthrough the mould-breakers had hoped for.)
Others: 24

We are giving a dinner party: Anneka Rice ('rear of the year' and lovely) & Nick Allott,‡ Sue & Peter Bowles (introduced to us by Peter Marsh and now good friends), Francesca & Adrian Gilpin.

Tuesday, 23 June 1987

I am reading the obituaries for Fred Astaire. They all quote the verdict on his first screen test: 'Can't act. Can't sing. Can dance a little.' I think, as a child, I wanted to *be* Fred Astaire, which is ludicrous as I have no feeling for music and can't dance at all. It is, I suppose, because he was Ma's great idol – and because his effortless dancing epitomises style. On screen (though he is not the least bit handsome) you cannot take your eyes off him.

The news of his death came through last night when I was on the set recording *Give Us a Clue* (Michael Parkinson, Lisa Goddard, Lennie Bennett, etc.). Lionel

---

* José Plácido Domingo Embil KBE (b.1941), Spanish operatic tenor.
† Sir Jeremy Hanley KCMG (b.1945), Conservative MP for Richmond and Barnes, 1983–97.
‡ Anneka Rice (b. Anne, 1958), TV presenter, won the accolade 'rear of the year' as the jump-suited 'skyrunner' on *Treasure Hunt* on Channel 4, 1983–8; married to theatre producer, Nicholas Allott, until 1992.

Blair burst into tears at the news and, blubbing, fled from the room. Wayne Sleep, also pretty nifty on his toes, raised a weary eyebrow. Eventually, Lionel returned and, with a supreme effort, bravely soldiered on.

Breakfast with Terence Stamp. The blue eyes are indeed wonderful and he was less *alarming* than I would have expected. He was rather gentle: he likes being a writer as much as being an actor – but I imagine his writing lacks the common touch. Supper with Joanna Lumley and Stephen Barlow.* He is a muso – and quite serious about it: he looks on Jo's show-folk friends with a degree of suspicion (and superiority?) – but I think he's decided to accept us. It was a very happy evening. We laughed a lot.

Friday, 26 June 1987

At TV-am this morning we said farewell to our weather girl Wincy Willis. I was dressed as a gorilla (naturally). We are just in from a congenial dinner down the road with Peter and Sue Bowles – generous and civilised. (Peter has a wonderful eye for good modern pictures.) Other guests: Camilla and Nigel Dempster† and Hilary and Michael Whitehall.‡ I like Dempster (I can afford to: he's done me no harm). I told him I could imagine no life more ghastly than his, grubbing around for dirt every day of your life. 'Oh,' he said, 'it's not like that at all – most people call *me* with their stories. They dish the dirt on themselves. They really do.' Michael Whitehall is almost as funny as Noel Davis, but a lot more waspish. He has respresented everybody *for a while*. They tend to move on . . . I think he and Martin Jarvis are no longer on speaking terms. He murmured that our host (Peter Bowles) is 'a fine actor, underrated, and not always easy to "place" because he has a reputation for being difficult. You know his nickname? "The irritable Bowles syndrome".' He said this as Peter stood immediately behind us, pouring the wine.

Tuesday, 7 July 1987

I organised an amusing event in the forecourt of Buckingham Palace today: the launch of the NPFA Million Mile Walk. I had a line-up of 'walkers' in novelty costumes and persuaded Prince Philip to inspect them as a kind of guard of

* Stephen Barlow (b.1954), English conductor and composer, married Joanna Lumley in 1986.
† Nigel Dempster (1941–2007), gossip columnist, best-known as the diarist in the *Daily Mail*, 1973–2001.
‡ Michael Whitehall, theatrical agent whose clients have ranged from Stewart Granger to Judi Dench.

honour. He raised a wary eyebrow, but went through with it – and played ball when it came to being photographed with the clown on stilts. Essentially, he lets the photographer get three shots of every set-up and then moves on. He told me, 'I have met a lot of photographers since I married the Queen. They only ever say one thing: "Just one more." But "just one more" is never enough.'

I have a new toy, a new video camera. In the garden tonight I filmed our guests before dinner: John Schlesinger, Pamela Harlech,* Noel Davis, Stefan Bednarczyk, Peter and Sue Bowles. Prompted by my morning at the Palace, Noel told lots of old royal stories – e.g. King George V out for a stroll in the gardens of Buckingham Palace, asking why his customary equerry was not in attendance. His Majesty was told the man was unwell. 'What's wrong with him?' asked the King. 'Oh, the usual complaint, sir.' Next day Queen Mary remarked to someone, 'I hear His Majesty's equerry is ill. What is the matter with him?' 'A bad attack of haemorrhoids, Ma'am,' was the reply. 'Oh?' said the Queen. 'Why did the King tell me it was the clap?'

Monday, 13 July 1987

Last night, dinner with Tim Heald & Alison, Peter Tinniswood & wife, and David Benedictus after lamentable Writers' Evening at Hatchard's in Richmond as part of the Richmond Festival. Other than the Festival Committee, the shop assistants, two drunks from the local newspaper and a couple of crones who quaffed the warm white wine but bought nothing, the place was deserted. M and I were pacing the streets searching for the bookshop when we came across Kenneth Robinson, looking haggard and unhappy, suffering terribly over his dismissal from *Start the Week*. (Only a radio programme, but to him everything.) He spoke at once of his unhappy marriage: 'If only I had murdered her when I first thought of it, I'd be out of prison by now.'

Wednesday, 15 July 1987

I am in Leeds doing the final of *Countdown* with Derek Nimmo. Our producer is a nightmare: a heavy drinker, a heavy smoker and the other day he was sub-poenaed as a witness in the trial of a notorious Leeds 'Madam'. As Derek said, '*Countdown* is such a cosy programme. If only the viewers knew!'

Derek is good value, always gregarious, always full of good stories. Today he told me about the Liverpool landlady who had recently had Frankie Howerd

---

* Born Pamela Colin (1935), American writer and editor; came to England as London editor of *Vogue* in 1964 and married Lord Harlech in 1969.

staying. 'Such a sad man,' she said, 'so lonely. He would have been all by himself, but as chance would have it, his cousin was in town – a Portuguese sailor – and he came to stay as well.'

Monday, 3 August 1987

Bodrum, Turkey

In a word, this holiday is a disaster. The night before we were due to fly out, Corfu Villas telephoned to say that, 'unfortunately', the gullet earmarked for us was no longer available. A larger party had come along and, for some reason still not clear to me, this larger party had to take priority. Corfu Villas would find us an alternative boat 'as soon as possible'.

Five days on we are still sweltering in the torrid heat of Bodrum. 'Bodrum equals badroom' is what they say around here. I am not surprised. The hotel is adequate, but it has no air conditioning and the heat is quite simply intolerable. We think we have now found a boat to go on. It isn't what we booked – a traditional gullet with plenty of cabin space and a proper deck to sunbathe and eat on. It is a motorboat – a mini-yacht, with a couple of tiny cabins, a tiny deck and a crew of two: the owner/captain, a large man in his fifties, and his little friend, wiry and monkey-like, who acts as mate and ship's cook. They speak no English, but are friendly. We had coffee with them after inspecting the boat in the marina. The captain kept pointing at me and my book and grinning, saying, 'Ernest Hemingway, Ernest Hemingway' – they appear to be the only English words he knows. Actually, I am reading Anthony Trollope, *The Way We Live Now*. It is only Trollope who is getting us through this. (M is reading it, too. When I finish a page, I tear it out and pass it to her. These are desperate times.) We have told the Corfu Villas rep that so long as we can sail in silence and all the music equipment comes off the boat (there are giant speakers taking up half the deck), we'll take it. Anything to get away from the hell of Bodrum.

Thursday, 6 August 1987

It could be worse, but not much. We have to keep the boat moving because we need 'the winters' to keep us relatively cool. ('The winters' meaning 'the wind' are the only other two English words the captain appears to know.) But, unfortunately, when the boat moves, M gets seasick. She has spent most of every day simply lying in our cabin with her eyes closed, moaning. She says she feels like death. She says she wants to die. We are not due to fly back until Wednesday. Tonight we are stopping off at Marmaris and taking dinner on shore.

Friday, 7 August 1987

This, I think, is very funny. Last night, we arrived in Marmaris. (Bodrum/badroom – Marmaris/marvellous.) The captain indicated that he would meet us on the quayside at 8.00 p.m. We emerged on time – M so grateful to be on dry land. We found the captain, but barely recognised him. Gone were his baggy shorts and T-shirt. He was cleanly shaven and dressed in an elegant white linen suit. We followed him into the town and, as we went, we noticed that people were looking at us. At first, I assumed they were British tourists who happened to be *Countdown* and TV-am viewers – but, very quickly, it became clear that it was the captain they recognised. He took us beyond the marina to a restaurant where the best table awaited us. As we arrived, other diners looked up and stared: some got to their feet and applauded. It turns out that the captain of our little boat is Turkey's Frank Sinatra.

In fact, he is Frank Sinatra and Cliff Richard combined – crooner and pop singer, Turkey's biggest singing star. It seems he comes to the London Palladium once a year and fills it with London's Turkish community. And every summer he spends a month on his boat with his oldest friend (our cook) cruising around the Mediterranean and writing songs. He writes a new album every summer – except this year it will be a little difficult because we ordered all his recording equipment off the boat! He has been happy to give up a week to take us cruising because the people from Corfu Villas told him I was a famous English writer. Indeed, he is under the misapprehension that I am England's Ernest Hemingway! We have not disabused him.

Friday, 4 September 1987

It's all happening in London. AIDS is rife – the Government is launching an explicit new advertising campaign. We are moving offices. I am about to become a director of a chain of wool shops. I have done a voice-over for Opal Fruits, finished *The Slippers that Talked*, chosen the Royal Britain merchandise, launched the Monopoly Championships in Belfast and recorded *I've Got a Secret* with Frankie Howerd. (He looked at me very warily, kept shifting his hairpiece.) We are now recovering with a weekend in the south of France with Simon and Beckie. Last night, champagne cocktails at the Hôtel Paris in Monte Carlo, followed by dinner at the Voile d'Or at Saint-Jean-Cap-Ferrat. Tonight, we are just in from a perfect meal at Roger Vergé's Moulin de Mougins, with the great man emerging from the kitchens and doing the rounds looking like a culinary Burl Ives.

Wednesday, 16 September 1987

Jeffrey [Archer] has invested £30,000 in our Royal Britain venture. I felt the least I could do was invest £1,000 in his play. Tonight we went to see it – the 'royal' preview' with Sarah York – and, to my astonishment, I think my money may be safe.* *Beyond Reasonable Doubt* is no masterpiece: you can see the joins, there are too many quotes from Dylan Thomas and far too many old chestnuts from the *Oxford Book of Legal Anecdotes*, but it *is* entertaining, it *does* hold you and M said she was more affected by Wendy Craig's death in this than Judi Dench's in *Antony and Cleopatra*.

This morning, tea and toast with Arthur Marx, son of the great Groucho. He looks like a cross between his father and mine and still has ambivalent, unresolved feelings about the old genius. But he confirmed that my favourite Groucho story is true. When he was hosting the game show, *You Bet Your Life*, he came face to face with a contestant – a Mrs Story – who had twenty-two children. 'I just love my husband,' she announced happily. 'I like my cigar too,' Groucho responded, 'but I take it out of my mouth once in a while.' (The exchange was edited out of the broadcast.)

At lunch-time, at the White Elephant in Curzon Street, I found myself sitting at the next table to King Hussein of Jordan. He and Queen Noor sat in silence watched over by three armed guards.

Monday, 28 September 1987

At the Epsom and Ewell Back Pain Association Tenth Anniversary Meeting (has it come to this?) I found myself sharing the platform with Edwina Currie MP, Parliamentary Under-Secretary of State for Health. I hadn't seen her since Oxford. She hasn't changed a bit – as bossy as ever and still thinking she's rather sexy. But I do like her and I was pleased to see her – though she arrived late, and in a state, and said she couldn't, *wouldn't* give a speech as promised. I gave the speech and we shared an Any Questions session. I was surprised Edwina didn't try to make more friends – the poor Mayor and Mayoress, the photographers, the old schoolfriend who hadn't seen Edwina for twenty-five years, etc., all got pretty short shrift.

---

* It was. *Beyond Reasonable Doubt*, starring Frank Finlay and Wendy Craig, repaid investors threefold. Jeffrey, by contrast, lost every penny of his investment in the 'Royal Britain' venture.

Wednesday, 7 October 1987

I am on the 10.30 a.m. shuttle to Belfast where I am presenting NPFA's £5,000 grants to a variety of Northern Ireland play schemes. In Northern Ireland, when building a playground, you have to build in 'protection money' to the contract or the playground will be vandalised. The sectarian divide is ingrained in the culture: the paramilitary (on both sides) have a hold on everything.

Happy start to the day at TV-am. Joe Bugner and Cathy Tyson were the guests. Bugner* is an amiable ox of a man, 6' 4", eighteen stone, 37, and about to earn a quarter of a million fighting Mike Tyson, win or lose. (Even so, I wouldn't do it.) Cathy Tyson† (no relation) is sweet and serious. Her claim to fame is playing the black prostitute in *Mona Lisa* with Bob Hoskins and Michael Caine. We had breakfast together and I told her how much I like and admire her husband, Craig Charles, and how I hope he won't dissipate his talent on fripperies when he is a writer with a distinctive voice and so much heart and charm. They could be a golden couple. She looked at me earnestly. 'Do you think so? I'm not sure I want that.'

Wednesday, 28 October 1987

Lunch at Jeffrey's. The usual gang: King Constantine, Lord Havers,‡ William Deedes, Peter Jay, Adam Faith, Barry Norman. At our end of the table we gossip about our host. Did he sleep with the prostitute? I say he didn't, but if he didn't, why shell out £2,000 to silence her? (£2,000 is called 'an Archer' now.) 'Because Jeffrey sees himself as a man of action,' is my answer. He consciously behaves like a character in one of his own novels. If a woman is making a nuisance of herself, sort it: pay her off. Sending emissaries with upturned collars to secret rendezvous with call-girls is the stuff of his kind of fiction. Remember: his telephone number contains the digits 007.

The lunch was fun. Much laughter at Peter Jay's expense when he had to disappear halfway through, summoned by telephone to his master's side. Jay is now 'chief of staff' to Robert Maxwell and when Captain Bob clicks his fingers Jay jumps. Maxwell is clearly a monster – but he gets away with it. At some gathering

---

* József Bugner (b.1950), Hungarian-born British-Australian boxer, twice British heavyweight champion; the bout with Tyson did not materialise.

† Cathy Tyson (b.1965), English actress, married to actor and comedian Craig Charles from 1984 to 1989.

‡ Robert Michael Havers (1923–92), Conservative MP, 1970–87; Lord Chancellor, June–October 1987.

in Scotland, he escorted the Queen and thought nothing of putting his arm around her.

Do we trust Adam Faith?* I'm not sure we do. He's a wide-boy wheeler-dealer who does his business from the American bar at the Savoy. Enough said. Do we think Lord Havers was up to being Lord Chancellor? We don't know, but we wonder if he's wise to be lunching with Jeffrey. There is something doubtful about this crowd.

Ex-King Constantine kindly gave me a lift back into town. I call him 'Your Majesty' and he likes that. (My feeling is, if you are going to do it, do it properly. Many, I notice, only half-curtsey to royalty. It's an unsatisfactory compromise. I observed recently that when the Duchess of Abercorn was presented to Prince Philip, she curtsied all the way to the ground.)

Thursday, 5 November 1987

Breakfast with Richard Briers. He makes me laugh because he is always working and always complaining that he has no work and what work he does have is all rubbish. Frantic morning moving the office from Kensington High Street to Britannia House, Hammersmith. 1.00 p.m. lunch with Jeffrey Archer at Sambuca in Sloane Square. I arrived a little early and sat at the window table looking out onto Sloane Square. At around 12.55 I saw Jeffrey's car coming round the square, but it didn't stop at the restaurant – it went on round the square. In all, the car circled Sloane Square three times – then Jeffrey got out, came into the restaurant and sat down. 'What was all that about?' I asked. 'What was all what about?' 'You, driving round and round Sloane Square.' He pointed to the clock above the door. 'What time is it?' 'One o'clock.' 'Exactly,' said Jeffrey. 'I am never early. I am never late. I am Jeffrey Archer.'

I told him I am looking for a new PA. He said, 'Go for the best. What do you pay the one you've got now? £10,000? You need to pay double. Don't go for a girl. Go for a woman who knows what she's doing.' I am going to take his advice.†

Returned to office refreshed, reinvigorated by Jeffrey's bounce. Went on to Colet Court [School] at 6.00 p.m. to hear Benet's poetry reading. He did Rupert Brooke's 'The Soldier' – and won the prize. (Well done, my boy.) Back for 7.00

---

* Adam Faith (b. Terence Nelhams-Wright, 1940–2003), chart-topping singer in the 1950s and 1960s, later actor, financial journalist and financial investments adviser; he was eventually declared bankrupt, owing a reported £32 million.
† He did. And, twenty-two years later, Jenny Noll is still working for GB.

p.m. and the family Guy Fawkes party in the garden – rockets, Roman candles and hot sausages: just right. And we have sparklers left over for tomorrow night's dinner with Jo [Lumley], Jane [Asher] and Co. It's all good.

Wednesday, 11 November 1987

Michèle is now convinced Jeffrey did go to the prostitute. Last night, after he had spoken *con brio* at the NPFA Local Authorities Conference dinner, he persuaded us to go on with him to Annabel's [the nightclub in Berkeley Square]. Michèle says that she saw the look in his eye: 'He's up for it. Any woman would recognise it.' I say, 'We all know about Andy [Andrina Colquhoun], but prostitutes?' 'Anything,' says M. 'Believe me, I saw the look. I know.'

At the dinner, Jeffrey's speech worked a treat. It always does. He speaks with passion, clarity and humour. He has a new section all about his mother, how amazing she is, how much he admires her, how she is taking her A Levels aged 83. He never refers to his father, but his mother he talks about all the time. Clearly he adores her. He says she gave him his love of theatre and his ability to write.

Saturday, 28 November 1987

Stratford-upon-Avon

Lunch at Armscote Manor with Fred and Amanda Docker. It is a beautiful Tudor manor house (with some sort of Guy Fawkes connection) and they have achieved it because Fred has a touch of genius, an original product (pre-cooked quality food for pubs and restaurants), ruthless ambition (charmingly concealed) and a readiness to work night and day. Tomorrow, lunch at Souldern Manor with Colin and Rosie Sanders – and it's the same story. Colin is a ruthless genius: he has created a sound desk that is now used in recording studios around the world. He knows what he wants and he goes out to get it – and he does it himself. Hands on.

This evening we went to see *Cymbeline* at The Other Place. Just as the play was about to start, Jeffrey Archer slipped into a seat alongside us. He is staying up the road at Alveston Manor, writing his book. He takes a room and simply writes, all day, undisturbed, with meals served when he wants them. He hadn't booked a ticket for *Cymbeline*. It's sold out, but somehow they found space for him. We went and had supper afterwards at the Greek place in Sheep Street. A very happy evening.

Shakespeare is a miracle worker. We all agreed that at our funerals, this has to be one of the readings:

The World is Changing

Fear no more the heat o' the sun,
Nor the furious winter's rages;
Thou thy worldly task hast done,
Home art gone, and ta'en thy wages;
Golden lads and girls all must,
As chimney-sweepers, come to dust.

Tuesday, 1 December 1987

The TV-am strike continues.* I am missing the place. I miss the building – it's a wonderful building (designed by Terry Farrell): it's a building that gives you energy. (It's the atrium that does it.) I miss the team. I miss the girls in make-up. And I am missing my 'breakfasts with the stars'. It's nothing grand: we just go to the canteen and line up for tea and toast (and bacon and baked beans). We've had a splurge of good guests recently: Eartha Kitt (I loved her when I was a child: I love her still: aged 60, she's still kittenish), Ken Dodd, Boy George (I like George and George likes me), Donny Osmond (I knocked, but there was no one there), Des O'Connor, Clive James – Clive said, not unkindly, 'Your jumpers – it's a neat substitute for an act' – Lenny Henry, Danny La Rue, Hank Marvin, Lorna Luft (yes, well . . . it's not her fault), Roy Castle, Kathy Botham (I really liked her: clearly she puts up with a lot), Peter Ustinov (still chuntering on), Carrie Fisher, Vanessa Redgrave – I was so pleased to see her. She's full of craziness, but it's all good-hearted – she is a good person as well as a great actress. Bruce [Gyngell] is determined to break the strike and I have a feeling he will. I don't especially like him: he is bronzed, brash, absurdly Australian, and has the glint in his eye of one 'born-again'. He belongs to the Movement of Spiritual Inner-Awareness. I don't warm to him, but I admire him and he knows what he is doing.

Wednesday, 9 December 1987

Garry Bennett† has committed suicide. He was the New College chaplain and I lived on his staircase, first in the room next door to his and then in the room

---

* At the end of November 1987, TV-am technicians belonging to the ACTT union went on strike for twenty-four hours and were subsequently locked out by the management. The dispute continued for twenty-two months, but the station resumed normal service in a matter of weeks, with the company's directors, managers and secretarial staff operating the cameras and technical equipment and Bruce Gyngell, the Australian managing director who had joined the station in 1984, directing the programme.
† Dr Gareth Bennett (1929–87), Chaplain and History Fellow at New College, Oxford.

above. Anonymously, he wrote a waspish foreword to *Crockford's Clerical Directory*, attacking the liberal hierarchy of the Church of England in general and the Archbishop of Canterbury, Robert Runcie, in particular. He was about to be outed as the author and it was all too much for him. He asphyxiated himself in his car, killing his cat first. (Perhaps he was also anxious that he was going to be outed as a homosexual. Why are so many conservative clergymen gay?)

I am in Leeds recording the *Countdown* final with Carol Thatcher. I told her her mother is changing the world. 'Yes,' said Carol, guffawing, 'that's what she thinks, too.'

Thursday, 17 December 1987

I did a speaking job for a company owned by Air France and was paid in kind — and generously. Even after our trip to the south of France I was £308 in credit, so last night M and I took Simon [Cadell] and Beckie out for dinner. We went to the Meridien in Piccadilly. It's owned by Air France. M and Beckie suggested we eat in the brasserie because it looked more fun. Simon wanted to dine in the 'more serious' Oak Room, so that's where we went. It was deadly, deserted and morgue-like in the way that grand restaurants in grand hotels so often are. The food was over-elaborate and served with ludicrous pomposity — silver lids simultaneously lifted from our plates with funereal solemnity. Simon rejected the proffered wine list — it ran to forty pages in a bound volume. He murmured to the sommelier confidentially, 'This used to be a British Railways hotel before Air France bought it. I'm sure you've got something extra-special lurking in the cellar . . .' By Jove, he had! The upshot is that the meal cost us all of the £308 we had in credit and we had to cough up £90 more. M was not amused (to put it mildly) and — wait for it — I am now in bed with food poisoning. We are not going to Jeffrey's champagne-and-shepherd's-pie party tonight. (M didn't want to go anyway.)

Thursday, 24 December 1987

Return to TV-am for one and all. And Rolf Harris too. (He was our strike-defying guest of the day. The Australians are sticking together: Tie me kangaroo down, sport.) The presenters have agreed to walk through the picket lines (it's quite exciting) and the studio is being manned by middle management. The lighting's dire and the camera work is a bit wobbly, but it'll get better. (Most people can do most things.) Bruce is directing the show — and loving it. There's a sense of defiance in the air: the show goes on. The age of the unions is over. The world has changed, completely. It really has. Merry Christmas, possums.

'It's a Disaster!'

January 1988 – June 1990

Monday, 11 January 1988

Went to Jeffrey's flat to be photographed with him, back to back, both of us grinning inanely, wearing red noses for Comic Relief.

Sunday, 17 January 1988

I am writing this lying flat on my back with my arms in the air. I can barely move. Last night I couldn't move at all. I came out of the bathroom at around 11.00 p.m. and, suddenly, as I was leaning over to get into bed, my back went – it went completely. I managed to fall to the floor by the bed, but I couldn't move. At all. I was in spasm. And in agony. M called Martin Scurr, Simon's GP. He came at midnight and gave me an injection. I am waiting for the osteopath now.

Later

Osteopath has been and gone. He's coming again tomorrow. We know why this has happened. As M says, this is how I was when she met me – doubled up. Nothing's changed. She says, 'Give something up' – but what? I am running NPFA day to day, but we are between directors so I have no choice. With Royal Britain, we are committed to raising the £5 million. We must. I have now taken on the chain of wool shops. I want to do it. And we are opening the Teddy Bear Museum – I saw the designer yesterday. (It's going to be enchanting.) And we have the books and diaries to create – we have no choice: that's how we earn our keep. The truth is I want to do more, not less. I want to achieve something.

It will work out. It always does.

Wednesday, 3 February 1988

Monday: 5th birthday of TV-am; completion of purchase of 19 Greenhill Street, Stratford-upon-Avon; train to Cardiff for the NPFA Play Awards for Wales; parents' meeting at Colet Court. Tuesday: TV-am (breakfast with Eddie

487

Kidd;* we talked motorbikes – my life's not all laughs); train to Leicester for
Newarke Wools meeting: I am liking life as a retailer; Saethryd's 11th birthday: I
love my daughter. If it's Wednesday (and it is) it must be Stratford-upon-Avon:
site meeting at 19 Greenhill Street. What we have bought was once a Tudor
farmhouse: it has a Victorian shopfront, but inside, upstairs, are all the original
beams. We are going to add a second staircase, have the shop on the ground floor
and turn the top two floors into the teddy bears' home. They will have a bedroom
and a playroom and a music room – and a library where we will display the works
of William Shakesbear (*Macbear*, *King Bear*, *Romeo and Paddington*) ... Nonsense,
but fun. I've a feeling it's going to work.

Tonight we went to *The Best of Friends* at the Apollo, directed by James
Roose-Evans, starring John Gielgud. Sir John is 83: this will be his farewell to the
stage. He lost his way once (as he does most nights, apparently), but it didn't
matter. He stamped his foot, screwed up his eyes and carried on. He still has a
quality that is unique. I must go to bed now. I have to be up in five hours for
TV-am (Greta Scacchi: she will be lovely we know – will she be nice?)† – then a
Royal Britain board meeting, a Victorama planning meeting, a meeting to clinch
the *AA Book of Games on the Go*, the Christie's Dolls and Teddy Bear Sale and a
speech in York ... On we go! On. On.‡

Wednesday, 23 March 1988

Breakfast with Russell Harty. Not his usual gay self – he uses the word in the
traditional sense: he does not like the modern usage. He looked drawn and

* Eddie Kidd (b.1959), English motorcycle stunt performer.
† She was. Greta Scacchi (b.1960), Italian-born Australian actress.
‡ GB's diary for the next four months runs to more than 50,000 words and records the devel-
opment of four business ventures: 1) the creation of the Teddy Bear Museum at Greenhill
Street in Stratford-upon-Avon; 2) the creation of the 'Royal Britain' exhibition at the
Barbican in London; 3) the rebranding and relaunching of the Newarke Wools shops as the
New for Knitting retail chain in thirty towns around England; 4) the transformation of the
Brandreths' publishing business, Victorama Ltd, into Complete Editions Ltd, under a new
managing director, Kate Dunning. GB also pursued his other interests – as chairman of the
National Playing Fields Association, organiser of the National Scrabble Championships,
etc. – and continued to appear on *Countdown* and TV-am, where his notable breakfast companions included the Bee Gees, Koo Stark ('she is lovely, even with her clothes on'), Joan
Baez, Peter Cushing ('he is still crushed by the loss of his wife; seventeen years on, he talks
of little else'), Eddie 'The Eagle' Edwards, Jackie Collins, Victoria Principal, Leo Sayer
and Billy Graham. 'He seemed to me to have an aura about him – or was it because I knew
he was Billy Graham that he seemed to me to have an aura about him?'

weary. He is fearful of being 'outed'. He feels 'hounded', he said. The tabloids are on to him. His boyfriend is half his age – and he has been seen with other boys. He sees no escape. They will get their 'pound of flesh'.*

Coffee with Sam Wanamaker† – at the site of the Globe. Except it isn't. It has been Sam's life's dream to recreate the Globe on the very spot where it stood in Shakespeare's day and now it transpires he is building it in the wrong place. He should be up the road and round the corner. He is philosophical about it. He just wants his theatre to happen – and it will. He is very gentle, but quite determined. 'If you know what you want, you get it in the end,' he said. 'I know what I want. I've wanted this since 1949. I formed the trust in 1970. We're getting there.'

Friday, 15 April 1988

This is so strange. I had lunch yesterday with Robert Booth [an old schoolfriend from Bedales]. I haven't seen him in years. I keep postponing him because I'm too busy (and lunch takes half the day), but yesterday we got together at the Brasserie in Brompton Road – and it was good. We talked about all the usual things we talk about – Bedales, life, love, Oscar Wilde. And then we talked about Kenneth Williams. I didn't realise that Robert knew Kenneth. I said, 'It's a while since we saw Kenneth. He behaved so badly the last time he came round.' And I told Robert about the sweet picture postcard that Kenneth had sent the other day – with on one side a still from a *Carry On* film with Kenneth peering into a periscope and, on the other, Kenneth's message: 'Is there life in Castelnau?' Anyway, we agreed that tomorrow – that's today – we'd phone Kenneth and fix to have lunch, the three of us. And I phoned first thing this morning and there was no reply. And now I've come in and just turned on the radio and heard the news. Kenneth has been found dead in his flat. He was 62.

Wednesday, 8 June 1988

Russell Harty has died. He was 53. It seems to be AIDS-related. We had Michael Parkinson on TV-am this morning and he did a generous tribute. Russell was a quirky individual and highly intelligent – and lucky to survive in television as a consequence. He had a very amusing way with him: he was fun. The party he gave for us at Settle was one of the happiest evenings I can remember. Thank you, old friend.

* They did, when he died of hepatitis ten weeks after this; a nude photograph of his partner, 26-year-old Irish novelist Jamie O'Neill, appeared on the front page of the *Sunday Mirror*.
† Sam Wanamaker (1919–93), American actor and director, whose vision of a recreated Shakespeare's Globe Theatre was finally realised four years after his death.

I doubt that Prince Philip knows who Russell Harty is or was. Yesterday, when he came to NPFA, and I told him I had had breakfast with Blake Carrington from *Dynasty* he said, 'I haven't the first idea what you're talking about. I had breakfast with the Queen.' When I told him there was now breakfast television, he seemed utterly appalled. He watches almost nothing – *A Question of Sport* and the News, that's about it. He reads the *Daily Telegraph*. I imagine he used to read *The Times* until Rupert Murdoch acquired it. He is open in his contempt for Murdoch, and he can't resist sarcastic digs at the expense of Prince Charles, but other than that, he is immensely tolerant. I've not noticed a trace of homophobia. I was told I'd find him grouchy and irascible. Perhaps he has mellowed with age: I find him liberal-minded, good-humoured and accepting. It's also incredible how, after all these years, he still seems to be *interested*.

I am writing this at TV-am, having coffee, overlooking Camden Lock. The sun is shining. On Monday I flew to Keighley to look at the design for our New for Knitting shops. I think it's going to work. We have now raised the money for Royal Britain and, at last, we have an opening date that looks to be realistic: 6 August. If Royal Britain works, I shall be rich. Won't that be nice? At 11.30 a.m. I am meeting M at the Royal Academy Summer Exhibition. At 1.15 p.m. we are having lunch at the Ritz. It is the prettiest room in London and I shall be with the prettiest girl. It is our 15th wedding anniversary. We met twenty years ago. Poor Russell Harty is dead and I am alive and truly blessed.

Monday, 4 July 1988

Yesterday, at 10.00 a.m. in Regent's Park, the Hon. Charles H. Price II, the United States Ambassador, formally launched the Teddy Bear Museum. Since this is the fourth of July and the teddy bear owes his name to Teddy Roosevelt, 25th US President, it seemed a good idea – and it was. There are good pictures – and plugs – in *The Times*, *Telegraph* and *Mirror* today. Mr Price is a genial cove who entered into the spirit of the event with gusto – surrounded by security men, their pockets bulging with handguns. We then drove straight on to Stratford and worked at the museum through the night – until 3.45 a.m. – adding the finishing touches. We are shattered but happy. The museum opened at 9.30 a.m. on the dot. It was still crowded when we left.

Monday, 11 July 1988

Yesterday I presided over the 18th National Scrabble Championships Final at the Connaught Rooms – it's a funny crowd that take part – and, in the evening, I heard the good news. In our first week at the Teddy Bear Museum, between 9.30

a.m. on 4 July and 6.00 p.m. on 10 July, we took a total of £3,979.42. A pleasing start.

Now I am going to Book House to be a judge at the Smarties Children's Book Prize. *Can't You Sleep, Little Bear?* is one of the titles. I shall see that it wins.*

Thursday, 21 July 1988

Breakfast with Pierce Brosnan, lunch at NPFA, supper with Benet's tutor. And, in between, publicity for Royal Britain (interviews, photos, etc.) and further disagreements with Adrian [Gilpin, the Royal Britain managing director] over the advertising. It has no heart, no warmth, it doesn't tell our story, it won't work. He simply repeats the mantra, 'You've got to trust your line manager.' Bollocks. You've got to trust your instinct. We are wasting hundreds of thousands on ads that won't work and Adrian is spewing out claptrap acquired on some poxy Institute of Directors management course. I am finding this very frustrating. I have responsibility without power. I brought in Adrian, he was my idea – we couldn't have got this far without him – but it's become his show, not mine. And there is nothing I can do about it.

Sunday, 24 July 1988

My back has gone. I cannot move.

Saturday, 6 August 1988

After three years and £5 million, Royal Britain finally opened its doors this morning. Almost nobody came.

Last night, at 10.00 p.m., Michèle went to walk the course. At 1.00 a.m. she returned, in tears. 'I don't think it's going to work,' she said. Six hours later we set off for the official opening. Adrian had sent a note to all the directors asking that his wife, Francesca, might be allowed to be the first visitor – in return for which she would supply hot coffee and croissants.

We arrived at 8.00 a.m. Workmen were still sweeping through. Adrian didn't want us to take a sneak preview, so we stood in the street outside, waiting . . . We waited for an hour. Sir Leslie [Porter, the chairman] paced up and down impatiently. Richard [Earl of Bradford, deputy chairman and principal investor] became increasingly tetchy. He had brought his family. They had been up since six. There was no sign of coffee or croissants – and no sign of the public either. At 9.00 a.m. we trooped in and trooped round the show. We all thought the same

* It did.

thing: 'Is this it? Is this what we've got for our £5 million?' But, interestingly, none of us said a thing. We just talked about Tuesday – the Big Launch – and the razzmatazz that will bring in the crowds.

Tuesday, 9 August 1988

A long day. It began well enough. My idea for the photocall worked – sort of. I had fifty 'stars of stage and screen' (well, you might have heard of some of them) dressed as England's fifty kings and queens, from King Edgar to George VI. The press concentrated on Anne Diamond as Queen Victoria. We'll get some coverage from that. The press parade was fine – the atmosphere was cheery – and during the day we had a handful of visitors – real, paying customers – trickling through. In the evening, we had the launch reception for family, friends, investors, the travel trade. One or two were enthusiastic: 'Gyles, it's brilliant – you'll make a fortune.' Most said nothing. Richard [Earl of Bradford] rushed about frantically saying 'It's a disaster, it's a disaster!' far too loudly.

Saturday, 13 August 1988

We have a £5 million disaster on our hands and I am flying to Hollywood first class. I am writing this on the plane. I am in first class because of my back: at least here I can lie in my seat. I am going to Hollywood because I am to be a guest on *The Late Show* on Fox TV. Millions watch it and the idea is I'm going to tell them all about Royal Britain. (The advantage of first class is that you feel safer than in steerage and you do touch down first. The disadvantage is that I am surrounded by out-of-control Arab children. Their obese parents are asleep and their nanny is very sensibly hiding back in business class.)

Monday, 15 August 1988

It is gone three in the morning and I am lying on my side in bed in my room at the Hotel Mondrian on Sunset Boulevard. This is what happened.

At 5.00 p.m. a stretch limo a street long (complete with darkened windows, cocktail cabinet and colour TV) swept me to the TV studio. We recorded 'as live' at seven, for transmission at 11.00 p.m. I was expected. My name was *painted* on my dressing-room door. I made myself at home, got out my costume (I brought King Canute's cloak and crown with me, to wear over a Royal Britain jumper – aiming to reinforce my message with visual aids) and began to run through my lines. 'Royal Britain is a roller-coaster ride through history, from the age of King Canute and King Arthur to the story of royalty in our times . . .'

With fifteen minutes to go, our host – Ross Shafer: he is going to be bigger than Johnny Carson, they say – put his head around the door. 'Great to meet you, Guy. I just love your accent.' I hadn't spoken yet. 'You're in the last quarter of the show. We keep the best to last. We've got a big, big audience tuning in to catch you tonight.'

Before I could say a word, he'd gone. I was whisked to make-up and returned to my room. I ran through my mental checklist of Royal Britain's finest features – the tableau of Richard the Lionheart at the Crusades, the animatronic of Elizabeth addressing the troops at Tilbury, the Christmas scene with Victoria and Albert – and then the monitor in the corner sprang to life, the opening credits started to roll, the studio audience burst into frenetic applause and Ross Shafer slid down the banister onto the set as his devotees squealed their admiration and delight. 'And on tonight's show,' I heard him cry, 'all the way from London, England, we'll have Guy Brandon, who is going to lift the veil on Bucking-ham Palace and dish the dirt on those raunchy royals. If you're watching, Fergie, watch out!'

But first, we had 'Dr Peebles', a trans-channeller, 'a medium rare' in Ross Shafer's deft phrase, a psychic who locked himself into a trance and brought amazing messages from the world beyond to individual members of the studio audience. He also brought the house down. They loved him. They loved him so much they extended his air time. Eventually, with just seven minutes of show left to run, the floor manager appeared at my door and led me down corridor after corridor to the studio. I stood in darkness at the edge of the set and watched and waited as the medium and his messages enjoyed their night of triumph. And then, suddenly, I heard our host announce, 'And now, yes – after that shattering, truly shattering experience – on a night to remember – I think you'll agree, ladies and gentlemen, this has been A Night to Remember!' – the moist-eyed audience whooped and cheered – 'before we go, let's look east to England and let's get at the truth. Here's the man who knows *all* the royal secrets – Guy Branson!' And on stumbled King Canute.

Ross had not been expecting the crown and cape, but he's a pro. He took them in his stride, with style, going down on one knee and saying 'Arise, Sir Guy!' as I flopped onto the studio sofa.

'We've only got sixty seconds, Guy, so let's get down to the nitty-gritty. Is it true that Chuck and Di don't do it any more?'

'I – er – I don't really know,' I countered lamely, mouth dry, heart pounding. 'All I can say is that at Royal Britain at London's Barbican you get a right-royal roller-coaster of kings and queens, from the reign of Edgar . . .'

And that was it. The music played, the credits rolled, and Ross was up, off and away to book Dr Peebles for a return engagement. I spent five minutes in hospitality and then departed. The limo that brought me back to the hotel was hardly stretched at all.

For dinner my minder (Rick Something, the local PR man who set up this whole fandango) took me out to Dudley Moore's restaurant at Venice Beach. I hoped Dudley might be there, but he wasn't. Rick consoled himself by sharing with anyone who caught his eye the exciting news that we had come fresh from *The Late Show*. Our fellow diners were not impressed. We didn't hurry back to the hotel. I did not want to turn on the TV much before 11.45 p.m. I couldn't face watching Dr Peebles's triumph twice in one night. In the event we sat down in Rick's room at around 11.50 – and we were still too early. Instead of *The Late Show* we found ourselves watching President Reagan addressing the Republican Party Convention, eloquently endorsing George Bush as his successor. *The Late Show* had been rescheduled. I finally hit the screen a little before 2.00 a.m. It was not an impressive sight, but it was certainly a man wearing a crown and a cape and, under the cape, if you looked very closely you could just about read 'OYAL BRI' on his half-hidden jumper.

If it weren't so pitiful, it would be quite funny. Goodnight.

Tuesday, 16 August 1988

I am on the plane flying back to London. I am amused by how much safer I feel in first class. I have spent three hours drafting a memo to the [Royal Britain] board. The essence of my message is that we haven't got the product quite right and we have got the marketing quite wrong. 'Action this day'. I am proposing a 'war cabinet' to meet every Monday at 8.00 a.m. to drive through all the changes.

Monday, 22 August 1988

8.00 a.m. Royal Britain Action Committee. We are going to turn this thing round, but it won't be easy. Adrian is exhausted, punch-drunk, drained, knocked sideways. We need action *now*, but nothing happens. We ask for flags in the street. They are promised. They don't appear. *Everything* takes so long. He is obsessed with systems, hierarchy, differentials, 'trusting your line manager', his status as leader. M says, 'He has to go.' She is right, but it's easier said than done.[*]

---

[*] Five months later, he was still there. Eventually, he left and the board was restructured, with Lord Bradford replacing Sir Leslie Porter as chairman and GB replacing Adrian Gilpin as managing director. A rights issue raised a further £2 million and a new design, marketing and public relations team were put in place. GB's full account of this experience runs to more than 200,000 words.

Tuesday, 27 September 1988

Breakfast with Kirk Douglas.* (It does set one up for the day. And he still looks the business. And does the business. He plays Kirk Douglas for you.) Morning on the Royal Britain accounts. It does not look good. Afternoon at the desk. Evening with Mike Ounsted of the Wildfowl Trust. The idea is simply this: at the back of our house, where the reservoirs are, we are going to create a wildfowl and wetland centre for London.

Tuesday, 15 November 1988

An amusing trio at TV-am this morning. Mary Hopkin,† Anthony Hopkins,‡ Gary Glitter.§ Mary is very gentle, very sweet; GG is an old trouper, ridiculous but good value; and Anthony Hopkins is something else . . . We went and had breakfast and talked Shakespeare and Wales – and he did his Olivier impression for me. It is better than the real thing.

On the way to Royal Britain, my taxi driver said to me, 'I was going to invest in your venture, but I didn't in the end. Do you know why? Not enough *executive* directors on the board.'

Thursday, 24 November 1988

6.00 a.m.	TV-am. On air at 6.20 a.m. Outside it's bleak midwinter. In here it's sunshine city. That's Bruce [Gyngell]'s genius: he has made us the sunshine station: he wears pink and yellow and insists we do too. Bright colours, bright smiles, brightness everywhere. (The girl who persisted in wearing black on screen was fired. He is ruthless.) Today is the first anniversary of the dispute. The unions have lost and Bruce has reduced the wage bill by three-quarters, from £8 million to £2 million. Perhaps he should be running Royal Britain?
9.00 a.m.	*Prima* magazine. I went to judge our Knit-a-Teddy-Bear competition. There were 1,300 entries – all there, and hideous, tumbling out of black plastic bags. We did our best to judge fairly – the editor insisted – but really . . .

* Kirk Douglas (b. Issur Danielovitch, 1916), American film star.
† Mary Hopkin (b.1950), Welsh folk singer best remembered for her 1968 hit, 'Those Were the Days'.
‡ Sir Philip Anthony Hopkins (b.1937), Welsh actor and film star.
§ Gary Glitter (b. Paul Gadd, 1944), English singer associated with 'glam rock'; later imprisoned for paedophile offences in Vietnam.

12 noon. Buckingham Palace. When I told Prince Philip what I had been doing this morning, he simply shook his head and sighed. 'And I thought I had to do some damned stupid things . . . Now let's get on with it.' He handed out the President's Certificates to the motley crowd we'd gathered for him, shook hands, nodded, chuntered on amiably, then wandered on his way. He has seven engagements like this today. 'I think it's clockmakers next,' he said. 'I like to be a bit on the late side for them.'

Lunch with Sandy Gilmour at Mark's Club. (I am never comfortable in these places. I play the part, but it's not me. They are all old friends of Lord Lucan.) On to meet Richard [Bradford] with Charles Fry [for more discussions on the Royal Britain finances]. Crossing Jermyn Street, I bumped into David Frost – 'A *joy*, Gyles, a *joy!*' – and then John Selwyn Gummer. 'When are you joining us in the House?' he asked. I felt like a character in one of Anthony Powell's novels. Life in Establishment England really is *A Dance to the Music of Time*.

Sunday, 1 January 1989

We saw in the New Year at Souldern Manor with Colin and Rosie Sanders. They gave a very generous party, with a good magician and wonderful fireworks. No one was introduced to anyone (which was probably a blessing), Aphra spilled Coca-Cola on the white carpet and Michèle sat on an antique chair which broke under her – apart from that, a fair time was had by all. The best part of the evening for me was the drive down, listening to a tape of James Villiers reading pieces by Patrick Campbell. We laughed out loud.

Today we've pottered, been for a long walk around Barnes and read our books by the fire. (Every winter I say I am going to light the drawing-room fire every Sunday – and I don't. Today I did.) I have been reading Kenneth [Williams]'s diaries – the originals. His solicitors sent over several years' worth for me to look at to help them come up with a valuation. I said £30,000. They aren't as revelatory as some of Kenneth's chums have feared, but there can be no doubt that Kenneth took his own life. The last words in the diary say it all: '– oh – what's the bloody point?' He was in pain ('this bloody ulcer and spastic colon'), he had given up smoking, he was waiting to go into hospital ('How I HATE those places'). He was frightened. And fed up. Personally and professionally, he had nowhere left to go. And he'd lost interest in Louie [his mother]. He was fed up with her, too.

Tonight I'm going to finish Melvyn Bragg's biography of Richard

Burton.* It's good, with solid slugs of Burton's own journal. (He was a much better writer than Kenneth.) Burton comes across as very likeable – despite the booze. Giving up alcohol is not one of my New Year resolutions, though 'moderation' I hope will be my 1989 watchword. I make no forecasts or predictions for the year ahead, though I'd like to *surprise* myself in '89.

Later

Re Kenneth, I think his gift as a raconteur added to his self-loathing. I have found the quote I was looking for. It's from Cyril Connolly: 'Most good talkers, when they have run down, are miserable. They know that they have betrayed themselves, that they have taken material which should have a life of its own to dispense it in noises upon the air.'

Wednesday, 4 January 1989

Tony Curtis† brought an atrocious painting in to TV-am this morning, but was very happy because we all told him how wonderful it was.

Thursday, 5 January 1989

It's 6.45 p.m. I'm at the Institute of Directors in Pall Mall, pretty shattered. Only five hours' sleep because Thursday is the day when my first slot at TV-am is at 6.15 a.m. Interviewing replacement Royal Britain marketing managers all afternoon. Not sure any of them is going to be right. Surprise lunch with Michèle at the Caprice. (Adrian failed to show due to food poisoning. He is overweight, overwrought and frantic to go. We must let him.) M and I talked about a new visitor attraction in the tradition of the Teddy Bear Museum, but in Chester. The Gingerbread House or Small World are my working titles – a cross between a Museum of Childhood and a Museum of Nostalgia. Simon Cadell called: his father's not well. I told Simon he'd been brilliant in the oh-so-clever-but-so-what? Tom Stoppard TV play on Sunday. He was happy about that. (We all need reassurance all the time.) Jo Lumley called – she's off to India as an escort on an upmarket tour: no fee, but all found. Now it's gone 7.00 p.m. Never mind the Himalayas, have I the strength to get to Hammersmith? We're having supper with Peter and Sue Bowles. Peter will have some good Richard Burton stories. I think that's exactly what I'm up for tonight.

* Richard Burton CBE (b. Richard Jenkins, 1925–84), Welsh actor and film star; *Rich* by Melvyn Bragg, 1988.
† Tony Curtis (b. Bernard Schwartz, 1925), American film star.

Tuesday, 17 January 1989

Breakfast with Jeremy Brett[*] – the definitive Sherlock Holmes. And he knows it. He lives the part. 'It's more difficult than Hamlet, believe you me. The concentration required – and I'm not like that at all.' He isn't: he is gregarious and full of easy charm. There is said to be a dark side, but he kept it well hidden over our mushrooms on toast.

Royal Britain board meeting. We are letting Adrian go and giving him a handsome settlement. (We have been very close for more than three years working on this. I doubt that I shall see him or speak to him again.)[†] We are going to go for a rights issue to raise an extra £2 million, with £1 million underwritten by Richard. I am taking over as managing director pro tem. It remains a good idea. I have simply got to work flat out to make it work.[‡] Onward.

Thursday, 2 March 1989

At TV-am I met Christine Keeler. She is 47 now. She has not worn well. Of course, it has been a rough life, but it is difficult to see even the trace of what the attraction might have been. She was young and available, I suppose, that's all. It certainly can't have been her conversation.

On to Benet's confirmation at St Paul's Cathedral. Benet was one of half a dozen of the boys who had to be baptised as well as confirmed. We chose not to have him christened when he was a baby. I now think that was a mistake: we should have got him good godparents, hugely wealthy old queens who could have left him all their money. (People who don't have children themselves are the

---

[*] Jeremy Brett (b. Peter Huggins, 1933–95), English actor, best remembered for playing Sherlock Holmes on television, 1984–95.

[†] He hasn't. Adrian Gilpin is now Chairman of the Institute of Human Development and author of *Unstoppable: The Pathway to Living an Inspired Life*, 2004.

[‡] He did; it didn't. GB's diary for the rest of 1989 is dominated by long hours spent at 'Royal Britain', where the product was improved, the overheads reduced and visitor numbers increased – but still the venture struggled. The New for Knitting retail chain struggled, too, having lost £300,000 in the second half of 1988. The 1989/90 recession was beginning to bite. Happily, the Teddy Bear Museum prospered and, as well as appearing on *Countdown* and *Blankety Blank*, GB hosted two new TV series, *Discovering Gardens*, and *Star Quality* which is now described on UKGameshows.com as 'Quite the worst game show ever made'. At TV-am his breakfast companions included John Mortimer and Jim Davidson ('an unlikely double act, both, for their ages, looking very much the worse for wear'), Britt Ekland, Susan Hampshire, Lulu, Jason Donovan, Roger Taylor and Brian May of Queen, Joan Collins and Debbie Reynolds ('I like a strong woman at breakfast: sort of sets you up for the day').

sort of people who should be godparents. I do feel bad that I am such a poor godfather. Not bad enough to do anything about it, of course.)

Saturday, 1 April 1989

I went with David Milne and Michael Ounsted to see Peter Scott at Slimbridge.*
We had tea in his sitting room looking directly out onto the wetlands. Mike Ounsted said to me, 'We'll make sure you have a view like this.' Sir Peter was very sweet, gentle, softly-spoken. I boomed rather: I was unnecessarily loud and brusque. I feel bad about it now. He is frail – and a great man. I was pleased to meet him – honoured. We talked about the Duke of Edinburgh and J. M. Barrie (Sir Peter's godfather – he was amused I knew) and we shook hands. I said, 'I am the chairman of the Barn Elms Protection Association. Let's save Barn Elms and create a Wildfowl and Wetlands Trust for London.' He said, 'Yes. It can be a memorial to us both. I'd like that.'

Sunday, 23 April 1989

A happy weekend taking part in the Shakespeare Birthday Celebrations in Stratford-upon-Avon. Yesterday, we had our own flag to unfurl in Bridge Street before parading to the Birthplace. Today we joined the Civic Procession from Holy Trinity to the Town Hall. At the reception, I made small-talk with Peggy Ashcroft, who wasn't much interested until she realised that Benet had been in *Madame Sousatzka*.† She became a woman transformed: Benet was a fellow player, another trouper, they had *acting* in common, a *film* in common. She chatted away to him merrily.

Wednesday, 10 May 1989

Yesterday, at TV-am, I met Shirley Temple‡ – a very smart cookie, savvy, charming, professional, and happy to provide a message for the Teddy Bear

---

* David Milne QC, amateur ornithologist, friend and neighbour of GB, and Michael Ounsted of the WWT, were driving forces behind the creation of the Wildfowl and Wetlands Centre at Barn Elms. Sir Peter Scott CH (1909–89) founded the Severn Wildfowl Trust (later the WWT) in 1948, with its headquarters in Slimbridge, Gloucestershire.

† Benet Brandreth, aged 13, and Michèle, played small parts, 'the new pupil' and his mother, in John Schlesinger's 1988 film, *Madame Sousatzka*. The stars were Shirley MacLaine and Peggy Ashcroft.

‡ Shirley Temple Black (b.1928), world-famous American child star in the 1930s and, later, US Ambassador and diplomat.

Museum. Today, I travelled to Manchester, to Granadaland, to host the Barbie Doll presentation, and, guess what, they were there: the original Ken and Barbie, in person, the children of Ruth Handler, sometime president of Mattel and creator of the Barbie doll. Yes, I have shaken the hands of Barbie and Ken. What more is there to say?

Tuesday, 23 May 1989

I sat down on the TV-am sofa next to Charlton Heston.* As I sat, I put my cup of tea on the table in front of us and immediately he picked it up and started drinking from it. It's fascinating to realise that The Star assumes that anything that comes within his orbit must automatically be for him. The moment he realised what he had done he was charmingly apologetic – and, five minutes later, when a coffee did arrive for him he told me I had missed a trick by not assuming it was for me. I liked him. He even managed to make the case for an American's right to bear arms seem reasonable. (Folksy charm is a useful weapon to have tucked in your armoury. His hairpiece wasn't so subtle, however.)

Thursday, 25 May 1989

To TV-am at 5.30 a.m. where I was persuaded into a pair of Australian shorts because of the heat-wave. With Rustie Lee (our Caribbean cook) and Bill Oddie (the depressive Goodie), I judged the TV-am Christmas card competition. (This is for *next* Christmas!) I had a good meeting with Bruce [Gyngell]. He likes my idea of turning Dan Dare into an animated cartoon.

On to Kensington Town Hall for the NPFA AGM. I have now formally succeeded Sandy [Gilmour] as chairman. Sandy took me to one side in a state of some distress to tell me that he has been offered an OBE. He is devastated. Of course, it's unimportant, but a knighthood would have transformed his life. A CBE, in truth, would have been about right. The idea of the OBE just appals him: he is hurt and disappointed. At first, when he got the letter, he accepted; then he wrote again – to the Prime Minister, personally – saying it was an insult to the charity he has served for twenty-six years . . . Poor Sandy. He is so unhappy about this.†

---

* Charlton Heston (b. John Charles Carter, 1923–2008), American film star.
† In due course, he was awarded a CVO, an honour the equivalent of a CBE but in the personal gift of the sovereign. GB's successor as NPFA chairman, Christopher Laing, was happy to accept an OBE.

Friday, 26 May 1989

Morning at the Stock Exchange making our presentation to the Mergers and Takeover panel to get the dispensation we need to allow Richard to put a further million into Royal Britain. Our overdraft stands at £750,000 and Frank Burrell [at the NatWest Bank] is saying he can't give us more without personal guarantees. Lunch with Paul Elliott, pantomime producer supreme – he has twenty-two shows on this Christmas and I have agreed to be in one of them. It's *Cinderella* at Guildford. I'm Baron Hardup (appropriately) to Bonnie Langford's Cinders. (Is this a ghastly mistake? Will I loathe the whole thing?)

Afternoon at Royal Britain, then evening at the Royal Opera House. Stephen Barlow was conducting *Turandot*. They lead the maestro by the hand all the way from his dressing room to the podium. Stephen looked the business (the shoulder-length hair helps) and did the business. He was wonderful. Glorious music, wholly seductive, and fabulous staging – a true treat and exciting to be in the maestro's dressing room sipping champagne with the maestro. Afterwards, we had a jolly supper at Rules with Stephen and Jo and family. Jo's mother and aunt played themselves as characters straight from the pages of Anthony Powell.

Wednesday, 28 June 1989

One of the perks of being chairman of NPFA is an invitation to the Royal Box at Wimbledon. We sat behind Queen Noor and the Lebanese and Egyptian ambassadors. The lunch was perfect and the tea even better. I spent most of the afternoon behind the box, in the private dining room, scoffing strawberries and cream with the Duchess of York [Sarah Ferguson]. Her Royal Highness is full of fun. The tennis, of course, is completely wasted on me – but the company and the food were fab.

Wednesday, 26 July 1989

Breakfast with Jeremy Irons. We talked about Simon and Sinead and Shakespeare. He is quite serious, but I think we amused one another.

At lunch, I was not amused at all. I went to the British Tourist Authority 'Welcome to Britain' Awards. I found myself sitting next to the Countess of Dartmouth (Lady Lewisham as was, Countess Spencer as is), daughter of Barbara Cartland, mother of William Lewisham, stepmother of Diana, etc.[*]

---

[*] Raine McCorquodale (b.1929), active in local government; married, first, to Gerald Legge, who became Viscount Lewisham and then Earl of Dartmouth; second, to Earl Spencer; finally, and briefly, to Comte Jean-François Pineton de Chambrun.

Done up to the nines 1950s-style, quite ludicrous and hugely self-opinionated, she would not stop talking – especially after lunch, when the awards ceremony itself began. I was trying to listen out in case we had won something – instead I had to sit pretending to be enthralled by her ladyship. Suddenly, from the far end of the room, I heard the words 'And the Come to Britain trophy goes to the Teddy Bear Museum, Stratford-upon-Avon' and, with great difficulty, I excused myself from the table and ran up to receive the award just in time. The silly cow had no idea. When I returned to the table in triumph she just carried on talking as if nothing had happened. I missed the citation. I missed the slide show. I missed my 'moment'. Ghastly baggage. (Every one else at the table found her great fun and immensely gracious.)

Friday, 4 August 1989

There is an English world beyond my world that I barely know exists. It is a good world, full of decent people leading good lives in wonderful settings. It is a calmer world, kinder. It is where I have spent this week, visiting fine houses and beautiful gardens in the West Country. This is Day 5 of filming our series, *Discovering Gardens*. We are doing a garden a day: Michèle is in the potting shed talking to the gardener, while I sit on the lawn with the cucumber sandwiches interviewing the owners and keeping the Labradors at bay. Yesterday, East Lambrook; today Clapton Court (Simon and Penny Loder – excellent people); tomorrow Tintinhull House with the celebrated Penelope Hobhouse. I am essentially a townie – I would get desperately restless here – but I can see the virtues and the charm of this world.

Tuesday, 5 September 1989

At breakfast, Max Bygraves[*] told me that the experience I had with Frankie Howerd is *exactly* the experience he had with Frank when they appeared in panto together almost forty years ago. 'He's doing it all the time,' said Max. 'And he always goes for married guys, that's the strange thing. It's as if he's looking for rejection.'

I am liking our new PR boys at Royal Britain: Eugen Beer and Mark Borkowski. They are nothing, if not inventive. This week's scam is to 'suspend' our court jester for telling inappropriate jokes about the modern royal family. 'He is supposed to be making jokes about Henry VIII, not the Duke of Edinburgh.' We do

[*] Max Bygraves OBE (b. Walter Bygraves, 1922), English singer, songwriter and entertainer.

it all for real. The jester tries to sell the story to a gossip column. Word gets out. I refuse to issue a statement, put down the phone when the journalists ring. The story grows. This one has worked: we have pix of the jester picketing the premises in the *Mirror* and the *Express* today. Next up, the ghost of Elvis will be sighted at Royal Britain – yes, 'The King is Back! Long live the King.'

Tuesday, 19 September 1989

First night of Jeffrey's play, *Exclusive*, at the Strand. The cast is strong – Paul Scofield, Eileen Atkins, Alec McCowen: Jeffrey has flawless judgement and real taste when it comes to actors and paintings – but the play is dire. At the party afterwards he is irrepressible. He struts about, dressed as a news-vendor giving out copies of a newspaper publicising the play. To his face we tease him. Behind his back we mock him. But I notice we don't stay away.

I didn't invest in this one and I am glad.

Tuesday, 28 November 1989

Between breakfast with Roy Castle and the boys from Wet Wet Wet at TV-am and lunch with Jeffrey Archer at the Caprice, I raced first to Royal Britain to plan our Christmas PR campaign, and then to the House of Commons where, in an upstairs committee room, I took part in the UK launch of the UN Convention on the Rights of the Child. I gave a good speech – about a child's right to play in freedom and safety, about a child's right to a childhood. I had something to say. (It makes a difference.) This is what I should be doing. Instead, it seems, I am going to Guildford to play Baron Hardup in *Cinderella*.

Tuesday, 5 December 1989

I began the day with Kylie Minogue (who is really sweet), dressed up as Buddy Holly (I looked quite convincing): I spent the rest of it with Bonnie Langford (who is really talented), playing her dad (I look all too convincing). This was the second day of our rehearsals. We're at the Dance Attic off Putney Bridge Road and I'm liking it. I like the team spirit. I like the fact that all these guys have done it before and know exactly what they're up to. Mark Curry (Buttons) told me (again) his story about the first time he appeared with Bonnie – they were children, the babes in *Babes in the Wood*. On the opening night, standing in the wings, waiting to go on, Mark was approached by Bonnie's mum, Babette. 'Now, Mark, when you get onto that stage, what are you going to do?' 'I don't know, Mrs Langford. Not stand in front of Bonnie? I don't know, Mrs Langford. What am I going to do?' 'Mark, when you get onto that stage, you're going to *sparkle*.'

Saturday, 13 January 1990

On Saturdays we do three shows: 11.00 a.m., 3.00 p.m., 7.00 p.m. By halfway through the third, we really have no idea where we are. Except Bonnie. Bonnie always knows where she is. I have loved watching her in this. I love the way when she makes her first entrance she always, *always*, ensures that her eyes scan every seat in the theatre, from the back row to the front. I love watching her dance: she gives every move that final, extra extension. And I find her rather sexy. This has been a happy experience. On the stage, I feel safe. No one can get at you there. And in my little dressing room here, I feel secure too.

Thursday, 1 February 1990

I hosted a dinner last night in honour of the 75th birthday of Sir Stanley Matthews.* He told me that at the height of his career he was earning £5 a week. Just before the speeches, when I told him we were going to show a short film of golden moments from his career, he said, 'If you don't mind, I won't look. I don't think I should.' When we showed the film, he simply stared down at his knees. He made no fuss about it. His lack of vanity was entirely real.

I am on the train to Edinburgh, on my way to launch *Puzzle World* on the unsuspecting Scots.†

Sunday, 15 April 1990

Anne Diamond is now doing Sunday mornings at TV-am and I am her sidekick. This morning our guest was the Reverend Jesse Jackson.‡ It was an alarming experience. His is a frightening presence. I took him to the canteen for breakfast and we sat together at a corner table, in near silence, closely surrounded by a semicircle of huge and menacing US security men. They stood bolt upright with their backs to us surveying the deserted canteen.

Tuesday, 1 May 1990

I spoke, not very well, at the London Playing Fields Society Centenary Dinner at the Savoy. I was seated next to the Chief of the Defence Staff, Field Marshal The Lord Bramall, whose terrible dandruff was wafted straight from his left

---

* Sir Stanley Matthews (1915–2000), legendary footballer, particularly associated with Blackpool and Stoke City.

† *Puzzle World* was a monthly magazine produced by GB's company for Sally Cartwright who went on to be the publisher of the rather more successful *Hello!* magazine.

‡ The Rev. Jesse Jackson Sr (b.1941), American civil rights leader and Baptist minister.

shoulder onto my *Petit tournedos de boeuf aux echalotes* every time a waiter breezed past. Colin Moynihan,[*] our diminutive Minister for Sport, spoke. As he left Colin said to me, 'When are you joining us at Westminster?' I said, 'I don't think I am,' but, of course, I want to.

Tuesday, 8 May 1990

On to Royal Britain and more crisis talks. Walk to the Savoy for the NPFA fund-raising lunch. Prince Philip (in his electric taxi) arrived ten minutes early, but *this* time (unlike last time when I was in the loo) I was on the doorstep ready and waiting. At the lunch – a smallish group, selected high-rollers (at least, that was the idea . . .) – HRH spoke well: no notes (certainly not the ones I'd provided!) and his usual trick of being sufficiently indiscreet to make his audience feel they were being 'let in' on something. Colin Sanders, bless him, offered £50,000 there and then. So did Roger Levitt.[†]

   Supper with Anne Maxwell[‡] in her basement flat in Labroke Grove. There's a touch of the Carol Thatcher good-hearted jolly-hockey-sticks about her, and, like Carol vis-à-vis Mrs T., Anne manages to be loyal to her awesome parent without apparently becoming his creature. I'm not sure the same can be said about brother Kevin who left the table at ten to return to the office: 'There's a lot still to do tonight. I've got to sign an Australian affidavit. It certainly can't wait till morning.'

Wednesday, 9 May 1990

At Royal Britain our overdraft has topped the million mark and is being extended little by little (guaranteed by Richard) while we search for extra funds and/or a buyer. John Broome, founder of Alton Towers, came today and declared that he would take it on – for a controlling interest. He'd pick up the overdraft and spend £2.5 million to give the show the 'wow' factor and jack up the marketing. Was it all bluff and bombast? We left it that he'll come again and take a closer look – when he gets back from his day trip to New York tomorrow . . .

   Lunch at the House of Lords with Lord Raglan,[§] Prince Philip's suggestion as

---

[*] Colin Moynihan (b.1955), Olympic cox, Conservative MP for Lewisham East, 1983–92, and Minister for Sport, 1987–90; now 4th Baron Moynihan.
[†] Financier and insurance salesman, soon to fall from grace.
[‡] Contemporary of GB's at Oxford, daughter of Robert Maxwell, soon to fall from boat.
[§] FitzRoy Somerset, 5th Baron Raglan, of Usk, Gwent (b.1927); Independent peer particularly involved with the Housing Association movement in Wales.

NPFA's man in Wales. Amiable, clear-thinking, amusing – *and* the name has a ring to it. Lord Longford pottered up and asked if I was still standing on my head. Then he tried to persuade me to show him there and then. I told Raglan Longford was the only man I knew who could embrace a totally naked woman and apparently not notice it.

Sunday, 13 May 1990

Took Benet [now 15] to see Charles Dance as a wonderful Coriolanus at the RSC yesterday: power politics and a fickle public. Glorious.

Today at TV-am Tony Holden told me a story told to him by Basil Boothroyd who was given an office at Buckingham Palace at the time he was writing his authorised biography of Prince Philip. Arriving for work one morning, crossing the courtyard, gravel scrunching underfoot, the eyes of a hundred tourists boring into him, Boothroyd encountered the Queen's Private Secretary coming the other way. Boothroyd paused to greet him. Pleasantries were exchanged. Courtesies were extended. The weather was discussed, the Queen's blooming health was touched on, the vigour and charm of the Queen Mother marvelled at, progress on Basil's book reported – then the Private Secretary threw in gently, 'If you'll forgive me, I must be on my way. I've had an urgent call to say my house is on fire.'

Thursday, 17 May 1990

I'm writing this on the train to Truro. We're off for three days' civilised filming [for the second series of *Discovering Gardens*]: Trewithian, Glendurgan, Mount Edgcumbe. There's a hilarious picture of John Selwyn Gummer [Agriculture Minister] on the front page of *The Times*: 'Where's the beef? Mr John Gummer pressing a burger on his reluctant daughter Cordelia, aged four, at Ipswich yesterday to underline his message that beef is safe.' Jim Henson and Sammy Davis Jr have died. The joy of a train journey like this is it gives you the time and space to read the obituaries with a clear conscience. Jim Henson is one of my heroes: a true innovator. He gave us the original Fozzie Bear to put on show at the Teddy Bear Museum.

Tuesday, 22 May 1990

Breakfast with Richard Harris, lunch with Wayne Sleep, late supper with Jo and Stevie. And in between all the laughter and campery, real anguish. Royal Britain is going to fail. Four years' endeavour going up in smoke. It'll cost us £100,000 plus. It'll cost poor Richard [Bradford] millions.

'It's a Disaster!'

The word from Bucharest: 'Mrs Edwina Currie, attired in bright red shoes and red polka-dot dress, walked into a Balkan-style controversy yesterday as she praised the conduct of an election won by a crypto-communist landslide that opposition politicians have likened to the vote-rigging practised under Nicolae Ceauşescu.'*

The word from the Barbican is similarly tragi-comic: J. Paul Getty Jr is not intrigued; John Broome calls to have another look round, but bows out by phone from Heathrow at 4.30 p.m. Richard battles valiantly with Frank (the bank manager) for an extra £50,000 to get us through the next fortnight. Richard: 'We've a man flying in from Canada on Sunday and tomorrow we're seeing Prince Rupert Lowenstein who manages the finances of the Rolling Stones.' (This last provokes a coughing spasm from Michèle and hysterical giggles from me.) Richard keeps going: 'A man is flying in from Canada, Frank. He's coming from Toronto. It's a long way to come to say "no"!'

Bank Holiday Monday, 28 May 1990

Twenty years to the week since I started my Finals at Oxford (Scholar, President of the Union, editor of *Isis*, *jeunesse dorée*, so much promise!) I find myself in a television studio at break of day (5.00 a.m.!), the early-morning toast of the ITV Telethon: standing on my head, unravelling the world's biggest jumper, leading the dawn sing-along with Rustie the Caribbean Cook. Something's gone wrong somewhere.

Wednesday, 30 May 1990

The Canadian saviour flew in and flew out. No go. It's all over. I'm now on the train to Cambridge for a meeting at Bidwells in Trumpington where we are gathering to discuss the timetable and details of the liquidation. If the bank had allowed us up to £1.5 million, with Richard's guarantee, we would have had the rest of the year to find a purchaser. The banks are bastards. Always have been. Always will be.

Saturday, 2 June 1990

A bleak week. Late on Wednesday afternoon I saw the staff at Royal Britain one by one and told them the news. I did it as well as I could and stayed pretty steady

---

* The MP for Derbyshire South was one of a team of parliamentary observers at Romania's elections.

until I got to the last of them who was so decent about it that I couldn't quite stop the tears welling and the lump in the throat. It was a good idea: we just got it wrong. The liquidators arrived on Friday morning, full of the jolly banter of the professional mortician. And last night we had a late consolation supper with Simon [Cadell] and Stevie [Barlow] and Jo [Lumley]. Jo was wonderful: 'Tchah! bah! baff! piff-paff! Away with despair, to hell with woe!'

Sunday, 3 June 1990

At TV-am Norman St John Stevas arrived as a complete self-parody: hooded eyes, luminous nose, teasing mouth. He murmured to Anne [Diamond], 'Gyles is very charming, isn't he?' 'Yes,' said Anne. 'Exactly.' Norman closed his eyes. 'That's why you mustn't trust him. Charming people are never to be trusted.' Edward Fox and David Owen[*] were the main guests. We invited them to test-taste the new range of British Rail sandwiches designed by Clement Freud and then turned to the overnight news: the sad death of Rex Harrison.[†] Because Edward had recently been appearing with Sir Rex in *The Admirable Crichton*, Anne looked to him for some appropriate actor-laddie reminiscences. The poor girl didn't get far.

> *Anne*: Did you know Rex Harrison?
> *Edward*: Yes.
> *Anne*: Did you like him?
> *Edward*: Yes. Ver' much.
> *Anne*: What was he like?
> *Edward*: Erm . . . er . . . a genius.
> *Anne*: What kind of genius?
> *Edward*: (*Pause*) A genius.
> *Anne*: But how did the genius manifest itself?
> *Edward*: (*Pause*) Either the sun shines. Or it doesn't.
> *Anne*: He was very much a stage actor?
> *Edward*: Yes.
> *Anne*: And films?
> *Edward*: Yes.

[*] David Owen (b.1938), MP for Plymouth Sutton, 1966–74, Plymouth Devonport, 1974–92; Labour Foreign Secretary, 1977–9; one of the founders of the Social Democrat Party, 1981, and its leader, 1983–7, 1988–90; later Lord Owen CH.
[†] Sir Reginald 'Rex' Harrison (1908–90), actor.

Afterwards, I joined David Owen for breakfast in the canteen. He prophesied that the general election will be very close, with Thatcher the victor by a narrow margin. I hoovered up the bacon and baked beans. He ate a single orange. It was an exciting conversation and it's left me thinking: if I don't stand in this election, I'm going to have to wait another five years. Go for it, boy.

Monday, 25 June 1990

On Friday I was at the Connaught Rooms for the Royal Britain creditors' meeting – a humiliation and a nightmare. On Saturday I was back at the Connaught Rooms presiding over the National Scrabble Championships Finals! I am described on the front page of today's *Times* as 'the high priest of trivia'. Michèle says, 'If your claim to fame is that you founded the Scrabble Championships and you go on wearing those silly jumpers, what do you expect? People will take you not for what you are, but for what they see. That's life.' Bah.

PART FIVE
Member of Parliament

The Candidate

August 1990 – April 1992

Thursday, 30 August 1990

This may be the day that changes my life.

This morning I took my courage in my hands and called Jeffrey Archer. 'Yes,' barked Jeffrey, 'it's about time. As I said to your mother, "If only he'd got on with it when I first told him to, he'd be in the Cabinet by now."' I don't know quite when Jeffrey can have met my mother, but never mind. The man I need to see is Tom Arnold,* son of the impresario, MP for Hazel Grove and vice chairman of the Party in charge of candidates.

I call Central Office right away. I speak to a terrifying young woman with a triple-barrelled surname and marshmallows in her mouth. But having discovered that Tom Arnold also went to Bedales, I write to him.

Friday, 7 September 1990

A letter arrives asking me to make an appointment 'at your convenience'. We're on our way! . . . Or so I think until I telephone Mrs Barnett Legh at Conservative Central Office who tells me (from a great height) that the earliest Sir Thomas can fit me in is Monday 5th November at 3.20 in the afternoon. An appointment two months down the road at twenty past the hour does not suggest an *urgent* desire to see me nor the prospect of an extended interview. Let's hope the election isn't called meanwhile.

I still haven't told Michèle what I'm up to.

Sunday, 9 September 1990

Mrs T. is on *Frost* saying she expects to be around for a good few years yet, certainly till she's 70. 'Some people *started* their administrations at seventy.' She's ridiculous, but wonderful.

---

* Sir Tom Arnold (b.1947), MP for Hazel Grove, 1974–97.

Saturday, 6 October 1990

Hot news: Britain is to join the European exchange rate mechanism on Monday when interest rates will be cut by 1% to 14%. Mrs T. is giving a press conference outside No. 10. 'Rejoice! Rejoice!' Naturally there's heated speculation about 'a dash to the polls' – and I haven't even had my frigging first interview yet!

Friday, 2 November 1990

Geoffrey Howe* has resigned in protest over Mrs T's attitude to Europe. 'I can no longer serve your government with honour.' There's a wonderful picture in *The Times* of the Thatcher Cabinet in 1979. Eleven years later and there's not one of them left. She's eaten every single one . . . By way of tribute at the Caprice at lunch with Colin Moynihan I chose steak tartare. I didn't ask him about Tom Arnold. If I don't get it nobody knows and then I can pretend (even to myself) it never happened.

Monday, 5 November 1990

'Thatcher moves to fight off Heseltine† threat' was today's headline. This I did not discuss this afternoon when I had my brief encounter with Sir Thomas Arnold MP. We exchanged pleasantries and then I came to the point. Sir Tom turned to gaze out of the window. 'Officially, the list *is* closed. It's all done and dusted,' he said. 'But . . . you never know.' He turned back to the desk and flashed a crinkly smile. 'Here are the forms. If you care to fill them in and let me have them back, we'll take it from there.' He opened his diary. 'Let's meet again on, say, 19 December at 6.30 p.m. Will that suit?' It won't suit at all, but I said, 'Yes, yes, of course, thank you, thank you so much.'

   I was out by three-thirty, the conversation was brief and straightforward, but the combination of Sir Tom's manner – the hushed tone, a certain urgency of delivery, a face with a touch of sadness in repose transformed by sudden brilliant smiles – and the smallness of the room itself gave the meeting an oddly conspiratorial quality. At Oxford I always felt a little hurt that no one had approached me about the possibility of joining MI6. I imagine the initial interview would have felt something like this afternoon's encounter.

* Richard Edward Geoffrey Howe (b.1926), MP between 1964 and 1992, and Mrs Thatcher's longest-serving Cabinet Minister: Chancellor of the Exchequer, Foreign Secretary, Leader of the House of Commons and Deputy Prime Minister; now Baron Howe of Aberavon CH.
† Michael Heseltine (b.1933), MP between 1966 and 2001, Baron Heseltine of Thenford, 2001, resigned from Mrs Thatcher's Government as Defence Secretary in 1986 and was now ready to stand against her for the leadership of the Conservative Party.

Saturday, 10 November 1990

'By-election disasters in Bradford and Bootle.' 'The recession will last until Spring.' Very cheery. Yet there is better news in Barnes: I've signed to do my first commercial (should total £20,000) and I've told Michèle what I'm up to on the political front. I think she thinks it won't happen. I think she's right.

Wednesday, 21 November 1990

Last night's vote [in the battle for the leadership of the Conservative Party]: Thatcher 204; Heseltine 152. She was four short of the 56-vote lead she needed to secure an outright win. The feeling seems to be it's all over.

Friday, 23 November 1990

There's a magnificent lead letter in *The Times* today. It runs to five words. 'Donkeys led by a lion.'

I watched her bravura performance later in the Commons. She was quite magnificent. 'I'm enjoying this! I'm enjoying this!' It was so impressive – whatever you thought of her – and rather moving, ditto.

Tuesday, 27 November 1990

I spent a long day at Shepperton making the Birdseye Waffle commercial: eight hours to shoot thirty seconds. In the real world Mrs Thatcher is now backing John Major. I'm backing Douglas Hurd.[*] In the world of Birdseye Waffles no one seems the least bit interested.

Later

The result is in. Major, 185; Heseltine, 131; Hurd, 56. John Major becomes the youngest Prime Minister since Lord Rosebery in 1894 and Michèle tells me that my man coming in last is a useful indication of the reliability of my political instincts.

Saturday, 1 December 1990

There are now no women in the Cabinet, but Ann Widdecombe[†] joins the Government for the first time. The paper describes her as 'a doughty fighter'. At Oxford she was a funny little thing. But mock not, Brandreth. She's in the Government. You aren't.

[*] Douglas Hurd (b.1930), MP, 1974–97, Home Secretary, 1985–9, Foreign Secretary, 1989–95; now Lord Hurd of Westwell CH.
[†] Ann Widdecombe (b.1947), MP for Maidstone since 1987.

Sunday, 9 December 1990

The Queen has given Mrs T. the Order of Merit and Denis gets a baronetcy. (In due course it'll be 'Arise Sir Mark . . .' That's the irony.) Tomorrow at 10 a.m. I'll be at the Dance Attic in Putney Bridge Road with a lordly title of mine own. It's Day One of the *Cinderella* rehearsals and I'm reviving my Baron Hardup. Bonnie Langford is Cinders and Barbara Windsor is the Fairy Queen.

Wednesday, 12 December 1990

Drinks with the Queen last night. When Her Majesty arrived, Michèle forgot to curtsey – and then remembered forty seconds into the small-talk and, without warning, bobbed right down and semi-toppled into the royal bosom. My performance was hardly more impressive. As the canapés came round I found myself stranded with Her Majesty, frantic for food but obliged to pass up on every tasty morsel that came past because the Queen wasn't partaking. My desultory attempt at conversation can best be described as jejune.

> *GB*: Had a busy day, Ma'am?
> *HM*: Yes. Very.
> *GB*: At the Palace?
> *HM*: Yes.
> *GB*: A lot of visitors?
> *HM*: Yes.
> (*Pause*)
> *GB*: The Prime Minister?
> *HM*: Yes.
> (*Pause*)
> *GB*: He's very nice.
> *HM*: Yes. Very.
> *GB*: The recession's bad.
> *HM* (*looking grave*): Yes.
> *GB*: Set to get worse, apparently.
> *HM* (*slight sigh*): Yes.
> *GB* (*trying to jolly it along*): I think this must be my third. Recession, that is.
> *HM*: Yes. We do seem to get them every few years – (*tinkly laugh*) – and none of my governments seem to know what to do about them!
> GB (*uproarious laughter*): Yes. Absolutely. Very good.
> (*Long pause. Trays of canapés come and go*)

GB: I've been to Wimbledon today.

HM (*brightening*): Oh, yes?

GB (*brightening too*): Yes.

HM (*We're both trying hard now*): I've been to Wimbledon too.

GB (*exhilarated*): Today?

HM: No.

GB (*Well, we tried*): No, of course not. (*Pause*) I wasn't at the tennis.

HM: No?

GB: No. I was at the theatre. (*Long pause*) Have you been to the theatre in Wimbledon?

(*Pause*)

HM: I imagine so.

(*Interminable pause*)

GB: You know, Ma'am, my wife's a vegetarian.

HM: That must be very dull.

GB: And my daughter's a vegetarian too.

HM: Oh dear.

Well, I had had a long day, and she has had a long reign.

Thursday, 20 December 1990

I had my second encounter with Tom Arnold last night. I knew I had to be in two places at the same time: on the stage of the Wimbledon Theatre and in Sir Tom's office at 32 Smith Square, SW1. Happily, the gods smiled on me and a moment or two before six, the supper-break was announced. I tore off my Baron Hardup costume, threw on my charcoal-grey suit, leapt into a cab and stepped into Tom Arnold's room on the dot of six-thirty. 'I appreciate I'm not on the list,' I said, 'but if a possibility crops up, would it be okay for me to throw my hat in the ring?' He glanced furtively to left and right and then leant forward and in a voice barely above a whisper said, 'I don't see why not.' He tapped the side of his nose and smiled again, and then opened up his diary. 'Let's see. We'll next meet on Wednesday 23rd January. Yes?' 'In the morning?' I said, as lightly as I could (I didn't mention the matinee at two). '11.00 a.m.?' 'Fine.'

At 7.03 p.m., on the stage of the Wimbledon Theatre the Lord Chamberlain (Ed 'Stewpot' Stewart) announced 'His Excellency the Baron Hardup of Hardup Hall' and I made my entrance – on cue, but in a charcoal-grey suit. The Ugly Sisters had a lot of fun with that.

Wednesday, 16 January 1991

Iraq rejects last-ditch peace moves as UN Gulf deadline expires. 'No choice but war,' says *The Times* leader. No choice but *Cinderella* at 2.30 and 7.30, says GB. We're cocooned backstage: out there there's the distant rumble of war – it could all have been scripted by J. B. Priestley. (He'd have enjoyed a moment with me last night. There's a small corner in the wings where I do several of my quick changes behind a makeshift screen. I was standing there in my knitted nightshirt when one of the dancers came round the screen, pulled off her top and stood naked for a moment. She looked at me and smiled. I tried to look at her face. 'Sorry,' she said, pulling on her top again. 'They're small, aren't they?' 'No. Yes. I mean they're charming.' And she'd gone. I can't help feeling a proper leading man would have handled the situation with rather more panache.)

Saturday, 19 January 1991

The Times reports: 'After just fifty days in office, Britain's youngest Prime Minister this century has been forced to become a war leader. His hardest passage so far came during the pre-dawn hours yesterday morning. John Major had slept no more than two hours during Wednesday night as he received intelligence briefings on the first sorties against Iraq.'

Will I get to meet him? Benny Hill is coming to the show today. That's who the cast here all want to meet. He's their kind of hero.

Wednesday, 23 January 1991

My third encounter with Tom Arnold, but this time I've come prepared. From my briefcase I produce a piece of paper:

To: Sir Thomas Arnold MP

Coming from a large family, and as the chairman of a national body with affiliated associations in every English county, and as a director of a retail chain with thirty branches, I can claim links with many parts of the country.

Specifically I have direct business or family ties with each of the following constituencies: Hertsmere, City of Chester, Croydon Central, Brighton Pavilion, Castle Point and Chingford. I live not far from Croydon, and my associations with Chester and Hertsmere are particularly close, as my father and his family come from the former and my sister and her family live in the latter.

(Okay, so my father came from Hoylake, but Chester's close. And if St Albans isn't in the Hertsmere constituency it ought to be. And desperate times call for desperate measures.)

The upshot is this: I can send my CV to the constituency chairmen at Chester, Croydon, Brighton, Castle Point and Chingford and Tom has said he will send my details to the Central Office agents in the relevant areas with his recommendation.

Friday, 1 February 1991

Iraq is getting dawn-to-dusk coverage on radio and TV, and most nights I tune in after the show. I didn't tonight because I went to an end-of-run celebration at Joe Allen's. War is not a topic much touched upon by the Wimbledon Theatre panto players.

Thursday, 21 February 1991

Hallelujah! A letter from the City of Chester Conservative Association inviting me to attend an interview on the weekend of 1st–3rd March. 'Questions from the chairman, a ten-minute speech without notes on a subject of my choice, followed by further questions from the Interviewing Panel.' It is simply signed, 'Vanessa. Agent.'

I ask to be booked in for the last slot of the weekend: 3.00 p.m. on Sunday the 3rd. I told Michèle about the interview and her *first* response was, 'It's fucking miles away!' There wasn't a second response.

Sunday, 3 March 1991

I was appallingly nervous.I booked myself into the Chester Grosvenor last night and just paced the room running and rerunning my speech. I played the local card for all it was worth, did the family stuff, the visionary stuff, why I am a Conservative. I went for a rallentando at the finish to tug at the heartstrings. 'I believe passionately in the values of our party. I know and love the City of Chester. We have such a great cause. This is such a special constituency. How I would love to be your candidate.' Well, I convinced myself anyway.

Sunday, 10 March 1991

It's Mothering Sunday and, if Chester went well, I've got to put it down to the mother of my children. At the Friday night drinks at the Grosvenor Hotel my darling girl worked the room. The chairman of the women's committee was Russian-born and Michèle even managed to charm her *in Russian*. I tried not to overdo it – not altogether successfully. I said to the Duke of Westminster [President of the

Chester Conservative Association], 'May I call you Gerald?' which was certainly a mistake. I don't think he'll be voting for me, but I felt the others might.

On Saturday the format was as before: fourteen inquisitors in a horseshoe around the candidate seated at a small card table. I was okay-ish on the questions – except I know nothing about farming. But that didn't seem to matter. The room was with me. When it was over I made for the loo and, when I emerged, they were all coming out of the interview room. A couple of the women whispered 'Well done!' as they passed, and the chairman – on crutches, he's ex-RAF, avuncular – came struggling up, rather embarrassed, and said, 'Good show – but I forgot to ask – anything I ought to know? – skeletons in the cupboard – that sort of thing – need your word.' 'I don't think so.' I tried to say it meekly. 'I think you'll be all right with me.'

Monday, 11 March 1991

Back home, we were still in bed with the early-morning tea when Sir Tom called. 'It's going well. But I think you ought to go and see Sir Peter Morrison.* I sense he's got one or two reservations . . .'

At five o'clock, on the dot, I rang the doorbell at 81 Cambridge Street, SW1. Sir Peter is tall, fat, effortlessly patrician, a non-stop smoker, a proper Tory grandee. He sat back on a sofa, glass in one hand, cigarette in the other. I struggled. I asked him about the constituency and he answered in vague generalities. I asked him about the local press. 'I never talk to them,' he said with satisfaction. I asked him why he was giving up (he looks 60, but he's only 46): 'When you've been a Minister of State, Deputy Chairman of the Party, worked with the Prime Minister at No. 10 and you know you're not going to get into the Cabinet – and I'm not – it's time to do something else. If I get out now I've got time for a second career. I'm going to make some money.' After about half an hour he was getting restless, so off I toddled. I don't know what was gained by the encounter, except he will have discovered I own at least one sober suit as well as all those ghastly jumpers.

Tuesday, 12 March 1991

Dear Gyles,

I am writing to confirm you are now down to the final three in our selection of a prospective candidate . . .

Vanessa. Agent.

---

* Sir Peter Morrison (1944–95), MP for the City of Chester, 1974–92; Minister of State for Energy in 1987, but, more significantly, PPS to Margaret Thatcher from 1990.

The Candidate

Saturday, 16 March 1991

Well, if that wasn't forty-eight hours that shook the world, it was certainly forty-eight hours that changed our lives.

On Wednesday night we went to St Paul's to see *Nicholas Nickleby* with Saethryd [now 14] as The Infant Phenomenon. She was gorgeous. When she was on, I concentrated. The rest of the time, my head whirred with my speech. On Thursday (M's birthday, poor thing) we set off for Chester early and ensconced ourselves in 'our' room at the Grosvenor. (This is proving an expensive business.) At 6.45 p.m. we were at Rowton Hall Hotel, stomachs churning, smiles fixed. The other candidates appeared equally daunted: Sir Peter's young man looked reassuringly unpromising, but Jacqui Lait* looked – and was – formidable. Vanessa said to me right away, 'Sorry, you can't go last this time. They're on to you. We're drawing lots.'

The lots were drawn. I was second on. The speech went well. It was a bit of a toe-curler, but it had as much local stuff as I could manage. The questions were a nightmare. Several I didn't understand *at all*. One of the first questions was about farm subsidies. I hadn't a clue.

My turn done, Jacqui Lait went in. Michèle went to the loo and when she came back she said, 'Don't be very disappointed if you lose. She's very, very good. She's talking about Europe and she knows her stuff.'

I must say Jacqui looked like a winner. She glowed. While they counted the votes, we stood around, laughing nervously, drinking coffee, making small-talk. Then, quite suddenly, the chairman was struggling in on his sticks. He paused, breathless, looked around the group then shot his hand in my direction: 'Congratulations. The vote was decisive. You are to be our prospective parliamentary candidate. Well done.' The others shrank back, faded instantly, began at once to make their excuses and go, as the chairman and Vanessa led us triumphantly back into the hall and a standing ovation. It felt very good.

What felt best of all was getting back to our room at the Grosvenor and collapsing over a bottle of ludicrously expensive house champagne. I raised my glass to my birthday girl and she raised her glass to me. By George, we'd done it!

Thursday, 21 March 1991

A 'briefing' from Peter Morrison. The conversation didn't exactly flow, but the gist of it was clear – and helpful: 'You'll need to spend about £2,000 a year of

---

* Jacqui Lait (b. Jacqueline Harkness, 1947), MP for Hastings and Rye, 1992–7, and the first woman to join the Conservative Whips' Office.

your own money on raffle tickets etc. and write an awful lot of notes. The troops like to get handwritten notes. Sometimes I do twenty a night. When the election's called I'll come down on Day One to give you a send-off, then I'll keep out of the way. If you want my advice, never talk politics in the constituency. On the great national issues, if you like, take the moral high ground. You can't go wrong. On local issues, keep your head down. And anything to do with planning, don't touch.'

Sunday, 14 April 1991

Of the past thirty days, I have spent twenty in Chester and ten on the run attempting to earn a living while proving to my would-be constituents that I'm all theirs. I'm going everywhere, doing the lot – from the King's School Lenten Service to the amateurs in *The Gypsy Baron*. The only oppressive part to date is the locals' obsession with my being local too. 'Where do you come from?' 'My father was born in Hoylake.' Slight reassurance. 'Where are your children at school?' 'London.' Faces fall. 'But, of course, when I'm elected I'll have to be in London much of the time and it's important to keep the family together.' Lips purse like a bitter walnut. 'And where are you living now?' 'In Whitefriars, Number 5 – next door to where Basil Nield and his sister used to live.' (Sir Basil was MP here in the late forties.) That reassures most of them – but the sharp ones with the angry little faces leave it a beat and then narrow their eyes and go in for the kill: 'Yes, that's where you're renting, but where's your *real* home?'

Tuesday, 14 May 1991

Last night we were invited for supper with the Deputy Chief Whip!* He has a charming house in Lord North Street, a charming wife called Cecilia (bird-like and delightful, with one of those deceptively daffy Kensington manners – don't be fooled by the tinkly laughter . . .), and a charming, disarming way with him. Lots of quiet chuckling. They couldn't have been more friendly or hospitable. He'd invited us because his is the constituency adjacent to 'mine' and he wanted to 'mark my card'. Also at supper was another Cheshire MP, Neil Hamilton.†
Dry and droll. I was on best behaviour: didn't drink, didn't talk too much, and didn't find it as alarming as I'd feared.

---

* Alastair Goodlad (b.1943), MP for Northwich, 1974–83, Eddisbury, 1983–99; later Chief Whip; now Baron Goodlad of Lincoln.
† Neil Hamilton (b.1949), MP for Tatton, 1983–97; Government Whip, 1990–2; Minister for Deregulation and Corporate Affairs, 1992–94; embroiled in the 'cash for questions' scandal thereafter.

Saturday, 18 May 1991

Weekend excitements: the Mill View Primary School May Fayre, the Chester Rugby Club Beer Festival (I've had to sponsor a barrel – £80! – and I hate the taste of beer), the Chester Festival of Transport and the Sponsored Walk for the Hospice . . . and I could face another year of this before polling day.

Yesterday one of our elderly activists sidled up to me. He must be in his seventies, small, stocky, cloth cap, bent, red nose with a drip at the tip.

'I don't think you're going to hold the seat, I'm sorry to say.' He looked *delighted* to be saying it.

'Oh,' I murmured, as cheerily as I could. 'Why not?'

'It's your handshake. It just isn't firm enough.' He put out his hand and I stupidly put out mine and he gripped my hand so hard I wanted to scream. 'That's what you need,' he said. 'You don't mind my telling you, do you?'

Thursday, 6 June 1991

The [NPFA] birthday lunch for Prince Philip was a complete success. It was Ladies Only (apart from HRH). I allowed myself to attend the drinks beforehand and HRH was genuinely amused by the women-only idea. I told him Jane Asher had done a special birthday cake . . . 'Didn't she used to go out with Paul McCartney?' 'Yes, but I don't think she likes to be reminded of that.' 'Pity. He's good news.' 'She's good news.' 'Yes, but Paul McCartney's quite special.' I was convinced the first thing he'd say to Jane was 'Didn't you used to go out with Paul McCartney?' but he didn't. When irritated (or sometimes, I suspect, just for the hell of it), he can be perverse.

Sunday, 8 September 1991

At 12 noon we gathered at Puddington for 'Peter Morrison's Annual Pimm's Party'. This is a gala event in the Association's calendar. Sir Peter provides the Pimm's and the Conservative ladies provide 'the bites'. Until I came to Chester I'd never heard of 'bites' – now I eat almost nothing else. Michèle got a message saying she was expected to bring sixty 'bites' to an event and what would she be bringing: sausages on sticks, celery filled with cream cheese, curried stuffed eggs? 'Stuff yours' was my darling wife's reaction. That's not what she said to them, of course. That's what she said to me. She also made me phone the hotel and order three trays of canapés as our contribution. We've not been asked for 'bites' since.

Thursday, 12 September 1991

Last night's Granada drama on the downfall of Mrs T. – *Thatcher: The Final Days* – was gripping stuff. For us, of course, the fascination was in the characterisation/demonisation of poor Peter Morrison. If it hadn't been for his ineffective campaign, she might have survived.

This helps explain why he's getting out. Of course, the programme didn't portray him as either a lush or an old queen, though we can see he's the one and we assume he's the other. I think Jeremy Hanley takes credit for coming up with the line – at the time of Peter's appointment as Mrs T.'s PPS – 'Ah, at last Margaret's got herself an aide who knows how to carry a handbag.'

Sunday, 6 October 1991

Peter invited me to sit in on his regular NFU meeting. On a Sunday morning about four times a year he has six to ten farmers from our part of Cheshire come to his house to tell him of their travails. Peter says whether it's eggs, wheat, beef, poultry, horticulture, they're never happy, but they always arrive in Jaguars.

This afternoon, I was working on my debut speech for the Party Conference. It's four minutes maximum. My spot is Thursday at 9.30 a.m.; my theme, the Citizen's Charter; and my position, considered adulation.

Monday, 7 October 1991

I spent two more hours fine-tuning my four minutes and then set off to be on parade for the Association's Autumn Lunch. Our guest of honour was William Hague,[*] PPS to Norman Lamont,[†] and excellent value: good jokes and a clear message. We think we know one another because I was President of the Union about ten years before he was and he seems to recall several of my older jokes. The activists know him because he wowed the Party Conference as a boy orator aged 15. He doesn't look much older now.

Friday, 11 October 1991

The Party Conference is an extraordinary phenomenon. It's only the activists who sit through the debates. Everyone else is junketing, non-stop. There's a nice freemasonry among the prospective candidates. I fell into conversation with one

---

[*] William Hague (b.1961), MP for Richmond, Yorkshire, since 1989; Leader of the Conservative Party, 1997–2001.

[†] Norman Lamont (b.1942), MP for Kingston-upon-Thames, 1972–97, Chancellor of the Exchequer, 1990–93; now Baron Lamont of Lerwick.

man who was standing in some godforsaken northern backwater. 'Do you live in the constituency?' I asked. 'Good God no,' he spluttered. 'Happiness is the constituency in the rear-view mirror.'

Jerry Hayes[*] bounded up to the podium on Thursday morning to give an apparently unscripted address on the wonders of the NHS and completely lost his way. 'Mr Madam Chairman,' he burbled, before concluding (with the rest of us), 'this must be the after-effect of a very bad night.' It made me feel my speech had been quite statesmanlike. I was appallingly nervous, but it was fine. I got a bit of an ovation in the hall, but wasn't much noticed beyond: as I began, we hit ten o'clock and the BBC TV Conference coverage was interrupted for *Watch with Mother*.

Last night I had my first close encounter with the Prime Minister. It was not an unqualified success. I had been asked to conduct the auction at the Conference Ball (and asked too to donate one of my 'famous jumpers' as an extra auction offering). Michèle and I arrived on time at the VIP reception and stood about making desultory small-talk. It was exactly like waiting for royalty. Cameras whirred, bulbs flashed, we all beamed and the PM and Norma worked the line, grinning resolutely all the way. As they got to us I was thrust forward clutching my 'famous jumper' – powder blue with 'MAJOR TALENT' boldly emblazoned on the chest – and as the Prime Minister caught sight of it I saw a danger signal flash behind his eyes. Whatever happened, he was not going to be photographed with that silly jumper. He started back, he grimaced, he gave a little cough, he muttered 'Good to see you' and moved firmly on.

Later

We have just watched the Prime Minister give his end-of-Conference address. It was exactly right: clear, uncomplicated, compelling. And best of all, at the end, when John and Norma went walkabout, what did we see? Picked out by the TV camera, the comely girl who last night bought and is today wearing a powder-blue jumper bearing the legend 'MAJOR TALENT'. So there.

Tuesday, 31 December 1991

199 firms a day are collapsing. We're behind in the polls. Our personal finances are pretty dire because I've spent a year walking the streets and treading water. But this is what I wanted to do and Michèle is supporting me without reproach. (Well, not quite without reproach: every time we're on the motorway for more

---

[*] Jeremy Hayes (b.1953), MP for Harlow, 1983–97.

than four hours trekking between here and Chester she hisses, 'You wouldn't wait, would you? You wouldn't see if something nearer London came up; you'd have walked over your dying granny to get it. I know you.' She does.)

Anyway, the year's done now. And there were good things too. Today Dirk Bogarde has a knighthood. And I have a brilliant wife and three good children and one fine cat and plenty of energy and ambition and *hope*. 1992, here we come!

Monday, 20 January 1992

This may be a 'key marginal' but as far as I can tell it's just me and Vanessa and our ageing activists against the world! That's not entirely fair. Central Office do send us visiting ministers – usually giving us all of seventy-two hours' notice. Today, for example, I took our Environment Minister[*] to Chester Zoo where I had to struggle to ensure that I ended up in the pictures with him when what the photographers really wanted was the Minister and the baby hippo. The trick is to make sure you are in *every shot* and in actual physical contact with the central figure in the picture. Appear in a couple of photographs, pop up on the local TV news, and the supporters purr, 'Oh, you've been busy!' Kill yourself from dawn till dusk doing good works but fail to have your picture in the paper and they look at you reproachfully, lips curling, 'We haven't seen much of you lately, have we?'

Saturday, 25 January 1992

I spent the morning 'saving' a nursery school and the afternoon learning about the severe financial challenges facing the Chester branch of the RNLI. Michèle is currently donning the appropriate glad rags as we ready ourselves for the Newton Branch Twenties Evening. We came up via Wilmslow last night and stayed with Neil and Christine Hamilton at their handsome Old Rectory at Nether Alderley. We were given the Barbara Cartland suite (pink and perfect) and, with due reverence, shown the very loo on which the Blessed Margaret had once sat. Christine is loud and splendid and winks a lot. Neil is very funny, and wicked. He's a Government Whip, but said: 'After the election I'll be a departmental minister of some sort. A couple of years in the Whips' Office and then you move on.' 'Aren't you ever moved out?' 'Oh no, the Whips' Office look after their own. That's the whole point.'

---

[*] Sir David Trippier (b.1945), MP for Rossendale, 1979–83, Rossendale and Darwen, 1983–92.

Friday, 14 February 1992

Today, from London, word has reached us along the crackling airwaves of 'Black Thursday', a bleak day of grim statistics, the worst of which is the sharp rise in unemployment, while here in Chester our schedule (on what my darling wife is describing as 'a high day of romance') has included breakfast at the Gateway Theatre, the Boughton branch Coffee Morning, lunch with the head-mistress at the Queen's School, tea with the Blacon Handbell Ringers, drinks with Tory grandee Lord Waddington in the Association Hall and eventually the razzle-dazzle of the Chester Nomads Hot Pot Supper at the Christleton Country Club.

Saturday, 22 February 1992

Yesterday I met the Foreign Secretary [Douglas Hurd] for the first time. Central Office told us we could have him for just forty-five minutes from 3.00 to 3.45, so we did a walkabout and a photocall down by the river. In all we must have encountered thirty to forty people: they all recognised him and were happy to shake his hand. I kept saying, 'Mr Hurd and I share a birthday, you know' and he kept saying, 'Gyles is a good chap' and that was about it. The photographers had us crouching on the banks of the Dee feeding the swans. The swans were rather reluctant to play ball, however, which meant that the Foreign Secretary and I had to spend a good fifteen minutes waddling on our haunches at the water's edge. Said Mr Hurd with a wan smile, 'I don't think Mr Gladstone did a lot of this, do you?'

This morning I had coffee with Sir Jack Temple,[*] Peter's predecessor. He's old and frail and blind, but he couldn't have been more courteous and sweet. I don't know that his years at Westminster had much impact on our island history, but he is clearly a good Cheshire man. His trademark was spotted ties – 'people knew who I was' – his canvassing advice was 'to get your driver to take you very slowly through all the villages – you sit on a rug on the bonnet and just wave at the people as you drive past – never stop – that way there are no damnfool questions.'

Tuesday, 10 March 1992

The high points of my Budget Day have been the Blacon Coffee Morning (in a house that smelled of urine and disinfectant – a smell I'd never encountered before getting this job, but one to which I find I'm now quite accustomed); sherry

---

[*] Sir Jack Temple (1910–94), MP for the City of Chester, 1956–74.

with the Dean,* a talk to some very elderly ladies at the Square One Youth Club; and the same talk to the Chester Glee Club. From what I can tell, the Budget looks ingenious: but what most of the crumblies really seem to want is a free TV licence.

Wednesday, 11 March 1992

While I was lunching with the Retired Masonic Fellowship at the Upton British Legion Club, the Prime Minister was closeted with Her Majesty at Buckingham Palace. Mr Major had a twenty-minute audience with the Queen and the election has been called for 9 April. The game's afoot. The race is on. The BBC's poll of fifty key marginals gives Labour a five-point lead, but that's bridgeable. We can win and, in Chester, we will.

Wednesday 18 March 1992

Today our star attraction has been Jeffrey Archer. We started off at the Quaker House where we imposed ourselves on a lip-reading lesson for the hard-of-hearing. Jeffrey stood in the middle of the room and boomed at them. He was so loud that they heard every word. Unfortunately, Jeffrey maintained the volume on our walkabout. He has become a caricature of himself, thrusting his hand out towards bemused tourists and barking: 'Jeffrey Archer. This is your candidate, Gyles Brandreth. Jeffrey Archer. Jeffrey Archer. Jeffrey Archer.' Michèle was so embarrassed she slipped home. I like Jeffrey. He's like Mr Toad, absurd but still a star. (And I don't forget: he put £30,000 into Royal Britain, lost every penny, and never said a word.)

Monday, 23 March 1992

Fun and games on the doorstep today. One woman dragged me into her sitting room and said, 'Sit down.'

'No, I can't stay,' I simpered. 'I just popped by to say hello.'

'Look, young man. If you want my vote, you'll sit there and listen to what I've got to say.'

I gave in. I had no choice. I was there for three-quarters of an hour agreeing on the importance of home births, the shameful undervaluing of midwives and the priority of pre-school play provision. As I left she said, 'I shall certainly be voting Labour.'

Later, in Boughton, one of our activists reprimanded me for shying away from

* Dr Stephen Smalley (b.1931), Dean of Chester Cathedral, 1987–2001.

a particularly ferocious dog. 'They can smell fear. You should go towards them and show them the back of your hand.' She did exactly that. I think she'll need stitches.

Tuesday, 31 March 1992

Mr Major brought his soapbox to Chester this morning and it was a triumph. We only had twenty-four hours' advance notice and strict instructions not to tell a soul about it. 'If we can't say he's coming, how's anyone going to know he's here?' was my question to Vanessa. 'We can alert the troops to the fact that we're expecting a very important visitor whose name we can't mention and let them draw their own conclusions.'

In the event, the police reckoned there were two thousand at least by the time the battle bus arrived. The door opened, we all roared, and the Prime Minister with a grin and a wave plunged into the throng. The crush was incredible. I managed to get right by him and stuck to him like a limpet as we moved through the heaving, cheering mass. We were surrounded by police, TV crews, cameramen, and at the Prime Minister's right hand throughout was Norman Fowler,[*] keeping up a running commentary: 'The soapbox is just to the right, John. Look towards the balcony now, see the camera, now wave. And now to the left, there's some girls at the window, another wave. That's it, good, good. It's going well. Nearly there.' Major then clambered onto the soapbox and made a proper speech. Here was the Prime Minister of the United Kingdom on a soapbox in the rain telling two thousand of the people of Chester what he wanted to do for his country.

Wednesday, 1 April 1992

Today's poll gives Labour a seven-point lead. They're on 42, we're on 35, the Lib Dems 19. I'm scuppered. I have just been watching Mr Kinnock[†] amid flashing lights and fireworks giving a triumphalist oration at a rally in Sheffield. He is so awful, and in ten days he'll be Prime Minister.

---

[*] Peter Norman Fowler (b.1938), MP, 1970–2001. In 1990, famously, he left Mrs Thatcher's Cabinet 'to spend more time with his family'; during the 1992 election he was John Major's special adviser and became Chairman of the Conservative Party after it, 1992–4; now Baron Fowler of Sutton Coldfield.
[†] Neil Kinnock (b.1942), MP, 1970–95, Leader of the Labour Party, 1983–92; later Baron Kinnock of Bedwellty and European Commissioner.

Friday, 3 April 1992

The Social Security Secretary Tony Newton[*] was our VIP yesterday and since nobody seemed to have heard of him Vanessa decided that we'd take him to a nursing home. We troop round, grinning inanely at uncomprehending faces. Let us hope the old dears will survive till polling day. (Vanessa has been brilliant with the nursing-home vote. The trick she says is to get the matron on your side. She's the one who fills out the postal and the proxy votes . . . Vanessa's also got me going to see the nuns in Curzon Park: 'You only need to nobble the Mother Superior. If she votes for us, they all will. It's called the rule of obedience.')

Tuesday, 7 April 1992

We've been parading our celebrity circus: Labour has come up with Simply Red, Nigel Kennedy and Steve Cram; we're fielding Ruth Madoc, Lynsey de Paul, Elaine Paige. Not bad. (We seem to be keeping Russell Grant and Bob Monkhouse under wraps.)

Thursday, 9 April 1992

Michèle and I voted first thing, up on St Mary's Hill, in the nursery school I saved (my one achievement to date!), and then spent the day visiting as many polling stations as we could manage. It's clear it's going to be a close-run thing. The Labour people are ruthless when it comes to getting out the vote: they turn up at the old folks' homes and shovel the old dears into charabancs. Our teams were mostly optimistic, but John Cliffe [one of the Conservative activists] may have been nearer the mark. Hangdog face, fag cupped in the palm of his hand, he shook his head mournfully. 'They're not coming out for you. You're too good for them. It's a crying shame.'

It's just gone ten. We're watching the box and it don't look good. Ask not for whom the exit poll tolls, it tolls for thee . . .

Friday, 10 April 1992

I am now the Member of Parliament for the City of Chester.

The leader of the Labour Group turned purple with anger and dismay. He wanted recount after recount, but eventually the moment came: the Returning Officer whispered the final figures to each of us in turn, we accepted them (the Lib

---

[*] Anthony Newton (b.1937), Conservative MP for Braintree, 1974–97; Leader of the House of Commons, 1992–7; now Baron Newton of Braintree.

Dem and the Green candidates with good grace; the Labour candidate through gritted teeth), and processed onto the stage.

Brandreth (Conservative): 23,411
Robinson (Labour): 22,310
Smith (Lib Dem): 6,867
Barker (Green): 448
Cross (Natural Law Party – we never saw him, but apparently he was always 'there'): 98

I've won. And it does feel good. And Michèle has been wonderful. After the count, I did radio and television and gabbled away to the local press and we went to the [Conservative] Club and caroused with the victorious troops, although I didn't have a celebratory drink. On Easter Sunday, however, we are lunching at the Caprice and, then, boy, will the champagne flow . . .

The Member for Chester

April 1992 – December 1993

Wednesday, 15 April 1992

I got back to Chester on the 11.23. There's a sackload of mail, including a hand-written note from the Foreign Secretary. 'Dear Gyles, Many congratulations – that's excellent news. I'm sure our stroll among the swans a month ago was decisive. Yours, Douglas.' I'm impressed – and pleased.

Thursday, 16 April 1992

The Queen came to Chester today to distribute the Royal Maundy at the Cathedral and to bestow upon us the gift of a Lord Mayoralty in a little ceremony at the Town Hall. When I arrived at the Council Chamber it was made clear to me that a Member of Parliament is of little significance on these occasions. I took my allotted place at the end of the third row back. Mayors past and present, Sheriffs, Councillors, city and county dignitaries by the score, processed with wonderful dignity to their places. Just as the Queen and the Lord Mayor followed by Prince Philip made to leave, Prince Philip caught my eye. He moved down the line towards the cheap seats.

'What are you doing here?'

'I'm the Member of Parliament.'

'Good God, are you really?'

It lasted only moments, but the effect on the Councillors was noticeable. And gratifying.

Monday, 20 April 1992

Frankie Howerd has died and I have started drinking. He was 75, which surprises me (he seemed younger), and I've raised several glasses to him because he was very funny and I was genuinely fond of him.

My first letter from the Prime Minister. A letter, too, from Michael Portillo[*]

[*] Michael Portillo (b.1953), MP for Enfield Southgate, 1984–92; Secretary of State for Employment, 1994–5; Defence Secretary, 1995–7; broadcaster and journalist.

whom I've never met. Has he written to all the new boys? Lord St John of Fawsley writes, in purple ink, 'My dear Gyles, You will be a wonderful MP but practise a little economy of personality in the Commons. They don't deserve to have too much too soon.'

Friday, 24 April 1992

As arranged, I presented myself at the St Stephen's entrance to the Palace of Westminster as Big Ben struck eleven. Tall, broad, beaming, Jeremy Hanley was waiting and gave me the most wonderful hour-long tour, starting at the Members' Entrance where he introduced me to the policeman. In the members' cloakroom there are 651 coat-hangers arranged in alphabetical order. Attached to each one is a small loop of pink ribbon: 'That's where you hang your sword!' When we went into the Commons chamber, Jeremy showed me two thin red lines woven into the green carpet in front of each of the front benches. 'When speaking in a debate, you must "toe the line". And the distance between those two lines is the exact distance between two outstretched arms and two full-length swords . . . At the House of Commons, sword-fighting is definitely not on. (*Pause*) *Back-stabbing* on the other hand is quite a different matter!'

Monday, 27 April 1992

It is difficult to describe quite how miserable I feel. The plain truth is, today has been my first full day at the House of Commons and I have hated it.

At 12.30, as arranged, I met Neil and Christine Hamilton in Central Lobby. Neil (now a junior minister at the DTI) and I set off to bag our places in the chamber. Neil said we should sit in the second row, just behind the Prime Minister. We reserved our seats and went off to lunch.

At 2.30 we were back in the chamber for the election of the Speaker. The place was packed. I sensed immediately that sitting, literally, at the Prime Minister's right ear, was wrong, preposterous, risible. I felt all eyes must be upon me and that every single person in the chamber must have felt contempt for me and my presumption. In fact, of course, I know that's hardly rational, no one was thinking about me at all, but I could feel nothing else. The whole amazing process of the election of the Speaker as good as passed me by. When the vote was announced – Boothroyd[*] 372, Brooke[†] 238 – the place erupted. History was

---

[*] Betty Boothroyd (b.1929), MP for West Bromwich, 1973–2000; Speaker, 1992–2000; now Baroness Boothroyd of Sandwell OM.

[†] Peter Brooke (b.1934), MP for the Cities of London and Westminster, 1977–2001; now Baron Brooke of Sutton Mandeville CH.

being made. The Commons has its 155th Speaker and she is the first woman. It was quite an occasion, but I loathed every minute of it. And it went on for two hours.

At 5.00 p.m. I made my way up to Committee Room 10 for the New Members' Meeting. All the Government Whips sat on the platform in a line and we new boys (plus the four new girls) sat, cowed, below at school desks – yes, school desks with ridges for your pencil and square holes for inkwells. It was exactly like a Dickensian school assembly photographed by David Lean in black and white. Even the jokes creaked: 'And when there is a three-line whip you will be here to vote – unless you can produce a doctor's certificate (*Pause*) showing you are dead.' As we shuffled out, my Whip[*] hauled me from the crowd. 'I don't know what you think you were doing sitting right behind the Prime Minister. Not a very good start. Don't let it happen again.'

Trembling with the shame of it (and thinking 'Fuck you' at the same time – it is all so stupid) I went down to Central Lobby for my assignation with Angela Eagle.[†] Smallish, youngish, short lank hair, pointy nose, blokeish manner, not my idea of a fun time (as Simon [Cadell] would say, 'She's happier in Holland')[‡] she's the victor at Wallasey and the person I'm hoping will provide my 'pair'. We went down to the bar in the basement to talk it over. I bought her a drink (was that a mistake? I imagine she *lives* for political correctness) and pleaded my cause – rather too desperately, I fancy. She's 'seeing one or two others', then she'll let me know. If I don't have a 'pair' I shall be stuck at the House of Commons every night for five years. I cannot believe what I've let myself in for.

Tuesday, 28 April 1992

At the centre of Matthew Parris's political sketch in *The Times* today we read: 'Though Mrs Currie returns to her post as Madam Limelight, Gyles Brandreth (C. Chester) who, *on his first day*, walked straight into the prime TV "doughnutting" space behind the PM and sat down, is already mounting a challenge.' This is exactly what I don't want.

---

[*] David Davis (b.1948), MP for Boothferry, and Haltemprice and Howden, since 1987; in the Whips' Office, 1990–93; soon to be nicknamed 'DD of the SS' by GB.
[†] Angela Eagle (b.1961), Labour MP for Wallasey since 1992; appointed Pensions Minister, 2009.
[‡] 'Where the dykes come from'. Ms Eagle 'came out' shortly after joining the Government in 1997.

Wednesday, 6 May 1992

Angela does not wish to pair with me. She's planning to be in the Commons for many years to come so she's looking for a 'pair' who is a little younger than I am and is likely to be in the House after the next election because he's got a safer seat than mine. The bitch.

This morning I was in my place (third row back, third seat in) at 11.25 for the State Opening. The House was packed. Black Rod came and did his stuff: 'The Queen commands the honourable House to attend Her Majesty immediately in the House of Peers.' Major and Kinnock led the way and we all trooped from our end of the building to the House of Lords. By the time tail-end charlies like me got there there was no room to get in so I watched the Queen reading her speech on one of the TV monitors in the Lords' lobby. At 2.30 we were back in our places for the 'proposing and seconding of the motion on the Loyal Address'. Kenneth Baker[*] kicked off and Kinnock was very good at his expense – 'He has seen the future – and it smirks' – 'He is adept at keeping one step ahead of his own debris'. Dennis Skinner,[†] heckling from below the gangway, was somewhat less subtle: 'He's the big fat slug on *Spitting Image*!'

It was about four when Paddy Ashdown[‡] got to his feet – and, as he rose to address the multitude, the whole House emptied. Literally. 'Is this normal?' I asked my neighbour. 'Oh yes, he's an utter bore. Even the Liberals despise him.'

Thursday, 7 May 1992

Marlene Dietrich has died, aged 90.

Mr Fletcher in the Fees' Office advises us that we should register London as our main residence (which it is anyway) because that'll work to our advantage with the mileage allowance. For travelling between London and the constituency it's 68.2p per mile if your vehicle is 2,301 cc and above, and 43.4p if you are between 1,301 and 2,300 cc. Our old Mercedes falls into the lower bracket. Mr Fletcher explained that a number of MPs upgrade their cars to take advantage of

---

* Kenneth Baker (b.1934), MP for Acton, 1968–70, St Marylebone, 1970–83, Mole Valley, 1982–97; Secretary of State for Education, 1986–9; Chancellor of the Duchy of Lancaster and Party Chairman, 1989–90; Home Secretary, 1990–92; now Baron Baker of Dorking.

† Dennis Skinner (b.1932), Labour MP for Bolsover since 1970.

‡ Jeremy 'Paddy' Ashdown (b.1941), MP, 1983–2001; Leader of the Liberal Democrats, 1988–99; High Representative of the International Community and EU Special Representative in Bosnia and Herzegovina, 2002–6; now Baron Ashdown of Norton-sub-Hamdon.

the higher mileage rate. I don't think we'll be doing that. My salary is going to be just £30,854 which is a nightmare. Michèle is not amused. 'You didn't think about the money, did you? You were so desperate to find yourself a seat you rushed in regardless.'

Tuesday, 12 May 1992

In a nearly deserted House, at exactly 5.35 p.m., I was called to give my maiden speech. I stuck to the formula recommended by DD of the SS: a couple of minutes in praise of your predecessor ('whatever they were like'), three or four in praise of your constituency, four or five on the issues under discussion – nothing too controversial, keep it under ten minutes. I opened with a couple of humorous sorties and then led into the challenges of being a 'new boy' at Westminster: 'Sitting in the right place is obviously vital. On the day of Madam Speaker's memorable election, I found myself innocently drawn to the spot immediately behind the Prime Minister – instinctively drawn there, I now realise, by the assumption that it was the correct place for the Member for the City of Chester because that is exactly where my predecessor, Sir Peter Morrison, was wont to sit when he served the Prime Minister's illustrious predecessor so ably and so loyally.' (Interestingly, doing my homework for my paragraph about Sir Peter, I came across this in *The Times* of 24 July 1990: 'The appointment of Peter Morrison as the Prime Minister's parliamentary private secretary may well prove to be as important as any of the ministerial jobs announced yesterday.' Mmm, yes, but perhaps not quite in the way intended.)

Thursday, 14 May 1992

Late this morning, DD of the SS found me and handed me a slip of paper. 'It's a question for the PM,' he smirked. 'You're asking it. This afternoon.'

My happy lunch with Michèle was ruined. At Prime Minister's Questions, I stood up – along with a hundred others. I thought, 'Please God, I'm not going to be called.' Mr Kinnock asked his questions, Mr Ashdown asked his, then suddenly I heard the Speaker say, 'Mr Gyles Brandreth.' 'Did my Right Honourable friend happen to see the punch-up in the Italian Parliament yesterday, when it was attempting to elect a new President? Does he see that as an example of the benefits of proportional representation or merely a dress rehearsal for the election of a new loser – er, so sorry – I mean a new *leader* of the Labour Party?' God, it was so cheap, so contrived, so graceless, but I spoke it as scripted, word for word.

Friday, 15 May 1992

Matthew Parris's verdict on my performance yesterday: 'Chester: *nul points.*'

Monday, 18 May 1992

At 6.00 p.m. an assignment with DD of the SS: 'You're doing well. I'm trying to get you onto a little group we have – good men who can be trusted. We meet in secret and look at ways we can undermine the Opposition. It's called the "Q" Committee – named after submarines used in the First World War. Don't mention it to anyone.'

Thursday, 21 May 1992

A nice letter from Windsor Castle [from Prince Philip]:

> Things have been a bit hectic recently, culminating with the Windsor Horse Show over this last weekend. Congratulations on your election. I should think Chester must be a delightful constituency. I cannot see any objection to your remaining as Chairman of NPFA as long as there is no clash between its interests and the policies of the Government. However, I am sure you will be able to steer a middle course!!

I wasn't in a state to steer anything this morning thanks to my sustained attendance in the chamber yesterday. The Maastricht debate (aka Second Reading of the European Communities (Amendment) Bill) began at 3.30 p.m. and concluded at 7.40 a.m.! When Edwina spoke at 5.55 a.m. she noted she was the 55th speaker called and thanked the Speaker 'for calling me in daylight'. She spoke rather well – notwithstanding repeated interruptions from Sir Nicholas Fairbairn* who is mad and brilliant and perpetually drunk. As he weaves his way into and out of the chamber, the tail-coated flunkies hover at the ready.

Friday, 22 May 1992

High drama last night. 22 of our side voted against the Government, ignoring Douglas Hurd's plea not to inflict 'a savage blow' to John Major's authority. Hurd was good. He's stylish. And Heath was a joy to watch: he is so arrogant. He didn't deign to mention Mrs T. by name, but he called her remarks about Germany 'rabid, bigoted and xenophobic'. He rumbled and he thundered, but, oddly, he didn't cut much ice.

---

* Sir Nicholas Fairbairn (1933–95), MP for Kinross and West Perthshire, 1974–83, Perth and Kinross, 1983–95.

Geoffrey Dickens,[*] who is gross but very jolly, is encouraging me to join 'the Currie Club' – 'we eat all the things Edwina's told us not to eat.'[†]

Thursday, 4 June 1992

At 5.30, with a group of 'arts-minded' colleagues, I went over to the Department of National Heritage. The new Secretary of State[‡] is an unlikely-looking specimen, but he's an enthusiast and he wants us to go out and spread the word. This clearly excited Patrick Cormack.[§] 'We'll be like unofficial ministers, will we?' he asked, puffing himself up at the prospect. In the tea room they call him the Bishop.

Monday, 29 June 1992

Lunch with the Foreign Secretary, tea with the Prime Minister. The PM patted my hand. Silence fell. I suddenly heard myself asking, 'What's happening in Yugoslavia?' Immediately he launched into a fifteen-minute impromptu masterclass on the tragedy of the Balkans. At one point he fished out his pen and on the back of a paper napkin drew a map of the territory around Sarajevo. He pinpointed the Serb and the Muslim encampments, he knew the names of villages, he seemed to know the names of the head men in those villages. And when he'd done, he tapped the table twice with the palms of his hands and got up to go. He had only taken a couple of sips of his tea and hadn't touched the teacake. Later I was telling Peter Tapsell[¶] this and he said, 'Yes, but he doesn't frighten anybody. When Margaret came into the tea room the teacups rattled.'

Wednesday, 1 July 1992

I came across Neil Hamilton and Michael Forsyth[**] swooning over pictures of Margaret Thatcher in her Baroness's togs. She was 'introduced' into the Lords

---

[*] Geoffrey Dickens (1931–95), MP for Huddersfield West, 1979–83, Littleborough and Saddleworth, 1983–95.

[†] As a junior health minister, 1986–8, Mrs Currie had been an outspoken champion of 'healthy eating', to the irritation of many of her parliamentary colleagues.

[‡] David Mellor (b.1949), MP for Putney, 1979–97.

[§] Sir Patrick Cormack (b.1939), MP for Cannock, 1970–74, Staffordshire South since 1974.

[¶] Sir Peter Tapsell (b.1930), MP for Nottingham West, 1959–64, Horncastle, 1966–83, Lindsey East since 1983.

[**] Michael Forsyth (b.1954), MP for Stirling, 1983–97; Secretary of State for Scotland, 1995–7; now Baron Forsyth of Drumlean.

yesterday. 'Her Iron Ladyship,' gurgled Forsyth. 'Isn't she beautiful?' cooed Neil. 'It's almost too wonderful to bear.'

Wednesday, 8 July 1992

Frankie Howerd's memorial service at St Martin-in-the-Fields. The best moment was Russ Conway accompanying the Graveney School Choir from Tooting singing 'Three Little Fishes'; the worst Cilla Black – only because she kept bursting into tears and when the performer cries the audience doesn't. Frank became a regular at Cilla's house every Sunday – 'always by invitation, usually his own'.

Wednesday, 15 July 1992

The pound is sagging, the Euro-nuts are rampant, Bosnia's in crisis, but what seems to be exercising the PM most is the rebellion on the Office Costs Allowance. Around forty of our side voted to increase our secretarial allowance by about £7,000 more than the Government wanted. The PM kept shaking his head and, of course, we toadies all followed our leader into the lobby, knowing that the rebels and the Opposition between them would give us the cash we need anyway. The new amount is £39,960 which – given the size of the mailbag and the level of constituency casework – is hardly excessive. I shall claim the full amount, or near it, and at the same time enjoy the plaudits that come from having voted for restraint.

Sunday, 19 July 1992

Forty-eight hours of relentless good works behind me, I'm on the train back to London. The story of the day is sensational: David Mellor, our Minister of Fun, caught with his trousers down and his pecker up. The object of his affections, according to the *People*, not the long-suffering Judith Mellor, but one Antonia de Sancha, 31, 'an unemployed actress'. What next?

Monday, 20 July 1992

It seems the *People* got its story by means of bugging La Sancha's Finborough Road love-nest. That has to be an invasion of privacy, doesn't it? No, according to Bill Hagerty, editor of the *People*. 'Mellor has complained he's been unable to write speeches because he's too tired. Now we know why . . . Mr Mellor's love-life has interfered with his effectiveness as a cabinet minister – and that's a matter of legitimate public interest.'

Monday, 27 July 1992

I went to the Department of National Heritage this afternoon to brief Robert Key,* Mellor's deputy, on playing fields. Tea was served, the Minister settled back into his armchair, said 'Fire away,' and then fell fast asleep. I burbled away and several times the Minister rallied, threw in an observation, and then gave up the unequal fight. After half an hour or so, I got up to go. The Minister got to his feet, rubbing his eyes, and thanked me profusely. I trust I left him refreshed.

Friday, 21 August 1992

We're at La Dulcinea, St Paul-de-Vence, staying with Colin and Rosie [Sanders]. We are going to be raising our glasses to the Duchess of York. She has been staying on the other side of our valley with her friend and financial adviser, John Bryan. Unfortunately, unbeknownst to them, lurking up in the hills, was an eagle-eyed jumbo-lensed freelance photographer who has taken a series of lurid snaps of Fergie, topless, cavorting with her buck at the poolside, tickling his fancy and – wait for it – sucking his toes. (This is not something Michèle has ever thought of doing – at least, so far as I know . . .) Anyway, these candid holiday snaps have now been relayed right round the globe and (courtesy of the *Daily Mirror*) have even landed on the breakfast table at Balmoral. Poor Fergie. Poor Queen.

Thursday, 27 August 1992

We flew into Heathrow to learn that Saddam Hussein has moved jet fighters to airfields just above the 32nd parallel and George Bush has declared a no-fly-zone just below it. We learn too that Norman Lamont is standing firm: 'There are going to be no devaluations, no leaving the ERM. It is at the centre of our policy.' But what's really got the nation's juices going has been an intimate telephone conversation between the Princess of Wales and a man called James. It is now available for all to hear, courtesy of the *Sun*'s 'royal hotline'.

Saturday, 19 September 1992

It seems we could have pulled out of the ERM on Tuesday night. Instead Lamont and Major decided to pour £15/20 billion of our foreign currency reserves into their doomed defence of our position. £15/20 billion down the drain!

If Norman goes, Major can regroup and soldier on. If Norman stays, the stench of failure will stick to the Government as a whole and the PM and the Chancellor in particular. We loyal foot soldiers won't smell too sweet either.

* Robert Key (b.1945), MP for Salisbury since 1983.

Thursday, 24 September 1992

There was a tangible sense of excitement in the tea room. There's nothing like a crisis for getting the adrenalin going. 'Isn't this fun?' squeaked [Michael] Fabricant.* Others, like Winterton,† who take themselves seriously (and, bless them, think others take them seriously too), were being rather more pompous about it. But no question: it's been a day of high stakes, high drama. And anticlimax. The PM survived, but he didn't do well. John Smith‡ was magnificent: dry, droll, devastating. We sat glumly and looked on as the poor PM went through the motions.

At 4.20 Paddy Ashdown got to his feet, the whole House groaned, got to *its* feet and set off for tea. And while I made for a rendezvous with a teacake, the beleaguered PM went to his room behind the Speaker's chair for a less happy encounter with the unfortunate Mr Mellor. Does he stay? Does he go? Can we save him? The tea room has decided: he goes, no question. Sir Marcus [Fox]§ made the point, of course, that had Mellor gone weeks ago, we'd have been spared a summer of silly headlines and the PM could indeed have concentrated one hundred per cent on his speech today. Anyway, Sir Marcus telephoned Mellor this morning and gave him the black spot. It's all over – bar the 'personal statement'. That's scheduled for 11.00 a.m. tomorrow.

Friday, 25 September 1992

Today's proceedings began at 9.30 with the debate on foreign policy – 'recent and proposed deployments in the Gulf and Yugoslavia'. Douglas [Hurd] was as smooth and impressive as ever. I sat next to Geoffrey Johnson-Smith¶ who muttered, 'Thank God for the grown-ups.'

Naturally, what the children had come to see wasn't Hurd at the despatch box: it was Mellor at the gallows. By custom, a personal statement interrupts proceedings, is heard in silence and takes ten minutes. As eleven approached, the *tricoteuses* dribbled in. We looked sorrowful, we put on our funeral faces, we wanted

---

* Michael Fabricant (b.1950), Conservative MP for Mid-Staffordshire and Lichfield since 1992.
† Sir Nicholas Winterton (b.1938), Conservative MP for Macclesfield since 1971.
‡ John Smith (1938–94), Labour MP for North Lanarkshire and Monklands East, 1970–94, had just succeeded Neil Kinnock as Leader of the Labour Party.
§ Sir Marcus Fox (1927–2002), Conservative MP for Shipley, 1970–97, vice chairman and chairman of the 1922 Committee of Conservative back-bench MPs, 1983–97.
¶ Sir Geoffrey Johnson-Smith (b.1924), Conservative MP, 1959–64, 1965–2001.

to show we cared. But in our hearts . . . (Stephen [Milligan]* said to me after-wards: 'Remember the Chinese saying? "There is no pleasure so great as watching a good friend fall off the roof." ')

Tuesday, 6 October 1992

This year I've got the measure of the Party Conference. The cognoscenti come for a couple of nights (max), show a face, take in only those parties where champagne is guaranteed, and make sure they have accepted a worthwhile dinner.

The talk of the town is Norman Tebbit's vulgar grandstanding barnstorming performance on Europe. He savaged Maastricht, poured scorn on monetary union, patronised the PM and brought the conference (or a good part of it) to its feet roaring for more. I know he's suffered for the cause of the party (his wife the more so), but there's something quite *nasty* about Tebbit.

Thursday, 8 October 1992

Last night we gave our little drinks party for the activists. We shared it with the Goodlads and Jonathan Aitken† – who is tall and handsome and charming and distant. (Talking of the tall and the distant, Heseltine stalked past me in a corridor at the Grand. I flattened myself against the wall like a good Filipino chambermaid. He glanced towards me, didn't flicker, stalked on. But, but – on the conference platform he's unbeatable: 'If John Smith is the answer, then what is the question?' They lapped it up.)

Friday, 9 October 1992

The great Denholm Elliott‡ has died (AIDS, alcohol and ulcers). Willy Brandt has died. Leslie Crowther,§ bless him, is struggling for his life. But the news from Brighton is that, on the fifth day of the Conservative Party Conference, the PM rose again. I have just been watching him and he's been magnificent.

---

* Stephen Milligan (1948–94), contemporary and friend of GB at Oxford, had recently become Conservative MP for Eastleigh.
† Jonathan Aitken (b.1942), journalist, biographer of Richard Nixon, Christian activist, Conservative MP for Thanet, 1974–97, Chief Secretary to the Treasury, 1994–95, imprisoned for perjury following an unsuccessful libel action against the *Guardian*, 1999. GB first met him during the Aitkens' association with TV-am in the 1980s.
‡ Denholm Elliott (1922–92), actor.
§ Leslie Crowther (1933–96), entertainer, had been injured in a car accident.

Monday, 26 October 1992

DD of the SS told me to present myself at the Lower Whips' Office at 5.30 p.m. 'We meet every Monday, just before Q. It's just half a dozen or so good men, ready to go over the top. We call the meeting Drinks. There aren't any, of course. It's a code word.'

In fact, wine was on offer, and nuts, and we sat in the corner, six of us huddled together on low sofas, and Bob Hughes[*] explained to us that we were 'sort of snipers', who had to be ready to lob in the odd grenade, torpedo the enemy, throw the Opposition off the scent. The metaphors were mixed, but the message was clear. Risk life and limb and, who knows, promotion could come your way . . .

Tuesday, 27 October 1992

The latest line from Admiralty House is that if we lose next Wednesday's vote [on the ratification of the Maastricht Treaty], it's the PM who goes. It's his job on the line. Back me or sack me. And the fix the [Euro-sceptic] rebels are in is this: lose Major and who do they get? Clarke?[†] Heseltine? It seems ingenious. Jeffrey [Archer] thinks it's brilliant. (Perhaps he thought of it?)

Wednesday, 4 November 1992

We survived thanks to the Lib Dems. When it all came right the whole place went berserk.

There's a rumour going round that it was rather closer than it needed to be. David Lightbown,[‡] all twenty stone of him, pursued one of the rebels into the lavatory and was so engrossed in the task of 'persuading' his prey to do the decent thing, he missed the vote himself!

Tuesday, 24 November 1992

We went to the lunch at Guildhall to mark the 40th anniversary of the Queen's accession. She gave the most wonderful speech – wry, personal and very moving – and, best of all, she spoke before the meal not after it! She talked about her

---

[*] Robert Hughes (b.1951), Conservative MP for Harrow West, 1987–97.

[†] Kenneth Clarke QC (b. 1940), Conservative MP for Rushcliffe since 1970; cabinet minister under Margaret Thatcher and John Major; Home Secretary, 1992–93; Chancellor of the Exchequer, 1993–97.

[‡] David Lightbown (1932–95), Conservative MP for Staffordshire South East, 1983–96; a Senior Whip.

annus horribilis. She didn't mention Anne's divorce, Andrew's separation, Charles's marriage on the rocks, but they were in her mind – and ours – and she talked about the weekend's fire at Windsor with a sense of pain and acute personal loss. She said, rather wistfully, that, of course, any institution must accept scrutiny and criticism, but couldn't it be done with a touch of humour, gentleness and understanding?

Wednesday, 2 December 1992

I have just come from drinks with the Princess of Wales in the Cholmondeley Room. Everyone said how wonderful she was looking. I thought (ungallantly) that her skin had rather gone to pot: a sort of light pebble-dash effect on her beaky nose. I thought the thing to do was try to make her laugh, so I talked about Norman Lamont. Of course, I should have thought it through. Diana is sympathetic to poor Norman! The papers have been rotten to him. Just as they have to her. 'They make things up, you know.' In the case of the Chancellor, it seems it was the Thresher's shop assistant who made it up. Norman was not to be found prowling the backstreets of Paddington in search of cheap fizz and fags: yes, he had visited Thresher's, but it was the Connaught Street branch, where he purchased Château Margaux at £ 9.49 the bottle.

In the tea room, unfair as it is, I'm afraid we do find the Chancellor's plight rather comical. 'Isn't it marvellous?' chortles Geoffrey Dickens, tucking into his toast and marmalade, leafing through the tabloids in search of more tasty titbits.

Geoffrey Johnson-Smith is more circumspect. 'What was it Napoleon used to ask of his generals? "Is he lucky?" I think we've got to concede that Norman has been very unlucky. He's a decent fellow, but it's become a bit of a chapter of accidents.' If Geoffrey's saying this, then Marcus'll be saying it too, and sooner rather than later they'll be handing poor Norman the dreaded black spot. There's genuine disquiet at the revelation that Norman's legal costs for evicting a 'sex therapist' from his house last year were covered in part by the Treasury, in part by Central Office. There's amazement that he allows his Access card to go over the limit and ignores the reminders. There's a general feeling he's too accident-prone – and too cavalier – for our liking.

Thursday, 3 December 1992

Lunch with the Chancellor in the flat at No. 11. When I arrived, William Hague was in the kitchen warming up the soup. I said I was sorry I hadn't brought a bottle, but Thresher's was closed and my Access was over the limit. Norman laughed. The only moment I misjudged it I think was when I stood looking out of the window, peering down onto Downing Street, and said 'Who'd have thought it? I'm standing here and you're Chancellor of the Exchequer!' That was a touch of *lèse-majesté* too far. It isn't amazing to Norman that he's Chancellor.

At 7.30 Jonathan Aitken gave a supper party in honour of Richard Nixon.* This was Nixon as hero, elder statesman and freedom fighter, rather than Tricky Dicky, fiend of Watergate. He gave a wonderful address, a *tour d'horizon*, without notes, with surprising dry humour. He's 80, but, on a night like tonight, the energy's still there. He said the energy's been drained from George Bush.† 'The voters have sensed it and moved on. You can smell a winner. Clinton is a formidable campaigner. I should know.' He was impressive. It was as Churchill said of his 'great contemporaries': 'One did feel after a talk with these men that things were simpler and easier.'

Wednesday, 9 December 1992

At 3.30 today the PM got to his feet to announce the separation of the Prince and Princess of Wales. John Smith was commendably brief. Paddy Ashdown less so. Ted Heath went way over the top. Then (this was truly bizarre) Bob Cryer‡ was on his feet asking us to remember divorcees everywhere and telling us that it's poor housing and unemployment that puts marriages under strain and it's all the Government's fault! Next up popped Dennis Skinner to tell us 'we don't need a monarchy anyroad'. He did not catch the mood of the House.

In the tea room William Hague was quite funny: 'At least this'll keep the Chancellor of the Exchequer off the front pages.'

Thursday, 14 January 1993

I went to another of Jonathan Aitken's 'thinking people's soirées'. He made me smile too, told me a story of how Hilaire Belloc, when he was an MP, was asked by an old boy at his club what he did for a living. 'I'm a Member of Parliament,' said Belloc. 'Good God,' spluttered the old boy, 'is that still going on?'

Monday, 18 January 1993

I returned from Chester to find Simon [Cadell] in the Harley Street Clinic (which doesn't sound good, but he was very airy about it) and George Bush using his last

---

* Richard M. Nixon (1913–94), US President, 1969–74.
† George H. W. Bush (b.1924), US President since 1989, had just been defeated in the presidential election by Bill Clinton (b.1946), US President, 1993–2001.
‡ Robert Cryer (1934–94), Labour MP for Keighley, 1974–83; MEP for Sheffield, 1984–9; MP for Bradford South, 1987–94.

weekend in the White House to fire off forty Cruise missiles in the direction of Baghdad's nuclear weapons sites. The Chancellor is equally gung-ho: as employment nears three million, the outlook, apparently, has rarely been rosier. That's not how it seems on the streets of Chester.

Wednesday, 3 February 1993

Good news. Malcolm [Rifkind, the Defence Secretary]* made a statement at 3.30: the proposed amalgamation of the Cheshire and Staffordshire regiments will not now proceed. We've saved the Cheshires! I hail it as a great victory for our campaign – which it is. I do believe all the lobbying did make a difference, although Colonel Bob Stewart and the Cheshires' deployment in Bosnia haven't been unhelpful either. Three cheers.

Rather less exciting is the fact that I've been dragooned onto the Standing Committee considering the Railways Bill. I wanted to be on the Lotteries Bill. My real mistake was letting slip to the Whip that I knew quite a bit about the lottery. I now realise it's *because* I'm keen and informed I'm the very last man they want.

Tuesday, 9 February 1993

I did my stuff at the Winter Ball. It turned out they asked me because they were weary of 'Jeffrey's hectoring tone'. I bet he raises more money though. I didn't do too badly, but it isn't much fun trying to raise £30,000 in under eight minutes flogging three items to four interested punters surrounded by nine hundred garrulous but non-bidding spectators. One good woman bought a bottle of champagne signed by the Prime Minister for £16,000. She deserves a peerage. (And I understand may get one.)

The best bit of the evening was encountering David Cameron,† special adviser to the Chancellor.

'Well done,' he purred, pink cheeks glowing. 'I hear you'll soon be joining us at the Treasury.'

'Really?' I tried to look as if I knew exactly what he was talking about while being far too discreet to let on. 'Tell me more.'

'PPS to the Financial Secretary. Can't be bad.'

---

* Sir Malcolm Rifkind (b.1946), Conservative MP for Edinburgh Pentlands, 1974–97; Foreign Secretary 1995–7; MP for Kensington and Chelsea since 2005.
† David Cameron (b.1966), special adviser to Norman Lamont at the Treasury; later, Conservative MP for Witney from 2001 and Leader of the Conservative Party from 2005.

GB and Michèle with the great
scorer, Sir Stanley Matthews,
31 January 1990

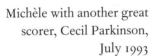

Michèle with another great
scorer, Cecil Parkinson,
July 1993

GB, former US President
Richard Nixon and
future Conservative
Party leader Iain Duncan
Smith, 3 December 1992

Work for Mad Hatters

3 November 1993.
'I've been told to
make a point of
order . . .' 'You'll
need the hat.'

17 *Unpalatable lesson: the truths of British political life* 19 *Sri Lanka: a father's search ends at a mass grave* 23 *How should rules on cross-media ownership be defined?*

THE INDEPENDENT

No 2,256 — WEDNESDAY 12 JANUARY 1994 — Published in London 50p

■ Thatcherites 'will back Clarke' ■ Caithness 'destroyed' marriage ■ MP's £200,000 loss wiped

Treasury scrubbed Brandreth debt

CHRIS BLACKHURST
Westminster Correspondent

THE DECISION to cancel a £200,000 debt of taxpayers' money owed by a company run by Gyles Brandreth, the Tory MP for Chester and Parliamentary Private Secretary to Stephen Dorrell, the Treasury minister, was taken within his own department.

Previously it was claimed that the grant, made by the English Tourist Board to Mr Brandreth's failed exhibition company, Unicorn Heritage plc, was written off by the National Heritage department. Labour then called for Mr Brandreth's resignation as PPS, but the *Independent* can reveal the slate was wiped clean by Treasury officials.

Under Whitehall accounting rules, the English Tourist Board has power to write-off debts up to £3,000 only. Officials at National Heritage can go up to £100,000. Above that, the Treasury decides.

Mr Brandreth was managing-director of Unicorn immediately prior to its demise in June 1990. When the company – set up to develop a "Royal Britain" exhibition at the Barbican Centre in London – received the grant in 1988, he was a director and shareholder, along with two of Britain's richest men: Sir Leslie Porter, former head of Tesco, and the Earl of Bradford. The exhibition flopped and the company went bust.

Mr Brandreth joined the Commons in April 1992 and was appointed PPS to Mr Dorrell last February. Three months later, on 12 May, National Heritage officials sent the Unicorn file to the Treasury.

A Treasury spokesman said the loan was investigated by an official in HE7, the division governing Home and Education expenditure, which includes National Heritage. He said it was the Treasury's job "to make absolutely certain there was no chance of the money being recovered". On 14 May the debt was scrubbed.

Unicorn's £200,000 was the largest single amount among £1m of tourist board grants deemed irrecoverable.

The Treasury official, whom the spokesman refused to name, reported to Andrew Turnbull, Second Permanent Secretary in charge of public spending. "It was the decision of an official, not a minister," said the spokesman.

Asked if there were similarities between Mr Brandreth's case and that of Norman Lamont, who had a legal bill paid by the Treasury when Chancellor of the Exchequer, the spokesman said the £200,000 "was treated as a company debt not a personal one".

Mr Brandreth said last night he could see no conflict between his position in the Treasury and the department's action. He added that from the present row broke, he had not discussed the debt with anyone from the tourist board, National Heritage or the Treasury.

Profile, page 3

12 January 1994. 'I toured the library and the tea room and the smoking room removing copies of the *Independent* – not only so that others mightn't see it, but so that I didn't have to see it either.'

Far left: GB with John Major, outside Number 10, 1993

Left: GB outside Number 12, the whips' office, with the prison-made ministerial box, 1995

Seconding the Loyal Address, 15 November 1995

At least it made them laugh . . .

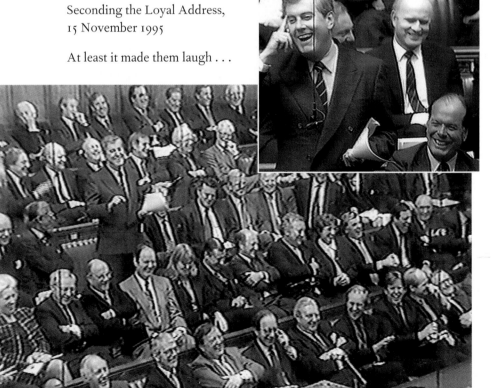

The Chancellor's room at the Treasury, 1993. From the left, seated: Stephen Dorrell (financial secretary), Kenneth Clarke (chancellor), Michael Portillo (chief secretary); standing: Tessa Keswick (special adviser), Andrew Mackay (Treasury whip), GB (PPS), Sir John Cope (paymaster general), Edward Heathcoat-Amory (Central Office), Anthony Nelson (economic secretary), David Ruffley (special adviser), Ian Twinn (PPS), Philip Oppenheim (PPS)

The Chancellor's room, four years later, 6 February 1997. 'Lunch at the Treasury these days is like an informal family picnic.' GB (Treasury whip) goes in search of another sandwich, Mark Robinson (PPS) serves the wine, Michael Fabricant (PPS) takes the picture

Fishing for votes

Facing the nation

The 1997 campaign: the
'activists' – knowing we're
going to lose . . .

GB and Michèle at the opening of the Teddy Bear Museum, 4 July 1988

With Dame Judi Dench and her bear in New York, 'in Marlon Brando's dressing room', 17 June 1999

Laughter and the love of friends, 1988. From left to right: Christopher Cazenove, Simon Cadell, Peter Bowles and GB conducting a raffle

Geoffrey Palmer, Donald Sinden, GB, in Ray Cooney's garden, 1999

Proud father. GB with Benet, 1995

Saethryd and Aphra, 1998

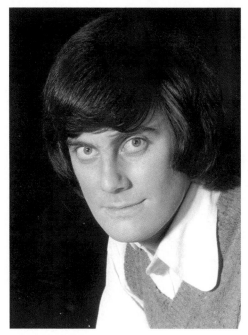

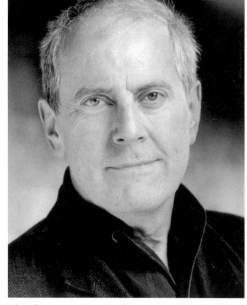

What a difference forty years make. Michèle: 'What happened to the hope – and the hair?'

Wouldn't it be wonderful if it were true? In case it isn't, I've not mentioned it to Michèle.

Wednesday, 10 February 1993

Just as I was wandering off from the six o'clock vote, Stephen Dorrell,[*] Financial Secretary to the Treasury, tapped me on the shoulder. 'Have you got time for a drink?'

We went to the Smoking Room, happily deserted, and sat in one of the deep, uncomfy leather sofas by the window. 'How would you feel about being my PPS?' He has an engaging way with him, shy, unconsciously charming. I said I'd be honoured. I heard myself saying, 'Well, if you're going to be a dogsbody you want to be one to a decent dog.' As we parted (we drained our orange juices swiftly), I compounded the infelicity with my parting shot:

'I'm sure we can have some fun.'

Stephen raised a dubious eyebrow: 'I'm not sure that *fun* is exactly what the Treasury has in mind.'

Monday, 22 February 1993

I was told to present myself at the Chancellor's room at 10.30 a.m. for Treasury Prayers.[†] The Chancellor came in last. He took his seat, folded his hands in his lap and closed his eyes. For a moment I thought, 'Goodness, we are going to say prayers,' but no, Norman was simply collecting his thoughts. And his first thought was a kind one, a word of welcome to me. 'At least the jokes should improve.' This pleasantry over, an eerie silence fell. I didn't say anything. The PPSs contribute when invited, after the ministers have had their say. This morning their 'say' didn't amount to much. Weak tea was brought in (with two sugar lumps in the saucer) and served in order of precedence. By the time I got mine and had burned my lip with the first sip, the meeting was over.

Thursday, 4 March 1993

Treasury Questions. For the first time since my first day I sit in the second row, immediately behind the Chancellor and the PM. This time, of course, it's kosher. The Treasury team don't do at all badly. The PM gets a much rougher ride. The

---

[*] Stephen Dorrell (b.1952), MP for Loughborough and Charnwood since 1979; Government Whip, 1987–90; Secretary of State for National Heritage, 1994–5, and for Health, 1995–7.
[†] 'Prayers': the name given to an informal meeting of ministers and parliamentary private secretaries (without civil servants being present), usually held at the start of the day.

moment Questions were over, he was up on his feet again, with a statement about the honours system. It's to be rewards on merit in future, no automatic knighthoods (suppressed cries of 'Shame!' from behind me).

Monday, 8 March 1993

We've lost [a minor amendment to the Maastricht bill]. And badly: 292 to 314. The Opposition benches broke into a frenzy. Skinner & Co. began jumping up and down, demanding the Government's resignation. The PM, ashen-faced, set off for his room. Soames* pushed his way through the crowd, barking at the Wintertons,† 'You're cunts – and ugly ones to boot.'

Thursday, 25 March 1993

On my way through the members' cloakroom, DD of the SS stops me. 'A word in your ear.' We huddle in a corner by the shoe-shine machine. 'There's something going round about you having financial difficulties. Anything in it?'

I am completely nonplussed.

Good Friday, 9 April 1993

A deeply unpleasant thirty-six hours. I am writing this in our bedroom, at the back of the house. We're being staked out by the *Sunday Express*.

Early on Wednesday evening I got a call from an *Express* reporter who said he wanted to talk to me about my interest in small businesses following my remarks last week on *Question Time*. I knew at once something was up and told him to call back.

When I got home Michèle told me that the reporter had been on to our accountants enquiring about Complete Editions. I telephoned Derek Sloane at Allen & Overy [solicitors] and we prepared a note to give to the reporter in the event that he turned up again.

This morning, first thing, the reporter rang the doorbell. Michèle opened the door and the reporter immediately placed his foot inside the door. He was holding a tape recorder. M gave him the note, bent down, picked up his leg and forcibly moved his foot outside the door. She closed the door and double locked it. And here we are, holed up inside.

---

* Nicholas Soames (b.1948), MP for Crawley and Mid-Sussex since 1983; son of Lord Soames, grandson of Sir Winston Churchill.
† Nicholas and his wife Ann Winterton (b.1941), MP for Congleton since 1983, were Euro-sceptics and Maastricht 'rebels'.

Mr Mellor would be marshalling his family for a photocall at the garden gate. Mary Archer would be serving them mugs of piping hot coffee and digestive biscuits. We are *hiding* in our own home. Why? Complete Editions is in good shape and, now Michèle is running it, doing better than ever. (Michèle's business philosophy: 'Turnover is vanity, profit is sanity.') If I go out there now, they've got their story: 'MP denies financial difficulties'. If I say nothing, if they don't see me, what have they got?

Easter Sunday, 11 April 1993

The tactic seems to have worked. The *Express*'s ruthless investigative reporter lurked outside for most of the day and then disappeared. At about eleven yesterday morning Michèle said, 'This is ridiculous, let's do something useful,' and we vanished into the basement and did the most almighty clear-out: a real spring clean. Who do these vermin think they are?

Thursday, 22 April 1993

The lead story in Londoner's Diary: 'Treasury man Gyles at a loss'. I got on to Allen & Overy at once. At 1.48 p.m. Tim House [solicitor] got hold of the *Standard* and told them the piece is defamatory.

I wrote a detailed note to my Whip telling him there was nothing in it and went over to the Treasury to see Stephen [Dorrell] to apologise to him – because, of course, they've dragged his name in. He couldn't have been sweeter, totally easy and relaxed about it. I ended up looking in on the Upper Whips' Office and David [Heathcoat-Amory]* said 'Join me for dinner', a kindness *much* appreciated.

Monday, 26 April 1993

A good day. On page 8 of the *Evening Standard*, Londoner's Diary: 'GYLES BRANDRETH – AN APOLOGY.' The photograph, I have to say, is one of the best I've seen. I look positively boyish. They're vermin, but we got the retraction, we got the costs, we got the damages, *we won*!

Monday, 10 May 1993

No. 10 for lunch. The PM began by offering us his 'analysis of why we're in the doldrums'. Nigel Forman,† eyes gently popping, wiry and cerebral, lamented the

---

* David Heathcoat-Amory (b.1949), Conservative MP for Wells since 1983.
† Francis Nigel Forman (b.1943), Conservative MP for Carshalton, 1976–97.

fact that 'we don't seem to have a lot to say. The think-tanks and the policy-making groups of the 1980s seem to have lost their cutting edge.' 'Yes,' said the PM, 'all their knives are now buried in my back.'

Thursday, 13 May 1993

It's fascinating the way the chamber sometimes can make a difference. I've just witnessed Kenneth Clarke [the Home Secretary] perform a spectacular U-turn and emerge a hero. We're rethinking the whole of the 1991 Criminal Justice Act ... it should have been a humiliating climb-down. Instead, the way Clarke played it, breezy, bluff, commonsensical, he came out triumphant. Blair* helped. Blair's dangerous. He could be one of us: public school, Oxford, decent, amiable, well-groomed, he's been scoring on law and order. Today Ken dismissed him as 'a tabloid politician', incapable of dealing with substance. It was a pleasure to watch.

Thursday, 20 May 1993

The Third Reading of the Maastricht Bill. Norman did well. Gordon Brown[†] had plenty of bark, but no bite. The Labour Party abstained so, inevitably, we won, but at least fifty of our side either voted against or abstained.

I said to DD of the SS, 'I'm not sure that we should be celebrating yet. The headlines aren't going to say "Maastricht Bill Achieved", they're going to trumpet "Tories' Biggest Ever Revolt".'

'I think not,' he said, with a sly grin. 'Haven't you heard? The Queen Mother has just been rushed to hospital. We're not sure if she'll last the night ...' Wolfish leer followed by conspiratorial chuckle.[‡]

Tuesday, 25 May 1993

Reshuffle fever is in the air. According to Portillo (his hair really is impressive at close quarters, a high sheen and not a touch of dandruff), since the Whitsun Recess begins on Friday, the reshuffle will happen on Thursday. That way, if you get the sack you can slink off home and don't have to face your apparently sympathetic (secretly gleeful) colleagues for a week or two.

* Anthony Blair (b.1953), Labour MP for Sedgefield, 1983–2007, Shadow Home Secretary, 1992–4; Leader of the Opposition, 1994–7; Prime Minister, 1997–2007.
† Gordon Brown (b.1951), Labour MP for Dunfermline East since 1983; Shadow Chancellor of the Exchequer, 1992–7; Chancellor, 1997–2007; Prime Minister from June 2007.
‡ In fact, the Queen Mother had suffered a minor injury to her foot. She was only in hospital briefly as a precaution.

Thursday, 27 May 1993

Well, well, Norman [Lamont] has gone, Michael Howard* is Home Secretary and Ken Clarke Chancellor. The Cabinet newcomer is John Redwood,† about whom I know nothing.

Wanting to see the action, I went into a deserted House for lunch. My first encounter was with Jeremy Hanley who had just emerged from No. 10 and was bubbling with justifiable excitement: Minister of State at Defence. I lunched with Michael Ancram‡ and teased him about his reshuffle haircut. He treated me to a large Bloody Mary. Before lunch was over the call had come through. He's going to Northern Ireland to replace Jeremy.

Friday, 28 May 1993

The reshuffle hasn't worked. No one seems any the happier – except for Ken Clarke who is pictured on the front page of half the papers, standing on the steps of the Treasury, beaming inanely, beer belly and Garrick Club tie to the fore. I've spent the evening enjoying the excellent hospitality of the Cheshire Regiment. I was invited to take the salute at Beating Retreat in the Castle Square. I turned up on time, but without a hat.

'Where's your hat?' gasped Colonel Ropes, red-faced, perspiring with anxiety. 'You can't take the salute without a hat.'

The Lord Lieutenant came to the rescue. The boot of his limousine was stuffed with hats – top hats, bowlers, berets, hats with plumes. Colonel Ropes selected a brown trilby which made me look at best like a bookie, at worst like a spiv.

I was driven onto the parade ground. I climbed the steps and stood there. Alone. Six feet away wretched Colonel Ropes *muttered* instructions, but I couldn't hear a word. As the massed bands marched to and fro, I doffed and donned my trilby with gay abandon. When the regimental goat came forward and bowed, I glanced towards my colonel and caught him looking at his knees. I decided to salute the goat on the grounds that it was wearing the regimental colours.

---

* Michael Howard (b.1941), Conservative MP for Folkestone and Hythe since 1983; Home Secretary, 1993–7; Leader of the Conservative Party, 2003–05.
† John Redwood (b.1951), Conservative MP for Wokingham since 1987; Secretary of State for Wales, 1993–5.
‡ Michael Kerr, now 13th Marquis of Lothian, known as Michael Ancram (b.1945); Conservative MP for Berwick and East Lothian, 1974, Edinburgh South, 1979–87, Devizes since 1992.

The ordeal over, I vowed never to wear a hat again and retired to the mess and drank a great deal.

Thursday, 3 June 1993

A week after the reshuffle and already it seems as bad as ever. There's a poll today showing the PM to be the least popular Prime Minister on record – less loved even than Neville Chamberlain in 1940.

Monday, 7 June 1993

In the Whips' Office they seem to have a firmer grip on what needs to be done. I arrived for 'Drinks' to be asked, 'What do you know about Gordon Brown? Is he gay? We need to nail the bugger. If there's dirt to dish, this is the week to dish it.'

The mood of the meeting was that Gordon ought to be gay, could indeed be gay, should in fact be gay, but maddeningly we have no evidence of any kind to suggest that he *is* gay!

Tuesday, 8 June 1993

This is Michèle's and my 20th wedding anniversary. I love my wife very much and the only thing I don't like about being an MP is that I'm always here – and she isn't. We had a celebratory lunch on Sunday with Simon [Cadell] and Veronica [Hodges], but the Finance Bill Committee has kiboshed the dinner I'd planned for tonight.

Wednesday, 9 June 1993

This morning, our first Prayers with the new Chancellor. It is going to be rather fun. This afternoon, the old Chancellor had some fun of his own. At 3.30 p.m., to a packed House, he made his resignation statement. It was fairly devastating stuff. 'We give the impression of being in office but not in power.'

The poor PM didn't flinch, but Norman's statement left the Opposition cock-a-hoop. When John Smith got to his peroration – 'a discredited government presided over by a discredited Prime Minister' – how they roared.

Thursday, 10 June 1993

I don't see how the poor PM can take much more of this. He's battered from dawn till dusk. PMQs was chaos. The PM did his best, but he played straight into Smith's hands:

PM: As one of my predecessors might have said, we've had a little local difficulty. We shall get over it. I am going on with the work in hand.

Smith: Doesn't the Prime Minister understand that when he announced business as usual this morning he caused apprehension throughout the land?

Tuesday, 15 June 1993

It's 9.30 on Tuesday night, Committee Room 10, where we are on Day 6 of our weary trudge through the fetid swamp of the 1993 Finance Bill. Michael Portillo is wishing he was at the Mansion House listening to the new Chancellor of the Exchequer making his debut. Michael *bought* white tie and tails for the occasion and then found that Harriet Hopeless* [Shadow Chief Secretary to the Treasury] wouldn't pair. She's a cow. (She's also an inexplicable half-inch away from being wonderfully attractive. In the right light she's almost gorgeous, but then she opens her mouth and suddenly you realise she's not that pretty, she's not that bright and – worst sin of all – she has no sense of humour.)

MP said that the Chancellor's Mansion House speech, at least in draft, had been quite unspecial. Stephen Dorrell told me that David Cameron has been sacked as a special adviser. This is a mistake. He may come from the Right, but he has astute political antennae and a fabulous turn of phrase.

In committee we are allowed to write, read correspondence, do paperwork, but books and newspapers are not allowed. I'm wanting to read the obituaries of Les Dawson and Bernard Bresslaw. I've got the papers with me, but I don't dare produce them. Old hands *photocopy* whole books in the library, and read their novels in committee, page by photocopied page.

Even later

It is five in the morning. Dawn is breaking across the Thames. The Chief Secretary to the Treasury has laid his head on his arm to sleep. Harriet Hopeless is sitting immediately opposite me, slumbering gently. Looking around it seems most of the committee is dozing fitfully. This is democracy in action.

---

* Harriet Harman (b.1950), Labour MP for Camberwell and Peckham since 1982. First female Solicitor General, 2001–5. From 2007, combined the posts of Lord Privy Seal, Leader of the House of Commons and Minister for Women with being Deputy Leader of the Party.

Tuesday, 22 June 1993

Michael Heseltine has had a heart attack in Venice. Interestingly, the tea-room reaction has been one of concern for the Government's dwindling majority rather than concern for Michael's health. People here admire him, but they don't appear to love – or even like – him very much.

Tuesday, 20 July 1993

I'm just back from the PM's end-of-term party at No. 10. It was one of those disconcerting occasions where everyone seemed to be muttering about the host behind his back. In fact, he was pretty chirpy, almost bouncy. He's now implying that if he loses on Thursday we all go. 'Back me – or I'll call a general election. And then we'll see who survives.'

Thursday, 22 July 1993

This has been an extraordinary day. The PM opened the debate quite brilliantly. He has never been better. He was simple, direct, passionate. We took the decision to join the Community over twenty years ago. It was the right decision. We must make the Community work in Britain's interests. 'I believe the ratification of the Maastricht Treaty is in the interests of our country. That is why I signed it.' He flattened Ashdown, who was at his most pompous (that's saying something). When he sat down at the finish we roared our approval.

The first vote was on the Opposition amendment – don't ratify the Treaty until we've agreed to accept the social chapter. This was the one we expected to win. In the event it was a tie. In accordance with precedent, the Speaker backed the Government with her casting vote. Scenting blood – and pints of it – the Opposition benches went berserk. There was an eerie silence on our side. Immediately, we returned to the lobbies for the second vote, this time knowing we were doomed.

We lost by eight votes. The moment the result was declared, the PM was on his feet telling us, quite calmly, that he's tabling a motion of confidence for tomorrow.

Friday, 23 July 1993

At breakfast there was much amusement at the discovery that last night the Wintertons were in different lobbies. Ann voted against the Government. Nicholas was with us. How come? 'Nick is frantic for a knighthood,' chortled Geoffrey Dickens, 'and our excellent Whips probably promised him one.' The two Whips at the table studied their grapefruit and said nothing.

The debate itself was a bit of an anticlimax. It was clear before we started that the rebels were going to come back onside. The PM was tired and it showed. John Smith, by contrast, sparkled. He was stylish, sarcastic and effective. Douglas Hurd was the genial archdeacon bringing balm and solace to a scratchy congregation. With the lame and the halt on parade, with the rebels back in line and the Unionists sticking with us, we coasted home with a majority of 40. And that's Parliament done and dusted till October.

Friday, 30 July 1993

We have lost Christchurch to the Liberals. Robert Adley's majority of 23,000 has been transformed into a Lib Dem majority of 16,400 – a swing against us of 35 per cent, the biggest anti-Government swing since the war.

Sunday 1 August 1993

It's going to be a good August, a 'working holiday', at the word processor all day, lots of treats in the evenings: plays, films, friends. Four weeks away from politics. Heaven.

Friday, 20 August 1993

Benet has secured his place at Cambridge, Magdalene College, Pepys's college. We celebrated at Tootsies (the young scholar feasted on a double double burger with a fried egg, cheese, bacon and tomato on top) and we're off to *Les Enfants du Paradis*. (When we first got Pepys's complete diary I began reading it to Michèle in bed. I never got through more than half a page before she was fast asleep.)

The Chester papers have arrived full of the good news about the £43 million investment at Chester Business Park, promising a thousand new jobs. My hastily faxed press releases – claiming a fair share of the credit for GB and the PM – have paid off. The national press is less encouraging. Cecil Parkinson has denounced a 'terrible twelve months of drift and dither.' Thank you, Cecil.

Saturday, 11 September 1993

This is so terrible I don't want to write it down. Simon [Cadell] is going to die.

We were in the kitchen having lunch. The phone went. Michèle answered. It was Simon. 'I'm in the Harley Street Clinic. It's not good news. I'm riddled with cancer. It could be just a matter of days. Of course, I'll want Gyles to do the address at the service.' He was so brave and several times he tried to be funny. When we had both talked to him (and been wonderfully British and brave too) we put down the phone and stood in the kitchen clinging onto one another, sobbing uncontrollably. It is so awful.

Tuesday, 14 September 1993

Simon's got it into his head that the press vultures are circling. We are drafting a press statement to pre-empt them.

He is being so brave and funny. A nurse whipped back the bedclothes to give him an injection. 'Just a little prick,' she said. Simon looked at her indignantly: 'There's no need to be insulting.'

Friday, 17 September 1993

Simon is the lead story on several front pages. 'I am dying says *Hi-de-Hi* star Simon' is the main headline in the *Mirror*, reducing the political story of the hour to a single column: 'Major knifes Lamont as No. 10 crisis deepens'.

It is so strange to see stills of my best friend's funny, lovely, lopsided face, alongside these stark headlines. It's an odd (macabre) thing to say, but I think he'll be quite pleased with the coverage.

Norman is bitter because he feels betrayed. He *was* betrayed. That's politics.

And I'm going to lose Simon. That's life. And I can't bear it.

Wednesday, 6 October 1993

At 6.30 p.m. I turned up at the Conference hotel 'autocue room' to rehearse the Chancellor's speech with him. Ken knows this sort of thing is necessary, but he can't bring himself to take it seriously. Just as he gets to the podium and is set to start, in comes Jeffrey Archer. It seems that *he* is expecting to rehearse the Chancellor. Ken reads the script. He manages to emphasise all the wrong words and he puts over the jokes in a curious one-note sing-song without any inflection at the finish so the audience has no idea if this is the point at which to laugh. I don't say any of this – or indeed anything – because Jeffrey is saying it all, and more. KC reads a chunk and pauses. Jeffrey offers his critique. Jeffrey is so joyously bombastic, so cocksure, it's terribly funny. When our time was up, Jeffrey sailed off, very pleased with his endeavours; the Chancellor, chuckling, rolled away in search of a pint.

Ken does not take Jeffrey seriously. Stephen [Dorrell] doesn't trust him and says I should steer clear of him. When it comes to Jeffrey, the wily ones (Dorrell, Clarke, Heseltine) keep their distance. They think the PM was naïve to give him a peerage.

Thursday, 7 October 1993

I drove up to Blackpool in time for the Chancellor's speech. He paid absolutely no regard to anything that Jeffrey or I had said and it worked. 'Any enemy of John Major is my enemy. Any enemy of John Major is no friend of the Conservative Party.'

Michèle and I went to the Conference Ball where I conducted a knockabout auction and the PM spoke informally to the troops. I think he's at his best off-the-cuff. We talked about tomorrow's speech. Clearly they're still dithering as to whether or not to mount a full-scale assault on the 'fringe lunatics'. I said, 'If you attack the people causing the divisions you make them the focus of the headlines. The Chancellor has done the call for unity.'

Friday, 8 October 1993

'It is time to return to the old core values . . . Time to get back to basics. Madam President, I believe that what this country needs is not less Conservatism. It is more Conservatism . . . It is time to return to our roots.'

It went down wonderfully well. I watched the PM from inside the Channel 4 commentary box, surrounded by professional cynics, but even they had to concede that he'd touched a chord with the faithful. They don't adore him as they adored Thatcher, but they love him and they share his nostalgic longing for Miss Marple's England.

Monday, 18 October 1993

As Mrs T. launches her memoirs, she tells us the PM is now back on 'the true path' and rejoices. At 'Drinks' in the Lower Whips' Office, we turn our minds to lower things: Steve Norris and his *five* mistresses. We are full of admiration, but it is utterly maddening for No. 10. 'Back to Basics' was never supposed to be about sexual morality.

Thursday, 28 October 1993

At lunch the Chancellor is in expansive mood – literally. Glass of wine in one hand, cheroot in the other, he leans back and a button bursts from his overstretched shirt front, wings its way past Portillo's ear and gently pings against a Treasury chandelier. The team look down at the table, the Chancellor giggles, and we carry on as if nothing has happened.

Wednesday, 3 November 1993

Yesterday we were here till two in the morning, struggling through the Lords' Amendments to the Railways Bill. Since it took five hours to get through barely fifty out of a total of five hundred, Tony Newton moved a guillotine motion to put a timetable to the proceedings. Uproar followed and tonight Labour mavericks have been seeking their revenge by lurking in the lavatories in the division lobbies so as to delay/obstruct/derail the votes. At about half past nine we were plodding through our lobby during the fifth division of the night when Greg Knight* suddenly pounced on me.

'You've got to make a point of order. Complain about the delaying tactics. Get the Speaker to order the Serjeant-at-Arms to clear the lobbies. *Now*.'

When the Whip speaks, you move. I stumbled into the chamber, where all was chaos, several hundred people milling all over the shop. I said to the Whip on the front bench, 'I've been told to make a point of order.'

'You'll need the hat.'

A collapsible black silk opera hat was produced from the clerk's table.

During a division the rule is that you can only speak when 'seated and covered'. Don't ask me why. I donned the ludicrous top hat and made my protest. Would the Deputy Speaker call the Serjeant-at-Arms to clear the lobbies and note the names of those members who were causing the obstruction? No, he would not.

Immensely relieved, I sat back and took off the hat. The Whip on the front bench whisked round and hissed, 'Put it back on. Try again. Go on. *Go on*. Now, man, *now*.'

On went the hat once more. I made a further protest, again to no effect. I passed the hat back to the Whip. Someone called for it from the other side of the chamber. It was flung over to Ernie Ross, tossed like a Frisbee. Then back it came to James Paice. Then it went shooting over to Mark Robinson. It whizzed here and there around the chamber like a ludicrous flying saucer. Suddenly it disappeared and John Marshall was calling for attention. We turned to look at him and there he was, the Honourable Member for Hendon, parliamentary private secretary to the Lord President of the Council, seated in the chamber of the House of Commons, with a knotted hanky on his head.

It's nearly two in the morning and I'm going home, but I just wanted posterity to know how we conduct our business here.

* Greg Knight (b.1949), Conservative MP for Derby North, 1983–97, East Yorkshire since 2001; Deputy Chief Whip, 1993–6.

Wednesday, 1 December 1993

The Budget was a triumph for KC. He is a wonderful operator and such a likeable man. He's had a superb press, although he said to me last night, 'It's a golden rule – a Budget that's acclaimed on the day doesn't fare so well in retrospect. Let's not get too cheerful too soon.'

I was up at dawn to fly to Manchester for the Waterstone's Literary Lunch with Fergie.* She had several pages of notes written out in a large and loopy hand. She rather overdid her undying devotion to the present Queen, but she was good-hearted and nicely flirtatious in a gosh-golly-girls-in-the-dorm kind of way.

I was planning to come back by train because it was going to be easier for me from Euston, but she said: 'Come on the plane. I've got two tickets.'

'Why?'

'I always get two . . . you never know.'

As a consequence of being seduced onto the plane, I arrived late for the charity do at St James's Palace. They were already à table. I went to apologise to our hostess, the Duchess of Gloucester,† knelt at her side and said, 'I'm so sorry I'm late.' She was not amused. I compounded my lèse-majesté by telling her (as Fergie insisted I should, absolutely insisted, 'You must, please, please. I don't see any of them now and I don't want to be frozen out') that I'd spent the day with the Duchess of York and 'Sarah particularly asked to be remembered to you.' The Danish Duchess said nothing, frowned ever-so-slightly to get her 'Who do you think you are?' message across, and returned her attention to her plate.

I should have remembered that she's not an easy ride. At the Roy Miles Gallery, at a private view, somehow we'd been left alone in the middle of a quite small room. I'd struggled with the small-talk long enough. She was saying nothing: I had nothing more to say. I moved slightly closer to her and, while I burbled some inanity in her ear, behind her back I frantically gestured to Michèle to come and rescue me. Suddenly I realised that Her Royal Highness was gazing over my left shoulder into the mirror that was facing her. She was staring at the awful reflection of me frantically waving – and drowning.

---

* The Duchess of York was promoting her book based on the journals and travels of Queen Victoria; GB was promoting his latest, Under the Jumper.
† HRH The Duchess of Gloucester (b. Birgitte Henriksen, 1946), Danish wife of Prince Richard, Duke of Gloucester, grandson of George V.

Wednesday, 8 December 1993

Last night at the Foreign Office party, in the newly refurbished and quite splendid Durbar Room, I met up with Liza Manningham-Buller, whom I last saw when she played the Fairy Queen in my production of *Cinderella* at Oxford twenty-six years ago. She's now one of our most senior spies, destined to be, if not already, the head of MI6. Extraordinary.

Tuesday, 14 December 1993

The PM came to mingle with his men in the tea room this afternoon and did well. He's engrossed in the Northern Ireland business and both his commitment and grasp of detail are impressive. He was busy sending out signals to reassure the Ulster Unionists, but he concedes there's been a 'chain of communication' between the Government and the IRA for years and there's no doubt we'll be talking to the terrorists face to face. What happens to our fragile majority then?

Monday, 27 December 1993

We are in Framlingham with Simon and Beckie [Cadell]. Simon seems to be in much better shape. Beckie is a saint. 'We don't know how long I've got,' says Simon, in his best Ralph Richardson voice, dropping a splash or two of *pêche* into our mid-morning champagne, 'so we'd better get on with it, eh, cockie?'

We've had a merry Christmas. I imagine the PM was feeling relatively festive too – until yesterday when the *News of the World* brought us its latest world exclusive. Tim Yeo,[*] our Minister for the Environment and the Countryside, has a love child! Michèle has been agin him since she saw him lolling on the front bench with his feet up against the despatch box. 'Arrogant sod.' I tried to explain that they all sit like that. 'No they don't. Mr Major doesn't. The sooner he goes the better.'

According to today's papers, the Prime Minister is taking a more charitable view. ' "This is a purely private matter," says PM.' Oh yes?

Thursday, 30 December 1993

Yesterday: lunch with the Hanleys. Jeremy told a funny story. Pretty young diary secretary comes in to see her minister.

Secretary: Well, Minister, there's good news and bad news.

Minister: Give me the good news.

Secretary: You're not infertile.

---

[*] Timothy Yeo (b.1945), Conservative MP for Suffolk South since 1983.

We're in Normandy, staying in what I'm choosing to call 'the valley of the Lilleys'. Peter* and Gail escape here whenever they can. We arrived to see Peter through the window, sitting at his laptop, engrossed: 'I'm looking for ways to reduce the social security bill.' It is good to be spending New Year with the most *thoughtful* member of the Government.

---

* Peter Lilley (b.1943), Conservative MP for Hitchin and Harpenden, and previously St Albans, since 1983; Secretary of State for Social Security, 1992–7.

Democracy in Action

January – December 1994

Thursday, 6 January 1994

Sometimes I feel I lead a double life. Not quite like Mr Yeo's, but a double life in the sense that who I am in Chester is so different there from here. I don't have the contempt for my constituents Alan Clark[*] clearly had for his – I rather like them – but last night was more my idea of a good time. We went to *She Stoops to Conquer*. It was a joy. We went on to supper at the Ivy: Donald, Diana [Mrs Sinden], Simon, Beckie [Cadell], Joanna [Lumley]. We were joined by Richard Gere who walked across the tables – on top of the tables – to reach us.

The news is that Tim Yeo has gone. His wife was ready to stand by him, but his officers weren't. Of course, if he'd gone on Boxing Day we'd have been spared a fortnight of nonsense.

Sunday, 9 January 1994

The Press Association have just called. They want my reaction to a story in tomorrow's *Guardian* 'about the government loan to your business being written off'.

Monday, 10 January 1994

I am so angry.

> The Government has written off a £200,000 debt to the taxpayer owed by a company set up by the Conservative MP Gyles Brandreth . . .

Yes, when we set up Royal Britain we applied for a grant and got it. When, two years later, we had to close, everyone lost their investment – me, the shareholders, the English Tourist Board, everybody. I assumed the grant was written off then.

---

[*] Alan Clark (1928–99), Conservative MP for Plymouth Sutton, 1974–92, Kensington and Chelsea, 1997–9. Minister of Trade, 1986–9, and Minister of State, Ministry of Defence, 1989–92. GB had been reading Clark's *Diaries*.

From that day to this, I have had no communication of any kind from either the ETB or the Department of National Heritage or the Treasury or anybody.

When IRN [Independent Radio News] called and said Mo Mowlam* was calling for my resignation I went berserk. I thought she was my friend. Because we chat, because we're friendly, because we've had a drink and a laugh, I thought I could trust her.

Fuck you, *Guardian*. Fuck you, Mo Mowlam.

Tuesday, 11 January 1994

Tony Newton was standing in for the PM at Questions. Dennis Skinner got in with the last question. Because I'm always in the chamber, he tends to treat me fairly gently, but this was too good to resist. 'How can the Government justify bailing out the Honourable Member for Chester at £200,000 when millions have been made redundant?' Tony was *fabulous*: 'Neither the company nor my Honourable Friend has been treated differently from any other company or any other individual in similar circumstances.'

Wednesday, 12 January 1994

There is a vast picture of yours truly on the front page of the *Independent*. The story shows that the decision to write-off the ETB grant was taken by a Treasury official. It never reached any minister. Absurdly, I toured the library and the tea room and the smoking room removing copies – not only so that others mightn't see it, but so that I didn't have to see it either.

Tuesday, 1 February 1994

In the tea room the leadership is the only thing anyone is talking about. Lamont is saying the PM is 'weak and hopeless' and, privately, all too many are ready to agree.

Friday, 4 February 1994

I'm just in from darling Saethryd's birthday supper at Riva† and full of the joys of chilled Frascati. Earlier a quick lunch in the tea room with Stephen [Milligan]. He spoke in the debate. He has the singleness of purpose of the properly ambitious, but it doesn't grate because he is so open about it. When we arrived and the *House* magazine asked us about our aspirations, creeps like me talked piously about the

---

* Marjorie Mowlam (1949–2005), Labour MP for Redcar, 1987–2001; Shadow National Heritage Secretary; later Northern Ireland Secretary, 1997–9.
† GB's elder daughter was 17.

fulfilment to be had as a good constituency member. Stephen came clean: 'I would like to be Foreign Secretary.'

Monday, 7 February 1994

This is truly appalling. Stephen [Milligan] has been found dead. Bill Cash* told me there's a rumour going round that it was some sort of sex killing. 'I don't think you'll like the details.'

Tuesday, 8 February 1994

When Stephen failed to show up, his secretary decided to go round to Black Lion Lane. There was no reply when she rang the bell and when she let herself in, she found him dead, lying on the floor in the kitchen, naked apart from a pair of stockings and a suspender belt, with a flex tied round his neck and a black plastic bag over his head.

It seems that, either alone or with a companion, he was playing some sort of bizarre sex game. A piece of orange was found in his mouth. Some kind of drug could have been in the orange. The bag was over his head and the flex was around his neck to restrict the amount of oxygen getting to his brain and so increase the sexual thrill.

I wrote to his parents this morning, simply saying how wonderful he was. I wrote to Jonathan Aitken too because I wanted Jonathan to know how much Stephen *loved* being his PPS.

Wednesday, 9 February 1994

Norman Fowler has just told me that when they arrived at Hammersmith police station on Monday night they had to join the queue at the desk, lining up with a prostitute, a vagrant and a busker – who favoured them with a song. I've just been listening to the poor PM on the radio saying Stephen must have been 'pretty unhappy'. I know he'll have meant well, but it's completely wrong. Stephen was gloriously happy. I imagine he went for his round of golf and came home and thought he'd play his little sex game as a weekend celebration.

Monday, 14 February 1994

The roller-coaster continues. Last week's tragedy is followed by this week's farce – or, as it turns out, this week's light romantic comedy. Hartley Booth,† Mrs T.'s

---

* William Cash (b.1940), Conservative MP for Stafford and Stone since 1984.
† Vernon Hartley Booth (b.1946), Conservative MP for Finchley, 1992–7.

soft-lipped wouldn't-say-boo-to-a-goose successor in Finchley, has resigned as Douglas Hogg's PPS following the revelations of his infatuation with a 22-year-old art college model-turned-political researcher. Apparently there was no affair, merely a *tendresse*.

Poor Hartley is a kindly, good-hearted fellow, never destined to go very far and now destined to go absolutely nowhere. I realise now that I could have walked in anywhere. There are scores of colleagues, in every part of the House, whom I would consider unelectable. Sitting ten feet away from me here in the library is a Labour member who is, without question, completely gaga.

Monday, 21 February 1994

O joy, O rapture! Dennis Skinner has been caught with his trousers down and his muffler up. It turns out the Beast of Bolsover has a wife at home and a mistress in London. He has been photographed, cap down over his eyes, woolly scarf up to his nose, in the bushes near their love-nest. The delight this has engendered at both ends of the tea room is palpable.

Tuesday, 22 February 1994

Last night the Palace of Westminster was surrounded by a marauding mob of gay rights protesters outraged at the failure of Edwina's attempt to introduce an equal age of consent in homosexual relationships. Choice quote of the night came from Sir Nicholas Fairbairn who probably scored a parliamentary first of some sort with his assertion, 'Putting your penis into another man's arsehole is a perverse act . . .' When I saw him later he could barely stand. 'I hear you were fairly forthright tonight,' I said. His eyes were closed, his head was lolling, but he managed to hiss, 'I thought getting back to basics was part of our policy.'

I adjourned to the smoking room for a drink. At about 11.30 I made my way out into Whitehall, calling 'I voted for sixteen! I voted for sixteen!' as the police let me through the gate. The rumble of the crowd turned instantly from jeers to cheers and they cleared a path for me. If they'd had them, I felt rose petals would have been strewn before me.

The gays in Chester will be happy; the activists will feel 'let down'. (That's the way they always put it when I do something they hate.) I've tried to explain that I'm wanting to decriminalise sex at sixteen, not promote it. Michèle thinks the age of consent should be fixed at 60 for all.

Thursday, 24 February 1994

Went down to Woodmancote for Stephen's funeral. Just a small party from Westminster: me and Michèle, Jonathan Aitken, Andrew Mackay (Stephen's Whip), Julie Kirkbride.* It was a lovely service – 'The Lord's my shepherd, I'll not want', 'He who would valiant be', an extraordinary address by Stephen's vicar from Hammersmith – and then we had to troop out into the graveyard for the interment. We were only a matter of thirty or forty feet from the hedge surrounding the churchyard and right along the lane, standing on stepladders, were the press. Stephen was laid to rest to the sound of clicking cameras.

At the eats afterwards Stephen's father was so brave. He's deaf so we shouted our condolences and he barked back. He insisted that we thank God for Stephen's life and achievement. I can think of nothing worse than losing your child in your own lifetime – nothing.

Tuesday, 12 April 1994

I invited John Gielgud to lunch to celebrate his 90th birthday. There were just the four of us: Sir John, Michèle, me and Glenda [Jackson].† (Glenda was Michèle's idea – and inspired. She looks so sour, but she was sweet and gossipy and exactly right for the occasion.) He arrived in Central Lobby at one, on the dot, twinkling and cherubic, amazingly upright and steady.

'It's a great honour that you should join us, Sir John,' I said.

'Oh, I'm delighted to have been asked. All my real friends are dead, you know.'

The stories just poured out of him. 'Marlene [Dietrich] invited me to hear her new record. We were in New York. We all went and gathered round the gramophone, and when we were settled the record was put on. It was simply an audience applauding her! We sat through the entire first side and then we listened to the other side: more of the same!'

He asked after Simon and said he remembered his grandmother, Jean Cadell, 'so well. She was a fine actress: she did *what she did* so well. She played Prism with

---

* Andrew Mackay (b.1949), Conservative MP for Birmingham Stechford, 1977–9, Bracknell from 1983; Julie Kirkbride (b.1960), journalist and Stephen Milligan's girlfriend; Conservative MP for Bromsgrove from 1997. Mackay and Kirkbride married in 1997 and, in 2009, announced their retirement from Parliament following allegations of abuse of parliamentary expenses.

† Glenda Jackson (b.1936), Oscar-winning actress and Labour MP for Hampstead and Highgate since 1992.

me in New York, when Margaret moved up to play Lady Bracknell instead of Edith.'*

'Why didn't Dame Edith play the part in America?'

'She was introduced to a blind devotee of the theatre who heard her speak and said to her, "You are much too beautiful to play Lady Bracknell," and that was that. Edith was very much concerned about her beauty, you know. Margaret agreed to move up from Miss Prism to play Lady Bracknell on condition she could model her performance entirely on Edith's. It was typically modest of her.' (Pause. Sip of wine. Twinkle.) 'Of course, Margaret's Lady Bracknell was very much the Lady Mayoress to Edith's Queen Mary.'

Monday, 25 April 1994

We've just returned from Raymond and Caroline Seitz's farewell party at the Ambassador's residence in Regent's Park.† Ray exemplifies 'discreet charm'. He's wooed and won the entire British Establishment, and they all seemed to be on parade tonight. A. N. Wilson and I shared high church memories: smells and bells at St Stephen's, Gloucester Road. Peter Ackroyd was fruity and very funny – and quite won me over: he said he'd loved my biography of Dan Leno. Michèle said, 'You could see he was drunk.' There was a lovely moment at the end, when we were lining up to take our leave. We were standing in the queue, just behind the Frosts – (David: 'Gyles, a *joy*, an absolute *joy*!') – and up strode the Heseltines, saw the length of the line, stalked grandly past us and went straight to the front. 'No line-jumping,' said Ray with a smile and back the humbled Heseltines came. Democracy in action. Michèle said, 'That man mustn't become Prime Minister.'

Friday, 6 May 1994

'A night of catastrophe for the Tories'. Lib Dems have been trouncing us everywhere. Rotherham has a new MP, swept in on a landslide. He's calling himself Denis MacShane . . . Can this be the Denis Matyjaszek I knew at Oxford?‡

---

* Gielgud's celebrated wartime production of Oscar Wilde's *The Importance of Being Earnest*, in which he played John Worthing, and, in London, Edith Evans played Lady Bracknell and Margaret Rutherford played Miss Prism.

† Raymond Seitz (b.1940), US Ambassador to the United Kingdom, 1991–4.

‡ It was.

Sunday, 8 May 1994

Here we go again. Poor Michael Brown[*] has been outed by the *News of the World*. They are bastards. And he is a fool. He took a young man on a Caribbean holiday. There's some dispute as to the boy's age, but he's certainly under 21 – and the 18-plus legislation doesn't come onto the statute book before the autumn. You've got to pity the poor PM too. As Michèle says, 'That's Back to Basics gone to buggery.'

Thursday, 12 May 1994

John Smith has died. The word spread round the whole Palace in minutes: people really did not know what to do. The Labour people stood around in twos and threes, the women hugged one another, and I noticed that every time one of our people passed one of theirs we instinctively touched a shoulder or an arm and said 'I'm so sorry', and I felt we meant it.

The PM opened the tributes and pitched it perfectly: it was simple, sincere, colloquial not oratorical – what he does best. Margaret Beckett[†] followed. I thought she was brilliant – moving and very brave. She was sitting next to the poor man at dinner only eighteen hours ago. She kept her tears at bay with a Herculean effort. Kinnock was good, passionate, strong; Ashdown just missed it, too wordy, too much about himself; I wasn't sure about Kaufman[‡] either. The best in a way was Tony Benn[§] – there was old-fashioned eloquence and two messages put across in under a minute: 'Inside John Smith burned the flame of anger against injustice, and the flame of hope that we can build a better world . . . He was a man who always said the same wherever he was. For that reason, he was trusted.'

Sunday, 5 June 1994

A Whitsun week of cultural treats. *King Lear* with Robert Stephens at the Barbican (*almost* as good as it gets); *Crazy for You* at Drury Lane (my kind of show!); Beating Retreat from Michael Ancram's window at the Northern Ireland Office; Kiri te Kanawa – on song and in the rain – at Hampton Court. Stevie

---

[*] Michael Brown (b.1951), Conservative MP for Brigg and Cleethorpes, 1979–97; Assistant Whip, 1993–4.
[†] Margaret Beckett (b.1943), Labour MP for Lincoln, 1974–9, Derby South since 1983; Acting Leader of the Labour Party; the first female Foreign Secretary, 2006–7.
[‡] Sir Gerald Kaufman (b.1930), MP for Manchester Ardwick and Gorton since 1970.
[§] Anthony Wedgwood Benn (b.1925), formerly 2nd Viscount Stansgate; Labour MP for Bristol South-East, 1950–61, 1963–83, Chesterfield, 1984–2001.

[Barlow] was conducting and introduced us to the diva – who is a Big Girl. Jo [Lumley] took us and Simon and Beckie and went to *so much* trouble with the picnic: dripping, shivering, we huddled together in our *impermeabile* pretending it was the golden summer evening it ought to have been. Bowen Wells[*] happened to be there and the highlight of the night for Michèle was when I went across to his wife as she emerged from the loo and gushed one of my unctuous and effusive greetings, only to be dismissed by Mrs Wells with a brisk, 'I'm so sorry, I haven't got time for new relationships.'

Friday, 10 June 1994

At the Albert Hall for 7.30: Brian Conley and Bob Hope.[†] Brian was the warm-up and brilliant. Bob Hope, alas, is gaga. He's 90. We expected a miracle. Instead we got a confused old man. The musical director kept him just about pointed in the right direction and whenever the poor old boy started tottering towards the wings or, worse, the edge of the stage, went off to retrieve him. It was a sad sight. The surprise was Dolores Hope: kept under wraps for forty years, she emerged from the shadows and stole the show.

Monday, 13 June 1994

For collectors of the truly ludicrous there's a treat in the pages of *The Times* today: Sir Antony Buck,[‡] looking like a terminally ill scarecrow, presents his new wife to the world. 'Tamara saw my picture in a Moscow newspaper and arrived at my doorstep unannounced.' Happily, the paper reminds us that Sir Antony's second marriage was to Bienvenida Perez-Blanco whose subsequent dalliance with the Chief of the Defence Staff brought his distinguished career to a rapid close. (Cue Michèle: 'Men! They're all the same . . .') When Tony and Bienvenida flew off on Concorde for a few days' honeymoon in Barbados, the happy groom was in prophetic vein: 'It's a long way to go for such a short time,' he said, 'but you only get married two or three times in a lifetime.'

When I first met him, years ago, I couldn't believe that such a complete tosser could find a place in the Government. But now I see how the system works.

---

[*] Petrie Bowen Wells (b.1935), Conservative MP for Hertford, 1979–2001; newly appointed to the Whips' Office in succession to Michael Brown.

[†] Brian Conley (b.1961), entertainer, had appeared in pantomime with GB; Bob Hope (1903–2003) was making his farewell UK appearance, with Dolores (b.1909), his second wife, whom he married in 1934.

[‡] Sir Philip Antony Buck (1928–2003), Conservative MP for Colchester, 1961–83, Colchester North, 1983–92; Minister for the Navy, 1972–4.

Wednesday, 15 June 1994

Long letter from HRH. He's sent me a photocopy of the serialisation of a book that's being published in Australia: 'Prince Philip's torrid sex life – famous lovers named.' They've thrown in everybody – Fergie's mum, Merle Oberon, Katie Boyle, Princess Alexandra, Patti Kluge. His only defence is to sue for libel, but as he says, never mind the cost, think of the additional publicity it gives the book. His idea is a sort of tribunal to which material like this could be referred. The author would then have to satisfy the tribunal that there was sufficient acceptable evidence to prove the truth of the statements.

It's maddening for the likes of HRH and Joanna that utter rubbish can appear in the press and be repeated endlessly and, short of litigation, there's nothing they can do about it. And, of course, if it's in the papers, it must be true. (I was at a party and, *within earshot of the Queen*, someone was muttering to me that Prince Andrew was really the son of Lord Carnarvon. I said, in a sort of desperate hushed whisper, 'Don't be so stupid.' The fellow continued, 'No, it's true. I read it somewhere.' I know that almost anything is possible in this world, but that the Queen has committed adultery is not.)

Thursday, 16 June 1994

It's going to be Blair. The remaining question: who gets the second spot? I'm backing Chester's son, John Prescott,[*] but Margaret Beckett has been quite impressive as acting leader these past few weeks.

Seb Coe[†] and I had dinner with the Chief Whip [Richard Ryder].[‡] Seb wanted to feed in his concerns that the Government is doing nothing that is likely to appeal to the younger voter; I wanted to remind the Chief of my charming presence, easy manner, natural eloquence, commitment and intelligence in the run-up to the reshuffle . . . I'm not sure either of us had much luck. Richard is quietly charming, but he wasn't interested in Seb's ideas and I was so busy being careful about what I said that I didn't say anything worth saying.

---

[*] John Prescott (b. 1938), Labour MP for Hull since 1970; Deputy Leader of the Labour Party, 1994–2007; Prescott's divorced parents were both constituents of GB.

[†] Sebastian Coe (b.1956), Olympic runner; Conservative MP for Falmouth and Camborne, 1992–7, Chairman of London Organising Committee for 2012 Olympic Games; now Lord Coe of Ranmore KBE.

[‡] Richard Ryder (b.1949), Conservative MP for Mid-Norfolk, 1983–97; Chief Whip, 1990–95; now Baron Ryder of Wensum.

Monday, 20 June 1994

All-Party Media Group Reception in the Jubilee Room. Amiable if desultory talk with Michael Grade, John Birt, Prince Edward. Grade asks, 'Who will be Party Chairman now that Heseltine's ruled himself out? Jeffrey Archer?' I pull a naughty face. 'I think *not*,' I say. The activists out in the sticks may want him, *do* want him, but there'd be a riot in the tea room.

Tuesday, 5 July 1994

Blair, not formally elected yet, is letting it be known that he is an admirer of Mrs Thatcher's leadership qualities. At least we can now be sure he isn't going to get Ted's vote.

Friday, 8 July 1994

'The millionaire novelist and Conservative peer Jeffrey Archer is at the centre of an official investigation into alleged insider share dealings in Anglia Television, of which his wife is a non-executive director.' O Jeffrey! Jeffrey! Jeffrey!

Sunday, 10 July 1994

This is bad. The *Sunday Times* (bastards) and their 'Insight team' (sanctimonious bastards) have successfully hanged, drawn and quartered Graham Riddick and David Treddinick[*] – naïve fools. An Insight journalist, masquerading as a businessman of some kind, contacted twenty MPs – ten of ours, ten Labour – and asked them to put down a parliamentary question on his behalf, offering them each a payment of £1,000 for their pains. Almost all gave variations of the response: 'No thank you – I can't help – contact your own MP etc.' Only two of the twenty – it had to be our two, of course – rose to the bait. '£1,000? That'll do nicely.'

Wednesday, 13 July 1994

Graham pitched it exactly right: a fulsome apology to one and all – to colleagues, to friends, to the PM, 'but most of all, I wish to apologise to you, Madam Speaker, for undermining – to whatever degree – the standing of the House.' From Tredinnick: silence.

The tragedy of all this is that out there in voter-land people will now be thinking that MPs do accept money for performing their everyday duties. The truth is, they don't.

[*] Graham Riddick (b.1955), Conservative MP for Colne Valley, 1987–97; David Tredinnick (b.1950), Conservative MP for Bosworth since 1987.

Thursday, 14 July 1994

I'm just in from the Blue Ball. Another night, another auction – and, yes, I managed to get through it without saying, 'And what am I bid for a parliamentary question? Any advance on £1,000?'

I sat with Norman Fowler and Angela Rumbold* and it was very jolly. The PM came up to our end of the table, very relaxed, very amiable: 'What are you three gossiping about?'

'We're discussing who should replace Norman as Party Chairman. We think we've got the answer. You tell him, Gyles.'

I ran through my spiel and, as I spoke, I watched the PM's grin broaden. 'Well, well, well,' he said. He looked positively impish.

Jeremy Hanley's got the job. That's certain.

Friday, 15 July 1994

The House is deserted. It is a very quiet Friday, just as I like it. Mid-morning, who should I bump into, but Jeremy Hanley? I was going to let him pass, then I couldn't resist it. 'You're going to be the next Chairman of the Conservative Party. I was with the PM last night. It's in the bag. You'll be brilliant.'

I left him looking truly perturbed.

Wednesday, 20 July 1994

Reshuffle Day. This is a day that makes a handful of people very happy and leaves several hundred others thoroughly fed up. I didn't really expect anything (I've had too much of the wrong kind of publicity and that's not what the Government needs now, I know) but I hoped, I hoped.

At 10.30 I walked over to the Treasury. Stephen [Dorrell] was in his room, alone, scrubbed, boyish, eager. He'd been 'summoned' for around 11.15. He looked up. 'What's the news?'

'Jeremy Hanley as Party Chairman,' I said. 'And you're going to National Heritage.'

'No.' He looked utterly appalled. 'Are you sure? I'd rather stay here. I'd rather carry on as Financial Secretary.'

I wanted to add, 'And remember who would be ideal as your junior minister' – and half did, but he wasn't listening. I said, 'I'll be back in an hour. Good luck.'

* Dame Angela Rumbold (b.1932), MP for Mitcham and Morden, 1982–97; Deputy Chairman of the Conservative Party 1992–7.

At 11.45 I returned to the Treasury. Stephen was in his room – surrounded by the team – champagne glasses in hand.

When they departed, Stephen closed the door. 'You were right. It's ghastly. I know nothing about the arts. Anything would have been better. Agriculture. Anything.'

'Did you discuss junior ministers?' I already knew the answer.

Thursday, 21 July 1994

It's an extraordinary system. Twenty-four hours ago Stephen was Financial Secretary, doing a job he understood. He is then, without even a line about why he's been given the new job, or what the PM hopes he may achieve, translated from one end of Whitehall to the other, or as Stephen sees it, from one world to another, from the centre of the universe to the realms of outer darkness.

Later

Stephen generously took us to celebrate his elevation to the Cabinet: he is very generous, very sweet, but his dismay at his predicament is rather disconcerting. We'd come on from the PM's reception at No. 10 – a peculiar affair: the promoted trying not to look smug, the demoted looking brave, the regularly overlooked looking resigned (and drinking steadily), the freshly ignored (*moi*) attempting to appear devil-may-care and perky. The PM was relaxed, friendly. 'What do you think?'

'Looks good. Jeremy's going to be excellent.'

'Yes. And Stephen?'

I didn't say, 'You tosser – Stephen's in the wrong job – and what about *me*, mate?'

Tony Blair is the new Leader of the Labour Party.

Thursday, 28 July 1994

A week in and Stephen is no happier. I've suggested he leaves sport entirely to Sproat, lets Astor (a Viscount, a proper lord, a chap with a castle)* look after 'the heritage' in all its glory, and concentrates himself on three or four areas where there's 'profile' and where he can make an impact: tourism, the arts, the lottery, broadcasting. He just doesn't see it.

---

* Iain Sproat (b.1938), Conservative MP for Aberdeen South, 1970–83, Harwich, 1992–7, and Viscount Astor (b.1951) were the two junior ministers under Stephen Dorrell at the Department of National Heritage.

Tuesday, 2 August 1994

Benet has set off for China, Saethryd is in Venice (en route for Florence, Sienna and Pisa), we have just seen Aphra off for her holiday on Cape Cod, Rhode Island and Manhattan.* It certainly beats a week in Broadstairs. (Michèle claims she only had one holiday as a child. I say, 'The world has changed.' She says, 'That's the one thing to be said for money. It keeps you in touch with your children.')

Long letter from the Chancellor (a good and kind man): 'I have no doubt you are disappointed not to be a minister and I think [Stephen] is a little unhappy with National Heritage. Both of you are rather impatient but your time will come! . . .'

These handwritten letters make a difference. I've said this to Stephen time and again. I replayed to him a story he'd told me about Helmut Kohl. Apparently, the German Chancellor has a list of the thousand most influential people in the country, and whenever he has an idle moment, being driven from A to B, he picks up the telephone and speaks to one of them, just touching base. I suggested to Stephen that he might try the same trick with, say, the director of Opera North . . . Stephen agrees with the theory, but I know it won't happen. He's conceded that I can organise some sandwich lunches. 'Oh God,' he shook his head despairingly, 'lunch with the luvvies!'

Thursday, 1 September 1994

We are going for a strawberry tea at Strawberry Hill House, the home of Horace Walpole. The news is that the IRA have declared a 'ceasefire'. If this can be made to last, if we can inch our way towards some sort of constitutional settlement, this will be the PM's great achievement.

Tuesday, 13 September 1994

Breakfast with Stephen at the Ritz. He is in much happier form. He likes Hayden [Phillips, the Permanent Secretary at the Department of National Heritage] (entirely *trusting* Hayden of course is quite another matter – the DNH under Hayden is *Yes, Minister* in spades), he likes his private office. We are going to do without a Special Adviser. I'm going to have his office.

Over properly poached eggs and mushrooms and *brilliantly* grilled bacon, we agreed that the summer hadn't been too bad – 'But – ' Stephen grinned from ear to ear – 'your friend Mr Hanley . . .'

---

* GB's three children were now 19, 17, 16.

It's got worse for Jeremy. The papers are producing full fat features listing the litany of his gaffes – being in Scotland and muddling up which party thinks what on devolution; inviting Jeffrey [Archer] to make a full statement on the Anglia shares business just when we'd all forgotten about it; telling the Chancellor he's had his last interest rate hike; telling the PM that he's got the job as Party Chairman for at least two and a half years . . . They're all tiny, trivial trip-ups – exactly the kind I know I'd make (admittedly the kind Ken Clarke wouldn't) – but one on top of another, and what do you end up with? Headline: 'Hanley fulfils deep foreboding.'

Wednesday, 12 October 1994

I am commuting to Bournemouth for the Party Conference. I saw Margaret Thatcher. She looks quite terrible: gaunt, pale, shrunken. She's lost at least a stone, and the mad glint in her eye had gone. She just looked sad. I saw Norman Lamont who has never looked happier! He's been making mischief on the fringe, telling us to reject a European superstate, and dismissing the PM's approach as 'simplistic'. Douglas Hurd is being magisterial, Geoffrey Howe is huffing and puffing in the wings, Norman Tebbit (now looking like a moth-eaten polecat) is adding his own touch of bile to the brew.

The news from the Conference platform is that the Michaels did well – Heseltine did his usual stuff and they stood and cheered; Portillo wrapped himself in the Union Jack, denounced Europe's 'crackpot schemes' and demanded 'clear blue water' between us and the Opposition. The really good news is that Jeremy's speech was a triumph – all is forgiven.

Friday, 14 October 1994

After our drinks 'do' for the activists last night, we climbed into the car under cover of darkness and raced home. (For sentimental reasons I was almost tempted to stay: we were at the Palace Court Hotel where, aged 21, I treated Michèle – more than once – to a slap-up dinner of lobster thermidor and chilled Sauternes!) This morning I drove back down again – alone. Sometimes, on a difficult day, I prefer to go it alone – I can concentrate on the task in hand, not worry about M – and then, if it's a success, I can report back, and, if it's a disaster, I can pretend it never happened.

I found my way to the makeshift green room behind the stage. I huddled in a corner with the PM. They were fiddling with his tie, which was fine, but what was absurd was they were still fiddling with his speech. Anyway, at 2.00 p.m. the moment was upon us. The martial music played and on we trooped – the party

hierarchy, me, the Cabinet. I did my stuff: a couple of jokes; praise for the activists (laid on with a trowel); knock the Opposition (compare/contrast our team
with theirs: mocking Prescott, Cook,* Beckett, Blair – looking at Hezza, 'Who
needs Bambi when we've got the Lion King?' – line kindly provided by Peter
Shepherd† who I bumped into on my way to the platform – it worked a treat);
encapsulate the policies they love best in three sentences; throw in a touch of
sentiment ('You do this not just for love of Party, but for love of country'); then
rack up the pace and the emotional charge for the peroration: 'Ours is the only
party that believes, that truly believes, in the United Kingdom. Ours is the only
party that understands . . . Ours is the only party etc., etc. . . . Onward and
upward!' Cue: sustained standing ovation – which, let's face it, is very nice.

In fact, both the PM and I did exactly what was required of us. I offered fifteen
minutes of rousing knockabout and he gave us an hour of what he is – intelligent,
thoughtful, middle-of-the-road, determined, honest.

Afterwards we returned to the green room for tea. I congratulated him on a
triumph. He said, 'I hope yours went well. I'm afraid I didn't catch it.'

I drove straight back to London. The traffic getting onto the motorway was
impossible. I realised there was a car next to mine with its horn honking. I looked
across. It was Portillo, leaning forward, with both thumbs up, mouthing, 'You
were brilliant, you were brilliant.'

Tuesday, 18 October 1994

At 3.15 p.m. it was Blair's first outing at PMQs – not at all bad. He paid tribute to
the PM's achievements in Northern Ireland and then went for our divisions over
the single currency. There was lots more warm guff about Ireland and just two
tricky moments: did Mark Thatcher make £12 million from the Al-Yamamah
arms negotiations? And doesn't Lord Archer owe the public an explanation on
his Anglia share dealings? The PM, on song, brushed both effortlessly aside.

Wednesday, 19 October 1994

I've just come from the chamber where Stuart Bell,‡ out of the blue, on a point of
order, got up and told the House that the *Guardian* is accusing Neil Hamilton and

* Robin Cook (1946–2005), Labour MP for Edinburgh Central, 1974–83, Livingston,
1983–2005; Foreign Secretary, 1997–2001, and subsequently Leader of the House of
Commons.
† City of Chester Conservative Association Treasurer.
‡ Sir Stuart Bell (b.1938), Labour MP for Middlesbrough since 1983.

Tim Smith of taking £2,000 a time to ask questions on behalf of Harrods. It beggars belief.

Thursday, 20 October 1994

What Mohammed Al-Fayed* says is this: 'I was approached by Ian Greer who offered to run a campaign. A fee of about £50,000 was mentioned. But then he said he would have to pay the MPs, Neil Hamilton and Tim Smith, who would ask the questions. Mr Greer said: "You need to rent an MP just like you need to rent a London taxi." I couldn't believe that in Britain, where Parliament has such a big reputation, you had to pay MPs. He said it would be £2,000 a question. Every month we got a bill for parliamentary services and it would vary from £8,000 to £10,000, depending on the number of questions. Then Mr Hamilton rang up and requested to stay at the Ritz Hotel in Paris with his wife. I agreed. I am a generous man, but he ran up such a big bill, even coming back for afternoon tea.'

This is truly horrendous. Tim I have known since Oxford. We might have gone into business together. He's got a ramrod back, a City background. And Neil and Christine are real friends. I can't believe it – and yet – I almost don't want to put this in writing – I know they did go to Paris at Fayed's expense. But a Paris freebie is one thing: 2,000 quid a question quite another.

Later

Tim Smith has resigned. Yes, he did have a 'business relationship' with Fayed and, yes, he failed to register it. Curtains. But Neil denies it all. Well, not quite all. Yes, he stayed at the Ritz, in Fayed's 'private rooms' and the bill topped £3,000, but he is adamant he accepted no fees, no 'cash for questions' of any kind.

Dinner with Bill Deedes† in Dining Room C. This is what we want: an evening of claret and anecdote – tales of the smoking room from the golden age of Supermac. He sees distinct parallels between now and 1963. And suggests we underestimate Blair at our peril. (I don't think we do underestimate Blair, but we

---

* Mohammed Fayed (b.1933), Egyptian entrepreneur who acquired Harrods, the Knightsbridge department store, in 1984. The acquisition was controversial, opposed, among others, by 'Tiny' Rowland, founder of Lonhro, and the subject of a DTI inquiry in 1987. Fayed, anxious both to retain his ownership of Harrods and to secure British citizenship (which he has still not been granted) sought support from Members of Parliament; he did so by retaining the services of Ian Greer Associates, parliamentary lobbyists.

† William Deedes (1913–2007), Conservative MP for Ashford, 1950–74; served in Harold Macmillan's Cabinet, 1962–4; editor of the *Daily Telegraph*, 1974–86; Baron Deedes of Aldington from 1986.

don't *rate* him. It's Cook we most respect. The tea-room line: if he didn't look like a garden gnome he'd be their leader – no question.)

Saturday, 22 October 1994

I have just left a 'chin-up' message on Neil's answering machine, but he's an idiot. He emerged from a school he was visiting in his constituency yesterday brandishing a biscuit that one of the children had baked and given him. 'Shall I declare it?' he enquired of the photographers at the gate. The inevitable has happened: the picture of Neil and his biscuit (a grinning Christine in the background) adorns the front pages. The PM will not be amused.

Tuesday, 25 October 1994

Neil has gone, protesting his innocence. The PM is setting up a 'committee on standards in public life' to be chaired by a judge, Lord Nolan. There's a lot of huffing and puffing in the tea room. An outside body scrutinising our behaviour? We don't like it.

Thursday, 27 October 1994

Jonathan [Aitken] has been magnificent. The *Guardian* splashed their story about his weekend in Paris (the bloody Ritz again!), Gordon Brown picked it up at Treasury Questions and Jonathan knocked him for six – the Cabinet Secretary has investigated and fully accepts Jonathan's version of events: he paid his own bill in full. Can we now have an end to this 'hysterical atmosphere of sleaze journalism'?

Saturday, 29 October 1994

The Aitken saga is rumbling on, but Jonathan is in the clear. His Association is standing by him. His chairman, Major John Thomas (there's a name to reckon with), is offering Jonathan 'unconditional support': 'As we all know, his integrity and his moral and Christian standards are above reproach.'

Tuesday, 1 November 1994

The entire day has had a weird Alice in Wonderland feel to it. We want to conduct the inquiry into 'cash for questions' in private, simply publishing the report at the end. Labour say the hearings should be held in public. Tony Benn (the Mad Hatter) is defying the Speaker (the Cook? the Duchess?), taking his little tape recorder into the sessions and producing his own minutes for distribution to the press. It's a shambles.

Wednesday, 23 November 1994

We are dancing the rumba on the foredeck of the *Titanic*. In the hope of bringing the rebels into line the entire Cabinet has agreed to resign en masse if Monday's vote on the European Finance Bill is lost. The Chancellor tells me, 'It's a fuss about nothing. The Party's got to pull itself together.'

In the tea room Edward Leigh* is telling us that Major hasn't lost his way because it's apparent he never had a way. In the smoking room Ted [Heath] is harrumphing that it's high time the Whips got to grips with the right-wing riff-raff and that we got ourselves a party chairman who knows what he's doing. 'It was different in my day. In my government nobody leaked. I wouldn't have it.'

Monday, 28 November 1994

We survived. Thanks to the Ulster Unionists, fairly comfortably. Ken gave a robust speech, the PM sitting glumly at his side. When it came to the vote, eight of our people rebelled and apparently they are to lose the whip, in which case Sir Richard Body† (who voted with us) will give up the whip as well by way of pro-test. Body is seriously strange. He's the one whose very name conjures up the sound of the flapping of white coats.

Hero of the hour: Lord James Douglas-Hamilton.‡ On Thursday night he succeeded to the Earldom of Selkirk. The Serjeant-at-Arms came to drag him from the chamber. This morning James did the decent thing and renounced the title so that he would be able to vote with us tonight. Soames: 'Lord James is a perfect gentleman. Gill§ is a perfect cunt.'

Technically we are now a minority government and the feeling in the tea room is that we are in terminal decline.

Tuesday, 29 November 1994

The Budget's been and gone. Ken was upbeat, 'a Budget for jobs', but the House dozed. (The other day Sir Peter Emery¶ was fast asleep on the front bench below the gangway. He had propped himself in Ted's corner seat. Ted arrived, Peter

---

* Edward Leigh (b.1950), Conservative MP for Gainsborough since 1983.
† Sir Richard Body (b.1927), Conservative MP for Billericay, 1955–9, Boston, 1966–2001.
‡ James Douglas-Hamilton (b.1942), Conservative MP for Edinburgh West, 1974–97; briefly 11th Earl of Selkirk; from 1997 Baron Selkirk of Douglas.
§ Christopher Gill (b.1936), Conservative MP for Ludlow, 1987–2001, and leading Euro-sceptic; now a member of the national executive of the UK Independence Party.
¶ Sir Peter Emery (1926–2004), Conservative MP for Reading, 1959–66, Honiton and East Devon, 1967–2001.

slumbered on. Ted prodded him, Peter stirred and then settled back again. From across the way Skinner barked, 'Wake up, Ted's here.' Sir Peter roused himself and shifted along the bench to make way for the Father of the House.)

Sunday, 4 December

We were at the Albert Hall as guests of the ever-generous Clelands.* John told us that Meatloaf had just given a concert in aid of the Prince's Trust. Prince Charles arrived, not looking forward to it. John hadn't been looking forward to it either, but it turned out to be sensational. Said John, 'All of Charles's people were there, a true cross-section of the British public, having a great time in aid of the Prince's Trust. And what did HRH do? He put in his earplugs and looked sad. As he left he said, "Dreadful, wasn't it?"'

Wednesday, 7 December 1994

Hartley Booth approached me. Incredibly, he is planning to produce an anthology of love poetry and wondered if I had any suggestions. I did not know what to say. Matthew Corbett came to lunch and fell foul of the security people. 'What have you got in this case, sir?' 'Sooty,' said Matthew. 'Now, don't try and be clever with us, sir.'

Thursday, 8 December 1994

KC was magnificent in the presentation of his mini-Budget restoring the lost billion from the negated VAT on fuel. (Clobber the motorist, drinker, smoker.) It wasn't the matter but the manner that swung it his way. It was a perfect example of how the right approach in the chamber can make all the difference. Gordon Brown failed to score. More chattering in the tea room: 'Why oh why isn't Ken Clarke our leader?' 'Because he's a Euro-nut. Otherwise he'd walk it.'

Friday, 16 December 1994

I'm on the train travelling to Chester, my last constituency weekend of the year. When I get to the other end I will step off the train and unveil a plaque marking the refurbishment of the station. I like unveiling plaques. I'm particularly chuffed at the one I unveiled in the old folks' home in Blacon. Once council run, it was taken over and revamped by a delightful Indian family. When I pulled the little rope, the curtains parted and I read the words: 'This plague was unveiled by Gyles Brandreth MP . . .' True.

---

* John Cleland, Chairman of the Albert Hall, and his wife Annie, friends of GB.

'I Hope You're Happy Now?'

January – December 1995

Tuesday, 10 January 1995

I had my postponed meeting with Hayden Phillips to discuss Honours. After the door had been securely closed, he murmured, 'This meeting isn't taking place, you understand.' 'Of course,' I murmured back.

Of the great mysteries of British society – how to get a table at the Ivy, who decides who features in *Who's Who* – none is more shrouded in secrecy than the honours system. For much of the meeting Hayden held his notes close to his chest – literally – and, when I mentioned a name, he would glance slyly down at his papers and then purr at me, 'Mmm – Alan Bates? Mmm, yes, I think we can help you there.' He played a funny cat-and-mouse game with a document which he eventually gave me, murmuring silkily, 'I shouldn't, I really shouldn't . . . but why not?' I presume he had intended to give me the paper – 'Honours In Confidence' – all along.

'I felt the "K" for Robert Stephens was right, didn't you? I saw his *Lear* and thought, "Yes, yes."'

'Isn't Donald Sinden on the list?'

He glanced down at his crib-sheet. 'Mmm, it works on the escalator principle. You can be on the escalator for a year or two before you reach the top. I don't think Donald Sinden's been on the escalator in my time.'

'I think he's one for the escalator, don't you?'

(Before he dies, Simon wants to see Don achieve his 'K' and, if it can be done, it will be.)

Tuesday, 7 February 1995

Jonathan Aitken preached at evensong at Hertford College Chapel on Sunday and he's sent me a copy of his address: 'My thesis to you tonight is that the gap between the Christian teachings and the honourable profession of politics is a narrow one, bridgeable by prayer.'

I like Jonathan more all the time. Stephen D. doesn't trust him.

Monday 20 February 1995

Michael Foot[*] (still wearing that same donkey jacket) has reassured us, 'I was never a Soviet agent.' Nicholas Fairbairn has died 'from liver complications', aged 61. 'Nicky liked his dram' is how the obituarists are putting it. Watching the poor man stumbling about the corridors here was pitiable, but even in his decrepitude there were still flashes of brilliance. He listed his recreations in *Who's Who*: 'making love, ends meet and people laugh.'

Wednesday, 22 February 1995

The PM was on a roll tonight, exhilarated by the triumph of the London–Dublin framework document. Paisley is ranting that Major has 'sold out the Union', Willie Ross[†] says it's 'unworkable', but in the chamber and the tea room it went down well.

The PM ended up at No. 10 for our reception for the London arts community. We were fearful that with all the Irish excitement he might have to give us short shrift. In the event, he was at his absolute best. I said to him, 'This is one of those days when you realise why you came into this, isn't it?' He grinned: 'Yes.' Then he checked himself, 'There's a long way to go, but at the end . . . just think of the prize.'

At the ridiculous end of the spectrum I found myself in a corner with a moist-eyed Andrew Lloyd Webber who, not having any idea who I was, said, 'Are you coming to Antigua for the weekend?' Lady Lloyd Webber turned to Nicholas Lloyd and Eve Pollard and cooed, 'Oh, do. It's just the Lloyd Webbers and the Frosts and the Saatchis – the home team.'

Donald Sinden was funny – as always. He asked Richard Eyre[‡] if it's true that Harriet Walter is to play Hamlet at the National. Before Eyre could answer, Don went on: 'I understand you approached Paul Scofield to play Claudius, but he said, "No – have you tried Miriam Margolyes?"'

Monday, 27 February 1995

I've just returned from No. 11. The Chancellor was late. He'd been in a huddle with Eddie George[§] in the wake of the Barings collapse. It seems a Barings trader, aged 26, managed to lose around £600 million trading in derivatives without anybody

[*] Michael Foot (b.1913), Labour MP for Devonport, 1945–55, Ebbw Vale, 1960–83, Blaenau Gwent, 1983–92; Leader of the Labour Party 1980–83.
[†] William Ross (b.1936), Ulster Unionist MP for Londonderry, 1974–2001.
[‡] Sir Richard Eyre (b.1943), director of the Royal National Theatre, 1988–97.
[§] Sir Edward George (1938–2009), Governor of the Bank of England, 1993–2003; Baron George of St Tudy from 2000.

knowing. I love the way Ken chuckles in the face of adversity. Bang goes Britain's oldest bank, 4,000 employees have lost their jobs, the pound's got the jitters, an international banking crisis is on the cards, but our Chancellor is still chortling.

Monday, 13 March 1995

As if he didn't have enough to do, the Prime Minister obliges colleagues by generously autographing bottles that can then be auctioned off at party functions. On a bad day there are *dozens* of bottles awaiting prime ministerial attention. Colleagues of the old school (and a more generous disposition) get brandy or malt whisky for the great man to sign. I'm opting for the Wickham Fumé at a fiver a bottle, despite the lordly reprimand I received from Sir Peter Tapsell: 'You cannot ask the British Prime Minister to autograph a bottle of English *table* wine! Good God, what is the party coming to?'

Thursday, 16 March 1995

I appear to have landed poor Fergie in the soup. She called. 'Children in Crisis' was in a crisis. They had a fund-raising dinner in the City and needed a speaker. Could I? *Please.* Yes, of course, but I have to be back at the Commons to vote at ten. So along I go. Sarah is in very jolly form, I sit on her right, we are cosy, gossipy, giggly (*slightly* excessively so). I get up and do my speech, going right over the top about Sarah's achievements, beauty, brilliance, pazazz. I say I've *got* to go now. Lots of huggy-kissy goodbyes and then, just as I'm slipping out, I have a bright idea. 'Look, why don't we find the richest man in the room and get him to take my place? He can sit next to you for coffee and you can seduce him. Before the brandy's arrived he'll have promised a nice fat donation for the cause. Go for it.'

And poor girl, she did. I've just had a call from the *Daily Mail.* The rich stranger sat next to Fergie. Then, to everyone's surprise, a prankster's auction ensued, in which people were persuaded to raise money by removing their clothing. The man who filled my seat was encouraged to drop his trousers – and just as he did so photographers appeared from the shadows. Flash, bang, wallop, there was dear old Fergie with a fellow she's never met before with his trousers round his ankles.

Wednesday, 22 March 1995

I have just returned from taking a delegation to the Department of Employment. She may look like a death-watch beetle, but Ann Widdecombe had my Chester people eating out of her hand. She understood exactly what they were after, told them precisely what she could and couldn't do, and when she makes a commitment you know she'll deliver.

Thursday, 30 March 1995

I had another meeting with Hayden on honours. Between us Danny Finkelstein[*]
and I had cobbled together a little list (literally on the back of an envelope) and as
well as the legit end of the business (Richard Curtis, John Cleland, Martin Jarvis,
Eileen Atkins, Alec McCowen etc.) we threw in some populist suggestions of the
'Arise Dame Cilla' variety: Norman Wisdom, Bruce Forsyth, Julie Goodyear,
Peggy Mount, Michael Elphick, Delia Smith. Danny (off the top of his head)
conjured up a raft of names for the sports list and, knowing I wouldn't have heard
of half of them, supplied thumbnail portraits: Ian Rush ('Liverpool soccer legend.
This is his testimonial season'), Fred Street ('for many years the England football
team's physiotherapist'), Martin Edwards ('Chairman of Manchester United. A
go-ahead sporting entrepreneur of the sort we are trying to encourage'), Len
Martin ('the best-known voice in Britain. He reads the football results on
BBC1').

Monday, 3 April 1995

We went to the Olivier Awards last night *in loco* the Secretary of State. It was
quite fun (we saw a number of chums, we sat with Sally Greene[†] and Diana Quick
– in my mind's eye still in that leather miniskirt – and Bill Nighy – whose half-
hesitant self-consciously sexy style M and I love and Simon [Cadell] *loathes*) –
but it doesn't work. If Stephen can't go/won't go, then it's better to send no one.
My turning up just advertises the fact he's failed to show – again. In the speeches
there was the customary mocking of Stephen and sneering at the Government.

Sunday, 9 April 1995

Palm Sunday. No hosannas. The *News of the World* strikes again. Last month, my
friend Bob Hughes.[‡] Today, my friend Richard Spring.[§] 'Tory MP, the Tycoon

---

[*] Daniel Finkelstein (b.1962), director of the Social Market Foundation and informal
adviser to GB and Stephen Dorrell at the Department of National Heritage; director of
the Conservative Research Department, 1995–7; now associate editor and chief leader
writer of *The Times*.
[†] Sally Greene (b.1957), theatre owner and producer.
[‡] Twice-married Hughes resigned as Parliamentary Secretary at the Office of Public
Service and Science on 4 March 1995 in anticipation of the *News of the World*'s report of his
extramarital relationship with his House of Commons secretary, Janet Oates. The paper
carried the story under the headline: 'Minister Got His Oates Morning, Noon and Night'.
[§] Richard Spring (b.1946), Conservative MP for Bury St Edmunds, 1992–7, Suffolk West
since 1997.

and the Sunday School Teacher. We expose three-in-a-bed sex session. Exclusive.' Richard, tall, likeable, languid, elegant in a Bertie-Woosterish, Newmarket-Races sort of a way, appears to have invited an acquaintance (a pensions company executive) and his girlfriend (Odette Nightingale, occasional Sunday school teacher – you couldn't make it up) to dinner last Sunday. The hospitality was generous, the conversation lively (it seems Richard thinks Portillo's quite fanciable, doesn't rate the PM but is ready to give Norma one anytime), and, evidently, chez Spring the post-prandial treats go well beyond *crème de menthe frappé* and a Bendicks bittermint.

Tuesday, 18 April 1995

SD: Gyles, have you got anything to do over the next three weeks?
GB: Er . . .
SD: Clear your desk – completely. Write the film policy.

The truth is we've got little time, little scope, little room for manoeuvre. What the industry wants are Irish-type tax breaks which the Chancellor can deliver, but we can't. But we can at least put our best food forward – and raid the lottery. I am seeing David Puttnam[*] at 7.00 p.m.

Later

The drink with David Puttnam was very funny. He's diminutive, friendly, eager and has the perfect solution to each and every problem on the planet. I rather hoped he'd be turning my children's books into movies. Dream on. He clearly can't wait to get out of movies into politics.

Tuesday, 25 April 1995

At PMQs Blair taunted the PM on the returning Euro-rebels. The PM countered by asking what Blair was going to do about his Clause IV rebels. Blair came back: 'There is one very big difference – I lead my party, he follows his.' The Labour benches went berserk. We sat sullenly, knowing it was true.

Later

I am in wine – and why not? I have just come from the Churchill Room where I have been embraced by Franco Zeffirelli![†] He does what I do: pretends to know

---

[*] David Puttnam (b.1941), film producer; knighted 1995; Lord Puttnam since 1997.
[†] Franco Zeffirelli (b. Gianfranco Corsi, 1923), Italian director of opera, theatre, film; a member of the Italian Senate.

everybody he meets so he doesn't give offence by failing to recognise someone he met in Padua thirty years ago who recalls the encounter vividly while Franco naturally can't remember it at all. I raved about his John Stride/Judi Dench *Romeo* and the Maggie Smith/Robert Stephens *Much Ado*, which made him think we must have worked together at the Old Vic in the sixties! He pressed me to come and stay in Amalfi. I *dragged* Stephen down there to meet him. I said, 'This is a great man – theatre, opera, movies.' Stephen looked bemused. 'And politics,' I said. 'He's a senator now.' 'Let's go,' said Stephen, grinning.

Monday, 1 May 1995

Howell James[*] came to the Marginals' Club dinner. Howell has been talking with Nicholas O'Shaughnessy[†] about ways to 'present' the PM. N. O'S. sees Major as a modern Baldwin. I think Major sees Major as a modern Baldwin.

Friday, 5 May 1995

I am sitting in bed with a bottle of Oddbins finest and a plate of Boots long-life chicken Madras curry (it's actually v tasty). I have just returned from *Ruddigore* at the King's School (the children play the minor parts, the head-master plays the lead!). My wife (whom I love) is in London, there is nothing on the box, so I am reading O'Shaughnessy's thoughts on Major and oratory. He makes all the points I've tried to make but much more tellingly: the PM aims at too many targets in his speeches, tries to persuade too many disparate groups, says too much. Baldwin's speeches were very short. He invented the sound bite. He used simple language, a simple message, short sentences, easy vocabulary.

N. O'S. is also fascinating on what he calls 'visual rhetoric'. He sent Howell a photo of Blair kneeling to lay a wreath at the spot where a policeman had been murdered. Blair's suit, the way he's kneeling, the look, the association with a fallen policeman – the picture delivers *everything*.

If Howell can deliver even some of this it could make a spectacular difference. We might even return to the vexed issue of *wunt* . . . the PM thinks it doesn't matter the way he pronounces a word. The truth is that 'wunt' is positively weird and gets in the way of what he's trying to say.

---

[*] Howell James, whom GB had known when he was press officer at TV-am, had just been appointed political secretary to John Major, 1995–7.
[†] From the Judge Institute of Management Studies at Cambridge University.

Monday, 22 May 1995

Poor Stephen has bombed in Cannes. He has been received by British film-makers with a predictable mixture of derision and contempt and he has not enhanced his reputation as a man of culture and self-confessed born-again *cinéaste* by assuming that the head of the festival jury, one Jeanne Moreau, is a man.

Wednesday, 24 May 1995

The House adjourned after we had listened to the tributes to Harold Wilson.* The best stories – and the most touching speeches – came from Tony Benn and Gerald Kaufman. Gerald told a story from the time when he was a junior minister at the Department of the Environment in charge of the government car service. Gerald received a minute from the Prime Minister – a rare thing for a junior minister – instructing him to write to all former prime ministers still living offering them a car and a chauffeur. 'I realised then that Harold had definitely decided to retire. He liked to plan ahead.'

Benn: 'Like all prime ministers, Harold Wilson worried about plots. I asked him once, when the plots were thickening, "Harold, what shall we do if you are knocked down by a bus?" Harold said, "Find out who was driving the bus."'

Monday, 12 June 1995

Mrs T. is rocking the boat. The Baroness has been on the radio, telling us what we really need is more Thatcherism – 'we must get back to Conservative policies'. The tea room is fairly deserted because the Whips seem to have organised a week of 'light business' and fairly early nights. They don't want the lads sitting around the watering holes grumbling and plotting.

Tuesday, 13 June 1995

I have just come from a convivial drink with the Chancellor. While we were downing the Rioja, it seems the PM has been being harangued by an unruly mob of right-wingers. Ken's view is that the 'the more you concede to these mad xenophobes' the more they'll want. The problem is, he's flirted with these people to keep them sweet, and now he won't deliver, they're turning ugly.

Thursday, 22 June 1995

At five o'clock, we shuffled in for the regular 1922 Committee meeting and Sir Marcus got up and made a bald announcement: the PM is stepping down as

* Lord Wilson of Rievaulx had died, aged 79.

leader, he continues as Prime Minister, election on Tuesday week. The PM will be a candidate and expects his opponents to 'put up or shut up'. We all sat there, speechless, then stumbled our way to the chamber. Assorted Labour rabble were hopping up and down hysterically. After an hour or so the fever subsided and the chamber emptied. The initial feeling here is that he's scored a brilliant coup. If he trounces any stalking-horse, and he will, then the sniping has to stop.

Monday, 26 June 1995

Redwood is the challenger. I've a feeling they may have kiboshed his campaign before it's even started. It wasn't what they said: it was how they looked – Teresa to the right of him in a hideous day-glo green and Marlow to the left in a quite ludicrous striped blazer.* Every picture tells a story.

I was standing behind the Speaker's chair just now, when a gangly Labour MP sidled up to me. I thought he was going to offer me some dirty postcards. I don't know his name, but he was at the Allied-Domecq do on Friday. 'Are you going to declare it in the register?' he asked, all sotto voce. 'If you don't, we won't.' There are some pretty tawdry types round here.

Wednesday, 28 June 1995

The official line is that a majority of one will be enough, but if Major only squeaks to victory, he's fatally wounded. I've spotted Gillian Shephard† in a couple of cosy corners. She's as loyal to the PM as they come, but if it goes to a second ballot . . . she'll be there for those who can't stomach Hezza. I reported this to Stephen. His jaw fell, '*Please* – spare us.'

Saturday, 1 July 1995

Norman Tebbit has clambered out of his coffin to urge us to vote for John Redwood, praising his 'brains, courage and humour'.

Monday, 3 July 1995

Ken Clarke is very funny: 'The party can't seriously be considering voting for this Martian.' 'I think he's supposed to be a Venusian, Ken. Or a Vulcan.' 'It's another planet, that's for sure.' But the man with green blood has fought a good

---

* John Redwood's supporters included Teresa Gorman (b.1931), Conservative MP for Billericay, 1987–2001, and Antony Marlow (b.1940), Conservative MP for Northampton North, 1979–97.
† Gillian Shephard (b.1940), Conservative MP for South West Norfolk, 1987–2005; Secretary of State for Education, 1994–7; now Baroness Shephard of Northwold.

campaign. Even if he doesn't make it tomorrow (and he won't), in the longer term he's positioned himself to overtake Portillo as the champion of the Right.

Later

Making small-talk with the PM is never easy. In such a night as this . . .

I found him [in the members' dining room] gazing blankly into the middle distance. He looked pasty-faced and weary.

'I think it's going pretty well,' I said.

'Do you? Do you?' He shook his head. 'I just don't know. I just don't know.' He thinks the *Daily Mail* is going to come out against him in the morning. The *Sun*, *The Times*, the *Telegraph*, they're all saying he should go. 'But the *Mail*? There you go . . . This time tomorrow, who knows?'

Silence fell. He looked at his plate. I burbled stupidly. He was monosyllabic. I burbled some more. Silence fell again. I thought, 'Poor sod, this could be his last night as Prime Minister and he's spending it with me, *like this*!' And then a gallant knight rode to the rescue. In came the Rt Hon. Peter Brooke CH and sat down beside me. He looked across at the PM and said he had just finished reading an article about a certain Surrey cricketer whose heyday was in the 1930s. The name meant nothing to me, but the PM brightened at once. Peter continued, describing some particularly memorable match from the glorious summer of '37, and within a minute the pall that had engulfed the table lifted and Peter and the PM talked cricket – talked 1930s cricket! – in extraordinary, animated, fascinated, happy detail. I sat silent in admiration.

Tuesday, 4 July 1995

He's done it:

> Major, 218
> Redwood , 89
> Abstentions, 22

I've just been on the radio hailing it as a 'resounding victory' for the PM. The truth is it allows the PM to carry on, but it shows the world that a third of the parliamentary party don't support him.

Later

Jonathan Aitken is resigning . . . to concentrate on his libel actions against the *Guardian* and *World in Action*. Heseltine was closeted at No. 10 for most of the morning and the buzz now is that he's going to become Deputy Prime Minister in return for having committed his men to the PM's cause. But if Hezza is promoted and Rifkind or Lang* get the Foreign Office rather than Howard, the Redwoodites will be spitting blood – and this within a matter of four hours of the election designed to resolve all our differences!

Wednesday, 5 July 1995

Stephen is the new Secretary of State for Health and he is so pleased it's almost comical. He can't stop grinning. I, on the other hand . . .

I began the day by making the pilgrimage to the stately home of the Heseltines. It is not at all as vulgar and arriviste as Alan Clark had led me to expect.† A touch of the uncomfortable French *salon* about the public rooms, but unquestionably a home fit for a *grand seigneur*. While Hezza himself was strutting into Downing Street as our new Deputy Prime Minister, I was doing my turn for the benefit of his Association ladies. Anne [Heseltine] was very gracious and rather sweet. 'Don't slim like Nigel Lawson. He looks so old and tired. You'd slip through the floorboards.' If only.

I got back mid-afternoon and found Stephen already ensconced at the Department of Health, gurgling with delight. I said, 'Who are the ministers going to be?'

He said, 'I'm not sure. Gerry's staying,‡ which is good. He's an ally. They want to move Julia Cumberlege.§ What do you think?'

'She knows the nurses and the midwives. I don't think you're going to want to spend a lot of time sweet-talking the midwives.'

'You're right. Let's hang on to her. I'll call Alastair.' Alastair is the new Chief Whip.¶ 'Alastair, if you can manage it, I'd like to keep Julia . . . She knows the midwives . . . Thanks.'

---

* Ian Lang (b.1940), Conservative MP for Galloway and Upper Nithsdale, 1979–97; Secretary of State for Scotland, 1990–95; President of the Board of Trade, 1995–7.
† See Alan Clark's *Diaries*, 17 November 1990.
‡ Peter Gerald Malone (b.1950), Conservative MP for Aberdeen South, 1983–7, Winchester, 1992–7; Minister of State at the Department of Health, 1994–7.
§ Julia Cumberlege (b.1943), Baroness Cumberlege of Newick since 1990; Parliamentary Under-Secretary of State for Health, 1992–7.
¶ Alastair Goodlad had been Minister of State at the Foreign Office, 1992–5; he had three spells in the Whips' Office: as an Assistant Whip and Lord Commissioner of the Treasury, 1981–4; as Comptroller of Her Majesty's Household and then Treasurer of HM Household and Deputy Chief Whip, 1989–92; and as Parliamentary Secretary to the Treasury and Chief Whip, 1995–7.

In the corner of the room, rather pathetically, I mouthed, 'What about Gyles?'

Crossing the members' lobby just now, I was stopped by a scurrying, breathless Greg Knight [Deputy Chief Whip]. 'Could we have a word – tomorrow?' he said.

This means I'm going to be let down lightly with a kindly word. Bah.

Thursday, 6 July 1995

All in all, it's not a bad line-up – except for one thing: it doesn't include me! I went to see Greg as instructed. 'I'm afraid it didn't work out for you this time. The PM has to reward his team and promote the women.'

At lunch-time, I said to Stephen that I thought he should get a new PPS. He was very sweet and said, 'No, no, no. I need you. I'd be heartbroken.' But the truth is that Health is of no interest to me – at Heritage he *did* need me and I could actually make a modest impact. I know it's only a game, but this minute, I do find it *very* galling.

Wednesday, 12 July 1995

The Chancellor is magnificent. We're halfway through the debate on the economy and he's at his chuckling, combative, blokeish best. He's been knocking Gordon Brown all over the shop. Gordon's always friendly in the tea room, infinitely more *real* than Blair, but what a windbag! The waffle and the gobbledygook, they just come tumbling out.

William [Waldegrave] is looking very chirrupy. It's a strange business this: a week ago he was our expert on agriculture, tonight he makes his debut as Chief Secretary with all the Treasury answers at his fingertips. As it turns out, Jonathan's departure may have been timely. The poor man is now contending with a prostitute who knew Jonathan fifteen years ago and has suddenly surfaced with the promise of a book of torrid revelations. In the tea room they're saying there's more to come. 'Some aspects of Jonathan's love-life are very dark indeed.'

Saturday, 15 July 1995

I'm in bed. Tea and Marmite toast, and I don't have to get up for an hour. If living in the moment is what we should be doing, this is a good moment in which to live. M is looking very beautiful and last night, at the Chester French Circle 15th anniversary dinner (!), she was quite wonderful.

Poor Peter Morrison has died and the obituaries are pretty uncharitable, concentrating on his time as Mrs T.'s PPS ('His part in her downfall') with a definite unpleasant nudge and wink in the direction of his 'bachelor' status and interest in 'young people'. He was found dead at the foot of the stairs. He was only 51. He looked 70.

Later

This afternoon's surgery was alarming. A fellow was booked in for 4.00 p.m. Yesterday his 'care worker' called to say he was dangerous and on no account should I see him. Unfortunately, we didn't have a number for him so we couldn't cancel. On the care worker's advice, I rearranged the office, so that the man would have to sit right inside the room and I could sit behind my desk right by the door. The care worker said, 'Whatever you do, when he's speaking don't interrupt him and look straight in his eye. And if he makes one false move, get out as fast as you can and call the police.' At four o'clock, when the poor unfortunate arrived, my stomach was churning. I manoeuvred him into the chair in the far corner of the room and hovered nervously by the open door. I gazed steadfastly at him as, very politely, his voice hardly above a whisper, he told me his problem: 'It's my care worker. He doesn't understand me.'

Tuesday, 18 July 1995

I have mastered the art of arriving at a Buckingham Palace Garden Party. The real time to reach the main gates is exactly 3.53 p.m. The riff-raff are already inside, so you have the pleasure of scrunching your way alone across the gravel, past the guardsmen, under the arch, across the deserted square, up the red-carpeted stairs and through. Proceeding at a leisurely pace, taking in the pictures, pausing to admire the porcelain, you will arrive at the bay windows leading out onto the garden at 3.59 on the dot. It's too late for the flunkies to push you out onto the lawn to join the crowds. You've got to stay where you are, in pole position, for Her Majesty's arrival under your very nose as the clock strikes four.

We took Aphra and Saethryd – it's Aphra's seventeeth birthday – and then went on to the end-of-term drinks at No. 10. I talked publishers with Norma[*] and the PM (good man) took the girls off to see the Cabinet Room. I said to Aphra, 'The Prime Minister has wished you a happy birthday – that's one for the diary.' She gave me one of her 'Oh-dad-how-can-you-be-so-embarrassing' looks.

[*] Norma Major had published a biography of Joan Sutherland and was writing a history of Chequers.

Wednesday, 26 July 1995

I've just come from a long session with Stephen at the DoH [Department of Health]. I advised him that he could probably get away with having Oliver Cromwell on the wall, but it would be a mistake to get rid of the drawing of Florence Nightingale. He is another one with the 'longer-term ambition'. And I'm backing him. (Michèle: 'God, poor man, he's doomed. You're the kiss of death. You know it.')

Wednesday, 11 October 1995

I reached Blackpool in time to hear Hezza's end-of-the-pier knockabout (all the old tricks, it creaks but it works) and Stephen's speech. Stephen did well, but the talk of the town is Portillo's effort yesterday. It was crude – awful mock heroics, cheap Brussels-bashing, wrapping himself in the Union Jack – but the activists stood and cheered and roared for more. Having paraded Nelson, Wellington and Churchill as his heroes/role models, he coasted to his climax on the coat-tails of the SAS. 'Who dares wins!' The PM had no alternative but to lead the ovation. I saw Michael at the Imperial. I said, 'How about you then!' He gave a wan smile. He knows he went too far.

Thursday, 12 October 1995

I went along to speak to Nick Hawkins's Association Ladies. As the car swept us into the car park, we were suddenly confronted by a seven-foot-tall chicken.

'What's that?' I squeaked.

'It's the chicken,' said Nick. 'It follows me everywhere. Ignore it.'

We jumped out of the car and marched briskly into the Conservative Club, pursued by the giant chicken squawking and flapping its wings.

Inside the club, Nick made no reference to the man-sized fowl, but as I stood there singing the Prime Minister's and Nick's praises, Nick standing po-faced at my side, I kept catching sight of the wretched chicken, bobbing up and down outside. It was agony.

The explanation? Nick has told Blackpool South, where he has a majority of 1,600, that he is looking for a safer seat.* The Labour Party are accusing him of being on the 'chicken run' and they've hired this costume to provide him with regular, and seemingly effective, embarrassment.

---

* He found one. Nicholas Hawkins (b.1957), Conservative MP for Blackpool South, 1992–7, and for Surrey Heath, 1997–2005, with a majority of 16,000.

Tuesday, 17 October 1995

We've only been back twenty-fours hours and it's all going wrong again. Michael Howard is in real trouble over his sacking of Derek Lewis.* The PM put up a so-so defence at PMQs, but Lewis is very plausible and there's the scent of blood in the air. So, Howard's on the ropes and Portillo's digging in. Michael P. is standing by his Conference speech – '*Je ne regrette rien*' – saying that he and the PM are singing from the same sheet while conceding he's singing fortissimo. Meanwhile the PM, poor bugger, is having to backtrack: he knew the general line the speech would take, he hadn't seen the wording.

But there's good news for someone: Douglas Hurd is to get £250,000 a year working a two-day week as deputy chairman of NatWest Markets.

I'm just in from St James's Palace, the Chester Cathedral fund-raising reception. My chat with the Prince of Wales consisted largely of manic barking laughter on both sides. Evidently we both felt that was the best way to get through it.

Thursday, 19 October 1995

A unique day. It began with the Home Secretary on the ropes, probably a goner. It's ended with him triumphant, as good as unassailable.

It was an Opposition motion – 'That this House deplores the unwillingness of the Secretary of State for the Home Department to accept responsibility for serious operational failures of the Prison Service' – and Jack Straw led the charge. He had a powerful case to deploy, but he was virtually sunk only five minutes in by a beautifully judged question from Bernard Jenkin:† 'Under the circumstances, would *he* have dismissed the Director General of the Prison Service?' It was a little hand grenade lightly lobbed, but its effect was devastating. Straw never recovered.

By the time Michael got to his feet, Straw was already in retreat. Michael scored again and again, both because he was so unrelenting – chillingly so – and because his mastery of the brief was absolute.

Blair kept nudging Straw, telling him what to say. Howard saw what was happening and began goading Blair – so that eventually he made the fatal mistake of getting to his feet, humiliating his man but completely failing to deliver any kind

---

* The Home Secretary dismissed the Director General of the Prison Service in the light of General Sir John Learmont's report into escapes from Parkhurst Prison in January 1995. The Home Secretary drew a distinction between 'policy matters', for which he had ultimate responsibility, and 'operational matters', which were the responsibility of the Prison Service.
† Bernard Jenkin (b.1959), Conservative MP for Colchester North and North Essex since 1992.

of blinding strike. It was an electric ninety minutes and when Michael finished, the roar from our side was incredible. Thanks to Straw's ineptitude and Michael's bravura performance, whatever the rights and wrongs of the case, Michael has set himself free. Amazing.

Tuesday, 7 November 1995

11.30 a.m. As instructed, I presented myself at 12 Downing Street. I arrived with Michael Jopling.* We were ushered into the Chief Whip's little study. We have been singled out for a signal honour: next Wednesday, when the Queen opens Parliament, we are to propose and second the Loyal Address. Michael is, I am sure, going to bottle out, I'm sure of it, but I've got to do this speech and, *come what may*, I've got to do it well.

Monday, 13 November 1995

Jopling has bottled out. It's now to be Douglas Hurd, which is so much better. Greg Knight was very funny: 'Remember, there'll be three hundred people in there all wanting you to fail. (*Pause*) And the Opposition won't want you to do that brilliantly either.'

Tuesday, 14 November 1995

At 6.20 p.m. I presented myself at No. 12. Douglas was already there. Drinks were handed round, banter exchanged. Douglas mentioned a school song that he might refer to. Alastair spluttered, 'Good God, you're not going to sing!' Douglas murmured reassurance. Greg Knight was perched on the edge of the sofa next to me. I passed him my speech. 'Looks fine,' he said.

Upstairs [at No. 10], in the main drawing room, the entire Government had assembled. This was the 'Eve of Session Reception'. The PM, in good humour, read out the Queen's Speech, word for word. Then Madam Speaker spoke – graciously and well, wishing us all the best in the coming session.

We quaffed, we sluiced, we made our way into the street. As we stepped out into Downing Street, Andrew Mitchell† (who did it so well in the year I arrived) caught up with me and put an arm around my shoulder. 'I know exactly how you're feeling. It's hell. But it'll be all right.'

* Michael Jopling (b.1930), Conservative MP for Westmoreland, 1964–97. Traditionally, the Loyal Address is proposed by a senior backbencher of distinction and seconded by a junior backbencher 'with prospects'.

† Andrew Mitchell (b.1956), Conservative MP for Gedling, 1987–97, Sutton Coldfield since 2001.

Wednesday, 15 November 1995

The butterflies were terrible. I must have gone for a pee at least three times between lunch and 2.30 p.m. I am an old hand, but I've never known anything like this.

Madam Speaker: 'I shall now call on Mr Douglas Hurd to move the Address, and Mr Gyles Brandreth will second it.'

Douglas got up – and made an immediate mistake by saying when he leaves the House it'll be his constituents not us he'll miss the most. And then he took us on a rural ride through Oxfordshire – we had the local school song, verse after verse of it – and while on our side we listened with respect, on their side they lost interest, the murmuring and shuffling began.

As I stood up and heard the groans and jeers from the benches opposite, my mouth was so dry I thought I might not be able to utter a sound. Madam Speaker, bless her, was sitting forward on the edge of her seat, willing me to keep my nerve. The rumbling opposite began to subside and I began extolling the virtues of the matchless City of Chester. 'It has two thousand years of history,' I said, and from the far end of the second row of the Labour benches Joe Ashton[*] cried, 'And a one thousand majority!' The House roared, and suddenly they were on my side. And from there on in there were no problems – even a couple of blissful moments. A joke at the expense of the Liberals united all but thirty members, a joke at Paddy Ashdown's expense united all but one.

Tuesday, 21 November 1995

I breakfasted with the only other person in the country who didn't watch the Princess of Wales being interviewed last night on *Panorama*. Stephen didn't watch because he really isn't interested. I didn't watch because I was in the chamber waiting for my adjournment debate on 'employment in Chester'. In the tearoom Fabricant was disappointed when I told him that I was pretty sure she met Hewitt nine months *after* Harry was born, not nine months before. Soames (Charles's fatman at Westminster) went over the top and is being sent a 'cool it' message from No. 10. However, I think we can take it that Soames's line that Diana's behaviour shows 'advanced stages of paranoia' reflects the true feelings of the Prince of Wales.

Tuesday, 28 November 1995

The Budget's been and gone. On the whole it's all very reasonable, very Ken, easy enough to defend on the doorstep. As the Chancellor sat down, from below

[*] Joseph Ashton (b.1933), Labour MP for Bassetlaw, 1968–2001.

the gangway Skinner called out, 'Is that it?' I suspect that may be the general verdict.

Potentially more exciting is news of the virtually unnoticed mini-mini-shuffle. The upshot is that there's a vacancy in the Whips' Office. I said to Stephen, 'This means there'll be a new Whip.' The penny dropped. 'I'll speak to Alastair,' he said.

Wednesday, 29 November 1995

President Clinton came to address both Houses of Parliament. At twelve noon we trooped into the Royal Gallery and took our places. We had the usual flummery: Black Rod, the Lord Chancellor, Madam Speaker, figures straight out of Gilbert & Sullivan. The fanfare sounded, trumpets from on high. In the middle of the stalls we'd come because we thought we should. He may be a Democrat, but he's still President. 'Be not too proud to be there.' But if we'd come to mock, we stayed to praise. He was sensational.

He looks good – tall, slim, handsome, his eye meets your eye – but the way he talks . . . His speech was just perfect. He saluted the PM's quest for peace in Northern Ireland, he affirmed the special relationship, he even announced that the US Navy's latest vessel is to be named the *Winston Churchill*. His speech did what oratory should, but he made it personal and intimate. There was none of the phoney theatrics you'd have got from Heseltine or Hague (or even me). It was the best speech of its kind I've ever heard.

Moments before the President made his entry, Greg Knight bustled down the central aisle, pointed at me, and said in an alarmingly loud stage whisper, 'The minute this is over the Chief needs to see you in his room.' Once we'd cheered the President on his way, I ankled round to the Chief's office.

'Ah,' said Alastair. 'Good, good.' He perched on one sofa. I perched on the other. 'The Prime Minister hopes you will accept your first ministerial appointment by joining the Whips' Office. It's the one job in government that you can only get with the full approval of your peers – so you're here because we wanted you. Lunch?'

Saturday, 2 December 1995

Clinton has had a remarkable week. He's delivered five major speeches in three days, by all accounts each one as powerful as the first. He must have a core of writers who understand the vocabulary and the *rhythm* he requires. In this country our senior politicians' speeches are simply cobbled together, usually at the last minute, invariably by young men in red braces.

And Brandreth hasn't had too bad a week either. Michèle said to me, 'I hope you're happy now?' She knows that we're going to lose the election, that's why she's content for me to stand again. This could be my one and only chance to be in government.

The upside: I get a salary, a car, a phonecard, a ministerial black box (Shana[*] explained, 'It'll take a few weeks to arrive – it's hand-made by prisoners') and, best of all, no more speeches. Whips mouth various procedural mantras in the chamber and on committee, but they don't ask questions, they don't make speeches, they don't have views.

The downside: I now have a pager strapped to my waist.

Wednesday, 6 December 1995

On a Wednesday, instead of our daily 2.30 p.m. meeting, the Whips meet at No. 12 for a marathon session from 10.30 a.m. to lunch. We sit around the large table, the Deputy at one end, his back facing the window onto St James's Park, the Chief at the other end, near the door to his study. The rest of us are arranged in a precise pecking order on either side.

The meeting includes a weekly assessment of the state of our sick and our troubled. The 'troubled' feature on a list marked U (for Unstable), the sick merely have their names read out. There is much banter, most of it directed at Liam [Fox] as our resident doctor.[†] 'I thought you said George Gardiner[‡] was going to be dead by Christmas. He's never looked fitter.' 'What do you make of Ted's ankles?' 'It's fluid retention, not a good sign.' 'They look like elephants' feet.' 'They *are* elephants' feet. Ted never forgets.'

At 12 noon champagne is served – in silver goblets. Bowen Wells, as Carriage and Social Whip, opens the champagne and pours it, partly onto the table, with luck into the goblets. As the Junior Whip, I follow him, altar boy behind the celebrant, offering orange juice to those who like their champagne diluted. To go with the champagne there are rather good, thick, scrunchy cheese straws.

As far as I can tell, my other duties are as follows:

1. At 10.30 a.m. on the dot, to close the double doors.
2. Before the meeting, to distribute the paperwork. After the meeting, to clear it away and destroy it.

---

[*] Shana Hole, Special Adviser to the Chief Whip.
[†] Liam Fox (b.1961), Conservative MP for Woodspring since 1992, was a GP before entering Parliament.
[‡] Sir George Gardiner (1935–2002), Conservative MP for Reigate, 1974–97; another committed Euro-sceptic.

3. At 11.59 a.m. to catch Bowen's eye, so that as the clock strikes twelve I can begin my perambulations with the silver goblets and he can begin faffing about with the champagne.

Extraordinary.

Tuesday, 12 December 1995

I saw the PM tonight. He looked quite chipper. The progress on Northern Ireland gives him a justified sense of achievement. Heseltine chairing all those Cabinet committees frees so much time. He was relatively sanguine about the shrinking majority: 'Perhaps it will concentrate the minds of some of our loose cannons.' Then he laughed, 'On second thoughts, perhaps it'll just encourage them.' He has been Prime Minister for five years. It hasn't spoilt him. Old hands say that after five years Mrs T. was well on the way to lift-off.

Tuesday, 19 December 1995

Last night: the Whips' Christmas party at No. 12. Quite jolly. Aphra said, 'Actually, dad, quite strange.' And it was an odd mix, from the lordly (the Heseltines) to the lowly (assorted secretaries, drivers et al.), wrinklies, teenagers, toddlers. Greg had persuaded Ray Alan[*] to provide a cabaret with Lord Charles (which made Greg and me laugh, even if it left others bemused) and Tim Wood[†] appeared as a mildly gauche Father Christmas.

Today, it's going to be touch and go. There is a series of EU documents relating to fishing quotas and regulations that somehow the House is obliged to 'take note of'. I don't understand a word of it, but I do know we're hauling in the lame and the halt and those who thought they might have been getting away for an early Christmas.

Later

A personal disaster. We won the first vote; we came to the main vote and we lost it by two. Cash and Cartiss[‡] voted against us and we had eleven abstentions – including one of mine, Peter Thurnham.[§] I had told the Deputy, 'You can count

---

[*] Ray Alan (b.1930), entertainer and ventriloquist who had appeared in pantomime with GB.
[†] Timothy Wood (b.1940), Conservative MP for Stevenage, 1983–97, Government Whip, 1992–7.
[‡] Michael Cartiss (b.1938), Conservative MP for Great Yarmouth, 1983–97.
[§] GB was 'Area Whip' for the North-West of England; his charges included Peter Thurnham (1938–2008), Conservative MP for Bolton North East, 1983–97.

on my lot.' In the first division, Thurnham came up to me with his Eeyore face and said he wasn't happy, but I said, glibly, 'You're doing the right thing.' He went back to his place in the chamber and, when the second vote came, he just sat there. As the doors were about to shut, the Deputy barked at me, 'Where's Thurnham?' It was too late to fetch him. Immediately the vote was announced, I ran up to him, distraught. 'I told you I wasn't happy,' he said, not looking at me. 'You didn't listen.'

At least we lost by a margin of two. If it had just been one, I'd have been suicidal.

Friday, 29 December 1995

Emma Nicholson[*] has defected to the Lib Dems. She did not feature on the list of the Unstable. We know that she's self-serving, self-regarding, and regularly misses the point not only because she's deaf, but also because she's not as bright as she thinks she is. None of this can we use to rubbish her. We *can* say – and Heseltine is going to – that she's a disappointed lady whose talents have been rudely overlooked. So what's our majority now? Three, two? And who's next? Thurnham? Happy New Year.

---

[*] Emma Nicholson (b.1941), MP for Torridge and West Devon, 1987–97; as Baroness Nicholson of Winterbourne, Liberal Democrat peer from 1997.

Over and Out

January 1996 – May 1997

Tuesday, 30 January 1996

Our voting procedure is absurd. This is what happens. A division is called. Two Government Whips and two Opposition Whips volunteer as tellers and give their names to the Speaker. Then one of our Whips and one of their Whips go and station themselves by the exit door of each of the voting lobbies. The members vote by filing past a clerk sitting at a desk on a raised stool (he ticks their name off on the register) and then exit, one by one. As they pass through the doors, the Government Whip counts them through, counting out loud, 'One – two – three – four – etc.', doing his best not to be distracted by the nudges, banter and asides of colleagues as they come shuffling through. The numbers counted, the Whips return to the chamber and hand the figures in to one of the clerks. The clerks then write the figures out on a form: 'Ayes to the right, so and so; Noes to the left, such and such.' The Senior Whip on the winning side then reads out the result of the vote to the House.

What I didn't realise until half an hour ago is this: the figure the Whip gives to the clerk is the figure that counts – and if he gets it wrong, too bad. Never mind what it says on the register, never mind how many people actually voted, what the Whip says goes. And last night it seems I miscounted by six! The Labour Party was not out in force and we had a comfortable majority, but had it been one of our tight ones we'd have lost – *thanks to me*. On nights when I'm on telling duty I shall have to lay off the *vino*.

Tuesday, 6 February 1996

Our tails are up. The PM is in cracking form. At PMQs he's outscoring Blair every time. Today he was outstanding. We're having fun with the Harriet Harpie hypocrisy charge[*] – and making it stick. Even the opinion polls are moving a

---

[*] Harriet Harman had chosen to send one of her children to a selective grammar school and had been openly criticised by her Shadow Cabinet colleague Clare Short, among others.

point or two our way. In the tea room we seem to have rediscovered the will to win. For about three weeks we've been on an almost even keel. Is this a record?

Friday, 23 February 1996

The papers do not make comforting reading. Thurnham is the lead story: 'Majority cut to two as Tory resigns whip.' Michèle said, 'He's one of yours, isn't he?' We tried to woo him every which way, but if someone is determined to be unhappy, what can you do? We wheeled in Michael Howard (his old friend from Cambridge), he saw Waldegrave, the PM saw his entire family! Indeed, when I left last night, the PM thought he might have done the trick. Peter had agreed to 'think it over'. He appears to have thought it over on his way to the *Newsnight* studio. Meanwhile, we won't have his vote on Monday – and if we lose on Monday there will be a confidence vote on Tuesday.

Monday, 26 February 1996

We won the vote – by one. We had a complete turn-out. I saw faces tonight I've never seen before. The lame, the halt, the gaga, the dying, we hauled them all in. Those that are too sick to stagger through the lobbies are allowed to sit in their ambulances in Speaker's Yard. Just before the vote, Whips from each side go to inspect them and report their presence within the precincts to the tellers. At 9.30 p.m., with one of the Labour Whips, I set off to carry out the identifications. I do now know everyone on our side by face and name, but there are still dozens of Labour members I couldn't name with certainty. We peered inside one ambulance (it had come all the way from Yorkshire). I had no idea who the poor unfortunate within was, but I nodded knowingly and said, 'Yes, that's him.' What a farce.

Thursday, 29 February 1996

I went to see Simon [Cadell] at the Harley Street Clinic. It can only be a matter of days now. He is beginning to look like my father looked, gaunt and beaky, unnaturally wide-eyed. He has been so brave. I would want to die at home, but I think he thinks it will be easier for Beckie and the boys if he's here. He was too tired to talk, so I just burbled on about what's happening at Westminster, and hugged him and kissed his funny bristly lopsided face and came away.

Sunday, 3 March 1996

M says Simon is much weaker, sleeping most of the time, can't really talk but gives a wan little smile when you peer into his face. It is so wretched.

I had a two-and-a-half-hour surgery. I had to keep shifting in my chair and jabbing my fingernails into the palm of my hand to stay awake. It was the usual mixture: housing, CSA [Child Support Agency], difficult neighbours, 'the school won't do anything for Darren – they think he's thick, but it's dyslexia.' The only diversion was to have two transvestites on the trot. One of them has been hoping for a sex-change operation for nearly thirty years. He/she comes to see me every six weeks or so, looking like a tragic drag queen, awful white make-up over his stubble. This time he brought his mum with him. She must have been 70, tiny, dotty, wearing a little fur hat, loaded down with carrier bags. She kept repeating, 'If that's what he wants, let him have it, let him have it.'

Thursday, 7 March 1996

Simon died last night. He was my oldest and best friend.

Friday, 8 March 1996

Simon gets a wonderful press. He claimed he never read his notices, but I think he'd have been pleased with these. It is my 48th birthday. Ma and Gin joined me and Michèle for lunch in the Strangers' Dining Room. It was a bit bleak. I couldn't concentrate.

Sunday, 10 March 1996

Drove to Honington for Simon's funeral. I read the lesson without tears or a crack in my voice – which is really all I wanted to achieve. The church is small and the nave quite narrow and when I walked back to my pew, I somehow brushed the coffin – and thought immediately of Pa. When he died I remember my mother stroking his coffin as it was carried into the church. She stroked it so tenderly. I've had that picture in my head all day.

Thursday, 14 March 1996

We have just had the statement on Dunblane. The horror of what happened is unbearable: sixteen children and their teacher murdered in cold blood. Michael Forsyth went up yesterday with George Robertson.[*] It's in Michael's constituency; he'd actually met the man at his surgery and said there was nothing about him that would have given you an inkling that he was capable of so terrible an act. Michael's statement was perfectly judged. He was deeply impressive – as was Robertson.

[*] George Robertson (b.1946), Labour MP for Hamilton, 1978–99; Shadow Scottish Secretary; later Defence Secretary, from which he resigned to become Secretary General to NATO, 1999–2004; now Baron Robertson of Port Ellen KT.

Friday, 15 March 1996

Last night we had M's birthday supper at a little Italian restaurant. It was just the two of us, a tiny candle-lit table in the corner. It was like going back twenty-five years. We had *moules* in a cream and white wine sauce and I don't think I have enjoyed a meal more *ever*. The whole meal cost less than half a starter at Le Manoir. 'This is what we like, isn't it?' said M. It is.

What she doesn't like is what we're embarking on now – a full 'constituency weekend', lunch with the Bishop, the Ellesmere Port Conservative Association dinner, the Cheshire Yeomanry *en fête* at the Town Hall. 'You're out five nights a week, sometimes six. The only night we know we'll have together is Sunday and then you're so shattered all you do is fall asleep in front of the box.' It's true. And it's one of the reasons why I'm reconciled to losing my seat.

Wednesday, 20 March 1996

All yesterday, all this morning Stephen worked on his BSE statement.[*] He clearly wants to be seen in the front-line. I said, 'I just don't see this as a winner. You've done the responsible thing today, getting it out into the open. Now lie low.' He wasn't listening.

Wednesday, 27 March 1996

The handling of the beef crisis is going from bad to worse. Our beef is now banned around the world. And no one in government – least of all the Agriculture Minister – seems to have a clear idea what to do.

Later

More news of mad cows . . . Neil and Christine [Hamilton] invited their friend Dame Barbara Cartland to dinner and asked Michèle and me to join the party. Dame Barbara was as ridiculous as ever: she seemed to have come dressed as the fairy queen in a Victorian pantomime. She was full of concern for the present Prince and Princess of Wales. 'Of course, you know where it all went wrong? She wouldn't do oral sex, she just wouldn't. Of *course* it all went wrong.'

---

[*] The Government was advised for the first time that there was a possibility that Bovine Spongiform Encephalopathy ('mad cow disease') could be transmitted from cattle to humans. Stephen Dorrell and Douglas Hogg (Agriculture Minister) came to the House with statements outlining the Government's proposed course of action in the light of the new scientific advice.

Over and Out

Saturday, 30 March 1996

I flew up to Chester yesterday morning and had a really good session with the farmers on BSE. They are profoundly worried, but remarkably calm. I've scored with them not because I have any of the answers, but because almost every day since this broke I have sent them the relevant pages from Hansard. They think I'm listening and that I care – and I am and I do.

Thursday, 4 April 1996

We're having Easter at home, the Hanleys for lunch on Saturday, Benet's organising a boat race party, and then we're off to Venice for five nights.

Ann Widdecombe came up to Chester with me this morning. We travelled together on the train, second class (Ann insisted). She's like Ken: she only says what she believes. You can't fault her. I asked her why she always sits on her own in the Aye lobby on days when she's got Questions. 'I'm there for forty-five minutes in case colleagues have any queries. All ministers are supposed to do it.' She is the only one who does.

She came to address the Presidents' Club. Of course, they were disappointed not to have a Cabinet minister, but in the event there was a *reasonable* crowd and they *were* impressed. She was good on the collapse of the 'moral consensus'. She told us about her first election campaign, in the run-up to which she had published a pamphlet called *Christian Principles*. She was going to do an open-air meeting. She'd set up her soapbox in the market square and then suddenly remembered she had left her pamphlets in the boot of her agent's car. She was to be seen running down Maidstone High Street shouting, 'Stop, stop! I've lost my *Christian Principles*!'

Tuesday, 16 April 1996

Lord Archer is wandering the corridors of Westminster urging us to take Sir James Goldsmith and his ludicrous Referendum Party seriously. Sir James (bronzed, rich, mad) is putting £20 million into his campaign. Jeffrey has produced a list of the seats most vulnerable to Goldsmith interference. Chester, naturally, is high on it.

Alastair Campbell* & Co. are going into overdrive in their desperation to gag

---

* Alastair Campbell (b.1957), former journalist, press secretary to Tony Blair as Leader of the Labour Party 1994–7; director of communications and strategy for the Prime Minister, 1997–2003.

Clare Short.* She's been yanked off the airwaves by the spin doctors and locked in a darkened, airless room. The truth is we should be as ruthless and determined to succeed as they are. But we aren't.

Sunday, 21 April 1996

We've just had the Whips' dinner with the PM, preceded by our annual 'assessment' of the Government. The exercise took three solid hours. There was joshing now and again ('If you could put Ann Widdecombe's brain inside Virginia Bottomley's body – think of it!' 'Yes, but what if it all went wrong and you got Virginia's brain inside Ann's body ...'), but on the whole the assessments seemed to me to be carefully made and well-judged.

As usual, the Chief said nothing, but his grunts said it all. When I was talking up Douglas French,† impatient clearing of the throat on my right made it evident I should move on and that poor Douglas's prospects are poor. When I was talking up Seb [Coe], there was a gentle, encouraging gobbling noise from the Chief's end of the table. Clearly Piers Merchant‡ has done something to upset somebody. His name produced splenetic spluttering all round.

Tuesday, 30 April 1996

Beef, Europe, the leadership – it's all as bad as ever. Chancellor Kohl lunched at No 10 and was served Aberdeen Angus. I said to the PM, 'Did he eat it?' The PM looked at me and half raised an eyebrow – which makes me think he didn't! The prospects for Thursday [the local government elections] are dire.

Thursday, 2 May 1996

A bad night. Five of our best Chester City councillers lost their seats. I went to the count and told them this was an opinion poll on the Government, not a reflection on them. They know it's true, but it doesn't make it any better. All afternoon I toured the committee rooms. Our activists are getting ever older, thinner on the ground and more demoralised.

Tomorrow the PM will issue his rallying cry – 'We fight on, we fight to win.

* Clare Short (b.1946), Labour MP for Birmingham Ladywood, 1983–2006; Secretary of State for International Development, 1997–2003, and subsequently Independent Labour MP.
† Douglas French (b.1944), Conservative MP for Gloucester, 1987–97; PPS to John Gummer; further advancement was not to be his.
‡ Piers Merchant (b.1951), Conservative MP for Newcastle Central, 1983–7, Beckenham, 1992–7; PPS to Peter Lilley; further advancement was not to be his either.

The election's a year away. The economy will turn it round for us, just you wait and see' – and we are charged with 'steadying the nerves, taking the temperature'.

I talked to Neil [Hamilton] who didn't appear to have registered that there were local elections going on. He is obsessed with his case to the exclusion of all else. He is hopeful that a Lords amendment to the Defamation Bill is going to enable him to pursue his case against the *Guardian* after all.

Wednesday, 5 June 1996

Good news. Sebastian Coe has joined the Whips' Office. It was to be another of the new intake but as we'd had word that he's been engaged in an extramarital dalliance (strenuously denied), the cards fell Seb's way. I like almost all my colleagues here, but we know that when we leave the place we'll rarely see one another. Seb is a proper friend.

Wednesday, 3 July 1996

We're not too happy with the PM because of his proposed Holy-Joe response to the recommendations of the Senior Salaries Review Body. It looks as if the SSRB are wisely suggesting a £9,000 hike for backbenchers (up to £43,000 from £34,000) and what amounts to a sweet £17,000 more for ministers. This is 26% plus-plus. The PM wants us to settle for 3%. We want the money – we particularly want it *now* because it'll mean enhanced pensions when we all lose our seats. It'll be a free vote, but the payroll [ministers and PPPs] will be whipped to support the Government's line and Blair and his acolytes will vote for restraint, so it's touch and go.

Thursday, 11 July 1996

At around ten past midnight the deed was done. Five divisions, each one going the way we wanted. I am now £17,000 better off. The PM is seriously displeased.

This morning's other excitement has been the visit by Nelson Mandela. When the trumpets sounded and the great man made his entrance I doubt there was a completely dry eye in the House. He is tall and handsome, but he's frail. He tottered down the steps. The Speaker had to hold his hand. I imagine it was the proudest moment of her life – and why not? As he passed he shook hands on either side. I was on the end of the aisle and he came right up to me – and then clasped the hand of the bugger behind. It was General de Gaulle all over again.

Tuesday, 16 July 1996

I met up with Jeffrey Archer for coffee in the Pugin Room (Jeffrey was tapping his watch when I arrived. 'I am *never* late!' he barked) and he took me through the key ingredients for making a successful novel – the shape of the book, the number of pages, the quality of paper, the type size, the number of lines on a page. It was both ludicrous and compelling – and he's done it, he's a world-class best-seller. But that's not what he wants. He wants to be in the Government – 'Minister of State, nothing more junior', and actually, as Arts Minister or Sports Minister, he'd give it energy, commitment, brio. But it won't happen. The activists would welcome it, the parliamentary party wouldn't wear it. The [Whips'] Office would regard it as 'a risk' and risks are not what we're taking now.

Thursday, 26 September 1996

I'm at the Ramada, Manchester. Saeths* is coming over for supper. I've done the Waterstone's lunch. Also on the bill: Peter Stringfellow.† 'Hello, ladies. You've read about me, haven't you? It was in the paper. It said I'd slept with four hundred women. (Pause) That was *last* year! (Nervous tittering from audience.) Mind you, I've had some good times in Manchester. Have I slept with any of you ladies? (He shades his eyes, scans the room.) Come on, ladies, own up.' At the back of the room a middle-aged matron raises a tentative arm. Throaty laugh from the platform.

I kid you not.

Tuesday, 1 October 1996

Neil Hamilton's case has collapsed. Today's *Guardian* headline reads: 'A liar and a cheat: official'.

Thursday, 10 October 1996

The PM's had a good press for his shirtsleeves question-and-answer session at the Conference today. And today is 'unity day'. Portillo has called for 'unity, unity, unity'. The Chancellor has wooed and won the faithful. And Hezza was at his ridiculous barnstorming best. It all feels quite good again. But then we go back into the real world.

---

* Saethryd, GB's elder daughter, was at Manchester University.
† Peter Stringfellow (b.1940), English nightclub owner.

Monday, 28 October 1996

Marginals' Club dinner with the PM. He's remarkably chipper, considering. I *assume* the Chief has told him about Barry Porter.[*] If Barry dies, our majority falls to one. And Barry, poor man, is going to die any day now. I speak to his wife and his mistress on alternate days. His wife (plus four, five children) is up in the constituency. His mistress, Angela, is nursing him in the flat down here. They are both coping remarkably.

Monday, 11 November 1996

I caught the 8.05 to Liverpool for Barry Porter's funeral. It was at St Xavier's, Oxton. The wake was across the road from the church, at a pub called the Bowler Hat. I travelled up with John Ward[†] who was representing the PM. John arrived at Euston, looking unusually anxious. He had seen mention of the Bowler Hat on the briefing note and, knowing Barry's Unionist sympathies, had spent the entire night worrying where he was going to find one.

Thursday, 21 November 1996

It's a shambles. We are six months away from a general election at most and the Prime Minister is being barracked by his own backbenchers. What the troops want is a debate on the floor of the House on the latest range of EU documents relating to EMU [European Monetary Union]. At PMQs the PM resisted – to open cries of 'Shame!' At 3.30 he stomped off, looking ashen, and angry, leaving Tony Newton to pick up the pieces. For the forty minutes of Business Questions the demands rained down on him. I sat right next to Tony. (I'm afraid I moved myself into the doughnut. If your constituents see you sitting there, amazingly, they think you're *doing* something.) His hands were shaking violently throughout. His voice trembled too, but his content was measured, courteous. He did his best, he held the line. Every time he sat down, he muttered, 'Was that all right?' 'It's fine,' I said. 'It's the wicket that's impossible.'

Monday, 25 November 1996

We have capitulated. The Chancellor is making a statement at 3.30 p.m. and we're going to find time for a debate after all. Five days of digging-in, mayhem

---

[*] Another of GB's charges, Barry Porter (1939–96), Conservative MP for Bebington and Wirral South, 1979–96.
[†] Sir John Ward (b.1925), Conservative MP for Poole, 1979–97; PPS to John Major, 1994–7.

and bloodshed all around, followed by total cave-in. Evidently we have a death wish.

Later

Ken was brilliant. He defused all the hostility. Make no mistake, the Government isn't frightened of debate. The Government welcomes debate, hungers for it. The man is a master.

Thursday, 5 December 1996

Yesterday Jon Sopel [BBC journalist] had lunch with Ken – and got the impression from the Chancellor that if there's any shift on our 'wait and see' policy on EMU, then he's off and a good chunk of the Government will be coming with him. Sopel ran the story – and all hell has broken loose.

Wednesday, 11 December 1996

David Willetts* has resigned. As a result, I become a Lord Commissioner of Her Majesty's Treasury† and – better still – assume the mantle of the Whip responsible for the First Secretary (aka Deputy Prime Minister), for the Chancellor of the Duchy of Lancaster, and for HM Treasury. My advancement is due entirely to my friend's misfortune.

Monday, 16 December 1996

The evening began with the Christmas party at No. 12. It was more relaxed than last year. I told Heseltine that I'm now the Whip designated to his domain. He glanced down at me briefly, nodded a wintry smile and immediately resumed his lofty survey of the room. Ann was rather more giving. I embraced her and introduced her to Michèle. Ann managed a good forty-five seconds of tinkly charm before moving on. (M said to me later, 'Don't bother, *really* don't bother. They're not interested in you, and they're *certainly* not interested in me.')

Contrasting Heseltine's common touch with Major's is fascinating. The PM

---

* David Willetts (b.1956), Conservative MP for Havant since 1992. He resigned as Paymaster General because of criticism by the Standards and Privileges Committee, who accused him of 'dissembling' in evidence he gave to an inquiry on the handling of the Neil Hamilton case. His fall from grace was short-lived.

† Constitutionally, the Treasury is governed by a Board of seven Lords Commissioners. The First Lord is the Prime Minister, the Second Lord is the Chancellor of the Exchequer and the remaining five are Government Whips.

arrived and the first person he saw was Sarah Box.* He clapped his hands with genuine delight. She giggled and was thrilled. He took her hands in his, they spun round together. He kissed her. The PM is attractive to women. The PM is attractive in a way Heseltine (superficially more handsome, a self-styled hero) could never be.

Howell [James], like a slightly camp royal equerry, kept a few paces behind the boss. I said to him, 'I think we should stop saying our policy on EMU is "wait and see". It sounds weak, indecisive, as if we don't know where we're going. Why don't we replace "wait and see" with "negotiate and decide"?' 'Excellent!' He called the PM back. 'Have you heard Gyles's idea?' The PM, beaming his nice beam, listened, laughed, agreed and moved on – in search (very sensibly) of something younger and prettier.

Wednesday, 18 December 1996

Breakfast at the Ritz. Stephen, Danny [Finkelstein], John K[ingman], Tim [Rycroft]. We raise our glasses of freshly squeezed orange juice to the excitements that lie ahead. Within the year Stephen sees himself as Leader of the Party – and why not? Of course, as I don't remind him, he is not alone. Heseltine, Clarke, Howard, Portillo, Rifkind, Forsyth, even Master Hague and Mrs Shephard are no doubt all harbouring the same fantasy – and, for all we know, hosting comparable breakfasts in other parts of town.

Wednesday, 1 January 1997

We're snowed in here [in Suffolk, staying with Simon Cadell's widow, Beckie, and their two sons] so we can't go back to London as planned. We're sitting by the fire drinking Simon's special peach and champagne cocktail instead. I'm reading Richard E. Grant's film diaries (my Christmas present from M – 'fucking fantastic – yeeeesssss!') and the new novel by Michael Dobbs. Beckie's done just the right lunch to go with the weather (roast chicken, roast potatoes, roast parsnips, glorious gravy, mellowing Burgundy), we've watched *Babe* on video with the boys (it's odd and sentimental, but eventually it works) and we've pondered the mysteries of the New Year's Honours. Still no knighthood for Donald Sinden. I took it up with the PM again before Christmas. 'I've been trying to get a knighthood for Alec Bedser,' he said. 'It isn't easy.' But it can be done. Today Bedser has his 'K' and the PM has a happy start to his year.

---

* The Chief Whip's assistant secretary, a civil servant, not a political appointee.

Thursday, 2 January 1997

Or does he? The lead headline in today's *Telegraph*: 'Dorrell urges Europe rethink'. The PM will not be amused

Friday, 3 January 1997

Stephen calls. The Prime Minister has been on the line, 'seriously dischuffed'. The poor PM has his New Year 'relaunch' all set up – *Frost on Sunday*, ad campaign on Monday, press conference on Tuesday – and what is today's helpful headline? 'Dorrell sparks Tory feud over leadership'.

The Deputy Prime Minister is in East Africa bird-watching. The Chancellor of the Exchequer, who is being 'kept in close touch', is in Mexico, also bird-watching. Unless health is the subject under discussion, the PM does not want or expect to hear Stephen on the airwaves for the foreseeable future.

Sunday, 5 January 1997

Today's headline beggars belief: 'TORY MP: MY LOVE FOR GAY TEENAGER'. The poor PM! He turns up for his New Year *Frost* interview, armed with his Dorrell answers, ready to lay into Labour, happy to assert that ours is the Party of the Family, and what does he find? The *News of the World* – and every other paper – packed with choice extracts from Jerry Hayes's passionate notes to an 18-year-old 'Young Conservative and Commons researcher': 'I've just been crying my eyes out. I can't help it. I love you with every fibre of my body.' Yup, it does make you want to weep.

Last night we had Noel [Davis], Harry [Audley], Joanna [Lumley] and Stevie [Barlow] for supper in the kitchen. Joanna gave us her story of a private dinner at the V & A at which, before dinner is served, the distinguished guests are invited to examine some of the museum's choicest treasures – exquisite boxes of ivory, silver and gold, designs by William Morris, sketches by Leonardo, the Thomas à Becket reliquary. At table, Joanna finds herself seated next to John Paul Getty Jr and asks him, 'If the lights had gone out when we'd been looking at all those fabulous treasures, what would you have been tempted to slip into your pocket?' 'I'd take the da Vinci notebooks,' says Getty. 'Why?' asks Jo. 'Oh,' says Getty, 'I could buy the rest.'

Wednesday, 15 January 1997

I had my first sighting of the Deputy Prime Minister's celebrated office today. 'It isn't a tennis court, is it?' said Lady Strathnaver [Michael Heseltine's special adviser] proudly. 'It's a football pitch!' Actually, what are big are the sofas – big and ridiculous. Either you perch right on the edge or you sit back and disappear. (We can assume this is where John Gummer has got to – he's slipped down the back.)

Thursday, 16 January 1997

The Chancellor was brilliant on the *Today* programme this morning – genial, sharp, on top of his brief, and they managed EIGHT WHOLE MINUTES without touching on Europe once!

Before Ken arrived, William [Waldegrave] was attempting to impose some order on the meeting. The moment Ken appears, the usual brouhaha breaks out. William shakes his head, the Chancellor winks at me, and the rest of the team all talk at once. They want to agree lines to take at Treasury Questions. 'We're going to say we've created two jobs a minute, aren't we?' 'Since when?' 'Since last year.' 'No, since '92.' 'Is that two jobs for every minute? Or for every working minute?' 'Are we using the European forty-eight-hour week?' 'I think it's better to say 10,000 jobs a week.' 'What's our line on Halewood?' 'Isn't it 15,000 jobs a week anyway?' Calculators are produced, banter is exchanged, but a definitive answer comes there none.

We've found Iain Mills* dead in his flat, surrounded by bottles. We're now a minority government. Suddenly 20 March looks more likely.

Friday, 17 January 1997

Watched *Dispatches* on Channel 4 last night: a hatchet job that rehashes all the worst slurs about Neil – the trips to the Paris Ritz, which he admits, and the brown envelopes stuffed with used notes, which he strenuously denies. Shots of Neil and Christine are intercut with shots of money being counted and champagne being poured. It's TV crucifixion and what's alarming is this: I know and like Neil and yet, as the slanders are repeated and repeated, even their best friends begin to wonder . . .

Monday, 20 January 1997

Christine has just been on the line, inarticulate with sobbing. 'We don't know what to do. They're killing us. We're alive, but only just. They keep on repeating these lies and what can we do? We've been found guilty without a trial. They've ruined us. I don't know how we can go on.'

---

* Iain Mills (1940–97), Conservative MP for Meriden, 1979–97.

Martin Redmond* has died, so we're back to level-pegging. Even so, there's a vote tonight that we expect to win comfortably, but we scrape home with a margin of one. In the Whips' Office nerves are a little frayed.

Tuesday, 21 January 1997

In Washington, Bill Clinton has been inaugurated for a second term. At Westminster, Gordon Brown has promised a public spending freeze, no income tax increases and no extension of VAT. In Kensington and Chelsea, Alan Clark has reached the shortlist. We live in an age of miracles.

At the Marginals' Club we swap stories about our appalling opponents. Someone mentions that his Labour PPC [Prospective Parliamentary Candidate] (chosen in a women-only shortlist, natch) is rumoured to be a witch and he's wondering how best to give the rumour wider currency. This prompts the story of Melford Stevenson (later Mr Justice Melford Stevenson) standing against Tom Driberg just after the war. Driberg, of course, was a notoriously promiscuous homosexual. At a public meeting at the start of the campaign, Melford Stevenson declared, 'I have heard the terrible rumours that are circulating about my opponent, Mr Driberg. I want to deny these scandalous and scurrilous rumours here and now. There is no truth in them whatsoever. Indeed I was at the Old Bailey on the very day Mr Driberg was found Not Guilty.'

Monday, 27 January 1997

A disaster of a day. Through a straightfoward cock-up, we lost the division by one vote. The PM was incandescent. Not a pretty sight.

Over dinner, Soames was booming. He appears to have a new baby: 'I like it to be handed to me like a machine gun, lightly oiled. There's a crisis back at base though 'cawse Nanny Caroline's gawn and the new gal doesn't arrive till Thursday. Cue for me to decamp on manoeuvres – four nights at the Dorchester, eh? Eh?'

Tuesday, 28 January 1997

Dinner with Ted Heath, the old boy at his most curmudgeonly. 'We need you to see John, Ted, he needs your advice.' 'Would he take it?' harrumphed Ted. Later, I pass another Grand Old Man in the corridor. Tony Benn is telling a young colleague: 'I don't understand what Blair thinks he's up to. You know, Clem would never have done it like this . . .'

---

* Martin Redmond (1937–97), Labour MP for Don Valley, 1983–97.

Incredibly, in the light of last night, one of our ministers has just missed a vote! I think we can guess where he is. A little earlier I heard him boasting: 'I've got some right high-class shank tonight. I'm going to take her home and knob her rigid.'

(When I got home just now I found that Michèle had left a sweet note and a consoling bottle of wine open on the kitchen table. She's heard about the miscounting of the vote on the News and assumed it must have been me.)

Thursday, 30 January 1997

At lunch, the Chancellor was so off-message on Europe that all you could do was gasp and laugh. William wanted to concentrate on ways of skewering Labour, but Ken, in swaggering mood, wanted to toast the Chairman of Toyota whose line this morning is that there'll be no new Toyota investment in the UK if we're not part of the single currency. Fortunately Ken's on the three-thirty to Geneva.

Thursday, 6 February 1997

Lunch at the Treasury these days is like an informal family picnic. While the Chancellor – nonchalantly lighting his cigar with EU matches – flicks through the *Express* – enjoying Mandelson's response to yesterday's hatchet job on Blair – others chat to one another, pick over the sandwiches, pour out more wine. You'd never think a general election was only a matter of weeks away. Philip Oppenheim says: 'The Conservative Party is united on only two issues. We all loathe Edwina and we all want the election on 1 May.' Plenty of chuckles.

Monday, 17 February 1997

Winston [Churchill]* is back from his mother's funeral in Washington. 'The two Presidents have been extraordinary. Chirac awarded her the highest rank of the *Légion d'honneur* – the only civilian ever to receive it posthumously. *"On a rien de plus!"* Clinton sent Air Force 2 to bring the body home. We had the Vice President to meet us and Bill gave the oration. What a woman!' The *Evening Standard* seems to concur, describing her as 'the greatest courtesan of the twentieth century'.

Tuesday, 25 February 1997

Winston was back from Paris. I had paged him on Thursday night. I'm impressed it works internationally. I suppose, with Winston, it needs to. One evening last

---

* Another of GB's charges, Winston Churchill (b.1940), the son of Randolph Churchill and Pamela Digby, later Pamela Harriman; Conservative MP for Stretford, 1970–83, Davyhulme, 1983–97.

summer we were coming through the division lobby together and I remarked on his unusually casual appearance. 'Yes,' he said, 'it's maddening. I've been running late since lunch. The service at the Cipriani was dreadfully slow today.'

Thursday, 27 February 1997

I arrived at No. 11 at 9.30 a.m. to find the Chancellor in mellow mood, bleary-eyed but well-scrubbed. It took ten minutes to sort out the coffee. 'Why won't it boil?' He hadn't switched on the kettle. 'We're out of milk – hold on.' He kept dashing out to the kitchen, into the hallway, but eventually we sat down and I outlined the strategy.

I reported that EDCP [the Cabinet Committee on presentation] hoped that he and the Foreign Secretary would be coordinating their two big speeches scheduled for next week. 'I'm going to be talking about the world,' said Ken, twinkling. 'What's he talking about?' 'The world,' I said. 'And they want our two worlds to be the same?' mused the Chancellor. 'Fair enough.'

Friday, 28 February 1997

The Wirral South result is entirely predictable: a 17% swing to Labour. We're doomed.

Monday, 3 March 1997

Interviewed by Jonathan Dimbleby, Stephen declared, 'We shan't be joining a single currency on January 1, 1999.' The headlines tell the story: 'TV blunder over pound spells crisis for Tories' (*Express*). 'Dorrell Does the Splits' (*Daily Mail*). 'Euro Gaffe Wrecks Tory Unity' (*Independent*). There's a sense today that we're in free fall.

Tuesday, 4 March 1997

For well over a year now, in dark corners, colleagues have been muttering about the succession. Now they talk of it openly. In the tea room a motley crew is running through the form: Redwood – 'no go, still the man from Mars'; Portillo – 'bruised and unreliable'; Howard – 'brilliant but bloodless'; Clarke – 'sensational, but his views on Europe make it impossible'; Rifkind – 'reality and dandruff are against him'; Dorrell – 'seemed a nice boy for a while, but it's all over'; Hague – '*please*, you can't be serious!'; Gillian – a round of mocking laughter. The consensus: it's got to be Hezza – with, wait for it, as a dark horse, a last-minute surprise runner: Jonathan Aitken.

Over and Out

Monday, 10 March 1997

I was rather dreading last night's 'showfolk party' for the PM at the Ivy. In the event, it was rather fun. There were about 150 in all – Barbara Windsor, Frank Bruno, Joan Collins, Anneka Rice, Ruth Madoc, Anita Harris, Mike Yarwood – more panto-land than *South Bank Show* – but the wine flowed and a good time was had by all. Cliff [Richard] looked the business – 'It's all off-the-peg and the shoes cost £55' and offered the PM crumbs of comfort: '*Heathcliff* got a terrible press and we got the biggest advance in history!'

The PM was funny. Donald Sinden was telling a fruity story. 'And then,' said Don, 'Lord Alfred Douglas turned to me and remarked . . .' The PM chipped in, 'At least you didn't say "And then Lord Alfred Douglas turned over to me and remarked . . ."'

Monday, 17 March 1997

It's coming through on the fax right now: 'The Prime Minister has today asked Her Majesty the Queen to proclaim the Dissolution of Parliament.'

I bump into a wild-eyed Neil Hamilton. 'Look, what am I going to do? Downey* isn't going to be able to report now before the election. I've got my AGM on Friday and I needed Downey to exonerate me.' Neil's fear, of course, is that despite one of the healthiest majorities in the land, he could still lose.

Tuesday, 18 March 1997

At yesterday's Cabinet, the Chancellor was late. The PM cast a withering glance at the empty chair and lifted his eyebrows before embarking on his announcement: the election would be on 1 May.

This morning it was all very playful in the tea room. Our boys were doing their ready-reckoning. 'Edwina's done for. Thank God!' 'Even her friends don't like her.' 'What friends?' 'She exudes sexuality,' said Winterton, mouth full of crumpet, 'oozes it, but she doesn't have any sex appeal at all.' 'Yes,' mused Fabricant, 'you can't really see yourself doing it with Edwina. Now I did once picture myself sleeping with Teresa Gorman.' Several of us made our excuses and left.

Thursday, 20 March 1997

At the Treasury we have a last sandwich lunch and the Chancellor makes a gracious little speech. 'Over the past few years we've built an economic recovery

---

* Sir Gordon Downey was the first Parliamentary Commissioner for Standards and charged with producing a report on the 'cash for questions' scandal.

round these sandwiches. The trouble is: the buggers out there aren't very grateful. This has been the best ministerial team I've had. And the best private office. Yes, Gyles, I know it seems a bit shambolic, but I don't like to take things too seriously for more than ten minutes at a time. I'm in the business of cheering ourselves up.'

There was a full turn-out for John Major's last PMQs. The cheering and the jeering were extraordinary – and he was at his best. We had tears in our eyes.

Monday, 24 March 1997

Two clerks from the Treasury caught up with me at 7 Millbank. They needed a Lord Commissioner to sign three Treasury Warrants. The first was for £215,096,760 and 90p. The next was for £1,554,472,000 – my first billion-pound cheque. The best was yet to come . . . in the foyer, witnessed by the security man and the lad on the switchboard, amid much giggling, I signed a warrant for £96,861,662,000! I was relieved to see that HM The Queen was my co-signatory and interested to note that her signature is as large and loopy as mine.

Thursday, 27 March 1997

News is coming in that Piers Merchant, 46-year-old husband, father and MP for Beckenham, is having an affair with a 17-year-old Soho nightclub hostess. You couldn't make it up! He's denying it, and wife, family and constituency are right behind him, of course – but I imagine by nightfall he'll be gone.

Friday, 28 March 1997

The farce is turning to tragedy. I've just been talking to an alarmingly volatile Christine Hamilton: 'The reptiles are back in force. I've just been out and screamed at them. I know it doesn't help, but we're at the end of our tethers. If Central Office start putting on any pressure, Neil can always stand as an Independent Conservative . . . It's all such a nightmare.' They're in a bad way.

Easter Day, 30 March 1997

The Beckenham constituency have backed Piers 43 to 3, so, as far as Piers is concerned, that's that. If the Duke of Wellington and Lloyd George and Steve Norris can get away with wholesale philandering, why should a hapless young man entrapped by the *Sun* have to fall on his sword?

And Neil, we know, is digging in. Teddy Taylor, John Townend, Jim Spicer have all been on the radio just now urging Neil to put Party before self, 'however unjust, however unfair'. Judging from my conversation with Christine, they're likely to be disappointed.

Over and Out

When I spoke to Alastair [Goodlad, the Chief Whip] yesterday I told him I was planning to go down to the river to watch the boat race. 'You couldn't contrive to rescue a couple of drowning oarsmen, could you? Create a bit of a diversion?' 'What if I have to give them the kiss of life?' 'Oh God! . . .'

Monday, 7 April 1997

All the front pages boast a double whammy of absurdity: Elton John, pomaded and perruqued, a perfect fright in silver and white, arriving for his 50th birthday fancy dress party, and the BBC's war correspondent, another fright in white, offering himself up as the anti-corruption candidate in Tatton!* Bell says he expects his career as a candidate to be the shortest on record because he hopes and expects Mr Hamilton to stand down. He has underestimated Mr Hamilton . . .

Tuesday, 8 April 1997

At 6.00 a.m. we left London.

At 11.00 a.m. we were on parade outside the Chester office. At quarter past, on the dot, the Foreign Secretary's limo rolled up. Malcolm was excellent – lots of crinkly charm and beady-eyed interest.

At 7.00 p.m. we went over to the hall for the adoption meeting. There was a full house, supportive, willing us to win. The faces were all familiar. Of course they were. That's our problem in a nutshell: many of my best people are now in their eighties and these are the good folk we call 'activists'!

We got home by ten and turned on the box for news of Cheshire's *other* adoption meeting. Neil secured the necessary endorsement: 182 in favour, 35 against, 4 official abstentions and 61 sitting on their hands. The media scrum outside the Dixon Arms was wholly predictable. Christine, dismissing a hack wanting Neil to speak into his tape recorder: 'We do not take orders from the *Observer*.' Neil: 'I feel like Liam Gallagher.'

Wednesday, 9 April 1997

The first day of the Brandreth campaign. The Association Chairman's wife is in charge of provisions and she's toured all the pubs we'll be visiting collecting the menus so that we can pre-order. I tell her she belongs to the Nick Soames school of canvassing: 'If you have taken a morale bash in the morning, it is important to have a good lunch.' (I don't share with her my favourite Soames story. A former

---

* Martin Bell OBE (b.1938), BBC foreign correspondent from 1962, Royal Television Society Reporter of the Year 1976 and 1992; Independent MP for Tatton, 1997–2001.

girlfriend is asked what it's like being made love to by Soames . . . 'Like having a large wardrobe fall on top of you with the key still in the lock.')

Sunday, 13 April 1997

Robert Atkins[*] calls and says the PM is tired, 'but much happier this weekend than last. I told him to remember Gordon Greenidge: it was when he started limping that he went on to score 100.'

My conscience is pricked. Mo Mowlam has been battling with a brain tumour. It's the steroids that have made her bulge and radiotherapy that forced her into a wig. Michèle has long said that I shouldn't make personal remarks.

Wednesday, 16 April 1997

The shambles continues. A couple of our tosspot junior ministers have come out against the single currency, but at this stage in the game what can the hapless PM do?

Friday, 18 April 1997

Oh dear. The PM, off-the-cuff, has offered a free Commons vote on EMU – but hasn't mentioned the idea in advance to Ken or Hezza, so they're both wrong-footed.

Monday, 21 April 1997

On my sortie to London yesterday, I caught up with Danny [Finkelstein]. According to Danny, our internal polling suggests we're 12/14 points down – not 19/20 – and it's coming our way. We gossiped about who had had a good campaign. Hezza – excellent. Howard – invisible. Clarke – 'too all over the place – and Europe kills him'. Hague – an early flourish, but nothing now. Portillo – excellent.

Thursday, 24 April 1997

Labour press officer quote of the day: 'Later today Tony Blair will be spontaneous. Tomorrow he will be passionate.'

Monday, 28 April 1997

Here in Chester I can only report a dismal day on the Brandreth campaign trail. Alternately it drizzles and sleets. The oomph has gone out of the activists and

---

* Sir Robert Atkins (b.1946), Conservative MP for Preston North and South Ribble, 1979–97.

nerves are getting frayed. My support manager (early fifties) and my road manager (early seventies) almost came to blows outside the mobile library in Guilden Sutton.

Wednesday, 30 April 1997

The crisis of the hour is that I've discovered a hole in the seat of my trousers – and I don't have another pair. I've been wearing one of my MP's suits day in day out through the campaign and finally it's given out – worn away. Is this a portent? Five years ago I had no idea what the election outcome would be. I hoped against hope, prayed the opinions polls would be wrong. They were. This time they can't be. What do I reckon the Chester result will be? Con: 20,000? Lab: 29,000? Lib Dem: 5,000? Others: 1,000?

Thursday, 1 May 1997

I wasn't far out: Con: 19,253. Lab: 29,806. Lib Dem: 5,353. Referendum: 1,487. Loony and A. N. Other: 358. End of era. Chester RIP.

We voted first thing and then spent the day touring the committee rooms, attempting to boost the flagging morale of our gallant troops. A policewoman noticed the hole in my trousers and mentioned it discreetly to Michèle. When I saw the Superintendent of Police at the count I commended his officer's vigilance.

We had supper with *Blackadder* in front of the box – and when ten o'clock came, readied ourselves for the exit poll. 'It's going to be a Labour landslide.'

A little after midnight we donned our glad rags, adjusted our brave faces, and made our way up the hill to the Town Hall. My opponent was standing on the stairs. I said to her at once, 'Congratulations.' She looked bemused. I wandered between the press room, the count, and the TV room where a large screen had been erected to display the results. It was so relentlessly bad for us, the other parties' supporters just looked on amazed. Of course, there were hurrahs for certain scalps – Neil Hamilton provoked a roar, Norman Lamont a jeer, and poor Portillo's defeat prompted a standing ovation.

Friday, 2 May 1997

Major has gone, and with some dignity. Mr Blair has arrived and already the messianic fervour is a little too rich for my taste. And as for Cherie . . .

I call Jeremy Hanley. 'This is the Job Centre. How may I help you?' Jeremy is funny, as ever – but devastated. 'I must tell you,' he chuckles, 'my three truly deranged constituents who come to every surgery – I've given each of them my successor's home telephone number . . .'

Saturday, 3 May 1997

We shop. (New Labour, new trousers.) We pack. We hoover through. By noon we're on our way. Lunch at Broxton Hall: poached salmon, salad, new potatoes, and a glass of Sancerre. The sun is shining. I'm 49. I weigh 12 st. 9 lb. I'm out of a job, but for the first time in years I'm beholden to no one. Cry freedom!

PART SIX
After the Fall

What Do We Do Now?

May 1997 – December 1998

Sunday, 18 May 1997

This is perfect. We are in Sicily, in Taormina, and the sun is shining. I am lying on a deckchair by the swimming pool. The season is only just beginning: there is hardly anyone else here. There is a gentle breeze and the smell of spring. It is eleven o'clock and my first cappuccino of the day has just been served.

M booked this for us during the campaign. She knew we'd lose. (She proposed putting our flat in Chester up for sale during the campaign, too. Seriously.) She is very happy with the outcome of the election. Everybody is. Britain is awash with hope. 'A new day has dawned, has it not?' The golden age of Blair is upon us. It'll all go wrong, of course. It always does. But that's not something that you can say out loud at the moment. Everyone (including my wife) believes that Saint Tony will lead us to the Promised Land and that the Conservative Party is not just down, but out – and probably out for good.

I am saying nothing. As an MP, you only meet two types of people: people with problems and people who are right. I marvel that everyone seems to have the answer to everything. What I discovered in Whitehall and Westminster is that, in truth, nobody really knows anything. (Even at the Treasury where, bless them, they really do think they know it all.)

It is so good to be here, away from all that. I can see Mount Etna in the distance. We are planning an expedition to Syracuse, where the boys come from. But first, lunch: *vitello tonnato* and a glass of Frascati, I think, don't you?

Friday, 30 May 1997

I am on the train, going to Leeds, to record *Countdown* – six episodes. (And, yes, madam, since you ask, they do feed you the words through an earpiece. But, no, I won't be wearing any wacky jumpers. 'Time for a change' and all that.) I am so lucky. I am picking up where I left off. *Countdown* called immediately after the election. CBS News called. LBC called. I have a contract for a new novel. I have work – and plenty of it. Many of my colleagues have nothing – *nothing* and no prospects. People like Derek Conway (who called just now) had huge majorities and still they lost – and now his children will have to be taken out of boarding school. People think there are 'directorships' and all sorts of goodies awaiting ex-MPs. Not so. What use is an ex-Tory MP to anyone? This is Blair's Britain. This is the age of New Labour. Old Tories have nothing to offer. Their contacts are outdated: their skills (such as they are!) irrelevant. It's fine for the few who are famous – e.g. Michael Portillo – but most of my former colleagues are shop-soiled, unknown, unfashionable and the wrong side of 50. The best they can hope for is something in the charity sector.*

Monday, 2 June 1997

Just before the election, in the tea room of the House of Commons, queuing up for a toasted teacake, I found myself standing next to Jack Straw. He was grinning from ear to ear. 'Why are you looking so cheerful?' I asked. 'Because I have been sitting here doing nothing for eighteen years – eighteen years! – and this time next month it looks as if I'll be Home Secretary.' And so he is. And well done him. (He beat me to it, after all.)

After lunch (sole off the bone, at Le Vendome in Dover Street, with Laurie Mansfield, agent to the stars, organiser of the Royal Variety Performance) I walked to Pimlico, to Stephen Dorrell's campaign headquarters. He hopes to be Leader of the Conservative Party – what's left of it. He is a good man, but it won't happen. He has no following – and I have no interest any more. Either you are in there or you're not. And I'm not. (They let you keep your ministerial box as a souvenir, but everything else – your pager, your pass, your office – you give up the *moment* you lose. When it's over, it really is over.)

Wednesday, 4 June 1997

Stephen has thrown in the towel. He's backing Ken [Clarke]. We went together to Ken's office this morning. John Gummer, David Curry, Michael Mates were there. They think their man's in with a chance. There was high excitement in the air. I felt the complete outsider. I shouldn't have gone.

---

* Derek Conway (b.1953), Conservative MP for Shrewsbury and Atcham, 1983–97, and a colleague of GB's in the Whips' Office, eventually found work as chief executive of the Cats' Protection League. He later returned to Parliament as Edward Heath's successor as MP for Old Bexley and Sidcup, 2001, falling from grace in 2008 over the misuse of parliamentary expenses.

What Do We Do Now?

Supper last night with Virginia and Peter Bottomley.* It was kind of them to ask us. Virginia is still fanciable (and thoroughly nice in a totally uninteresting way), but Peter is an oddity. Michèle was seated next to him at dinner. He told her a long and rather rambling story and then, five minutes later, told her the same long, rambling story all over again. She doesn't think his mind is going: she thinks he did it deliberately to see if she would say anything. She didn't.

I am just in from lunch at The Ivy with Trevor McDonald. Trevor enjoys lunch. He enjoys life. He likes being part of the Establishment. I think he's relished his time chairing the Better English campaign.† I think he knows it will lead to a knighthood. He'll like that. (He didn't altogether like the fact that Andrew Lloyd Webber had the 'best' table, the table at the top of the room. He made a joke about it, but I think he was thinking, 'Why aren't we sitting there?')

Thursday, 19 June 1997

William Hague has defeated Ken Clarke by twenty-two votes and, at 36, has become the youngest leader of the Conservative Party since Pitt the Younger. 'Much good will it do him,' says Michèle. 'No one is interested in your lot any more. The people have spoken, Gyles. Listen to the people.'

I do. I have. This week I am writing a children's book: *The Adventures of Mouse Village*. Next week I start my novel: *Venice Midnight*. (Jo Lumley gave me the title. I was calling it *Venice at Midnight*. She said, '*Venice Midnight* is much more intriguing.') I am getting on with life in the real world. My friend Seb Coe, by contrast, has thrown in his lot with William. He is already his right-hand man. 'What's the point?' asks M. 'If he sticks with it,' I reply, 'he'll be offered the first safe seat that comes up or a place in the House of Lords.' 'Do you think so?' 'I know so. I know how the system works.' 'Is that what you want?' she asks – and I don't reply. The truth is: I'm not sure. (Actually, the truth is I can't *afford* to play at politics. I have a living to earn.)

*In 1967 Virginia Garnett (b.1948), now Baroness Bottomley of Nettlestone, Conservative MP for South West Surrey, 1984–2005, married Peter Bottomley (b.1944), Conservative MP for Eltham, 1975–97, and subsequently for Worthing West.
† Sir Trevor McDonald (b.1939), reporter and newsreader, joined ITN in 1973; in 1996 GB persuaded him to become chairman of the Better English campaign set up by Gillian Shephard, the Secretary of State for Education.

Saturday, 28 June 1997

We went to Cambridge to watch Benet take his degree. We went on afterwards to the Master's drinks at Magdalene. The sun shone. The young people looked so happy. We parents looked so proud. This is what life is about.

Sunday, 20 July 1997

We are in south-west France, about an hour from Montpellier. I'm not sure exactly where we are. We are staying with Simon [Cadell]'s mother and we are just in from supper at Le Cocagne with Antonia Byatt.* She has a funny, strangulated voice, but a nice way with her and she and Gill have become good friends because each of them has lost a son. ASB kindly let me use her fax machine this afternoon. I was admiring it when I heard her say, 'I bought it with the Booker Prize money.' I was a little surprised, then I realised she thought I was looking at her swimming pool.

Sunday, 31 August 1997

I came down into the kitchen to make the early-morning tea and turned on the television and heard the news. Princess Diana is dead. I called Michèle and we just stood there watching. We just stood there. It was quite difficult to take in. I went out to buy the papers and, amazingly, the *News of the World* had produced a 6.00 a.m. 'shock issue': 'DIANA DEAD. Princess Diana died just after 3 a.m. London time today after a horrific car crash in Paris. Her boyfriend Dodi al Fayed and the driver of their Mercedes were killed instantly when the car slammed into a wall in a tunnel along the Seine river near the Champs-Elysées.'

Later

It's wall-to-wall Diana. Charles has gone to Paris to collect the body. William and Harry are at Balmoral with the Queen and Prince Philip. Blair has been on the box and brilliant – if you like that sort of thing. William [Hague] botched it utterly.

Monday, 1 September 1997

Last night Saethryd went over to Kensington Palace and joined the crowds. They came in all shapes and sizes – a lot of black people, a lot of gays – and they all brought flowers to lay at the palace gates. The outpouring of emotion is extra-

---

* Dame Antonia Byatt (b.1936), British novelist; her best-known novel, *Possession*, won the Booker Prize in 1990; her son, Charles, was killed by a drunken driver in 1972.

ordinary. There are pictures in the paper of William and Harry being driven to church with Charles yesterday: no tears there, just stiff upper lips. But the rest of the world is awash. And they have all got something to say: Mother Teresa, Lady Thatcher, Bill Clinton, Nelson Mandela. Even James Hewitt's mother Shirley has thrown in her two cents' worth: 'He's in a state of shock.'[*]

I am sorry for Diana, of course. And for her sons. This is a tragedy – but it is their tragedy, not mine. I cannot say that I am feeling this personally as the rest of the world seems to be doing. I am out of step with the rest of mankind. Mr Blair has his finger on the national pulse: 'She was the people's princess and that is how she will remain in our hearts and our memories for ever.'

Friday, 5 September 1997

It's completely out of hand. The world has lost the plot. The issue of the hour appears to be the Buckingham Palace flagpole. As anyone who knows anything knows, the flagpole is traditionally bare except when the sovereign is in residence when the Royal Standard is flown. And the Royal Standard is never flown at half mast, even on the death of a sovereign. But the tabloids are having none of that – they are baying for blood. Actually they are baying for tears. 'Show us you care, Ma'am!' Well, the Queen doesn't cry – and certainly not in public – but she has bowed to public opinion and the union flag is now flying over Buckingham Palace at half mast.

Later

I have just watched the Queen's live broadcast. It was perfectly judged. It will have diffused the anger. She did not say anything she did not mean. She did not go over the top. But she did enough.

Saturday, 6 September 1997

We sat in the kitchen and watched Diana's funeral. Tony Blair's over-emotional reading of the lesson was an embarrassment, but other than that it all worked. Charles Spencer's tribute to his sister was very touching – even if it didn't quite make sense. (Prince Charles and the royals are William and Harry's 'blood family' too, surely?) When he'd finished, the crowd outside applauded – and the applause was taken up by the congregation inside the Abbey. 'The people's princess' indeed. I imagine the Queen is utterly bewildered by it all.

---

[*] James Hewitt (b.1958), former British household cavalry officer and lover of the Princess of Wales.

Later

Interesting call just now. I was surprised to see Prince Philip in the formal funeral procession, walking behind the gun-carriage bearing Diana's coffin along the route to Westminster Abbey, but I have now learnt why he was there. Prince Charles and Charles Spencer were expected to walk, with the boys, but it seems that Prince Harry and, in particular, Prince William were initially reluctant. The Duke of Edinburgh, who had not planned to walk (he is merely the ex-father-in-law, after all), said to William, 'If you don't walk, you may regret it later. I think you should do it. If I walk, will you walk with me?'

Thursday, 9 October 1997

Yesterday, I wasted half a day reworking the peroration for William Hague's end-of-conference speech. I have just faxed it over to them. It won't be used – and William doesn't need help from outsiders anyway. This kind of thing comes naturally to him. Far (far) too much time is spent on the leader's speech at Conference. (My favourite conference speech story is John Whittingdale's[*] about Mrs T. and the Monty Python parrot sketch. They had drafted a paragraph for her in which the Liberal Party was likened to the dead parrot – 'This is an ex-Party' etc. Mrs T. didn't get it. They explained to her: 'It's a joke, Prime Minister, from Monty Python. It's very funny. It will work. Trust us.' Reluctantly, she went along with it, but she had her reservations to the last. Even as she was approaching the podium to deliver the speech, she said to John Whittingdale: 'This Monty Python – is he one of us?')

Thursday, 16 October 1997

A new John Gielgud story, told to me tonight by David Hemmings – once so beautiful, now blown up like a bullfrog, but funny and delightful and brilliant. In the story, we are on location, filming *The Charge of the Light Brigade* – directed by Tony Richardson and starring Jill Bennett, among others. Mr Richardson is rumoured to be having a dalliance with Miss Bennett at the time – even though he is married to Vanessa Redgrave (also in the film) and Jill Bennett is married to John Osborne (who wrote the script). It is early afternoon on the Anatolian plain. Miss Bennett is in her tent, having her siesta. Mr Richardson is nowhere to be seen . . . John Gielgud (playing Lord Raglan) and David Hemmings (playing Captain

---

[*] John Whittingdale OBE (b.1959), Conservative MP for South Colchester and Maldon, 1992–97, and Maldon and East Chelmsford subsequently; political secretary to Margaret Thatcher, 1988–92.

Nolan) are near the tent, by a tea urn, getting themselves some refreshment. Not far from them, chained to a wooden post, is a large, live Russian dancing bear. The bear is required for the next sequence of filming. The sun is high, the afternoon is hot, the bear is restless. The bear is tugging at its moorings and, eventually, succeeds in free-ing itself from its post. It lumbers towards Miss Bennett's tent, where it gets caught up in the guy ropes. The tent begins to collapse and Miss Bennett emerges, dis-traught and in her negligée. Squealing, the poor lady flees across the Anatolian plain, hotly pursued by the gigantic Russian bear . . . At which point, Sir John Gielgud looks up from the tea urn, spies the scene and, waving a reproving finger, cries: 'Tut-tut, Mr Richardson – how could you? And in your motoring coat, too!'

Saturday, 29 November 1997

'I, Gyles Brandreth, have undertaken to act as Godparent on behalf of William Edward Charles Dorrell, baptised on November 29th 1997 at Worcester Cathedral. My Christian responsibility as a Godparent means that I should 1) pray regularly for him, 2) set him an example of Christian living . . .' And on it goes. Why can I not learn to say 'No'? The service was nicely done and I *mean* to be a good godfather, but I know I'll fail.

I will have to follow Noël Coward's example and send my godchildren a present on *my* birthday rather than theirs.

Tuesday 9 December 1997

At the Garrick Club lunch to celebrate Donald Sinden's knighthood I sat next to Mary Archer. She was amazingly jolly, much less the ice maiden than she used to be. I still can't fathom the marriage. She gives him credibility, with the freedom to do as he pleases, but what does she get out of it? Money? A more exciting ride? It's not a mere marriage of convenience: when they are together they do still seem to be in love: they certainly enjoy each other's company. My psychiatrist friend says, 'they share a life-lie'.

Wednesday, 24 December 1997

It is Christmas Eve and we have brought our children to the Taj Mahal. (No, not the restaurant in the Balls Pond Road: the real thing.) We flew to Delhi yester-day. As we reached the final ticket barrier to board the plane, the children went ahead of us. We saw Benet reach the other side and begin to punch the air. He had been upgraded. Saethryd went next and she was upgraded, too. More jubilation. Finally, Aphra went through and got upgraded as well. I'm ashamed to say our hearts rather sank: three upgrades already, there'll be none for us, we thought.

But there were. Yes, they upgraded all five of us. To them that hath . . . (Thank you, Air India.)

The drive to Agra this morning was extraordinary. The dusty streets are full of cars and cows and camels – and on the motorway the notion of 'lanes' is merely nominal. And the Taj Mahal itself? Well, let's simply say that it does not disappoint. (And, yes, we sat on what they call 'Diana's bench'. *Every* visitor now wants to be photographed sitting there.)

Wednesday, 28 January 1998

Last night we were in the kitchen, having supper, watching TV, when the telephone rang. We didn't answer. We don't. (It's usually Radio Wales wanting to know if I'd like to talk about teddy bears on their breakfast programme.) The phone kept on ringing and we kept on ignoring it – and then, this morning, I was standing in the bathroom and I opened the *Telegraph* and I read about the helicopter crash in Oxfordshire last night. It said 'a businessman' was killed. I knew at once it was Colin [Sanders].

He was a month away from his 51st birthday. He made a fortune (£50 million plus) and it bought him the helicopter that killed him. He was coming back from a night-flying lesson. They think he became disorientated and crashed into the ground when he thought he was lifting up into the air. Poor man. He loved life. Poor Rosie.

Wednesday, 18 February 1998

Supper with David Hemmings and Lucy. On the mantelpiece, within his eyeline from his place at table, he keeps a card with, in large letters, the names and dates of birth of all his children. Alongside each child's name is the name of the mother. 'They get upset when I get them muddled,' he explained.

The Duke of Edinburgh told me that when he and the Queen dined with Ronald Reagan, he was amused to see that Reagan had a card in front of him telling him who was who and where they were sitting. An arrow pointed to the right: 'Elizabeth II – Queen of England. Call her "Your Majesty".'

Sunday, 8 March 1998

This is my 50th birthday. I don't feel 50. I feel 28. (And when I was 28, I felt 14. The truth is I still feel 14. As M would say, 'Yes . . . er . . . well, I think we see the problem.') My darling wife has brought me to Madrid. We are staying at the Ritz. We are dining at Botin, the oldest restaurant in Europe, so it claims (*Casa fundada en 1725*). Roast baby lamb is the speciality. I'm desperate for it. That's the only downside of Spain: they really don't eat before 10.00 p.m. (How do the American tourists manage?)

Thursday, 12 March 1998

We took the train to Oxford for Colin's memorial service at St Mary the Virgin. A good turn-out: the expected (George Martin)[*] and the unexpected (Judge Tumim)[†] and those funny family members that turn up at weddings and funerals: middle-aged men with pony-tails and sandals, rough-looking women with clattery high heels and lipstick that's too loud. Wonderful music – starting with Procul Harum's 'A Whiter Shade of Pale' (Colin was involved in the original recording) and, at the front of the service sheet, a photograph of Colin looking so young and happy that just to glance at it brought tears to the eyes. And oddly affecting, too, at the back of the service sheet, this sentimental verse:

> In times of deepest sorrow
> When tears may cloud our eyes
> It seems our grief is endless
> But then we realise
> That sorrow is the memory
> Of a happy yesterday
> And memories live on and on
> While sorrows fade away

I gave an address (I'm getting used to this) and likened Colin to one of his own firework displays – brilliant, colourful, dazzling, difficult to define, suddenly over. I talked about his generosity (how he flew us to Verona in his own plane and when we got to the Arena di Verona complained that there were no elephants in *Aida* – '*Aida* isn't *Aida* without elephants') and his genius. He told me his real legacy was to have invented the plastic clip-on thingy that you fix onto the side of your plate to hold your wine glass in at stand-up parties.

The moment the service was done, I raced to the station. (This is my life: racing to the station!) I missed the train – but I had warned them. I was giving the Prince Philip Lecture at the Royal Society of Arts: I'd said if I didn't turn up, Jo [Lumley] would read it on my behalf. As, heart pounding, I stumbled up the steps in the nick of time, HRH said: 'This is disappointing. We'd all hoped that Joanna

---

[*] Sir George Martin (b.1926), record producer, most celebrated as the Beatles' producer.
[†] Sir Stephen Tumim (1930–2003), judge, chief inspector of prisons, 1987–95.

was going to read it for you, then those who didn't want to listen would at least have something decent to look at.' He was in larky form. Before we trooped into the lecture hall, we assembled in an anteroom and viewed a large modern portrait of the Queen, all blue and orange. Gazing at it, HRH pulled a very funny face: 'My lips are sealed,' he said.

Lecture done (I called it 'Child's Play': I think it worked okay) we went upstairs for dinner. M and Jo sat either side of HRH: he is good company. The girls say he's the best: flattering, intelligent, flirtatious, attentive. But he did his stuff too – led a discussion on how we could take forward some of the ideas in the lecture. I said the problem now isn't so much playing fields and places for play and sport – it's people. Getting good adult volunteers to give their time – that's the challenge. I said he should start a new scheme to find volunteer youth leaders. He said he was too old: 'I've done enough.'

Saturday, 18 April 1998

I am on the plane to Miami, on my way to the Bahamas. Last night I went back to the Oxford Union for the 175th anniversary dinner. It didn't quite take flight. Hague, Heseltine, Heath (squeezed into a white dinner jacket, he looked like a cross between a band leader and an African dictator), all a bit predictable. Robin Day barking as we got into line for the group photograph – 'Back here, Brandreth – the front row's for the senior people.' I teamed up with Ann Widdecombe. I was pleased to find her there.

Tonight we stay overnight at the Miami Airport hotel. (I know Miami Airport well: it is the obesity capital of the world, full of huge gum-chewing Americans in hideous brightly coloured boiler suits going round and round in circles.) Tomorrow night we arrive at Hamilton House on Windermere Island, Eleuthera. We are joining Sandy Gilmour and friends: the house belongs to his cousin, the Duke of Abercorn. The Mountbattens have their holiday home next door.

Saturday, 25 April 1998

Michèle says this has been her best-ever holiday. It is idyllic here: pale sand, blue sea, clear skies, and easy company. The house is simple, but just right. We are in the room Prince Philip uses. They say he's to be seen here, walking along the beach with the Duchess of Abercorn, hand in hand. We say: why not?

Tuesday, 28 April 1998

In advance of next week's referendum, I took part in the *Evening Standard/ Newsnight* 'debate on London'. We don't need a Mayor for London. We certainly don't need a new 'Assembly'. I thought we Conservatives were supposed to believe in less bureaucracy, not more; in containing public expenditure, not extending it; in encouraging grass-roots democracy, not imposing additional tiers of know-it-all, top-down government. We have elected members in thirty-two London boroughs already. Enough's enough. And as for Jeffrey [Archer] promising to work 'nineteen hours a day, 364 days a year' running the capital, heaven forfend! I said some of this tonight, not very well and to little effect. What I didn't say is that I have already been approached about the possibility of becoming the Conservative mayoral candidate – not because they want me, but because they want *anyone* but Jeffrey. I know they've tried to persuade Seb [Coe], too. The approach was not altogether flattering: 'Don't worry, you won't win. London votes Labour. We expect to lose, but let's lose quietly and with dignity – that means without Jeffrey.'

Sunday, 10 May 1998

Late night, lots of laughs: Joanna and Stevie, Biggins and Neil [Sinclair, his partner] Nikko Grace* and Ian [Jeffs], Lynda Bellingham.† Non-stop laughter, in fact. (Can't remember what about, but it was good for the soul.) Early start: *Breakfast with Frost* at 11 Downing Street. I told David Joanna would like to be asked to his summer party: she will be. I told the Chancellor [Gordon Brown] it was good to be back in Downing Street: he said he'd been amused to read my articles about my time at the Treasury. 'You lot seemed to do a lot of eating and drinking and telling jokes. We don't tell jokes.' I can believe it. He is grouchily amiable, but so earnest – and still biting his fingernails to the quick. After the show, he took us upstairs to his flat. He lives above No. 10, while Blair and family are in the No. 11 duplex which is bigger and more like a proper house. I was intrigued that when he took us into his bedroom, the Chancellor rather ostentatiously opened the built-in wardrobes as if he wanted us to see the women's frocks that were hanging in there. They looked quite large, but I don't think they belong to Gordon. I assume they belong to his girlfriend.‡ I presume he was keen for us to know that he has one – and that she's not a 'beard'. I don't think he does anything without calculation.

* Nickolas Grace (b.1947), English actor, still remembered as Anthony Blanche in *Brideshead Revisited*.
† Lynda Bellingham (b.1948), English actress, still remembered as the mum in the Oxo commercials.
‡ Sarah Macaulay (b.1963) married Gordon Brown at his home in Fife on 3 August 2000.

Tuesday, 12 May 1998

This morning I was on the radio being touted as a possible mayoral candidate. I pointed out to the listeners that last week's referendum showed that three-quarters of Londoners either don't want a Mayor or don't care. I said that if I stand and if I'm elected, I'll do *nothing*: no press conferences, no initiatives, no grandiose strategies, nothing. Best of all, I'll even give the money back. (The Mayor and Assembly are going to cost £20 million p.a. minimum. It's truly appalling.)

This afternoon, tea at the House of Commons with Virginia Bottomley. We talked about the mysteries of the honours system and her plans for the future. She's going to be a head-hunter. Afterwards, as I was walking through Central Lobby, I bumped into Benazir Bhutto.[*] I greeted her like a long-lost buddy – which she is – but clearly my cheery informality was not what was expected. I remember her being rather fun at Oxford in the seventies. She took herself very seriously today. I tried to disarm her. 'It's only me,' I said. 'So I see,' she replied. 'It's just us, Benazir,' I persisted. 'We are in the Palace of Westminster,' she answered crisply. 'A certain decorum is called for.'

Monday, 8 June 1998

This is our 25th wedding anniversary and we have come to Bruges to celebrate. A mistake. The Eurostar was wonderful. Bruges is not. Well, it may be okay when the sun is shining, but it's bucketing down outside – the rain is torrential and the hotel is dreary: small and sepulchral, the dining room so hushed you dare not speak above a whisper. Bugger Brugge.

Friday, 26 June 1998

Lunch in Stratford-upon-Avon with Sarah Kennedy.[†] She came to help us celebrate the Teddy Bear Museum's 10th birthday. She was a triumph: people really love her. She has energy and warmth. (If you want to be loved, warmth is essential. If you want to succeed, energy is everything. When I had supper with Lord King of British Airways,[‡] I asked him to what he attributed his success. 'Energy,' he said, 'using my own, and harnessing that of other people.')

---

[*] Benazir Bhutto (1953–2007), Pakistani politician, President of the Oxford Union, 1976. The first woman elected to lead a Muslim state, she was twice Prime Minister of Pakistan (1988–90, 1993–6); assassinated at an election rally in Rawalpindi.
[†] Sarah Kennedy MBE (b.1950), British broadcaster, who has hosted *Dawn Patrol* on BBC Radio 2 since 1993.
[‡] John King (1917–2005), famously dubbed 'Mrs Thatcher's favourite businessman', chairman of British Airways, 1981–93; Baron King of Wartnaby from 1983.

Dinner at The Ivy with Eileen Atkins and Bill Shepherd.* 'I met Bill in a lift, you know. I held open the door and said, "Where are you going?" And he said, "I'm going wherever you are." He asked me to marry him within three days. I thought, "You're pissed and you're going to be terribly upset when you wake up tomorrow because I'm going to say 'Yes' and see what happens." It was a truly insane thing to do.' She talks about Bill as if he wasn't there. He listens to it all with a happy smile on his face. They have been married more than twenty years – 'with a lot of broken crockery along the way'.

Eileen is our least-known best actress. She wins all the awards, but people don't recognise her in the street. (She hasn't done a telly series.) I love her. (I really love her.) She is 64 and a bundle of energy. And intelligence. Tonight she talked a lot about Virginia Woolf. (She usually does.) And Alec Guinness: 'He's a prickly old bastard – with a secret life, I'm sure, but nobody knows what it is.' The reason Eileen became friends with Alec Guinness is that, one day at rehearsals, he heard her say, 'I hate my mother', and he said, 'I've never heard anybody say that before.' He had great difficulties with his own mother.

Eileen's mother couldn't understand Eileen. Another actress once said to her, 'Your mother looks as if she's accidentally hatched a snake.' 'I come from a family that has never stopped being disappointed in what I do.' That's why she did Jeffrey's last play [*Exclusive*]. 'Jeffrey is my brother's favourite author. For once, I thought, my family won't look at me and wonder, "God, what have you put us through this evening?"'

Monday, 27 July 1998

By coincidence, lunch with Norman Lamont and tea with Julian Clary.† I didn't mention one to the other. I don't think they have met since the notorious night when Julian announced on live TV‡ that he had 'just been fisting Norman Lamont . . . talk about a red box . . .' The audience roared and I doubt that Norman minded, but it played badly in the press and, for a while, derailed Julian's career.

Five years on, they are both doing fine, even if the glory days are gone. Norman is stouter, but still fun – *obsessed* with the dangers of the euro, still brooding on the injustice done to him by John Major, and he appears to have mislaid his nice wife along the way. Julian is tall and slim and beautiful – the

* Dame Eileen Atkins (b.1934), English actress, married film producer Bill Shepherd in 1978.
† Julian Clary (b.1959), English camp comedian and writer.
‡ At the British Comedy Awards in December 1993; both Lamont and Clary were presenting awards that night.

beauty of his face is extraordinary. But he is about to turn 40 and needs to do something new, hence our meeting. I told him about the bizarre life of Henry Paget, 5th Marquess of Anglesey – 'the dancing marquess'. He died young in 1905, celebrated for his beauty, notorious for his extravagance, his eccentricity (he would lie naked in a coffin covered only in jewels), his non-consummated marriage (he was gay), his love of theatre. He put on his own shows and starred in them, with the estate staff as extras. There's a film in this – it has everything: love, heartache, skulduggery, buggery, Monte Carlo and bust – and, if beautifully written, could be a break-out vehicle for Julian. Except, I don't think he was very interested. And I'm not sure he can act.

Saturday, 1 August 1998

Went to the Royal Military Academy, Sandhurst, to watch Benet's passing-out parade.* It was one of the proudest moments of my life. And M's. Benet has found it very tough. He was in contention for the baton of honour – but it went to a girl, a driven vegan, Sally Glazebrook. After the parade, we walked over to lunch with the commanding officer (we were honoured with a place at his table) and I overheard Sally asking him how and where she should display the baton. He said, 'You mustn't display it. You can give it to your parents. They can look after it for you. And, after today, you must never refer to it again.'

Tuesday, 18 August 1998

'I did not have sexual relations with that woman, Miss Lewinsky.' Ever since he said it, men all over the globe have been hoping not to have sexual relations with their wives, girlfriends, passing interns. 'Sexual relations' is intercourse, according to the White House lawyers; 'not sexual relations' is a blow-job. (I love Maureen Lipman's line: 'What's the worst thing about oral sex? The view.') Last night we got the latest twist in the Zippergate scandal – President Clinton's televised confession to the American people: 'I did have a relationship with Miss Lewinsky that was not appropriate. In fact, it was wrong. It constituted a critical lapse in judgement and a personal failure on my part for which I am solely and completely responsible.' This morning I have been on CBS News, live, essentially sharing Michèle's message with the world: 'Men, they're all the same . . .' Clinton is asking for privacy and throwing himself on the mercy of his wife, his

---

* GB's son, aged 23 in 1998, had joined the Territorial Army and was commissioned into the Fourth Battalion Royal Green Jackets (Volunteers).

daughter and 'our God'. He is hoping that a humble look, a hair shirt and a series of high-profile prayer breakfasts may save him from impeachment.*

Wednesday, 9 September 1998

The Foyle's lunch to mark the publication of my novel, *Venice Midnight*. It was a rather sad affair. Miss Foyle is ancient and her empire is crumbling.† As she reminded me, once upon a time, a thousand people came to the Foyle's lunches and General de Gaulle and Bernard Shaw and H. G. Wells addressed the throng. (It was at a Foyle's lunch that Bertrand Russell made his famous remark: 'Words make the difference. No matter how eloquently a dog may bark, he cannot tell that his parents were poor but honest.') Today we had a hundred and twenty elderly folk, Miss Foyle, yours truly and the Earl of Bradford. It was fine, but it was not 'an event'.

Thursday, 17 September 1998

In younger and happier days, I became reasonably accustomed to rebuffing advances from older men. Never from younger women, alas – until today. And today, I have to admit, was not entirely flattering. She may be a household name, but she is only a year younger than me and she was drop-down drunk – and on the cabbage diet. Indeed, she appears to be subsisting on boiled red cabbage and alcohol. I went to her flat: she was already weaving about the place. We went round the corner for lunch: she fell down in the street twice. (I was terrified that paparazzi would jump out from behind dustbins and snap her in the gutter.) As I ate, she drank. One bottle, then a second. With difficulty, I got her back to her flat, where she had a sudden burst of energy and pursued me from room to room until I found the front door and fled.

I imagine she won't remember any of it. If I had the courage – and I were her true friend – I would send her a note today telling her to join AA and giving her Hes's number.‡ She'd get on well with Hes. AA is the only way. One day at a time.

---

* They didn't, but, after a twenty-day impeachment trial in the US Senate, he was acquitted of all charges of perjury and obstruction of justice.

† She was 87 and died the following year; her nephew, Christopher Foyle, took over the business, modernised and transformed it, restoring the lunches to some of their former glory; coincidentally, he also bought GB's former house in Campden Hill Gardens.

‡ GB's sister, Hester, was an active and open member of Alcoholics Anonymous.

Tuesday, 20 October 1998

Today I was attendant upon the Queen and Prince Philip at Holy Trinity, Sloane Street. It was a service of thanksgiving to mark the Duke of Edinburgh's half-century of service to the National Playing Fields Association. I am not sure whose idea the service was – perhaps it was the Queen's. People don't realise that, while she is driven by duty, she is sustained by faith. The Church of England's hold on the British people may be slipping, but the Church – and church-going – remain central to the Queen's life. You might think we'd cele-brate fifty years of HRH's presidency of the Playing Fields with something sports-orientated, something on a playing field even, but, no, we go to church. And I watch the Queen as she prays: she concentrates, her eyes shut tight. Holy Trinity turns out to be High Anglican, all smells and bells. As we arrived, and the incense was wafted in his direction, the Duke began to wave it away: 'I thought this was supposed to be my celebration, not my cremation.'

Friday, 30 October 1998

Tim Pigott-Smith* and Pam have bought the Cadell family's old house in Highgate. We went there for dinner tonight. Selina [Cadell] and Michael Thomas [her actor husband] came too. It was a happy evening, but very odd to be back in the house that was so much part of my childhood. It looked exactly the same but felt quite different. Selina hoped for ghosts, but there were none.

At one point in the evening, Tim disappeared for ten minutes. He returned, looking puffed and a mite dishevelled. He did not say anything, but I think he had run down the road for more wine.

Wednesday, 16 December 1998

The National Portrait Gallery's primary collection, covering six centuries, hon-ours in all no more than 7,000 people, and of the Gallery's forty or so annual acquisitions only half a dozen are likely to be portraits of living individuals. I know this because this morning (still recovering from Anthony and Georgina Andrews's charming party last night and after a jolly breakfast with Edwina Currie at the Savoy at 9.45 a.m. I went to the NPG to interview its smooth and cunning director, Charles Saumarez Smith† – 44, tall, thin, pasty-faced, not gay

---

* Tim Pigott-Smith (b.1946), English actor who, like Simon Cadell, trained at the Bristol Old Vic Theatre School.

† Charles Saumarez Smith CBE (b.1954), art historian, director of the National Portrait Gallery, 1994–2002; director of the National Gallery, 2002–07; chief executive of the Royal Academy of Arts since 2007.

but with an odd, slightly lisping manner of speech. 'The Gallery is about history not about art, and about the status of the sitter rather than the quality or character of a particular image.'

How do you get to be included in the nation's hall of fame? 'Temporary notoriety or short-term fashionable prestige is not enough.' The Beatles are in, so is Mick Jagger, but the Spice Girls 'have yet to prove their lasting importance and historical interest'. Sir Elton John, it seems, has already proved his, but Sir Cliff Richard has yet to come up to snuff. (They are snobs at the NPG, that's what it amounts to.)

Given the criteria for eligibility ('Is the person pre-eminent within a particular field of endeavour? Are they in the *Dictionary of National Biography*? Will members of the public be interested in them in fifty years' time?'), are we surprised to learn that this year's entries include Melvyn Bragg, Michael Palin and the clothes designer Paul Smith? I did guffaw somewhat when told of the recent inclusion of Harold Evans and Tina Brown. Said Saumarez Smith silkily: 'They stand as icons to the fact that glossy magazines are now the fastest route into the halls of fame.' (Bollocks to that.) According to the NPG rule book, commissions are only undertaken of figures whose 'eminence is beyond reasonable doubt' – but it's the Merchant Ivory school of eminence, with touches of New Labour modishness and upmarket camp. Helen Mirren (painted by Ishbel Myerscough) and Helena Bonham Carter (photographed by John Swannell) are in, but Joanna Lumley is not. Jeffrey Archer and Catherine Cookson can dominate the best-seller lists, but the writers who top the charts at the NPG are Beryl Bainbridge, Salman Rushdie and A. S. Byatt.

'The collection demonstrates public culture not popular culture,' says SS, explaining why the 'brilliant artist, film-maker, writer and gardener' Derek Jarman is represented (oil on card by Michael Clark, 'done at the Soho patisserie, Maison Bertaux, just before Jarman's death from AIDS') while neither the cast of *Coronation Street* nor of the *Carry On* films gets a look-in. When he said, 'I would not rule out Kenneth Williams,' I volunteered that there's a fine, quite early portrait of Kenneth by John Bratby currently available. There was no response. The truth is, had Kenneth been painted by Maggi Hambling he'd have romped in. (The rule is that the artist is a secondary consideration, but a marginal candidate depicted by a right-on artist will find the scales tipping in his favour. George Melly has just arrived, again by Maggi Hambling.)

There is something very irritating about England's elitist (though-they-deny-it) intellectual establishment. These people bring out the worst in me. But I liked SS and when I said, as I was going, that children's writers are shamefully under-represented at the NPG – and that the UK's contribution to children's literature is one of the country's greatest contributions to world culture – he took the message on board at once and said, 'Perhaps you should curate an exhibition for us?' Perhaps I will.[*]

Thursday, 17 December 1998

I have decided to like Cherie Blair, partly because others seem to despise her (she doesn't take a good photograph: mouth like a letter-box), but mainly because she has been very helpful and friendly, lending me 'Tony Blair's Teddy Bear' to put on display at the museum. The bear is called Lynton (as in Anthony Charles Lynton Blair) and today, after his long holiday with us in Stratford, I took the little fellow back to Downing Street. As Iraq was being bombed,[†] I stood in the hallway of No. 10, holding the bear in my arms, waiting for Cherie, when who should come marching into the building but John Prescott. I said, 'Hello, John.' He simply glowered. His face turned purple with suppressed rage. Anger, rudeness, resentment are his stock-in-trade. (And yet, apparently, he stills gets the girls. It's almost incredible, but they say it's so. There were hacks haunting Chester when I was there, digging for dirt about JP. Poor Pauline. What she puts up with.)

Tuesday, 22 December 1998

Britt Ekland[‡] was once one of the world's great beauties – and so famous, too. I had a cup of tea with her this afternoon in her dressing room. She is playing the Fairy Queen in the Wimbledon panto. She was quite sanguine about her lot. 'I have to earn a living, you know. Pantomime – that's the reality of showbusiness. What else is one to do?'

Speaking of Swedish beauties, I saw Ulrika[§] the other day. When I first knew her, at TV-am in the eighties, she was truly the loveliest creature on the planet –

---

[*] He did. The exhibition, 'Beatrix Potter to Harry Potter: Portraits of Children's Writers', curated by GB and Michèle Brown, opened at the National Portrait Gallery in May 2002.

[†] From 16 to 19 December 1998, in response to Iraq's failure to comply with certain United Nations Security Council resolutions, US and UK forces bombed Iraqi targets in an operation code-named Desert Fox.

[‡] Britt Ekland (b.1942), Swedish actress who appeared in *The Man with the Golden Gun*, 1974, and was married to Peter Sellers, 1964–8.

[§] Eva Ulrika Jonsson (b.1967), Swedish television presenter who came to fame as the weather girl at TV-am in the late 1980s.

beyond belief beautiful and very sweet. She is still sweet, but, suddenly, the looks have gone and the bust has dropped alarmingly. (Cue Michèle: 'You're not looking so cute yourself, baldie.') Of course, I've reached the age when anything under 30 looks appealing (it's heart-breaking), but am I *fundamentally* ageist? No. Jo [Lumley] came to supper tonight. She is two years older than me and I think (truly) that she is more attractive than she's ever been. (With Jo, it's the energy that's the allure, the life force.)

Wednesday, 30 December 1998

I am having coffee and a Chocolate Oliver biscuit – a Christmas present from Aphra. (A perfect Christmas present: all I want now are Chocolate Olivers and socks for Christmas.) In an hour we are setting off for Framlingham for the New Year [to stay with Beckie, Simon Cadell's widow, and her family]. It's a long drive. (There are times when I think life's too short for East Anglia.)

Last night Eileen Atkins and Bill came for supper in the kitchen. Eileen brought me a wonderful present: *A Moment's Liberty: The Shorter Diary of Virginia Woolf*. Eileen adores VW. 'I read her diary every day. She says *fabulous* stuff.' She has reams by heart. 'Life for both sexes is arduous, difficult, a perpetual struggle. It calls for gigantic courage, and strength. More than anything, perhaps – creatures of illusion as we are – it calls for confidence in oneself.'

Eileen said, 'The joy of the diary is that there's a gem on every page', and proved her point by opening the book at random and putting her finger on the entry for 18 May 1930: 'The thing is now to live with energy and mastery, desperately. To despatch each day high handedly . . . So not to dawdle and dwindle, contemplating this and that . . . No more regrets and indecisions. That is the right way to deal with life now that I am 48: and to make it more and more important and vivid as one grows old.'

That's my philosophy for 1999 sorted.

The Pursuit of Happiness

January 1999 – January 2000

Tuesday, 12 January 1999

Good news. Saethryd (three weeks away from her 22nd birthday) has had her tonsils out at St Luke's, Fitzroy Square. She's sore and tired, but fine.

Good news. Benet (Public Speaking Champion of the World – again)[*] got in from the Philippines at 4.45 a.m. He's sore and tired too – long flight. (Wonderful how these young people now travel the world. When I was their age, Vietnam was a war zone. Now they go there to top up their tans.)

Good news. Rowan Atkinson[†] has sent us Mr Bean's bear (with personal message) to display at the Teddy Bear Museum. (I don't find Mr Bean remotely amusing, but in France and Albania they adore him. I never laughed at Norman Wisdom either. Or Charlie Chaplin. But I don't argue with success. Mr Bean is an international phenomenon. We are proud and grateful to have his bear.)

Wednesday, 27 January 1999

Dinner party: Joanna [Lumley], Anthony Palliser, Charles and Romilly Saumarez Smith, David and Lucy Hemmings, Sarah Butterfield (David was tied up at the House of Commons – not literally, I don't think.)[‡] Hemmings (off the sauce) arrived with his own herbal concoction tucked under his arm and his hands splayed out in front of him as though he were trying (with difficulty) to suppress a huge erection. He walked around like this for quite a while, muttering: 'It's the Viagra – haven't got the dosage quite right yet.'

All jolly, though the object of the evening was not achieved. Anthony is a wonderful painter. Twenty-five years ago the National Portrait Gallery acquired his portrait of Graham Greene. Since then, nothing. We wanted to introduce him

[*] GB's son Benet, now a barrister and lecturer on rhetoric, was then 23 and taking part in international student debating and public-speaking competitions.
[†] Rowan Atkinson (b.1955), British comedian and actor; he created the hapless comic character Mr Bean in 1989.
[‡] Sarah Butterfield (b.1963), artist, married to David Willetts MP.

to Charles SS. We did – but nothing will come of it. Charles made polite noises, but his eyes stayed cold: Anthony isn't 'in', isn't hip, isn't Maggi Hambling. And he lives in Paris, a million miles away from Charles Saatchi, the White Cube etc. He is nevertheless a superb artist who has stuck to his last for thirty years and whose worth will one day be recognised. Anthony knows it. I showed him this line that I had come across in the introduction to the script of *A Funny Thing Happened on the Way to the Forum*: 'Irwin Shaw once advised all writers, in order to withstand criticism from without and compromise from within, to be vain about their work.'

Monday, 1 February 1999

An evening among the fallen – rather jolly, as it happens. Supper with Neil and Christine Hamilton at their flat on Albert Bridge Road. They fight on – they fight to win.* They are like things possessed: Neil drinking too much, Christine on manic overdrive. But they are still fun, still friends, and Christine is a fine cook and a generous hostess. Also of the party: a remarkably sanguine Jonathan Aitken. He thinks prison is a possibility. He seems quite ready for it.†

Tuesday, 2 February 1999

Jane McCulloch, theatre director, poet, daughter of the celebrated Joseph McCulloch, sometime rector of St Mary-le-Bow, told me today how, once, she was at a private dinner party with the Queen. After dinner, when almost everyone had gone, the Queen kicked her shoes off and sat on the sofa, with her feet tucked up under her. It really is difficult to envisage the Queen with her feet tucked up under her.

Just in from Pizza on the Park. We went with Jo. Steve Ross, Sheridan Morley and Patricia Hodge did a Coward cabaret. Hodge started singing offstage, unexpectedly. She walked in from the back of the restaurant, singing 'Someday I'll Find You'. It was wonderful. She has the best voice for Coward in the world.

---

* In the event, Neil Hamilton, having already dropped his libel action against the *Guardian* over the 'cash for questions' affair, lost his libel action against Mohammed al Fayed in December 1999 and lost the appeal in December 2000. Unable to pay his legal fees, he was declared bankrupt in May 2001 and discharged from bankruptcy three years later.
† Following his unsuccessful libel action against the *Guardian*, in 1999 Jonathan Aitken was charged with perjury and perverting the cause of justice and sentenced to eighteen months' imprisonment, of which he served seven.

Tuesday, 23 February 1999

Mark Borkowski brought Uri Geller to see us today.[*] I think I like him: I can't say for sure because he's impossible to know: he is unfathomable. His manner is as smooth as his skin – and both seem not quite real. He wanted to sell us his novel. We wanted him to bend spoons. Generously, he obliged. He left the tea tray positively littered with bent cutlery.

M recalled that years ago, when, on TV, he said he could stop people's watches, hers, at home, stopped at that very moment. I said, if the power of his mind is so amazing, why can't he persuade us to publish his novel?

Thursday, 18 March 1999

I am in the Presidential Suite at the St David's Hotel in Cardiff Bay. The luxury of it is completely absurd. I have a bedroom, a sitting room, a study and a bathroom that's a 'wet-room': there is no conventional shower: hot water simply cascades over you and then, miraculously, drains away. Downstairs, the vast, deserted lobby is awash with tail-coated flunkies. I seem to be the only paying guest – and apparently I'm getting the suite at a tenth the asking price. The hotel is Rocco Forte's dreamchild.[†] Can it possibly work? In Cardiff?

I am here to address the Welsh Conservative Party Conference dinner. I imagine the conference delegates are all staying at assorted guest houses up the road. Were he alive, that's where Lord Forte would be staying, too. (I remember going to see Rocco a few years ago, on behalf of NPFA. I went by Underground and, coming up the escalator at Tottenham Court Road station, I found I was standing just behind Lord Forte. The old boy must have been about 80. I followed him as he trudged, briefcase in hand, from the tube station to Forte Towers. As we arrived, Rocco swept up beside us – in his chocolate-coloured Bentley.)

Wednesday, 31 March 1999

I am sitting in the Palm Court of the Ritz Hotel. I am waiting for a cappuccino. I have just walked here from Buckingham Palace where I have spent the morning

---

[*] Uri Geller (b.1946), Israeli-British performer, writer and self-styled 'mystifier'. Michèle was then working as a publisher for André Deutsch Ltd. GB was a consultant to the company.

[†] Sir Rocco Forte (b.1945), hotelier son of Baron Forte (1908–2007). In his lifetime, from almost nothing, Charles Forte built up a huge international hotel and catering business, passing control to his son in 1993. In 1996, after a hostile bid, Granada succeeded in acquiring the Forte Group and Rocco Forte subsequently developed a series of luxury hotels, among them the St David's in Cardiff Bay.

interviewing the Duke of Edinburgh for the *Sunday Telegraph*. I think it's probably the first 'personal' interview he has given. I had planned to record it, but at the last minute I lost my nerve and stuffed the recorder back into my briefcase. I thought its presence on the table might inhibit him.

We met in his library. It is a large room on the first floor, at the right-hand side of the building. It's his sort of room: serviceable not cosy. As he arrived, he said, 'Remind me, why am I doing this?'

'It's a favour to me, sir,' I said. I tried not to gush. I know it irritates him. I said I wanted to write something celebratory, saluting his achievements over half a century of public service and challenging one or two of the myths that have grown up over the years. He sat down, sniffed and looked at me, doubtfully.

We were alone in the room. We sat on firm sofas facing one another. I opened my notebook. 'How do you think you're seen?'

He frowned. 'I don't know.' Long pause. 'Refugee husband, I suppose.'

Another pause. 'And your achievements?' I asked. He snorted. He spread his hands across the sofa and sighed.

Silence fell again. I filled the air with sound. 'Stupid question,' I said, gazing down at my notes. 'You're involved in at least 837 organisations. You're a colonel-in-chief, admiral, what-have-you, forty-two times over. The first achievement is simply to have survived fifty-two years of it – parades, processions, receiving lines, receptions, lunches, dinners, more than 20,000 official engagements.'

Still he said nothing. On I gushed. 'You've measured out your life in handshakes and small-talk.' A slow sigh from HRH. More gushing from yours truly: 'And to keep your sanity, alongside all the surface stuff – necessary, unavoidable – you've got stuck into a range of particular projects where in-depth involvement has given you the satisfaction of a worthwhile job well done.'

He shrugged. At least he didn't disagree. I thought, I am getting nowhere. I thought, I am going to come out of here with nothing – *nothing*.

I struggled on. 'I've made a list of achievements – and myths – half a dozen of each.' I read out my list of 'achievements', starting with 'Supporting the Queen'. He smiled a wintry smile, but he said nothing. 'That's what it's all been about,' I persisted. 'Absolutely,' he said. That was all.

On I ploughed, rattling through the Duke of Edinburgh's Award Scheme, the International Equestrian Federation, the World Wide Fund for Nature, the Commonwealth Study Conferences . . . Still nothing, or next to nothing. Eventually, he leant forward: 'What about these myths then?'

I looked at my notebook. I was glad I had it. If I hadn't had an agenda to work through, I'd have been lost by now. 'Well, Myth Number One,' I said, 'is that it's been a life of frustration, that you've always regretted that you weren't able to pursue your naval career—'

At last, he seemed engaged. 'In 1947 [the year of his marriage] I thought I was going to have a career in the Navy, but it became obvious there was no hope. The royal family then was just the King and the Queen and the two Princesses. The only other male member was the Duke of Gloucester. There was no choice. It just happened.'

I said I knew that his friend Lord Lewin (former First Sea Lord, former Chief of the Defence Staff) used to say that if he had stayed in the Navy he'd have gone right to the top.

Crisply: 'No. Given the way of the British press, I wouldn't have got very far. Every promotion would have been seen as me being treated as a special case. The late King died in February 1952 and that effectively brought my naval career to an end.'

'That was disappointing?'

He's a perverse sod. He won't concede it. 'You have to make compromises,' he said. 'That's life. I accepted it. I tried to make the best of it.'

'When the King died, did you know what to expect?'

'No. There were plenty of people telling me what *not* to do. "You mustn't interfere with this." "Keep out." I had to try to support the Queen as best I could, without getting in the way. The difficulty was to find things that might be useful.'

'But there was the example of the Prince Consort, you'd read biographies—'

'Oh, yes.' A slightly exasperated sigh. 'The Prince Consort . . . The Prince Consort's position was quite different. Queen Victoria was an executive sovereign, following in a long line of executive sovereigns. The Prince Consort was effectively Victoria's private secretary. But after Victoria, the monarchy changed. It became an institution. I had to fit into the institution. I had to avoid getting at cross-purposes, usurping others' authority. In most cases that was no problem. I did my own thing. Got involved in organisations where I thought I could be useful. The Federation of London Boys' Clubs, the Royal Yachting Association, the MCC. Of course, as long as they were going all right, there wasn't much for me to do. But if an organisation was going bankrupt or had some crisis, then I'd help. The fund-raising never stops.'

'Has much of it been fun?'

A puzzled look – almost contemptuous. 'I don't think I think very much about "fun". The Variety Club events were fun. The cricket matches for the Playing Fields were fun. The polo was *entirely* fun!'

It had begun to move. I kept going. 'The second myth is that you're a stick-in-the mud, old-fashioned. In fact, I think you're a moderniser—'

A more explosive interruption. This man likes to disagree. To get him to say anything, you have to provoke him. He is in the business of being contrary. 'No, no, not for the sake of modernising, like some bloody Blairite, not for the sake of buggering about with things. I'm anxious to get things done.'

(I'm not a proper journalist, am I? Already I know that I'm going to remove the Blairite reference. HRH said it, on the record: I was there to interview him, notebook in hand. To quote him would be entirely legitimate, but if I use the line, that's the story. 'Duke attacks "bloody Blair".' I mustn't mention it to Dominic.[*] If I do, he'll run with it. He's ruthless. And a proper journalist.)

The next myth, I suggested, is that he's curmudgeonly. He looked quite hurt. 'I don't think I have ever got up to make a speech of any kind, anywhere, ever, and not made the audience laugh at least once. You arrive somewhere and you go down that receiving line. I get two or three of them to laugh. Always. Occasionally I get fed up, going to visit a factory, when I'm being shown round by the chairman who clearly hasn't got a clue, and I try to get hold of the factory manager but I can't because the chairman wants to make sure he's the one in all the photographs.'

I pleased him by saying what I believe: 'You've got a reputation for not suffering fools gladly, but in fact you've been suffering fools willingly for over fifty years.'

He grinned. 'I have suffered fools . . . with . . . patience.'

I suggested that long before Diana came on to the scene as the unstuffy tactile people-friendly princess, he had been the true pioneer of royal informality.

'Yes, yes, but . . . You won't remember this, but in the first years of the Queen's reign, the level of adulation – you wouldn't believe it. You really wouldn't. It could have been corroding. It would have been very easy to play to the gallery, but I took a conscious decision not to do that. Safer not to be too popular. You can't fall too far.'

Suddenly he was full of energy, leaning forward, peering over my notebook. 'What's next? "Tactless overseas"? Is that on your list?'

---

[*] Dominic Lawson (b.1956), journalist, editor of the *Sunday Telegraph*, 1995–2005.

Happily it was. In my notes, in large letters I had written the words 'Slitty eyes'.[*] I want to nail that one for him if I can.

Since 1952, HRH has taken part in 586 overseas visits to 137 different countries. 'Now,' he said wearily, 'I am desperate if I find there are British press on a foreign visit. I know they'll wreck the thing if they possibly can.'

I suggested that some of the problems with the press are of his making. He was the one who gave the first interview. 'Yes, I made a conscious decision to talk to the media – but not about me, only about what I'm doing, what I'm supporting.'

'The trouble is, talk about the Commonwealth Study Conferences and after three lines people are yawning. They want what's sexy, they want personalities.'

'The press have turned us into a soap opera.' There was something despairing about his laugh. He glanced at my notebook again. 'Any more?'

'Diana.' I stared down at the pad. I thought: Am I going to get away with this? 'The public view, for what it's worth, is of a grouchy old man, unsympathetic to his daughter-in-law.' I paused and looked up. 'But I happen to know that, when things were difficult, you wrote to Diana – kind letters, concerned, fatherly, loving, caring letters from Pa, explaining how you knew, first hand, the difficulties involved in marrying into the royal family.'

He smiled his wintry smile and said nothing. I blundered on. 'The impression the public have got is unfair.'

He shrugged. 'I've just got to live with it. It happens to a lot of people.'

'And Sarah? There's a knee-jerk reaction out there that if the Duchess of York isn't being treated generously, somehow you're behind it.'

He shook his head. 'I try to keep out of these things as much as possible.' He pulled a funny face. 'Her behaviour was a bit odd.' A sigh. 'But I'm not vindictive. I am not vindictive . . . I don't see her because I don't see the point. But the children come and stay. Our children come and stay. We are a family.'

---

[*] On 16 October 1986, in Beijing, when the Queen and the Duke were on a state visit to China, Prince Philip met a group of British students studying at the Northwest University in Xian. The Duke was interested in the students because they came from Edinburgh University (he has been Chancellor of four universities: Edinburgh since 1952). Chatting to them (with neither Chinese nor press present), he expressed surprise when he discovered that they were spending a whole year in China – long enough 'to go native and come home slit-eyed'. Because one of the students later gave a friendly account of the conversation to a journalist, an inconsequential private aside was turned into banner headlines around the world. 'The great wally of China' said the *Mirror*; 'The Duke gets it wrong' said the *Sun*.

'And what about being at odds with Prince Charles? People say how different you are. I think you are remarkably similar, in mannerisms, in interests—'

A final interruption. Dramatic. 'Yes, but with one great difference. He's a Romantic – and I'm a pragmatist. That means we do see things differently.' Another pause. 'And because I don't see things as a Romantic would, I'm *unfeeling*.' Another laugh. Another shrug.

I think I've got enough. I am going to go home now and bash it all out on the word processor. I'll shape it later. I want to do him justice without being over-sycophantic. I know he won't do an autobiography ('Why look back?'), but I floated the idea of a collection of correspondence – letters to and from him. He didn't dismiss it out of hand. I asked him about the future. Where does he see the monarchy fifty years down the road? 'I'm not going to be drawn into speculating on that. All I'll say is that I've tried to help keep it going while I've been here.' He's a good man, dealt a bizarre hand which he's played pretty flawlessly.

Friday, 9 April 1999

M has gone off to the Bologna Book Fair. I'm home alone, laughing at myself at the end of a wretched day. At 12 noon, Dominic [Lawson] called. He'd just heard that John Gielgud had died. He said, 'I'm going to need 2,000 words for the Review front by six o'clock.'[*] I said, 'I don't think I can do it.' He said, 'You must.' At one, he called again: 'Have you started? I must have 2,000 words by 6.00 p.m. We want something very personal and revealing. This is your subject, Gyles.' I hate writing against the clock – I *hate* it. I think my brain is going to burst. I'm caught in the headlights, paralysed. But I did it. I turned off the telephone, I locked the study door, and, between one and 5.45, head thumping, for four and three-quarter hellish hours I toiled away. At 5.45 p.m. I called Dominic. 'I'm nearly there. Give me half an hour more to revise it and it's yours. It's nearly killed me.' 'Oh,' answered Dominic, lightly. 'Haven't you heard? False alarm. He's not dead at all. I think we tried to call you at lunch-time, but you weren't answering the phone. We won't need the piece now. Sorry.'

Saturday, 10 April 1999

I went with Jo [Lumley] to the Oscar Wilde play at the Gielgud. It was 'The Trials' all over again – okay, but not extraordinary. The moment the house lights went down, Jo fell fast asleep. I just about roused her for the interval. She said she hadn't enjoyed a show so much in years. We went on for supper to the Bluebird

[*] From 1999 to 2003, GB was editor-at-large on the *Sunday Telegraph* Review.

Café in King's Road. (It was a garage in the 1950s when we lived in Oakley Street. I remember coming to it with Pa on Saturday mornings to fill the Volkswagen with petrol.) The restaurant was packed, and clattery, but, because it was Jo, they found us a table. As we ate, above the hubbub, we worked on Jo's 'poem' for David Frost's 60th-birthday bash. We were rather pleased with our endeavours.

Monday, 12 April 1999

Jo has just called. Our 'poem' was a wow – but, somehow, all the credit for it went to Tom Stoppard!

Aphra has got her internship with Kleinwort Benson.[*]

Thursday, 15 April 1999

Went to the Globe Theatre in Southwark to interview Richard Olivier: round-faced, bearded, 30-something son of Sir Laurence, and still living entirely in his father's shadow. By every account (especially John Schlesinger's), the old man was a domestic monster. Why? I asked Richard. 'Dad lived for his work. The National Theatre was his real child – we were just stepchildren living in Brighton. He saw us at weekends, but we could never really get his attention. He was either too tired or reading scripts. He was never as "alive" with me as he was on a stage or a film set.'

As a boy, Richard was lonely, isolated, unhappy. When he got married, he found he was behaving like his father – working all the time as a means of avoiding proper personal relationships. (Does this ring bells?) When his father died, ten years ago, it got worse for Richard, then better. 'I was bitter, resentful, angry, until I joined a men's group and went into therapy.'

I don't think 'a men's group' is quite my scene. Apparently, it involves blokes tramping through the forest in search of trees to hug. But I mustn't knock it because I haven't tried it and Richard found it helpful – 'magical' even. Now, he's not angry and he is using what he has learnt to give leadership lessons to business groups based around *Henry V*.

I felt guilty, of course, because ostensibly I was there to talk to Richard about his work, but all I really wanted to talk about was his father. That's been the story of his life.

---

[*] With a BA and MSc in Economics from University College London, she eventually went on to join the civil service as an environmental economist.

While I was at the Globe I had a cup of tea with Mark Rylance.[*] Now he *is* magical. He is a beautiful actor and an extraordinary human being – actually he's not quite human: he's like a spirit, he's Peter Pan high on Shakespeare. (And he looks like Dan Leno. I am going to send him my Dan Leno biography. It's my last copy – my only copy. But he swept me away. He just talked about the Sonnets. I can't recall a word, but I came away *enchanted*. I'd assumed he was gay, but he introduced me to his wife. I am not unhappy with my lot, but *his* achievement, his peculiar genius, I do envy.)

Sunday, 2 May 1999

Supper at the Caprice with Sally Bulloch[†] and Richard Dreyfuss.[‡] Sally was awash with champagne and nicotine. (She is bereft of malice: she is the sweetest, most generous person in the world.) Richard is too normal to be a wholly convincing movie star. He must have read my mind because he said, out of the blue: 'I was the real deal once – then I gave up drink and drugs.' He said he is quite comfortable around alcohol these days: others can drink and he won't crave it. 'But if there was a line of coke on this table right now, you would need six strong men to keep me from it. I would have to be dragged screaming into the street. I could not resist it. Coke is *wonderful*.'

Tuesday, 4 May 1999

Spoke at the Royal Society of Portrait Painters' dinner. Not an easy acoustic, but they laughed. I like them: they know they're a bit old-fashioned, they know the NPG doesn't rate them, but they keep going. Looking out at them as I spoke, I felt I was watching a slighty faded print of a 1950s English comedy. Sir Robert Fellowes[§] was there, looking and behaving just like Richard Wattis.[¶] He let slip that he has persuaded the Queen to sit for Lucian Freud. 'His usual pose?' I

---

[*] David Mark Rylance Waters (b.1960), actor and director; artistic director of Shakespeare's Globe, 1995–2005.

[†] Sally Bulloch (1948–2008), English child actress-turned-hotelier, for twenty years executive manager of the Athenaeum Hotel, Piccadilly. A close friend of GB, she was a regular guest on his Sunday-afternoon programme on LBC, 1999–2003.

[‡] Richard Dreyfuss (b.1947), US Oscar-winning film and stage actor, best known for *The Goodbye Girl*, *Jaws* and *Close Encounters of the Third Kind*.

[§] Sir Robert Fellowes (b.1941), now Baron Fellowes of Shotesham, private secretary to the Queen, 1990–99, and brother-in-law to Diana, Princess of Wales.

[¶] Richard Wattis (1912–75), bespectacled British character actor, noted for playing officials and civil servants.

asked. Sir Robert became suddenly alarmed. 'This is absolutely confidential,' he murmured. But he is clearly excited – and understandably. I think he reckons it could be *the* portrait of the reign. 'If she's starkers,' said Andrew Festing, 'it certainly will be.'

Thursday, 3 June 1999

Went to the Dorchester to interview Kenneth Branagh.* It was one of those absurd conveyor-belt interviews favoured by the movie industry: the star sits on a sofa in the middle of a vast hotel suite while, at fifteen-minute intervals, hacks are led forward to squat briefly at the feet of the deity. Normally, the vacuous PR girl remains in heavy attendance. Kenneth said, kindly, 'I know Gyles,' so we were left in peace. We had a cup of tea and stood by the window looking out onto Hyde Park. I gushed about his *Hamlet* – not surprisingly. He gushed about *Venice Midnight* – which was good of him. It's about an actor exactly like him. (I want him to make the movie.) He said he particularly liked the three rules of charm – the three Cs: Be courteous. Be carefree. And concentrate. He said, 'I'm trying to adopt them.'

Wednesday, 16 June 1999

We flew to Newark from Gatwick courtesy of Continental Airlines (now sponsors of the Teddy Bear Museum) and arrived in New York City elated but exhausted. Heavy with jet lag we made our way to the hottest ticket in town and slept soundly throughout. I exaggerate, but *The Iceman Cometh* lasts *four and a half hours*: it was good (wasn't it?), Tim Pigott-Smith was wonderful (genuinely), but the evening is too long. It really is. Fortunately we got a sort of second wind for the after-show supper with Tim and Pam at Café Leux on W70 and Broadway . . . it was gone midnight when we arrived and, when we left, dawn was close to breaking and only Francesca Annis and Ralph Fiennes remained (canoodling at a corner table). Tim was understandably high – the show is a colossal hit. President Clinton has just been – but having the President in the house is a mixed blessing: it's an honour, of course, but a nuisance too: the audience spends the entire evening looking at *him*.

Thursday, 17 June 1999

The good people just keep going. They never give up. We went to see Twiggy yesterday, off-Broadway, in a revamped version of Sheridan [Morley]'s *Noël and*

* Kenneth Branagh (b.1960), Northern Irish actor and film director.

Gertie. (Sheridan doesn't give up either: he seems to be *commuting* to the show on a weekly basis. The cost will kill him, if the jet lag doesn't. He is not a well man.) Twigs gave me a cracking interview after the show, full of energy. 'They said I was finished at seventeen, Gyles. Well, I'm still here.' I love a trouper.

This morning I interviewed Ms Judith Ré, of the 'JR Academy', expert on 'Social Savvy'. She is giving etiquette classes to Midwesterners staying at the New York Palace. Apparently, they have no idea how to use a knife and fork, let alone where to tuck their napkin.

This afternoon we went to meet up with Judi Dench at the Barrymore Theater. 'I am in Marlon Brando's dressing room,' she told us, tears pricking her eyes. 'The one he had for *Streetcar Named Desire*. Can you believe it?' She is amazing: truly unspoiled by success. Ned Sherrin told me that she never reads a script before accepting a part. She just says yes if it 'feels right'. Ned said (and he's directed her more than once I think) that she does it all by instinct – 'hasn't the first idea what she's saying, but somehow it comes out exactly right.' (It could be true. I remember seeing Olivier, when a very old man, reading poetry to Patrick Garland on the box.* Patrick gave him something to read – a Philip Larkin, I think – and Olivier read it, sight unseen, flawlessly. It was incredibly powerful and moving. When he'd finished, Olivier handed the piece of paper back to Patrick and, after a moment's pause, asked, 'What the fuck was that about?')

Tonight, I addressed the Trollope Society of America and did my best to do justice to the setting: the Knickerbocker Club, on Fifth Avenue and East 62nd – one of New York's oldest and finest gentlemen's clubs: John Jacob Astor, the Rockefellers, the Roosevelts, they were all members of 'The Knick'. It was a happy occasion – what Douglas Hurd would have called 'another of life's memorable cul-de-sacs'.

Speaking of which, tomorrow we go to an upstairs room in an uptown branch of the New York Public Library to see the original Winnie-the-Pooh. The original Eeyore, Piglet, Kanga and Tigger are there, too. (They are in New York because neither Milne nor Christopher Robin wanted them at home. AAM gave them to his New York publisher who left them to the Library.) Whenever I think of Milne, the title of his autobiography comes looming into my mind: *It's Too Late Now*.

Enough. No time for lamentation now. Bed. M is emerging from the bathroom in her white fluffy bathrobe. They are wonderful, all-enveloping bathrobes and

---

* Patrick Garland (b.1935), theatre and television director; he produced the thanksgiving service for Laurence Olivier at Westminster Abbey in 1989.

we are each going to take one home, *having bought them*. I can't remember who it was who said if you travel on a bus after 30, you've failed, but M says the definition of having grown up is leaving a hotel without stealing the soap.

Sunday, 4 July 1999

Thought for the day. On 4 July 1911, Robert Baden-Powell wrote this in a letter to a friend: 'I know my weak points and am only thankful that I have managed to get along in spite of them! I think that's the policy for this world: Be glad of what you have got, and not miserable about what you would like to have had, and not over-anxious about what the future will bring.'

Thursday, 15 July 1999

I've come with Benet to the Ways with Words Literary Festival at Dartington Hall, near Totnes. It's my kind of audience: they're all members of the National Trust. We did a reading of the trials of Oscar Wilde – with me as Wilde and Benet, in his wig and gown, playing the various prosecuting counsel. I introduced the proceedings, telling my story of meeting Mr Badley at Bedales, explaining that I'd shaken the hand that shook the hand of Oscar Wilde. From behind me, Benet piped up. 'Can I say something, Dad? I had a tutor at Cambridge who had had an affair with Lord Alfred Douglas, so I can say I've shaken the hand that shook the hand that shook something else of Oscar Wilde . . .'

Friday 23 July 1999

Breakfast with Jeffrey in the Archer embankment penthouse. I went to interview him for the *Sunday Telegraph*. He wants to be Mayor of London – the first. He is campaigning hard. 'It's going well, Gyles. I don't want anything to go wrong. I've got to be careful. I know I can trust you.' We are not alone. It is 8.20 a.m. and already, up in the gallery, Jeffrey's PA is fielding phone calls. Joseph, the butler (of Middle European extraction and riper years, straight from Central Casting), pads discreetly in and out. While Jeffrey and I tuck in (for the master, a boiled egg, timed to the second; for me, crunchy brown toast and the crispest bacon), two of the mayoral campaign team sit quietly in attendance. They do not eat. Or speak. Jeffrey runs his life as though he's a character in one of his own novels.

I know almost no one who doesn't mock him, but I know few so successful – at least in monetary terms. What is his secret? 'Boundless energy. Determination. And when I see something, I go for it. Longfellow said, "The heights that great men reached and kept were not attained by sudden flight, but they, while their companions slept, toiled ever upward through the night."' Later he offered me another gem: 'Energy plus talent, you'll be a king; energy and no talent, you'll be a prince; talent and no energy, you'll be a pauper.'

What fuelled his ambition?

'I didn't do well at school. I failed. I was a disaster. I remember canvassing in Edinburgh with Malcolm Rifkind. We passed his old school and I said, "I bet you were a prefect." He said, "No, I wasn't actually," and then he told me how, for fun, he had done a test on the Cabinet and three-quarters of the Cabinet had failed to become prefects too. I've often thought failure to succeed at school drives you to want to succeed afterwards. It's ironic how few school captains appear to go on to do anything else. It's almost as if they've achieved what they want to achieve. I still want to achieve.'

I mentioned a line of Aristotle Onassis: 'I must keep aiming higher and higher – even though I know how silly it is.'

Jeffrey chuckled, 'That's good. The line I love of Aristotle Onassis is: "If you can count it, you haven't got any."'

He gave me plenty of good stuff. And, towards the end, I managed to confront him with the Walter Mitty side of his nature. To my surprise, he acknowledged that telling the truth has been a problem in the past, but says Mary has made him face up to it and he claims he has changed. That's the line I am going to run with. Archer – the changed man. Toad for Mayor! Poop-poop!

Wednesday, 11 August 1999

The day of the solar eclipse.

I am writing this in the sitting room of Clive Syddall's cottage at Portloe in Cornwall. We travelled down yesterday. We left Paddington at 11.00 a.m. We reached St Austell after 4.00 p.m. (I believe it was quicker in Queen Victoria's day.) Terry's Taxis met us and brought us to this hinterland. Clare's Café supplied our supper. This morning we rose at dawn to ready ourselves for the momentous event: the first total solar eclipse visible from the United Kingdom mainland for more than seventy years – and we were in pole position. At 11.11 a.m. we raised our eyes and gazed at the clouded sky. There was a bit of a darkened moment and, in the distance, some birds squawked. And that was that. (At least, we tried. And, apparently, the fast train from St Austell only takes five hours. And the buffet should be on today.)

But who cares? We have news of our own son. Benet has passed his Bar finals and won the Du Cann Prize for Advocacy – £1,500.

Monday, 23 August 1999

Tea with Donald Sinden. In under an hour he smoked nine cigarettes. He is 76 and has the constitution of an ox. I told him how I had been to see his play in Norwich on Saturday and, during the interval, overheard two elderly ladies discussing him. One said, 'He's what you'd call a *proper* theatrical knight, isn't he?' 'Oh, yes,' cooed her friend, 'he's the real thing.' Don beamed and gurgled. 'Oh, I like that. That's rather good.' 'Wait,' I said, 'I haven't finished. The first lady then added, "I always thought a knighthood was rather wasted on Derek Jacobi."' Don *exploded* with pleasure. 'Oh – ah – ee!' Cigarette ash sprayed around the room. He was hooting with happiness. 'I'm wicked. We actors are not as generous towards one another as we should be. Did I ever tell you about the television programme I did with Edith Evans and John Gielgud? We were shown clips of the great players of yesteryear and asked for our reactions. During the bit of Ellen Terry, Edith nodded off – *nodded off* during Ellen Terry! And when they showed a bit of Olivier's *Othello* and asked Gielgud what he made of it, John didn't know what to do: "Oh, no, no, no, no, no, no." That was all he could say.'

I love Don's stories. New stuff today (well, new to me):

'A dear friend of Donald Wolfit's wrote to him to congratulate him on his knighthood and added, facetiously, "I do hope I'm still going to be able to call you Donald." Wolfit replied, "My dear fellow, we've known each other for forty-five years, you must certainly continue to call me Donald. [*Pause*] Of course, I cannot answer for Lady Wolfit."'

'The first master comedian I learnt from was Lawrence O'Madden – forgotten now, but, oh, his timing! He'd be beside me on stage and under his breath he'd say, "Wait for it, w-a-i-t for it, wait – for – it . . . *Now!*" A laugh is like the roof of a house. It starts under the eaves and works its way to the top and then rolls down the other side. You wait till it's halfway down the far side before you move on. I am fascinated by the craft, by how it works. It was Ralph [Richardson] who told me, "You've got to have a least five consonants in a tag line. You can't get a laugh on a vowel." I once asked John G., "What are the most essential things about acting?" With hardly a pause he replied, "Feeling and timing," and then, head erect, his eyes twinkled to the side as he added, "I understand it is the same in many walks of life."'

I told him that, over the years, I've recorded a lot of his stories in my diary. He said at once, 'Do you know the story of the young actor in rep who kept a diary? He *loathed* his leading man. He confided the details of his obsession to his diary.

"Tonight, he killed my exit round." "Tonight, he ruined my finest scene." Then came, "Monday, 6.15 p.m. Dear Diary, Tonight I believe I am going to get the better of him. We open a new play and I have a speech ten minutes long. Downstage. In the light. Facing out front. And *he* is upstage, seated at a desk, with his back to the audience. I think I must win . . ." Later, a slightly drunken hand added, "11.45 p.m. HE DRANK THE INK!"'

I told Don that we'd been staying with Beckie [Simon Cadell's widow]. We talked about Simon. I asked him if he brooded about Jeremy.* 'No, no, not at all,' he said simply. '"If it be now, 'tis not to come; if it be not to come, it will be now; if it be not now, yet it will come: the readiness is all." '

Friday, 3 September 1999

I am writing this in the drawing room of Chalet Coward, the Swiss home of Noël Coward, the self-styled 'Master', playboy of the West End world, the twentieth century's foremost theatrical entertainer. And I'm amazed. There are splendid signed photographs in silver frames on top of the piano, but photos apart, it is all so – well – *ordinary*. Yes, the house is halfway up a mountain, with views across Lake Montreux, and cow bells are clinking in the distance, and Dame Joan Sutherland lives next door, but the house – its architecture, furnishings, feel – are (dare I say it?) *mundane*.

Later

But the photographs were fabulous. They were all there: Marlene, Tallulah, Nureyev and Fonteyn, Dickie Mountbatten, Larry and Viv. And across the room, on the mantelpiece, on her own, in pride of place, the dear, darling Queen Mother. We've had a memorable day. I am writing a piece to mark the Coward centenary. He was born in Teddington, Middlesex, on 16 December 1899. I've come to Montreux to meet Graham Payn, his lover, companion and friend, the last living link with the legend. Graham is 81, spry, bright-eyed, self-deprecating, and, like the house, unexpected: cosy, unpretentious, as ungrand as you can imagine.

'We weren't grand. It's hard for people to believe what a simple life we led. Some people don't *want* to believe there was a domestic side to Noël Coward, but there you are. I am sorry to shatter the illusion, but the cigarette holder and the Sulka dressing gowns were just props. Noël's standard wardrobe was modest, off

---

* Three years before, Sir Donald's elder son, Jeremy, also an actor, had died of cancer, aged 45.

the peg. All that brittle, sophisticated stuff was just a cover. Professionally, he was tough as old boots. Personally, he was quite vulnerable.'

I am sitting in our room at the Hôtel Eden au Lac, writing up my notes. M is in the bath recovering from the excitement of having her lunch seated in the Master's chair. We're going over to have supper at Harry's Bar at the Montreux Palace. Lunch was delicious – caviare and sour cream, fillet of beef, home-made strawberry and raspberry ice cream – all prepared and served by Jean-René, who came to Chalet Coward thirty-one years ago as Noël's masseur. He's versatile. (He drove us to and from the station, too.)

Lots of Queen Mum talk. 'Noël always preferred the Yorks, long before there was any thought they might be King and Queen. He used to visit them quite often, much to the irritation of Queen Mary who felt her eldest [the Prince of Wales, later Edward VIII and Duke of Windsor] was being upstaged. Let's face it, the Windsors were not exactly joy unconfined. The Duchess was a lot quicker and wittier than her husband. The Duke, to be honest, was an extremely dull man. Noël said he even danced a boring Charleston, which is no mean feat.'

I managed to ask about the younger brother, the Duke of Kent. 'Did he and Noël have a fling?'

'Oh no. We can put the record straight on that. I asked Noël about it and he was quite clear. "We did *not* get over-friendly." ' (I wonder.)

Writing the piece isn't going to be easy because, while Graham doesn't drink now (hasn't for three years), his face bears witness to past excess and he does not remember a lot! I asked him if he had a favourite 'Noël Coward story'. He looked quite thrown. 'Oh goodness, I'm not sure that I do.' I offered him one of mine. Noël goes to a Swiss clinic, a sort of health farm for the stars, where their most famous treatment is a rejuvenating serum taken from sheep's glands. As he drives up to the clinic, he passes a field full of sheep and, right in the middle of the flock, he spies a single black sheep. Excited, he points to it and says, 'Ah, I see Paul Robeson is here already.'

'Oh, that's *wonderful*. I've never heard that story. But Noël certainly went to the clinic. He didn't like getting older. He didn't like *looking* older. The clinic's over at Vevey. They all went there, Marlene, Vivien . . . I'm not sure about Paul Robeson. It cost a bomb. I don't think it did much good. That's *such* a good story. You tell it so well. And you do the voice. Oh, do another.'

It was absurd. I sat at Noël Coward's dining table with Noël Coward's lover, telling Noël Coward stories in a Noël Coward voice – and our charming host chuckled and nodded and assured me he hadn't heard *any* of them.

Monday, 6 September 1999

I am making two films for ITN: one about the nature of leadership, the other about the future of the Conservative Party – is there life after death? I went down to Alfriston in Sussex to see Denis Healey and get some historical perspective. The joy with Denis is that, though he is now 82 and beginning to shrink, he remains so certain about everything. Sitting in his handsome mock-Lutyens sun lounge, weighing Clement Attlee and Margaret Thatcher in the scales, the name of the Leader of the Opposition cropped up. 'William Hague?' snorted Denis. 'William Hague? He's a twerp. A twerp. There's nothing more to be said. Forget him, forget it. Move on.' Denis is not troubled by self-doubt. And he is blessed in Edna. I like her approach to life. As she brought in the coffee and ginger cake, I said, 'How are you?' She replied, pleasantly: 'You don't need to know. If you've got worries, keep them to yourself. A trouble shared is a trouble doubled.'

Friday, 10 September 1999

I have been granted the pre-conference interview with the Leader of the Opposition. (Perhaps no one else wanted it?) I went to see him at Central Office in Smith Square. The foyer is now New Conservative: colour scheme by Gap, Sky News on the TV, the *Independent* the one newspaper on the coffee table. The only vestige of William's predecessors is a small bust of Winston Churchill, the last bald leader of the party. Beneath a huge portrait of a purposive Master Hague, finger pointing to the future, is a yellow flyer inviting the faithful to sign up for a seminar at which 'leading professional consultants' will provide 'an excellent opportunity to perfect your skills in three key areas: presentation, personal development, interview technique.' (A four-hour session: £10 including lunch.)

I had a good hour with William, but I came away with nothing. Because of yesterday's excitement,[*] I felt obliged to ask him all sorts of impertinent questions. Was he gay? Had he ever had any homosexual experiences? Would he mind if his children were gay? He played it all with a straight bat. I moved on to confront him, rather rudely, with his failure to make an impact. He answered, genially, 'Time will tell.' I confronted him with his critics: 'The unkind ones picture you as a foetus in a baseball cap,' I said, 'the others see you as an old man in

---

[*] On 9 September 1999, in an interview with *The Times*, Michael Portillo, who was hoping to become the Conservative candidate in the forthcoming Kensington and Chelsea by-election, admitted to 'some homosexual experiences as a young person'.

a young man's body, an odd-looking political nerd reading Hansard at the age of seven. What do you say to that?' He said something anodyne.

Interviewing a safe pair of hands like William will never be easy. He won't drop catches. I asked him if he had a favourite maxim. 'I think Willie Whitelaw said, I think he actually said to me, "Nothing is ever so good or so bad as it first seems in politics." '

Seb (who sat in attendance at the interview, with the glossy-lipped Amanda Platell)* claims his boss is 'the most qualified man who ever wanted to be Prime Minister'. Denis Healey says he's a twerp. I reckon the Whitelaw maxim may be nearer the mark. William is 38, a considerable achiever, likeable, clear-headed, quick-witted, rational, reasonable, intelligent, articulate, thoughtful, shrewd. But something's missing. I was impressed, I wasn't moved. I was charmed, but not inspired. In theatrical terms, he is a first-class leading man: he knows the lines, he won't bump into the furniture, he'll never miss a performance. But he isn't a star in the way Blair is. He won't be Prime Minister. (Foreign Secretary perhaps, twenty years from now, in our next administration.)

Sunday, 12 September 1999

It's 2.00 p.m. I am writing this sitting in the atrium of the ITN building on the Gray's Inn Road. It's a Norman Foster building and, thanks to the atrium, one of my favourite places in the world. I am all alone in this vast space, having tea and a ham and salad sandwich. This is where, from 4.00 p.m. to 7.00 p.m. every Sunday, I do my show for LBC. I don't know if anyone is listening (I don't think many are), but I like doing it: I almost *love* doing it. I produce it myself: I choose my own guests. I have good names – Joel Grey, the Duke of Edinburgh, Charlton Heston, Ken Livingstone, Deborah Bull, to name but a few from recent weeks – and complete freedom. It's the freedom I like.

M accepts me doing it, which is good of her, a) because the money isn't marvellous (though it all adds up) and b) because (ever since I can remember) she has been asking that we take one day off a week and (ever since I can remember) I have been promising to do so . . . But it hasn't quite happened yet.

I've come in early today because I am awaiting the arrival of Michael Aspel and crew.† My star guest on the show today is my friend Martin Jarvis and Mr

* Amanda Platell (b.1957), Australian journalist, press secretary to William Hague, 1997–2001.
† Michael Aspel OBE (b.1933), English television presenter, host of the biographical tribute programme *This Is Your Life*, 1994–2003. In 2003, GB was one of the last people to be featured on the programme.

Aspel is going to 'surprise' him live on air. 'Yes, Martin Jarvis, actor, This Is Your Life!' Michael A. is going to be in the corner of the studio, hiding in a cupboard (literally), until the moment of discovery.

Thursday, 16 September 1999

We are on the train from Madrid to Granada. Michèle is taking us to see the Alhambra. The sun is shining brilliantly and I am blessed. If it wasn't for Michèle this wouldn't be happening. She makes *everything* happen – holidays, home, happiness. I am a totally serviced human being. Yes, I sometimes fill the dishwasher, I sometimes empty it. I *always* wipe the kitchen surfaces last thing and I almost always remember to check the back door. Apart from that, nothing. (I do occasionally remember to bring home flowers for the hallway. I am going to be better about that.)

Monday, 4 October 1999

Everything I do seems to hark back to my childhood. M says it all the time – and it's true. (It wouldn't surprise Dr Freud, of course. 'Happiness is the deferred fulfilment of a prehistoric wish. That is why wealth brings so little happiness: money is not an infantile wish.' Discuss.) Today I went to interview Vanessa and Corin Redgrave. I was supposed to be talking to them about them: inevitably we talked mostly about their father. I now have the full story of the whereabouts of Michael's ashes. Corin (for £600) had bought a plot for them in Highgate Cemetery. Lynn wrote to her brother, 'I quite understand that you would like to bury Dad's ashes near Karl Marx. I should have preferred St Paul's, the actors' church in Covent Garden, and so would Mum I think. But your choice means more to you than ours would to us, so you should go ahead.' He didn't. For nine years the ashes remained unclaimed at Mortlake Crematorium. Eventually, Corin collected them and, for several weeks, they kept him company in the boot of his car. 'Strange as it might seem, I felt comforted by them. After a while I began to wonder how I had ever managed without them. Alone in my car I would play music to them, and even sing to them. Sometimes they would sing back, a distant, clear, pure, baritone – "every valley shall be exalted". Once, when Radio 3 was playing Haydn's "Miracle" Symphony, I could hear them laughing. It couldn't last, of course, and it didn't.' One day Rachel said, 'I must take Michael's ashes to St Paul's, I've promised Lynn I would.' So that's where they now are.

And Rachel, 90, is living with Vanessa. Lynn is still living in America. She is divorcing her husband of thirty-two years. Last November, while she was preparing the turkey for the family's Thanksgiving dinner, he confessed to her that he had been 'a naughty boy'. Some years ago, unknown to Lynn, he fathered a child by his personal assistant – who subsequently grew up and married his and Lynn's only son! (How lovely it is to lead an uncomplicated life.)

Wednesday, 6 October 1999

I am in Blackpool for the Conservative Party Conference. I stood at the back of the hall to listen to Jeffrey's speech. Our mayoral candidate scored a conference triumph. As he and Mary emerged afterwards I hugged them and they beamed. The activists adore him. They love him for what he is: a gung-ho no-nonsense tub-thumping rallier to the cause. They love his loyalty. They love his certainty. They love his energy. They feel he is a winner. Of course, what they don't know is that the hierachy of the Conservative Party would rather have had anyone – *anyone* – other than Jeffrey as candidate for Mayor. But the activists have the final say, so they've been lumbered with Jeffrey and now they've got to back him to the hilt.

I am having dinner with Adam Boulton.[*] He is very jolly and gets fatter every time I meet him. (I have just seen Tim Rice. Ditto.)

Wednesday, 13 October 1999

Went to Birmingham to be the MC and warm-up act for John Major. He is on tour with his Memoirs. He put a nice inscription in my copy, but whenever I see him nowadays, I feel he is looking at me warily, as though he thinks I know something I shouldn't, as though he can't entirely trust me.[†] (Norma was lovely. Fastidious, intelligent, normal. As ever.)

Tuesday, 19 October 1999

For our film on leadership, we went to Plumstead this afternoon to interview a self-styled 'gangster' named Dave Courtney.[‡] He claims to be an old associate of the Krays and spoke luridly of the 'fear' they instinctively instilled. The more he played the villain the less seriously I took him. He seemed to be a thoroughly nice

---

[*] Adam Boulton (b.1959), English journalist, political editor of Sky News since 1989.
[†] Though a friend of Edwina Currie since their university days, GB had no inkling of her affair with John Major. In March 1997, GB had reported in his diary John Major remarking that he imagined Edwina was then knocking on 'quite a few publishers' doors', but he did not realise the significance of the observation until the publication of her *Diaries: 1987–92* in 2002.
[‡] David Courtney (b.1959), Bermondsey-born author of a series of autobiographical accounts of his life as a hard man of crime.

family man. (There were women and children crawling all over the place.) 'Dodgy Dave' implied that he'd been a killer in his time and assured me that now I am a friend of his I can count on his 'protection'.

Monday, 1 November 1999

I am on the train coming back from Salisbury. I have been interviewing Ted Heath. His Queen Anne house in the Cathedral Close is quite perfect. 'When Roy Jenkins came to lunch he looked out of the drawing-room window and said, "Ted, this must be one of the ten finest views in Britain." I said, "Oh really, which do you think are the other nine?"' As he told me the story, Ted's shoulders heaved with happiness. The old monster was in mellow mood. He showed me some of his treasures: his orchids (a present from Fidel Castro), the dish that once belonged to Disraeli, the Richard Strauss manuscript, the Churchill paintings. 'This is the one I prefer. It's got two signatures. Winston signed it when he painted it and then signed it again when he gave it to me.'

'What will you have? Tea, gin, whisky, champagne?' It was not yet four o'clock, so I settled for tea. My proposed theme was the qualities required for successful political leadership. He seemed happy with that. 'You suggest some and I'll respond.'

'Energy,' I began.

'Yes.'

'Stamina.'

'Yes.'

'An ability to perceive reality efficiently and tolerate uncertainty.'

'Hmm. Yes.'

'An ability to inspire loyalty and maintain discipline.'

'Yes, but it depends how it's done. Political leadership is different from military leadership. In politics you can't just lay down the law and expect people to follow it. We see an attempt being made to operate in that way in the Conservative Party now. Hague says, "I'll do it my way!" That's not political leadership. It's an attempt to impose a particular point of view. True political leadership is about persuasion, and about listening to and taking account of others.'

'But also about having a clear personal vision, knowing where you want to go?'

'Yes.'

'And to that end you have to be determined, single-minded, to have what Napoleon admired, the mental power "*de fixer les objets longtemps sans être fatigué*"?'

'Yes, yes, absolutely.' (I knew I'd score with that one.) 'The great leaders will always concentrate on the big picture, not get too bogged down in the day-to-day. I remember, in the middle of one crisis [in 1958] – three ministers, including the Chancellor of the Exchequer, had just resigned – I went to see Macmillan in his room at Number Ten to talk to him about the timing of the announcement of their replacements. I found him sitting in his armchair with his feet up on a stool, reading in front of the fire. He agreed to what I proposed and then said, "But please don't worry me any more. Can't you see that I'm trying to finish *Dombey and Son* before I go off on this foreign tour tomorrow morning?"'

'Would that approach be possible today?'

'Yes, perfectly. It was that approach that allowed me my music, my concerts; it allowed me my sailing in the spring and the summer. It's a question of how you handle the job. I didn't interfere with departmental ministers just for the sake of it. I only became involved if something appeared to be going wrong.'

'When did that style of government begin to change?'

'With Harold Wilson. He was a workaholic. He had a small group around him and they met constantly, working into the early hours. They say Wilson was a great operator, but to what effect? There's nothing left of Wilson now.'

'And, of course, Mrs Thatcher only needed five hours' sleep and never stopped.'

'Hmm, yes, well. One saw the consequences.'

He gave me plenty of good stuff – scorning Thatcher and Reagan; dismissing Mandela; praising Castro and Chairman Mao. He doesn't care. And mock him as we may, he has his place in history. On 24 January 1972, Ted signed the Treaty of Accession in Brussels. There's no turning back. 'It was the proudest moment of my life.'

Friday, 5 November 1999

I am at Dublin Airport, awaiting my cheapo Ryan Air flight back to London. I have had a wonderful day – in pursuit of happiness with Professor Anthony Clare.* He is a complete delight: wiry, beady-eyed, engaging: Gabriel Byrne meets Kermit the Frog. I want to spend more days like this with people like him – the combination of easy charm and high intelligence is irresistible.

He is medical director of St Patrick's Hospital, Ireland's first mental hospital, founded by Jonathan Swift in 1757. To reach his office from reception I was

---

* Anthony Clare (1942–2007), Irish psychiatrist, writer and broadcaster; presenter of *In the Psychiatrist's Chair* on BBC Radio 4, 1982–2001.

escorted through a labyrinth of corridors and stairwells, past sullen young women with eating disorders, alcoholics and depressives, shuffling figures muttering to themselves, and rows and rows of old people sitting sadly in armchairs gazing vacantly into the middle-distance.

His welcome could not have been warmer – or more courteous. 'I love your articles. I read your piece on Jeffrey Archer. You think he's changed, do you? . . . I have never met him so I can't comment, but in my experience, people don't change. A liar remains a liar, a philanderer a philanderer and so on. In the case of Mr Clinton, Miss Lewinsky is very unlikely to be an isolated incident.'

We gossiped, then we got down to business. We spent three hours talking about happiness. Freud thought 'to love and to work' were the essential elements of happiness. To be happy you need to have people to love and work that satisfies. Good health is important, but you can be happy without it. 'Being reasonably attractive is a help. People come towards you, warm to you. But you can be too beautiful. Extremes are difficult for human beings to cope with. Marilyn Monroe wasn't very happy.' There is no evidence that money buys happiness. In fact, there's some to suggest the reverse. Firstborns have a tendency to happiness, so do children with two parents, and men who are married. You can be happy in war because there is comradeship and a sense of common purpose. 'Those engaged in war are testing themselves. That seems to be important. Happy people are rarely sitting around. They are usually involved in some ongoing interchange with life.'

He gave me plenty of science – stuff on seratonins and endogenous opioids – and plenty on Jung and R. D. Laing. And, ultimately, he delivered what I wanted – the 7 Steps to Happiness. I said: 'This is the bit I and my readers are going to cut out and stick on the fridge door.'

'Oh God,' he sighed. He closed his eyes. He rubbed his thumb against his forefinger and pondered. 'Okay,' he said eventually. 'Here goes. Number one: *cultivate a passion*. How important it seems to me in my model of happiness is having something that you enjoy doing. The challenge for a school is to find in every kid some kind of passion – something that will see them through the troughs. That's why I'm in favour of the broadest curriculum you can get.

'Next, *be a leaf on a tree*. You have to be both an individual – you have to have a sense that you are unique and you matter – and, at the same time, you need to be connected to a bigger organism, a family, a community, a hospital, a company. You need to be part of something bigger than yourself. A leaf *off* a tree has the advantage that it floats about a bit, but it's disconnected and it dies.'

He said that the people who are best protected against certain physical diseases – cancer and heart disease, for example – in addition to doing all the other things they should do, seem to be much more likely to be part of a community, socially involved. If you ask them to enumerate the people that they feel close to and connect and communicate with, those who name the most seem to be happiest. 'Of course, there may be a circular argument here. If you are a rather complicated person, people may avoid you. If, on the other hand, you are a centre of good feeling people will come to you. I see the tragedy here in this room where some people may sit in that chair and say they don't think they've got very many friends and the truth is they are so introspective they've become difficult to make friends with. Put them in a social group and they tend to talk about themselves. It puts other people off. So that's my third rule: *avoid introspection.*

'Next, *don't resist change.* Change is important. People who are fearful of change are rarely happy. I don't mean massive change, but enough to keep your life stimulated. People are wary of change, particularly when things are going reasonably well because they don't want to rock the boat, but a little rocking can be good for you. It's the salt in the soup. Uniformity is a tremendous threat to happiness, as are too much predictability and control and order. You need variety, flexibility, the unexpected, because they'll challenge you.

'*Live in the moment.* Look at the things that you want to do and you keep postponing. Postpone less of what you want to do, or what you think is worthwhile. Don't get hidebound by the day-to-day demands. Spend less time working on the family finances and more time working out what makes you happy. If going to the cinema is a pleasure, then do it. If going to the opera is a pain, then don't do it.

'*Audit your happiness.* How much of each day are you spending doing something that doesn't make you happy? Check it out and if more than half of what you're doing makes you unhappy, then change it.

'And, finally, Gyles, if you want to be happy, *Be Happy.* Act it, play the part, put on a happy face. Start thinking differently. If you are feeling negative, say "I am going to be positive," and that, in itself, can trigger a change in how you feel.'

He slapped his hands on his desk and laughed. 'That's it.'

'And it works?'

'Well, it's something for the fridge door.'

Tuesday, 9 November 1999

I am back at the New York Palace, writing up my notes on my morning with Walter Cronkite.[*] Yes, the twentieth century is drawing to a close and I have

---

[*] Walter Cronkite (1916–2009), America's most celebrated broadcast journalist.

come to meet the man who reported it – the face of CBS News, the original 'anchorman' (the word was coined for him), the first newsman to be honoured with the Presidential Medal of Freedom.

'Jeez, you're meeting Uncle Walter? I don't believe it. Uncle Walter, man, whoa!' My cab driver spoke for the American people. According to opinion polls, Cronkite is still 'the most trusted man in America'.

On the nineteenth floor of the CBS building sits 'The Cronkite Unit'. The great man is 83 now, it is eighteen years since he last presented the evening news, but a staff of five are in attendance. 'Does he really need all this?' I asked one of the assistants. She looked at me quite dewy-eyed: 'With someone of Mr Cronkite's integrity, standing and stature, you can't let things drop, you simply can't.' Clearly this was the Emerald City and I was Dorothy on my way to meet the mighty Oz.

'Mr Cronkite will see you now.'

And, suddenly, there he was – the man who broke the news of Kennedy's assassination – and, of course, he wasn't terrifying at all. Seated behind his desk, sucking a throat lozenge, he was Bert Lahr as the Cowardly Lion: avuncular, benign, almost bashful: 'Oh, for gosh sakes, come in, have you been kept waiting?' He was eager to please and happy to help. He swallowed the lozenge.

Somehow I've got to write this up big 'cos it cost a lot to get me here, it's an exclusive, and we are hoping for syndication. I asked Mr Cronkite to name the most significant event of the twentieth century.

'Man's landing on the moon. Without a question of a doubt.'

'You put the lunar landing ahead of the discovery of penicillin, contraception, the computer—'

'Or even the splitting of the atom, yes, for heaven's sakes. The development of vaccines, the X-ray, all the rest, fall in some way behind. Of course, the advent of the birth control pill has changed the whole societal relationship between the genders and helped to elevate women to an equal role with men, but the landing on the moon is in a different league – not because I was there to report it, but because it marks man's first escape from his environment on earth. One of the few dates the modern American child knows is 12 October 1492, the day Columbus landed in the New World. One day people will be living on other moons, flitting about at the speed of light, and they will look back to a time they can barely imagine when three men climbed into a funny little vehicle they called a spaceship and took almost four days to reach their destination. Five hundred years from now the one year of our century that will be memorised by school-children – if they are still going to school, they may be getting their education by osmosis, who knows? – but the one year they'll know is 1969, when man first walked on the moon.'

Which US presidents will be remembered one hundred years from now?

'The wartime presidents, Wilson and FDR. One of the reasons we remember wartime presidents is that so much of the democratic procedure is suspended in wartime. They can act on their own initiative, do more or less as they please.

'I wouldn't want to put the presidents I've known in a particular order. Any of us close to power see the clay feet. I remember Truman for his courage and his cocky certainty that he was right. Eisenhower said his intention was to calm the nation down and he succeeded. He said his plan was to do nothing, literally nothing, to let the war wounds settle. He could not utter a single sentence that parsed, but you knew what he meant and he meant well.

'Cut short as it was, the Kennedy presidency has left little that's noteworthy for the history books, but Jack's charm, his style and his rhetoric captured the imagination of a generation of Americans to a degree unmatched by any other occupant of the White House this century, even including the Roosevelts, Franklin and Theodore. And, yes, he showed courage in the Missile Crisis in 1962 when we didn't know how that would come out.

'Lyndon Johnson lived up to that bromide that he was bigger than life. He really was. Hard to describe, he was hard to live with. The first time he came for an interview, he produced a sheaf of papers from his pocket. "Boys, here are the questions you'll ask me." I explained that we didn't use prearranged questions. "That's all right with me," he said, and he took back the papers and walked right out the door. His achievement as President was to get the civil rights legislation through Congress. I don't think Kennedy could have done that.

'I got along rather well with Nixon. He was stiff, uncomfortable, totally incapable of even halfway sensible small-talk, and we all know that he had a psychological problem, no question, but he showed amazing political courage in following Kissinger's lead and opening up China. Gerald Ford, who succeeded him, was a nice man who played a good game of golf.

'Now this may surprise you: of all the presidents I have known since Herbert Hoover, the best brain was possessed by Jimmy Carter. His accomplishments were few, but his mind was remarkable. Reagan had a personality that could sell almost anything. Every visitor to the Oval Office left impressed with the Reagan modus operandi. Before answering questions or introducing new topics, he slid his top desk drawer open just enough to read from a set of pre-prepared cards. But, by golly, he was affable. After our last interview, when I'd announced I was stepping down from the CBS Evening News, he invited me into the Oval Office with some of his key people. We had cake and champagne and spent two hours in a hilarious exchange of stories – most of them dirty.

'The problem for President Bush was that his party affiliations prevented him from acting as his heart would have wanted to. His instincts were liberal, but he was forced into positions on the Right. And that brings us up to Bill Clinton, who we've had now for almost eight years – an extraordinary individual. The moral burden he has carried will ensure that he is an asterisk in history – there for ever, for that reason alone.'

Wednesday, 10 November 1999

We are just back from lunch with Quentin Crisp.[*] We met in the Bowery Bar, on the Lower East Side, for crab cakes and whisky. He came because we asked him. 'I never say "no" to anything because I recognise that, as I lie dying on an iron bedstead in a rented room, I shall regret what I didn't do, not what I did.' He says he likes meeting strangers: 'They are so much more reliable than friends.' He wore his trademark hat and chiffon scarf and lilac eyeshadow. Knowing he lives alone in a small room he never cleans in the heart of Hell's Angels country ('You can't get any lower and that's a comfort'), I was surprised to find, as I helped him off and on with his coat, that his pale silk shirt, though frayed, was quite fresh, his jacket, though old, was newly pressed. He explained that some nuns live nearby and they do his laundry. He looked immaculate, like an Edwardian dandy: Max Beerbohm meets Hetty King. I helped him on to the banquette by the window: 'Mr Crisp's usual table,' said the waitress. He is 90: mentally alert, physically frail. It was a curious experience: for two hours we sat and gazed at an old man with mauve hair, the self-styled 'stately homo of England', as – head held high and almost always in profile – he talked, in a gravelly, lilting voice, almost without pause. I asked him if I could record the conversation. He said: 'Of course. You must.' He didn't ask us anything, he almost never looked our way: he simply talked. It was a one-man show for an audience of two.

He told us his life story. He was born in 1908. His father was a suburban solicitor (without a sense of humour), his mother a housewife (with pretensions). 'I went to church as a child, but even as a child I recognised it was merely a social occasion. We were dressed in starched shirts and sailor suits and knew it had nothing to do with You Know Who.' With an elegant turn of his one good wrist, he waved his fork towards the sky. 'When I was in Ireland performing my one-man show – I don't really act, I just say what I think – I told the audience I was

---

[*] Quentin Crisp (b. Denis Pratt, 1908–99), English artist's model, author and performer.

an atheist and a woman got up and said, "Yes, but is it the God of the Catholics or the God of the Protestants in whom you do not believe?" I don't believe in God and He doesn't believe in me. I wanted to call my life story *I Reign in Hell*, but Jonathan Cape decided that wouldn't do, so when it was published in 1968 it was called *The Naked Civil Servant* and now, everywhere I go, I have to explain I was never a civil servant.'

As a child, he was a misfit. As soon as he could walk, he took to wearing his mother's clothes and imagining himself as a fairy-tale princess. At school he was beaten. As a young man, walking through London, asserting his individuality with hennaed hair, 'blind with mascara and dumb with lipstick', he was beaten up. He changed his name: he was once Denis Pratt. He tried to join the Army, but was declared 'totally exempt, suffering from sexual perversion'. In 1942, he became an art school model and for the next thirty years worked in virtually every art school in and around London, usually posing naked. His crucifixion pose was his favourite. He asked himself the question, 'Who would you be if there was no praise and no blame?' and then tried to live according to his answer. His favourite line belongs to Blanche DuBois in Tennessee Williams's *A Streetcar Named Desire*: 'I never lied in my heart.'

'I have made only two decisions in my life. The first was to leave home, the second was to live in America. I left home when I was 22 because I felt I couldn't really go on eating my parents' food and taking their shelter and never doing a thing they asked. It was very difficult because I had no money and I had to live in the worst parts of London – in King's Cross and Clerkenwell.' He rolls the names around his mouth and spits them out with haughty theatrical disdain. 'In America, everybody is your friend. In England, nobody is your friend. In England, if you like something you don't mention it, if you don't you do. In America, if you don't like something you don't mention it. What you do like you mention – so the air is full of praise, which is nice.

'The secret of how to be happy is to remember that happiness is never out there, it's always in here.' He looked at me directly (for only the second time) and cupped his hands around his heart. 'And, also, to live alone. I had no opinions about cohabitation until the last four or five years, but recently I have become a kind of mail-order guru, and people come to see me and tell me their problems. And all the problems concern the person they live with, so to be happy you have to live alone. Usually I eat alone. I go to most places alone. When I receive an invitation I go, and if you can live on peanuts and champagne you need never buy food in New York. I like people, but any people will do. I have my friends, but I'm *mad* about strangers because they haven't heard it all before.'

He made us laugh a lot – and he laughed too. He said, 'The secret of success as a performer is to make the audience like you. That's all you have to do.' We liked him at once. After lunch, we found a cab and dropped him off outside his rooming house. I asked about his fellow tenants. 'They're nice. They carry my letters up for me because I can only go up and down the stairs once a day now my heart's so bad. My neighbours are kind, except for one of them who puts dead mice under my door. I think he wants to me to go. He probably wants my room.'

We shook hands and told him what a privilege it had been being his strangers for today. 'Thank you,' he said, almost looking at us. 'It's been fun.'

Later

My favourite Crisp lines:

'If at first you don't succeed, failure may be your style.'

'Never keep up with the Joneses. Drag them down to your level.'

'There is no need for housework, just keep your nerve. After the first four years, the dirt doesn't get any worse.'

'For flavour, Instant Sex will never supersede the stuff you had to peel and cook.'

'People who are lonely are those who do not know what to do with the time when they are alone.'

'Life was a funny thing that happened to me on the way to the grave.'

Saturday, 13 November 1999

We're at Newark, awaiting the flight home. At the birthplace of Theodore Roosevelt yesterday morning, I bought two huge biographies of the great man. Will I ever read either of them? Probably not. But I am pleased to have them nonetheless.

We had tea yesterday with Kate Ganz. She glowed. Not entirely unsurprisingly: her parents' art collection sold for $206.5 million dollars. She is also content that her marriage is over. Not so Tony Holden. We had supper with him at Café dell'Arte – lots of laughter (he is the best company), but he is heartbroken because it seems his marriage to Cindy is coming to an end. She is in London. He is here. He has been here for a year working on his book at the New York Public Library. I'd have thought it pretty obvious that if you're apart a year it will put a strain on a marriage, but Tony seems genuinely surprised.[*]

---

[*] Kate Ganz (b.1946), New York art gallery owner, daughter of noted twentieth-century art collectors Victor and Sally Ganz, was married to the art critic of the *Daily Telegraph*, Richard Dorment. Their children and GB's had been at school together. Tony Holden was married to the American writer Cindy Blake.

Thursday, 18 November 1999

Just in from recording *Have I Got News for You.** Not a very jolly experience. I survived. I had one or two good moments, but whether they make it to the final cut is anybody's guess. They record one hundred minutes of material and use twenty-nine. It's okay for Hislop and Merton: they know the form and have slave cameras. Merton does very little during the course of the evening, because he knows that whatever he does offer will be used. From start to finish, the rest of us are whirling about like dervishes trying to come up with something vaguely amusing. It was exhausting.

I've no doubt that, as ever, I tried too hard. Hislop was friendly, but the atmosphere is cold. Nobody seems to like anybody else very much. Hislop and Merton clearly both depise Angus Deayton – who is very good. And the more the audience warm to Deayton, the more they loathe him. That was quite funny to watch, but, overall, I rather hated the whole thing. Of course, you can't say that: this is a show everyone loves. Don't knock it. It's like saying that Mo Mowlam is a self-regarding, self-indulgent, over-rated old bat – it just can't be done. Anyway, there's a decent fee, there's good exposure and it's done now. But I wouldn't want to do it again. It looks like a happy show, but it's not a happy place.†

Sunday, 21 November 1999

It's all over. 'Jeffrey Archer destroyed' is the *Sunday Telegraph* headline. The *News of the World* has nailed him as a liar who was prepared to commit perjury in his libel action in 1986. The feeling is he'll end up in jail. Three to five years they reckon. Michèle says I have been naïve. Jeffrey's father was a womaniser, a fraudster, a convicted felon – and a Conservative councillor. 'It's in the genes,' says M. 'He's got self-deception written through him like the word Blackpool in a stick of rock.'

The papers are devastating. The collapse is complete. There is no bouncing back from this. Between 2.00 p.m. and 5.00 p.m. yesterday I managed to write a thousand-word piece for Dominic. Then we had supper with Jo and Stevie. Jo

---

* *Have I Got News for You*, humorous quiz programme based on the week's news, made by Hat Trick Productions and broadcast by the BBC since 1990, hosted by Angus Deayton (b.1956) until 2002, with Ian Hislop (b.1960), editor of *Private Eye*, and Paul Merton (b.1957), comedian, as team captains.

† In fact, GB has returned to the programme on a number of occasions, both as a team member and as guest host.

and I were more sympathetic to Jeffrey than our spouses. 'He's a con man,' said Stevie. 'He took you in. That's what con men do.'

I am going to write to Jeffrey now.

Monday, 22 November 1999

The press are going to town: 'Lying Archer may face jail: scandal returns to haunt Conservatives' – *Guardian*; 'Archer faces criminal charges: Hague's judgement questioned as sleaze returns to Tory Party' – *Times*. On the front page of the *Telegraph* there's a huge picture of Andy Colquhoun [Archer's former mistress and personal assistant], in floods of tears, running the gauntlet of newsmen outside her home. It's a cruel world.

And a ridiculous one. This afternoon I made my way to Kensington Fire Station to film Michael Portillo and William Hague on the hustings. William didn't turn up. Michael did – and, as he arrived, he was ambushed by Peter Tatchell and friends.* In the scrum that followed, I was knocked over. I carried on reporting. Flat on my back from the pavement's edge I declared: 'I'm in the gutter, but I am still looking at the stars!' Maddeningly, the cameraman had stopped rolling. My gem was lost. ('Twas ever thus.)

Also today: Cherie Blair is pregnant, aged 45. I did a piece about it for CBS News. The hapless Leader of the Opposition is childless, friendless, sleaze-ridden, but our sainted Prime Minister just goes from strength to strength. Where does he get the time? And the energy? (He *is* the father: we can be certain of that.)

Also, on all the front pages, news of the death of Quentin Crisp. He told us his doctor had said he shouldn't fly, but he said he was going to anyway. He flew over on Saturday and died in Manchester on Sunday morning. I am so glad I had the chance to meet him.

Monday, 29 November 1999

A handwritten note from Mary Archer, in reply to my letter to Jeffrey:

Dear Gyles,

You may choose to hunt with the prey or sympathise with the quarry. You cannot do both.

Yours sincerely,

Mary

* Peter Tatchell (b.1952), Australian-born political campaigner and gay rights activist.

Tuesday, 7 December 1999

Coffee with Christopher Lee,[*] at 6′ 5″ the tallest leading actor in the history of cinema. Also, I discovered, the most long-winded. I met up with him at a discreet hotel behind Sloane Square (11 Cadogan Gardens). I got out my recording equipment and, at a little after eleven, I asked him my first question. At a little after twelve, he was still answering it. Fifty minutes later, when he was just getting into his stride with his answer to my second question, I interrupted (which I know was rude), made my excuses and left.

Lunch at the Gay Hussar with Geoffrey Atkinson. He produces the Rory Bremner show[†] and his commitment is humbling. He really cares about politics. (He is more serious about politics than almost any politician I know.) He sees his programme doing what the Opposition ought to be doing but isn't: with in-depth research, analysis and understanding, calling the government of the day to account.

Tea with Paul Burrell.[‡] His devotion to Diana is not in question, but I do wonder if he was quite as intimate as he implies.

Monday, 13 December 1999

I might tonight have been at Jeffrey's champagne and shepherd's pie party in his penthouse by the Thames. Invitations were sent out a while back, but last week a letter came from our host (in his own hand) saying, with regret, he had decided to cancel. So, instead, tonight I made my way to 14 Cottesmore Gardens, W8, to the gala bash given by Mr and Mrs Conrad Black.[§] It was generously done, but the crush was incredible: the Establishment was out in force, braying smugly at one another and gushing over our shiny and complacent host and his glamorous wife. (I mock, but I gushed and gurgled with the worst of them.) I was pleased to be there: it made an amusing scene: but though, I suppose, I *am* part of it, I don't

---

[*] Sir Christopher Lee (b.1922), leading English film actor, particularly associated with horror films.

[†] Geoffrey Atkinson produced *Rory Bremner, Who Else?* from 1993 and, from 1999, *Bremner, Bird and Fortune.*

[‡] Paul Burrell RVM (b.1958), former footman to the Queen and butler to Diana, Princess of Wales.

[§] Conrad Black (b.1944), Baron Black of Crossharbour, Canadian-born newspaper publisher and author, sentenced in 2007 to 78 months' imprisonment on charges of fraud and obstruction of justice; married, as her fourth husband, to Barbara Amiel (b.1940), British-Canadian journalist.

feel part of it at all. I don't like these events: I don't like these people (certainly not en masse): why do I go? I suppose I feel I can't not be there.

Tuesday, 21 December 1999

This afternoon I went to Hackney to be photographed with Miss United Kingdom. She was very pretty (I have met a lot of these beauty queens: often they aren't) and very sweet and consequently I did my best to hold my stomach in throughout. (Identifying her is going to be one of the challenges in my *Sunday Telegraph* Christmas quiz.) This evening I went to the Garrick Club for what promised to be rather a special occasion.

Sproatie [Iain Sproat, former MP] phoned a month back. 'We are having a dinner at the Garrick in honour of Anthony Powell* on his 94th birthday – a select group, Tony Quinton in the chair, should be quite special. Would you and Michèle like to come?' We said we'd love to. (Though of a different generation, having lived the life I've lived, I recognise every element of *A Dance to the Music of Time*: every phrase rings true.) Thrilled to be asked ourselves, we thought about it and realised it was the kind of event that Jo would love too. I called Sproatie back. 'Our friend Joanna Lumley is a huge fan of Anthony Powell's. They've corresponded by postcard. I know she'd be excited to come to the dinner. Would there be room?' 'All the places have gone,' said Sproatie. 'Everyone wants to be there. But since it's Miss Lumley, let's squeeze her in.'

And tonight was the night. We all gathered at the Garrick at 7.30 p.m., as planned – in the Milne Room. Some had brought first editions to be autographed; others had come with gifts for the great man. Jo arrived bearing a present, a home-made birthday card and a special hand-picked posy for Mr Powell. We stood around, clutching our gifts, having drinks, making small-talk, feeling oddly nervous and excited, waiting for 'the arrival'. At eight o'clock, Sproatie turned to the room and announced, 'Dinner is served. Take your places, if you please.' A hush fell.

'It's only just eight,' said Jo. 'Shouldn't we wait for the guest of honour?'

Sproatie laughed. 'Anthony Powell's not coming,' he said. 'He's ninety-four.'

'I know,' I said, blanching, 'that's why we're here.'

'You didn't think he was coming, did you?'

Well, yes, we did, rather . . .

---

* Anthony Powell CH CBE (1905–2000), English novelist and critic, best known for his twelve-volume work *A Dance to the Music of Time*, published between 1951 and 1975.

We sat down, speechless. The dinner was not unjolly. Once I'd regained my equilibrium I quite enjoyed it. After it, Tony Quinton – whom I hadn't seen since he interviewed me for my Oxford scholarship thirty-three years ago – led a discussion on the great man's works. During it, Sproatie spent a lot of time talking about the edition of the *Complete Works of Pushkin* that he is publishing – under the auspices of Mrs Gorbachev. I think he's flogging them at around £1,200 apiece. I think I heard Joanna, somewhat hysterically, agreeing to buy a set. (I am surprised she didn't buy two.) You couldn't make it up.

Thursday, 30 December 1999

Our family is dispersing for the dawn of the new millennium. (Yes, I know it's not due for a year yet, but everyone seems to think the century ends tomorrow, so we're going with the flow.) Benet will be the furthest flung and the first to reach the year 2000. He is in Australia and plans to witness the festivities in Sydney Harbour. I envy him. We will not be joining the Queen at the Millennium Dome. (The Dome is a disaster. It has no heart. It's all contrived. I did warn them, right at the outset, when I was at the Department of National Heritage. I really did. I knew it wouldn't work, couldn't work, and for a reason: yes, the team that gave you Royal Britain has laid its dead hand on the Millennium Experience, also.)[*] I think I'd have quite liked to stay at home for the millennium, watch the video of *The Court Jester* that Simon [Cadell] gave me and then catch the fireworks from our bedroom balcony . . . but M says we should go to Framlingham: 'That's what we do for New Year.' Certainly, it's what we did when Simon was alive. And I'm happy to go. Indeed, I'm grateful to be asked. The Crofts are giving a family party. It'll be fine. It'll be fun. ('Nothing matters very much and most things don't matter at all.' Arthur Balfour.)

Saturday, 1 January 2000

Framlingham, Suffolk

Dear Simon,

How are you? Stupid question, of course. You're dead. All the same, I thought I'd write to you today because it's the first day of a new year – some say it's the first day of a new millennium – and I'm here, sitting on your old sofa in your old home, thinking of you.

---

[*] Gary Withers and Imagination, the designers of GB's failed venture at the Barbican, were involved in aspects of the creation of the Millennium Experience on the Greenwich Peninsula.

The Pursuit of Happiness

We have had a memorable night, thanks to your in-laws. We went over to Honington Hall where they wined us (royally) and dined us (splendidly) and then entertained us with a special showing of Inspector Gadget *– possibly the worst film in the history of cinema. (I don't think you could have sat through it: you'd have twitched until you exploded.) The children enjoyed the movie while the adults drank steadily. As midnight approached, the film ended and we switched to TV. That's when the real horror began. The poor Queen had been dragged from Sandringham to take part in the 'festivities' at the Millennium Dome. As midnight tolled, she was obliged to stand in line holding hands with Tony Blair, singing 'Auld Lang Syne'. It was truly the sight of the century – Her Majesty, with barely concealed disgust, allowing her Prime Minister to take hold of the tips of her fingers and yank her arm up and down in time to the music. It said everything we needed to know about Blair's Britain at the dawn of the twenty-first century.*

And if we'd had any lingering doubts, they were washed away when we switched to live coverage of the millennium fireworks. As Big Ben finished striking the hour, we had been promised a spectacular 'River of Fire' – two-hundred-foot flames rising above the Thames and sweeping, surging, leaping, coursing at 775 mph, in just ten seconds, from Tower Bridge to Vauxhall. Alas, it was not to be: the spin out-performed the delivery: we held our breath and nothing happened: the River of Fire turned out to be a dribble. It was so feeble it was funny. In fact, it was all so ghastly, I rather enjoyed it. I suspect it would have made you very angry.

But you'd have enjoyed the party. David and Anne [Croft] are lovely people and generous hosts – none more so. (We need more generosity in this mean-spirited world.) Your extended family was all there. We talked about you. (Well, some of us did.)

And you will be pleased to know, even though it's nearly four years since you died, you have not been entirely forgotten by the wider public either. Predictably, it's not for your stage work that they remember you: your Mercutio, your Hamlet, Oswald in Ghosts, *that archetypal silly-ass in* Tons of Money *at the National, Elyot in* Private Lives *(those would be my top five), not even for your award-winning performance in* Travels With My Aunt. *No, your immortality, such as it is, seems to rest on your portrayal of the holiday camp manager in the TV sitcom* Hi-de-Hi. *(You are allowed to smile. If I am remembered at all, it will be as the man who wore silly jumpers on breakfast TV.)*

We still get plenty of Hi-de-Hi *repeats on the box. And because, for so long, you were one of the masters of the commercial voice-over, you still crop up in unexpected places. The other morning I stepped out of the London Underground at Bank Station and, suddenly, over the loudspeaker system, I heard you booming at me: 'Mind the gap!' It's not much of a line, but you do it brilliantly. (Do you remember how, at school, Rachel loved to quote Stanislavsky: 'There are no small parts, only small actors'?) I stood on the station platform and let three trains come and go just to listen to you. I could picture you in the recording studio: a small cigar in your right hand, left hand cupped behind your ear, your lopsided mouth close to the microphone, taking such pleasure in pitching it so perfectly. It was good to hear that voice again: crisp, energetic, fruity, lived-in.*

Where are you, old friend? It's 12 noon. You should be in here serving me a glass of champagne with crème de pêche. *That's what we do on New Year's Day. (Actually, any day will do.) Do you realise it's thirty-five years since we met – in 1964, when the Beatles and the Rolling Stones were all the rage, but you and I (bless us) were living in another era. Our heroes were Gerald du Maurier and Jack Buchanan. I played you my Noël Coward records: you played me your Flanagan and Allen. We spoke of Sir Ralph and Sir John, Sir Michael and Dame Peggy as though we knew them – and, as it happens, one day we would. (We took that for granted.)*

I see now what a quaint couple we must have seemed: an absurd pair of prematurely middle-aged teenagers who thought they knew it all. In fact, while I had long sensed (at least since I was 7) that I understood everything – absolutely and completely – when I met you I had to concede that, in terms of sophistication and a thorough understanding of the ways of the world and the pleasures of the flesh, you were the undoubted master.

At 13, you could blow perfect smoke rings (at that stage you preferred Gitanes to Gauloises); at 14, you could tell the difference between a Chablis and a Montrachet at a hundred paces; at 15, girls would do things for you that the rest of adolescent Britain could only dream of. (Do you remember that brief dalliance I had with the nurse in the sanatorium? I suppose I was 17 and she was 23. It seemed to me to be the most thrilling thing that had happened in the long history of desire – until I gave you the details and you explained to me, quite kindly, that, by your standards, my tentative kissing and cuddling was very thin beer indeed.)

Why did our friendship work?

We had common interests and shared values. We were equally narcissistic, self-absorbed, ambitious, but never in competition with one another. We were never critical of one another either. In time, our wives might tell us to spend less, drink less, improve our posture, hold our stomachs in, but we simply accepted each other, exactly as we were, without qualification, without question. Neither of us was ever judgemental. If you had reservations about my politics (which you did) you never said so. If I had reservations about your women (and the assortment was varied) I never spoke a word.

Our friendship may have been profound, but our conversation wasn't. We avoided introspection. (That's one of the secrets of happiness: my new friend, Professor Anthony Clare, has just told me so.) We didn't discuss our feelings, ever, not even when you were dying, possibly because we were middle-class Englishmen of a certain vintage, but perhaps, too, because, instinctively, each knew how the other felt and there really wasn't any need. We never had a cross word — not once in thirty-five years.

Our relationship was totally secure and wonderfully uncomplicated. There was no jealousy, no envy, no confusing desire. That's the joy of friendship: sex never gets in the way. A love affair is fun, thrilling (the highs so high), but it's unsettling, dangerous, exhausting too; and, if you've been around the block, you know it always ends in tears. Marriage (I think I understood this better than you) is magnificent — fundamental, essential, and, when it works (thank you, Lord), a blessing like none other — but it isn't easy. Living a lifetime with your lover/husband/wife calls for energy, staying power, infinite care, eternal compromise. Ours was an altogether easier lot. A friendship that begins in childhood is simply a favourite cardigan: you don't need to keep it in good repair, you simply need to slip it on.

We were good companions, you and I. We made each other laugh (without fail), telling the same stories in the same funny voices, year after year. We had awarded ourselves a special licence (irrevocable) to quaff (the best champagne), to scoff (the finest caviare), to gossip until dawn.

We both went along with the Noël Coward line that 'on the whole work is more fun than fun'. That doesn't mean to say that we didn't take our pleasures where we found them. (Do you remember the menu gourmand at the Hôtel du Cap at Antibes? Our wives said, 'Eleven courses and a different wine with every course? You can't!' We did.) But, essentially, we were defined by our work rather than by our family lives or our relationships. Our careers came first. Yours was more satisfactory, of course, because you never had any doubt about what you wanted to do. I've meandered: that's been a mistake. Being an actor was your life: you were most alive in a studio or on a stage. You relished and understood your craft. (You were also very ready to share your experience.

When I was an MP and a Government Whip, you and I discussed John Major's distracting way with words, his curious sing-song speaking voice and his annoying way of saying 'want' as 'wunt'. You suggested I suggest to the PM that you give him some help with his pronunciation. Did I tell you that I did? Mr Major was not amused.)

There was an unspoken conspiracy between us, wasn't there? It was our world and whatever we wanted of it could be, would be, must be ours. Do you remember one summer turning up in the south of France at the villa your parents had rented and finding the sky hopelessly overcast? You opened a bottle of champagne and stood there, glass in hand, glaring at the heavens, commanding the clouds to part. Of course, they were happy — they were honoured — to oblige.

We thought we were invincible and then, one day, we had our comeuppance. On the morning of Saturday 11 September 1993 — I can tell you the date: I keep a diary, as you know: I am writing this in my diary now — I was standing in the kitchen at home, squeezing the orange juice when the telephone rang. 'You are going to have to be brave,' you said. 'I'm in the Harley Street Clinic. It's not good news . . . Of course I'll want you to do the address at the service. We must talk about that. And the music. I think a combination of Charles Trenet and the Battle Hymn of the Republic, don't you?'

In the event, you struggled on for two and a half years, with such grace and style and indomitable joie de vivre. *John Wells (who followed you all too quickly to the grave) put it perfectly: 'Simon showed us how to live and then taught us how to die.'*

Four years on, what's the news at this end? Not much: Tony Blair is Prime Minister; John Birt is a lord, Henry Cooper is a knight and Shirley Bassey and Julie Andrews are dames (I kid you not: all as of yesterday); and, apart from Frasier *and repeats of* Inspector Morse, *there's still nothing worth watching on the box.*

On the domestic front, the big news is that your wife has a new man. Don't worry. He's okay. In fact, he's lovely. She often says you must have sent him. He's younger than you, taller, better-looking, better-read, calmer, easier-to-live-with. (He isn't an actor, so he must be. Actors are impossible. We know that.) I like him a lot now, but at first I found it difficult to be in the room with him. It was nothing personal. He's intelligent, thoughtful and kind. I just couldn't bear to see him sitting in your chair, drinking from your glass.

He is wonderful with your sons. He does those dad-like things with them (watching football, playing games) that you (and I) were never very good at.

The Pursuit of Happiness

The boys seem happy: the tension that was in the air during the years when you were dying has gradually disappeared. They are 12 and 14 now, looking good, growing tall, winning prizes. You've got plenty to be proud of. (So have I. My children are the light of my life.)

Your mother is pretty perky too. In truth, she's the one I feel for. I can imagine nothing worse in all the world than losing your child. At her house in France, she created a glorious sundial in your memory. You'd love it, and you'd be proud, too, if you could see the way she soldiers on. No doubt, in the still watches of the night she feels quite bleak, but she's British and she's brave and she doesn't let it show.

And how am I? I'm fine. I lost my seat at the general election — a relief really. Michèle hated the life. I could have gone back. I was offered a crack at the first by-election that came along — a safe seat, too. But I couldn't do it to her. She has given me her life. I owe her something. (In truth, I owe her everything.) And ten years in opposition? Fifteen, maybe? And then what? Secretary of State for Hairpins — or possibly the Arts. No, I shan't be Prime Minister: I missed the boat — too busy faffing about on the quayside. But I'm not downcast: a new millennium dawns and I have plans . . . a novel, a play, a film — I am going to get one thing right, completely right, *before I'm done. I shall make my pitch for immortality.*

Meanwhile, here I am, starting 2000 at the forefront of the second division. I don't complain. I'm a hack but a happy one: doing radio, TV, journalism. Working all day, every day. It's fun. I'm well paid. I travel the world meeting interesting people. I pursue my projects. I make my plans. I've lost weight. I drink less. I even exercise now and again. And the curse of cholesterol means I've given up the pâté de foie gras. It's all okay. It's really very good. I want for nothing and I surround myself with famous, funny and delightful people. Oh yes, there's still laughter at my end of the table — but, old friend, let's face it: without you it isn't quite the same.

Yours ever, Gyles

Acknowledgements

I am indebted to everyone who has crossed my path since the late spring of 1959. I hope that those who feature in these diaries will not feel that I have treated them unfairly. They will have their own recollection of the events described, I know. Tony Benn told me that he and two fellow Labour MPs and diarists, Richard Crossman and Tam Dalyell, once compared diary entries of an evening they had spent together. Each had recorded a quite different highlight. The only common factor, according to Tony Benn, was the way 'we had each insulted the other for not listening properly or understanding the case we were trying to put.'

Editing these diaries for publication has not been an easy or comfortable experience. To see so clearly so many opportunities missed or wasted has been distressing. But it's done now and I am grateful to all those who have helped me with the enterprise, notably my daughter Saethryd who, with considerable patience, great good humour and very few cries of 'Oh Dad, how could you?', has sorted and filed more than forty substantial boxes of my memorabilia. I am grateful, too, to my publisher, Kate Parkin, for editing the material in Part Five. She and her colleagues at John Murray – principally Roland Philipps, James Spackman, Amanda Jones, Sara Marafini, Caroline Westmore, Victoria Murray-Browne, Bernard Dive and Shona Abhyankar – have been unstinting in their encouragement and support. Considerable thanks are due to my copy-editor Jane Birkett, proofreader Nick de Somogyi and indexer Geraldine Beare. As ever, I am indebted (and to the tune of more than fifteen per cent) to my literary agent Ed Victor, and to his team, particularly Charlie Campbell and Linda Van. Finally, I should like to add a special word of thanks to my old schoolteachers. Even in the earliest entries in the original diaries, while there may have been an excess of exclamation marks, I did not come across a single spelling mistake or significant error in punctuation.

Thanks, also, are due to David Kremer, David Rarrell, Bill Potter, Philip Ingram, Francis Loney, Michael Gell, Sydney Harris, Geoff Wilding, Roy Granger, Greg Knight, Fatimah Namdhar, the *Daily Mirror*, the *Evening Standard*, the *Independent*, the *Sun*, *The Times* and the Press Association for permission to reproduce their photographs and cartoons.

Index